THE OSAGES
Children of the Middle Waters

The

Children of the

UNIVERSITY OF OKLAHOMA PRESS

Osages

Middle Waters

JOHN JOSEPH MATHEWS

NORMAN

By John Joseph Mathews

Wah'Kon-Tah: The Osage and the White Man's Road
  (Norman, 1932)
Sundown (New York, 1935)
Talking to the Moon (Chicago, 1945)
Life and Death of an Oilman: The Career of E. W. Marland
  (Norman, 1951)
The Osages: Children of the Middle Waters (Norman,
  1961)

Library of Congress Catalog Card Number: 61–9006

Copyright 1961 by the University of Oklahoma Press,
Publishing Division of the University.
Composed and printed at Norman, Oklahoma, U. S. A.,
by the University of Oklahoma Press.
First edition, August, 1961.
Second printing, October, 1961.

To *A-Ci'n-Ga,* the Big Hill girl of the Buffalo gens who became my great-grandmother, and to Elizabeth Palmour, who became my wife.

Introduction

THE SPANIARDS OF THE LOUISIANA TERRITORY had a population vacuum which disturbed them deeply.

They were afraid that the English would come down from the north and fill it; therefore, they invited some American families over from the east side of the Mississippi to fill the vacuum, so that they could build up a resistance to English infiltration. They were selective, and did not invite the wandering "free men" who had no serious intentions of settling anywhere. They invited substantial citizens and offered them land and aid.

Thus, about 1795, Zenon Trudeau, commandant of St. Louis, invited Joseph Williams, my great-great grandfather to settle west of the Mississippi in Spanish Louisiana, granting him land along the southern bank of the Missouri River, opposite San Carlos, which was later to become St. Charles, Missouri.

One of Joseph's sons was a red-haired, raw-boned man, who became a missionary to the Osages at their villages on the modern Osage River. He lived with the Osages and married an Osage girl. He became interpreter for the missionaries of Harmony Mission, and translated the Bible into Osage for them. He was interpreter at the second treaty of 1825 between the United States and the Osages. After his wife died, he sent his two daughters away to school in Kentucky, and he himself disappeared into the Rocky Mountains. He was William Shirley Williams.

One of his daughters, Mary, married John Mathews from Kentucky, and after her death, he married her sister Sarah. He had trading posts among the Indians: one at Fort Gibson, one at the Osage Mission, and one at the place which the Osages called *Mo'n-Ce-Gaxe-To-Wo'n,* Metal-Makers-Town. His blacksmiths repaired their guns and shod their horses, and therefore he became Metal-Maker. This is the modern Oswego, Kansas.

John Mathews and Sarah Williams Mathews were my father's parents. My father came to the last reservation of the Osages with the Big Hills in 1872.

My father's house stood on a sandstone hill; a ridge-finger around which Bird Creek flowed in a large bow. At the bottom of the ridge, in the rich alluvium valley, were the sandstone buildings of the Osage agency. Also, from my father's house one could look away to the east and see the rounded lodges of the Thorny-Valley People, and at night one could hear the giant pulse-beats of the kettledrum when they danced the *I'n-lon-schka.* This would be during the June distribution of annuities.

The elongated valley was also the home of the Little Osages, the Down-Below People, who had moved from their homes near Mission and Rock creeks to live with the Thorny-Valley People of the Great Osages.

When the quarterly payments were made (per capita payments of interest from the trust created from the proceeds from the sale of their reservation in Kansas), the Thorny-Valley People and the Down-Below People and the Hearts-Stay People were not compelled to travel to the agency. However, the Upland-Forest People and the Big Hills must travel from twenty-five to thirty miles from their villages in the southern and southwestern parts of the reservation. The Big Hills camped on the bank of Bird Creek during these visits.

I learned all this later, but they were the source of my first memory.

I was a very small boy when the seed which was to disturb me all of my life was planted. I had probably been moved from my mother's bedroom because of the arrival of my second younger sister, and being the only boy in the family, I had a room to myself. At least I was alone and certainly afraid.

I might have lain all night obediently silent, but I remember the hour before dawn, when the silence was the heaviest. There floated up to my room through the open window which overlooked the valley, a long, drawn-out chant broken by weeping. I could even hear the sobbing. It was like the song of the wolf and yet like the highest pitch of the bull wapiti's moonlight challenge, and it broke, too, not with the terminal grunt of the wapiti's challenge, but with a soul-stirring sob.

I heard it many times later as I grew up and up until the time I entered high school, and I have never been able to describe it to myself; it was indescribable, and there is nothing with which to compare it. It filled my little boy's soul with fear and bittersweetness, and exotic yearning, and when it had ended and I lay there in my exultant fear-trance, I hoped fervently that there would be more of it, and yet was afraid that there might be.

It seemed to me later, after I had begun to reason, that this prayer-song, this chant, this soul-stirring petition, always ended before it was finished, in a sob of frustration.

It was Neolithic man talking to God.

Later, when I became a man, quite unconsciously I searched for the continuation of that which had ended before it was finished. I searched for it in the call of the muezzin from the tower of a desert mosque, searched for it in the overwhelming fervency built into Gothic cathedrals, and I tried to find it in a Mexican Indian pilgrimage to Chalma.

It seemed to me that the muezzin simply restated a creed, as the Christians did in the Apostles' Creed. The Indians streaming down from the mountain passes and up the canyons to pay homage to *El Señor de Chalma* later danced Spaniard-taught pastorals in the nave of the stark, lonely church at the head of a wild mountain canyon.

When I arrived back home, back to my hills, after ten years away, I found that most of the old men of the tribe with whom I had talked had passed on to Spiritland, but there were a few left, and when I talked with them, I realized that I was not conscious of obtaining information for a book but for the satisfaction of something within myself, and I set down that which I learned as a sort of expansion of my diary. The idea of a book came to me when I noted that the old men talked more eagerly and with more patience to me than they had ever done before. It couldn't have been deference to my age, since I was still a young man. Then I suddenly realized that they were worried; they were worried about the disruption of their father-to-son history. They were worried about the end of their own gentile and tribal importance, and that the sheet water of oblivion might wash their moccasin prints from the earth. Their only chance now of immortality was to live in the word symbols of the Heavy Eyebrows, the white man. So they talked eagerly, with precision and with meticulous care, preserving the sanctity of every word that had been handed down to them from their fathers.

I became almost at once aware of the importance of oral history, which I have called in this book, tribal or gentile "memory," since that is what my informants believed it to be. I at first experienced a European or Amer-European impatience when, during every visit to the old men, I had to listen again, word for word, to that which had been told me before. Then suddenly it occurred to me that if there were fabrications or misinterpretations in the history I was hearing, they might be from two to three hundred years old, and the very atmosphere they bore would be of great value to me. Certainly they would not be disturbed by "new light" thrown on them. About these stories handed down from father to son, this oral history of a people, there was, I began to note, a biblical atmosphere, but with the advantage of never having been written down. There could be no later interpretation because of religious taboo, and each word had a certain sanctity. The history was a part of them, of the informants and the tribe, and they could not be detached from their narrative as were literate Europeans detached from their written narratives.

Since their oral history was a part of them, and they themselves were children of *Wah'Kon-Tah,* it could not be colored by struggle-interest as it related to the pre-Columbian period, when they were in harmony with the natural balance. Later, it may have been tainted with vindictiveness and injured innocence, after the enemy god had become dominant.

This knowledge put me on guard when I read the Amer-European and European documents. One had to keep constantly in mind the basic interest of the writers of military reports, trappers' letters and stories, Spanish, French, and American official reports, and missionary journals and letters home. One had to make allowances for the smugness of the traveler whose interest was chiefly academic. No matter how sincere, honest, and objective the Europeans and the Amer-Europeans were, their unconscious economic, political, military, social, and religious interests often nullified all three. One had to know something of the background of the writers of private letters, official reports, verbal witnesses, and travelers, both scientific and those who traveled for pleasure or adventure.

Ambition to advance one's personal interests, either politically or economically; military ambitions and Christian intolerance and the settlers' struggle for existence could not live with untainted academic interest, and practically all European frustrations in a variety of interests were easily and credibly projected to the reticent "savage."

The documents were invaluable, and in them were facts that could be set against the criteria of Osage nature, their phraseology, their God-concept, and their earth-harmony. One had to know that the Europeans' and Amer-Europeans' actions were natural under the circumstances and nearly always trustworthy as history, while their documents were often unconscious smoke screens for the protection of their illusions about themselves, despite the valuable facts they contained.

Also, one had to understand that the fate of the Neolithic man along the Missouri River was written when the Europeans first landed on the North American shores, and that there was no Right or Wrong concerning the European invasion; it was only a biological incident as far as Neolithic man was concerned.

Besides taking the biological view of the conflict between civilized European and the Neolithic man, and knowing the culture of both, setting one against the other to attain the truths, one had to be aware at all times of the difference between "instinctive knowledge" and fiction. With one's family associated with the Osages for 150 years and one's awareness of one's own personal experiences, there was always the danger of confusing the two.

But there were incidents in which fiction had to be employed. I had seen the marriage festivities, just as I had seen a mourning dance, yet in the description of the marriage of Bloody Hands and The Light I used fictitious names for all the people who took part, even though the ceremony itself was authentic. I did this because the ancient ceremony was described to me by two different women; one *Mo'n-Si-Sah-Qui* of the Bear gens of the Little Osages and the other *La-Ta-Sah* of the Big Hills. They varied only in small details, but I had no choice but to use fictitious names, since my ceremony was not descriptive of a specific one.

Again, in the meeting of the Osages with the first Europeans, the "instinctive knowledge" would overbalance the isolated facts of oral history. This was also the case in the story of Braddock's defeat and in other minor incidents.

So, in setting out to write about the Osages, especially in my search for information about them, I thought of myself as a paleontologist searching for a lost femur, a lost tarsus, several vertebrae, or ribs. In assembling the fact-bones for my reproduction, I had to supply the missing ones with the plaster of "instinctive knowledge." I had much more than merely a jaw bone and a femur: I had bones from every part of the skeleton. More than that, when covering the finally reproduced skeleton with flesh and hide, I could use the material of my personal experiences and the experiences of my father and grandfathers, and I, myself, had seen my dinosaur walking.

To name all of the people who have given me information would result in a long list, which would by its very length nullify the importance I would desire to give them. For the same reasons, I have decided not to name any of the many curators of museums, librarians and directors of historical societies, or any of the many museums, archives, libraries, and historical collections which I have visited over the last thirty years. To write simply that I am deeply grateful to all of them and will long remember their graciousness and courteous attention must suffice. Most of the Osages with whom I have talked through the years I have named in the bibliography, since they were very important sources of information, as were the books and documents I have listed there.

Naming those who gave extremely important aid in another category makes only a short list, a paragraph: in 1939, I received a John Simon Guggenheim Memorial Foundation Fellowship, for which I express deep appreciation. Just after the war of 1941–45, I found my income not adequate for the research I had to do. While my income varies periodically, I felt I couldn't wait until it became adequate again, so I accepted financial aid from my friend, the late Frank Phillips of the Phillips Petroleum Company, and from my friend Allen G. Olliphant, oil producer, and the late W. G. Skelly of the Skelly Oil Company. This aid made the publication of this book possible perhaps two years sooner than if I had not received it, and I express my deep appreciation.

JOHN JOSEPH MATHEWS

The Blackjacks
Pawhuska, Oklahoma
April 20, 1961

Contents

xix

Maps

xx

BEFORE THE EUROPEANS

"And our name in time shall be forgotten,
And no man shall have any remembrance of our work."

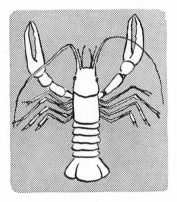

—Wisd. of Sol. 2:4

I.   People from the Stars

If a snake were slithering along in definite search for food, and suddenly he became aware of the shadow cast by the wings of a red-tail hawk, high-circling, he would draw his head back and retract his body until it formed into a series of half-loops, then he would freeze, with only his forked tongue darting for messages. He would be like a carelessly dropped rope; like a new rope that had not the kinks stretched out of it.

That is the way the Osage River of central Missouri and eastern Kansas looks, as it comes down from the high prairie to flow through the wooded hills. It lies shining there, among the hills, like a snake under the shadow of wings, or like one that had been touched on the end of the nose by a snake stick.

It has looked like that ever since the last Ice Age; that period in earth's history when an ice sheet crept down from the north and seemed to try an escape down what became the Mississippi Valley. Near its mouth was the point of an ice wedge, the nose that felt out the terrain for the least resistance as the mass crept down over what is now the modern states of Minnesota, Wisconsin, Iowa, eastern Nebraska, northern and northeastern Missouri, and the extreme tip of northeastern Kansas.

But the conditions that made the great ice sheet possible became static and the relentless flow stopped, and there the nose or wedge remained, until the ice began to recede by melting. Muddy, milky

3

waters ran from its front, and rolled in angry spate as they gathered into streams and tumbled forward into the great central drainage that flowed south, and that later became known as the Mississippi River.

But the river much later called Osage by the Europeans did not empty its waters into this milky flood, but into a stream that came out of the west. This stream had its source from the west in the Rocky Mountains, two of its ultimate sources in what later became known as the Yellowstone National Park. This stream started off north in heedless, youthful frenzy, but the great ice sheet bent it southeastward and made it flow along the edges of the glacier, and forced its swirling, muddy, foaming waters into the continental drainage ditch called the Mississippi. This mighty stream from the Rockies not only received other streams from the mountains but also had the glacial waters to carry off.

This made a wild flood of angry waters, spreading over a great flood plain. It dashed down out of the mountains, excited and in high spirits, but soon came onto the plains, and here it had to become calmer and more sedate. Even so it rushed at the face of the great glacier, but had to give up its youthful ambitions and flow along the edges of the ice, eventually pouring itself into the glacial-milk waters of the Mississippi. Fed by the glacial water, it had regained some of its early, boisterous frenzy but had lost its careless joy and clean exuberance.

Its early frustrations seem to have made it maniacally angry and it has been angry ever since, changing land from modern Iowa to modern Nebraska and back again, trading land between Missouri farmers, eating away at the Dakotas, tearing at the pines of the Rockies, eating the soil away from the roots of the elms and the sycamores, and bending the sandbar willows, carrying the uprooted trees downstream during spate, or leaving them mud-anchored to bob in the current, sometimes planting them upside down in its own bed.

Flowing from the hills south of this mad river, this diabolically whimsical river called the Missouri by the immigrant Europeans, is the river that looks like a stunned or fearful snake. This river called Osage had not been scooped out by the ice sheet, and the hills through which it took its lower course were actually the reason for the formation of the ice sheet's wedge, since they were old Ordovician hills when the Pleistocene glacier crept over the land, seeking as does water the terrain of least resistance.

The Arctic fox might have hunted along this river, and the bull caribou might have sent his challenge over the dwarf birch, since there must have been paper birch and dwarf willows and funereal winter tamaracks. Certainly there would not have been great elms, syca-mores, hackberries, walnuts, and long-armed white oaks. But there might have been men living here then, at the edge of the ice sheet. They were living elsewhere in this period called Pleistocene, because they have left their record in bones and flint scrapers, and arrow-heads and spearheads, and their desires and dreams and God fears through pictures on cave walls in Spain and France and elsewhere, along with their fetishes and skull fragments, teeth and refuse heaps.

And thus the ice sheet crept forward for centuries perhaps, seek-ing the depressions, the drainage courses, nosing south, scraping the land level; grinding, cracking, groaning, glinting savagely under the moon; sending out fingers of milky, muddy water, that canalized and began to roar and foam. Then the ice began to melt and retreat to the north, leaving the flourlike soil it had ground and the boulders it had carried from the north; the great granite boulders it had sculpted from fragments it had picked up from the northern granitic shield.

It left long ridges of terrain, like military breastworks, and lodge-shaped piles of earth and frustrated rivers, and the depressions it had scooped out of the earth became lakes and marshes strung on chains of sluggish rivers. The angry Missouri carried off the waters and dumped them into the continental drainage ditch, the Mississippi, but never since has tried to flow north.

The birch, the willows called Arctic, the winter tamarack, the shaggy musk oxen, the white fox, the gigantic beaver had been gone for centuries, and now there were great timber wolves sending their hair-raising hunting song across the hills, and white-tail deer climb-ing up the bluffs from watering in the river, looking back over their shoulders. There were black, shaggy strings of buffalo coming down from the hills to the river in single file, swinging their heads in rhythm. After drinking with little caution and with much splashing and sniffing and pushing, they would graze on the lush bottom

5

grasses or scratch themselves against the rough bark of the hackberry. In July the bulls would roar and paw the earth and thrash the sapplings with their horns, and the roars were like thunder bouncing back from the river's walls.

And there was the black bear with the white spot in his chest, which was later to become a symbol of the hunters who would claim the river for their own.

The hills were covered with hardwood growths now and the river bottoms were dark and cool under the whispering foliage of the gigantic sycamores, the black walnuts, hackberries, ashes, and regal red oaks. In the Ordovician hills through which it flowed for half of its course, the river that looked like a fear-frozen snake was hidden by the creases of the hills, and by the timber that was like the hair of the earth, but the three-forked tail of the snake was on the limestone prairie where there were few trees, except in the alluvium. And there at the forks, the river had been sluggish for centuries, discouraged by the flooding Missouri and backed up by it, had spilled over its banks and filled depressions, and here were marshes and spongy earth and lazy water in the sun, sparkling as it had sparkled for centuries. The trees had followed the river to the edge of the high prairie.

Here to the marshes and the mirrors of water came the trumpeter swans and the white pelicans like smug old men to nest and dream and preen. The tall sandhill cranes hunted for frogs, ever alert but standing for hours, dreaming, becoming restive in the autumn, to fly above the lenses of water threaded by the river; high above the frozen snake's tail croaking in tremolo, seemingly befuddled. In the spring they danced on the high prairie, away from the swans and the pelicans.

Thus it was at the head of the river, where the trees became timid and did not venture boldly. On the lower river, where the trees were like the earth's pelage, the golden eagle circled over the hills, watching for gravid does that wandered away from the band, dipping down to throw his shadow over the panther lying on an escarpment also interested in the restless does.

At sunset and after, there was a constant roar of the wings of passenger pigeons, coming in to roost, and far into the nights there would be the cracking of limbs of the elms and hackberries under the weight of their millions. And here in the spring the wild gobblers made distant thunder with their strutting, and their gobbling bounced back from the cliffs.

But the wolves and the buffalo and the eagles and the pelicans and the swans, the panther, the bear, the beaver, the deer, and the wapiti; the trees, the fishes, the water striders, and the river that ran into the mad river of the ice sheet and looped like a fear-frozen snake had no names. Not even the earth and the sky had names until the Children of the Middle Waters came. But when they came, this was one of the first things they did; they gave all these animals and birds and insects names because they would use them as symbols, and transmute their special powers which *Wah'Kon-Tah* had given them, and had not given the Children of the Middle Waters. The Children would transmute these powers through the agency of prayer-song, and use them vicariously, making them a part of their own bodies and spirit, even charging them with their dreams and their fears and their urges, so that the symbols might give back to them that with which they had been charged.

The Children of the Middle Waters had begun to reason long before they came to build fantasies upon the foundations of their biological instincts and upon their mysterious urges. They had begun long before to fumble toward the Light which their mental development would demand that they recognize. They felt more now than the urges of food-getting and mating; there was the third urge that came with thought. This was *Wah'Kon,* the Mystery Force, and in their urgency to come to some understanding of this life-force, they knew great fear and confusion, and they could only build their own framework into which they would try to fit this *Wah'Kon* and therefore bring it within the boundaries of their conception. They had been busy for perhaps centuries building a ritualistic cage for this *Wah'Kon,* the Mystery Force, that they might have it under control, materialize it out of the world of abstractions, so that they might know relief or protection from their own fears and uncertainties.

Long before the Europeans found them, they had named the animals, the fishes, the trees, the plants, and the birds, and had named themselves, *Ni-U-Ko'n-Ska,* Children of the Middle Waters. They

7

also knew how they got there and why they were there, and they also had fumbled towards an understanding of the *Wah'Kon,* and had a very comforting interpretation under which they dwelt.

When they first came to make their homes near the forks of the river that was like a snake, which they called Place-of-the-Many-Swans, they were noble and clean and guiltless of Caddoan blood, and carried no hair of the European on their spears, and they knew no fear of the Sac and Fox canoes creeping along the river banks in the darkness. This was in the beginning, before they knew these people, even though later one division of the Pawnees, whom they called *Pa-I'N,* Long-Hair People, might have been the "enemy," along with other Caddoan people they referred to so often in organizing their religion.

They were pure and clean and noble because they had just come from the stars—from among the stars, say the holy men. They were all *Tzi-Sho* then; all Sky People, but when they descended to earth, the Sacred One, they found her divided into land and water, over which the Great Mysteries chose to send the wind howling like wolves, and to send down balls of ice to pound their heads, and breathe snow across the land, and cover the Sacred One with it, and to send screaming winds to steal the song-prayers from the Children's lips and clutch at the bodies beneath the buffalo robes with long, icy fingers. The Great Mysteries dropped funnel-shaped clouds from the sky and sent them dancing over the land, carrying away man and his pitiful little things into oblivion. Waters fell from the sky and the foaming water of the river swirled and sucked and roared, carrying dead buffalo on its back, and making the riverside walnuts and elms shake in fear. Surely at this time they must have made their first songs of death and mourning and supplication, cowering in their caves.

From the first dim dream, the first abstract thought, these people who called themselves Children of the Middle Waters began to create their own world, reducing their fears, their urges, their fumbling placations to concrete and practical forms, so that they could know comfort and security from the results of their own fumbling. All tribal memories of the dark centuries when they fought, hunted and mated; all the struggles, the food-getting, the adjustment to carnivorous animals, to poisonous reptiles, and to cold and heat, and poison-ous plants seem to have been flooded and obscured in the first grow-ing light of their mental development. Instead of employing the light to illuminate the long dark centuries of their development up to the time of the man erect and sapient, the man pre-eminent, they began to create a fantastic, conceivable, and comfortable world of their own. They began to dream and create Great Mysteries of their own instead of probing those of which they were a part.

The Little Old Men of today are sufficiently realistic to admit that the Sky People were befuddled when they first descended to earth, the Sacred One, but there is never a hint as to why they descended to the tragedy of long adjustment to earth and its disorder. Did *Wah'-Kon-Tah* send them down in Jehovian anger, because they trans-gressed his laws? They have never intimated that there was an express reason for their descent.

They were quite modest before the mighty manifestations of the Great Mysteries, and meek before earth's anger and whims, and re-ferred to themselves as the Little Ones. But still they had a ponderous self-esteem, and it would be in harmony with this self-importance if *Wah'Kon-Tah* had really sent them down as caretakers of the Sacred One. Certainly much later, when the immigrant European noted their military activities and commented on them, he might have been led to believe that they could have had just such a commission, since there did seem to be a species of Arabic fervency in their military aggressions.

But they came from the sky, say the Little Old Men; from among and of the stars. They were children up there as well, of Grandfather the Sun, and as they say, noble and clean and shy and befuddled and inquisitive, just as might be expected, and immediately they began to explore.

They were also disorganized, but there was order in the descent to earth, since they were from the orderly sky. They said they had no organization when they first came to the Sacred One; that they had only *ga-ni-tha,* which means chaos. They came to earth in three groups or divisions, but these did not constitute the whole tribe. There was one division indigenous to earth.

9

THE OSAGES

When the Children of the Middle Waters, who in their humility called themselves the Little Ones, came down from the stars, they floated down into a red oak tree, and as they alighted they loosened acorns which clattered down among the leaves, bounced from the limbs and branches. They must have come down singly or in small groups, with the People of the Waters leading. They floated down from the sky with their legs outstretched to the tree tops, and their arms up like the wings of an alighting eagle, since it is this great bird's landing which they later imitated in their creation dances.

The fringes along the outseam of their buckskin leggings, which they have always worn, were in imitation of the golden eagle's tarsal feathers that grow like heavy, hairlike mold to the toes. The rattling of the dislodged acorns, they later imitated with the ceremonial gourd rattles, and the falling hail of acorns later symbolized the many children they needed to keep the tribe at fighting strength.

Since they dislodged acorns so easily, one supposes that the time must have been autumnal, and almost immediately they must have been face to face with the temperamental madness of the prairie-plains or prairie-woodland winter. But it is not known by the modern Little Old Men when the three divisions, the People of the Waters, the People of the Sky, and the People of the Land came upon the earthly village of the Isolated Earth People. There seems to be little hint of the seasonal changes in the genesis of the Little Ones which the Little Old Men have handed down. Perhaps such things, such disagreeable things, as blizzards and tornadoes and floods have no place in man's creations, desiring, as he must do, to attain a feeling of comfort in ignoring them, except when he wishes to stress a moral.

So these children from the sky divided into three groups, which were to be organized and named later after they had walked upon the Sacred One seeking. They walked in order: the People of the Water led, then came the People of the Land, and the People of the Sky last.

Much time passed during these wanderings, and they had to learn to protect themselves immediately from animals, and to do this they were compelled to kill. They had to learn to flake a flint and to sharpen a stick, through scraping the charred end to a point, and to make slings for defense. One must assume that these celestial people had appetites and must eat, and they must find edible plants and animals, and had to capture fire and hold it in control.

Before they left the Sky Lodge, *Tzi-Sho,* Grandfather the Sun, had called them to him and had pointed out to them the thirteen rays that radiate from him in the mornings and again in the evenings during certain atmospheric conditions. He asked them to note their straightness, and to note that there were six of these rays on the left side and seven on the right side, and that further there was a glow on the left side that was the shape of the soft under tail-feather of the golden eagle. These things would have great significance in their lives on the Sacred One, he warned them. He then showed them how to make arrow shafts from the dogwood and the ash tree as straight as his own rays, and he fashioned a bow from the Osage orange tree, and another from the antler of the wapiti.

The Little Ones were well armed now, and soon they had furs to keep them warm, and plenty of meat from the generosity of the buffalo. They met him one day and he gave them four colors of maize, and instructed them in the use of his hide, fat, sinew, and horns, and he gave them the squash. They met the crayfish, who brought up from the earth the four sacred colors, dark, red, blue, and yellow. They met the cedar and the evergreen water sedge, the symbols of life everlasting. A panther showed them the lotus fruit which they have ever used for food, and the roots of the water lily.

So as they wandered over the Sacred One, they had plenty of food and clothing and they had spears and slingshots and bows and arrows with which to protect themselves.

Wah'Kon-Tah struck the long grass of the late summer or early spring with his crooked firelance and the flames raced, and the Little Ones learned about fire. At night they would sit about their own captured fire and look up at their brothers who had remained in the sky, gradually becoming aware of the seasonal changes and of the various positions of the Big Dipper, as he wheeled about the North Star. They called the Morning Star the Male Star and the Evening Star the Female Star.

They took notice immediately of the seasons. The season when life

11

began again, when the little earth-hugging flowers came, they called *Be*. The season during which the buffalo bulls pawed the earth, throwing clods of earth or smoky dust over their backs, roaring with their tongues out and with mouths close to the earth, so that the Sacred One would carry their challenge far, the Children called *Do-Ge*. The season when the maples and the oaks stood like warriors painted for the war movement, they called *To'n*, which means "standing." When the winds howled and burnt their faces with ice, and the Little Ones had to find shelter under the keening trees of the bottoms or in the canyons, they called *Ba-The*.

Then one day as the three groups traveled over the land, the Land People and the Sky People were dawdling when the Water People came to a river. The water of the river was happily singing and talking and whispering over the rocks and the gravel. The great sycamores and elms, the chinquapin oaks, the hackberries and red oaks and black walnuts leaned over from the bank to listen to what the river was saying, listening to the song he was singing and trying to hear the mysteries he was whispering. And as the leader of the Water People stood watching and listening, he saw a man standing in the middle of the river with the waters wrinkling against his belly.

The leader knew at once who he was, and he turned to his followers and said to them: "Here stands *Wah-Sha-She*, whose body is the waters of the earth." The river spoke to the Water People through its embodiment, *Wah-Sha-She*, and said in the liquid tones of the cowbird: "Oh, Little Ones, if you make your body of me it will be difficult for death to overtake you, and you will make clean and purify all that comes to you. When you come from your home in the sky to make the flowers grow, Grandfather will paint your face with many colors [rainbow] and smile upon the Little Ones."

The leader talked with the others and they henceforth called themselves *Wah-Sha-She*, Name Givers. The River embodiment, *Wah-Sha-She*, had named the Water People with his name, *Wah-Sha-She*, and they would symbolize all the waters of the earth.

The Name Givers then named the Land People, *Hunkah*, the Sacred One, and the Sky People, *Tzi-Sho*, Sky Lodge. But they were not complete; they must search for the group who were indigenous to the Sacred One who called themselves the Isolated Earth People. On finding them, the Children would be a tribe, a unit of men symbolizing the universe.

They resumed their wanderings, the Water People leading, the Land People behind them, and behind the Land People, the Sky People, but this time they had a definite objective; the finding of the *U-Tah-No'n-Dsi,* the Isolated Earth People.

One day the *Wah-Sha-She* came to a village. The scene as handed down through generations of Little Old Men is quite clear-cut and realistic, even though the houses or lodges were never described. The essentials that had to be brought out to characterize these people of the village were startlingly stark and realistic.

The three groups were afraid to approach the village, so they stopped at a distance and sent a messenger forward. He crossed several valleys, and after crossing the last one he stopped on a ridge above the village and concealed himself. He could smell the village odors, and they made him sick.

He saw some of the people. The men had bangs and were tattooed about the eyes and the mouth. He watched from his hiding place all day. The women were almost naked, wearing only an apron of deerskin and a robe that was allowed to slide from their shoulders when the sun grew warm. The girls were bold and walked in pairs followed by several young men acting like dogs and coyotes. The girls would stop and pick up rocks to throw at the young men, who would dodge them. The girls were like she wolves, growling and rushing bare-fanged at the following males. Their robes were half open and their breasts were tattooed.

The messenger returned and guided the Water People, *Wah-Sha-She,* the Name Givers, to the village, but the *Tzi-Sho,* Sky People, and *Hunkah,* the Land People, followed reluctantly. They looked back over their shoulders to the clean prairie under the whispering winds.

When they came to the village, the leader of the Water People looked back at his people and said: "We have come to the village of strange people." This was the village which the Children sought, the *U-Tah-No'n-Dsi,* the Isolated Earth People.

When the leader of the *Wah-Sha-She* said back over his shoulder to his people that they had come to the village of a strange people, his followers stood waiting, but the other two groups, the Land People, called *Hunkah,* and the Sky People, called *Tzi-Sho,* turned away in disgust, walking away holding their noses.

They had seen the bones of many animals and men around the village, and had seen the wolves and the coyotes waiting, and the turkey vultures circling in rhythm high over the prairie. The little winds had brought to them the odor of decay and charred grass. The great crawling mass of buffalo intestines was musical with flies.

At the edge of the trail that led downhill to the village, a pair were coupling. At the edge of the village, two men were fighting with war clubs, and a man in woman's clothing was running away frightened. Among the lodges, a man lay dead, and standing over him was his brother, wiping the blood from his war club.

Here in the village of the Isolated Earth People was death, decay, disease, and waste, and the bones of men along with the bones of animals. This is what one might expect of earth without the influence of the sky.

But the chief of the Isolated Earth People sent a messenger to the leader of the *Wah-Sha-She,* and he went into the village to smoke the pipe with the chief. When they had passed the pipe between them, the leader of the *Wah-Sha-She* said to the chief, "Who are you?" and the chief answered, "I am of the earth people and the red boulder is our symbol. It is red like the dawn and it is life everlasting. When they come to it the enemy war parties must divide and pass on each side; all things move aside for the great red boulder."

The leader of the *Wah-Sha-She,* the Water People, said: "Our bodies are of the red clay pipe which we are smoking. We are Water People, and all things come to us for purification."

As they smoked, the Isolated Earth People and the Water People found kinship: the one symbolized by the red boulder, which had the color of the sacred sun and its durability and was passed by the war parties without molestation; the other symbolized by the purifying smoke of the pipe and the cleansing water.

The chief of the Isolated Earth People listened to the leader of the

14

Water People, and made his village ready to move to another country. They would leave the place of the bones of animals and men, so
that the yellow flowers could grow there and hide the ugliness forever. The Isolated Earth People would leave death and disease and
ga-ni-tha, disorder, to seek homes in a new country, guided by the
people from the sky. Water would fall from the sky and wash clean
the village site and the sun would look down upon it and smile and
from his smile would spring the flowers, and thereafter the site would
be called the Place-Where-the-Yellow-Flowers-Grow. Under this
beneficent influence of the sky, the Isolated Earth People would know
other things besides death and chaos.

The *Wah-Sha-She* led the Isolated Earth People to the *Hunkah,*
the Land People, and to the *Tzi-Sho,* the Sky People, and they all sat
down in a place far away from the village of the Isolated Earth People
and smoked the pipe prayerfully, and knew with great contentment
that they were one people. Henceforth the two grand divisions of the
tribe would be *Tzi-Sho,* the Sky People, and *Hunkah,* the Earth
People, but *Hunkah,* the Earth People, must be divided into land
and water, and the *Hunkah,* who had come from the sky, would symbolize the land of the earth, and *Wah-Sha-She* would symbolize the
waters, and these would become subdivisions of the Grand Hunkah,
the Earth People. Thus would the *Ni-U-Ko'n-Ska,* the Children of
the Middle Waters, symbolize the universe of sky and earth and land
and water.

The tribe as a whole and each individual member became both
Tzi-Sho and *Hunkah,* and have a home both in *Tzi-Sho (Tzi-Shiu),*
the Sky Lodge, and on *Hunkah,* the Sacred One. Each man, woman,
and child would be both sacred and profane, both spiritual and material, and in his dreams and in his thoughts, and in his songs and in
his yearnings, he could lift himself out of his *Hunkah* existence and
become his *Tzi-Sho* self to wander above the necessities and demands
of the earth, and with the borrowed virtues and prowess of animals
and birds, he would create a world that would harmonize more comfortably with his particular stage of mental development. Under the
disturbing urges of reason, he assumed that he was the man pre-
eminent. However, he was befogging the dawn of thought, and he

would continue to befog his thought as his reasoning developed, and he would never reach the stage in mental development where he could throw the light of reasoning back to the centuries of animal darkness and attempt to understand them as they were, as one might light a Cro-Magnon cave with an electric bulb.

So when their first thoughts came, they built a world of their own, materializing the mysteries, so that they would remain within the boundaries of their understanding, and they could communicate with them and reason with them and sometimes even influence them, by creating amulets, fetishes, and symbols, such as the fresh-water mussel, from the skins of birds and animals, and by embodying them in the wapiti and the buffalo and recording them in tribal memory, in magic words and rituals which would give back to them encouragement and comfort in lieu of the chaotic fears with which they had charged them. Under this created magic, they could feel some importance and much comfort, and would no longer feel the hopelessness of their insignificance when the tornado danced, the thunder roared, lightning lanced the prairie, and maniacal winds screamed, or when the *we-lu-schka,* the Little Mystery People, came into their stomachs or their limbs or their heads, to take away their remaining years.

But all this creation was under the constant fear of *Wah'Kon-Tah,* and they attributed to him their own pride and vanity; giving him all their own attributes, except, perhaps, lust. Feeling that they might have gone too far in their assumptions, they eagerly stressed the fact that they themselves were the Little Ones, so as not to offend his warrior pride.

They built up mysticism around the primary urges of food-getting and mating, as well as under the influence of *Wah'Kon,* the Mystery Force, but the bases of the former two life-forces were understandable, and the fear element was absent, except when the scarcity of buffalo became a religious matter completely. These two urges, food-getting and mating, were older urges in their existence, having been with them during the long dark centuries before thought, or perhaps reason, appeared. However, when the first dim reasoning dawned, it threw a light on food-getting and mating, and there developed a superstructure of dramatics and romance, accompanied by fetishes and filters and symbolical orgies and intricate nuptial ceremonies, but understanding them in their practical, earthy minds, they never felt the necessity to create a new world under their influence. They only embellished them beyond the nuptial displays of birds and animals.

Dreams, however, are supposed to be impossible except as they are based on some experience or reality, so that when the Children of the Middle Waters tried to create a new world for their own comfort and security, they could not make it completely out of gossamer, and they had to build upon the two primary laws of nature which they understood and under which they had developed. Therefore, in creating their mystical world, they made the sun male and the moon female, the Morning Star male and the Evening Star female, the earth female, and the sun, again, male. They really got as far away from earthly reality in their artificial, spiritual ornamentation as the ancient Greeks, when they arranged the mating of the sun and the moon to produce the sacred hawk. However, the girls of the Little Ones were never ravished by the Male Star or the sun.

They elevated the tricks and the antics of the animals and birds in their preying on others, or in being preyed upon, to mysticism; and courage and bravery and fleetness and deception and bluff, all of which having been employed by them from the beginning of time for their own survival, were used in their creations when fumbling for understanding, through the impetus of their reason-inspired awe of *Wah'Kon,* the Mystery Force.

After the Water People, the *Wah-Sha-She,* the Land People, the sub-*Hunkah,* the Sky People, the *Tzi-Sho,* and the Isolated Earth People, the grand division of the *Hunkah,* got together, they were a tribe and symbolized the universe as they knew it. They made their arrows of ash and dogwood and straight like the rays of Grandfather the Sun, just as he had instructed them, and they took the hide of the large animal, the buffalo, the hide of the yellow animal, the wapiti, and the hide of the little animal, the deer, and made of them their clothing, their lodges, and of the black bear, skin for their beds. From the horns of the large animal they made their spoons, and again from his hide, their boats and their shields, and from his heart sac and stomach, bags and pots, and they took sinews from his back. They made bows from the antlers of the yellow animal and hooks upon which to hang things, and hoes from his shoulder blades, as well as some scrapers. From their little animal they made their moccasins and their leggings, and from his antlers their battens for weaving. Many other things they took from these three sacred animals besides food.

In the first years of their earth-dwelling, they had little time for anything except the maintaining of themselves: the growing of their food, their hunting, the making of utensils and weapons and the weaving of cattail stems and leaves for the siding of their lodges, as well as their constant wars of survival with both animal and man and nature. But when they had their lodges full of food and their enemies were far away and Grandfather the Sun smiled on them they had time to think and to realize that they had no order.

When they were fighting to keep their place on earth, and fighting with unnamed enemies, who seem to have always come from the west, they had little time for anything except the crudest of symbols and the simplest of rituals. Their enemies then might have been the Caddoan tribes. They do not in their tribal and religious memory fail to mention pre-European enemies. They had then to live with all the gentes in five closely grouped villages, since in great numbers they could better protect their prairie-plains and woodland domain, and these great numbers had to be maintained chiefly by the hunt, and to be able to maintain themselves in one region for a very long time, game had to be plentiful. Theoretically, meat-eaters among the species cannot anchor themselves permanently unless they become agriculturists or become pastoral.

The buffalo were about the villages then, and even wintered in the woods down the river, during certain seasons when conditions were favorable.

The Little Ones have always said that the buffalo were independent, and were "just doing that," which is their name for the month of March and could be translated as "capricious." The buffalo, being very prominent earth people, had never come under the direct influence of the orderliness of the sky.

The deer were always standing with ears forward like sound detectors, or watching their fires with phosphorescent eyes, or flashing their fantastic, uplifted tail flags. The bull wapiti in the first full moon of September came prodding up their river, challenging.

Their corn grew waist high and bent over their footprints, and their pumpkins lay like just-above-the-horizon full moons.

2. The Little Old Men

THE ENEMIES FAR AWAY, the lodges full of meat and lotus fruits and lily roots and corn and wild beans and blazing star bulbs, the nuts and squashes, the people's thoughts became ornamental and their dreams were longer. At such times of plenty and idleness, the women would sew little useless bunches of porcupine quills with thread from the linden or the pawpaw tree on their men's shirts, or string necklaces of the ivory teeth that grow in pairs in the mouths of the wapiti. The young men made whistles from the wing bone of the trumpeter swan, and courting flutes from the cedar and the sumac.

The idle men began piercing their ears with an awl made from the wing bone of the golden eagle, using a small piece of peeled hickory as a stop, then suspending from the puncture shortened porcupine quills.

At such times young men would walk up and down the village ways extravagantly painted, carrying war clubs and with black squirrel tails attached to the heels of their moccasins. Sometimes they would follow another young man with woman's paint on his face, wearing woman's clothing, down the village ways, laughing and shouting obscenities. This disgusted the older men, and they thought this energy of youth ought to be turned into other channels. This was the *ga-ni-tha* of the Isolated Earth People.

The old men sat in the shade of the elms that had ventured up the river to the edge of the prairie, and were troubled by the thought that *ga-ni-tha* had come with the Earth People. Soon they began to study the stars and talk of the constancy of the sun, the wheeling of the Big Dipper; of the moon and the Morning and Evening Stars, and of the Pleiades, which they called Deer Head, and the Galaxy.

They talked of the swiftness of the bank swallows and of the courage and ferocity of the striking falcon; of the old-wise-man look of the tranquil pelican, who traveled slowly and unafraid across the loops and swamps and oxbows and crescent moon-shaped lakes abandoned by the whimsical river. When he stood for hours, he seemed to be musing on the mysteries of existence, and even to have solved them. He was the embodiment of spiritual contentment.

They watched the black bear dig grubs, and when he turned toward them they saw the white spot on his chest, like a moon peeping between black clouds.

The old men became intrigued with their own observations and soon they could see hints from *Wah'Kon-Tah* in them, and soon they moved a little farther from the noise of the village and met each day during periods of tranquility under the shade of an elm. Soon they were called wise men, and during the hours of peace and full stomachs all through the centuries, these wise men, called the Little Old Men, with their inquisitive groping, created a formal religion, an organized buffalo hunt, an organized war movement, and a civil government.

The Little Old Men thus came into being and they were called *No'n-Ho'n-Shinkah,* which means just that, Little Old Men. The term *shinkah,* meaning "son" or "little," is a term of endearment as well as a diminutive, and *shinkah* is used as a suffix to imply such endearment just as the Spaniards use the diminutive as a suffix for that purpose.

The Little Old Men soon became sacred, but of course they were never little, and certainly characteristically tall. They were older men within whom the fires of mating and hunting and war had been banked, and with the still-coursing life-force exigent, they canalized it, not impounding it with the fat of easier living. They hung no porcupine quills from their ears or other *wah-don-skas* made by the sated, whimsical women and girls or by the professional bow maker.

Their unused energy went into ornamental thinking and creation. When the tribe lived in plenty and the enemies were far away, the skies were clear, and they for the moment were not compelled to concentrate on their enemies skulking behind trees or as part of the willows of the sandbars. At such times as there were no dust tails above the plains, the Little Old Men sat and compared ideas from their thinking, and there was consensus that whatever order they might attain, it must certainly come from the sky. Every day was the same there, even behind the clouds. The sun and the moon and the stars behaved in perfect order. They said among themselves that the sun would come every morning and that the moon might change her form, but she always appeared. Even when she appeared during the reign of the sun sometimes, they knew that she was only a woman who had forgotten something and had been allowed to come back for it under the indulgence of Grandfather the Sun.

The falling stars were merely brothers of their former life, traveling, and the comets were long-tailed stars leaving the Sky Lodge. Thus were the gods of the sky in perfect order in their movements— the sun and the moon and the stars never making a mistake, and the Big Dipper wheeling, and Polaris always there to guide the Little Ones.

And these Old Men who had banked the fires of youth, and who for the moment felt no need to worry about the food and shelter for the season, sat together to discuss these things which they observed. They sat for days making their guttural speech sounds, accompanied by the very graceful movements of their long-fingered, copper-colored hands. Here was the sky full of order and the earth also indicating some kind of rhythm, but still not as dependable as the sky, and since the three groups from the sky, the *Tzi-Sho,* the *Hunkah* and the *Wah-Sha-She* had taken the Grand *Hunkah,* the Earth People, into "new country," away from the bones and charred symbols of earth-death, there was still the disorder of earth to be dealt with; disorder and death, and *Wah'Kon-Tah* was showing the Little Ones the complete harmony in the sky. These things the Little Old Men told each other, as they sat the day through waiting for juicy ribs to be brought to them from the fire. It was an honor to bring special, juicy ribs to them, and the young girls vied with each other for this honor. Those who had passed pubescence must not come near the holy men during menstruation, nor would the women be allowed to take part in the cookery during such periods.

There must be order in the war movement, both in defense and in offense, they told each other. There must be leaders so that the young men trying to win honors would not walk out onto the plain in their war paint to kill detached members of the tribes to the west, whose medicine was strong, thereby bringing an attack upon the village of the Little Ones. And there must be order when the Little Ones went out to hunt the buffalo. There must be honored men appointed to say when the hunters must converge in a wide circle upon the grazing herd, and when they might begin their yells and wear their devil's grimaces at the proper signal. No young man hiding in the creases of the plains must rise in his fantastic paint to frighten the buffalo toward the cliffs before the *Ah-ḳi-ta,* the especially appointed one, had given the signal. The young men must set fire to their weed piles on each side of the narrowing neck of the gourd-shaped drive only on the signal from the *Ah-ḳi-ta.*

These things the Little Old Men told each other. And further, they assured each other, the young men must not marry whom they might choose, but if they were *Hunḳah,* they ought to marry girls from the *Tzi-Sho,* so that the blood would not run thin and weaken the medicine of the Little Ones. The overpowering of girls strayed from the camp was the spirit of the Isolated Earth People in complete control of the young men. The marriages between the *Hunḳah* and the *Tzi-Sho* would symbolize the marriage again of Sky and Earth.

Each day the Little Old Men would rise and slowly draw their buffalo robes about them, singing their Rising Song, and say among themselves that they had now learned the will of *Wah'Kon-Tah,* and they would ask him to help them attain the order which he himself maintained in the sky. They would make certain songs and dances and create recitations for ritualistic use, so that *Wah'Kon-Tah,* the creator of order, could understand them and their desires and aid them in prolonging life through a plenitude of food and the bravery of their warriors. Their conversations with *Wah'Kon-Tah* would be formalized, and this he could better understand.

And so during the long hours of tranquility, when the benign sun of early autumn shone on strips of buffalo hanging like elongated autumnal pin-oak leaves from the drying poles; when the camp smoke from a hundred fires floated like prayer-smoke from the pipe; and dogs lay everywhere with bellies distended, the latter moving in and out like lazy bellows as their owners whimpered in dream-fright, the Little Old Men formalized their understanding with the Great Mysteries.

They observed the antics of the bold girls, and the young men parading with polished war clubs and black squirrel tails attached to their heels, and they studied the clever crows who sat in the trees waiting in silence, and the vultures circling like aerial skaters around and around monotonously and soporifically. Their interest was ever with the wise-old-man-appearing pelican down in the river valley, standing in the marsh among the mirrors of trapped water. For hours he would stand thus, contemplating the vicissitudes of existence.

It was at such times that the Little Old Men created a universe for their people, so that man, pre-eminent, could be as comfortable as possible in a mutual understanding with *Wah'Kon-Tah*. It was during such times of tranquility and plenty that the Little Old Men began their organization of the people, but there must have been thousands of such periods during hundreds of years and many generations of Little Old Men before the order was attained. And there were many interruptions.

These Neolithic people had not yet known the necessity for making the adjustment to their natural environment that would anchor them to a certain patch of earth, where they would plant their crops and store their harvest, thus assuring themselves food for the lean periods and create property and jealousy and envy and greed.

They accepted food as a gift, and depended upon a harmonious relationship with *Wah'Kon-Tah* for replacement when they had gorged their present supply. They built no pallisades or trenches to protect their villages and camps, except in hunting camps, where buffalo stampeded even though the people selected such sites with military defense and hunting strategy in mind. They depended on their scouts and their constant readiness for war, and on mobility for their protection, and were readily adjustable to the whim of nature when Arctic winds hurled snow over the plains and woods and drove game out of their range. They could sit for days while the winds whistled over their rounded lodges, the dung-fires smoldering, buffalo robes over their heads and their eyes shut, waiting in majestic silence. They didn't pray to *Wah'Kon-Tah* at such times, because they had too much respect for him. Later, after the winds had passed on, the Little Ones might ask the panther for his stealth and power in finding game, or ask the aid of the white-tail buck, the bull wapiti, or the buffalo in giving them the location of their "people."

During times of stress, and always during the buffalo hunts, the Little Old Men must leave their world-making for the spiritual comfort of man pre-eminent, and take part in tribal activity in order to assure man pre-eminent's physical comfort. If they were old, they helped the women. This was before they had organization, when old men were only a hindrance. After the organization effected by themselves, they had ornamental places of high honor, and all must come to them.

At that pre-organization period, they sometimes helped with the butchering of the animals, when the shaggy beasts fell coughing at the foot of the cliffs, frantic with fear and pugnacity, and even, under necessity, forming a part of the long line in antlike procession, carrying the meat to the temporary hunting camp, or scolding and disentangling the pack dogs, raising the pitch of their voices if need be, since the dogs understood only strident women. They did this if time was important and there was great necessity; if there was a blue-black cloud on the northwestern horizon, or the wolves had come in great, starving hordes on the heels of the migrating buffalo, or if the scouts had warned the people of Caddoan moccasin prints. No night guard, even with brush fires surrounding the bloody place of slaughter at the foot of the cliffs, could keep the hungry wolves from entering the flaming circle to the feast.

If in a hurry, the older men must climb to camp with their chunks of meat, along with the women and pack dogs, while the hunters were still hamstringing the broken bulls and cows, whose tongues flapped from their mouths as their eyes rolled. And they sometimes had to work hard and fast, returning time after time with the women and the panting dogs; these old men, these philosophical systematizers with the supernatural. They had to act with the tribe when tribal survival was the necessity. From the beginning of time there were no insurgents, since the law that was the very tribe itself could not be broken without total disaster for the individual. The man pre-eminent, walking the earth erect, with his war club, his spear, and his bow, and his control of fire, must put his ego aside when the tribe was in danger.

The hunters and warriors, after the last coughing bull had been dispatched, would sit with their bellies moving in and out, with the sweat making runnels in the dust of their bodies, as they wiped the blood from the flint or granite heads of their axes with a patch of mallard-hen skin which they carried about their persons; never the green neck of the mallard drake, since he was sacred. (His neck feathers were wrapped around the pipe stem, just below where it joined the bit.)

During the periods of adversity due to the capricious nature of the earth, and during the buffalo hunts, and when the scouts reported the finding of Caddoan moccasin prints, the Little Old Men could not divide their minds; one-half for dreams and one-half for exigent realities.

Finally they met no more under the red oak or the elm tree, close to the capricious smoke of the campfires, but a kindly man gave them permission to meet in his lodge, and soon, much to the self-satisfaction of the donor, this particular lodge was called the Lodge of Mystery, and soon the Little Old Men became holy through a long period of time and the Lodge of Mystery became a holy place, and in the ritualistic recitations it was given honor, as most of the recitations began with the words, "It has been said in this lodge."

As the years, and even the centuries flowed on, other men took the place of the Little Old Men almost each generation and added new thoughts to the fumblings toward an understanding of *Wah'Kon,*

26

the Mystery Force, until there was a most intricate organization, including endless ceremonials, songs of supplication, and very rich but baffling symbolism. The generations of Little Old Men had been so impressed by the orderliness of the sky that each new generation of them became more and more hopelessly involved in labyrinthine ritual in their attempts to bring earth's mysteries and whimsicalities, plus man's frailties, into harmony with sky-order, for the comfort of man pre-eminent.

When they came face to face with problems too big to be fitted into the cage which they were building for the constant urgings of *Wah'Kon* to be understood, they sent men out to fast, or went out themselves, and through fasting for four or seven days they could come back with verities revealed to them through hunger-dreams. They often got their answers to their song-prayers from the manner in which a duck hawk fell upon a teal, or a prairie falcon struck the arrow-flight bird, the prairie chicken. In the hunger visions, perhaps slightly fevered at times, they might find their answer from the buffalo bull himself, through the interpretation of a cough, or from the falsetto challenge of the rutting bull wapiti, or even from the manner in which a wolf worried a calving cow, or through the restive tail of a hunting panther. The faster might find his answer in a diurnal skunk nonchalantly turning buffalo chips, or at night in the number of times *ito'n,* the great horned owl, called from the black line of river trees; or from the song of a lone wolf or a dog coyote. A solitary wasp falling to the ground with his victim cicada might give the answer, or it might come from a spider on his perfect, lacey web. He would not inspire the faster from the camp of the Little Ones, as he once inspired Bruce, since his message to the faster would not be entirely symbolical but mystical.

The faster would stumble back to the camp or the village and with the stain from the sacred earth he had placed on his forehead still visible, his ribs like a washboard, he would tell the Little Old Men of his experiences and his vision, not knowing the difference now between illusion and reality, making no effort to know.

And so the Little Old Men became men of mystery, and the lodge in which they sat became the Lodge of Mystery as they talked and gesticulated in the middle of the lodge around a fireplace. Even their language became mystical, and only a few could understand them when they wished to be mystically obscure; only a few of the men and no women at all, except, as some say, perhaps the Bear women. The more mystical they became, and the more they used meaning-less words to screen the meaning of the holy words, the more holy they became in the minds of the people.

The Little Old Men themselves, in their thinking, learned nothing whatever of the origin and the nature of the Little Ones, and of course attained little of the order of the sky in the organization of their people, but in their attempts, like all men pre-eminent, befogged themselves with satisfying, mystical, and elaborate ritual. And even-tually, like all men buoyed on the fear-emotions and greed of the people, began to believe in their own holiness and superiority; from some of them, much later, in the historical periods, developed the dark-minded medicine men.

The natural environment colored the people's concept of *Wah'Kon*, and the whole organization of the tribe and its relationship with *Wah'Kon-Tah* were created from the observations by the Little Old Men of the character of the region wherein they had their permanent villages. The organization of the Children of the Middle Waters was a reflection of the region where they lived, its contours, its fauna and flora, and its climate. The tribal organization and the tribal concept of God show very plainly that they lived where a lazy, winding river had abandoned successive channels many times and left lenses of water and oxbows and crescents and marshes, refilling them during the overflows. And no matter where they lived in the beginning of dawn-thought, and no matter what dim tribal memory indicates about their coming from the southeast, their religion reflecting the earth indicates a region of river-abandoned water in general, exactly like the region at the forks of the river now called Osage in modern Bates and Vernon counties, Missouri. If they had lived in the vague prehistoric times at the head of the Mississippi River, where there are lakes—glacial, not river-abandoned—and lazy meandering rivers and marshes and lenses of water, one might expect to find the moose and the loon among their life symbols, and if they had lived in the vague

Southeast, they ought to have a word for the sea. The centuries could have erased such tribal memories, even from carefully guarded religious symbolism and ritual, one must suppose, even though one knows that the bull moose would have impressed them deeply with his importance, perhaps more than did the bull wapiti of their plains-prairie-woodland home.

Their God-concept and their organization indicates as well that they lived in a region that had long periods of lush tranquility, and that water fowl and water animals abounded; that they lived at the contact line between the prairie-plains and the woodland, in a region where the Arctic air found no barriers to its savage rush and would periodically meet the dog-breath air from the Gulf to spawn disaster, which gave dramatic proof of *Wah'Kon,* the Mystery Force.

For food they had abundant white-tail deer, wild turkeys, prairie chickens, wapiti, buffalo, skunk, fish, lotus, pawpaws, haws, grapes, persimmons, hickory nuts, walnuts, hackberries, pecans, and acorns, besides their cultivated crops of varicolored maize, squashes, beans, and pumpkins, and *do,* the wild potato.

In all the regions in the Western Hemisphere where there were indigenous peoples, there could not be found a more fortunate tribe than the *Ni-U-Ko'n-Ska,* the Children of the Middle Waters. People living in such a region of plenty where the jungle air of the Gulf came floating over, only to be pushed back by the cold masses of air out of the Arctic, spawning tornadoes and causing a bombardment of earth by balls of ice, must adjust themselves to such crises with the same suddenness with which they came. On the plains, where there were no north or south barriers, nature went periodically mad and struck as a stealthy enemy might strike, without warning, except perhaps a smudge on the northwestern horizon, or the behavior of the smoke from the campfires, lying close to earth. They must ever be ready for an attack from the elements out of the north, or from the Caddoans out of the south or the west and southwest.

Through their constant alertness and their prowess, they could hold their lush land, and from their prowess and the lushness which it protected, they seemed to have found that rare boon among ancient hunters, leisure. They found sufficient leisure to create their own elaborate protection from the real world of mystery, by evolving a comprehensive mystery of their own.

There was no volcanic activity in their domain from which they might have created a hell, and there was little tribal tradition about the trembling of the Sacred One.

3. The Fireplaces

THE GRAND DIVISIONS of the Little Ones, were the *Tzi-Sho,* the Sky People, and *Hunkah,* the Earth People. The *Tzi-Sho* had no sub-divisions, but the *Hunkah* had two; the sub-*Hunkah* and the *Wah-Sha-She,* representing the land and the water respectively. This was symbolical of the universe.

But there was more to the universe than sky, earth, land, and water. There were the stars, the groups of stars, that must have special meaning, and the animals and the plants and the insects and the birds; and winds and thunder and lightning. So the Little Old Men divided the *Tzi-Sho* grand division into seven fireplaces, or gentes. They gave the grand division *Hunkah* one gens or fireplace, but divided this grand division into two subdivisions, and then divided each subdivision into seven gentes or fireplaces each. Each fireplace or gens would have its own life symbol, and a sub-gens symbol as well. These were the original gentes, these twenty-two, and the Little Old Men sent each gens out under its leader to find a suitable symbol from among the animals, plants, insects, stars, birds, etc.

These gens can be visualized walking over the earth in their very careful search for suitable symbols. They must be cautious and make no mistake in the selection of their symbols, since a bad choice might damn them forever. They had to be especially careful, since it was assumed that to become a symbol of one of the gentes of the Children of the Middle Waters was a very great honor, and the leaders of the gens would be stopped constantly by "little people" asking for the honor despite the fact that they might be highly unsuitable. However they stopped and questioned every one of the "little people" whom they met, since they must not only have symbols for the twenty-two gentes, but there must be symbols for each sub-gens, and this would mean that practically all the animals, birds, plants, insects, fishes, and stars with the desirable characteristics would be chosen, and thus highly honored.

The first gens of the *Tzi-Sho* grand division was called *Wah'Kon-Ta-No'n-Paw-be,* which means *Wah'Kon-Tah* is feared by all, and refers to the life symbol, the sun. The sub-gens was called *Wah-Bah-Hi,* the Awakeners. The sub-gens contributed the messenger for the gens, called the *shoka.* Messengers were in constant use by the Little Old Men and in all the ceremonies. It was below the dignity of the leaders to go in search for anyone; they sat and waited for all things and people to come to them by request of the *shoka.* This messenger of the Awakeners could demand prompt action from all the messengers of the other gentes.

This gens had very little searching to do, and they chose for their symbol the most desirable of all, the sun. They simply chanted to *Wah'Kon-Tah* for inspiration: "Oh, Grandfather, we have nothing that we can use as a proper symbol for the first gens of the Sky People." And Grandfather heard them and said: "I am a person fit for the symbol you desire, since I am the god of day."

They believed themselves honored. They built their fires that night and they sang above the chorus of the wolves, and the Moon Woman answered them and suggested that they also take her as a symbol along with the sun, saying, "I am the goddess of night, and I too am eternal, and if you make your bodies of me you will reach old age, and the Little Ones will live forever."

The next morning, when they came out from their robes to sing their prayers to Grandfather, the Morning Star, the male star, heard them and he suggested to them that he was also immortal, and if they chose to live to old age they must choose him as well.

All day they traveled toward the west as the Little Old Men had instructed them, and that evening when they were again singing above the chorus of the distant wolves, the Evening Star, the female star, asked them to also take her as a symbol. Here were the people of the sky, gods and goddesses all, offering themselves as symbols to this gens of the grand *Tzi-Sho*.

The next day they traveled on to the west, singing in their great pride, until Grandfather the Sun went down, then he showed the thirteen rays, seven on the right side and six on the left, and they immediately cut thirteen sticks from the willow to use as sticks to count their *o-do'n,* war honors.

They followed the sun many days to the west, and after counting many valleys, and just as the sun had left the sky, they were attacked by tall, light-skinned people who wore buffalo horns on their heads and tails made of buffalo hide. These tall pale-skinned warriors were fierce fighters, and were piercing the buffalo hide shields cut from the left side, the *Tzi-Sho* side, of the bull buffalo, which the gens wore on their left arms. Just then the Moon Woman came out, and the tall warriors fled back to the west.

The gens turned back to the east toward their village. Late that afternoon about their fire, they talked of the things that had happened. They were unhappy that the Moon Woman had to intercede in their fight with the pale, tall men from the west. As they talked, a pileated woodpecker flew to the red oak under which they sat and shouted "kuk-kuk-kuk-kuk-kuk," and the people of the gens looked up at him and saw that he carried the color of night and the color of day, and his head was the color of Father Fire. They suddenly realized that they had no sacred thing with them when they were fighting the pale, tall people. Here was the bird with the red of fire, the white of day, and the black of night.

The leader immediately blunted one of the arrows in the fire, as one did the arrows the little boys used for birds, then he shot the woodpecker and skinned him, and by this time one of the women had a little woven rush shrine ready for the skin. Now they need never fear the roads to the west. The leader hung the shrine from his neck and in order to assure himself completely, he told his people that again when they came west following the road of Grandfather, they would prevail against their enemies.

33

These people of the *Tzi-Sho* also suspended the head of the pileated woodpecker from the sacred pipe; only the skin of the beautiful red-crested head of course. Not only this gens of the *Tzi-Sho*, but all the people of all the gentes had to have some fetish when they followed the road of Grandfather onto the plains, where the enemy roamed.

Not all tribal or gentile travels to the west were military. They could not exist without salt and they had to get their *mo'n-ka-ska*, gypsum, and their salt from the red plains of the Permian to the southwest. They traveled to a place on the high plain which they called Salt-Low-Land-Forest on the Big Salt River for their salt, and to the red Permian buttes for their gypsum. These places are now in the modern state of Oklahoma. The Salt-Low-Land-Forest is the Great Salt Plains, and the Big Salt River, the modern Salt Fork of the Arkansas, with its thick growth of brush and occasional cotton-woods. They have described well the glitter of the selenite chips on the red buttes and pinnacles of the eroded Permian Red Beds. They used the gypsum to whiten the deer sinew employed in the making of arrows.

The second gens of the Grand *Tzi-Sho* were the *Ci'n-Dse-A-Gthe*, with a sub-gens called the Dog People. The Dog Star was their life symbol. This included all the "dog people" of the prairie plains and the woodlands; the camp dogs, the timber wolf down river, the lobo of the plains, and the coyote. These were the true awakeners, and more importantly they were monitors. The coyote yapped when the atmospheric pressure was low, and often in winter a low pressure presaged the coming of a mass of air from the Arctic, and in summer, cold air from the north that sometimes met the air from the Gulf and created disturbances menacing to the lives of the Little Ones. The coyote also heralded often the forthcoming of Grandfather the Sun, warning the Little Ones to throw back their robes and come out of their lodges to stand and mourn their prayers to him. The coyote also greeted the Moon Woman. The camp dogs howled at the approach of the enemy, and the wolves sang certain meaningful songs of frustration which might indicate the nearness of the enemy.

This second gens of the Grand *Tzi-Sho* could easily see that the willow was a death-resisting tree. The storm winds bent it almost to

34

the ground, and yet it sprang back from death. The swirling flood of the Smoky Waters, the mad river of the glacier's edge when in spate, rushed through the branches of the willow, yet it sprang back when the waters receded, with the smile of Grandfather the Sun on it.

From the willow, this gens made its sacred club, then painted it red with the wet earth from the Permian Plains mixed with bear fat. This gens, instead of going out to search for a symbol, had stayed in camp with the camp dogs and the wolves around them and the Dog Star above them. They gave the sacred club to a messenger and sent him out exploring. He traveled four valleys and awakened one morning after a long dream, and found himself looking into the face of a large buffalo bull. The bull sniffed and stared. It was the Buffalo-Bull-Pawing-Earth Moon, and the young man was afraid to move. After the bull went away roaring across the plains, he arose and trotted back to camp looking neither to the *Tzi-Sho* nor the *Hunkah* side, pushing away all thoughts except those relating to his experience, fearing to lose some of the emotion that suffused him.

When he told his gens of his experience, they immediately said that Buffalo-Bull-Face would be an honored name among them, and that they would give it as a symbol to another gens of the *Tzi-Sho*. They said among themselves that in the search for this important person, they would always take the road traveled by the sun.

The third gens consisted of the people who called themselves the Gentle *Tzi-Sho*. They said of themselves that they were a gens before the descent to the Sacred One, and that they had sent a messenger down to make reconnaissance before they descended to the red oak. Their family group had become a gens in the sky, and after they descended to the Sacred One, it was to them that the buffalo had given the four kinds of corn: the red, the white, the blue, and the yellow; the two kinds of medicine: the blazing star and the poppy mallow; and the three kinds of squash.

Each family group that had become a gens pridefully took much credit to itself, but the story of the Gentle *Tzi-Sho* was interesting. They say that when they climbed down from the red oak tree, they went along the roads of the earth, and they came upon the red cedar and the evergreen sedge, symbols of life everlasting, and they knew they were on the trail to the village of the Isolated Earth People when they came upon a dead animal left to rot. But they did not see these Isolated Earth People until they had joined their Grand Division the *Tzi-Sho*.

This was during the Yellow-Flower Moon, they said, and from this came the season of yellow and lilac and mauve, when the rays of Grandfather the Sun are lazy with haze. Thus they took their symbol, and called themselves Gentle *Tzi-Sho*. This was the time of the lazy hum of the insects and the sad insect chorus from the grass roots and the lethargic circling of the red-tailed hawk. All these things their symbol included, and under the influence of this hazy tranquility, they called themselves the Peacemakers.

They also claimed the sand-hill crane. He was almost as tall as a man and saw everything that moved on the prairie, and they took one of their dances from this bird's nuptial dance in the spring. When peace lay somnolently over the prairie, the great crane stood dreaming, but when he took a few steps and launched himself into the air flapping heavily in a circle, trumpeting in annoyance, the Little Ones knew that an enemy scout was near.

It was the fourth gens to whom the Gentle *Tzi-Sho* gave their experience with the face of the buffalo bull, and they accepted and called themselves Buffalo-Face-People. This gens was in some mystical manner associated with the first gens, and they were necessary to make the seven fireplaces of the *Tzi-Sho* and division complete, despite the fact they sat silently during the ceremonials of the Little Ones. This gens had chosen only the face of the buffalo bull, and this angered the bull, who had given so much to the Little Ones. His dignity was hurt, and later he caused trouble.

The role of this gens is a silent one, and it has the duty of ceremonially cutting from the buffalo hide that part from which the symbolic moccasins were made, which are worn by the *xoka,* the priest, and *shoka,* the messenger, in the involved degrees of the war rites.

The fifth gens was the Sun Carriers, the *Mi-Ki'n-Wa'no,* who had chosen as their symbol that mystical power that carried all the bodies of the sky. Even the heavenly bodies, the manifestations of the supernatural must be supported by something, despite uninhibited mysticism.

They would not accept the possibility, no matter what myths they might build about the sun and the moon and the stars, that even they could sustain themselves in space, so this gens of the *Tzi-Sho* took as their symbol the invisible and incomprehensible carrier of the heavenly bodies. Things did not float without some sort of support—not even the seeds from the cottonwood and the milkweed, or the long glistening strands of the spider during Yellow-Flower Moon. Even the smoke from the camp fires or the smoke from the tops of the lodges fell to earth when the atmospheric pressure was low, warning the Little Ones, along with the coyotes and the wolves, of the approaching storm.

The balloon of imagination of the later immigrant Europeans had had its earth placental cable cut long before these whites came in contact with the Little Ones, but that of the Little Ones was still captive, though buffeted by the mysteries of the sky.

The sixth gens of the Grand *Tzi-Sho* was the *Ho'n-Niki-Shinkah,* Children of the Night, or Night People. A gens of the *Tzi-Sho,* the Sky People must have as a symbol the very important, powerful and very mysterious phase called night, which was ruled over by one of the heavenly bodies, called Moon Woman. The black bear was chosen by these people as a symbol within a symbol, since he is black like the night, and the little white spot in his chest is the moon.

This is the time, the night, when the panther lies near the rock covered by lichen, waiting by the deer trails; the time when the lobo breaks the night silences with his song, and *i'to,* the great horned owl, frightens the "little people" of the weed stems, and *ca'xe,* the crow, tries to grow small against his limb.

The seventh gens of the Grand *Tzi-Sho* named themselves the Last *Tzi-Sho* since they were the last of the peaceful sky people to set out in search of a symbol. There not only now seemed to be a dearth of symbols suitable to a peaceful sky people, but this particular gens seemed to lack imagination, since the only symbol they could think of was the very important, but much used black bear. They chose him not because he was the color of the sacred charcoal, or because he

37

cleverly robbed them or tore up ant hills and shattered decaying logs in search of food, or even because he was very sensible and hibernated. They chose him, and to be different, painted him red, calling him the red black bear, and they chose him not for his courage, his good sense, his cunning, his strength, the great importance of his fat, his hide, or his body as food, but because the wrinkles of his neck and feet and the under parts of his body were symbolical of old age. Survival to attain old age was an obsession of the Little Ones, and was biological progression speaking through man's creative dreaming. Survival of the tribe and the individual was nature's obsession as well.

It is odd that the buffalo bull should become a symbol of a gens of the Gentle Sky People, since he was a lustful, pugnacious disturber of tranquility, walking up and down the plains roaring, challenging the world. In June and July, the Buffalo-Pawing-Earth-Moon and the Buffalo-Mating-Moon, the Little Ones must be very careful about walking out alone onto the plains when the bulls held their heads close to the earth, roaring like a Highland stag or a leopard. At such times they lifted the whitish dust over their backs like a cloud or hurled pieces of muddy sod high like rising birds.

The Little Old Men explain the inclusion of the buffalo bull as a symbol of one of the *Tzi-Sho* gentes in this manner. They were sitting in the long lodge, which was the Lodge of Mystery, as they worked over the tribal symbol, which must be got ready before another attack from the enemy. This symbol was the symbol of all the gentes. It was the skin of a hawk. The hawk had finally been chosen for this highest of honors, because of all the animals and birds which the Little Old Men had watched and studied carefully, he had appeared oftener in their hunger dreams. He alone was stainless, the perfect symbol for man, pre-eminent.

As they sat one day in the Mystery Lodge, preparing the skins and waiting for the women to weave the rush shrine, they were startled by an explosive cough, and then by an angry roar. They looked toward the *shoka,* the messenger, then indicated the door with pursed mouths. The *shoka* went to the flap and lifted it, and there stood an angry bull. His eyes rolled and his tufted tail stood erect. As the *shoka* stood staring at the bull, the Little Old Men became alarmed.

The bull roared and pawed the earth, throwing clouds of dust into the air. The stricken *shoka* asked, "Who are you?" and the bull replied, "I am *Tho-Xe* the buffalo bull; lift up your heads."

At that moment a terrific crash of thunder shook the earth. The Little Old Men were frightened and one of them picked up the skin of the hawk that had not yet become sacred and threw it to the bull. He was not an ordinary bull, say the Little Old Men, but there was something about him; he was apparently *Wah'Kon-Tah*-touched. When he saw the hawk skin, he looked at it and ceased roaring, then lowered his tail and became friendly, and at the same moment the great cumulus-nimbus cloud that had stealthily crept up in the northwest slid off to the southeast, and the sun came out to smile on the scene, and the thunder that had made the earth tremble only growled with contentment in the distance as the cloud vanished.

The bull and the thunder had been jealous and angered since they had not been chosen by the *Tzi-Sho,* the Sky People as symbols, so they had appeared to demand the honor, after the seventh symbol had been chosen.

Since the buffalo bull had been one of the first "people" the Little Ones had met after their descent from the sky, and since he had given them corn and squash and sinew and robes and bedding and lodges and food and utensils, they had thought of him as part of *Wah'Kon-Tah*'s manifestations, and had assumed that he was like Grandfather the Sun, an integral part of the manifestations, taken by the first gens of the *Tzi-Sho* as their symbol. Now they realized that in his jealousy he was demanding specific honors that went with his power, and they must placate him. He had called forth the thunder with his roaring and they knew that the thunder, the mightiest manifestation of *Wah'-Kon-Tah*'s anger, which hurled the crooked fire to earth, must be placated as well. So the Little Old Men gave the *Tzi-Sho* two extra fireplaces, or gentes, and named them, Those-Last-To-Come, and they were given the office jointly of caring for the most sacred of fetishes, the *wah'hopeh,* or hawk shrine.

And this is the reason the earthy, raging, challenging buffalo bull became a symbol in the Grand *Tzi-Sho* division, the gentle Sky People. The thunder, of course, belonged there properly.

The Little Old Men had learned early in their earth-dwelling that they would enjoy their "remaining days," if they allied themselves with power. The Little Old Men also say that thunder brought the birds from the sky to earth, and retained the swallow as its messenger. When the blue-black curtain creeps up the northwestern horizon and its edges are like the smoked old and tattered lodge covering, then the *ni-shku-shku,* the swallows, swarm above the prairie grass, here and there, circling, twittering, telling the Little Ones to prepare for wind and rain and cracking thunder.

The Grand *Tzi-Sho* had completed their search for life symbols for their seven fireplaces and had added two gentes by command of earthly and heavenly power, and at the same time the Grand *Hunkah* was searching for a symbol for its only gens, as were its two divisions, the sub-*Hunkah* and the *Wah-Sha-She,* for their seven symbols each.

The Grand *Hunkah,* the *U-Ta-No'n-Dsi,* the Isolated Earth People, who had not descended from the sky with the others, but were found by them living in the squalor and lechery and disease inherent in a people existing without the influence of the sky, also had set out to find a suitable symbol for their gens.

They traveled many valleys in their searching. The V-shaped gorges of the Ordovician hills of the lower Osage River, the river of the Little Ones, and the saber-cut gashes of the plains were taken as milestones by them; these rather than the ridges, since their pedestrian travel was along the main streams, to which the feeder streams ran almost at right angles. Hence one traveled so many valleys.

Naturally, many animals and birds and insects and manifestations of *Wah'Kon-Tah's* power, both beneficent and maleficent, presented themselves for the honor of symbolizing this grand division of men pre-eminent, but their leader walked on, crossing many valleys and building many fires.

They had searched the prairie and the plains and had turned back down the river, and one day, as they passed along a deer trail leading down across the bottoms among the buckeye and the red buds, the pawpaws and the willows, the leader pursed his mouth in the direction of a bluff, and the people stopped dead still. The leader very slowly felt for an arrow, and very slowly notched it, then step by cautious step he went forward along the trail, his eyes on the white-tail buck standing over his daytime bed from which he had just risen with movements so slow that they were scarcely perceptible. As the leader moved almost imperceptibly along the trail to an opening, his face was suddenly smeared with a clinging, tenacious gossamer. The spider climbed to the top of his web and waited and the leader clawed at his face, and the buck's white flag floated away through the brush like a phantom.

The people snickered, but the leader was angry. He picked the last strand of the clinging web from his face and, scowling at the spider, said, "You little black thing, *pi'she*." This was one of the only two swear words in the language of the Little Ones and means "bad." The leader struck at the spider with the end of his bow, but the spider only moved aside.

Again the leader said, *"pi'she,"* and lifted his bow again, but the little spider lifted his arms in defense and said, "Where do you go that you cannot see." The leader answered, "We are the children of the Grand *Hunkah* of the Children of the Middle Waters, and we search for a symbol."

"You have come to the end of your search," said the spider. "Take me for your symbol."

The people hid their smiles with their hands, and the leader had difficulty keeping his dignity. The leader then assumed a stern and interested expression and asked if the spider had the stealth and courage of the panther, the strength and symbolism of the bear, the dignity of the wapiti, and so on. And the spider had to answer that he hadn't, but he said, "Where I build my house, all things come to it and break their necks therein." The leader remembered that the people would have no meat that evening at camp because of the spider's house, but also that even an enemy might thus be frustrated, and certainly all things came to the spider, since he had only to wait.

The spider clinging to his shattered web finally convinced the leader of the one gens of the Grand Division, Isolated Earth People, that he would make a proper symbol for them since he was symbolical himself of ambush and earth-cupidity. Thus they adopted him forthwith. Still, however, he was ugly and small and had no aggressive power, so after adopting him, they continued to travel the paths of the earth searching for other strategists of the dark, merciless earth struggle.

They met the short snake, the water moccasin, resembling a piece of grapevine that had fallen into the water. They met the gentle bull-snake, who hissed his warning when the feet of the Little Ones came near him, and the gentle blacksnake, who "hears" the faintest cry of the flicker's nestlings, and lastly they came upon the "great snake." The leader of the gens jumped back and fell against his people, for there in front of him "listening" with his tongue was the rattlesnake. As he raised his head above the grasses, he looked like a fallen branch-let profuse with lichen, and he spoke thus: "I send many things into the Spiritland, but first I warn all things and send my challenge chur-ring through the grass and stab men's hearts. Even though I send the careless-footed one into the Spiritland, they shall always with my aid bring themselves back to consciousness."

These snakes were symbolical of the earth's merciless killing, but they were also symbolical of eternal life, since they "died" each win-ter and came back to life each spring.

The sub-*Hunkah,* one of the divisions of the Grand *Hunkah,* had seven gentes, the first of which was called *Hunkah A-Hiu-To'n,* the winged *Hunkah,* and referred to the golden eagle. This sub-*Hunkah,* People of the Land, knew that the eagle was a robber of crows, stand-ing regally on leftovers of the buffalo drives, while crows and ravens and great vultures stood by like respectful subjects.

Yet they called him "the stainless one," in the same spirit in which the later immigrant politician was addressed as "the honorable" when he attained high office. This great bird attained heights as well and circled under the eyes of Grandfather the Sun, and was therefore well known and must be recognized despite his weaknesses. His known virtues of valor and ruthlessness and his ability to remain in the eye of the sun were not acceptable to the Little Old Men as a tribal sym-bol after they had watched the clean, swift courage of the clean-killing falcon, but for the People of the Land, he would be a glorious symbol for one of their gentes, since they need not be concerned with the purity of the sky in their choosing.

When this gens saw the golden eagle circling with majestic indolence immediately under the eye of Grandfather, they knew that they would always be noticed by *Wah'Kon-Tah* if they adopted such a symbol. Also, he as well as the black bear carried the color of the sacred charcoal on parts of his body and talons and beak tip.

And now the second gens of the sub-*Hunkah* gives the black bear his important place as a symbol, since he is properly of the earth. They make him a symbol within a symbol, or as a trope painted red. He was a very important symbol, and they recognized this fact in making the symbol of their sub-gens, a trope called *wah-sabe-skah*, the white black bear, to go along with another symbol, the white trumpeter swan. Surely the "white black bear" was a trope, since for ceremonial purposes the albino bear would have been too scarce, if such ever appeared.

The trumpeter swan was a very important bird, and really belonged to the People of the Waters, the *Wah-Sha-She*, but apparently since they failed to choose him, the People of the Land did so. The trumpeter embodied beauty and endurance and strength. All little people grew fatigued and breathless after long runs or flights; even the panther was known for his short wind. The swan flew on and on without tiring. He stood with dignity on the mud of the lake margin or swam with incredible grace and beauty like a dry sycamore leaf before the breathing of the late summer wind, and always in each generation, despite the warnings of his elders, some little boy suffered a broken arm from the wing strokes of the swan protecting his nest. He had dignity and grace on water and land and in the air, and no enemy could come near his home. Later the Little Old Men, aware of his virtues, would borrow him from this sub-gens as a military tribal symbol.

Wah-sabe, the black bear, did symbolize the sacred charcoal as well as very good sense and jocularity. He could be a great and very skillful hunter with power, and yet a peaceful planter of persimmons and blackberries as he wandered far and scattered his droppings over the earth. He was a clown and had a great sense of humor. He was like a resting warrior talking jestingly of his narrow escapes.

He furnished the Little Ones with clothes and meat and cooking

43

grease and medicine and beds, and they dipped sycamore splinters into his tallow and made torches, and they mixed his fat with clay to make paint, and his claws became amulets to be worn around the neck by warriors. He could climb trees like a scout and stand like a man.

The gens that took *i'n-gro'n-ḳah,* the panther, considered themselves very important because of the importance of their life symbol. The fireplace of the black bear gens and the fireplace of the panther were close together, and they were considered as being a unit, with one sub-gens between them.

The panther is closely associated with Grandfather the Sun, but the modern Little Old Men do not seem to know why. He discovered for the Little Ones several useful plants, bringing to them first the root of the *ci'n,* and they politely said that it would not do for food, but they could put it to another use. Then from the lake he brought the *tse-wa-the,* the food they depended upon always, the lotus fruit. He also brought them the root of the *do* which they depended upon for food, and then the wild bean, *ho'n-bthi'n-cu.*

The people attributed many noble deeds to the panther, especially the discovery of the roots of plants growing on the margin and in lake ooze which had to be dug up. This should have been the bear's province. However, the panther's discovery of the wild bean to the Little Ones was logical since he was a very skillful turkey hunter. Turkeys always come to growths of these beans.

And the Little Ones of the sub-*Hunḳah* gens who chose him for a symbol knew that he was no coward. He was a yellow-gray ghost with belly to the ground sneaking away, and part of a limb or rock when immobile, and not even the gods knew him from limb or rock, and when he lay waiting near the deer trails, the Moon Woman looked for him in vain. He was no coward, say the Little Old Men, because he slunk away from men, but wise. He was interested in living in order to attain old age and he had the valor to protect his life, and the strength and swiftness to kill his own food, avoiding leftovers and the bloated bodies of animals lying in the trail. He was an expert swimmer, say the Little Old Men, and the Little Ones sang to him for aid in crossing the Smoky Water during mild spate.

44

O'po'n, the wapiti, belonged as a symbol to the third gens of the sub-*Hunkah.* They made the body of the wapiti into the symbol of the earth upon which they walked. They said he discovered to them the four colors of the earth: dark, red, yellow, and blue clays, and here they disagree with the next gens of the sub-*Hunkah* and the Little Old Men as well, who say that it was the crayfish who brought up from the earth the four sacred colors of clay.

The Children of the Land say that when they first came near the great wapiti, the *o'po'n tonkah,* he stood and gazed at them, his antlers like the branches of a winter hickory. Then he turned and trotted off with knees high, and as he splashed through the edge of the water, his great bull hooves slashed the mud exposing the sacred colors of clay.

On seeing this, they followed him through the trees, then he stood and waited for them and offered himself as their symbol. They might see, he suggested to them, that when he threw himself upon the earth, he left hairs, and these hairs became the grasses of the land. He turned and asked them to note his rounded buttocks. Those humps, he said, were the rounded prairie hills; and the right side of his body was the level land, the plains; the ridge on his back, the land ridges; and the gaps in the ridges were represented by the downward curve of his neck between his head and the hump of his shoulders. The tip of his nose would be the peaks of the earth, and the knobby base of his antlers, the rocks strewn over the land. The large tines of his antlers were the river systems, and the smaller tines the creeks.

The next gens chose the crayfish. When this particular gens of the Children of the Land came along the roads of the earth looking for a symbol, the crayfish raised his arms and stopped them, offering himself. Of course they put their hands to their mouths, to restrain themselves. He saw them laughing silently behind their hands, and he became annoyed and went into the earth, then after some time came up carrying the four sacred colors of clay, one at a time. First he came up with the dark clay, then the red, the yellow, and the blue. Then, as if not sure he would be accepted, he raised his cloven hand and said that it symbolized the forked pole which supported the drying poles when they hung their meat to dry.

This gens took as its sub-gens symbol the Little Sacred One, the immature golden eagle, and it has to do with *i-ba-tse ta'dse,* the winds, since the immature eagle must first conquer the funneled winds of the deep canyons when he leaves his home high in the cliffs. The winds of the earth were important; they brought the snow and the ice slanting across the plains, bent the trees and made them angry, held the vulture motionless in the sky, tore at the lodge coverings, whispered in the prairie grass, and screamed like a crazy woman. They sent the fire across the prairie, causing the Little Ones to flee, or sent the crazy dancer, the tornado, down from the clouds, frightening the Little Ones to the sumac and oak saplings, to cling tightly to these plant people, who only bent to the fury of the wind.

The winds were both *Tzi-Sho* and *Hunkah;* they were peaceful and gentle, and yet they could scream in madness and send the lodge coverings across the prairie. They aided the hunter, even bringing to him the scent of the buffalo musk, and they brought secret messages to the camp dogs. They hid the noise of the hunter's approach as well as that of the warriors. They brought the odor of the campfire to the weary hunter, and they lifted the dust of the travois high into the air like smoke, and this could serve as a signal to the enemy or the searching kinsman.

The north winds brought snow and sleet and sent the Little Ones to cover, and the east wind chilled them to the marrow of their bones. The south wind swept the land clean of snow and whispered of spring, and the west wind was gentle, and when the Little Ones had it in their faces as they followed the path of Grandfather the Sun, they knew there would be no rain.

The Children of the Waters, the *Wah-Sha-She,* the Name Givers, the other division of the Grand *Hunkah,* would go to the oxbows, the marshes, the lazy waters, and the lakes for their symbols. But they too had met the panther and had admired his courage and his ferocious silence and arrow-swiftness, so one of their gentes chose him as a life symbol for a sub-gens. They named the sub-gens, Panther-in-the-Water, and the gens itself took for its symbol the fresh-water mussel and called it the *wah-sha-she-skah,* the white-name-giver. This sluggish mussel, lying hour after hour in the shallow ripples, was extremely important to the *Wah-Sha-She*. They sent this gens to wade the waters, or sit along the banks of the rivers, or on the marges of the lakes and marshes, in search of a proper symbol. At the confluence of the two chief forks, which the Little Ones called the Place-of-the-Many-Swans, they watched the dragonflies, the water striders, the frogs, the water beetles, the stately swans, the tall egrets, their bodies the white of day and the legs the color of night. They studied the whooping crane and the great blue heron that stood for hours like the splinter of a water-edge stump, waiting.

However, it was while wading the ripples of the river that they found the suitable symbol. They watched him jet water, they saw the wrinkles on his shell, and these wrinkles to them were the symbols of old age, and to attain wrinkles one had to live through many dangers, and they talked among themselves. "If we choose *tsiu-ge,* the fresh-water mussel, with the wrinkles of old age on his shell, we shall live to see old age." The mussel, much flattered by their attention, said, "I have passed successfully the seven bends of the river [River of Life], and in my travels the very gods themselves are unable to follow the trail, and your trails, Oh, Little Ones, will like mine be invisible."

The leader of the gens opened the shell and there shone brightly the pearly light of the god of day, and out of the shell they carved a gorget, round and shining, and in it made two slits, through which they passed the string made from the hide of *ta,* the buck deer, and tied the gorget close about their necks, and thereafter this was the sun, the god of day. This would also be worn by *xoka,* the initiator of the rites.

Another gens of the *Wah-Sha-She* sat long on the marge of the lake and finally chose the cattail as their symbol. Like the silent, utilitarian cattail, this gens remained silent in the ceremonies. They sat during the rituals in order to fill out the seven fireplaces. They used the cattail leaves and the stems in their lodge building.

The *Wah-Tse-Tsi,* the Star-That-Came-to-Earth gens, had as their sub-gens the bald eagle. The *"star that came to earth"* would be the star that the clear, still water reflected, and this gens of the Water People might have both a *Tzi-Sho* and a *Hunkah* symbol. Certainly as they wandered along the water courses and along the marge of the lakes, searching for a symbol of their element, they would be very much intrigued by the stars reflected in the water.

For the symbol of their sub-gens, which contributed the *shoka,* they chose the bald eagle. Although he apparently is one of the mighty hunters of the earth, he belongs equally to the water, since he is much more the fisherman than the hunter and is found near large bodies of water. Since he became a symbol of this sub-gens of the Water People, they overlooked his frailties, just as did the gens of the *Hunkah* who had chosen the golden eagle for their symbol, comforting themselves by calling him "the stainless one." However, in the bald eagle this gens of the Water People had much more to wink at.

While the golden eagle would gladly accept leftovers, and perhaps even take carrion if he were savagely hungry, he was a killer of his own prey most of the time, and his food in the spring was the fawns of the deer and the calves of the wapiti and the buffalo, while the bald eagle was a habitual robber and dead-fish eater. Nothing shone in the pre-mechanical world more brightly in the sun than quartz or selenite, but next to them surely would be a dead fish washed ashore by the wavelets of the lake. From his hunting station high above the waters, the royal one with the white head of old age and dignity would volplane and land heavily on mud or sand and eat his odorous dinner. Or he might wait for an osprey to make a difficult catch, then bluff him into giving up his prey.

The people of the Star-That-Comes-to-Earth gens admired the bald eagle for his strategy in robbing the osprey of his fish, but both birds appear in their rituals.

The gens who called themselves the Children-of-the-Deer, the *Ta-i-Nika-Shinkah,* seemed to have stayed in camp when they should have been out searching for a symbol, and also they seem to have chosen an animal, the deer, or "small animal," that might have belonged to one of the gens of the sub-*Hunkah,* since he was not of the water. One of the gentes of the Water People had already taken the panther and made of him an expert and voluntary swimmer, but this

48

gens made no attempt to make of the white-tail deer a water animal for ritualistic convenience, even though he is a real swimmer and will go to the water as a sanctuary when hard pressed. These characteristics are not mentioned in the songs of the gens about him. They only mention that he too carries the symbol of life everlasting, the charcoal, on the tip of his nose and the tip of his ears.

The story goes that this gens remained in camp and did not compete with the other gentes of the *Wah-Sha-She* for the more desirable symbols pertaining to water. As they sat indolently, a white-tail buck came bounding into the camp seeking refuge from the hunters. He bounded among the lodges, darting between them, dodging around them, clearing the cooking fires, then bounding untouched away. During this time the hunters had loosed their arrows at him, but no arrow had touched him, though several of them quivered from the lodge coverings, as the women scolded stridently and the dogs mouthed.

The indolent gens immediately chose the white-tail buck as their symbol. Through his cleverness in taking refuge in the very home of one of his enemies, through the artfulness of his dodging, and through his speed, he escaped unhurt. When they went on the warpath, or when they hunted as a gens, they sang his song, and asked his permission to take to themselves some of his fleetness, his cleverness, and his artfulness in foiling his enemies.

When this gens hunted the deer "people," the deer themselves advised these People of the Deer where they might find their "brothers." Under the white oak, where the earth is cut by sharp hooves and the grass worn away, but where the acorns lay; under the red oak, where the ground was disturbed by sharp hoof-cutting, but where the acorns lay; and under the twisted oak and the stunted oak (the blackjack), where the ground was cut and the grass worn, but where the acorns lay.

The *Wah-Sha-She Wa'no'n* gens took the snapping turtle as a symbol of their gens, and the cottonwood as the symbol of their sub-gens. The snapping turtle has a tail with seven serrations, and these became in the minds of the gens symbolical of the seven *o'do'n* or war honors, suggested by the rays of the sun on the right, or *Hunkah,* side. Also his carapace is impenetrable to arrows. The little boys first learned this in shooting at him, since their arrows were deflected.

The cottonwood trees were often the only large trees that would follow the rivers onto the high plains. They furnished light and fuel, as well as shade, for the Little Ones, and they pointed out the head-waters of the prairie rivers to them when they trudged wearily across the plains.

Ho-I-Nika-Shinkah were the Fish People, and they were also known as the exclusive owners of the bow, since it was their duty to make the ceremonial bow and arrows. Black as symbolized by char-coal was the everlasting evidence of irresistible fire, and red the sym-bol of dawn and sunset. Thus were the arrows for the war ceremonials painted, one black and one red, and the bow was painted black on the back and red on the inside. Red is also the color of day and black the color of night, and the pattern of day and night was never broken and thus was used as a symbol of life everlasting.

The Fish People gens of the *Wah-Sha-She* not only chose the little fish people as their symbol but chose also the beaver, the otter, and the willow tree, and they gave the tribe the right to ask the aid of their symbols, the beaver and the otter, when they desired to cross rivers in spate. The Little Ones stood on the slippery banks and sang their prayers to *Wah'Kon-Tah,* but they petitioned through the bea-ver, the otter, the turtle, and the eel, all empowered with ability which *Wah'Kon-Tah* had not given the Little Ones, but which, with permission from the empowered ones, they could use vicariously.

This gens of the *Wah-Sha-She* chose the red perch and the black perch as their symbols of life everlasting, since they bore the colors of life everlasting night and day. The otter, they chose because of his swiftness, and his skin became sacred and they made it into a tail-piece which the dancers wore. Also they made bandeaux of his skin, as they did with that of the beaver. The otter symbolized jocularity, relentlessness, and courage. He enjoyed life so intensely that he must always be doing something about it; he played tag in the water, ran up and down the banks of the rivers, chased another in circles both in the water and on the banks, and he made slides down the steep banks of the rivers. He would start at the top and slide down into the water, then clamber back up and repeat the slide. The drip from his fur kept the slide slick.

It was the beaver who presented the Little Ones of the *Wah-Sha-She* with the willow as a symbol of resistance and long life. It grew where the flood waters whirled about and over it, and was sucked under in the muddy waters, but always sprang back into life after the floods had receded—the beaver whose trail is straight through the water, leaving ripples on each side of him which are symbolical of the wrinkles of old age which it is one's duty to attain.

He swam to the first bend of the river and brought back willow saplings, then cut them into counting sticks, so that this gens of the Water People could keep their records. He swam successively to the seven bends of the river and each time brought back willow saplings, and cut them into counting sticks for the people of this gens so that they could count their *o'do'n,* or war honors, and other things, such as the days and the hours and the number of songs in the ceremonials. He gave them food and fur, and he would warn them with the splank of his tail on the water when man or animal disturbed him in his work or at his lodge or his home in the bank.

The last gens of the Water People named themselves They-Who-Clear-the-Way. This must have referred back to the travel order of the three groups from the sky when they first descended to the earth and began their search for the fourth group, the Isolated Earth People. It was the *Wah-Sha-She,* the Water People, who led the way, and this last gens of the Water People must have had that honored office of clearing the way from the beginning. Their name and their symbol seem to refer to the making of the way through the river bottoms overgrown with saplings and briers and entangling vines.

O-cu-ga-xe, They-Who-Clear-the-Way. *O-cu* means "tall weeds and lowland growths of saplings"; and *ga-xe* is the word for "make." This term "make" in the language of the Little Ones implies more than just the making of things. It may signify the destruction of things or the transmutation of things. In order to make lodge coverings and bullboats and shields and utensils and robes, you had to destroy the buffalo; and to make charcoal, you had to destroy the redbud tree; and to "make" tall weeds and lowland tangled growths, you destroyed enough of it to make a trail for the Little Ones.

The sub-gens of this gens called themselves Walkers-in-the-Mist, which would certainly lead one to believe that the gens was devoted to guiding. In the fogs and the mists, the Little Ones depended upon the moss of the trees and the stones, and the compass weed whose leaves point north and south, with the flat surfaces turned to the east and the sun and the west and the sun.

Even when there was no sun, the compass plant showed the Little Ones the way. Its bloom is of the yellow color which they loved, since yellow flowers were predominant during the Yellow-Flower Moon, the tranquil peacemaker season. The main stem of the compass plant exudes a gummy substance which the children of the Little Ones chewed.

4. "Move to a New Country"

WHEN THE newly-arrived-upon-earth children of the sky, represented by the *Wah-Sha-She,* the Water People, the sub-*Hunkah,* the Land People, and the grand division the *Tzi-Sho,* the Sky People, came upon the Isolated Earth People, the indigenous ones, the four groups formed a tribal unit, and were anxious to lead the Isolated Earth People away from the earth-ugliness of their village, saying that they were thus taking them to a "new country." This leading the Isolated Earth People, who became the Grand *Hunkah,* symbolizing the earth, away from the chaos of their earth dwelling was the "first move to a new country," and the second and third moves came as the Little Old Men organized the tribe. They spoke of these moves as one might speak of changing camping places, and each organizational step was a step away from the old, just as they walked away from the disorder of the old campsites, with their stamped grass, fire holes, cracked bones, and tattered bits of hide, horns, and hooves, bones of camp dogs, and ash ridges that sometimes circled the campsite. They left these places to grow up in yellow flowers.

The Little Old Men had begun to believe that the former Isolated Earth People, now called the Grand *Hunkah,* had not been influenced sufficiently by its sub-divisions, the Water People and the Land People, and might, if not controlled, bring about degeneration of the tribe, perhaps similar to their own degeneracy when the people from the sky first came upon them. Dividing the four groups into twenty-two original gentes, each with its living symbol, contributed little to order. Young men from the Black Bear gens, or from the Panther gens, or of the Wapiti of the sub-*Hunkah,* would violate the girls of the Peacemakers or the gentle *Tzi-Sho.* The young men in the fire of their youth and under mating urges pranced like the swollen-necked buck, or danced with knees high like the rutting wapiti bull under the September moon. They used the sacred paints to paint their faces fantastically, or hung lynx skins from their shoulders. They made necklaces and anklets of scarlet tanager feathers, or of the feathers of the cardinal and the parakeet.

They strutted among the lodges with their war clubs decorated into uselessness, as they themselves were too encumbered with decoration to be of any military use. They walked abreast, taunting, shouting obscenities to the girls and the women, laughing, clowning, exhibiting.

They often got together in groups and with war clubs and bows and spears walked out upon the plains in search of excitement, painted diabolically and burdened with their decorations, with not one thing sacred to *Wah'Kon-Tah* among them. They would attack anyone or any group on sight.

These young men vied with each other in the buffalo drives, and in their eagerness to perform some outstanding feat they might set fire to their brush piles too soon or wave a robe too soon, thus turning the frantic herd away from the gourd-shaped drive's important neck. They might single out a bull and wait for him with their spears and arrows, forgetting the drive in their emotion of self-glorification.

But the first move to a "new country" must have to do with the war movement, since self-preservation must come first, no matter the needs for other reformations.

The Little Old Men held long conversations about the condition of chaos, and they decided that, first, there must be more tribal authority, and that the bloody, disorganized power of the former Isolated Earth People, the Grand *Hunkah,* must be diminished, and the power of the *Tzi-Sho* must be increased until the two were equal. This could be done by appointing two grand chiefs of equal power for the tribe, one from the *Tzi-Sho* and one from the Grand *Hunkah,* and they would rule together, each with his province of action and each with his prerogatives, just as the earth and sky co-operate. They not only gave certain sacred offices to the two grand divisions, but gave special responsibilities to some of the gentes. The *Hunkah* grand division was given the honor of keeping the lodge where the naming ceremony was to take place. Here to this lodge, as they attained the proper age, the children of the various gentes were led to be named formally. This was very important, since they must have sacred names which would be protective and honor their gentile symbols. This was an earthly matter, since it was the things of the earth that were trying constantly to take away the people's "remaining days."

The sub-*Hunkah* was given the authority over the lodge wherein the war ceremony was performed, and given specifically in charge of the Black Bear and the Panther gentes. The black bear was a cunning hunter and a very powerful one, and the panther was the ultimate in stealth, ruthlessness, and protective coloration. However, these earth-prowling gentes were only in charge of the lodge of the war ceremonies, while the incitement of any war movement had to be under the supervision of the Black Bear gens, separated from his partner in mischief making, the Panther.

The Black Bear gens of the sub-*Hunkah* was associated in this authority with the *Wah-Sha-She* subdivision of the Grand *Hunkah*, the Grand *Hunkah*, and the *Tzi-Sho*, and each took a phase of the golden eagle for this special war symbol: the Grand *Hunkah*, the mottled, immature eagle; and the *Tzi-Sho* the eagle colored by dawn red, called "red eagle."

These four were empowered to punish any group of young men who might go out to attack a scouting party of the enemy and draw their anger to the camp of the Little Ones. There would be no war movement and no hunting movement, except for individual hunting with bow and arrow and spear when there was no community drive, without the consent of the organization authorized by the three divisions and the one gens. There must be order, and the *ga-ni-tha* of the earth must be displaced by sky order.

But only the first steps were taken toward the organization of the war movement, and later it would have to be expanded, but first there must be authority, and the establishment of this would constitute another "move to a new country."

The Little Old Men had chosen two principal chiefs for the Little Ones from two important gentes of the tribe. The *Hunkah* chief was chosen from the *Wah-Tse-Tsi*, Star-That-Came-to-Earth gens of the *Wah-Sha-She*, the Water People, and the *Tzi-Sho* chief was chosen from the most important gens of the *Tzi-Sho* grand division, the *Tzi-Sho Wa-No'n*, the Children of the Sun and the Moon and the Heavenly Bodies.

The office of this dual chieftainship was hereditary, except where the heir was temperamentally unsuited or indifferent to the tribal laws and customs, or one who might try to make a "move to a new country" without the consent of the Little Old Men.

The gentes from which these two grand chiefs were chosen were now honored and an honorary name was attached to each of them; they were known as *Wah-Shta-Ge,* meaning "gentle," and when these two gentes were mentioned, the title "gentle" was given. The *Wah-Sha-She* gens, so honored, was sometimes referred to as the *Po'n-Ka Wah-Shta-Ge*, Gentle Head Man, and the *Tzi-Sho* gens, which had given the *Tzi-Sho* chief, was called *Tzi-Sho Wah-Bi'n I-Ta-She,* Those-Who-Do-Not-Touch-Blood.

Naturally the *Tzi-Sho* chief was the peace chief and the *Hunkah* the war chief. In all the ceremonials, the *Tzi-Sho* chief took the left side and the *Hunkah* chief the right side from orientation. In the Lodge of Mystery, the path of Grandfather the Sun would be left between the *Tzi-Sho* side and the *Hunkah* side, running from east to west, and the *Tzi-Sho* would be on the north of this path and the *Hunkah* on the south, or on the left and the right respectively, with the symbolical warrior facing east.

When the Little Old Men chose the chiefs, they instructed that they must go out alone and fast for seven days and six nights to await a message of approval from *Wah'Kon-Tah.* They were to listen and watch for signs from the supernatural, concerning plants to be used for food and for medicinal purposes; especially would this be the province of the peace chief, the *Tzi-Sho,* while the *Hunkah* chief would listen for advice about war and hunting and earth utilitarianism.

The *Hunkah* chief set out with the downy feather from the under tail-feathers of the golden eagle attached to the right side of his head, so that *Wah'Kon-Tah* would know who he was. He set out strong and brisk, and his voice carried over the prairie as he sang his prayer to *Wah'Kon-Tah*. During the day, when Grandfather was directly overhead, he sat down to meditate, then he would resume his journey, and at night he would watch the sun go down and give up hope for that day that there would be a sign. He would rub the dark earth from his head where he had smeared it that morning, and with his head bent to the right, he would go to sleep.

Day after day he did this. He would be awakened by the sun in his face or by the morning star, then he would stand and chant his morning prayer to *Wah'Kon-Tah,* find some dark earth again, and, placing it on his head, set out over the prairie singing his prayer.

Then it was evening of the fifth day and there had been no sign from *Wah'Kon-Tah.* When he bent his head to the right, the *Hunkah* side, he fell into a sleep. During the next day's wandering over the prairie, sometimes he stumbled over tussocks or up-tilted limestone, as he grew weaker and weaker from hunger. He had had no food, only water from the prairie seepages and abandoned pools in the ravines. He became illusioned, and small patches of dwarf-plum thicket far out on the prairie became bears digging grubs and ant hills in groups, and the marsh hawk hunting down the ravines over the maze of fieldmice trails became two birds, separating, then merging. The prairie breeze that sprang up when Grandfather was well above the prairie tore the prayer-song from his lips, and it seemed that the pulsing drum rhythm of the earth had suddenly stopped, only to begin again, like the pulsing song of the katydid, the sticker-to-women's-breasts.

But Grandfather the Sun turned away his ears and there was no sign. The downy under tail-feather of the golden eagle was blown from the right side of his head, the *Hunkah* side of his head so that it bent to the left side, the *Tzi-Sho* side, and he had to hold it on the

57

right side as he walked along and sang his prayer to Grandfather. He must not do the least thing wrong, so he must hold the eagle feather upright on the right side, so that *Wah'Kon-Tah* would have no trouble recognizing him as the Grand Division chief chosen from the *Wah-Tse-Tsi* gens, the Star-That-Came-to-Earth gens of the *Wah-Sha-She*.

Grandfather seemed to grow weary too and dawdled along his path across the sky, but finally he sank in the west. The prairie breezes died and the talk in the grasses was stilled. The prairie chickens, the arrow-flight travelers, flew from the feeding ground to the roosting ground in clouds across the face of the sun, who was now red and sinking to his bed. A scout *ca-xe*, a crow, left the flock which were flapping across the prairie to their timber roost along the ridges. The *ca-xe* circled over the weary chief alone in boundless space, then, satisfying himself, he swung upward and flapped back to the flock as silently as he had come.

Grandfather sank behind the prairie-plains swells, and behind the cliffs to the west; behind the *Mo'n-Ha,* which was the name for both the cliffs and the west. The headwaters of the Osage River have cut deeply into the Carboniferous limestone, and farther west were the Permian cliffs and gorges where the swallow, the storm messenger, built his nest, and still farther west, the Rocky Mountains have disturbed the Permian, which rises in greater cliffs and buttes and is ever dressed in the sacred red. Thus, to the Little Ones, the west and cliffs are the same.

As the sun set, the last notes of the chief's prayer-song broke with a spiritless mumble. A wolf sang quaveringly, but this wolf song meant little to this child of the Star-That-Came-to-Earth gens. The chief looked at his willow sticks and saw that this was the evening of the sixth day. He sat on the prairie braced by his right arm. He wiped the vigil symbol from his head, since it would be bad medicine to leave it on all night when he was not praying. He lay on his right side, the *Hunkah* side, and groaned, since his joints were sore from five nights of lying on the hard prairie earth.

Suddenly the sign came in his hunger-dreaming, but the modern Little Old Men say that it was not a dream. The very old man did come to stand before the chief in his withered flesh, the modern sage ones say. His fingers clutching the willow staff were like the talons of the red-tailed hawk resting on a small limb. He was too old and shaky to pull his face hairs, and there were the scraggly patches of beard, grayed like the hair of the wolf. His buffalo robe was blackened from the smoke of many fires.

But his voice was strong. "My son," he said, "I have heard your cry and I have come to give myself to your people. I am Old Age." He extended a trembling hand and touched the chief. "When the Grandfather comes out of the prairie to look at you, go to that stream you see in the distance; walk up that stream and you will see a high bank, and under that bank where the winds cannot come, you will find me standing by the calm water." He disappeared.

Grandfather was just peeping over the prairie hills the next morning. This was the seventh day. The chief looked for the dark earth to put on his head again, but it was too dry. He stood facing the east until Grandfather flooded him with dawn red, then began his prayer, and the tears ran down his cheeks, and with his tears he wet the dark earth on his face and made it stick. When he had finished his morning prayer to *Wah'Kon-Tah,* he turned up the little prairie stream and again began the prayer-song he had been singing for six days. He turned upstream and walked until he saw the high bank. There, standing as the old man said he would be, was He-Who-Becomes-Aged-While-Still-Traveling, the white pelican, the philosopher of old age, he who, even when old, travels on the strong wings of youth.

The chief knew that the pelican was the very old man who had come to him the night before. Realizing this, he spoke courteously: "Oh, father, the Little Ones have nothing of which to make their bodies strong against old age."

The pelican replied: "When the Little Ones make of me their bodies, they shall always live to see old age." The chief immediately declared for his *Hunkah* people the signs of vicarious old age which the pelican exemplifies, a state difficult to achieve in the constant violent earth struggle of club and spear and fang, of lightning and tornado and *weh-lush-ka,* the little "people" who come with insects and with throat-rattler, the frost, and can't be seen.

There was no sound except the prairie breeze in the willows, and the chief and the pelican looked at each other. Then the pelican said: "Look at my shoulders with their slope of old age, but they work my strong wings tirelessly. And look at my wings; take seven of the feathers from the right one, and from them make awls for the Little Ones, and when they use the awls made from my wing feathers, the talk of their tattooing will be recognized at all times by *Wah'Kon-Tah*.

The chief took seven feathers from the right wing of the pelican, the *Hunkah* side, and thanked him and left. He felt stronger now and thought only of getting back to the village and food and rest, but as he stumbled along in his weakness, he came face to face with a very aged golden eagle. He stood on some drift left by the spring spate, where he had fallen from his last flight, old and weak now, after many moons flying under the eye of Grandfather—moons beyond the counting of the willow sticks of the Little Ones. But nothing had brought him to earth during all these moons; nothing could take away his remaining days, and now he had attained very old age, and there were no more moons remaining.

He turned his head to the chief and said: "The Little Ones shall make of me their bodies." He did this with great dignity. "Take back to them my wing feathers, so that they can make awls of the bones and use them to bring the Little Ones back from Spiritland [cupping]."

The eagle then gave the chief a downy feather from under his tail, and this was to be the symbol of old age softness and gentleness, and when stained red with pokeberry juice would be the symbol of the kindness of the *Tzi-Sho*. The red feather itself represents the odd red glow on the left side of the rising sun, a noticeable feather-shaped glow within the widespread dawn blush.

When the chief reached the village, he called the people together; he called together the people of both the grand divisions, the *Hunkah* and the *Tzi-Sho*, and told them of his experiences. This, of course, after he had eaten well and had slept for many hours. The people turned their ears toward him and the children sat silently like little owls, or wandered away quietly to play as their elders sat absorbed by the promises of long life vicariously from the pelican.

Almost immediately the pelican became a sacred symbol of peace and longevity, and as such he must have a shrine, like that of the sacred hawk, the war symbol. It would be larger but not more important, although it would be called the *Wah-hopeh Tonkah,* the Great Sacred Shrine.

The *Tzi-Sho* chief took a different direction from that taken by the *Hunkah,* but he chanted his prayer as he walked just as the *Hunkah* had done. He sang his prayer as he walked with uplifted face to Grandfather the Sun, and the tears wet his face.

Soon, he too became very tired and very hungry, and strange images came to him, and when he looked away from the sun, all colors of the spectrum flashed before his eyes, and certain geometrical patterns formed in his brain and remained for minutes. These he would remember so that they could be woven into the sacred shrines.

When the sun had gone into the prairie swells, he fell to the earth, leaning his head to the *Tzi-Sho* side, the left, and there lay in his robe until the sun appeared again to give the prairie-plains a red glow. Each morning as the sun appeared over the prairie, he would stand with outstretched arms and cry his prayer. When finished, he would resume his wandering, again wailing his song of supplication.

Buffalo bulls raised their shaggy heads from grazing and stood, black and immobile in the distance, looking at him intently. But they kept their tails of anger down, with only the prairie breeze playing with their beards and ruffling the hump-rib hair. In his hunger-illusions, the bulls would seem to move in un-buffalo-like lateral jerks, and sometimes they seemed to be talking to him, but he paid little attention to them since they were not the symbols of his gens.

The modern Little Old Men do not mention the prairie flowers, the voices of spring or summer, nor yet the weather; they mentioned the crow, the wolf, the bears, the marsh hawk, and the prairie chickens in the wanderings of the *Hunkah,* and only the buffalo bulls and the song of the coyotes during the wanderings of the *Tzi-Sho.*

As Grandfather went to his robes on the sixth day of the *Tzi-Sho* chief's vigil and the chief was removing the earth from his head, the coyotes sang like women doing the tremolo when the warriors dance, one far on the right, the *Hunkah* side, answering as if he had the blue earth of mourning on his head. But for the *Tzi-Sho* chief who was of the *Tzi-Sho Wa'no'n* gens, whose symbol was the sun himself, they had no message.

The coyotes ceased their laughing, their tremolo, their keening, and the prairie breeze died with the light, and strange dreams came to the chief. Then through the silence of early night he heard footsteps which grew louder, and soon a man stood before him, and he stood in an aura as if in the light of day. He spoke in a very strong voice but he was very old, balancing by the willow staff which his hawklike fingers clutched: "I have heard your cry. I am a person who can heal all the pains and the illnesses of your people, when the Little Ones make of me their bodies. They then shall live to see old age. In the morning, when the mists have cleared, go to that stream you see there in the distance, and follow it until you come to a bend, and there in the middle of the bend you will see me standing in the midst of the prairie winds. I am *Mo'n-Ko'n-Nika-Shinkah,* Little Man Medicine."[1]

When Grandfather appeared to glorify the prairie with a red glow, the chief wailed his morning prayer to him, then reached down and found some dark earth, and wetting it put it on his head, then, resuming his supplications, walked wearily toward the stream. He came to the bend indicated by the old man of his dream, and there, where the soil had been torn away by the angry water, stood Little Man Medicine.

The chief removed the soil from the root that looks like a little man, and was careful not to break it. This was the seventh day, and now he could return to the village, which was far down the stream, where the water stood all summer. He stumbled over the limestone rocks that the stream in its madness had rolled, and he struggled through the drift which it had left. He sat down often on the blue shale ledges along the banks, and as he rested he looked up and saw another bank from which the angry waters had torn the soil, and

1 The classical name for this plant is *Cucurbita perennis.*

there in the middle he saw another Little Man Medicine. He climbed up with the loose soil flowing down behind him, and very carefully dug the root. Its manlike legs were shorter than the first one, but it was thick through the hips, and he knew it was a female *Mo'n-Ko'n-Nika-Shinkah*.

The chief stumbled on downstream and soon the cottonwoods and the elms, like fingers from the downriver forest, welcomed him, and soon he saw the smoke from the fires of the village.

As the *Hunkah* chief had done, he called all the people together, both *Tzi-Sho* and *Hunkah,* and told them of his experience, and straightway the Little Old Men began to plan a shrine for the sacred root.

5. The Sacred Hawk

In their thin skins, the Little Ones would have frozen in winter, and during the summer the mosquitoes would have sucked their lives from them as they killed the summer caribou on the barrens of the north. The wind-blown sand in the plains part of their domain would have kept them cowed in their caves for days. Those things which *Wah'Kon-Tah* had given the buffalo, the wapiti, the deer, and the bear for protection against the elements, and did not give to the Little Ones, they took with permission from these animals through prayer and ritual. And through prayer and ritual they petitioned for the prowess of the little people. Thus did they pray through the panther, the buffalo, the turtle, the beaver, the otter, and the eel, as well as through the hawk and the eagle, and even the lowly spider, for arts and abilities which *Wah'Kon-Tah* had not seen fit to give them, the Little Ones. They needed the ability of the eel, the beaver, and the otter to aid them in crossing streams in spate, and the ability of the otter made childbirth easier for women. When they prayed they wore bits of skin and feathers, and whole skins of both animals and birds to whom they sang their prayers.

They sought the aid of all-devouring and devastating fire when they blackened their faces with his charcoal, and the leaders of the war movement wore the skin of the falcon about their necks.

The Little Old Men had sat long and watched the falcon in his hunting. Anyone who has ever watched a falcon hunting, either on his own or as flown from a hunter's wrist, knows that there is nothing more inspiring. There must have been a long period of indecision, however, before they chose him over the eagle and the osprey and the red-tailed hawk, the last named with the dawn of Grandfather the Sun on his tail. But apparently, after a long season of observation, they became convinced, as have many others, that, of all the animals and birds, the falcon is the most admirable, in savage courage, with a swiftness so great that one had not time in which to defend himself against its attack, and with a ruthlessness that is fascinating in its silence and cleanliness. To the ancient Little Old Men, and to some modern ones, the falcon seemed to have a very long life, since through all their years of close observation they had never seen a falcon defeated or destroyed by his enemies. The osprey was bullied out of his prey by the bald eagle, but never the swift, sure, arrogant falcon. They noted too that the prairie falcon came back year after year to the same nesting spot, and they had piles of willow sticks as a record of these returns. The fact that they had no way of knowing whether the returning pair were the same pair year after year or their offspring taking over the old home was of little concern. If certain knowledge had favored the eventual taking over of the nest by offspring or a strange pair, they still might have shut their eyes when discussing it, in order to keep the satisfying illusion from escaping them. They must have a double-edged symbol for the two most important necessities of their existence: military adequacy and the longevity of the individual and the tribe.

But there is evidence, even so, that the *Wah-Sha-She,* the Water People, wanted to adopt the osprey, since he was of the water, really, and lived on fish. According to the modern Little Old Men, especially those of the *Wah-Sha-She,* they had liked the way in which the osprey splashed the surface of the water and came up with a fish, and the nervous fright he inspired among the others of the water. The grackles feeding along the marge of the lake, and the blue-winged teal feeding among the reeds would rise and circle in reconnaissance, and coots would run on the water, splashing their way into the air. The frogs leapt from their hunting stations and the turtles rolled off their logs. All this indicated the great importance of the osprey, but still he feared the bald eagle.

But when the Little Old Men watched the prairie falcon take a passenger pigeon on the wing or a duck hawk outfly a blue-winged teal, without disturbing very much the other members of the flock, they finally made their choice. As a matter of fact, they had seen the prairie falcon or the duck hawk strike such terror in the heart of a passenger pigeon that he would fly in fright into the lodges of the Little Ones, and they had seen these two falcons attack birds bigger than themselves.

They chose the smaller falcon over the bald eagle as the most important of symbols after they had seen the big fellow magnificently steal a fish from the osprey, because later they had seen him alight heavily at the lake's edge to eat the stinking dead fish washed ashore. They chose the hawk over the golden eagle because they had seen this great bird, who circled with regal dignity just below Grandfather the Sun, glide from his high throne-cliffs to chase the ravens and the crows away from the bloody leavings of the Little One's buffalo drives, shaking his head like any earth person to rid himself of the swarming green flies.

The falcon was not a slave of the Sacred One, the Earth, whom he symbolized, but spent much of his time winging his way across the sky, always with arrow swiftness. The Little Old Men said he must be born of heaven, the child of Grandfather the Sun and the Moon Woman, and they straightway made him so, and they gave him a shrine of three coverings. They said the valor of the falcon must be the valor of the men of the tribe, so that the tribe could not be overcome by their enemies, and it must be this valor, speed, ruthlessness, alertness, and freedom from the bonds that bind the little ones of the earth that would keep intact to the Little Ones their remaining days.

The hawk became a being somewhere between the Sacred One and the Sky Lodge, favored of both and a son of both.

The gentes had chosen a great variety of life symbols, from the graceful white trumpeter swan to the little black spider; from the powerful, arrogant buffalo bull to the crayfish. All but a few of these had military significance. However, it was the swan who was chosen for a war standard.

The Little Old Men had a sort of bishop's crook made from a

hickory limb, six or eight feet in length, seasoned over the fire to effect the recurving for the crook. About this crook, they wrapped the plucked skins of the trumpeter swan; skins plucked of the coarse feathers only. After wrapping the hickory crook completely, they suspended the tail-feathers of the golden eagle from it by a bit of rawhide thong, so that the feathers would be agitated in the wind. There were three tail-feathers suspended from the tip end of the crook, two from the upper part of the staff, two from the middle part, and two from the bottom, just above the sharpened end which was stuck into the ground. This was the standard of the Little Ones, their pennon, their flag, and the leader carried it on ceremonial military forays, stuck it into the ground and fought for its protection.

They chose the swan for this office because he was beautiful, very graceful, and more dignified than any other bird or animal, even the bull wapiti, they believed. The pelican was the symbol of philosophy and the sagacity of old age, the one who continued to travel strongly even in old age, but the trumpeter swan was the symbol of youth and beauty and grace and dignity and strength, and not even *sho-mi-ḳasé,* the coyote, dared come near his nest on the prairie marshes. The blow from his wing was a terrific one and quite often disabling.

Thus did this life symbol of the sub-gens of the Black Bear gens of the sub-*Hunḳah* become a tribal military standard. There were also other fetishes for the dangerous enterprises of the war movement. There was, of course, the sacred charcoal made from the redbud tree with which the warriors blackened their faces, and there were the wolf songs, taken vicariously from the real wolf song of the plains and the timber, and there were the special songs of the different gentes; the song-prayers to the panther, the bear, the eagle, the pileated woodpecker, and the white-tail buck, but the falcon embodied all the virtues which the tribal warriors assumed for themselves. They saw themselves as falcons, swift and sure and ruthless, coming back to their village with their victory and with no fear of retaliation. This swift arrow-flight out of the sun to the prey, the savage courage to strike without hesitation over the size of prey or enemy, or the circumstance, and the silence and dignity and arrogance and indestructibility were characteristics which *Wah'Kon-Tah* had not given the

Little Ones, and when they found them in the falcon, they straightway assumed them, by prayer-song to the one who had them.

Apparently man universally, and from the beginning of civilization, has admired the falcon through a species of warrior-hunter-observer self-identification with flight, courage, daring, and ruthlessness, along with swift and effective retreat.

When the Little Old Men made the fetish, they cut the skin down the back for the extraction of the body. When the skin was dried, they placed it in a woven buffalo-hair bag. This, in turn, was placed inside a deerskin bag and the whole placed within a woven rush bag and tied. From the carrying strap of deerskin was suspended a scalp-lock contributed by the Black Bear or Panther gens, and also from the strap was suspended an eagle's tarsus with outspread claw. This was hung below the woven rush outer covering, or shrine cover, and represented the hunting eagle, who was always with outstretched, ready talons, and the scalplock represented the defeat of the enemy.

At first, the dried skin of the hawk was wrapped in the buffalo-hair bag and the deerskin covering, thus honoring the buffalo and the deer, but one afternoon when a party of the *Wah-Sha-She* were coming across the prairie on their return from a scout, a blue-black cloud rose out of the northwest and, without spitting one drop of rain, shot forth a crooked lance of lightning, killing several of the party. Their leader was carrying the *wah-hopeh,* the sacred hawk skin in its buffalo-hair bag with the buckskin covering, but this did not protect the scouts.

The survivors came into the village carrying their comrades and singing the song of death. The Little Old Men looked at the sky in fear, then fanned away the evil spirit from the bodies with an eagle-tail fan, as the dead warriors sat limp, tied to trees, with their heads on their chests. The women keened and the Little Old Men walked to the Lodge of Mystery to get some message from *Wah'Kon-Tah.*

After long hours of prayer-song, it came. The sacred bundle, the *wah-hopeh,* was not properly covered, and since the scouts were of the *Wah-Sha-She,* the Water People, the deerskin was not completely protective obviously; there must be something else from these people.

The women relatives of the dead warriors were not yet finished putting the blue earth of mourning on their foreheads when the Little Old Men sent out the first messengers to gather a suitable rush belonging to the Water People for the weaving of a rush covering for the sacred bundle.

One of the messengers came back to the village from the limestone prairie with some bluestem grass in his hand, but the Little Old Men said, "Younger brother, this will not serve." Another came with red grass, and again they said, "This will not serve." They said this with great courtesy, even though the messengers were quite young men. Another came in with the marsh reed from the borders of a half-moon lake, but this was not the proper rush, so he came back with a ribbed reed from the same lake, noting the Little Old Men's interest in the shape of the lake. When they turned the ribbed reed down, the messenger came back with the large rush. When he was assured that this was not the proper reed, he went back to the lake and pulled off his clout and his moccasins and waded out to the center of the lake, where grew a thin rush which was later called *ca-shinkah,* and which was the same size from the bottom to the top of the stem. The messenger came before the Little Old Men with the slightest belt of miniature flotsam about his middle. The Little Old men accepted this perfect rush immediately, and the young man was so proud that he only stood and looked into the distance menacingly, to veil his emotion, as the holy men praised him.

This would do for the woof of the weave, now there must be something for the warp. This must be stronger, and they thought of the linden tree, from the bark of which the Little Ones made some of their strings and some of their ropes. They also used the wood for the making of their bowls. This tree was an old friend of the Little Ones and gladly gave up its fiber and bark and wood to the messenger of the Little Old Men, but the Little Old Men thought the fiber just a bit too rough for the warp of the sacred bundle. The messenger went back into the deep woods to the east, and there he found a small linden, a sapling, but its fibers were too tender, and he sought out the various growths and brought them to the Little Old Men, but still they said they would not do, first for one reason and then for another.

The eager messenger wanted the honor of discovering the right rush or fiber, and he wandered further into the woods along the lower river, and there he found the pawpaw, from which the Little Ones got their most delicious fruit, but the fibers of this tree were not quite the thing for the sacred shrine.

The messenger was disappointed, and the Little Old Men themselves wanted to honor these two old friends from the downstream forest, since they were useful, but not only that, they gave deep pleasure to the Little Ones; one in the spring or early summer, the other in the early autumn, as it brought forth its long, mushy fruits. In the spring, the linden sent its perfume through the woods on subtle little currents, searching out the Little Ones as they moved through the trees.

Finally the messenger came back with the nettle weed, which was found suitable by the Little Old Men, and again they gave praise to the "young brother" who brought it.

Now, with the outer covering made of woven rushes, all the four divisions would be represented. The Grand *Tzi-Sho* would be represented by the covering made of buffalo hair, and the Grand *Hunkah* by the skin of the hawk itself; the sub-*Hunkah* would be represented by the outspread eagle talons and the scalplock given by the Panther and the Black Bear gentes; and now the *Wah-Sha-She* would be represented not only by the deerskin wrapping but by the outer covering made of rushes of the water province, and the whole would be under the direction of the *Wah-Sha-She,* and the making of the shrine was in the hands of three of the gentes of the *Wah-Sha-She:* the *Wah-Sha-She Wa-no'n,* or Elder, Turtle, and the Cattail gentes.

Wah'Kon-Tah ought now to be pleased and strike the warriors and hunters of the Little Ones no more when they carried the sacred hawk about their necks. Even the messengers which the Little Old Men had sent in search of suitable rushes, up and down the river and into the woods, were young men of the *Wah-Sha-She,* and the woman they called in to weave the shrine was of the *Wah-Sha-She.*

The Little Old Men sat gravely, when their minds were finally made up concerning the designs to be woven into the rush covering. There must be designs representing the clouds between the earth and the sky, since the sacred hawk was symbolically between earth and sky, and there must be a pocket in the weaving for the hawk skin, and this pocket must be made from the weave by folding the bottom up about a third the length of the weave and fastening the ends with fiber from the linden tree or with deerhide thongs. On this pocket must be designs representing both the sky and the earth. The tying of the ends to make the pocket of the folded part must be done with ceremony. One end must have seven ties, representing the *Hunkah,* and this end would point toward the south and right, when the bundle was placed with its length at right angles to the east. South is the direction to which the hawk's head would point. The other end would have six ties and point to the north and left, since the long side of the bundle faced east. This of course would be the *Tzi-Sho* side.

The Little Old Men sent *shoka,* the messenger, to bring the shy and honored woman to them. She came in silently behind the *shoka* and looked about the Lodge of Mystery with quick, cornered-coyote glances and sat down on the packed earth floor at the farthest point from the Little Old Men. They presented her with a buffalo robe with the hair on it and a black bear skin, and told her she must follow their instructions about the symbolical designs they had visualized, and they had the *shoka* sing the song for her which they had made for the occasion. She was to sing this song as she worked before her loom; a wailing song about death and the loved ones who had gone away, a lamentation.

The woman's loom was a primitive affair of two stakes and two slats, the latter perforated to hold the *ha-do-ga,* the nettle weed used for the warp, and the tine of a deer antler was used for the shuttle to run the woof made from *ca-shinkah,* the little rush. A deer tine was also used as a batten.

The woman must not be disturbed in her sacred weaving or in her singing, and her relatives must not see her at her work, hence it was necessary to build a small lodge by the side of her family lodge, and there she entered with an armload of nettles and rushes, her stakes and her slats and her deer antlers. After she had arranged all the material just so, she went to her robes and slept until the Male Star, the Morning Star, shone brightly in the east, then she stepped outside her lodge and took up some dark earth, moistened it, and rubbed

71

it on each side of her forehead, the left for the *Tzi-Sho* and the right for the *Hunkah*. She must have chanted her prayer to *Wah'Kon-Tah* as was the custom, but the modern Little Old Men are not sure of this.

Anyway she re-entered and put on the buffalo robe, then spread the bear skin and sat on it, with her legs together and straight out in front of her. Then, with the stakes stuck in the earthen floor on each side of her and the warp fixed to the perforated slats, she began her work, all the while singing her song of lamentation. She took no food, and when the dark earth dried on her forehead, she renewed it.

For four days she wove and sang, sometimes weeping when she remembered the members of her family who had gone away, and in her song were sobs that turned into wails of inconsolable grief.

On the fourth day she took her weaving to the Little Old Men, hollow-eyed and very shy. The woman temper had gone from her, and there were only fear and tension with tears and wailing just under the surface.

The holy ones took the weaving and approved of it, and the woman looked at her moccasins. They folded the lower end to form the pocket, and used their eagle-wing awl to punch holes for the linden fiber or the deer thongs, seven on one end and six on the other. As they did this, they recited the prayers which they called *wi-gi-e*.

When the pocket was made, the Little Old Men placed the hawk's skin in it, in its wrappings of buffalo-hair weave and buckskin covering. The other part of the rush weaving represented the flap which would be wrapped around the pocket. There is sometimes a deerskin tobacco pouch, but always the scalplock and the eagle's talon attached to the folded bundle, which has been tied with a buffalo hair rope, *wi-gi-es* being recited during every move until the bundle is completed.

Now it belongs to all the children of the four groups, the two grand divisions and the two subdivisions. It is sacred and must not be touched by anyone who has not the proper authority. When it is opened, it must be opened only by him who has that authority, and the skin of the hawk must always be brought out of the wrappings with an upward and forward movement, head first in simulation of birth. Nothing must be taken out with the backward movement, since Grandfather the Sun never moves backward. Only the crayfish and a few others of the little people can move backward, because it is obvious that he is only retreating strategically, even as the warrior may retreat with face to the enemy.

After the *wi-gi-es* of the perforating ceremony and the making of the pocket, and before the weaving is folded over, a black pipestone pipe is filled and handed to the head of the *Wa-no'n,* or Elder, gens of the *Wah-Sha-She,* and as he smokes he offers prayers for all the people of all the gentes. The smoke ascending carries the prayers of all the people up to *Wah'Kon-Tah,* then he tells the long story of the finding of the Little One's "tobacco."

He goes on and on monotonously, and the listeners let their heads fall forward and shut their eyes. He tells in a monotone how the young men from his gens, the *Wa-no'n,* were sent out to find a plant which could be smoked, and they came back with a variety of plants, and each time the leader of the gens and the Little Old Men would with deep courtesy say, "This will not do." And the "younger brothers" would try again. One messenger came back with a plant which the European late-comers called "Indian tobacco," and others brought in others. There was a plant brought in with leaves like the ear of the bull wapiti, but even with this significance, the Little Old Men grimaced when they inhaled the smoke. The compass weed was brought in, and they wanted to use it, since this weed, along with the moss, the lichen, the stars, and the sun, gave the Little Ones the directions, but they grimaced and spat, waving the messenger away to try again.

This same messenger left the prairie where the compass weed grows and wandered along the river into the forests to the east. He searched at the edge of the water and found nothing, then he looked up into the elm and there saw a great ball of mistletoe. This, he thought, must be a hint from *Wah'Kon-Tah,* bringing his eyes up to that ball. He climbed the tree and knocked the plant loose and it fell to the bank of the river. He carried it back to the Little Old Men with great pride. He told them that the plant had been pointed out to him by a sign, pulling his eyes up from the bank of the river where he had been searching, and the Little Old Men upon hearing this

73

believed that he might have the thing for which they had been searching. However, when they put it in their pipe and smoked it, they made wry faces and coughed and said that the stuff could not be inhaled.

Then the chief messenger, the *shoka,* went out to search, but he walked up the river onto the prairie. His eyes were drawn to the side of a ravine, where a patch of sandstone formed an escarpment and there seemed to be blood seeping from the wounded earth. He came closer and found a small bush with red leaves. He gathered some of them and took them back, saying to himself, "Surely this can be inhaled." But when the Little Old Men smoked it, they said it wouldn't burn long enough and that the *shoka* must find the brother to it. The *shoka* climbed to the top of the hill, and there stood the other sumac. He gathered the leaves and brought them back. The Little Old Men dried them and smoked them and said, "This is what we have been looking for; the smoke of this brother shall represent the prayers of all the people."

They then made many pipes, some of the red pipestone clay and the black pipestone clay which they got from their kinsmen, the *Wa-Zho-Xtha,* by the later European called Otoes, who lived near the Blue Earth Country up the Big Water. They fastened the stem to the bowl with a deerhide string on which they had strung little shells.

6.   The Commandments

In the traditions of the Little Ones, organization of the war movement and the precious fetish the sacred hawk was a "move to a new country." But soon the necessity to move again grew out of the last. The Little Old Men, reacting from the *ga-ni-tha* of the spirit and energy of the young men, had really bound the war movement so effectively in ceremonial that when the scouts came in to say that the "enemy out of the west" were seen, the eager young men, smeared with charcoal and wearing shields and carrying spears, stood about waiting for authority to counterattack. The *wah-tsde-pia'n,* the town crier, ran wildly up and down the village ways beating his pronghorn-skin drum, weeping and mourning his alarm chant. The appointed ones of the three divisions and the one gens leader failed to get together with sufficient speed, and the Little Ones had to go out against the enemy in the old Isolated Earth People manner, while the women herded the children to the thicket of the ravine's bottom, keening.

The enemy were finally driven away, with the Little Ones advancing over them like a prairie fire, and several of the wild-eyed young men came back leading captives with their captive-straps. They were bound and tied to trees, and there was no law to protect them. The women taunted them and the children threw stones at them, and the camp dogs bristled and barked at them and lifted their legs against them when they found them bound and harmless. The little boys shot at them with their fire-blunted arrows.

Those who had been killed were left lying where they had fallen and the crows came to quarrel over them, and it was said that when they were sated, one of them left a black feather in the open mouth of one of the fallen enemy. Some of the people stood watching the crows come, two and three and four or five at a time, to fight above the bodies, and they made a song, the famous *Ca-xe Wah-T'ho'n,* the Crow Song, which was later adopted and sung ceremonially.

But they didn't know what to do with the captives, so they killed them and cut off their heads and placed them on poles and on trees around the camp, so that the enemy scouts could see them.

The Little Old Men stood and watched, and they said among themselves, "This is *ga-ni-tha;* we must make another move to a new country." After several days in the long Lodge of Mystery, they called the people together and said that hereafter the various gentes of the tribe could organize war parties, but they could not carry the *wah-hopeh,* the sacred war bundle, the skin of the sacred hawk. Any of the gentes of either of the grand divisions could form a war party, under the authority of the division chief. A small war party was authorized, composed of one or more of the gentes of either of the grand divisions, and in a third category, a war party could be organized by one single gens.

This made speedy retaliation possible, but it also gave a gens leader who might have a rather small sense of responsibility licence to go out looking for trouble. Sometimes a leader or chieftain of one of the *Hunkah* gentes might feel more obligated to the symbol of his gens than to tribal or divisional authority in a circumstance where the tribal unit was not in danger.

As a matter of fact, it has been said by a member of the *Wah-Sha-She* subdivision that once upon a time, a leader of the Wapiti gens of the sub-*Hunkah* came under the influence of his symbol one moonlit night in September, the rutting season of the wapiti. He dressed in his war paint, fastened the antlers of a spike bull wapiti to his wapiti-skin headpiece, and came out of his lodge dancing, with his knees high like a trotting bull. He threw back his head and challenged in a very good imitation of the bull wapiti's high-pitched challenge, even to the terminal grunt, as if the high intensity of his emotion had snapped.

Naturally people came to watch him. He advanced with his high-kneed dancing toward a group of girls and women, and they fled, giggling. There was one there who stood fascinated in a sort of submissive glow as he danced around her. Then suddenly grunting like an enamoured bull, he took hold of her, but she didn't pull back, and he led her to his lodge. The women came back, and cutting their eyes at his lodge, they broke out in explosive giggles.

That night the crazy leader of the Wapiti gens took a number of his young men on the war movement after killing the husband of the girl.

The relatives of the slain man waited for his return, and the Little Old Men said among themselves that something must be done. The war movement had been organized, and the great tribal buffalo drives were being systematized under the new divisional chiefs, but now they must leave their organization of the buffalo hunts and go immediately to a "new country" to escape the spirit of the Isolated Earth People. There must be civil law, and they sat long in the Lodge of Mystery, and their thoughts were on this leader of the Wapiti gens and on the relatives of the slain husband. The relatives carried their war clubs in the folds of their robes, and were sullen, and all day their scout sat in the forks of a great cottonwood gazing across the shimmering plains.

Then, after a night of counciling, the Little Old Men came from the Lodge of Mystery to join the people of the village as they stood in front of their lodges and sang their prayers to Grandfather the Sun as he peeped over the forest to the east.

After the wailing and the mourning prayer of the people had ended and the camp dogs had stopped their howling and crept back to their leaf beds under the wind, *wah-tsde-pia'n,* the town crier, went up and down the village ways singing that there would be a meeting of the leaders of all the fireplaces in the Lodge of Mystery. There the Little Old Men told the leaders of the "new road" they had taken. "It has been said in this lodge," they said, "when two men fight and

77

threaten to kill, the chiefs shall make them stop. When murder is committed and the relatives of the murdered man are not satisfied with the peace-gift and want to take the life of the murderer in compensation, the chiefs shall cause the relatives to keep the peace. If the leader of the relatives persists in his intention to lead his kinsmen against the murderer, the chiefs shall expel him from the tribe." This was perhaps the harshest punishment within the authority of the chiefs, since in this Neolithic society, unit protection was imperative for the individual.

"If the relatives accept the offer, the pipe is handed to the leader of the relatives by one of the principal chiefs. If he smokes the pipe and then in a fit of anger and remembered wrongs, he kills the murderer anyway, the chief may order his death.

"If the relatives of the murderer refuse to bring peace-gifts to the murdered man's relatives, the people of the village may be called upon to do so; then the leader of the murderer's relatives must be expelled.

"If a man is threatened by another and his life is in danger, he may flee to the lodge of the *Tzi-Sho,* the peace chief, and there enjoy complete sanctuary. The lodge of the *Tzi-Sho* chief as well as the lodge of the *Hunkah* chief have opposing openings, one facing the east and one the west, so that the road of Grandfather the Sun may run through without obstruction. In the center of each of the lodges, between the two openings, are the sacred fireplaces, one in each lodge, and both of these are sacred peace fireplaces and dedicated to the peacefulness and the tranquility and order of Grandfather the Sun.

"The man threatened with murder may come from the east on the road that Grandfather takes daily, and walk into the lodge of the chief, and no one dares to enter there to take him. Even a stranger may have this sanctuary, even though he may be a man from the bitterest enemy of the Little Ones."

The Little Old Men thought of the captives who were decapitated and desecrated, and they made a law. When, they decreed, the war party comes home with captives, the chiefs may, as they see fit, save their lives and make them members of the tribe. This is the office of

Tzi-Sho Wa-Shta-Ge, the gentle *Tzi-Sho,* the Givers-of-Life, symbolized by the life-giving sky and the sun.

As the leaders of the gentes went back to their lodges, there was probably no discussion about the Little Old Men's omission of rape and adultery in their "ten commandments." Nor was there any mention of theft or covetous eyes on the property of others. While there was at this time no mention of rape, there were old women appointed to act as *dueñas* in each gens, and they carried weapons like a body guard, and along with the weapons they carried respect and embodied taboos.

7.   The Tribal Hunt

WHEN THE LEADERS of the gentes left the Lodge of Mystery, the Little Old Men went back to their meditations about the organization of the buffalo drives. There was no desire on their part to restrict the hunting of the individual with bow and spear, if he went for deer or wapiti or even buffalo; they simply came to the conclusion that the drives must be a communal effort, like war. The organization of the tribal hunt was the organization of tribal economics, and there was no place for individual exhibitions of bravery or marksmanship, or other histrionics to which the young men, by their very nature, were prone.

The Little Ones who hunted for sport and out of necessity could not hope to supply the villages or the camps with food, lodge coverings, cooking utensils, robes, beds, shields and bullboats, no matter how well they hunted or how plentiful the game. So the Little Old Men organized the buffalo drives. First, scouts would be sent to locate the herd, then the principal chiefs, the *Tzi-Sho* and the *Hunkah,* would go out to choose a location for the hunting camp. They must take into consideration many things. They must consider the terrain and the water supply, and a camp, no matter whether it were to be semi-permanent or just temporary, must be a military one in all respects. It must not be capable of being surprised, since, like wolves, the tribes of men must also follow the buffalo, and where one found the buffalo, one also found men and wolves and coyotes and crows and ravens and, in the spring and summer, vultures.

There must be terrain which would facilitate escape. The chiefs must consider the temper of the herd. Were they restless? If so, was this restlessness due to the conditions of water and grazing or to barometric conditions that made the smoke of the campfires hug the earth and not ascend in columns? Also, what were the coyotes saying? Was there a storm coming? If so, the Little Ones must hurry.

The two principal chiefs then led certain members of each of the gentes to the place which they had selected as a hunting camp. It may have taken them a day or two days or even three to reach the place from their village. A man may walk four miles an hour, but the scouts of the Little Ones could make much better time than this since they traveled in a wolf-trot, and could perhaps make six or seven miles an hour. A man may walk four miles an hour, but only if he is alone or with others also unburdened. However, a hunting-camp movement meant that the women and the children and the dogs and impedimenta must go along. Travois would be overturned, and there would be vicious dog fights and stops, and camping places had to be carefully selected on the way, each one named for terrain, topographic features, a lone tree on the plains, a death, an old buffalo bull driven away from the herd by the younger bulls, a growth of certain flowers, a certain type of water, color of the earth, a humorous incident, or a young man's prank.

From the permanent village to the first camp stop, both the grand chiefs were in authority, but thereafter they alternated; one day the *Tzi-Sho* was in charge and the next day the *Hunkah,* and on the last day of the return journey, when the village was the objective, both chiefs had equal authority again.

For the carrying out of his orders the *Tzi-Sho* chief appointed five warriors from both grand divisions as *a'ki-da,* soldiers, and the *Hunkah* also appointed five from both divisions. These were men who had counted many *o'do'n,* military honors, and this was a citation. The *Tzi-Sho* gentes so honored were the People-Who-Were-Last-to-Come, the Mystery gens, or Thunder People, and the Buffalo Bull gentes. These choices were obvious. The thunder had to be placated, and they had to be in favor with the buffalo bull. The other gentes of the *Tzi-Sho* were the Sun and Moon gens, the Buffalo Face gens and the Carriers of the Sun and Moon, including, of course, the sub-gens of the Sun and Moon gens, the Awakeners.

All these are obvious selections. First, the heavenly bodies and the sub-gens the Awakeners; they needed the favor of the one and to be constantly alerted by the other. And, of course, the Carriers of the Sun and Moon, or as it was referred to, Carrier-of-the-Heavenly-Bodies must be present, and the Buffalo Face as well.

For the *Hunkah* five *a'ki-da,* there was one each from the Black Bear gens and Panther gens counted as one, one from the Deer People, the Wapiti gens, the Eagle gens and the Isolated Earth People's one gens, the Spider, with its symbolism of all things coming to its house and breaking their necks therein.

These were also obvious choices. The cunning of the black bear with his coat symbolizing in its desolation phase the all-conquering fire, combined with the stealth, straight-to-the-objective, and silence of the panther were necessary. The reason for including the Deer People gens representative on a buffalo drive is not quite clear, but the winged one, the eagle scouting power, and the spider power of the grand *Hunkah,* the erstwhile Isolated Earth People, were essential. Also, the wapiti in his body conformation and color was symbolical of the yellow plains and the contours and rivers and stones.

There must be leaders of the ten *a'ki-da,* said the Little Old Men, so they designated the leaders of the *a'ki-da* from three of the gentes: one from the Black Bear gens, inevitably; one from the Deer gens; and one from the Thunder gens of the *Tzi-Sho.* These leaders of the *a'ki-da* became very special soldiers and were honored with special titles.

The soldier leader from the Thunder gens of the *Tzi-Sho* was given the title of Chief Soldier, the one from the Deer gens was given the title of Little Soldier, and the one from the Black Bear–Panther gentes was called Big Soldier.

After noting the quality of the grazing, the water, and the restiveness or tranquility of the herd, the chiefs and the leaders had to note the nature of the drainage and the erosion. The security of a very busy camp must be considered, since a hunting camp was very busy, and the enemy, taking advantage of the busyness, would make a sneak attack. There must be valleys and washes that offered escape. This was the military aspect; but besides this, there must be deep canyons bordered by abrupt escarpments, so that the herd would fall over the edge through the gourd's neck of the drive.

The Little Old Men decreed that there must be perfect order, a reflection of the order of the sky. Each man knew his duty under the direction of the *a'ki-das,* who in turn carried out the order of the chiefs. There were certain men who must approach the herd down wind, so that the herd might scent the men even before seeing them, keeping the scent of the men in their noses, with their eyes for the down-wind front [they ran almost invariably into the wind] however upon first scenting the men, they had already entered the gourd-shaped drive, and were moving toward the neck. Forming the periphery were men behind stone cairns which they had built or behind piles of broomweed or other available prairie weeds. These they set fire to at the exact moment when their yells and robe-waving seemed unlikely to veer the herd so that they would stay within the periphery and flow toward the neck. The men in these positions did not wish to frighten the animals and perhaps stampede them, so they simply showed themselves and waved their robes, and if necessary set fire to the weed piles. However, the men stationed along the neck were painted like demons, and at the right time they danced and waved their robes with demoniac yells, and lit their weed piles on a signal from one of the *a'ki-da,* and by this time the herd might have become panic stricken and lunged along the only way open to them. As the leaders saw the escarpment, they would set their feet as hook brakes, lowering their heads. This was of no avail; the irresistible mass behind them pushed them over the cliff, and all of them the drivers had managed to keep within the boundaries of the gourd-shaped drive tumbled to the canyon floor, in clouds of dust, where the tribal members assigned to this special work began to cut the hamstrings and use lances and clubs, and arrows when necessary, but the last were used only on those that seemed to be getting away. Arrows shot in excitement could be very dangerous.

Here in the canyon bottom under the escarpment the animals were butchered "on the skin," one man butchering while one held a front leg and another a hind leg and another the head.

The skin was cut from the chin to the base of the tail, then each leg was skinned out to the hoof and the skin peeled down to form a clean place for the meat, which was sliced from the body in laminae. The ribs were then cut from the backbone and laid to one side on the skin.

The viscera were taken out of the carcass piecemeal. The intestines were dragged out a little way from the carcass, as one might handle a hose, and the contents squeezed out, and the tube then turned back upon itself, so that it could dry and be washed. The paunch was taken out and emptied away from the carcass, and turned inside out to be washed, then it was filled with melted tallow and placed almost immediately into a hole dug out of clay, and clay was padded about it so that the filled paunch fitted perfectly and there were no humps or irregularities. This was done at the camp, where the women had already dug the holes in the clay. Little boys were called and directed to carry the paunch as quickly as possible to the women in camp. The heart sac was treated much the same way. When the tallow hardened and the paunch dried, it was taken out, leaving the shaped and dried paunch as a vessel.

Soon the meat was cut from the bones, and was in natural thin strips ready for smoking, and the bones were ready to be roasted and cracked for the marrow. The brains were carefully saved for the tanning, the hooves for glue, the horns for spoons and other utensils, and the sinews along the backbone became cord and thread and bow-strings when many of them were twisted together.

When they were through with the butchering, the men would carry the ribs up to the camp, and they immediately set about cooking them. They were busy cooking the ribs as the long line of old men, women, and boys, and dogs, formed an antlike procession, carrying the meat to the camp out of the canyon. This was tradition; on the hunts, the men cooked the ribs while the women were busy with the meat and hides.

The modern Little Old Men of twenty years ago brought tribal and gentile memory to their service, even to the most trivial things, like a woman laughing or crying or the way a wolf howled, but they seem to have retained little of the camping plan or the plan of the villages, so that one can be sure only that the typical lodge of the Little Ones was made of a cagelike framework of hickory. The ends of peeled saplings of perhaps fifteen or twenty feet in height were stuck in the ground to form a circle or an oblong. These were bent together and tied at the top with perhaps linden fiber or buffalo-hide thongs. These sapling poles were then strengthened by transverse hickory saplings of smaller size, reaching completely around them from top to bottom, tied to the upright poles and to each other. Over this the buffalo skins were thrown, leaving a smoke hole at the very top center and an opening to the east as a door. Sometimes they wove cattail stems and made walls of them, especially for the bottoms of the lodges. These lodges could be made circular and small, or oblong and as long as forty or fifty feet and quite high enough for the men of the Little Ones, who were often six feet, six inches tall. The Lodge of Mystery was of the oblong type, and the chief's lodges were often large and always with two doorways, one opening to the east and one opening to the west.

The hunting camps seem to have had no formal arrangement at all, at least much later in historical times. For ceremonial purposes, the Little Old Men arranged the lodges in sevens: seven long and seven wide for each of the grand divisions, the *Tzi-Sho* and the *Hunkah*. Between the *Tzi-Sho* on the north and the *Hunkah* on the south, there was always a clear avenue running east and west. Standing in this avenue between the two chiefs' lodges, which were opposite each other and were in the middle of the first line of lodges, facing east, one found the *Tzi-Sho* group of lodges on his left to the north, and the *Hunkah* group on his right to the south. The north is the direction of consistent light, and the direction of the periodic play of the Aurora Borealis even on the thirty-eighth parallel. So *Tzi-Sho,* the peace people, were ever associated with the north, whence came constant light, and ever therefore associated with the left from orientation, while the *Hunkah* were ever associated with the south and the right. The formal camp plan is shown in the diagram on page 86.

North - Tzi Sho

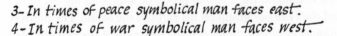

Tzi Sho chief's lodge | Hunkah chief's lodge

South - Hunkah

3- In times of peace symbolical man faces east.
4- In times of war symbolical man faces west.

All the openings of the lodges, except the chiefs', which had both east and west openings, were to the east, and on every sunrise the occupants came out of their lodges and stood by their doorways, and wailed their prayers to *Wah'Kon-Tah*.

86

8.   Kinsmen and Enemies

||||||||||||||||||||||||||||||||||||||||||||||||||||||||||||||||||||||||||||||||||||||||||||||||||||||||||||||||||||||||||||||||||||||||||||||||||||||||||||||||||||

BUT THESE PEOPLE who called themselves the Little Ones, had great height, consummate artistry in bluff and aggressiveness, and could hold their rich domain against all invaders. They could keep their enemies from crossing the Big Waters, the Mississippi, from the east and from crossing the Smoky Waters, the Missouri, from the north through the aid of two tribes, one of whom had once been a part of them. The *Ko'n-Za* gens had left the Little Ones because of a quarrel over buffalo sinew. After the drives there was a division of all useful parts of the buffalo among the gentes, or a division according to need, since the whole tribe had taken part in the drive and the carcasses were community property. In some manner this particular gens thought the division unfair. They must have had a very proud and independent leader or chieftain, since they left the tribe in anger and went off making much trouble and shouting insults. They went away to camp by themselves, and thereafter were known as a separate tribe. The split became permanent, even though they kept all the rituals of the parent Little Ones. In the language of the Little Ones they were called *Ko'n-Za* from this separation, which means They-Desire-to-Run or Noisy People and may even relate to the yapping of coyotes or, as some have said, to the boasting of the wind.

The Konzas, as spelled by the Europeans later, and much later known as the Kaws, though a small tribe, were ever great warriors, and even though they might have had skirmishes with the parent

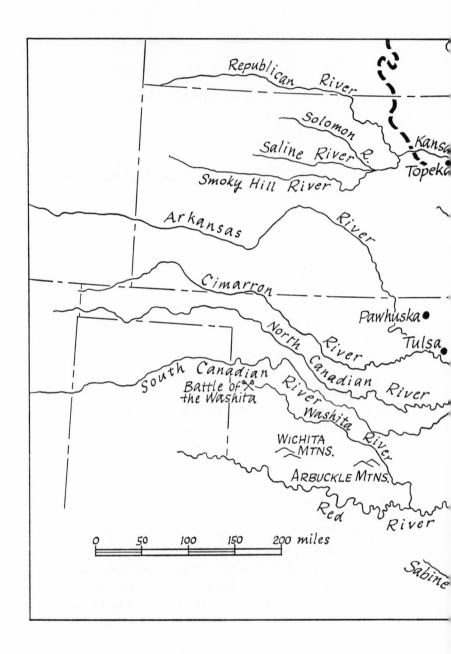

OSAGE AREA OF CONTROL, PRE-COLUMBIAN TO 1808

tribe, they usually allied themselves with them in serious trouble. These people lived in different spots along the *Ni-Sho-'Dse,* Missouri River, north of the Little Ones, and at one time above where the Missouri turns northwest and on the river running into the Smoky Waters from the west to which they gave their name, the modern Kaw or Kansas.

The other tribe related, linguistically, to the Little Ones lived also on the Smoky Waters, chiefly along the lower river in the forest and at times a little way up the *Ni-U-Tonkah,* the Big Waters, Mississippi River. They were a woodland people, and part of their name seems lost completely. They were called *Ni-Sho'Dse,* Smoky Water People, by the Little Ones.

The Little Ones, except for short, and often bloodless skirmishes with their splinter tribe, the Konza, and with the other Siouan tribe, The Smoky Water People, the Missouria or Missouri, lived amicably with them. They must have been on good terms or the Little Ones would not have allowed them to live so close to them, even though they lived on the fringes of the boundaries of the Little One's domain, the boundaries of the domain they claimed as their own.

Except for skirmishes, the Little Ones also lived amicably with the *U-Ga-Xpa,* the Pushed-off-the-Hill People, the Arkansas or Quapaws, who were also closely related to them and lived at the mouth of the *Ni-Shu-Dse,* Red Waters, the Arkansas River. They may have been of some aid to the Little Ones in keeping the Chickasaws to the east side of the Big Waters, the Mississippi River.

The Little Ones themselves had probably splintered from the Dakotas far back in dim prehistoric time. At least they spoke the Siouan tongue, and they could understand each other, with the slight aid of sign language. There were no amicable relations between them, and they called the Dakotas *Pa-Ba-Wa-Xo'n,* which means Head-Cutters, which in itself may hint of their relations.

They had kinsmen all along the Mississippi, from the mouth of the Arkansas to beyond the headwaters, and along the Missouri up to the Big Bend, where the Missouri had run rushing against the glacier and had to flow southeasterly. Those kinsmen north of the Missouri were ever being pressed westward by the Algonkians, it would seem. The people who spoke the Siouan tongue were powerful in numbers and with few exceptions aggressive by nature, occupying at one time or another and simultaneously the modern states of Minnesota, North and South Dakota, Nebraska, Iowa, Missouri, Kansas, Arkansas, and part of Oklahoma. They might have withstood the Algonkians who pushed them toward the west even into the historical period and the Iroquois who might have pushed them westward in prehistoric times if they had formed a confederacy similar to that of the Iroquois, especially if they had formed such a confederation after they came to the Big Waters and the Smoky Waters. Instead of confederation, however, there was almost constant war among them. There were seven fireplaces dividing the Dakotas, and these fireplaces became semi-independent tribes, one of them at least, the Assiniboines, becoming allied with their ancient enemy, the Algonkians.

Many of these semi-independent tribes had their own names and retained little from the mighty Sioux except their language and their aggressiveness, along with their pride and insolence, and some of their religious formulae and symbolism.

The Little Ones could not look to their swarming kinsmen along the upper Smoky Waters and the upper Big Waters for aid in keeping their rich domain. They could not expect aid from a very powerful tribe that had splintered from them, whom they called *U-Mo'n-Ho'n* (Omaha), Dwellers-on-the-Bluff, who lived along the upper Big Waters and later the middle Smoky Waters. This tribe had once been a part of the Little Ones, and represented several gentes, perhaps of the sub-*Hunkah* division. Several of the gentes of the sub-*Hunkah* had quarreled with the *Tzi-Sho* grand division over something that has been completely forgotten, and after persuading as many members as possible of the several sub-*Hunkah* gentes to go with them, they struck their lodges, and vociferating much as the Konzas had done, traveled up the Big Waters to make their home on a bluff above the river, not far from the pipestone quarries. They carried with them the rituals and the symbolism and the organization of the Little Ones.

There had been warfare and quarrels among the Siouan tribes even before the balance was completely destroyed by the introduction of firearms from the east and horses from the west.

The traditional Caddoan enemies of the Little Ones were more sedentary than the Siouans, and gave hint of having at one time been in touch with, or mildly affected by, a higher civilization. But they did seem to be constantly on the prowl, and were ever too close to the villages of the Little Ones. The Pawnees had torn the living hearts from many a captive maiden of the Little Ones in an Aztec-like sacrifice to the Morning Star, and the Little Ones walked in fear of them, and the women began keening when the scouts reported Pawnee moccasin prints.

The Pawnees, along with the other Caddoans, were possibly the enemies of the Little Ones from the time the latter first settled at the Place-of-the-Many-Swans—*Pa-I'n,* the Little Ones called them, Long-Haired People, and the division later called the Loup Pawnees, who lived on the Loup River near where it flowed into the *Ni-Btha-Ska,* Waters-Flat-White, Platte, they called *Pa-I'n Ma-ha* (*Pa-I'n,* Long Hair; *Ma-ha,* [Lodges] from-River-Bank People). The Little Ones hunted them as people might hunt animals who preyed upon them.

Hatred of the Little Ones seemed to burn in all Caddoans, and the forays into the domain of the Little Ones seemed to have had retaliatory motives. If the early mound builders of the Mississippi Valley were Caddoans, then it is not improbable that the Siouan Little Ones crossing the Mississippi from the east in dim pre-European times might have taken their domain from the Caddoan inhabitants, and the latter's hatred might have had its source in tribal memory. Later, in historical times, the Cheyennes had migrated from the north and east, the Shoshonean Commanches had migrated from the north, and the Kiowas from the northwest, and they apparently became Plains tribes with no desire to occupy the prairie-plains forested-hills domain of the Little Ones. Certainly there were many battles with all these, including the Athapascan Apaches and another Algonkian tribe of the plains, the Arapahoes, but apparently these skirmishes had a sportive or chivalric quality that was not apparent in the almost constant and bloody struggles with the Caddoans, especially the three

Pawnee tribes and the Wichitas. This hint is found in the stories of
the modern Little Old Men, in the inflection of their voices, in the
impish expressions of their faces as they speak of these people of the
Plains. They talk of coups on chiefs of these tribes and the number of
horses they took and the manner in which they outwitted them and
the number of scalps they waved from their spear points or which
fluttered from their ceremonial shirts. However, when they talk of
the Pawnees, and the Caddoans in general, there are no impish expressions, and their voices are monotoned, their long-fingered hands
agitated, plucking their blankets, when they talk from tribal memory.

Because of the necessity for protecting their domain and making
their claim to such a vast area an honored one, they fought with their
enemies constantly and with capriciously mad nature, and remained
virile and energetic and powerful.

Wah'Kon-Tah knew just which of his children were of the *Hunkah* and which of the *Tzi-Sho,* because in hunting camp where the
lodges, sometimes at least, were placed by whim, the *Tzi-Sho* children
had to wear certain symbols on the left side and the *Hunkah* on the
right. Among the men who were allowed to wear them, the downy
eagle feather, stained red with pokeberry juice, was worn on the left
side of the head by the *Tzi-Sho,* and its softness symbolized the softness of the peace people of the sky, the *Tzi-Sho* division.

Blessed with strong enemies in the pedestrian days—the Caddoan
tribes perhaps—and with a crazy woman climate that kept the Little
Ones ever alert and virile, they did not quite smother themselves in
their own ornamental creations made possible by the leisure which
their abundance allowed them. Their domain between the high plain
and the woodlands, with water standing white in the light of day,
was teeming with the animals of both plains and woodlands, and
with fruits of both provinces.

With the leisure which their prowess and their prowess-protected
abundance gave them, they had much time to create their own comfortable world, until their rituals and their songs and their long, long
repetitious ritualistic recitations which they called *wi-gi-es* were almost like some parasitic vine sapping the life of a great, deep-rooted
tree, but not quite. Useless ornamentation could also have been an
enemy.

93

One who has never sat out a tornado in a tent or lying flat and ignominiously in the mud clinging to a sapling, one who has never been caught by a vicious storm on a night-black prairie and heard the lightning pop around him or has never sensed the roaring flood creeping toward him in the blackness of night, may wonder why the Little Old Men were never quite satisfied with their creations, their songs, their sacred dancing, their wailing prayers, their fetishes, and why they must repeat and repeat and add and add to the incomprehensible intricacies of their ritualistic fumblings toward a mutual understanding with *Wah'Kon-Tah*. Each new manifestation of *Wah'Kon-Tah*'s wrath sent the Little Old Men into conference to amend the inadequacies, or rather amend by adding to their rituals. They were like a Christian telling his beads over and over until the dawn, when, in the prosaic reality of daylight, he might have a feeling of inadequacy and frustration and decide to walk on his knees to a hallowed place, as he tells them again.

From their sacred songs and recitations, words became sacred since they became charged with all the intensity and hope and fear and mystery in their souls. A word repeated many times absorbed an incredible sanctity, and became so revered that the Little Old Men began to use meaningless and coined words in their places to protect their sanctity from the women and the profane laymen, the result being that this obscurity, added to the already befuddling repetition and hyberbole, makes interpretation of what is inherently a rather reasonable and down-to-earth protective creation almost impossible.

This charging of words with sanctity, along with the semi-independence of the gentes and the self-esteem of their chieftains or gens leaders and the unfettered ambitions of Nobodies to strut before the alien uninformed, was an important weakness of the Little Ones when the aggressive adventurer and trader of the Europeans should arrive.

THE HEAVY EYEBROWS

"The Osages are the worst two tribes that we have on the Missouri and at the same time the strongest, the more so if they unite. For this reason it is necessary to temporize with them to some extent, handle them as tactfully as possible in order to restrain their excesses, as the few forces in the country do not permit anything else."—Pérez to Miró, March 7, 1790.

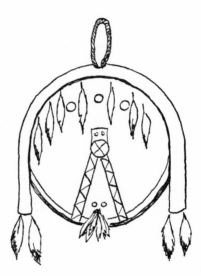

9. First Meetings with Europeans

THE LITTLE ONES had no explanation for the prairie, the plains, the forest, the rivers, not even for *Wah'Kon-Tah*–tinted Permian buttes and canyon walls of the west. They had never been concerned about their earth origin. Like the sun and the moon and the stars, they were there. Like all men even much past the dawn of reasoning, they were only concerned with themselves, with their fears and their self-preservation. They had never said that *Wah'Kon-Tah* made the prairies and the plains and the rivers, and in their struggle-dependence on every whim of the earth and the precise order of the sky—every movement and sound, every stirring of leaf and grass blade, and every alarm note of bird and animal, every shift of the wind and every shape of the clouds—they might have allowed him much more than seven days for the creation, even though the shepherds of man-swarming regions and earth-detached men swarming the marketplaces and temples might consider seven days adequate.

They were satisfied with the fact that earth, sky, land, and water were there: the sky orderly, the earth whimsical, often chaotic and often maleficent, and acceptable only under the discipline of the sky. They knew that it had little order when they came to it from the stars, and they had found on it only *ga-ni-tha,* disorder.

Whence came the European seemed to disturb them very little. He was an off-brand whom they had not seen before who came paddling up their river. He was not of them, then he was a potential enemy, even if not one at the moment. But he was of breath-stopping interest to them. When they first saw him, they had no idea that this pale, hairy man would later overrun their domain, as no other had ever been able to do. At the time of meeting, they were still the men pre-eminent.

In the latter part of the seventeenth century, the European came to them. He came up their river just as the Sacs and Foxes would do later to attack their villages, and just as the *Ni-Sho-Dse,* the Smoky Water People, their relatives, had done many times. Rivers have al-ways aided men's enemies, but their river would one day aid the Little Ones in bringing them guns before their urgent enemies had them.

On this certain day, the history thereof garbled in tribal memory, two pale men came up the river with two of the *Ni-Sho-Dse* war-riors. They had hair on the backs of their hands and on their faces, and hair glistened in the sun as it showed itself from the V of their Algonkian buckskin shirts. Their eyes and their mouths were almost hidden by hair. Their mouths were like the den of an old, male, bank beaver overhung by rootlets.

They wore the buckskin leggings and moccasins of the *Ni-Sho-Dse* with whom they had lived for two snows on the Smoky Waters. The Little Ones knew they were with the *Ni-Sho-Dse* because two hunters of the *U-Dse-Tsa* (Little Osages), a physical division of the Little Ones, had seen them. They, the *U-Dse-Tsa* had stood apart, and the strange men could easily see that they were different from the *Ni-Sho-Dse,* the Smoky Water People, in dress and manners. One wore the headskin and antlers of a buck deer, and neither would be wearing shirts. Algonkian or Iroquoian shirts would come later with trade and through imitation.

During the two snows, the strange men would have taken *Ni-Sho-Dse* women, and the women would have been proud, as the others stood about and watched them flesh the hides with fleshers and scrapers, which the Little Ones would later call *mo'n-ce* (metal). There was no story of guns at this first sight of the hairy ones.

The two hunters of the *U-Dse-Tsa* (Little Osages) would stand apart alert and bluff-scowling, watching every move of the strangers, but when these hunters of the *U-Dse-Tsa* would arrive back at the village, they would be important, and describe everything they saw to the Little Old Men, and to the chief of the Grand *Hunkah*. The *shoka* would be sent to report on the village of Smoky Water People, north and east of the Place-of-the-Many-Swans, and with him and perhaps following him would go many others, and they would verify the stories of the hunters, and especially they would talk of two miracles: the strangers with hair like the black bear and the *mo'n-ce*. There would be long discussions about these stories, but strangest in all their minds would be the men with heavy hair over the eyes, and secondly the metal scrapers. Not knowing what to call these strangers, they would refer to them as *I'n-Shta-Heh,* Heavy Eyebrows.

So when these strange men appeared in their tree that had been hollowed out by fire and chipping, on the river below the village, they were already identified as Heavy Eyebrows.

The Little Ones were not frightened, but nervous. The women would look at them from the darkness of the lodges, and the children peek at them from around their mother's buckskin skirts. The men stood waiting, bluff-scowling and silent.

The Heavy Eyebrows asked for the *Ki-He-Kah,* the "*Roi,*" they would say in their language, since they knew only about kings. After a long wait, the *shoka* would appear, and the *Ni-Sho-Dse* interpreters would ask if these pale men could see the Grand *Tzi-Sho,* since they had gifts for him. The *shoka* would act as if he had happened to come down to the river aimlessly. The two chiefs and the Little Old Men had known of the arrival, but remained within their lodges and sent *shoka* to investigate.

The *Tzi-Sho* chief would be waiting in his best leggings and moccasins, his roach being of dawn-tinted deer-tail hair with wild turkey gobbler "beard" bristles quaking above his head. In his roach, or to the side of it and tied to his residue natural hair, would be the soft under tail-feather of the golden eagle. This would be on the *Tzi-Sho* side, the left. He would sit ready with gifts and the pipe, his back straight, with an air that would be much more than one of dignity, but would also imply a haughty generosity and a superiority that needed no criterion for evaluation.

The *Hunkah* chief would not receive the Heavy Eyebrows, but would wait for the *shoka* to tell him if all he had heard about them was true: that they had scrapers and fleshers and awls and war clubs that glinted in the sun. The *Hunkah* would probably be consumed by curiosity, but would not disturb the poise of his dignity. But, just in case he might be seen, he would be dressed in his gypsum-rubbed deerskin leggings and his roach of deer-tail hair and turkey gobbler's beard attached to the only hair left on his close-shaven head. This residue of natural hair was a lock beginning back from his brow about the center of his head and reaching to the nape of his neck, then hanging down like the tail of the buffalo, which the tail part of it represented. This natural lock was a perpetual challenge to his enemies. Attached to the right side of his lock would be his eagle feather, a hard tail-feather of the golden eagle, the white margin tinted dawn-color. The hardness of the tail-feather would signify war hardness, not the softness of peace which the under tail-feather of *Tzi-Sho* represented. His war standard of trumpeter swan skin wrapped about a crook would be within his reach.

Neither of the chiefs would be impressed by the Heavy Eyebrows. The very name given them as by concensus would indicate that *I'n-Shta-Heh,* "Heavy Eyebrows," had no dignity and was a name both personal and quite informal. One could not possibly attach dignity to it. It was like the names little boys in their play gave each other, having to do with characteristics both physical and mental, or having to do with an incident, chiefly a ridiculous one. They, according to the nature of the incident or some salient characteristic of a boy, might call one of their number "Eats Grass," "Big Thing," "Spoils-the-Spring," or "Crosses-His-Mother"—the last having to do with a boy who, when younger, would run around his mother, then stop in front of her so that he could nurse, when he was much too old to do so.

Also, the odor of the Heavy Eyebrows became a tribal memory, because it was so very different from anything the Little Ones had ever known before. The Heavy Eyebrows with their dried sweat and armpit odors made some of the Little Ones sick, and were nauseating to many of the others. This European odor was certainly no stronger than the odor of drying hides and other odors of the village, but it

was strange to them. Until recently they have wondered why the
I'n-Shta-Heh, now referring to white men in general, kept their body
odors imprisoned by collars and trousers.

The people along with the chiefs would believe that the strangers
could have no dignity, and must represent a tribe of little dignity,
therefore of little importance. In the village they flashed their eyes
everywhere and let them rest for long moments on the women and
girls. There were grease swipes from their fingers on their buckskin
leggings. They were like camp dogs who wag their tails and slaver
when there is fresh meat to be trimmed, and the same cajoling ex-
pectancy was in their laughs. They stood long to look at the buffalo
robes, piled and waiting to be tanned.

They would be too much afraid to sneer at the pagan temple, as
they might call it. It was a lodge a little way off from the other lodges,
and like the others with a framework made of saplings, but not covered with buffalo skins or cattail leaves or stems like the others, but
with other hides. They would have noticed it particularly because of
the very beautiful skins with which it was covered, all with the hair
intact and carefully prepared. On one side there was a wapiti skin,
on the east side. On another side was the skin with pelage intact of
the black bear, and on the third side the skin of the panther, while
covering the smoke vent was the skin of a trumpeter swan in full
feather. The *coureurs de bois* would have been fascinated but afraid
to go near this lodge apart, since from within would come the earth-
rhythm beats of the drum, and there would be chanting so primitive
that it might hold them by its strange power.

This would be the Little Old Men singing their Rising Song in
the Lodge of Mystery, rising from their counciling after trying to
resolve the problem of the presence of these hairy strangers. To the
coureurs de bois the Rising Song would be the chant of lost angels.
They would make the sign of the cross, and turn away.

These Heavy Eyebrows had seemed so eager to please that the men
who had watched them land in the hollow tree and who had followed
them as they climbed the ridge to the village, talking with the Smoky
Water interpreter, wondered if they ought not be killed before they
reached the *Tzi-Sho* lodge of sanctuary. From behind their backs

these men of the Bear gens would wet their index fingers in their mouths and point to them. This was the sign to kill.

It is not known what the Heavy Eyebrows brought to the *Tzi-Sho* as a gift, or what he gave them in return, after smoking the pipe.

After smoking with the *Tzi-Sho* and flashing their quick Latin eyes about the lodge as they talked through the interpreter, since the *Tzi-Sho* would make no attempt to understand their few words of the Siouan tongue, they would rise from their special buffalo robe and find themselves looking up into the chief's face, as they again took his limp hand in turn.

On the way down from the village to the river's edge, they might say to each other, "*Mon Dieu,* what height has this king of the *sauvage!*" As they compared notes in their own language, the little boys would follow behind like coyotes, ready to run or freeze.

When the pirogue had disappeared downriver, the Little Ones would relax, and the women would take up their routine duties and laugh among themselves about certain things the Heavy Eyebrows had done, and they would put their right hands over their mouths in surprise and incredulity, as they talked of the hair on the backs of the *I'n-Shta-Heh*'s hands. The men would laugh over a witticism about these hairy ones making the long sleep like the bear. One of the little boys might hold bits of scrap buffalo hair above each eye and walk about examining things, as the others followed and laughed heartily.

10. Flood on the Smoky Waters

THE LATTER PART of June, 1673, the three ultimate forks of the Smoky Waters far to the northwest in the mountains were pouring their snow water into this mad river, and farther down, the long river of the *Kaw-Thu-Wah* (the Kiowa Indians), later called Yellowstone, was pouring its snow water into the mad one, and this mad one, the Smoky Waters, was roaring and foaming in frenzy, as if it could remember its frustrations of the Pleistocene times. It carried tree-length splinters of lodgepole pine and whole cottonwood trees and dead buffalo, and swirled and sucked and loosened large masses of loess and alluvium, which fell into it lazily, like a buffalo falling onto its side from the kneeling position after a fatal wound. It swirled through the high plains where the buffalo bulls roared and pawed the white dust over their backs like smoke, the roaring from thousands of throats drowning the noise of the mad waters. It raged through fantastic buttes and "white castles," twisting angrily through high plains, falling so deep in its own gorges in certain places that one couldn't even guess its presence from a short distance away, save for the tops of the waterside cottonwoods.

It dashed around the bend where the wedge of the ancient glacier had forced it southeastward, then farther down it raged past the rounded earth lodges and palisades of the Mandans and the Arikaras, the ancient enemies living close together. It foamed by the bluffs where one day would be the earth lodges of the Omahas, and farther

103

down before it turned east, and after turning it flowed past the lodges of the Konzas, and foamed by the lodges of the Missourias. It backed its muddy waters far up the Waters of the Konza (Kaw River). White Waters, the river of the Little Ones, then vomited the cottonwoods, the walnuts, the pines, the sycamores which it had not left anchored upstream, and the buffalo chips and the dead buffalo which it had not lodged against trees and driftwood, into the Big Waters, the Mississippi, its waters maintaining their character for miles along the right bank of the Big Waters, side by side with clear waters from the Mississippi's headwaters.

During this early summer madness in the latter part of June, 1673, which the Little Ones called Buffalo-Bull-Pawing-Earth-Moon, Father Jacques Marquette, a Recollect Franciscan, and a French trader, one Louis Jolliet, floated into the spew of the mad river. They were in two canoes and had with them five paddlers.

The enthusiastic father was not looking for furs, but for souls, and adventure, both exploratory. He was apparently a man of some culture and of intelligence. Like Frenchmen in general he had avidly learned the Indian languages and was perhaps proficient in Algonkian, and when he stopped with the Illini on or near the Des Moines River, he inspired confidence with his Algonkian words and his black robe. He and his followers naïvely followed an Illini trail from the river to their village, and he had stood some way from the village and had shouted. From them he first received knowledge of the Little Ones and their location on their river, and of the Missourias on the Missouri and of the Otoes and Konzas, and meticulously he made his little sketch map with the drainage from the west and placed each village as he imagined it from his talk with the Illini.

He must have been frightened of the wide, savage Mississippi from the time he floated onto it from the willow-screened sluggish Wisconsin and felt his canoe bumped by a Mississippi River catfish.

When he floated into the muddy, angry waters of the Missouri, his fear was ascendant: ". . . we heard the noise of a rapid, into which we were about to run. I have seen nothing more dreadful. An accumulation of large and entire trees, branches, and floating islands was issuing from the mouth of the river Pekitanoui, with such impetu-

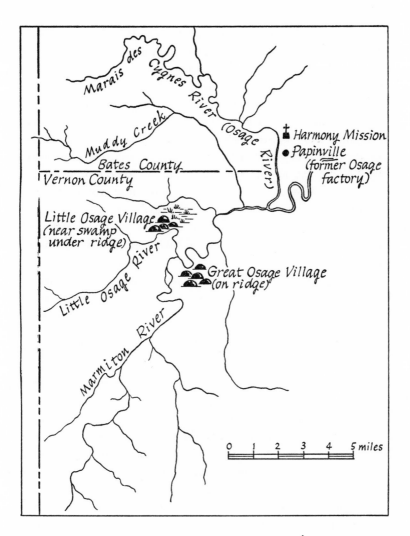

OSAGE VILLAGES IN PRESENT MISSOURI NOTED BY PÈRE MARQUETTE
IN 1673

osity that we could not without great danger risk passing through it. So great was its agitation that the water was so very muddy, and could not become clear." After writing down meticulously a name for the Smoky Waters, *"la rivière Pekitanoui,"* the river of the "Oumissouries," the true explorer was on the surface as he wrote: "Several villages of savages are located along this river, and I hope by means of it to make discovery of the Vermillion Sea or California," and he wrote further, "and I do not despair of discovering it some day, if God grant me the grace and the health to do so in order that I may preach Gospel to all the peoples of the new world who have so long groveled in the darkness of infidelity."

Here was a spirit of adventure, hunger for geographical knowledge, and missionary faith that should have made all of North America the New France.

Perhaps one or more of the "five men who were quite determined to do anything for such a glorious expedition" could speak a few words of the Siouan tongue; they had come through the Winnebago country, the kinsmen whom the Little Ones called Big-Fish-People, along the marge of Green Bay, on their way to the Fox River and portage to the Wisconsin.

A knowledge of the tongue could have been picked up by Père Marquette or trader Jolliet, since the latter had spent some time in the Lake Superior region looking for copper and the missionary might have come in contact with the Sioux near Sault Ste Marie. Many *sauvages* had come to the raising of the gigantic cross there in June, 1671, when Père Marquette was stationed at St. Ignace Mission.

The *coureurs de bois* living with the Smoky Water People apparently did not see Marquette, and he fails to mention *coureurs de bois* at the Illini village, so the enthusiastic explorer-missionary must have got his information from the Illini, who were well acquainted with the Missouri River tribes; and since his information seemed to be accurate, one assumes that his Algonkian was adequate. It was better than his Siouan, although he could have got much from the Otoes.

The modern Little Old Men do not know who gave the name for the subdivision of the Grand *Hunkah,* called *Wah-Sha-She,* known as the Water People and Name Givers, to the Heavy Eyebrows as the name for the *Ni-U-Ko'n-Ska,* the tribe whose name means "Children of the Middle Waters." They can't say whether it was the Smoky Water People or the Illini who gave the Heavy Eyebrows the wrong name for the tribe, but they know how it happened. It came about through the Deer gens of the *Wah-Sha-She,* who spent much time hunting along the Smoky Waters and were on friendly trading terms with the Illini, or it came about through the village of a band of Little Ones, later called Little Osages, who lived downriver from the Smoky Water People. These Little Ones who lived in a village on the Missouri were only a physical division, and most of the gentes were represented within their unit.

It is said by the Little Old Men that when the Illini came to trade, they asked the name of the people with whom they were trading, what they called themselves; and since the people with whom they were trading happened to be the Deer gens of the *Wah-Sha-She* subdivision of the Children of the Middle Waters, the Deer People proudly said, "We are the Deer People of the *Wah-Sha-She,*" and this name the Illini had remembered and had carried back with them, and when Père Marquette came up their trail shouting and being welcomed, stayed with them, and asked for information about the people living along the Pekitanoui, the Illini had described the Little Ones and called them *"Wah-Sha-She."*

The eager missionary wrote the name very carefully, but what he wrote was the result of phonetics. To him, the Frenchman, the *Wah* could only be written *Oua,* the *Sha, Zha,* and the *She, jhi* or *ghi,* so that when he lifted his quill, he would have for the first *"sauvage"* living up the Pekitanoui—not exactly on the river but on a tributary —the name *Ouazhaghi* or something similar.

Thus did the *Wah-Sha-She* subdivision of the Grand *Hunkah* of the *Ni-U-Ko'n-Ska* become identified as the tribe. They, the Water People of the Children of the Middle Waters, also known as Name Givers, unwittingly played their inherent role.

The English of the Atlantic Coast south of the St. Lawrence River were jealous of the venturing of the French into the wilderness of mystery by way of the waterways, and eagerly picked up every tidbit of information. When the trader Jolliet was wrecked on the lakes on his way back to New France, he had the geographical information he and Père Marquette had gathered, and the English learned of the sketch map the missionary had made; and the name *Wah-Sha-She,* which suffering from phonetics had become *Ouazhaghi,* suffered again from phonetics. To the English the *Oua* of *Ouazhaghi* must be pronounced *O,* the *zha* became *za,* with the *ghi* becoming *zge,* which came out as *Ozazge.* Finally, after many variations from the tongues and pens of many, everyone, including the Little Ones, settled for "Osage."

Both the French and the English as well as the Dutch had got a foothold on the Atlantic Coast during the early part of the seventeenth century and the Spaniards had been for some time in the Southwest, centering in that area which is now included within the boundaries of the present-day New Mexico, but according to the modern Little Old Men the French were the first of the Europeans to come in contact with the Little Ones. This was due to topography and to the differing national characteristics of the European colonizers and to their political struggles. The French were searching for a river that would lead to the "Vermillion Sea or California" and ultimately to China, and the Spaniards, after the chimera of Quivira and Cibola, were searching later for a river which would lead to a "South Sea" or one that would lead to a "North Sea." The English were interested through jealousy of France, but were compelled in their probing toward the Mississippi River to use game trails and later the Tennessee-Ohio rivers to the great river, setting out from the colony of Carolina.

The French had highways, as definite and almost as well marked as the modern concrete ones. They had the St. Lawrence and the Ottawa rivers through Lake Nipissing to the Great Lakes, thence over the divide between the Fox falling into Green Bay and the Wisconsin which ran many-fingered and through willows into the Mississippi under the bluffs of modern Iowa. They also had the portage between Lake Michigan and the Illinois River which ran into the Mississippi from the east just above the mouth of the Missouri from the west. The French did not really control the St. Lawrence highway to the lakes at this time, since Champlain's battle with the Iroquois near the lake which was named for him.

The *voyageurs* used birchbark in the country of birches for their canoes, hides in the country of the buffalo, and cane in the country of canes.

The Spaniards had to cross over from the headwaters of the Pecos River and pick up the faint and unlikely beginnings of the Canadian and the Cimarron rivers or jeopardize their horses and themselves probing for the Arkansas and the South Platte rivers in an immensity of windswept sky and land which was like a calm sea solidified. No matter what their theoretical objective, they were deflected by sand dunes, waterless leagues, one of which looked exactly like the others, solidified spew of ancient volcanoes and earth fissures. Their horses must have grazing and water, and all these things determined their course. The headwaters of the Red River were much more pronounced in Palo Duro Canyon, but from the headwaters of the Pecos it was a long way across the plains, and between these two rivers were the Apaches and later the Comanches. They didn't explore the lower waters of their own Río Grande until 1747.

They had an alternate way to the Arkansas and to the headwaters of the Platte. This was their trail up the Río Grande through the San Luis Valley, from which they could go over Medano Pass in the Sangre de Cristo mountains to the Huerfano River, thence down it to the Arkansas, or go over the Pancha Pass, cross the Arkansas to go up Trout Creek and over the divide to the headwaters of the South Platte.

Also, about the time the Frenchmen came to the Osages, the Spaniards were having trouble with their anchored, corn-planting, pottery-shaping Basket Weavers, who were horrifying the Franciscans by reviving their ancient dances and soon would be chasing the Spaniards back down the Río Grande, washing the contaminating touch of the Franciscans from their bodies in the river and desecrating the mission churches which they had labored to build, freeing themselves from Spanish rule for a dozen years.

The missionary Marquette and the commercial adventurer Jolliet were restive and made no attempt to visit the villages of the Little Ones. They placed them on the map as they did the villages of the Pawnees, the Missourias, the Konzas, the Otoes, and others; then

109

floated on down the frightful Mississippi, watching the west bank for an inflowing stream that might lead to the "Vermillion Sea."

On the east bank the little party passed the mouth of a very large river which they called the "Ouabachi" or the Rivière de St. Jerome, the modern Ohio, and Marquette put off the buckskins of the explorer and put on again the black robe of Christian charity, as he became much disturbed about the fate of an Algonkian tribe who lived a little way up the river Ouabachi and were called in their own language *Chaouanons,* People-of-the-South. Père Marquette was worried over the possibility that the Iroquois, who had chased them from their homes farther east, would find them and burn them. These people were later called Shawnees.

The missionary and the trader-explorer finally arrived at the mouth of a river flowing from the west. They landed at this swampy, marshy place, and here they found a Siouan tribe, the people whom the Little Ones called *U-Ga-Xpa,* Pushed-off-the-Hill-People, and the river from the west with a marshy mouth which they called *Ni-Shu-Dse,* Red Waters. The name *U-Ga-Xpa* was Gallicized and Anglicized much as the name *Wah-Sha-She* had been, and finally became both "Quapaw" and "Arkansas." Looked at closely, one might find the original *U-Ga-Xpa* in both.

These people at the time of the separation were supposed to have been called Down-River-People, and the Omahas called Up-River-People, since one after separation went downriver and the other upriver. However, there is no part of *U-Ga-Xpa* which refers either to water or river.

The travelers got along beautifully with the Quapaws, and they seemed for Siouans to have been rather mild, and it was said that they were afraid to go upriver to hunt the buffalo, but it is very likely that their importance suffered in the fracturing of the adventurers' illusions about the "Vermillion Sea" and the road to China. Here in the fetid swamps at the mouth of the Red Waters, now called the Arkansas River, Père Marquette and his companion lost hope. They learned that the Mississippi ran into the Gulf at Latitude 31 degrees, 40 minutes, and that they could float to it within three or four days.

They decided to return home by way of the Illinois River and not try for it.

Then on March 14, 1682, another Frenchman came to the mouth of the Arkansas.

Sieur de la Salle had a grant in New France called La Chine, but he got exploration fever and went to France to obtain permission to explore the Mississippi and establish forts, after formally claiming the valley for the French crown.

While in France he met a tough, one-armed gentleman Italian soldier called Henri de Tonti, and brought him back with him. They came down the Mississippi in 1681 with twenty Frenchmen and eighteen Algonkians accompanied by ten native women and their children, and naturally they brought along a Recollect missionary, one known as Zanobius Membre.

They stopped at the mouth of the Arkansas to raise a cross and the arms of Louis XIV, and took possession of the country in the name of the King. Father Membre in his black robe raised his hands and his eyes to heaven and prayed and the *Vexilla* was chanted, while the wild Quapaws stood and watched.

Father Membre wrote: "I took occasion to explain something of the truth of God and the mysteries of our redemption, of which they saw the arms."

Tonti was given a seigneury comprising an area at the mouth of the river which he would call St. Louis, when his fort was finished.

The explorers moved on down the great river, and then on April 9, 1682, claimed the mouth of the river and the whole drainage for France, and called it "Louisiana" in honor of Louis XIV, *"le Grand Monarque."*

Here again the cross was raised and again the arms of Louis, and the *Vexilla* and *Domine Salvum fac Regem* were sung by all, but it is not known whether a wild tribe of Caddoans were present. After the chanting came shouts of *"Vive le Roi!"*

The Little Ones now lived in a wide land called Louisiana, and the Sacred One and the Middle Waters would be claimed by kings from another world; only the Sky Lodge was left to them. But these things they would not know for a long time.

II.   *Coureurs de Bois* and *Voyageurs*

THE FRENCH TRAPPERS and unofficial explorers who visited the Osage villages above the Place-of-the-Many-Swans very likely could neither read nor write, even though they were subjects of the most dazzling civilization in Europe, and were possibly more ignorant of the earth, its denizens, and themselves than the Little Ones. Certainly they were more ignorant of the earth. When they were told by their Smoky Water hosts, the Missourias, that spirits guarded the door of the Lodge of Mystery of the Little Ones, where the Little Old Men counciled, they might first visualize anthropomorphic materializations, winged and spear-bearing, but they would almost immediately realize that at the door of a pagan temple this could not be. There would be some relief for them when told that these spirits were of the black bear, the wapiti, the lynx, and the panther. They might smile indulgently when told that these four spirit doorkeepers of the Lodge of Mystery could read the minds of those about to enter and frustrate their sinister purposes. Hearing this ridiculous bit of pagan belief about lowly beasts of the fields, they would experience more comfort the next time they visited the villages and heard the Rising Song of the Little Old Men.

These ignorant, questing men would undoubtedly believe all that had been handed down to them from the Medieval bestiaries, since theology still dominated the lives and thoughts of men in general. They would believe, no matter how many skins they might rip from the black bear, that the black bear gave birth to a ball of pulp during hibernation and licked it into body shape with legs and head, until it became a bear. Even the English poet Alexander Pope must have believed this, judging from his lines in the *Dunciad*.

Also, these trappers from the most civilized country in Europe might believe that the panther was sweet tempered and had only one enemy in all the world, the dragon, and that when he went to sleep after gorging, then after three days awoke and walked about, belching with a ringing sound, his sweet breath would permeate the forests, and other animals hearing and scenting would follow him about with love in their hearts.

The dragon, on the other hand, would hide in the deepest cave in craven fear.

They might believe these things traditionally, along with thousands of their countrymen back in France, without knowing their origin in the ancient association of the panther and Christ, although they would know that the dragon symbolized the devil.

The earth-detached philosophers and "realists" who were beginning to awaken the political and social hopes of the lowly ones in Louis's scintillating, ornamental civilization by their writings, or were having their theories taken up as fashionable fads in the sated courts of Louis XIV and XV, might even have believed these natural history stories from the Medieval bestiaries, since there was no social or political reason for investigating them.

These *coureurs de bois,* who would rarely get a shot at a panther and would be interested in their skins only, might also believe with the Medieval Christians that the female panther had kittens only once in a lifetime, since in their eagerness to be born, the kittens would snarl and scratch and spit until they had torn the womb and made their escape. After that the female could have no more kittens.

The third guard of the Lodge of Mystery, the wapiti, they would call "elk," because the English in their ignorance thought he might be the elk of Norway, not having learned from the Algonkians that the elk of America was called "moose."

The fourth guardian would be regarded with contempt, since according to the story which would have been handed down to them, a lynx's urine hardens into a precious stone, but the devil in his heart causes the lynx to cover his urine by scratching sand over it with his hind feet, so that good Christians were unable to find the later-developed gem.

The *coureurs de bois* would believe that their living with Missouria and Osage women was not a sin to be confessed, since obviously these women were pagans, but the offspring of such cohabitation were quite another category; they were souls to be saved and to do nothing about the saving of them would be a mortal sin.

They had a beautiful faith which their social and intellectual superiors were perhaps losing in the new philosophy of realism that was growing during the last years of Louis XIV's reign to bloom during the Regency and the reign of Louis XV. They had the faith that had erected the incomparable prayers in stone over Europe and England. Stone by stone, men like them had built the Gothic cathedrals, making their spires lead the eye and the thoughts to heaven. They, themselves, or under the influence and leadership of gentlemen adventurers and missionaries of culture, had brought nothing except the old *ga-ni-tha,* the disorder of the Isolated Earth People, back to the Little Ones.

They also had a rollicking, carefree sense of humor, the very type that could be appreciated by the Little Ones. As a matter of fact, their humor had the same basis as that of the Little Ones: dignity made ridiculous. There is nothing an Osage appreciates more than a disastrous climax to the strutting of a man who creates war honors for himself, just as nothing amuses the Frenchman more than the picture of a romantic lover being forced to leave the boudoir by a window, half-clad.

It was this type of boisterous *coureur de bois* or *voyageur* with a surprising sense of poetry who named the lake in the Champlain country of New York "Scarron" (now called Schroon) because it had the shape of the body of Louis XIV's most noted mistress, Madame Scarron, who became the Marquise de Maintenon, and eventually queen after Marie Térèse's death.

The French even in the seventeenth century seemed to have the empire idea through expansion of colonies, especially after 1663, when the royal government took over from the companies. At least their nature seemed better fitted to such an idea than to one of agriculture, under the inspiring energy of the intendants of this period, especially under Talon and certainly under the leadership of the magnificent Count Frontenac. They could have anchored in rich glacial soil somewhere in their New France even if they could not make a go of agriculture in the geologically and climatically harsh Quebec and Three Rivers area along the north bank of the St. Lawrence River.

But the gentlemen adventurers, the seekers for gold and silver and copper, the bourgeois enterprisers and adventurers, the trappers and the missionaries all were restive and all had the light of adventure in their eyes, and they ventured up their water highways and over the lakes and down the Mississippi, and they came around Florida and fumbled for the mouth of the Mississippi. They questioned the natives, learned their languages, and made maps and dreamed dreams.

Also the waterways up the Ottawa, to Lake Nipissing, to Georgian Bay, along the shores of Lakes Huron and Michigan were highways to freedom, an escape for the transplanted peasant from feudal responsibility, and for the criminal, freedom from Louis's terrible galleys.

The grants in New France had been made to the gentlemen and ambitious bourgeois of France, and to favorites of the king or Colbert, and these seigneuries were enfeoffed to the common man or peasant and former soldiers, in queer longitudinal strips, reaching to the St. Lawrence, with small houses at the river end of the strip. In the middle of the primordial forests these little farmsteads were like houses in some modern resettlement area of utilitarian ugliness, forlorn and unimaginative. Sometimes these formed a parish, and man, insignificant in the immensity of savage river and lake and forest, went his potty little European way under the authority of the lord, the governor, the intendant, and the Bishop, each watching the other for transgressions of traditional precedent. Talon, the prototype of Chauvin, disliked Bishop Laval because he was a Jesuit.

The peasant of spirit had no desire to stay and was ever watchful for chances to escape from this familiar social and political suppression which he had so long known in France. A mischance, and he went to the galleys along with a group of passive enemy Iroquois, where he might be forgotten and stay for the rest of his life, long past the period of his sentence.

Once away on the rivers and lakes, he might be free forever from the longitudinal strips of land belonging to his lord, and from severe frowns from the church and the atmosphere of "perpetual Lent."

The Jesuits were champions of the natives along the St. Lawrence and in the Lake Champlain region. They fought bitterly with the traders over the matter of trading spirits to the natives for furs, and they even had many of the Iroquois slaves returned from the galleys, even though they were dedicated enemies of the French. The traders defended this practice of trading spirits for furs on the grounds that if they did not do so, they would soon lose their trade to the English and the Dutch, who they said had no such scruples.

It has been suggested that Champlain's defeat of the Iroquois earlier was a mistake, and that if they had made friends with the Iroquois instead of with the Algonkians, the struggle for the Continent with the English later in the eighteenth century might have come to a different conclusion. The Algonkians were closer to the Quebec and Three Rivers settlements, and the domain claimed by the Iroquois gave them the position as buffer between the French north of the St. Lawrence and the English south of it. Also, with Dutch guns, the Five Nations were too strong for the Algonkians and forced them up the Ottawa, to the shores of the lakes and beyond and into conflict with the mighty Siouan tribes.

The French fraternized with the tribes, learned their languages, ate their food, married their women, and in general treated them in harmony with the new thought being born in scintillating France concerning the importance of the common man. This might have been due to an atmospheric influence rather than to a seepage from the intellectuals of the mother country. The proud Count de Frontenac met with both his Algonkian allies and his Iroquoian enemies in council, painted and dressed as they dressed.

The church encouraged large families so that the colony would have a large population and therefore power. When women were brought to New France as wives for the settlers and there were settlers still unmated, interracial marriages were encouraged.

Thus it was the exploring spirit of the French missionaries and the gentlemen adventurers and the spirit of the freedom-loving common man, along with the energetic traders and explorers and trappers, that brought the Heavy Eyebrows up the river that lay in the sun like a stunned snake to the villages of the Little Ones before they met the English or became well acquainted with the Spaniards. It was the effervescence and the sense of humor, the Gallic verve and adjustability and sincere spirit of fraternization that inspired friendly relations with the Little Ones and made them allies for over a century.

This despite the fact that within this period many a scalp of the *I'n-Shta-Heh,* the Heavy Eyebrows, would wave from the coup stick of the Little Ones, and there would be many a buckskin shirt handed down decorated with the scalps of *I'n-Shta-Heh.*

12. *I-Spa-Tho* and Long Knives

It seems now to have been rather fortunate for the Little Ones that they did meet the French first and became allied with them since their attitude and colonial philosophy were what they were. The attitude of the English on the Atlantic Coast and the Spaniards on the headwaters of the Río Grande might have been more disturbing. But still, either of these powers might also have been attenuated by the time they might have tried to embrace the domain of the Children of the Middle Waters, as was the French power. However, it appears for the other reasons that the Little Ones were lucky.

An Indian chief, possibly one of the chiefs of one of the Iroquoian tribes, was courteously invited to "sit above the salt" in Puritan households, while his followers "sat below the salt" with the servants and other visitors of inferior degree. The food was the same at both ends of the table, however. Those "below the salt" did not talk with those "above the salt," unless questioned. This would seem to be a reasonable relationship, but the English, especially the Puritans, grew tired of trying to teach the Indians, and in despair it was suggested that it might be a rather effective defensive action against the fact of their existence if trade blankets could be infected with smallpox virus. This idea was acceptable to Sir Jeffrey Amherst, and when one Elliot went forth to preach to the natives, his wife sent his lunch along.

When the Spaniards first came to America, they had a tremendous struggle with their consciences about just how the Indian ought to be classified.

He was an animal because he ate food and mated, but the Spaniard shared these habits with him. On the other hand, he seemed to care little for gold and did not know God, and therein lay the dilemma. If he spurned gold and knew not God, then obviously he could not be classed as a human being, or if so, he might be in the category of Aristotle's born slaves, with degrees of reasoning above that of an animal. If he could by chance be classed as a human being, then he must have a soul; and in order to save their own souls, the conquerors must baptize him and teach him the love of God. However, in the process he could be useful as a sort of ward of the landowners and the administrators and become a part of the encomienda system.

Emperor Charles V back in Spain was made happy when he could know definitely that the natives were human beings and therefore bearers of souls, and he probably would have enjoyed self-flagellation for allowing the doubt to be presented to him. He would have quite a sufficient burden on his immortal soul without adding to it by making a mistake about the category of the Indian.

It had been definitely decided that they were human beings some time before the Little Ones met their first Europeans, and the sedentary Río Grande natives had become the obedient wards in the encomienda system, sweating out their paganism in the fields and carrying timbers and stones for the construction of the administrative and ecclesiastical buildings, their souls salvaged but protected from Satan's clutches by the ever watchful overseers. They were under two majesties, the Church and the King, and both had tried to protect them from the landowners and the administrators, but both had failed.

They owed their status as human beings to the Franciscan missionaries and to the King, the former having fought stubbornly for them against the administrators and the crystallized mentality of the universal soldier. They, like the French missionaries, had fought to ban spirits from barter with them, and lost, even though the Spanish trader couldn't bring up the argument which the French in New France used concerning English and Dutch competition.

The Spaniards had a code of regulations which had as their object the prevention of exploitation and extermination of the native populations which were superior to anything the colonial French or English had. Since the natives, anchored and sedentary, were as virtual slaves, they were also a necessary basis for Spanish colonial economics; naturally, these sedentary, agriculturists-weavers the Spaniard had to save.

There were no nuclei of anchored agriculturists as a basis for slavery out on the immensurable plains, to make possible the extension of the Spanish colony; there were only, as Castañeda said, "sky and cows," and since Quivira of the sixteenth century had proved to be a chimera, explorers on the plains had come to the conclusion that there was no place there where one might become rich.

That had been the object of most of the conquerors, according to Bernal Díaz, who wrote, "We came to worship God and also to get rich," and the great Cortés himself had said, "but I came to get gold, not to till the soil like a peasant."

The Franciscan missionaries were just as dedicated to the saving of savage souls as their brothers in New France on the St. Lawrence, but they seem to have been more contented with the salvaging of the lost souls of those among whom they lived, only going out with large parties upon the plains as representatives of one of the "Two Majesties." They rode mules or flop-eared burros, or, walking, held their cassocks from the chollo and pear cactus. They seemed to have little urge to venture as Père Marquette and the other French missionaries had done, from their missions on Lake Michigan and on the St. Lawrence; learning first Algonkian then Siouan, pushing far into the wilderness.

The granitic harshness of the north shore of the St. Lawrence River and the winters that were like the determined attacks by an implacable enemy inspired adventure and activity, while the sun hung on one's back much of the year on the upper Río Grande, which made the cool, adobe shade a luxury and filled men with cat-like contentment and love-yearning. There were no white waters tumbling out of wild, dark, mysterious forests, suggesting adventure or a means of escape for the common man.

The Río Grande, except where it trickled with brooklike modesty near its sources, often tried to hide itself from the sun by cutting down into the lava and basaltic plateaus. Only to the north, where it came down between saber gashes, almost hidden by blue spruce and firs and pines, was it of the mysterious forests. To the west were lava and basaltic plateaus, and to the east the limitless plains, and there was no beckoning mystery under the bowl of the sky, where you could see a picket-pin gopher from the distance of half a mile and see the sky under the bellies of the buffalo. When you set out, you rode horseback on the plains, especially when alone or as a member of a small party, since to walk would reduce one to the ridiculous insignificance of an upright beetle. If you were a common soldier or a native slave or an ascetic priest, you might walk as a member of a large party.

Even if you were a member of a large party, you were stopped by great black lava flows like pulled black toffee, grassless plains and sand dunes, quicksands in the treeless rivers, and sandstorms; and even on tranquil days the peaceful winds played with the fetlocks of your horses.

If you set off up the Río Grande, you finally found yourself in canyons that led only to passes. In the summer there were the wild Utes and Comanches, and in the winter snow barriers and starvation, but you could go all the way to the headwaters of the South Platte, the highway to the Missouri River.

It has been stated that upon examining the maps, one might conclude that between 1535 and 1706 no explorer passed all the way through the Great Plains from east to west, or from west to east. A line can be drawn, it is stated, from Canada to the Río Grande, between the 96th and the 101st meridians without crossing the path of a single Spanish explorer. If this be true, the Spaniards of the headwaters of the Río Grande may not have visited the Little Ones in their villages during the seventeenth century.

The Little Ones have no documents, naturally, and no tribal memory of meeting any European before they met the French, and this is borne out by the name which they gave the Spaniards. They simply tried to pronounce the name as they heard it from others, indicating that they had known about the Spaniards long before they came in contact with them. They called them *I-Spa-Tho,* which is obviously an attempt to pronounce the word *"Español,"* or the French *"Espagnol,"* since it is not likely that they had ever heard the English, "Spanish."

If they had come face to face with the Spaniards in their chain mail, their helmets, and, above all, mounted on *shonka tonkah,* the "great dog," they certainly would have had something to hand down as tribal memory. The two dirty, ingratiating Frenchmen coming up their river in a dugout are certainly a part of tribal memory, though hazy, and a much more dramatic meeting with the Spaniards would certainly have been handed down.

It is quite likely they would have fled, even if they had heard of the big dog ridden by men, and this very fact would have grooved the impact of the meeting. The tribal memory is replete with strange meetings with "little bad people," black men who lived in the water, and dragons.

The fact that the Little Ones tried to pronounce *Espagnol* might bear out the statement of those who analyze the old maps. They have not tried to characterize them from some incident or physical characteristic as they did in the cases of the French and the English—the Heavy Eyebrows and the Long Knives respectively. Certainly, if the panoplied, mounted Spaniards had appeared at their village or camps, they might have called them Riders-of-the-Mystery Dog, or Sun-on-Heads, or Sun-on-Shields, or Shining Breasts, or for some incident which, in the case of mounted Spaniards, would have been terrifyingly dramatic.

And the Little Ones even in their pedestrian days were wide wanderers, and there is no reason to believe that their moccasin prints could not have been found past the 101st meridian before 1706 as their horse's hoofprints were certainly found there after 1700 at least. They have stories, the locale of which could be nowhere else than far past the 101st meridian. It is reasonable to believe that even in their wanderings, following Grandfather the Sun to the Cliffs (the west), they did not meet up with the Spaniard during the seventeenth century.

Parallel with the *coureurs de bois* of the French, there might have been a few English rangers along the game trails or floating down the Tennessee River from Carolina; certainly there were English rangers on the headwaters of the Ohio River, but apparently there were no *corredores del llanos.*

The attitude of each of these three European nations feeling for footholds on the new continent was based on the necessities of each. Spain had to have a nuclei of earth-attached natives, and therefore made the best regulations concerning their relationship with the natives. The English wanted to christianize the natives in a rather a thing-to-do spirit, but when they became tired of the native's failure to understand the stocks on Boston Common, ordinances against bare female breasts, metal buttons, and long hair and the confusion of differing credos, they seemed to think he might as well be eliminated entirely. They razed his forests, drove his game back into the deep forests, plowed up his land, and shot at friend or foe when they became nervous, especially after the French of the St. Lawrence began paying the Algonkians a bounty for their hair.

The Virginians didn't want to end the wars with the natives "because the way of conquering them is much more easy than the way of civilizing them by fair means, besides that, a conquest may be of many and at once whereas civility is particular and slow."

It seemed that the object of the English colonists was to anchor along the Atlantic Coast, then creep into the interior, felling the game and eliminating the native if he interfered by his simple presence, even if he was not active in defense of his domain.

Thus did the attitude toward the native and the philosophy of each of the European powers grow out of their economic necessity, and it was fortunate for the Little Ones that they were truly Children of the Middle Waters, and the French missionary and trader-explorers, the *voyageurs* and the *coureurs de bois* came to them attenuated in strength, far from Quebec and Natchez and New Orleans, with only trade in furs and trade with the Spaniards and the "Vermillion Sea" and China and later the "Western Sea" in their minds, their two agricultural attempts far away on the St. Lawrence and the lower Mississippi. Also the French were lucky that they brought eagerness for fur and trade and souls and the Gallic spirit for fraternization to the

123

Middle Waters, that they lived with native women and eagerly learned the language of each tribe with whom they came in contact, and could bow grandly to the *Tzi-Sho* and the Grand *Hunkah* of the Little Ones who held dignity and falcon-swift courage above property, and lastly because they could paint their faces and dance around the fire in a circle, arm linked in arm, to their own ballads.

Perhaps the personalities who influenced the Little Ones, or at least whose activities affected them more than either Père Marquette or La Salle, were the Lemoyne brothers. They were members of one of the most remarkable families of North America of that time or any time, and were Canadians.

They were the Sieur de Bienville and Sieur d'Iberville. They had sailed around to the Gulf, and had felt blindly in tropical rainstorms for the mouth of the Mississippi, and in so doing had kept in mind two possibilities: one, the trade with Spain up the "Marne," the later Arkansas; and the other, the possible probing of the English from Carolina. Both Spain and England had to be kept at a distance from the great river and its valley. They established the post at Biloxi and then at Mobile and Natchez about 1700, after entering the mouth of the Mississippi, which they were calling the "Colbert," in 1699.

To them came several energetic and aggressive Canadians whose names would be associated with Louisiana for years, two who came later would give the first written account of the Little Ones, stressing their *méfiance*. This was a term employed by the French to characterize any tribe of Indians who were strong enough to frustrate their designs.

One of these men was Charles Claude du Tisne and the other Bernard de la Harpe, who came to Louisiana for adventure. Among the others were Le Page du Pratz and Father Pierre François Xavier de Charlevoix, whose writings are of the greatest importance. There were also Sieur de Boisbriant, who would become the commander of the Illinois country, and Juchereau de St. Denis, right out of a picaresque novel, who founded Natchitoches, then left it under the command of Du Tisne to go romancing and trading across modern Texas, to open up trade with the Spaniards across drainage, using the Red River to make his start. He arrived at the Río Grande, and was put under "comfortable arrest" by the commandant, Ramón. Later he married the granddaughter of Ramón and brought back to Louisiana shoes, ribbons, laces, and silk stockings. However, there were still the barriers up the Arkansas and the Red rivers, as well as the Missouri, in the form of the Padoucas, the Apaches, and the Pawnees, and the "Louisiana Plan" must be carried out, which meant the placing of forts strategically to protect the claims of the French from both the Spaniards and the English, and making allies of the Plains Indians.

This activity by the brothers was retarded by the War of the Spanish Succession from about 1701 to 1713, and the Little Ones and the other Siouans of the Missouri were not energetically molested, but they were for the first time affected by European political balancing.

13. Horses

THE LITTLE ONES met the *A-Pa-Tsi* and fought them before 1700, and they fought the *Pa-Do'n-Ka* until after the coming of the Americans. The present-day *A-Pa-Tsi,* or Apaches, built at that time frail little cone-shaped houses from willow stems and leaves, sparse grasses, and reeds from the desert. They were so small that when the giant Osages explored them for loot after defeating the owners, they had to stoop to enter. They named these short bowlegged people of the desert and the semi-arid plains, *A-Pa-Tsi,* [Lodge] Makes-Us-Stoop People. There were people on the plains they called *Pa-Do'n-Ka,* or Wet Nose People. The name *Pa-Do'n-Ka* was Hispaniolized or Gallicized into "Padouca," who some say were the modern Comanches.

The Little Ones knew and fought both these people in their own domains on the plains and named them, and still apparently knew little of the Spaniards until in the eighteenth century, when they began to raid them.

But it has been said rather definitely that both the Pawnees and the Missourias had horses in 1682, the year they all came under the protection of Louis XIV. If the classical enemy of the Little Ones, the Pawnees, had horses at this time, and if their kinsmen the Missourias had horses at this date, they, the Little Ones, must have had them. They came often in contact with their ancient enemy both by accident and by design, and each tribe held prisoners of the other, at all times, and pumped them as any military intelligence officer might pump a captive.

The Little Ones must have known about horses long before they saw them, and after seeing them, they must have acquired them either by capture from the Pawnees or got them in trade with the Missourias and the Kiowas.

The modern Little Old Men have a drusy tribal memory that they got their first horses from the Kiowas. It has been suggested that the Little Ones named the horse in honor of the Kiowa, since they call him *ka-wa,* but they called the Kiowas originally *Ka-Thu-Wah,* or *Kaw-Thu-Wah.* It is also suggested that they called the horse *ka-wa* in an attempt to say *caballo.* Since the Little Ones through the years have grown lazy in the matter of pronunciation and have shortened many words, as English-speaking peoples would leave out syllables or shorten verb endings, *ka-wa* could easily have been shortened from *Kaw-Thu-Wah.* It is probable that they had not met up with the Spaniards before they acquired their horses, that they got them from the Kiowas, and that *ka-wa* is not an attempt to pronounce *caballo.*

It is almost certain that the Little Ones had their horses before the beginning of the eighteenth century and that they came indirectly from the Spaniards on the Río Grande, but there is no tribal memory concerning this highly dramatic meeting of the Little Ones with the horse, and their pedestrian days seemed to have flowed into their cavalier days, the juncture smoothed over by the absence of tribal memory or by clouded mouth-to-ear traditions.

They were probably mounted before their kinsmen, except the Missourias and perhaps the Konzas, and this only magnified their prowess and gave them definite security in their domain. In the next century, the eighteenth, they would ride wildly against their enemies of the west—the Pawnees, the Apaches, and the Caddoans of the Red River—and against the Kiowas when they came south from the Black Hills and the Comanches when they came south after splintering from their Shoshonean folk.[1] Added to these enemies in the west

[1] George E. Hyde, in *Indians of the High Plains* (p. 28 ff.), identifies the Padoucas as "various tribes of the Apaches," saying that "the Comanches, now

would be the Arapahoes and the Cheyennes and other westward-migrating Algonkians; and though they have little in their traditions concerning the Cut-Heads, their kinsmen the Sioux of the north, they clashed with them after they acquired the mobility of mounted warriors.

While there is little or nothing in the traditions of the Little Ones about their dramatic acquisition of the horse, there is drama in the meeting of a splinter tribe of the Little Ones with the horse, and this might well serve as an example of what might have happened on their first sighting of the "mystery dog." The Siouan tribes of the north had no horses until perhaps fifty years after the Little Ones were skilled horsemen.

As had been mentioned, the Omahas had splintered from the Little Ones, and by thus splitting from the tribe, had unitized several gentes of the *Hunkah* divisions, and they went up the Mississippi as an independent tribe to live near the pipestone deposits. Here the Cut-Heads, the Yankton Sioux, triumphant with guns from the English of Hudson Bay through the Crees and the Assiniboines, but still with no horses, drove them out, and they settled at the mouth of the Little Sioux. The Cut-Heads, the Yanktons, also drove their kinsmen, the *Paw-Xo-Dse,* the Iowas (Snow-Heads[2]), and the *Wah-Zho-Xthe,* the Otoes, from the Blue Earth River country, also in modern Minnesota. Of the three tribes of fugitive kinsmen, only the Iowas had guns, and none had horses.

The musket-happy Cut-Heads followed and harassed the three tribes to the Missouri River, and the Omahas and the Iowas settled near the *Ni-U-Skah,* the White River, and while there, one of the gentes which had belonged to the *Hunkah* of the Little Ones before unitizing with others to become the Omaha tribe, became frightened and left under their leader.

This was the dissident fraction of the Star-That-Came-to-Earth gens of the *Wah-Sha-She* division of the Grand *Hunkah* of the Little

---

living in the old Padouca country, were confused with the tribe they had driven out and were given the name of that tribe."

[2] The Osages say that at some traditional separation from the Iowas the latter walked off with snow falling on their heads.

Ones; the gens which furnished the *Hunkah* chief, and they were very proud. Because of this fact they clung to the highly honored title of *Paw-Hah'n Wah-Shta-Ge* of their original condition with the Little Ones, which means "Gentle Headmen" or "Gentle Leaders."

After the Omahas had been driven to the White River by the Cut-Heads, their medicine seemed weak and they joined the Iowas, but the *Paw-Hah'n Wah-Shta-Ge* left them, assuming again their once honored name of Gentle Headmen, and they traveled up the Missouri and sought sanctuary with the Arikaras, a Caddoan tribe, long earth-house dwellers on the southeastern limb of the Big Bend of the Missouri River. Soon the *Paw-Hah'n* became "Ponca," and the *Wah-Shta-Ge* was dropped by the other tribes, and they themselves gradually accepted the name Ponca.

There is a river which runs from the apron of the Black Hills to the Missouri, and the Little Ones and other Siouans call it *Ni-Pische,* meaning "Bad Waters" or "Bad River."

The Ponca went up this Bad Waters hunting with their Caddoan protectors. They were far out on the plains, with the Black Hills looming ahead of them like a cloud, when out of the cloud of alkali dust emerged an apparition. It materialized into a party of Kiowa hunters mounted.

Both the Arikaras and the Poncas fled in terror down the Bad Waters from these then unidentified people riding mystery dogs. They hid themselves when they could find sufficient cover, but apparently the Kiowas were not on the warpath, and rode casually on down the river, flushing groups of Poncas and Arikaras, who fled weeping.

14. Guns

SOME TIME AFTER THE PLANS (inspired by La Salle, Iberville, and Bienville) were being carried out along the Mississippi and the Illinois rivers and their, France's, mission-forts were being constructed, and just as the Little Ones were becoming accustomed to the *wah-don-skas* of metal, such as awls and fleshers and hatchets and knives and tattoo needles, more and more Frenchmen came to live at the forts. And those at Cahokia, just below the mouth of the Missouri on the left bank of the Mississippi, the Little Ones visited quite often. This mission-fort at Cahokia was a gesture to the Jesuits, but it also served as one of the string of forts and settlements to discourage the English. It was called Tamarois Mission as well as Cahokia, and was built also with the idea that it would become a center of activity and trade for all the natives of the lower Missouri River, despite the fact that it was across the river in Illini country from them.

It was founded in March, 1699, and Father Limoges, a Jesuit, arrived from upriver and with enthusiasm made known his plans for planting the cross all along the Missouri River. He felt it was time to raise a cross at the village of the fierce pagan giants known as the *Ouazha-she*. These people, who called themselves Little Ones when *Wah'Kon-Tah* was listening, were needed for the French plan because of their prowess and their domination of the lower part of the Missouri River, and their souls were important since they had already become sinners by killing and scalping a few French trappers, and there would be more rejoicing in heaven over the salvage of one sinner than a host of sinless ones.

So there was another mission planted at the mouth of the Des Pères River where the city of St. Louis now stands. Father Cosmé had celebrated mass there in company with Henri de Tonti in December, 1698, and the mission was established late in 1700 when the Kaskaskia Indians of the Illinois confederation of Algonkians came down from the Illinois River to the mouth of the Des Pères. This mission lasted only two years, and the Bear gens of the Little Ones have a story which might have a connection with this mission's short life. It was apparently on the right side of the river to serve the people of the lower Missouri, but yet on the wrong side.

After building a string of forts with the English in mind, the French then turned their thoughts to the Spaniards. The commandant Iberville also became suspicious of the Spaniards, and despite the fact that La Salle had taken the western drainage of the Mississippi for Louis XIV, the French knew little of what lay west of the river above the Red River.

Coureurs de bois were sent out up the Mississippi to find what they might. In these explorations they passed the mouths of the Osage, Grand, and Kansas rivers, and reached the Platte. They turned off each of these feeder rivers, especially the Osage, which they knew quite well by now, and apparently did not go farther than the mouth of the Platte. It is not known whether these illiterate *coureurs de bois* saw any evidence of Spanish penetration.

However, they carried muskets for their protection, in case they did come upon a Spanish settlement far up the Pekitanoui, river of mystery. By this time they were not using the matchlock, but the more advanced musket which had a flint attached to the hammer which struck sparks on the grooved steel of the pan and thereby set off the priming. This improved musket they called a fusil, and even though it had been improved and was much lighter than the old matchlock, wherein a match made of twisted cotton boiled in saltpeter had been employed to set off the priming, it was still cumbersome and would not fire every time, especially on days of high humidity or fog or on rainy days, unless the priming was protected or changed often. Also the Frenchmen sometimes carried a forked stick as a rest.

The fusil was not a sporting rifle, but was an instrument of war, and the *coureurs de bois* found it useful for killing game with which to sustain themselves in the primordial forests and on the plains, and to kill Spaniards if necessary. Anyone who opposed them in carrying out the "Louisiana Plan," whether Spaniard or Indian tribe, was said to be *méfiant,* which term applied to others also implied French virtue.

One day a party of *coureurs de bois,* exploring the new land for the commandant, were camped on the Osage River, opposite where the waters were deflected by a high limestone bluff.

The Little Ones were accustomed to seeing signs of these parties or meeting them on the river or along the wapiti trails, and groups from all the gentes had at one time or another visited Cahokia, where they had met the Black Robes. This would have been about 1700, and they had met their first Heavy Eyebrows between seventeen and twenty-five years before. When a hunting party of the Eagle gens saw the smoke of the *coureurs de bois*'s fire, they came to it. They were not hungry, but they had seen the sun glint on a long *wah-don-ska* leaning against a tree.

They had smelled the smoke of the campfire, and a scout had told them of every detail and of the number of Heavy Eyebrows present, and it was his story of the glinting *wah-don-ska* leaning against the tree that brought them to the fire of the Heavy Eyebrows.

The party of Heavy Eyebrows was a rather large one and outnumbered the Little Ones, so the greeting from these Frenchmen was not effusive. Also, the Little Ones were a hunting party and had no furs with them.

The Little Ones stood about as if waiting for something to happen. They never took the initiative under such circumstances, but saw and interpreted every gesture of the campers, as well as every expression, and wondered at every explosive laugh. Such laughter was always a mystery to them and often shocked them into immobility and vague fear, as it did the bear and the wapiti and the panther. Ebullient Frenchmen often whistled, and this caused the Little Ones to fear greatly, since only ghosts whistled. They always had this secret worry when they met with Frenchmen: that one might start whistling.

This standing about silently waiting always gave the Heavy Eyebrows confidence in their latent assumption of superiority, and they mistook this primitive caution or good manners as a sign of peasant fealty, even though they might not dare to act on their assumption.

But the Little Ones were curious, and the sun-glinting *wah-don-ska* leaning against the tree kept shouting to them, urging them to come closer and touch.

Finally, one of the Little Ones walked over and held his hand out to touch the fusil, and several of the Heavy Eyebrows jumped up and one took it. This was pure impudence, since the Little Ones were fewer than they, and they decided to show the *sauvages* what power they had with this long thing, inspiring a little more respect. One of them walked away to a tree and placed against it the bleached skull of a buffalo. Just as the forked stick was ready as a rest, a band of white-tail deer came cautiously down from the other side of the river to drink. They stood under the bluffs and stared at the fire and kept their ears forward to get the sound of talking.

The Heavy Eyebrows with the fusil moved his forked stick and rested it again, taking long aim across the river at the deer. There was a terrific blast, and the smoke hung so thick that the deer could not be seen. There was only the noise of the band scrambling up the flank of the bluff, as if they were running in the night, and the pitiful screaming of the one that had been the target. The scream came out of the smoke like the cry of a spirit, but the Little Ones stood stolidly, since they knew it was the deer.

The smoke lifted. The deer was down in the back, the ball (ten to the pound) was soft and large and had entered the sacral region. The deer continued to scream until one of the hunters walked to the edge of the river and finished it with an arrow since the Heavy Eyebrows made no move as they did not wish to waste another shot.

The Gallic pride of race was inflated and the *voyageurs* watched the faces of the Little Ones, and the Little Ones could only stare at the long *wah-don-ska*, again leaning against the tree, but they made no move to come near it.

Finally they wandered off upriver among the red oaks and walnuts, following the snakelike loops. They walked until darkness overtook them, then they built their fire and stuck pieces of venison on sharp sticks, and set them in the ground slanted toward the fire.

After eating, they talked desultorily of the *wah-don-ska* that killed the deer across the river. There was consensus that the thing that held the flint was like a skunk's leg, and they named it that. They talked more of the long *wah-don-ska*, lazily, as if it had no interest for them, but it had absorbed all other thoughts like the black bass in the summer pools of the prairie canyon, as they would say, who eats all the others and keeps the shallow water muddy. So were their thoughts muddied, and no little thoughts could live in their heads.

They were naturally poetic and were not concerned half so much about the sudden explosion and the power which killed the deer across the river as about the scream of the deer coming out of the smoke fog. If they had been terribly impressed by the blast and the wonder of the smoke the *wah-don-ska* belched, they might have called it a "smoke stick" or a "thunder stick," but the poetic Little Ones kept saying among themselves, "It-causes-things-to-cry-out," and that is what they named the first gun they had ever seen, it-causes-things-to-cry-out, *wa-ho-to'n-the,* and that is their name for a rifle. When they speak of the hammer of a rifle, they must say, "the-skunk-leg-of-it-causes-things-to-cry-out."

15. To Control a Continent

Now THE HEAVY EYEBROWS had begun to talk about tin and lead mines as well as about furs, and sent small parties up the Missouri to explore and to determine the closeness of the Spaniards, and one explorer, Le Sueur in the summer of 1700 assured himself that the meaning of the term Missouri was "canoe," and that the people who bore that name were "people of the canoes," and he noted the continual war between the Osages and the Pawnees.

Another, Father Marest of the Kaskaskia Mission, wrote to Iberville, who was on the Isle Dauphin, concerning the geographical information which he had been able to come by. He said that the Missouri (still calling it the Pekitanoui) was as long and as large as the Mississippi, and he wrote of the Konzas and the Pawnees, stating definitely that they carried on commerce with the Spaniards and had Spanish horses. He also mentioned the Sioux and the Iowas as being allied, and also mentioned the Otoes, all linguistic relatives of the Little Ones and except for the Sioux in close touch with them. He stated that neither he nor any of the French had yet been among the tribes of the Missouri, except the people called the Missourias and the people called Osages. He wanted very much to be accurate in writing to his commandant, so he assured him that while he believed in what he had been told, he must hasten to assure Monsieur the Commandant that the details were had from the *sauvage* Osages themselves, "a people who could not tell exactly the distance of or from each vil-

135

lage"—possibly in French leagues. They could have told accurately the number of valleys. He could say, however, "It is the country of the beaver."

Two years later the Black Robe, Father Bergier, successor to Father Cosmé of Cahokia, was interested in establishing missions immediately among the *sauvages* of the Missouri, especially among the Konzas and the Pawnees, and he applied for permission from Quebec and Paris. He seemed to dismiss the Little Ones, since even at this early date they were apparently appreciating their importance in the plans of Iberville and Bienville, and were beginning to be haughty and demanding, periodically parading in their great height with their faces painted by their women with bluff paint. These patient and prideful artists applied the traditional designs in redbud charcoal and pigments from the Red Beds and limonite deposits from the Mississippian limestone, all mixed with bear fat. Self-confident men of more than six feet, heightened by the roach of turkey gobbler "beard" and deer-tail hair, with faces diabolically painted, swarming the forest, even if they came only with furs, could very well wait for salvation, since humility, the very basic state for the reception of Christ, was dramatically absent.

The Father definitely decided that the numerous and prideful Osages were not ready for his ministrations, nor were the Missourias, who had been reduced to harmlessness and in their weakness of medicine were trying to attach themselves to the Konzas and the Little Ones.

The Little Ones say that any number of disasters might have caused the weakening of the once strong medicine of the Missourias. They know that the Sac and Foxes (possibly about 1701) had crept along the left bank of the Missouri in the darkness, in a string of canoes, and had taken the Missouria village unawares, killing more than half of them. They also say that the Missourias would not kill the Heavy Eyebrows and allowed each trader or trapper or Bohème to stay and even gave them their most beautiful women. Soon, they say, the *we-lu-schka,* the little mystery people living in the semen of some of the wandering Heavy Eyebrows, had killed off many of the

Missourias, and now they must camp close to the Little Ones or the Konzas.

Then Iberville nurtured the idea of opening up commercial relations with the Spaniards, who were vaguely conceived to be somewhere near the vaguely conceived headwaters of the Missouri River and eventually reaching California. Within the first ten years of the eighteenth century, despite the War of the Spanish Succession in Europe, several expeditions went up the Missouri, but possibly not more than four hundred leagues, which in miles would be about one thousand. They questioned bands of people from the Osage, Konza, Pawnee, and Iowa and other tribes and often made their stories fit their preconceived ideas of Pawnee, Apache, and Spanish *méfiance*. By this time the Padoucas, the *Pa-Do'n-Ka* of the Little Ones, had raided down from the Kaw River and were active in the area later called Comanchería, which includes the southeastern part of modern Colorado, the southwestern part of modern Kansas, extreme eastern New Mexico, and the Panhandles of Oklahoma and Texas. This movement to the southern plains seemed as by design to cause the Heavy Eyebrows more difficulty in carrying out their plans.

One Derbanne, in 1706 and 1707, had boasted that he and his small party were the first Frenchmen to go far up the Missouri and that the fact that they had seen Spanish horses would be sufficient evidence that there had been Spanish penetration.

Iberville had some idea of exploring the *Ni-Zhu-Dse,* Red Waters, of the Little Ones, called by the French "Marne," later called "Napestle" and by other names, and finally the Arkansas River. He even had the idea of moving some of the friendly Indians there to form a buffer between the French and the Spaniards. The immigrant Padoucas would soon, after they took root, become this buffer, but unfortunately they were the enemies of the Little Ones and the Konzas and the Pawnees.

This would be the first attempt by European commercial interests to use the tribes as pawns other than military—at least in the Mississippi Valley, and even this scheme was also military strategy.

The Little Ones have no memory of this, even though they, being the most powerful of the French allies, must have been approached. It is likely that they were still too well organized under the authority (loose though it may have been through gentile pride and the vanity of perhaps twenty-two chieftains or leaders) of the Grand *Tzi-Sho* and the Grand *Hunkah*.

The people of the plains, whom the Little Ones called *Pa-Do'n-Ka* because their noses sweated, and whom the French and Spaniards called Padouca, were called *Komanteia* by their mountain neighbors the Utes, and this name, which meant in Ute "Anyone-Who-Wants-to-Fight-Me-All-the-Time," finally became Comanches.

They became the real buffer between the Spaniards and the French, along with the Apaches, from whom they had taken their domain. The Pawnees were enemies of both the French and the vigorous Padoucas at this time, and the Little Ones, while extremely important as pipe-talk allies at least, were also a very important factor in keeping the Padoucas confined to their domain, as well as keeping the English-favoring Sac and Foxes north of the Missouri and the Pawnees fully occupied.

And this necessity of the French—to keep the wild Centaurs of the plains, the Padoucas, confined to a range which sometimes extended far up the Kaw and the Arkansas, leaving only the Missouri River highway open for the French fur trade and for prospecting for minerals—made pampering of the Little Ones a policy.

This necessitous pampering was the beginning of the haughty insolence which characterized the Little Ones for a century and a half. They received fusils in trade with the French and horses in trade with the Kiowas and the Konzas and by theft from the Pawnees and the Padoucas and the Apaches. They had the musket first among the tribes of the lower Missouri because they had the power to open the water tradeways of the Missouri, as no other tribe, with the exception of the across-the-Missouri Sac and Foxes, dared trespass on their domain. After they got their horses, they controlled the lower Missouri, their own river, the Osage, the Gasconade, the Konza (the modern Kaw River) with the aid of their splinter, the Konza tribe, and the Arkansas, possibly to a wavering line of range domination between them and the Padoucas; and later they would chase the Caddoan tribes across the Red River. They crossed to the south of the Arkansas also west of the hundredth Meridian at will into the domain of the Padoucas and hunted on the Republican River in territory claimed by the Pawnees.

The modern Republican River, which runs out of Colorado into Kansas, then into Nebraska, thence into Kansas again to become a fork of the Kaw River, was always a magnet for buffalo. During the long summer hours they stood under the scattered cottonwoods where the prairie breezes discouraged the flies, and here they ruminated by the thousands, lying or standing like statues, indolently leaving their droppings through the centuries. The Little Ones called this river Buffalo-Dung Waters, as did the Pawnees. It was on the Buffalo-Dung Waters that the Little Ones circled a band of gunless Loup Pawnees (*Pa-I'n Ma-Ha*) and killed them all. They tugged a dead, fallen cottonwood with a spikelike end and replanted it with the grisly head of a Pawnee stuck on the end. Long Hair [Lodges] from-River-Bank People were worthy foes, and they made a song about this incident.

Because of the lure of the Mississippi and the Missouri rivers for adventurers and traders and trappers and prospectors, and because of their significance in European politics, and because the Little Ones and the Missourias and the Konzas lived on the highway that was the Missouri River, they were not only the first Missouri River tribes met with by the exploring French, but were of great importance to their plans. In this way, since the French were eager to learn all they could about the prospects of trade in furs and trade with the Spaniards and about mining, the Little Ones especially had the honor of giving their names to many of the rivers and to the other tribes. The names many of these tribes called themselves have been lost, and they carry those given to them by the Little Ones which were recorded by the French.

Of the Siouan tribes, the *Ko'n-Za* became the Kansas and eventually the Kaws, their modern name. This tribe may have the honor of being the first Siouan tribe met by the Europeans, and the name the

Little Ones gave their *Hunkah* splinter might have been Hispaniolized as "Quaes" about 1520 or 1521, when Coronado met a people
whose name he interpreted as "Quaes."

The splinter tribe represented by unitized gentes of the *Hunkah*
division of the Little Ones, called by them the *U-Mo'n-Ho'n*, Dwellers-on-the-Bluff, became the Omahas, and the *U-Ga-Xpa* became the
Quapaws. The *Paw-Hah'n* became the Poncas. The Caddoan enemy,
the *Pa-I'n* became the Pawnees, and the *Wi-Tsi-Ta* became the Wichitas, and the Athapascan people of the southern plains, called *A-Pa-
Tsi* by the Little Ones, became the Apaches, and the *Pa-Do'n-Ka* became the Padoucas long before they were known as Comanches. And
across the Mississippi, living along the Ohio River in the modern state
of Kentucky, was an Algonkian tribe who had been driven out of the
northeast by the Iroquois and out of the southeast, to which they had
fled, by the Iroquoian Cherokees, who called themselves *Chaouanon*,
People-of-the-South. These Algonkians were rather more developed
than the buffalo tribes of the plains, and it seems that the Little Ones
traded with them across the Mississippi, bringing them buffalo robes
to trade for maple sugar and syrup. The Little Ones called them
Zho-Ni, meaning Water [Sap]-from-Wood-People, or *zho*, wood,
and *ni*, water. The name by which these people are now known is
Shawnee.

Some of the names which the Little Ones gave the French they did
not attempt to Gallicize, but translated. The forks of the Osage River
near where they lived, the Little Ones called The-Place-of-the-Many-
Swans, and the French translated it into Marais des Cygnes. They
called the river near whose mouth they lived *Wa-Tsi-Uzi*. It might
have been the name for the whole Osage River system originally and
meant Snake-with-Mouth-Open, since the mouth of the Osage River
is wide like the mouth of a striking snake. However, the Heavy Eyebrows called this branch of the Osage River, the Marmiton.

When they placed their fingers on sketches they had made in the
dust and asked, "How does this river call itself," the Little Ones
would say, "*Ni-Btha-Ska*, Water-Flat-White," which the French
translated into La Platte, but the name remained in the modern state
of Nebraska. The river of the *Ko'n-Za*, became the Kansas or the

Kaw, and the name has been preserved in the modern state of Kansas.

This was what the French were busily doing during the first decade of the eighteenth century. They were also learning the language of the Little Ones and using it as a lingua franca, as the early missionaries and traders on the St. Lawrence were using the Algonkian tongue. They were pointing to each tribe between them and the Spaniards and each tribe living along the Missouri River and asking, "These people, what do they call themselves?" The Little Ones didn't know what they called themselves, but had their name for each one of them, and these names represented certain incidents or physical or mental characteristics, as they did among the little boys at play or the young men exuberantly at hunting or at war. These names they gave to the Heavy Eyebrows.

The French had no academic interest in the people or the places, but rather intense commercial and political interest, and the information they received was expressly for commercial and political enlightenment.

As the Heavy Eyebrows became more and more familiar with their giant allies, they noted that they did not all live in one village, but in several villages. There was a village on a high ridge on the south fork of the White Waters or Snake-with-Mouth-Open Waters, which they now called the Osage River, just below the mouth of the Snake-with-Mouth-Open-Waters or the river they called the Marmiton, which seemed to be the main village, and this was where the Grand *Hunkah* and the Grand *Tzi-Sho* lived. However, on the same fork of the Osage River almost at river level near a marsh, there was another village of Little Ones, and they knew that there was another village on the Missouri River proper, and still another village up the ridge from the main one. They wondered about these villages and asked first about the village on the river near the marsh at a lower elevation than the main village on the ridge. There was also a village on the Snake-with-Mouth-Open-Waters, the Marmiton.

These Little Ones who live near the marsh under the ridge are the *U-Dse-Tsa,* the people tried to tell them, the *U-Dse-Tsa,* the Down-Below-People. But the Heavy Eyebrows couldn't understand why they were called thus. Weren't they a part of the *Wazhazhe?* The people assured them they were, but they were also called *U-Dse-Ta.* The Heavy Eyebrows could not understand, so the Little Ones resorted to sign language, and bending, lowered the hand with the palm downward indicating below. Ah, at last the Heavy Eyebrows seemed to understand; that lowered hand would be the manner in which they would indicate smallness, a petite something, and they assured themselves that the Little Ones living down under the ridges near the marshes must be the *Petit Wazhazhe,* or the Little Osages, and this is what this physical division of the Little Ones have always been called. Naturally, most of the men of the Down-Below-People of the Little Ones were six feet and over, but the French interpretation stuck.

16. The Little Ones Had a Traditional Flood

THE LITTLE ONES know well the details of the physical division of the tribe, a division that has nothing whatever to do with the gentile organization, except that the five physical divisions, the *U-Dse-Ta,* the Down-Below-People, called Little Osages, did have a chieftain over the gentile leaders. He might belong to the Eagle or the Bear or some other gens, but still would be leader of the village unit, the Little Osages.

The physical division of the tribe happened in a time no one knows and on a large river, but no one knows which large river. According to the tribal memory, it was a river capable of spreading over wide areas when in full spate, and any one of the four rivers associated with the history of the Little Ones could qualify. It might have been the Ohio, the Mississippi, the Missouri, or the Little Ones' own river, the Osage.

Whatever river it was, the Little Ones were living as a tribal unit along its banks, with the fireplaces of all the gentes intact and the civil and military organizations complete.

The Little Old Men had added ritual to ritual to safeguard the tribe against all the whimsical manifestations of *Wah'Kon-Tah* as they had experienced them, by propitiation. Since the *wah-hopeh* shrine had been made for the sacred hawk, there had been no hunters or warriors killed by the jagged lightning spear of *Wah'Kon-Tah* while carrying it, and he seemed to be pleased with the Little Ones and was listening to their prayer-songs and to their dance-prayers; and to the fasting Little Old Men and the fasting chieftains and leaders, he seemed to send the proper messengers to respond to their petitions.

But suddenly the rains began. For days the rain fell, and the river became discolored, then the foam swirled on it as it climbed into the willows and gurgled about the roots of the sycamores. It climbed higher and began to roar, and walnuts slanted over the waters that were as brown as the buffalo cow in the summer, and finally fell and were carried off, and the elms shivered. The waters began to feel with their brown-yellow fingers up the feeder canyons and to spread out in lenses over the ancient flood plain.

The Little Ones watched, and when some large red oak or hackberry or walnut or sycamore fell, they hissed through their teeth. Here and there women began to keen, and the dogs became nervous, and occasionally there arose a wolflike howl, long drawn out and mournful, and after this more women would keen. The *Wah-Sha-She,* the Water People, especially the Turtle gens, would sing a prayer, and when this was not effective, they prayed through the beaver and otter and deer and panther.

But still the rains came, and the waters the color of the cow in the summer rose higher and higher and the roar became steady and a purposeful thing of destruction, as little by little the waters crept up to the village of the Little Ones, and the trees on the other side became like bushes, and there were treetops in the water bowing and disappearing, then emerging.

Then one morning, after a night when there was no sound except the roar of the river, the Little Old Men began to take the sacred skins covering the Lodge of Mystery. There was no song of the wolf or the coyote and no hunting call of *ito'n* the great horned owl, to give the Little Ones comfort, and the Little Old Men cut their Rising Song short and warned the people.

They had to flee pell-mell as a sudden flood wave lapped at their lodges. They ran for the high ridge and the bluffs back of the river. Members of families in their fright were separated, only the children belonging to each being kept grouped. Each of the gentes had members distributed among the five groups the people formed into, and *Tzi-Sho* could be found with *Hunkah,* and leadership of the frightened ones seemed to fall to the most fleet and purposeful.

One group climbed the bluffs and stopped and watched from the hills, and many of them climbed trees. A second group stopped on the plateau, which was forested, and there during a lull in the rain started their fires and began to dry their things, casting retreating wolf looks at the flood below. The first group, those who climbed above the bluff to the hills and there climbed the trees, were thereafter called *Pa-Ci-U-Gthi'n,* now *Pa Solé,* Top-of-the-Tree-Sitters, or Big Hills. And those who stopped on the plateau above the bluffs to dry their clothing were called *Co'n-Dse-U-Gthi'n* now *Sa'n Solé,* Upper-Forest-Sitters, or Upland-Forest People; and the group who ran up the broad valley of a feeder stream, and stopped high up in the valley were thereafter called *Wah-Ho-Ka-Li,* Sitters-in-the-Locusts, or Thorny-Thicket People, since the upper valley of the feeder stream was covered with water locusts with long spurs like the spurs of walks-on-wings, the turkey cock.

The fourth group, because of impedimenta or because of many small children, were unable to climb the bluff quickly, and stopped under the bluff and watched the flood abate. Here they established their camp, and were called Down-Below-People, and later, through French misinterpretation of the sign language, were called Little Osages.

The fifth group stayed in the flooded village, gathered on some high ground like the back of a floating turtle, and there chanted and sang, weeping; a terrific cacophony of keening women, men singing their prayers, and the dogs howling, with the stench of flotsam and mud and decaying organic matter as the waters receded and the summer sun shone to make steam of the air. These people were called *No'n-Dse-Waspi,* the Heart-Stays-People.

The people of the different groups who had climbed the cliffs and had stayed under the cliffs and had fled up the broad feeder valley came back to the fetid village, and each family claimed their own. While they were doing this and the Heart-Stays-People were cleaning out their lodges preparing to stay, the Little Old Men came among them and said that they would send two leaders out to fast for seven days to determine what *Wah'Kon-Tah* wanted them to do, and in the meantime they must stay where they had built their drying fires until they could know the will of *Wah'Kon-Tah*.

The chieftain of the Heavenly Bodies gens of the *Tzi-Sho* division was chosen to go out and fast, and the chieftain of the Eagle gens of the *Hunkah* division was chosen for the hunger-vision.

The Heavenly Bodies leader placed the soft under tail-feather of the eagle on the left side of his head and put the dark earth on the left temple. The symbolical man was facing east, since this was a peaceful activity, and the Heavenly Bodies leader of the *Tzi-Sho* went to the north, the left from orientation, after walking to the left around the village four times. The Eagle gens leader placed the long tail-feather of the eagle on the right side of his head and put the dark earth on his right temple. He, after walking four times around the village to the right, went to the south, the *Hunkah* side, and right from orientation; thus the two fasters would go in diametrically opposite directions, each singing his prayer-songs to *Wah'Kon-Tah*.

When the songs had died in the distance, the others went back to their slimy work. Late that afternoon the river had shrunk by half, and the wolves sang, and the coyotes yelped, and close by from the top of a dead burr oak, *ito'n,* the great horned owl, gave comfort again with his talk, and from the prairies back of the woods came the sad-sweet cry of the curlew, and the Little Ones knew that the rains were over. Ever since that tragic time the curlew has been associated with happiness, despite his mournful song.

Tribal memory recalls this physical division of the Little Ones in smallest detail in regard to the effects of the least incident upon the people, such as the wolf song and the coyotes and the owl, and the welcome sadness of the curlew and the talk of the wild waters, and their color and their odor, and the emotions of the people; but there is nothing about the experiences of the two fasters. Usually these experiences are given in recitations or songs and in that way remembered, but this time there seems to be nothing. They say only that the two wiped the dark earth from their heads and after seven days came back, bathed, and were fed, and after a long sleep came before the Little Old Men.

Soon the town crier walked along the slippery ways singing the message from the Little Old Men, that *Wah'Kon-Tah* had spoken. He raised his voice to a high pitch, then held it on one note like a lone winter wolf, then in diminuendo gave the message.

Soon the five groups were gathered in one place around the Little Old Men, who told the people that the reason *Wah'Kon-Tah* would not listen to them when they asked for the water to stop rising was now clear. *Wah'Kon-Tah* had desired that the Little Ones break up into five villages, so that one village would not grow to be too large, and if the enemy struck one village suddenly, the others would be free to come to their aid, and also each village would be a scout or guard for all.

The Little Old Men here manifested their ingenuity. They saved face since their petitions had been of no effect when the water was rising, and were now saying that the scattering of the people in groups had been *Wah'Kon-Tah*'s plan, and thereafter, just as no two young people of the same gens could marry each other, no two people of the same gens within the same physical division could marry each other, and the boy must go to the girl's village to live.

But of these five groups only the *U-Dse-Ta*, the Down-Below People, the campers under the cliff (at the bottom of the cliff), became almost as distinguished as a splinter tribe because of the special questioning by the Heavy Eyebrows and because the terrain of their village under the cliffs must be so conspicuously different from the ridge or hill dwellings of two of the groups, or plateau or high valley dwellings of the others. The Heart-Stays People seemed to be the smallest group of the lot.

Obedient to *Wah'Kon-Tah*'s wishes, the five groups ever after lived on the type of topography to which they fled that day long ago. They settled in the places where they had camped with their drying fires, and when they migrated, each group chose a spot most closely resembling the topographical features where they had taken refuge— the hill people on the hills, the plateau people on the plateau, the thorn people in a broad valley, the down-below people under the cliffs or the ridges, and the heart-stays people in beautiful low valleys on the edge of a stream. The large village of the Little Ones just below the mouth of the modern Marmiton River in modern Vernon County, Missouri, was really on a ridge above the river and was a combination of hill, plateau, and thorn villages when Du Tisne visited it in 1719. The *U-Dse-Ta,* the Little Osage, village was on the same south fork of the river also in modern Vernon County, Missouri, but above the mouth of the Marmiton and, of course, under the ridge by a marsh.

17. The Down-Below People Meet the Cliff Dwellers

As DID THE TRIBE AS A WHOLE, the *U-Dse-Ta,* the Little Osages, virile and energetic, rode afar in search of excitement. They too felt their great importance to the Heavy Eyebrows and became arrogant and whimsical.

One day a group of them set out across the prairie-plains to the west and southwest. The leader carried the *wah-hopeh,* the sacred hawk, and they all wore their red fetish shields and were armed with a few fusils, but all carried their bows and arrows and with them they had the ceremonial arrows, one red and one black.

They set out on the road which Grandfather takes every day when he goes home. They had gone up the south fork of the Osage River, thence across the prairie-swell divide to the Neosho River, and down it to the river they called Red Waters, the Arkansas. They traveled up this river until they came to the mouth of the modern Huerfano River, then up this river to the south fork called Cucharas River, thence up this river to the pass in the Culebra Range of the Sangre de Cristo Mountains called La Veta. This was an old Spanish trail, and these questing Little Osages might have met either Spaniards or Comanches or even Utes in the San Luis valley. The Spanish Peaks were the last definite landmark given by Traveling Rain of that time long ago, or else definite description did not reach the ear of the late chief of the Little Osages; faded before they got to him.

They either picked up the modern Río Grande and traveled down,

149

or they went up this river and passed over the Continental Divide at Wolf Creek Pass and thence down the San Juan River. They were going toward the Cliffs, the west again, and they had crossed many valleys and their counting-sticks of willow were growing into a bundle.

Horses must have inspired in them a spirit not unlike the spirit of the eleventh-century crusaders or knights but without definite objective, certainly without romantic objective. They rode on and noted the harshness of the Sacred One. The sun glinted from mica and disintegrated quartz, and cacti stood like lost men in the distances. They kept close to the bed of the river where water was found in lenses.

And then these venturing cavaliers, looking for an enemy, met only the dragon. He was much smaller than the dragons of chivalry, and they were hungry, so that their approach was not in the least romantic. They had seen no game, only dancing heat. They would not have caught one of their own prairie dogs or a gopher, since they carried evil, but this thing they cornered, and *Wa-K'o'n-Tsi-E,* One Who-Triumphs, picked it up. It didn't bite like a snake, but caught his hand and seemed to chew falling over on its back, grinding poison into his veins, and the others had to kill it before they could get it detached, and they then had no stomach for it.

They cut One-Who-Triumphs' wound, but did not try sucking out the poison, and they looked about for pear cactus stem so that they could stop the bleeding, after they believed the poison to be gone. There was no narrow-leafed purple cone flower there as antidote.

They were in sight of some distant mountains. One-Who-Triumphs became nervous and sweated so copiously that the dry air seemed unable to absorb it. He became frightened and, as was characteristic of the Little Ones when they came face to face with menaces which they could not understand, he gave up and fell from his horse. The others watched him die, then set the body upright facing west and piled sun-hot stones about it. They spent an hour singing the Song of Death, but the song that carried over the prairie-plains or bounced from the limestone bluffs of their lower river seemed to be smothered as it left their mouths here in this land of no water. They rode on, taking his horse with them. The mountains were dulled by heat haze, but they were coming close to them, and in them they would find water. When they referred to the Gila monster, they called him "When-He-Bites-You-Die-Before-You-Reach-the-Mountain."

The late chief of the Little Osages could not place his finger on a spot in modern Colorado or Arizona or New Mexico and say this is the place where we met *I'n-Ba-Pa-We-Tsi'n,* Hits-Head-with-Stone People. Traveling Rain, his long-ago ancestor, had never described every stream or mountain, and definite description had never come down to the late chief.

The Hits-Head-with-Stone People were really Sling-Shot people, since the sling shot was their weapon, and they were short and burned almost black by the sun of the desert. Their lodges were like the lodges of the cliff swallow high up in the face of a cliff, and down below they had their corn patches. Traveling Rain had handed down the incident through six chiefs of the Little Osages, and as the late chief told of it, there was the impression that it had happened yesterday, even though this happened more than two hundred years ago from the time of the telling in 1934, if one allows thirty-three years to each generation.

"We rode toward these short, sun-blackened people," he said. "They wore their hair cut in bangs, and they sent some out to menace the horses. They were not afraid of horses. Their faces were not bluff-painted, but they wore masks which were representative of faces twisted and snarling in anger, and as they approached, they chanted."

The *U-Dse-Ta* on their horses felt secure, and they carried a few fusils as well as their other armament. They put their horses into a slow lope and rode past the men in masks, and they stepped aside, and the people working in the field fled toward the cliffs, but the Osages overtook them and cut them off. They stood defiantly and began loading their sling shots as the Little Ones rode among them. However, as they lifted their new French axes to strike, the short people crouched out of range, but rose as a man when the Osages were riding past before turning their horses, and each man grabbed a horse by the tail with his left hand, and with his right let fly his stone from the sling shot, aimed at the backs of the Osage heads.

151

Several fell from their horses, and others wobbled but clung to the befeathered manes.

Even when they put their horses into a run, the short men clung for as long as possible. Past the short men the Osages turned and stood in line, stringing their arrows, and the short men stood reloading their sling shots. The Osages, instead of rushing them, stood guard while several of them began rounding up the two horses from which the riders had fallen. They were nibbling at the stunted corn as if nothing had happened. They bluff-rushed the short men away from their dazed comrades, then pulled them up and rode off some distance.

The short men began to run toward the cliffs, and already people were high on the face of the cliffs like ants in a sinuous string. The Osages then began to circle the fleeing people who had not reached the base of the cliffs, each warrior trying to determine which one of them might be the chief or leader. To count coup on him would be a signal honor. However, they seemed to be all alike, these stocky, sun-blackened men, and they killed three of them before they arrived at the base of the cliffs. The killer of each man counted his coup by striking the dead body with his bow end or with a coup stick if he happened to have one along. He was followed by the one who arrived at the body first. They had only one spear among them, so they tied all three scalps to the spear, and the leader carried it uplifted, but in the desert air the scalps hung limp, and their song fell flat and died in the heat-dance.

They were not far from junipers, and they rested in the shade of them and allowed their wounded to rest, but one of them, *U-Ki-Pa-To'n,* Rolls Himself, began talking about strange things, and when he rose to walk, he fell, and again talked about strange things. They waited there for him to die. They piled stones about his sitting form, facing the way Grandfather travels when he leaves the Sacred One. They sang the Song of Death again, then rode on.

When they got into the high mountains again, they found the bundle of willow sticks, which represented the valleys they had crossed, cumbersome, so they cut several branch ends of the pine, and thereafter until they reached the Red Waters, the Arkansas, they counted the valleys by the long leaves, pulling one after each valley crossed.

18. Slaves and Spirits

THE LITTLE ONES WERE NOW FAMILIAR not only with the illiterate and jolly fugitives from church and fief on the St. Lawrence, with their gay *chansons* and their very funny dancing with arms locked, circling a fire, but with builders of forts, second sons of France, gay adventurers and noblemen of culture, but most of them seemed interested only in furs and mines and trade with the Spaniards, and the Little Ones were a means to all these things. The only other interest they had in the Little Ones had to do with their women. They all took the widows or married the girls.

The Black Robes had not yet succeeded in winning back from the devil the imperious souls of the Little Ones, so they remained with their own religion, civil government, and military organization intact, and the only change which the Heavy Eyebrows had brought about in them was to make them arrogant, imperious warriors, pampered liars (where the sacred word had not been given), slavers, and impudent negotiators.

It seemed that there were always several gens under their leaders riding the woodlands and the prairie-plains, taking horses, killing the Heavy Eyebrows on their way to trade with tribes other than themselves, killing the whole party if they carried guns to trade to the Pawnees or other Caddoans. Then they lied their way out when the Heavy Eyebrows accused them of infidelity.

They appreciated their position as buffer and balance of power between the French and the Spaniards, and they realized that the furs they brought to trade with the Heavy Eyebrows were the best, since they came from their lush domain.

Typical was their creeping upon the camp of eleven *voyageurs* who had many trade fusils. This was typical of the Black Bear–Panther gentes, and they have a story which describes a like incident, if not this one. When they came near the camp, say the Black Bear gens raconteurs, they saw that the Heavy Eyebrows were fewer in number than they, so they rode boldly up to them. Under such circumstances when outnumbered, the Heavy Eyebrows were very effusive in their greeting to their allies, and began lying about the trade fusils for the Caddoans.

Apparently the Black Bear warriors didn't intend to kill their Heavy Eyebrows allies, but simply take their fusils and other trade goods, but when the Heavy Eyebrows became so effusive and tried to pat the leader on the back, the gens seemed to act in unison, and they had soon killed the eleven *voyageurs*.

The letter from the governor-general of Louisiana, Bienville, to the commandant of the Illinois country implies that the Little Ones reflected Latin chicanery and that they used Latin tactics.

"The Osage, according to the advice which they have had from the Missouri that Monsieur Dartaguiette had resolved to send the nations against them to avenge the death, have charged the traders who were at the Missouris to make excuses to him in their behalf, and of assuring him that they had no thought of killing Frenchmen, and that they would submit to all satisfaction required of them. Not content with that, they have been to the Arkansas [Arkansas Post among the Quapaws] to bear their excuses to the officer who commands there—that I do not believe it suits the state of our affairs to push this matter any further. We do not need to seek new wars."

Obviously the Little Ones had no intention of doing any of the above things, but they aided the Heavy Eyebrows in saving face, knowing before they killed the *voyageurs* that the Heavy Eyebrows would be compelled to make the usual bluff about "sending the nations against them." These nations the Little Ones knew well; they were the Caddoans who fled across the Red River when the word

"Osage" was mentioned. The Caddoan tribe with the dangerously strong medicine, the Pawnees, were enemies of the Heavy Eyebrows most of the time and were not to be controlled by them.

The Little Ones, proud and virile as pedestrians, were now as cavaliers even more imperious, restive, and whimsical, and they still placed bravery above all other virtues. They never, albeit, seemed to accord the Heavy Eyebrows the same status as they accorded the Pawnees, the Apaches, the Padoucas, and later the Sac and Foxes and the Cheyenne-Arapahoes. They cast no pearls of bravery before the amiable, sinuous Latins, who imprisoned body odors within the buckskin Algonkian shirts and whose chief mission in life was the bringing of *mo'n-ce* miracles down the Mississippi, and lately up the Mississippi.

There was little romance in their relationship, and seldom were there exciting, romantic skirmishes where a warrior leader might display his courage by riding up and down before the enemy.

The Heavy Eyebrows were prosaic business partners, who supplied them with fusils and hatchets and knives and scrapers and fleshers and awls, for which they traded slaves and furs.

And business was ruining romance, and ceremonial as well. Now they didn't think of the traditional counting of coups when they met the Pawnees, but of taking them alive to be traded to the Heavy Eyebrows as slaves. A live Pawnee to be traded meant more fusils, until almost every warrior of the more energetic gentes had one, and soon there was a difference between the war parties which rode out to count coups and take scalps and those which rode out slave raiding.

They used more yellow in their face painting now, since yellow was the mark of the captive, and the yellow paint on the face of the Little Ones was a sign that they were on a raid for slaves. Each warrior carried a captive-strap cut ceremonially from the left or right hind leg of the buffalo hide, according to whether it was to be carried by some gens of the *Tzi-Sho* or by a gens of one of the *Hunkah* divisions. This captive-strap was carried ceremonially in the treated heart sac of the buffalo. Hanging from the warrior's buffalo-skin belt made from the skin of a calf, and which supported his clout, was his buckskin pouch, decorated with flattened porcupine quills. In this pouch among other things he carried paint made from the four colors of the earth—dark, blue, yellow, and red—to be used at the proper times. On raids he carried limonite.

When they came into the villages or camps with their captives, there were no scalps waving from their spears, and their song, "We have met our enemy and now our brother can enter the Spiritland," had no meaning. The dejected captives walked in front of them, and the women came out to meet them shouting maledictions and brandishing knives, if the captives happened to be from an enemy people of strong medicine. The warriors protected their captives, their merchandise. The women must forget traditional rituals, and they were not allowed to come near them. If one of them remembered a father, a husband, a son who had not come back with the others from a skirmish with this enemy, then she must be contented to go out alone, place the blue of mourning on her forehead, and mourn to *Wah'-Kon-Tah*.

The captives meant fusils, and the fusils meant power, and this power meant more captives and fewer of the Little Ones scalped by the Pawnees or the Padoucas, who were still almost gunless, as were the other enemies, the Red River Caddoans and the Apaches.

When the Little Ones explained to the Heavy Eyebrows that the more fusils meant the more captives to be taken down the river, they took the limit off the number of fusils to be traded to their whimsical allies.

Slave trading, since they captured only the enemy, soon occurred to the Little Ones as being just another manner of defeating their enemies, even though their traditional songs and their tradition of saving the life of the bravest of their captives, and the carrying back to village or camp the hair of the defeated ones did not harmonize with their songs and ceremonials. Apparently *Wah'Kon-Tah* gave no sign of his displeasure.

But Bienville did disapprove of Indian slavery, and the Heavy Eyebrows traders would meet the Little Ones at some designated spot away from the eyes of the officials and the missionaries, and here they traded the bright fusils, powder, lead, weaving, axes, fleshers, needles for tattooing, knives, and beads. The traders would look the captives over carefully, then put their own value on them. They captured no women for this purpose, according to tribal memory of the Little Ones.

There was always the white oak barrel of *pe-tsa-ni,* firewater, in the form of rum perhaps. The Star-That-Came-to-Earth gens say that the leader always appointed *a'ki-da,* soldiers, to see that no one became drunk before the trading was over. These men had the traditional power to whip anyone who failed to conduct himself properly, and anyone killing an especially appointed *a'ki-da,* would in turn be killed by the gens.

The Heavy Eyebrows must have liked this organization, since they would want no wild-beast-slobbering drunkenness. They might, however, believe that it might be advantageous if the Little Ones took just enough of the spirits to drown their shrewdness in fumes, so that their already tremendous profits could be even greater. They need worry little about the trading shrewdness of the Little Ones, since they had practically none. When they wanted a thing badly, they must have it at all costs.

The Little Ones did become insanely drunk after the Heavy Eyebrows had taken their captives downriver to meet a boat on the Mississippi or the Missouri, which took them to Natchez and thence to the Caribbean Islands to be sold as slaves to the French landowners.

They would not stop until they had drunk the barrel dry. They sometimes cut each other with their French hatchets, even killing each other before the *a'ki-da* could intervene, but even insanely drunk the *a'ki-da* could keep them from riding off to commit murder in their exaggerated bravado.

But they did get away from the control of the *a'ki-da* occasionally and run their horses wildly over the prairie or through the woods until they fell dead. Once they killed a Bohème, a vagabond, harmless, with only his pack and his stick and his pipe; then two of the mad party killed each other over his scalp, with all traditions controlling such matters drowned completely.

There is much more in the tribal memory of the modern Little Old Men concerning the correctness of the ancient Little Ones and their virtues, no matter what gens is giving the information, than there is of questionable activities which the modern white men might cluck at and deplore. It is difficult to get a mouth-to-ear account of the slaving activities and the killing of hunters and trappers and traders from any of the modern gentile leaders. When drinking is mentioned, the modern Little Ones stress the appointment of the *a'ki-da,* with the air which implies, "That's the way we did it in the old days." There could well be a tribal memory of drunken fights and rapings, as well as anger-crying and hair-pulling among the women, since tragedies might often have followed mad, mouth-foaming drunkenness, where there were no inhibitions whatever.

It is also difficult to determine just what effect the slave trade might have had on the religious ceremonials and traditions of the Little Ones, especially those having to do with going on the war movement, since this phase would be the one directly concerned. No gens with characteristic self-esteem would admit having such tribal or gentile memories to parade before the criteria of white-man virtues.

It is not known whether slaving was an activity of only a few of the gentes or whether it had the sanction of the whole tribe. Customarily the *Tzi-Sho* would intervene to "give life back" to the unfortunate captives, especially if they had stood their ground and fought bravely. There is no one to say what did happen to the Padoucas or the Pawnees who stood to fight bravely, even taunting the Little Ones when hopelessly surrounded by these giants with yellow paint on their faces. During the last forty years there is no one who will say. It is known that certain gentes of the Little Ones did ride out under the traditional ceremonies of the war movement to take captives to sell to the Heavy Eyebrows as slaves.

There were the customary gentile preparations for the war movement, and the taking of captives for the slave trade might have been sanctioned by the Little Old Men as military defensive action or under the aegis of religion. This would have been strikingly European in its illogical and hypocritical spirit.

When the sun, disease, and the lash had killed great numbers of the Indian slaves in the West Indies or on the lower Mississippi, the Heavy Eyebrows would come to the villages of the Little Ones to tell them that they needed more and more captives, and there would be a feast given by one of the chieftains of one of the sub-*Hunkah* or the *Wah-Sha-She* gentes. The chieftain would sit apart, straight and dignified, with his otter and gray fox-skin quiver, his best buffalo robe hanging from one shoulder, his shell gorget tied close around his neck, his eagle tail-feather stuck on the right side of his head, his tattooed chest visible, the gifts for the Heavy Eyebrows around him, and at the right time he would designate several young men to distribute them, after the pipe had been circulated from his left.

Inspired by the marketplace obsequiousness of the Heavy Eyebrows and their eulogies to the bravery of the Little Ones and to the greatness of their virtues, the Little Ones would then choose *Do-Do'n Hunkah,* the Sacred-One-of-the-War Movement. The warriors would call upon the *Wah-No'n* gens of the *Wah-Sha-She* to lay before the council the sacred pipe, which was held in custody by the chief of this gens. They then went through the ceremony of the war movement.

They danced. None of the modern Little Old Men know what dances they danced when they readied themselves for the slave raids on the Pawnees or the Padoucas, but it is quite likely that they did not dance the mourning dance, although the women did put blue clay on the tops of their heads, since it symbolized pre-mourning as well as mourning. This was because death was certain to come to some of the raiders on such an expedition.

Even though such expeditions might have little of tradition, and therefore less religious significance than those which followed the mourning dances, they would certainly face death at the hands of their enemies. And this meant that they must go through rituals of the war movement with the usual meticulous attention. Carelessness in ritualistic preparation might mean not only death, but exposure. Each warrior knew that over the prairie and plains to the west there would be swallows and dragonflies to spy on him and expose remissness or cowardice.

One knew that swallows, both cliff and barn swallows, will circle above even a single man on horseback to pick off the insects which the horse disturbs from the grasses, and often at certain times of the year the dragonflies swarm and bounce over the prairie, rather aimlessly it seems, just as if they had no other business than to bear tales. The same is true with the assumed but classical purposelessness of butterflies, except in the case of the monarchs in migration. Almost as soon as the Little Ones rode onto the prairie, the little people came to spy on them. If there were among them the members of the Thunder gens of the *Tzi-Sho,* they must make some sign of recognition of the swallows particularly, since they were messengers of that gens, appearing before summer storms as harbingers of the thunder.

The eight leaders took the *wah-hopeh,* the sacred hawk, out of the shrine, and straightened the spread eagle talon, the *hi-ca-da,* which was tied to the bottom of the buckskin wrapping, symbolizing the outspread, readied talon of the golden eagle; they smoothed the Pawnee scalplock attached to it. The warriors gathered around the returned leader of the war movement as he let the sacred hawk fall. If it fell on its breast with its head pointed to the west, the whole village chanted the song of the *wah-hopeh.* The west was the road of Grandfather and war, and when the sacred hawk "looked" to the west, there would be no difficulty about the approval of *Wah'Kon-Tah.* When the Little Ones desired the war movement, one assumes that the leader might influence a little the fallen position of the hawk, since if he fell "looking" to the east, the direction of peace, the war spirit would fade in the hearts of the warriors, and they would ride out upon the prairie heavy with fear. Some of them might even expose themselves to the enemy unnecessarily, not out of bravado, but out of complete resignation inspired by fear not of the enemy but of the omen of the hawk's position. They were like the mustangs they rode, full of spirit and challenge and fight, but suddenly giving up under manhandling. The Little Ones gave up under unknown menaces and under the frown of *Wah'Kon-Tah.*

They left the village singing, or at least the leader sang again the song he had sung to Grandfather as he asked for approval: "I go to learn if I shall go— To make the enemy lie reddened on the earth— To make their scalplocks to wave in the wind," just as if they were setting out on a sacred conflict with the enemy.

There would be no reddened, blackened enemies lying on the earth, except those accidently killed in the effort to take captives.

The earth would not be brown with enemy dead, and there would be no whitened bones or scalplocks waving in the wind. They covered their deceits with their law, their religion, and self-delusion, much like the Europeans.

They would ride out of the village under the eight war leaders and the three "soldiers" over all. The *wah-hopeh* bundle would be hanging from the neck of the leader, down his back, and each warrior would carry his fetish shield so that it covered his breast. This shield was made from the right or the left side of the buffalo skin, the *Hunkah* or *Tzi-Sho* side. It was circular and painted red, and was protective because of its sacred powers, while the shield that actually turned the arrows of the enemy was also round, but was cut from the tough neck skin of the buffalo bull and stretched on a hickory framework when the skin was green. It was sewed on the rim of the hickory framework, with the sinews from the backbone of the buffalo. On each side of the spinal column of the buffalo there was a strong sinew, but for the thread which the Little Ones used for sewing the green neck hide of the bull buffalo to the hickory frame, the sinew on the left side of the column, the *Tzi-Sho* side, and the sinew from the right side of the column, the *Hunkah* side, were twisted together, not only to make the thread much stronger, but also as symbolical of the merging of the *Hunkah* and the *Tzi-Sho*. The red fetish shield was small because it must not be allowed to interfere with the military actions of the warriors, while the practical shield was larger and was carried on the forearm. They also gave to this shield some sacred power by attaching eagle tail-feathers to the lower edge. The golden eagle was a war and earth symbol of the tribe as well as a gens symbol.

Some of the warriors carried trade war hatchets, murderous things made by the French for the Missouri River trade, often decorated almost into uselessness for quick maneuver in the Frenchman's attempt to please and appeal to the vanity of the Little Ones.

Many of them carried fusils, and their buckskin bags contained bullets and shavings from arrow-shaft making, from the dogwood and white ash which they used as wadding. They also had their paint bags, and each carried a bow and arrow, the leaders carrying spears as well. They could shoot several arrows during the time it might take fusil shooters to ram home the shot and powder and wadding and prime the pan.

Thus they might set out as if on a crusade, but actually on a commercial venture. The women would follow a little way, clutching the manes of their husbands', brothers', fathers', or uncles' horses, singing of victory, but here and there one would break into sobbing and would sing the Song of Death, when she suddenly remembered a son or a husband, father or uncle who had ridden toward *Mo'n'ha,* the Cliffs, the West and Spiritland.

19. *Coureurs de Bois,* Vagabonds, and Sac and Foxes

THERE WERE NOW Frenchmen living with their Osage women without benefit of Jesuit, some of them married by Osage formula and some just sharing their robes with venturing widows. Besides the trappers and *coureurs de bois,* there would be an occasional dog-faced Bohème, a vagabond who had attached himself to a trading party after escaping from church and seigneury on the St. Lawrence, or from one of the post-missions on the Great Lakes or even Tonti's fort and settlement at the mouth of the Arkansas River. The Little Ones called these Bohèmes or vagabonds, Walkers-over-the-Earth.

One or more would take up residence with the Little Ones and try to imitate them in their talk, gestures, and dress. Because they had no dignity, they were accorded the role of court fool, with the privileges of court fools. They painted their faces in imitation of the Little Ones and dressed in leggings and breechclouts, but were not allowed to wear the eagle feathers symbolizing distinction. They had the Gallic urge to be histrionic, and they invariably overdid it. They semed to have been a little afraid and a little obsequious, but burned with a desire to be noticed. Their great hour came when they could strut in reflected glory, using their short-fingered hands to make the stories which the long fingers of the Little Ones accomplished so poetically in telling of incidents or when giving information to the newcomers to the village. Some of the inaccuracies in nomenclature of the lower Mississippi River and the Missouri River are due to these strutting Bohèmes, but being Europeans, they were given some status as informers by official Europeans.

The town crier of the Little Ones was called *wah-tsde-pia'n,* the humble one. He had special privileges, and was usually a born exhibitionist and parader. He was privileged to tell lies, to make jokes at the expense of the most dignified, even about the Grand *Hunkah* or the Grand *Tzi-Sho.* It was he who cried to the village or the camp all the messages from the Little Old Men or the chiefs, and he had privileges even above the official ceremonial messengers, the *shokas.* He wore skins hanging from his shoulders that had no significance. He might hang the skin of the coyote on his back, and a bobcat skin down the front. He painted his face as he chose, always striving to appear unique, fearsome, and especially esoteric.

He must have a good voice, since he walked around the village crying his message, and he must be heard by all. He cried the dancers together, holding his voice at a high pitch for perhaps twenty seconds, like a wolf, then breaking into diminuendo with the message.

There was the same tolerance of the Bohème in the camps and villages as there was of the town crier, but the latter took great pride in his lies and his jesting and his privileges, while the Bohème took himself seriously and his lies were only lies of illusion and were for the express purpose of contributing to his self-importance. He dared not jest, but his posturings served the same purpose, no matter how serious he might be in his imitations.

A Bohème away from the villages and the camps was in constant danger from the wandering gentes, especially the Black Bear–Panther people. These twin gentes imitating the lethal jocularity of the black bear and the curiosity of the panther might kill the tattered one with hair up to his eyes simply because he became frightened by their menacing play.

Frenchmen observing the Little Ones dance would have been held fascinated, and perhaps would have become vaguely uneasy, as they watched the painted giants with their bodies bare above the waist, the turkey gobbler beard of their roaches quivering, and the eagle feather bouncing with the rhythm of their steps; the wild, dedicated singing of the drummers, the tremolo of the women watching the warriors in their superb grace, as the moccasined feet seemed to bounce from the sentient earth packed hard under the willow-branch covering of the dance structure.

The dancers bent forward and traced the "trail of the enemy" with their coup sticks, or they twisted with eyes upon the floor like foraging eagles; they crept swiftly around the drummer-singers like the panther or lumbered like the bear. Some stood by their places where each buffalo robe was spread, moving their feet in rhythm, but standing like the solitary buffalo bull out on the plains. Some danced with knees high in imitation of the trot of the bull wapiti in rut.

They carried the old war clubs made of hickory and flint or glacial granite and the new hatchets of the French trade, and they had begun to tie hawkbells, which the French were quick to see they might find better than the terrapin shells filled with pebbles, around their legs just below the knee. This made a wonderfully sharp sound in the rhythm of the dancing, much like the almost metallic insect chorus from the summer grass roots. Long after the dancers had gone to their robes, you could hear the bells and feel the rhythm in the grass roots chorusing. Some of them carried quill-decorated coup sticks in one hand and their eagle-tail fans in the other.

The women were now decorating the handles of the coup sticks and the handles of the gourd rattles, as well as the moccasins, with trade beads to replace the flattened porcupine quills.

Some of the dancers were bare-legged as well as bare-backed, wearing only clouts tucked in front and back under their belts, the clouts of buckskin and the belts woven from the hair of the buffalo calf. Some wore the buckskin leggings with the fringe symbolical of the tarsus and tibia feathers of the golden eagle.

The rhythm was the rhythm of the earth, as if the drumbeats were heart beats, and the songs the drummers sang all seemed to have an orison-like quality, as if the centuries-old prayer-songs had colored their voices. Some of the songs of the drummer-singers were slow like some military drumbeat for the dead, and the dancers danced upright and solemnly around the singers, and there was no tremolo from the women. Some of the dances were gay and fast, and smiles might come to the dancers' faces. Then there were those which had the intensity of high emotion, which grew to the point of breaking as the dancers circled and gestured with their hatchets and seemed to be emotionalizing themselves beyond all inhibitions.

The women would sit as if stunned and fascinated, for there was sex lure in the dances, even when they were social or military. The dancers in the social dances might imitate walks-on-wings, the turkey gobbler, and the arrow-flight traveler, the cock prairie chicken, in his nuptial dance. They also seemed even to fluff their feathers like the burnished cock passenger pigeon. The French onlookers might feel the atrophied hackles prickle the backs of their necks or "feel in their souls savage exultation"; and a stray Bohème might be on the verge of bursting with reflected glory, the focus of eyes, because as the dancers rested and the water boys came with the gourd dippers, they might be assisted by the Bohème, who would hold the gourd to the dancer's mouth, contributing to the self-esteem of both.

More and more of the Heavy Eyebrows came up the river of the Little Ones, watched the dances of the warriors, asked them questions, drew maps in the sand, the unaccustomed ones nervous at all times, fleeing back down the river when the Little Ones seemed displeased but forming with them stronger and stronger alliances, so that when their commandant at Fort Detroit, one Dubrisson, was attacked by the Fox Indians of the Great Lakes region and was seriously besieged, the Heavy Eyebrows took along with them up the Illinois River most of the Missourias, who seemed so eager now to attach themselves to strong medicine, and at least one gens of the Little Ones. The Wapiti gens of the Little Ones and members of some unknown gentes went along with the Heavy Eyebrows soldiers to break the siege, not knowing why they were going perhaps, except to get at their enemies the Foxes. This was in the year 1712.

This expedition up the Illinois River along the shores of the modern Lake Michigan and thence across to the straits must have taken many days. There is only faint tribal or gentile memory of this expedition to the relief of Fort Detroit, but there is a personality in the tribal memory. There, with their allies the Heavy Eyebrows and the Missourias, they met one of the most interesting and able, and at the same time one of the most romantic and whimsical of the French adventurers. He was Étienne Veniard, Sieur de Bourgmont. He had been a *coureur de bois* and had come over the lakes to the straits, and had because of his energy and ability become in 1706 commandant of Fort Detroit, taking over several years earlier from the equally remarkable Henri de Tonti, the gentleman. Bourgmont was still at the fort when the Foxes attacked, but not in command. Something had happened.

When he saw the tall Osages accompanying the Missourias and the tattered French soldiers from the forts along the Illinois and Mississippi rivers, he declared them to be the most alert of the Indian nations. The Little Ones, on the other hand, seemed to have been drawn to him, and when the siege was lifted, he deserted his post and in Gallic enthusiasm followed the tall, alert people back to the Missouri and the Osage rivers. He, on his part, seemed to have been fascinated by both the Little Ones and the Missourias, and there is a vague gentile memory of an effervescent, sparkly eyed Heavy Eyebrows who lived with the Wapiti of the sub-*Hunkah* and the Crayfish gens of the *Wah-Sha-She.*

He was one of the few Europeans who had the characteristics which the Little Ones admired, and they remembered him. He may have been the well-remembered Heavy Eyebrows whom they called *U-Ga-Sho'n,* the Wanderer. This was the name given by the Wapiti gens to some Heavy Eyebrows who lived for some time among the Wapiti, and they might have named him for the single bull wapiti that might wander over many valleys.

He was a man of education and wrote of his personal experiences, along with a description of the route that must be followed if one wished to ascend *"la rivière du Missouri."* This was a sort of diary of his activities in 1714.

Whether he married an Osage woman is not known, but he stayed with the Osages, and he either went through the ceremonies of marriage or lived with one or more. He spent some time tracing the snakelike coils of their river, so that it could appear on Vermale's map which appeared in 1717, and Le Page du Pratz wrote later that he went up the Missouri for eight hundred leagues.

He later married a Missouria girl, or at least lived with a daughter

168

of the principal chief, after fathering several children among the Little Ones.

In 1718, Bienville requested from the King, now Louis XV under the regency of the Duc d'Orléans, the Cross of St. Louis for him. He had been of great service to his country, but even occupied with discovery and exploration and planning, he had time to mention the fact that the Little Ones had the best furs in the Missouri region and that their blood was good. He suggested that the best route to Spanish trade and eventually to the sea was through the country of the Little Ones and the Missourias; up the Missouri River, up the Osage River, and up the Kaw or Kansas River. He suggested that the route up the Arkansas River would be made difficult through the activities of the Padoucas and the Apaches, who even if won over as allies of the French would ever be made unstable in their loyalties through Spanish influence and trade. On the other hand, his countrymen need worry little about the Osages, since they were alert, very energetic, and had the power along with their splinter, the *Ko'n-Za,* to keep the lower Missouri open. Later one might influence the Little Ones and their traditional enemy the Pawnees to make peace, and peace could be made with their other enemies, the Padoucas and the Apaches.

The way down the Missouri for furs and the future metals would be kept open by the Little Ones, and the *Ko'n-Za,* and the five posts ordered by Louis XIV in 1714 would discourage others. Natchez would be the *magazin* to which the trappers and traders would send their furs.

When the Little Ones went to Fort Detroit with their allies, the Heavy Eyebrows, to raise the siege, they met in battle one of their bitterest and most powerful enemies. They had known them before. They had come wandering down to the north bank of the Missouri River, restive, like many of the Algonkians who had been disturbed by the Iroquois and the European invaders. They called these handsome, able warriors, *Ca-Ge-Wa,* Hard-to-Kill People, but the Heavy Eyebrows called them Reynards (Foxes), and when allied and integrated with the Sauk, they became known later as Sac and Foxes.

They were one of the few tribes in the region to whom the French did not point and ask of the Little Ones, "The people there, what do they call themselves?" They knew them before the Little Ones knew them, since they had met them on Lake Michigan, and they were distinctive in that they were one of the western Algonkians not allied with the French, but leaned to the English.

However, the Heavy Eyebrows had made the same mistake in naming them as they had made in naming the Little Ones; they had named the tribe for one of the bands, but had translated the band name *Wagosh,* which means "Red Fox" into the French, *Reynard.* The tribal name was the Red-Earth People, while the Sauk tribal name was Yellow-Earth People. These Sac and Foxes were lake people before they came wandering, and they made dugouts and came in them down the Mississippi. The Little Ones wouldn't allow them to settle on the southern bank of the Missouri, so they wandered up and down the north bank, crossing over on raids. Later, they used bull-hide boats as well.

If the Little Ones had ever met their match in cunning and flash bravery, it must have been this Algonkian tribe, a canoe and dugout people, who were planters and bark-lodge dwellers. They were not earth-proud, and did not easily become attached to some particular geometrical bit of planting, yet they wandered up and down the Mississippi between the mouth of the Missouri and the mouth of the Des Moines, and along the north bank of the Missouri to beyond the mouth of the Grand.

They were fierce and handsome and tall, say the Little Ones, and they came out of the reeds along the river during the night and across the Missouri and up the Osage, the river of the Little Ones. They moved in the darkness in their dugouts along the banks of the rivers where the Little Ones were camped, and there was only the tinkle of water, such as is made by bank-foraging catfish or a carp, or a turtle or a fishing raccoon. They moved through the reeds in darkness to the attack just before dawn, and that is why the Little Ones called them Hard-to-Kill People.

The horses of the Little Ones were useless against them, since they seldom came out of the reeds or the marshes or the alluvial forests. The Pawnees, the Little Ones could ride against, horseman against horseman, with the Little Ones having the advantage of many fusils, but the Sac and Foxes had many English muskets and no horses. When they grew tired of fighting, they made their way across the Missouri to safety. The *Wah-Sha-She* say that when they were fleeing from a superior number of the Little Ones and didn't have time to gain their dugouts or canoes, they would disappear in the smoky waters of the Missouri. The Little Ones waiting and watching along the bank could see nothing, but sometimes there was something not quite right about some fine black rootlets floating just under the bank, and if they stayed and watched very closely, they might find that the rootlets were Sac and Fox hair. They say they could never discover the bronze noses among the roots, but just the very fine rootlike hair.

There can be no vacuum; every square inch of earth is filled if that square inch can nurture some species by itself, but if it is harsh desert, then it may take a square foot or a square mile to nourish one species, but every square inch will be under the control of some form of life.

The military activities of the Iroquoians and the unbalance caused by the English, French, and Dutch of the Atlantic Coast had exerted pressure on the Algonkians, and they were forced west and wandered here and there searching for new homes. The pressure originating along the Atlantic Coast became a chain pressure, whereby the Europeans and the Iroquoians disturbed the Algonkians, and as they were forced west, they pressed the Siouans, and this chain pressure reached all the way to the Rockies.

If this chain pressure had caused the tribes to turn down the Mississippi to the Missouri instead of debouching them onto the Great Plains, perhaps the history of the Little Ones might not have been so pleasant, but on the other hand their untouched domain might have been a power center rather than just an enclave resulting from topography. It is easy to believe that it was the former, a power center around which the displaced people flowed, since there were no topographical barriers and there were a plentitude of game, rich soil, and two inviting highways, the Missouri and the Osage rivers, not to mention the Mississippi.

Anyway, the Kiowas left their river and came down to the plains after having been driven from the Black Hills by the Sioux. The

Padoucas and the Apaches remained on the plains. The Cheyennes, the handsome fighting men, who the Little Ones say had the color of a tanned deer hide after the first rubbing with gypsum, moved around them circling down the plains. While the Little Ones had named the *A-Pa-Tsi,* the Apaches, [Lodges]-Make-Us-Stoop People, and the *Pa-Do'n-Ka,* Wet Noses, the Sioux had named the Cheyennes, before they came to the southern plains, People-Speaking-Tongue-Not-Understood. However, the Little Ones did have their own name for them: they called them *To'n-Se-Moie,* Walking-on-Prairie-People.

These chain-pressure disturbed and displaced ones, who included the Arapahoes and the Sac and Foxes, flowed north of the domain of the Little Ones to become enemies. These enemies, the Kiowas and Cheyennes and Arapahoes rather mild ones as far as the Little Ones were concerned, were added to the traditional *Pa-I'n,* the Pawnees, the Wichitas, and *Pa-I'n Ma-Ha* of Loup River, and the other Caddoans of the Red River, who were themselves able to keep the Little Ones constantly in the war movement; and with fusils and horses they became eager and overweening. Pampered by the Heavy Eyebrows and with the imperiousness which the horse gives to all men, they rode in gentile groups south and west chiefly, carrying their sacred falcon, their sacred redbud charcoal, their red fetish shields, their utility shields, their spears, their bows and arrows, and their fusils. The red shield, the charcoal, and the falcon became more sacred and more powerful as they gained victory after victory.

They rode across the prairie and the plains, slipping their robes from their shoulders and tying them around their waists when the sun became hot, their *Hunkah* eagle feathers in their scalplocks spinning in the wind and the roach quivering, the *wah-hopeh* songs torn from their lips by the prairie winds, as were the Songs of the Crow, picturing the crows quarreling above the enemy dead, and the Songs of the Wolf imaging a pack of black, yellow, gray, or white wolves loping over the plains. The prairie breezes hissed through their horses' tails and their manes waved like Pawnee scalps, while their dust gave a message they wanted all to see. Even their own splinter the *Ko'n-Za* sent their scouts out to see what the Little Ones had in mind, and the heavy-faced Pawnee scout would watch them from the tall grass

172

of a hill, going behind it out of sight to wave his robe-message to his party.

The Heavy Eyebrows were doing well in furs and slaves, but they really preferred sudden wealth, and always there was the dream of gold; and just as their ancestors had created a spiritual world for their own comfort and comprehension very much as the Little Old Men had done, they went farther and began to create a material world out of their dreams. They created gold mines, and they knew they must be up the Missouri somewhere, "closer to the Spaniard." They must build a fort on the Missouri River above the mouth of the Osage River. From here they could explore the mines of the unknown country "which are more precious than those of lead." They even associated the Spaniards with dream wealth. Since the conquest of Mexico and Peru, the Spaniards had been associated with wealth and romance.

About these things they would ask the Little Ones. The Wapiti people would tell them one thing, and the Bear and the Deer and the Buffalo-Face or the Heavenly Bodies, or the Crayfish, the Turtle, the Beaver, the Cattail, or the Spider would tell them quite different things. Each gens would answer their direct questions in a manner which they believed would please them. When a dream or an image had become quite mature and they wanted so badly for it to be true, they would ask anyone who might appear to be important. The intentness in the face of the Heavy Eyebrows would be so noticeable and their desire so written there that the Little Ones would answer their questions in the affirmative to please them.

The Little Ones were not lying, but being extremely courteous.

One Hubert wanted to reassure his countrymen that they must know quite definitely about the distances and the inhabitants along the Missouri. He assured them that the mines were to be found only a short distance up the Missouri. He named the rivers in succession as one ascended: The Osage was 35 leagues, then 14 leagues farther Rivière à la Barque, and 5 farther the Rivière à la Mine de Plomb, and 7 leagues farther the Rivière au Portchicore, and 11 leagues from this river, the village of the Missourias. From this village to the River of the Kansa was 30 leagues, and at 120 leagues up that river, it forked to the northwest, where there were a variety of mines, and that it was only a short distance from the branches of the upper Kansas River to the drainage of the Arkansas and the country of the Padoucas who traded with the Spaniards.

Trading was not quite the term to describe the relationship between the Spaniards and the Padoucas. The Padoucas usually took what they wanted from the Spanish settlements and left nothing in return except bodies and broken corrals and high excitement.

Following the advice of Bourgmont, who had gone to France to receive his honors, leaving his Missouria wife but taking his mixed-blood son with him, the French began making gestures of peace with the Padoucas. A few hardy *coureurs de bois* under instructions from Bienville urged members of the Black Bear gens to go with them into the Padouca country.

The Little Ones seemed to have been impressed by the horsemanship of the Wet Noses. They say the Padoucas seemed to carry their few guns as a bluff, since they fired no shot at them. But they came at them with arrows flying, and they stuck to their horses like the spider, they said, and shot at the Little Ones from under the horses' necks. The Little Ones had learned from the French that they must not fire all their fusils at the same time, one third firing then loading while another third fired. However, in the excitement of the clash, with the short-legged men riding all over their horses and yelling in a strange manner, the Little Ones became excited and fired in volley. The Little Ones say that when they used their bows and arrows against the bows and arrows of the Padoucas, one of the Padoucas jumped from his horse and began waving his robe. He waved it three times, which meant peace or truce. They wanted to talk to the strange white men with the Little Ones; they had never seen white men like these before. The Padoucas, the Little Ones, and the Heavy Eyebrows sat for a long time talking in sign language, then they exchanged presents and each party went his own way. The horsemanship of the short-legged men became a gentile memory.

20. The Company of the Indies

IF THE GREAT PLAINS had not been open for the chain-pressured Algonkians and the northern Siouans, if the modern Dakotas and western
Minnesota had been blocked by a strong indigeous tribe or tribes, and
these pressure-wanderers had been forced down the Mississippi and
up the Missouri, and if they in some power federation might have
been able to dislodge the Little Ones, the history of both mid-America
and the Little Ones might have been quite different. So might their
history have been different if John Law's dreams had come true.

Louis XIV finally died in 1715, with his soul saved in the end by
the dedicated fervency of Maintenon, his second queen, his bag of
earthly desires empty as was his treasury. As his great-grandson,
Louis XV, was only a pettish little boy, the Duc d'Orléans must become Regent. He was cynical, a sated Age of Reason disciple who had
been "bored with himself from birth." His sexual orgies and his
gambling had been conspicuous even in Paris of the day, but he had
more than a spark of understanding of state finances and the need
for roads and other civic improvements, and for all his notorious im-
morality had sense enough to listen to John Law.

In the year 1671, just two years before the Little Ones came to recorded history through Père Marquette's map, a boy was born in
Edinburgh, Scotland, who, through his energy, his brilliance, and
even perhaps his handsomeness, was to have great effect on the lives
of the Little Ones. He would organize the activities of the Heavy Eye-

brows in the Mississippi Valley, giving the colony an agricultural base.

He was a goldsmith's son, and had been brought up as a wealthy child and young man. He was a poet and at the same time a financial genius and mathematician. His studies had made him a master of the principles of private and public credit, all the while writing poetry and studying political economy and taxation.

He went to London as a quite young man and was taken up by London society on account of his handsomeness and his cleverness. He became a dedicated gambler and a racing enthusiast and a lover of other men's wives. To have manifested constantly his brilliance, his graces, and the simple fact of his physical attraction were sufficient reasons for inspiring hatred among the drab men of the patricians of William and Mary's reign.

The idle women of society flocked about him, and he eventually had to fight a duel and was tried for murder. He was condemned to death, but was pardoned by the crown, and one might suppose that there might have been a woman in this as well. However, the brother of the deceased duelist took an appeal, and while this was pending before the King's Bench, John Law escaped to Holland, and there could have been a woman in this also.

Holland was the business nation of Europe, and here Law had the nation as a library for his research. He returned to his native city of Edinburgh and attempted to sell Scotland his ideas, which embraced the issuing of notes on the land to one-half or two-thirds of the value. The paper currency thus issued would have the same value as that issued on gold, which fluctuated in value.

Naturally he failed. He was too handsome, too quick, and too glib for the Scotsmen, and he had to go to France to find a kindred spirit. This kindred spirit he found in the person of the Duc d'Orléans, Regent of France.

He first got entrée into the circle of the Regent through the intro-duction of a gambling game which he had invented, called faro. They played the new game together, as well as an older game with eager women of the court. They drank and watched the horses run, and gradually John Law had the Regent interested in the greatest gamble of all: his scheme for the financial revival of France.

But there was the Council, and the Regent tried to convince the Council of the soundness of the scheme, but the Council in turn were advised by the leading merchants and financiers. Some of them had idle and beautiful wives who were eager to be fashionable and imitate the ladies of the court in extra-marital diversions and venturing, so that they might boast in relaying bon mots to each other from the great and the conspicuous ones.

The merchants and financiers distrusted both the Regent and Law.

But Law had studied France, and if Holland had been his library, France would be his laboratory. France's financiers preyed upon France instead of gaining their wealth from industry. Here was a rich land agriculturally, upon which notes could be issued, and besides that, there was the whole Mississippi Valley to be developed. The wealth of the nation would be the wealth of the people, and there would be no more starving and simple poverty, and France would no longer have to live on loans carrying usurious interest.

There would be no more hoarding, since there would be no reason for the hoarding of paper. The people would be liberated from their crushing, brutalizing poverty, the noblemen could pay their debts. Law's scheme was a financial straw in the flood of taxation and usury, but the Council distrusted him and his sponsor, the Duc d'Orléans.

He then established his own bank, and when it caught on, he established the Company of the West for the development of the Mississippi Valley; and Antoine Crozat, the merchant who had the monopoly for trade in the lower Mississippi Valley, was glad to hand over his concession to the company in 1717. The company, after absorbing several other companies, became in 1719 the Company of the Indies, whose soul and heart and inspiration and energy and ideas were those of John Law.

It was this energy of one man which sent the first official Frenchmen to visit the chief village of the Little Ones. And it was this spirit and energy of a man far across the ocean that sent the first European cutpurses and criminals to the lower Mississippi in significant numbers, and the first Negroes, who would later come in contact with the Little Ones.

The official visitor was Charles Claude du Tisne, a personable man, as most of the Frenchmen with whom the Little Ones had come in unofficial contact had been. He was in the Bourgmont mold, except that he was born a gentleman. He was gay and witty and laughed like Bourgmont, but perhaps more delicately about things that plagued men both red and white.

Du Tisne not only was the first official visitor to the Little Ones, but was literate, and he wrote about them, and what he thought about them will be remembered and will always be of extreme importance. The earlier, unofficial *coureurs de bois* visitors to the villages, the men in greasy, smoke-stained buckskins, not only could not write, but many of them quite possibly could not read, although they with the occasional Bohème carried more knowledge of the Little Ones into oblivion with them than could appear in the writing of the gentleman Du Tisne.

However, he seemed to have had the same eye for the pretty girls; and the gentleman's sensitivity to the odors of rendered buffalo fat, hardwood smoke and horse mint, calamus root and black perfume (columbine seed) disturbed him as little as they did the *coureurs de bois* and the Bohèmes. The horse mint, the calamus root, and the columbine seed were used by the women and girls as perfume, and they were much more effective than French perfumes of the age, since they were applied to bodies washed in the river every day both summer and winter. Bathing had religious significance since it was one way of doing away with evil; the final ceremony after induced sweating and the taking of emetics.

Du Tisne had been born in Canada, and perhaps his Old World chivalric taboos might have become weakened in the primeval forests. His conscience allowed him plenty of latitude. While with the Little Ones he had some visiting Mentos, Caddoans from the Arkansas River, sell some Indian slaves for him south of the mouth of the Arkansas.

Representatives of the Company of the Indies seemed to have some freedom in such matters, but the company was quite upset when it was learned that the tribes on the Illinois, the Missouri, and the Arkansas rivers were being urged into war by the *voyageurs* so that they could trade for the captives and take them downriver as slaves. This was contrary to the wishes of the King through the Regent, which might not have meant much if it had not also been considered a jeopardy to the commerce of the company. However, Du Tisne did sell his slaves in the personal colony of John Law in southeastern Arkansas.

Du Tisne had started out from Fort Kaskaskia in the Illinois country with his party. He made his way up the Missouri River about forty leagues according to his reckoning, and there he turned into the mouth of the Osage and labored with his dugouts to the Place-of-the-Many-Swans and thence to the village of the Little Ones, whom the French were now calling Grand Ouazhazhe, to distinguish them from the Down-Below-People, whom they called the Petit Ouazhazhe.

This village was eighty leagues from the mouth of the Osage River. In miles, according to his reckoning, from the mouth of the Missouri to the mouth of the Osage would be one hundred miles and from the mouth of the Osage to the village of the Grand Osages, two hundred miles.

He arrived and perhaps might have expected some recognized form of hospitality tinted with obsequiousness. He was an officer in the King's service. But he had very likely not realized that the spring sun had brought sweat to his shirt, which quite possibly he had not changed more than once during his long, difficult journey. He had very likely been afraid of some baleful disease in the waters of the Missouri and the Osage and had not bathed. He possibly didn't realize that along with his men he would have the same European odor which the *coureurs* had, and was perhaps just as hairy. There was nothing in the appearance of this hairy, sweaty party of Heavy Eyebrows to indicate their importance, except a document indicating delegated authority, which the *Tzi-Sho* couldn't read. Like the *coureurs,* the *voyageurs,* and the Bohèmes, this malodorous party were detached from the great sailing ships the Little Ones had never seen, and couldn't possibly be associated with the Gothic cathedrals or the palatial architecture of Versailles, heavy draperies, Gobelin hunting scenes, swings in formal gardens, ladies sportive in silks, and oil paintings. They were *I'n-Shta-Heh,* Heavy Eyebrows, and were not many at that. They had no horses but carried fusils, and most certainly their chief importance lay in the dugouts in the form of presents or various *wah-don-skas* for trade. It would be the Little Ones themselves who would have the importance; they were two hundred warriors strong in one village alone, and had many of the very best horses taken from the horse-proud Pawnees, and fusils and the more rapid bows and arrows.

Du Tisne wrote that he was well received and that the Ouazhazhe had plenty of horses, "which they steal from the Pani [and] can be bought from them." He explained his intentions to them like a good officer carrying out orders from his superiors, with the expectation that they would be obeyed. The Little Ones were pleased with the plans as they pertained to themselves, the men pre-eminent, because they meant more fusils traded for Pawnee and Padouca captives and for furs and robes. After the officer of the King's service, with his instructions from the company, had made clear his plans, they were to him as good as carried out, and naturally he expected approval by the Little Old Men and the chieftains.

Then he made a mistake, chiefly because he needed a guide from the Little Ones. He laid before them the company's plan for making peace with the Pawnees, carrying trade fusils to them. It is likely that he did not expect objections to his plan, but he got them in the form of a threat, not just talk. The Little Ones couldn't let the Pawnees have fusils, and if the Heavy Eyebrows made peace with them, what would the Little Ones do for captives and scalps?

The Grand *Hunkah* came into the disturbed council. His exalted position would not suffer defeat in any form, so he grandly told the council of chieftains and Little Old Men that they were right, that the Heavy Eyebrows chief was their guest and their ally and no harm would come to him as long as he stayed in the village, but he could not trade guns to the Pawnees so that they could kill the Little Ones.

Du Tisne told the council that Bienville himself would be annoyed with them if they did not let him carry out Bienville's plans. He intimated that the King himself would be angered if they stopped his officer from doing his duty. The *Hunkah* knew that if Bienville became annoyed with the Little Ones, this might mean the end of *mo'n-ce* and *wah-don-skas* from down the Big Waters, so he very sedately, after a long speech about the friendship between the Heavy Eyebrows and the Little Ones, said that their brother Du Tisne might go to the Pawnees, but only if he went with his interpreter, carrying trade goods and three fusils, and the white flag of truce.

In Du Tisne's account, he said he stood firm, and told the council that he would go in spite of their refusal. The fact that he really left the village of the Little Ones with only an interpreter and trade goods they could carry would appear to make his boast a little face-saver. The Little Ones were worried about the possibility of Bienville's stopping the flow of presents and trade goods, but Du Tisne took this yielding as an appreciation of the importance of the governor of Louisiana. He seems to have made himself believe that this was the reason for the yielding of the *Hunkah,* since his pride urged this interpretation.

He followed the well-worn trail up the south fork of the Osage River, thence up the *We-Ts'a-U-Zhi,* Snake-with-Open-Mouth Waters, which the Heavy Eyebrows called Marmiton. The Marmiton debouched into the Little Osage River with wide mouth like a striking snake; but the French called it "Marmiton," meaning really Town Crier or Scullion River, this being their translation of the Osage *wah-dse-pa-i'n,* or town crier. Then he traveled over the prairie divide to the *Ni-U-Sho,* Waters-[Colored]-Like-Cows-Hide, to the *Wa-Ce-To'n-Xo-E,* Gray-Green-Bark Waters,[1] translated by the Heavy Eyebrows as "Verdigris." It took him and his interpreter four days to make the journey from the Place-of-the-Many-Swans to the villages of the Pawnees on the Gray-Green-Bark Waters, which he described as being "situated on the bank of a stream on a slope held together by raised prairie to the southwest of which there is a wood which is very useful to them."

He counted one hundred earth houses and guessed they had about two hundred warriors. He also described another village north of the

[1] This refers to the bark of the sycamore tree.

first which was greater. Between the villages they had three hundred horses, "and of which they do not wish to get rid." He said they were very brutal, but he was sure they could be tamed by trade in fusils, since they had only six. Here may have been one reason why the well-armed Little Ones had been so successful in capturing slaves from their powerful traditional enemies, and the chief reason why the name "Pani" and slave had become synonymous during this period. The Little Ones, living on one of the water highways of the venturing Heavy Eyebrows and being powerful, had the advantage of trade fusils, while the equally powerful Pawnees of the backlands through which the much less important Verdigris ran had at this late date only six fusils for several hundred warriors.

With the same Gallic aplomb as he had laid his plans before the Little Ones, Du Tisne told the Pawnees that he wished to go to the Padoucas. They were as obdurate as the Little Ones about the possibility of putting fusils into the hands of their enemies, and they flatly refused to allow this representative of the King and the company to go among their enemies with trade goods, especially fusils. There was apparently no compromise, as there had been with the Little Ones.

Du Tisne promised them fusils so that they could fight on equal terms with their ancient enemies, the Osages, and after planting a white flag of truce in the middle of their village, he left them with great expectations and well pleased with his visit. He must have felt that he had accomplished much, since on his arrival at the village they had threatened him twice with a war club, which he called a "tomahawk." But, he writes, "because of the boldness with which I faced them," they consented "to make an alliance with us, and traded generously with me." He traded them the three fusils and some powder, hammers, and knives, for two horses and a Spanish mule.

The Little Ones knew that he could trade only the three fusils to their enemies, but they were annoyed anyway because their ally had gone to their enemies, and they were jealous, and had sent scouts down to the Pawnee villages ahead of Du Tisne to say that he was really coming to make slaves of them. This was the reason for the Pawnee hostility; they welcomed trade in much-needed firearms.

When he arrived back at the Osage village, he found the Little Ones surly, and his companions were frightened and were quite ready to leave. The Little Ones would not give him a guide back to the Illinois country.

To make matters worse, he had horses now, and would not be able to follow the well-marked water highways down the Osage River to the Missouri and up the Mississippi to the Illinois, where one could not possibly become lost. With his horses he had to cross the north fork of the Osage River, which they called White Waters and which the Heavy Eyebrows were calling Marais des Cygnes, Marsh-of-the-Swans. He went north to a village of the Missourias, where he swam his horses across and floated his impedimenta across on cane mats, the construction of which were a Missouria specialty.

He had only his compass and fourteen horses and one mule. The *U-Dse-Ta,* the Little Osages, say that he rode the mule out of the village of the Grand Osages, and this was dangerous. It detracted from his importance in the eyes of the Little Ones, and it was said that one of the *Hunkah* gentes of the Little Ones wanted to follow and kill him and his party, but were restrained by the Grand *Hunkah,* even though all agreed that this lack of dignity made his word and his agreements questionable.

On the way back to the Illinois country he lost six of his horses, but he deplored only the loss of the nine hundred pounds of furs and baggage which they carried.

The Little Ones had their horses and their fusils and their new and very profitable slaving enterprise, and the Heavy Eyebrows had their excitement. There had been no gold discovered, but Gallic optimism knew that there would be, and there were, of course, stories about secret mines found by exploring *coureurs de bois,* their location kept secret for fear that the new company might take over, and there were rumors that the Spaniards were receiving gold from the upper Missouri River tribes in trade, which the natives believed to be copper.

Also there was the constant fear that the Spaniards would move toward the Mississippi River, and nothing could stop them more effectively than the Little Ones and the Pawnees, and then if lucky the French might even effect a peace with the Padoucas and make allies of them also.

Permission had been asked by Bienville to build a post on the Missouri River, so that the new-formed company could take advantage of the mines and the fur and slave trade all the way from the Missouri River to the Río Grande. What then could stop the new spirit of development, with a fort on the Missouri and three of the mightiest warrior tribes of the lower Missouri, the Arkansas, and the Kansas rivers as allies?

First, there must be no Spanish invasion if the great dream were to be carried out, and this involved control of the Arkansas and the Missouri rivers especially, from their mouths to their sources, which, of course, in the case of both rivers was mystical. The French had their post at the mouth of the Arkansas, and they must have a post on the lower Missouri. Here would come the Jesuits to save the souls of the *sauvages* before they could be saved by the Spanish Franciscans.

The gesture toward the Jesuits was good business on the part of the Duc d'Orléans and John Law. It was not a matter with them of asking for their Company of the Indies the aid of God through Jesuit good offices, to make them strong against their enemy the Spaniards, as the Little Ones might ask such aid of *Wah'Kon-Tah* in their dance-prayers, but chicanery of the marketplace. The cynical Duc d'Orléans and the brilliant John Law, the businessmen expansionists, would use as instruments the rather blind fervency of the Jesuits as well as the chivalric glee and vindictiveness of the Little Ones.

One feels that the years 1719 and 1720 were exciting ones along the lower Mississippi and the Missouri, and men seemed to be effervescent with dreams. One feels the impending glory—a vague glory of the future with which all enterprisers seem to infuse themselves to a point beyond all poetic fantasy. But in their plans the French found themselves in a dilemma. They made allies of the Siouan people of the lower Missouri; the Osages, the Missourias, the Konzas, the Otoes, and one division of the Caddoan Pawnees. They had furnished the Osages and the Konzas with guns for the purpose of slave taking from the Padoucas and the *Pa I'n-Sabe,* which might have been that division of the original enemies of the Osages whom Du Tisne had visited in their villages on the Verdigris River, at a spot which is now near the modern town of Chelsea, Oklahoma.

In their plans the French had to have the Pawnees as allies, and to make allies of the Padoucas appeared to them to be imperative. The problem was that there seemed no way of making alliances with the Pawnees and the Padoucas with their right hand and with their left trade fusils and hatchets and powder and ball and metal arrowheads to the Osages, so that they could furnish Padoucas and Pawnee captives to be made into slaves for the planters. It was said that the Konzas and Otoes alone had taken some 250 captives from the Padoucas, and the Osages were so busy raiding the villages of the Pawnees of the Verdigris and of the Republican and Loup rivers for captives and running off their finest horses that the Gallicized name for the Osages' *Pa-I'n-Sabe* became *"Pani Noir,"* with the *"Pani"* becoming synonymous with Indian slave. Many of the shifty-eyed and secretive French traders referred to all Indian slaves received from the Osages and the Konzas and the Otoes as *"Pani."* So many bolts of weaving, so many hatchets, or so many knives or awls or fleshers for so many *"Panis."*

If the French allowed the Osages and the allied Siouans to carry on with their eager raids on their old enemies, the Pawnees, and the new ones, the Padoucas, how could they ever hope to reach New Mexico either for trade with the Spaniards or to occupy vast *llanos* which the adobe-shade-loving Spaniards could not hold once the Padoucas, the Pawnees, and the Apaches were French allies and not enemy buffers? Obviously slave capturing, exciting and profitable sport that it was for the *sauvages,* must stop. But how? They had a bear by the tail, just as they had on the St. Lawrence when the Franciscans and the Jesuits tried to stop the trading of spirits to the Algonkians.

In that dilemma the Algonkians would take their furs elsewhere, *Mon Dieu,* even to the English, and in this dilemma of the slaves, the Siouans, *Mon Dieu,* would take their captives to the Sac and Fox agents of the encroaching English. Already the Osages had begun to trade captives to the Sac and Foxes when they became jealous of the French gestures to the Pawnees after Du Tisne. Padouca captives traded to the Sac and Foxes for English goods along the muddy shores of the Missouri made them trade friends for a short time.

The only way out of this dilemma was to allow the original allies, the powerful, willful Osages, whom they called loyal and friends, to continue to bring in captives to be sold into slavery, winking at their transactions with the shady Frenchmen while pretending to the Jesuits and themselves that the horrible business had been stopped.

After Bourgmont's activities on the lower Missouri and his exploratory trip to the mouth of the Platte, rumors had seeped to the Río Grande about his influence with the Osages and the Missourias, and the Spaniards got the wind up about the time he had been called back to France in 1719 and perhaps decided to act during his absence. There was also Du Tisne's treaty with the Pawnees and his visit to the Great Osages, and they knew about the Company of the Indies and the personal energy of John Law behind it. They also knew about the French flirtation with the Padoucas. The Padoucas and the Apaches might be enemies, but they were also enemies of the French and their allies, and they were buffers along with the limitless space of "cows and sky," where one was guided by water and terrain and not by compass and desire.

In the early summer of 1720, the Spaniards sent Captain Pedro de Villasur out from Santa Fe with forty-two soldiers accompanied by a party of settlers and others. There was a renegade Frenchman with the party, an enemy of Tonti because he had aided in the murder of Tonti's very good friend and leader, La Salle, on the lower Mississippi.

He was now a Spanish subject, and his name was L'Archeveque and it is very likely he planned the campaign, as far as objectives were concerned. He knew the important balance-of-power tribe, the Osages, quite well; and he might have reasoned justly that a try at negotiations with the excited slave catchers, closely allied with the French for forty years, would be no good. Also, he knew there could be little gained in trying for an understanding with the Padoucas, who had a rather good thing in stolen Spanish horses which could be traded to the Plains Indians.

So the expedition took the long way across the empty plains. They did not have to wait for a favorable whim of nature as the French had to do on their river highways. Here on the plains nature's whims were tantrums worse than Missouri River floods, but summer was the best time for travel across them, albeit nothing changed to make the going easier and the heat waves danced and the wind blew. The only change was in the grouping of the real "cows" and the fantastic "castles" and rampant "horses" and "dragons" and cones of "cream" formed by the cumulous clouds.

They traveled east of north. They crossed the dry beds of the river which the Little Ones called *Ni-Shu-Dse-Btha-Tha,* Flat-Red-Waters, and the *Ni-Ckiu-E Ga-Shki-Bi,* Cut-Rock-Salt-Waters, which are now called the Canadian and the Cimarron respectively. They crossed the *Ni-Shu-Dse* of the Little Ones, now called the Arkansas, and finally came to the *Ni-Btha-Ska,* Waters-Flat-White, called by the French "La Platte." Here on a feeder river seeping out of the sandhills to the northwest and flowing clean and sinuously into the Platte on its north bank is the river called by the French the Loup, and at the junction of its valley with that of a feeder called Beaver was a prehistoric village of the Pawnees. It is likely that the Pawnees, later called Skidi or Loup Pawnees, lived there then.

Villasur and his company had come to the South Platte, crossed it, and gave it their own name, Río Jesús María, then crossed the North Platte and called it the St. Laurent. They followed down the north shore level with the strings of white water, all but absorbed by the sand, and came to a point "where the river Jesús María unites with this stream," and there they camped. On the tenth of August they came opposite the Pawnee village.

They advanced to talk, but the Pawnees were surly, and the Spaniards recrossed the North Platte. This was August 13.

The Spaniards must have brought gifts and trade goods with them, since they were essential in dealing with the tribes, but as often happened, the interpreter, who could have been the turncoat L'Archeveque, might have misinterpreted the Spanish spokesman. The interpreter could have misinterpreted the intentions of the Spaniards, through his paucity of synonyms in either the French or the Spanish language, or he could have misinterpreted them intentionally. Also it is an Indian trait, whether he be Algonkian, Siouan, or Caddoan, when acting as an interpreter with all eyes on him, suddenly to become suffused with his own importance and make a long speech of his own, filled with imaginary grievances or colored by remembered tribal glory, leaving the treacly words of the Spanish spokesman uninterpreted.

When the Pawnees seemed to have become moved by the inter-preter's words, Villasur put the North Fork of the Platte between the village and his party. However, on the fourteenth, just before dawn, the Pawnees attacked, Villasur was killed, and only thirteen of the Spanish expedition escaped back to Santa Fe—some wounded, all leaderless, retreating dramatically across the shimmering plains, dodging bands of the Padoucas, bands of the Konzas, and the Paw-nees of the Republican River.

The Spaniards, to salve their wounds, said that there were French-men in the village of the Pawnees, hidden during the parleys but present at the dawn attack. They said they were dressed as Pawnees.

John Law and his company were out for more than furs and trade and mines: the Mississippi Valley had to be made to produce, and in order to have agriculture, there must be population. Colonists were reluctant to sign up and the Huguenots were not allowed to settle by order of the King, so the company's men scoured France for colonists. Heretofore most of the French in the great valley had been gentlemen adventurers with their servants and followers, *voyageurs* and *coureurs de bois,* trappers, traders, and missionaries: men who had come with Iberville and Bienville, with La Salle and Tonti, followers of St. Denis and Du Tisne and La Harpe. But within a period of five years, seven thousand nondescript people came to Louisiana. They had been taken from jails, asylums, from dark side streets of Paris, swept up from the gutters, and from the salt mines, and girls were kidnapped by men in masks and put aboard ships. There were impoverished people who would go anywhere and do anything to free themselves of their intolerable existences. The company settled Germans on Law's grant in what is modern southeastern Arkansas.

They also brought over six hundred Africans for agricultural labor. Two of these black men were the first the Osages had ever seen. They were with La Harpe.

Bernard de la Harpe was commandant over several of the Caddoan tribes of the Red River, and after establishing relations with a num-ber of the tribes up the river, he set out to explore the western drain-age of the Mississippi in order to clear the way toward the Spanish settlements through making friends with the intervening tribes, and perhaps to find a shorter way to New Mexico overland to the upper Arkansas and the Missouri rivers, rather than by the roundabout way up the Mississippi to their respective mouths.

He set out from the big bend of the Red River and traveled through the mountains of what is now southeastern Oklahoma, along the backbone of the drainage between the Kiamichi and the Little rivers.

The Osages were allies of the French, as every member of the La Harpe party knew well, but every blue haze they saw in the tops of the pines, and every odor of smoke, and every strange hoofprint put the men on guard. La Harpe had with him several Caddoan guides, and of course his Frenchmen, and also two Negro slaves from Law's colony.

His Caddoan guides were filled with fear, and his Frenchmen were nervous, since no one knew just what the pampered Osages might do. The Kiamichi[1] Mountains might be a long way from their villages on Osage River on the edge of the Ozark plateau, but they had horses and they had hunting camps on the Arkansas, Neosho, and Verdigris. Their horses were the best the horse-loving Pawnees could breed. The Little Ones seemed to be ubiquitous. They rode in gentile groups with a chieftain who seemed to have little responsibility to the *Tzi-Sho* and the *Hunkah* grand chiefs, but to the Frenchman the chieftains represented the authority of the tribe, and the tribe was blamed for the bloody and whimsical sportiveness of some of the *Hunkah* division gentes.

The eagle feather on the right side of their scalplocks would identify them as a *Hunkah* gens, either of the *Wah-Sha-She* or the sub-*Hunkah* divisions, and the manner in which their faces were painted would tell much more. If they were painted with redbud charcoal and yellow limonite, then they might be on a slaving expedition. This yellow might be the only difference between slave raiding and sacred mourning in search of an enemy scalp, in which case the face would be black with perhaps a little blue—the black on the upper face down to the upper lip, with the blue of mourning covering the lower face.

However, the group of horsemen La Harpe's scouts saw on the twentieth day of August, 1719, were twenty in number, and this

[1] *Ki-La-Ma-She,* meaning "Twin Peaks."

would not be a mourning party after an enemy scalp, since mourning parties usually rode in fours, and it was not likely that a mourning party would have ridden so far south of the Place-of-the-Many-Swans far up in the modern state of Missouri. This group was seen in an area wherein lies the modern town of Hartshorne, Oklahoma.

The scouts hurried back to La Harpe and reported with great fear. The Osages were following their trail to the main party, boldly, haughtily, without trying to conceal themselves. They had recognized the scouts as the despised Caddoans.

"They were some Osages," says La Harpe. "Although they are friends of the French, this nation is treacherous, and it is good to be on one's guard. The party approached carrying the tomahawk; our savages wished to flee, but I assured them that if they took this action they were lost, and that there were some other ways to extricate them. We kept our countenance and the Osages appeared, on their part, to be getting ready to attack us. In this perplexity, I advanced to them with three Frenchmen well armed, one of which was the soldier of the garrison, who understood several languages. This hostile party surprised by our boldness offered us the Peace Pipe. They explained to us that they knew of our nation and that we were their friends but they were pretending to scalp our guides. I opposed their schemes, and I said to them that if they persisted in their demands I should find myself forced to fight with them. This resolution made them change their attitude. They reflected among themselves and agreed to let us pass in peace. I gave them some presents after which they withdrew, without approaching our guides, who had remained with the rest of our people on guard."

La Harpe had set out for the fort of Natchitoches with fifty Frenchmen, Caddoan guides, and the two Negro slaves, but the number he had with him when he met the Osages in the mountains of modern Oklahoma is not known.

However, the actions of the Osages reflect much. They wouldn't have come face to face with La Harpe and his party if they had been bent on taking captives or scalps. Standing face to face with the party, they might have noted that they themselves were superior in number or fewer in number than the French and might have whimsically decided to wipe out the expedition. There were probably more Frenchmen and Caddoans than Osages, and therefore the latter accepted gifts and had their Black Bear fun in pretending to scalp the Caddoans. Also the Frenchmen were the source of the fusils and the war hatchets, and they must be careful not to disturb the relationship to the extent of rupturing it. They undoubtedly bluffed the gifts out of La Harpe.

They at times had a bluff-painting for the face, when they especially wanted to frighten others. This was a pattern of black and yellow or orange, but so applied that it was neither a sacred design nor a captive-hunting design, but merely for bluff.

Of the *Nika-Sabe,* the black men with La Harpe, there is little gentile memory chaining back to that meeting with the Heavy Eyebrows who had with him the strange black ones.

The very next day La Harpe saw a "unicorn," the fantasy of the Bible and Medieval Europe. It was being smoked by a Caddoan tribe he called "Naouydiches," who lived on the Canadian River in what is now the state of Oklahoma and near the town of Eufaula. The Europeans believed in the existence of the unicorn, and it was not a matter of attributing speech and character to a fanciful animal as in fables. He was in the natural histories of the Medieval period, and Europeans and Amer-Europeans believed in his existence far into the nineteenth century. The Medievalists had a method for hunting him. They led a virgin into the wood where the unicorn lived and left her alone as a decoy, and the unicorn came to her. "He soon leaps into her lap when he sees her, and embraces her, and hence he gets caught."

La Harpe's Caddoans could have told him that what he saw was a spike wapiti (young bull) with one spike knocked off.

He visited the Touacaras in a very fertile valley along the Arkansas River which he thought to be the most fertile of the whole colony. This would be a perfect valley for an agricultural colony, and therefore it could become strategic. Further, since it was near the spot on the Arkansas where the two rivers flowing down from the Osage country came into it, he thought an entrepôt might be established here for the concentration of all furs and minerals.

John Law's commissioners divided the Louisiana country into nine judicial districts, but the Arkansas and the Illinois district concerned the Little Ones, and the Company of the Indies had intended to establish some sort of law here.

Bienville sent Bernard de la Harpe exploring again, this time up the Arkansas in 1721 and 1722. He was to make friends with the tribes he might meet, and if by chance he met Spaniards, he was to oppose them and remind them that they were trespassing, "showing them that we have made the discovery of these parts before him; that further more these rivers since they flow into the Mississippi, are dependent upon the government of the province."

He carried with him beads, hatchets, knives, and red pigment. But apparently the Little Ones were still masters of this region in fact, despite the carved arms of the King left at the Touacaras village, all the grand proclamations, and the ceremony of the cross-raising for the approval of God.

Still, in 1721, La Harpe was more concerned about meeting with his allies the Little Ones than with the Spaniards. The French feared them more than they feared the Padoucas and the Apaches. They could not depend upon the new allies which Du Tisne had made for them, the Pawnees, since these people had begun to move from their villages on the Verdigris up the Arkansas and to the Kansa River and the Republican River. The Little Ones, with their constant horse taking and slave hunting, as well as their ample supply of fusils, had caused the Pawnees to wander northwestward.

This time La Harpe had only sixteen soldiers with him and some Caddoan guides, and each member of the party seemed to have been constantly on the lookout for Osage scouts. As they ascended the Arkansas, each member of the party watched the shores nervously. They had been instructed by Bienville to note the character of the river, to learn something of the natives who lived along its banks, and to go as far up the river as they were able to do in pirogues.

The equestrian Little Ones were constantly along the Arkansas, wandering and questing like knights. They seemed to control it from the mouth, the Quapaws notwithstanding, to an oscillating skirmish line, perhaps in western Kansas or eastern Colorado. The Osages describe Fountain Creek flowing into the Arkansas at Pueblo, Colorado.

They tried to keep the raiding Padoucas south of the Arkansas in that region. The Pawnees were leaving the Verdigris, and the Wichitas were fleeing north up the Arkansas into modern Kansas to the mouth of the river which the Little Ones called the Little-Red-Waters, the Little Arkansas, near where the modern city of Wichita, Kansas, now throbs and clanks on the plains. The other Caddoans had fled before the Little Ones across the Red River.

The Caddoan Mentos who had been on friendly terms with the Little Ones when Du Tisne had visited them and who conveyed slaves for him to be sold in the John Law personal grant in southeastern Arkansas, were now cowering. When La Harpe approached for slave trading, they refused him, saying that the Osages were jealous. When Richard Pockert had been sent previously to trade for horses with the Mentos, he and his party of five were attacked by the Little Ones and their horses and trade property taken from them.

And now La Harpe was moving cautiously and conscientiously up the Arkansas River. The shadows of the wind-swayed branches of the tall walnuts and hackberries and red oaks and elms might be Osages. The great horned owl at dusk might be an Osage signaling, or the call of the *coucou* during the early daylight; or in the darkness of the midnight river bottom the mew of the hunting raccoon might be a close-by signal. The members of the party awoke before dawn to wait and listen.

"On the sixteenth of April, 1722, we left at five o'clock in the morning. After two leagues of traveling we heard two gun shots to the left; we took them to be from Zauyoouy hunters; however, fearing the Osages, we redoubled our attention on being on guard." They saw no signs of the Little Ones.

La Harpe liked the "rock" on the Arkansas for which the modern city of Little Rock was named later, and he liked the forks of the Canadian and the Arkansas as a good place for the establishment of posts. He had been especially interested in the "rock," since rumor had it that it was of emerald. He even explored fifty leagues (125 miles) by land searching for it, and in his greed (or was its discovery part of his orders from the company?) he might have searched farther, but his men complained and he had heard about La Salle.

There was a change in the ideas concerning further exploration of the Arkansas within the council representing the company in Louisiana, who seemed to think that they were spreading themselves a little thin especially to the west at this particular time and ought to consolidate along the Mississippi for the present. It did seem also that the Osages were more whimsical and unrestrained on the far-away Arkansas than they were on the Missouri and the Osage rivers closer to the authority of the Grand *Hunkah* and the Grand *Tzi-Sho*.

La Harpe expressed his opinion of the Osages after describing their village and their domain: "One sees some very beautiful prairies, wooded by little thickets, and some very beautiful lands, suitable to put the plow there. The Osage village is situated on an elevation, to a league and a half from the river to the northwest. That village is composed of a hundred huts and some two hundred warriors; they remain at their village as the Missourias passing the winter hunting buffalo which are abundant in these quarters. One trades some horses with them which they steal from the Pawnees, some roe skins [whitetail deer] and buffalo robes. These Indians [*suavages*] are well made and deceitful; there are several chiefs of the bands but few absolute; generally they are treacherous and violate their word easily. They are lead mines 12 leagues from their home, of which they do not know the usage."

21. Fort d'Orleans

THE BUILDING OF FORTS AND POSTS began along the Mississippi, the Illinois, and the Missouri. For the Mississippi and the Illinois, it was only a continuation, but for the Missouri it was something new.

The post that had become the village of New Orleans honored in its name the cynical Duc d'Orléans, and now a fort-post on the lower Missouri was to be named in his honor as well. When Bourgmont established his fort among his wife's people, the Missourias, on the north bank of the Missouri River in 1723, he called it Fort d'Orléans. This spot is in modern Carroll County, Missouri.

The Osages and the Missourias liked him, and he had no trouble with them, but when he had gone back to France to be decorated in 1719, he was given a royal commission as *"Commandant de la Rivière du Missouri,"* and was promised a reward and royal rank on condition that he establish a fort on the Missouri within two years' time and make treaties with the Padouca and the Konza tribes. This elevation of a former *voyageur* created jealousy, and when he arrived in New Orleans in 1722, he found that no preparation had been made for his trip up the Mississippi and the Missouri. He finally got together forty men and as much material as he could, and set out for the Missouria village far up the Missouri.

Jealousy had caused whisperings in the ears of the Duc d'Orléans and John Law, perhaps in the form of stories about Bourgmont's great influence with the powerful Osages and his relationship with the Missourias. Certainly anyone with great influence over the Osages, the balance of power on the lower Missouri, could very well destroy the company's plans for expansion. The company advised the King through d'Orléans that Bourgmont might need watching, and as a consequence he had to take two commissioners up the Mississippi and the Missouri with him.

The commissioners were envious. They immediately realized Bourgmont's influence with the Osages and the Missourias, and although they soon chose Missouria women for themselves, they perhaps kept reminding themselves that Bourgmont was not really a gentleman for all his royal honors. They, for example, did not marry their robe mates.

The contemptuous commissioners had the men put to work building their individual houses, leaving the commandant only his personal servant and three of his men to build the fort proper, and while directing the work, he had to live in "a hut made of sticks with a grass roof," perhaps like the lodges the Missourias then built. This was in the river-reed and sapling and cattail country, and the Missourias, like the Osages, built their lodges of the materials available in the region in which they found themselves. Out on the edge of the plains they could have covered their lodges with buffalo hide.

This treatment of the newly appointed *Commandant de la Rivière du Missouri* might indicate that the commissioners were personal representatives of the boy king through d'Orléans, and had the duties of the modern Soviet commissars during Russia's war with Finland.

But they couldn't destroy the enthusiasm or the work of Bourgmont. He finally got personal quarters built for himself, a church and shelter for the priest, barracks, an armourer's cabin, and an excavation in which to store ice. He built no fortifications since he didn't have the force to man them, and anyway he was in the middle of the Missouria country and married to the grand chief's daughter. South of the river the giant Osages had complete control, and they too were his friends.

After threatening to return to France to lay his problems before the King, he received the men and the supplies he required.

But the fact that Bourgmont was encouraged to carry on with the building of forts on the Missouri indicates that the council at last had settled on the Missouri as the highway to riches and trade with the Spaniards and as the proper approach to the Padoucas and the Apaches.

The fort in the Missouria country on the north bank of the Missouri River finished, Bourgmont called it Fort d'Orléans, honoring the Regent. This was in the autumn of 1723, and he was now free and ready to carry out his second commission: to make a treaty with the Padoucas. However, ice formed on the river that year, and he had to adjust his plans to this important circumstance.

While waiting in the fort, restlessly, one can assume, he heard that the Otoes and the Iowas had made an alliance with the Sac and Foxes and with the Sioux, both of whom were bitter enemies of the French. This, Frenchmen knew, would be the work of the English.

Bourgmont made the trip to the Otoe country overland, and there was able to bribe the Otoes and the Iowas to break the alliance. This was hard winter's work in a land where there are no barriers to the Arctic cold and whimsies.

In June, 1724, he was ready to set out for the camps of the Padoucas. He sent St. Ange upriver, and he led a party up the north bank of the river, the two parties planning to meet at the upper village of the Konza. He actually left Fort d'Orléans July 3, 1724, with eight Frenchmen, one hundred Missourias, and sixty-four Osages.

The head chief of the Missourias, possibly the father-in-law of Bourgmont, led the Missourias; and very likely a chieftain, the leader of the *Tzi-Sho Wa'no'n,* was at the head of the Osages, since they would be a part of a peace-making expedition. The tough, enthusiastic and popular Bourgmont was leader of the whole expedition, naturally, and he had his little mixed-blood Missouria son along with him. The boy must have had ten or twelve years of age at this time.

The heat was the usual heat of the region during the summer, and therefore they got away early each day to take advantage of the cool morning air. The Little Ones complained when they must start before they had made their chant to Grandfather the Sun or the Morning Star. They rested at midday, then took up the march at two in the afternoon. It was very hot, and the small feeder streams flowing from the north into the Missouri River, having received no rain recently, became a series of little lenses of stagnant water from which mosquitoes rose like tiny wraiths when members of the party lay on their bellies to drink. On the fourth of July the hunters killed twenty "roe" deer and some turkeys. "The bucks are there in herds."

On the sixth of July they met the Konza scouts, sent out to inform Bourgmont that a delegation awaited him on an elevation in the middle of the open prairie. The Osages, the Konzas, and the Missourias always made rendezvous with other tribes and the Heavy Eyebrows on a lense of open, elevated prairie, so that they could see in all directions. From such a point of view they could see just how many there were in the party. This was supplementary to the scouts' report. But what the scouts wouldn't know was the party's mood, and from their point of view they could sense the mood of the approaching ones, note how they were armed, and what they brought as smoke-gifts.

That afternoon the expedition met the chief of the Konzas and several others of the Konza people, and according to the writer, "The calumet to the wind with great rejoicing." They had a great feast prepared and had the mats spread and brought the red and the black peace pipes, and handed them one at a time to Bourgmont, and then they honored the chief of the Missourias and the leader of the Osages, who with his followers numbering sixty-four was only a chieftain, temporarily leading one or more of the *Tzi-Sho* gentes.

When the pipe was accepted, there would be gifts, possibly a horse from the leader of the Little Ones and perhaps the same from the Missourias and a fusil from Bourgmont.

They danced. The Frenchmen danced in a circle with locked arms singing a ditty, and the natives danced one of their social dances, with singers about the drums in the center of the dance ground.

The Padouca captives which the Osages and the Missourias had with them were brought along for a purpose, and would be returned to their people with grand gestures by Bourgmont. This had diplomatic importance and had nothing whatever to do with humanity or conscience, even though the transfer would be made under the banner of friendship. The return of the captives would put the Padoucas in a much better frame of mind for allying themselves with such kind-hearted people.

Bourgmont knew the Indian nature very well, since he had made knowing Indians his business and since he lived with them and spoke his wife's Siouan tongue. He wanted as large a delegation as possible to meet with the Padoucas, and had tried for a large delegation of Osages since the Padoucas would undoubtedly be impressed by their strong medicine. However, not only did he have only sixty-four Osages with him, but they were of the *Tzi-Sho,* and soon they were discontented and became more and more whimsical.

Even though it was July and they traveled cross-drainage on the bluffs of the Missouri River above the twisting, sometimes narrow flood plain, dipping into the limestone canyons and climbing out bathed in sweat and tormented by insects, they would dance some-time during the night's encampment and fire their fusils in joy shots. They had no need to take precautions; their party was a large one, and they were in Osage-Konza–dominated country. The familiar keg of spirits was not mentioned in the journal.

They camped on the high lenses of prairie, among the trees where night winds might discourage the mosquitoes. Soon the fires would cast jagged, animated shadows. The Osages, the Konzas, and the Missourias would dress in their dance clothes and paint their faces from their paint bags and dance a social dance they all knew; a dance something of the nature of but not of the same source as the modern *i'n-lon-schka,* which was intertribal. The singers would beat the rhythm on a drum and sing the Siouan songs they all knew well. They would be bare from the waist up, and they would wear hawk-bells stitched to a band which was tied about the leg just below the knee. These bells sounded in earth rhythm, and the fantastic hatchets they got in trade with the French were held in the striking position.

Long after the encampment grew quiet, the grass-roots insect sing-ers would continue the rhythm and even the metallic tone of the bells. The warriors could go to sleep to their own rhythm of well-being.

The next day they traveled all day and reached the banks of the Missouri River where it bends to the north. They had not really just then reached the banks of the Missouri since they had been traveling along its northern banks ever since they left Fort d'Orléans, but here the sudden turn to the north stopped their westerly traveling. However, just across the river in a broad valley was the Konza village. They camped where they were stopped on this especially hot day. The breeze had vanished, and the journal mentions the suffering.

They crossed the Missouri the next morning at eight, by three methods. There was a large pirogue for Bourgmont's use, and in this the warriors placed their fusils and shields, and the leader of the Little Ones placed therein the sacred hawk, the *wah-hopeh,* and these things were in the care of Bourgmont's cadets. Usually the Little Ones would shoot their arrows across a stream they were about to ford, then with bows in their mouths slip down off the rump of their horses and take them by the tails. Even an unaccustomed horse, which might become frightened and rise up pawing water frantically with his front feet, could often be encouraged to swim across if caught by the tail.

The Missourias were experts at making floats out of cane, and they were pulled across on these floats by their horses or by the young men who held a rawhide thong in their mouths as they swam. Dogs were sometimes trained to do this.

They camped within "the distance of a gun shot from the Konza village." This was perhaps the lower village. Soon the people came with a peace pipe, and after this food was brought and speeches were made, and in their praise of their visitors the Konzas did not neglect their own greatness. They assured Bourgmont that all the young men who might wish to go with the French chief could go with him to the Padoucas, saying to him that these were warriors "who have no other wish than yours." This assurance out-Latined the Latin, and was just as sincere, but it is also un-Siouan and highly suspect.

The Konzas accorded the chief of the French a courtesy which they must have imitated; perhaps they had seen the Pawnees perform it, since their close kin, the Siouans, did not practice it. The Pawnees, like most of the Caddoans, were advanced a little beyond the Siouans since they were more agricultural, and had more intricate rituals with some refinements in human sacrifice the Siouans had never dreamed of. Since human sacrifice implies elaborate cere-

200

mony, such ceremony seemed to have spilled over into other phases
of their culture.

Anyway the Konzas carried Bourgmont on a buffalo robe to the
lodge of the principal chief, who sat like a large bronze bust in kingly
dignity, among piled up gift furs and provisions. The chief made a
speech of welcome, which was followed by other speeches, and gifts
were finally distributed.

A messenger came from St. Ange, who had come upriver in a
pirogue, to the effect that several of his men had contracted fever and
must be taken back downriver. Bourgmont sent them back to Fort
d'Orléans, along with five Missourias who were to go to the Otoes to
enlist their aid. The greater number of strong allies of the French
for the Padoucas to see, so much the better.

On July 20, the Osages became restive and worried. They had heard
about the men under St. Ange who had fever, and they had seen the
Missourias pull several of the Padouca captives across the river on
their mats. They had lain on their backs, and were very sick with
fever.

The Little Ones, ever alert and ever cautious, camped apart from
the others thereafter. They noted that more and more of the party
become ill with fever. This was probably typhoid or malaria, and not
the *we-lu-schka,* the little mystery person which made *wah-don-skas*
on the face and gave an overpowering odor, the *we-lu-schka* that left
the Little Ones blackening on the earth.

In their fright they became sullen, and on this day they left without ceremony, and some of the Missourias left with them. The Bourgmont party were camped about eight miles north of the Konza River,
and about ten days from the place where they expected to find the
Padoucas.

When Bourgmont contracted fever, he sent Konzas, Missourias,
and Frenchmen to the village of the Padoucas on a scouting expedition, and on August 4, 1724, the scouts traded a certain band of the
Padoucas their first fusil for a horse and robe—the first fusil this particular band had possessed.

Then he sent fifty Konzas to the Padoucas for a courtesy visit, and
they made such an impression that five of the Padoucas came back

with them as a return courtesy. At this time one of the Padouca captives died of the fever, and since apparently she was very important among the Padoucas, this unlucky incident made Bourgmont nervous, but the visiting Padoucas mourned for her and manifested no other emotion except a formal grief.

One night the Otoes, the Konzas, the Missourias, and the Iowas, the last having joined the expedition with the Otoes, danced in honor of the five visiting Padoucas. The Padoucas joined them, and they danced for an hour and a half.

Bourgmont had to return to Fort d'Orléans on the Missouri on account of his illness; and when he was recovered, he set out again for the villages of the Padoucas, leaving the Konza village October 8, 1724. His guide lost his way on the plains, and the company traveled too far south, and since they came upon volcanic tufa and obsidian, they must have been on the headwaters of the Cimarron River in the extreme northwestern corner of the Panhandle of modern Oklahoma or in extreme northeastern modern New Mexico or extreme southeastern Colorado.

When they finally traveled west and north again and came to the Padouca village, the Padouca captives with the expedition waved their robes three times above their heads as a friendly signal.

This was October 18, 1724. Bourgmont told the Padoucas that the French had as allies some of the strongest tribes on the Missouri River, each having strong medicine. They were the Osages, the Otoes, the Missourias, the Konzas, the Iowas, and recently the Pawnees. Now the French wanted to add another tribe with strong medicine to their allies.

He presented a French flag to the chief, and made the usual gifts to him, but the chief was embarrassed by the small number of Spanish horses they had in the village at that time and assured Bourgmont that this situation would be remedied on the next trip across the Sangre de Cristo Mountains.

The French tried to outdo the Spaniards who came out to trade with the Padoucas once every spring, who brought horses and knives but no guns. The French had brought guns, swords, hatchets, powder, bullets, Limbourg (cloth) red and blue. They brought Flemish knives and other knives, scissors and combs, and shirts, flintlocks, awls, vermillion, needles, boilers and hawkbells, beads, brass wire, and a variety of ornaments.

The Padoucas were overwhelmed. It was similar to a modern television sponsor's giving away a car or a trip to Bermuda.

Again the Little Ones left Bourgmont on the trail back. This time they were in a hurry to get back for the tribal autumnal buffalo hunt. Bourgmont arrived back at his fort on the Missouri on November 5, 1724.

Now the ambitious, energetic former *coureur de bois* and son of bourgeois parents, who inspired jealousy among the gentlemen adventurers of France because of his social status and because of his gaining the honors of a gentleman and because he was very successful in his relations with the powerful tribes of the Missouri, had only one more duty to his king under the current orders, namely, "that the above mentioned Sieur de Bourgmont will be able to engage some chiefs of the principal tribes to pass in France with him in order to give them an idea of the power of the French, and the above mentioned Sieur de Boisbriant and the Council of the Colony will provide the things that will be necessary to him to that effect."

On December 15, 1724, an intertribal council was held. Bourgmont stood before the council and made his plans known. All listened very intently because they had faith in him, but the Otoes refused to send representatives of the tribe to France because, as they said, they "had no warriors to lose." This put a new light on the adventure when the Little Ones did their thinking about it. He who might be delegated by the Grand *Tzi-Sho* to go with Bourgmont across the sea would be in a much more precarious position than one going into battle. In battle he would be under the eye of *Wah'Kon-Tah,* the approving eye since he would have the sacred hawk, the *wah-hopeh* with him and his red shield hung on his chest, and would have sung his prayers to Grandfather the Sun, sung his Crow Songs and his Wolf Songs. But there down the Big Waters, far past the mouths of the Smoky Waters and the Red Waters and the waters of the *Hi'n-Sha* (modern Red River), the Caddos would be the same as singing his death song. The Osage name for the Caddos, *Hi'n-Sha,* means Dark-Faces-That-Glow.

203

There were four Osages, five Missourias, and four Illini, among the latter a chief of the Metchegami, called Chicague. These were the ones chosen. The Missourias had chosen four chieftains and the daughter of the principal chief. Some have thought that she might have been the mother of Bourgmont's son. There is no hint through gentile memory or tribal memory about her identity. Not even Traveling-Rain, the chief of the Little Osages of about that time, has handed down mouth-to-ear information to the late chief of that physical division of the tribe.

There was much made of this council and the appointment of the several natives who were to accompany Bourgmont to France so that they could bring back stories of the magnificence and the powerful medicine of the Heavy Eyebrows. The French slanted the speeches of the Missourias in the following manner, in which there was nothing more un-Siouan and nothing more French: "We love the French Nation and hate the Spanish and English" was the way Bourgmont's interpreter translated the speech of the chief, and this sentiment was recorded by the French as the consensus of the other tribes.

There is no word picture of the delegates of the Little Ones standing wooden-faced waiting to enter the pirogues that would carry them down the Missouri to the Big Waters, the Mississippi; past the Waters of the Caddos into heart-stopping adventure, and then perhaps into Spiritland. However, the Missourias broke into wailing as their tribesmen stood waiting. They said, "We will cry for you a little while in order not to dream of you, if you should die on your journey."

All of them seemed to feel some comfort in the fact that Bourgmont's little Missouria mixed-blood son had made the trip to France and back to the Missouria village safely, and that the Heavy Eyebrows themselves had made the trip many times. The Little Ones and the Missourias both said to the departing ones, above the keening of the women, that they would mourn for fifteen moons, and if after that period they did not return, they would count them dead, and they hoped that if they did not go to Spiritland and did return, they would not come back naked and with empty hands.

Even if there had been someone along on this strange journey who could have seen into the hearts of these native Americans, he would have smeared his expression with treacly sentiments of the period or burdened it with the silly back-to-nature poetic philosophy of that French period. Probably it is just as well.

When the queer party landed at New Orleans after their long trip down the Mississippi, Bourgmont found that the company had suddenly become very economical, and had his usual trouble with jealousy, and was not allowed to take all of his *sauvages*. As a matter of fact, he was allowed to take only one from each tribe, and these included the chief Chicague, the daughter of the Missouria chief, and the nameless Osage.

They arrived in France September 20, 1725. Great interest surrounded them, and the people swarmed to see them, and the court and its followers were always ready for novelty, and these American *sauvages* were novelty of the most romantic kind.

They would meet everybody, including the boy king, Louis XV, but they would not meet the Duc d'Orléans or John Law. D'Orléans had fallen over onto the lap of a frail beauty of his set while sitting before the fire and had died in December, 1723. John Law, after scrambling the classes of France through the enrichment of the butcher, the baker, and the candlestick maker, wiping out mortgages for the nobility, robbing Peter to pay Paul, left France much as she had been before his System, not more impoverished by the bursting of his bubble. The Company of the Indies, even after he had been compelled to flee, carried on, and directors of the company met the party of *sauvages* and Bourgmont when they arrived in France. With the directors were the Duc de Bourbon, who had taken the position of first minister, after the termination of the Regency when the King had become thirteen a few months before the death of d'Orléans. He was one-eyed and brutish, and came along with his Duchess and perhaps with his mistress, Madame de Prie, and certainly accompanied by the Duchess d'Orléans. This was the party that met the romantic *sauvages* from the Missouri and the Illinois rivers in far-away America. Already Frenchmen who had ventured in America among the *sauvages* had created frontier histrionics, and in making their heroism seem more romantic at home had elevated the "Peau Rouge" to a highly romantic position in the minds of Europeans.

The Duchess d'Orléans was possibly not as depraved as her daughters and her husband, but she was more stupid, and this made her amours less attractive, and it must be assumed that she perhaps needed diversion badly at the moment. The Peau Rouge and the "Princess" of the Missouri especially became a vogue, and this was a happier vogue than the suicides which followed the failure of the Law System. Actresses in powder and patches carefully arranged had plunged dramatically into the Seine. A ruined gentleman walked off the embankment with sword in one hand and a golden-headed walking stick in the other.

The *sauvages* were taken to the Bois de Boulogne and allowed to run down a deer. They were given coats trimmed in gold and fitted with cock hats, and they all danced at the Italian Theatre. They went to masked balls, and women cooed over Chief Chicague and the other red men, who quite likely knew well some of the better bed chambers. Such visitations would have been a unique novelty to the ladies. "The scandals of the Regency were the outcome of fashion rather than passion. . . . Great ladies surrendered themselves to the Duke of Richelieu, not because they were enamoured of his silly oval face or brutal impudence, but because their reputation in the smart set depended on their being the heroines of his anecdotes of his bonnes fortunes." The *sauvages* would probably not consider such matters worthy of their boasting, but the ladies might find themselves more interesting.

The Duchess d'Orléans found a new diversion and a plaything in the Missouria girl, the "Princess" of the Missouri. She arranged the baptism of the girl in Notre Dame de Paris, and stood as her godmother, and *La Belle Sauvage* was given gifts by the King and the members of the court, one a repeating watch set with diamonds. The Duchess gave Chicague a snuffbox, and gifts were made to the others, but have not been recorded.

Later, there was another diversionary buzz when the excited Duchess arranged the marriage between the "Princess" of the Missouri and Sargent DuBois, who was of the party from the Missouri, and there were more presents from the King and ladies of the court.

22. "Louisiana Has Never Been in Open War with the Osages"

PERHAPS THE REASONS why La Harpe was not further encouraged in his explorations up the Arkansas and the reasons why the fort on the Missouri called Orléans was allowed to become neglected were based on international relations and not on the local conditions. It is perhaps true that the fort had little effect on the activities of the Little Ones. They intercepted French traders who were packing merchandise to be traded to Pawnees, Padoucas, or any tribe of the Missouri Siouans. The French traders even went to live with the Missourias, believing the tribe to be a refuge, since they were on friendly terms with the Little Ones most of the time.

The Little Ones confiscated trade goods being carried to their enemies, and they killed Frenchmen when they could do so with impunity. And they were clever: if they must kill Frenchmen, they chose the members of a trading expedition, whom they knew to be of little importance to the governor of the Illinois or to Bienville in New Orleans. But they made every effort to count coup on the important men of the Pawnees or others of their native enemies, and despite the fact that the scalps of the leaders and chiefs were much more important than the scalps of ordinary warriors, they seldom killed the leader of the French trading or exploring expeditions. When reports came to Bienville that the Osages had killed another Frenchman or Frenchmen, the first and most important consideration in the minds of the members of the council of the Company of the Indies in Paris was the maintaining of good relationships with the whimsical and energetic Osages. They had never needed strong allies more than since the Treaty of Utrecht in 1713 which ended the War of the Spanish Succession and had changed conditions in the balance of colonial power in America. France had been obliged to give up Newfoundland, Acadia (Nova Scotia), and Hudson Bay. When this treaty was signed, the French of Louisiana and later the Company of the Indies and the King back in Paris realized that England had won a stronger foothold on the American continent and that the struggle for a continent was really just beginning.

The Heavy Eyebrows would need the Little Ones and their power, as they would need the Algonkians to train against the English-favoring Iroquois. When the time came, they would even need the Spaniards.

Thus did the Little Ones become a factor in the balance of power among European nations, as the Algonkians and the Iroquoians had been long before them. The Little Ones had been a balance between the Spaniards on the Río Grande and the French on the Mississippi, but now, in the French sense of urgency to protect their boundary along the Mississippi and the Illinois and the St. Lawrence, and to withdraw their protective barriers and trade stepping-stones on the Missouri, the Little Ones became quite important in international balance.

The documents indicating their bloody whimsies are many, and the excuses the French made for them—to themselves—are sometimes ingenious. On April 22, 1734, Bienville wrote in explanation of the murder of eleven Frenchmen by the Osages: "The news that I have had the honor of sending to Your Excellency concerning the letters I have received about the murder of eleven *voyageurs* of which the Osages have been accused has been only partly confirmed. It is true that they killed a slave and a Bohème [vagabond] *engagé* with the hunter whom they mistook for a savage. The others, who were away when the blow was struck, were frightened when they returned to the *cabanage* where the murder had been committed, and not daring to trust any nation, they decided to go to the Illinois by land, where they arrived after two months march. Thus the officer who commanded at Arkansas, not seeing them return, judged that they had been killed and advised me of it."

The story here is not only the glossing over of the incident by Bienville, but the very fact that the subjects of the most powerful nation in Europe had to flee, frightened, "to the Illinois by land." This meant they could not even use their own highways, the rivers, through fear of their allies, the Little Ones.

And by this time there was no more Fort d'Orléans. Its power had been sapped by concentrations along the Mississippi and the Illinois against the English. In a letter from the Company of the Indies, in Paris, which was sent to Governor Perrier in 1727, there was an order for the abandonment of the fort which Bourgmont had labored so conscientiously to build. The soldiers were to be withdrawn and only the missionary left "if he believes he can make some progress in the preaching of the gospel among the savages," and the commander of the post was ordered through Perrier "to have his garrison carry back to Illinois all the effects of the company which are worthy of transportation."

The missionary, Father Jean Baptiste Mercier, worked on for fourteen months after the company's abandonment of the fort, but in 1732 he wrote that there was no protection for missionaries and that a mission to the Missouri Indians was out of the question. He suggested that he needed missionaries to work among the Osages and the Missourias, but since none had been sent out, what could he do, a lone missionary, with no flock except savages to support him and the mission? He wrote also that the Osages and the Missourias had asked for missionaries. The Missourias were a little insecure because of decimation by disease and perhaps attacks by the Sac and Foxes, and they were very agreeable at this time to any suggestion; but if the Little Ones asked for missionaries, it would be for the purpose of keeping the Heavy Eyebrows well disposed toward them, so that there would be no cessation of fusils and *mo'n-ce wah-don-skas* coming up the Great Waters. They were not analytical and had no academic interest in the beliefs of the Heavy Eyebrows, their own concept of *Wah'Kon-Tah* remaining intact. The Heavy Eyebrows had not yet actually proved themselves more powerful than the Little

Ones; therefore, why adopt Christianity, even though they might be careful to pay the usual respect to the Heavy Eyebrows holy men, who might do them mystic harm?

Governor Perrier wrote from New Orleans in 1729 that he had relieved Fort d'Orléans, a fort which had "caused considerable expense to the company." As a matter of fact, he believed that all the Frenchmen who had been killed had been on their way to the Missouri, "where it was easy for the Foxes to surprise them."

It seems odd that the Frenchmen going upriver to the fort must travel the north bank of the Missouri River, dominated by the Sac and Foxes, when they could have traveled up the river of the Osages and then have gone overland to the fort. Or they might have paddled up the river along the south bank, which was Osage and Konza dominated. The Sac and Foxes could have made the fort untenable, as could the Osages, as could also the urgency of the French to meet colonial conditions after the Treaty of Utrecht.

In a memoir of 1729, the company deemed it imperative that the French form alliances with all the Indian tribes between New Orleans and Illinois and distribute soldiers among all the posts from Natchitoches to Fort Louisburg on Cape Breton Island.

Thus, while the French were preparing for the inevitable contest with the English for control of the continent, their allies the Osages seemed to sense their position, and they began to be less meticulous about the importance of the Frenchmen they killed and did not restrict themselves to unimportant Bohèmes and unlicensed *coureurs de bois* and slaves.

Letters traveled both ways across the Atlantic about them, those traveling east to Paris softening the stark incidents of hair-taking, so that they might harmonize with the company's policy of keeping intact the important alliance. The letters traveling west across the Atlantic to New Orleans were documents of gracious tolerance and face-saving, such as the letter from the Minister replying from Versailles, September, 1738, to Bienville's letters on the usual subject of Osage whimsicalities: "If the Osages bring to Bussonière the authors of the deed perpetrated by that nation upon the Frenchmen of the Arkansas River, this will be an indication that the nations will have disapproved of this act of treachery, and that will terminate the matter." But he also warned the commandants; and more than that, he ordered them to refrain from doing anything that might anger the Osage tribe and result in war; just see that "the authority does not suffer." Later Bienville, in a letter to Versailles in 1738, wrote in "regard to the coup struck by the Osages upon our hunter of the Arkansas River, the nation is not yet prepared to give satisfaction for it." They were very likely never "prepared." And in any case it was probably not the nation's (tribal) problem, but the problem of one or two gentes of the subdivision of the *Hunkah,* during a time when the tribe as a whole were dancing ceremonially and singing their prayers each sunrise far away from the Arkansas River, on a ridge above their own river, the Place-of-the-Many-Swans, and were quite unaware of the coup.

In 1740, the commanding officer of the Illinois, Jean Baptiste Benoit, Sieur de St. Claire, learned that a Missouri River Indian had killed a Frenchman named La Grillade, who had lived with the Osages or the Missourias for eight or nine years, and after the killing, presumably by the Panther or the Bear gens of the Little Ones, the Missourias had not dared cross to the Illinois for their "needed goods."

An Illini had reported to the commandant that the Osages, in order to boast of their prowess and their contempt for the medicine of the Heavy Eyebrows, had brought some French heads to the Illini village.

At first, the French had pampered the Little Ones as a necessary buffer between themselves and the Spaniards and as efficient slavers for the traders, and now they must pamper them because they must turn their backs to them and the Missouri and prepare for the war to control the continent, although they did not know they were preparing for the war with the English. This turning of the back on the Missouri and trade with the Spaniards and the dream-riches of the headwaters of the Missouri and the Arkansas was only a military face-about; the spirit of trade and exploration did not die. As a matter of fact, the French seemed at this period to begin to realize some of their commercial dreams.

There is tribal and gentile memory of raids into the country of the Utes and the *I-Spa-Tho,* the Spaniards, and even after the gesture of friendship under the leadership of their friend Bourgmont, the Little Ones considered the Padoucas their enemy. It is possible that this enmity might have retarded French commercial relations with the Spaniards, since in their jealousy the Little Ones would prevent French traders from trading with the Padoucas, especially if they used Fort d'Orléans as a starting point. This might have been indirectly the cause, or one cause, of the failure of Fort d'Orléans; this and the Sac and Fox marauders.

There is much evidence besides the gentile and tribal memory that not only the Little Ones but the Pawnees joined the Padoucas and the Apaches in raiding Spanish settlements along the Río Grande. This, of course, was not concerted action; each tribe made its raids independently. In the fact that their allies, the Little Ones, were raiding the Spaniards with whom they wished to trade, the French faced another problem, not less important than the old slavery problem.

However, the Padouca barrier was broken in 1739 by the famed Mallet brothers, Pierre and Paul. They went up the Platte River, thence down the south fork, over Trout Creek Pass into the Arkansas drainage, then over Poncha Pass and down the Río Grande to Taos and Santa Fe. They apparently didn't go through the heart of the Padouca country, but through the country of the Utes. After being detained in Santa Fe by the suspicious Spaniards, they returned by way of the Canadian and the Arkansas rivers.

This successful breaking of the Padouca barrier inspired Bienville, and he sent Fabry de la Bruyère to make the try, guided by four members of the Mallet party. He was instructed to go up the Arkansas, and to observe astronomy, botany, and geography and other natural features of the country. But somehow he set off up the Canadian, leaving the Arkansas at the mouth of the Canadian. He set out in September, a month in which the Canadian tries to flow under its own sand bed, and naturally he got only about, or a little more than, one hundred miles above the mouth by January of 1742.

He had been watched by a group of one or more gentes of the Little Ones, the party numbering thirty-five. They were on a slaving expedition, either against the Caddoan Mentos or the Pawnee-Piques (Picts) of Red River; and since they were not a mourning party or war party, they were less ill tempered than curious about the Heavy Eyebrows who were trying to float their dugouts on the wet sand.

Fabry de la Bruyère was afraid of his giant allies just as most French traders and explorers were, and he tried to be friendly with them. They sat their horses and wondered at the trade goods, and wondered for whom they were meant. They realized that it might be some time before the Heavy Eyebrows could navigate the river and that they would have plenty of time. Perhaps they could even talk this Heavy Eyebrows leader out of some of his trade fusils and powder and ball.

Realizing that the Heavy Eyebrows were not going anywhere until the water came down the river from the Padouca country, the chieftain asked La Bruyère to come across the river and camp with them. He became characteristically amiable when he noted the party's circumstance and he became talkative. He told La Bruyère that there were at that time six Heavy Eyebrows traders in the villages of the Little Ones, and what could one make of that? One could only say that the Heavy Eyebrows and the Little Ones were certainly allies and friends. The wily chieftain also informed La Bruyère that there was a great one of the Heavy Eyebrows staying with the Missourias, and called Chevalier de Villiers.

La Bruyère maintained alert guard during the night; the men listening to the great horned owls, the mewing of raccoons, and the certain foxlike yaps of the coyotes, all of which night talk they knew quite well the Little Ones used as signaling notes. The next day they seemed to be filled with gratitude, and when the chieftain demanded knives and gunpowder and bullets and fusils, he got what he demanded except for the guns, La Bruyère suggesting that fusils were for trade for horses only.

The Little Ones seemed to understand this, and they said that they would return from their expedition with both horses and slaves.

They kept their word. This was the kind of word given which the Little Old Men had endowed with sanctity—the kind of word which once given did not longer belong to the giver until he had carried out his promise. Then he might get his word back, and would be able to use it again. They did not speak of "breaking" their word, but thought of it as something given another as a sort of hostage until the agreed-upon action was performed.

La Bruyère knew well that they would be back, and instead of being happy, even though he needed horses, he fortified his camp.

The Little Ones had met the Mentos and had taken their horses and the one pack mule, leaving the Mentos afoot, and for good measure they had a couple of scalps. They had only seven horses and the one always useful mule, but they noted the fortifications. La Bruyère was effusive with his explanation that the fortifications were against the Pawnee-Piques. However, the chieftain knew exactly the location of the Pawnee bands, and knew that La Bruyère could not have been frightened by them, since they would have come to him only in friendship and great expectations of trading horses, of which they always had many, for fusils, of which they always had too few. As a matter of fact, one of the chief interests of the Little Ones was to keep the Heavy Eyebrows from trading fusils and powder and lead to the Pawnees.

The Little Ones had come back for the sacred word they had given, and this Heavy Eyebrows chief had fortified his camp. It was obvious now that he wanted horses so that he could carry his trade goods, and especially his trade fusils, to the Pawnees and the Padoucas. This Canadian River up which he was trying to float his cargo, which the Little Ones called Flat-Red-Waters, had its source in the land of the Padoucas. They also knew that without horses he could not make it until the rains came in the spring. This was February.

They refused to trade their stolen horses, since the commander refused to admit that he had trade fusils, which the Little Ones knew he had. Now they didn't have to ask for their word back, since the word of the Heavy Eyebrows had "fallen to the earth."

If the chieftain of the Little Ones had been less imaginative, there certainly would have been trouble since La Bruyère had a detachment of only fifteen men.

But he apparently was imaginative and very shrewd. The chieftains of the gentes were often very able and were often superior in intelligence to the grand division chiefs, the *Tzi-Sho* and the *Hun-kah*. They had much more latitude in employing their shrewdness, since the traditional restrictions did not apply with such force to them. They, the chieftains, leaders of the gentes, need not walk or ride in great dignity, the symbols of generosity and sanctuary. They knew they were constantly in view of *Wah'Kon-Tah* and his messengers, such as the swallows and the dragonflies from March to September and the bluejays in the winter, yet he didn't expect as much of them as he expected of the Grand *Tzi-Sho* and the Grand *Hunkah;* he could laugh at their frailties.

Only seventeen of the original thirty-five Little Ones returned to the Canadian camp of the Heavy Eyebrows, and this fact might have much to do with the chieftain's decision not to make trouble as La Bruyère placed a neat little pile of lies before him. He said he needed the horses now which he had refused to buy from the Little Ones when he first met with them, because at that time there had been no Pawnees skulking about, and he needed the horses now to escape from their country. Also—and this was quite true—he was on his way to meet his brothers, the Spaniards, since the Spaniards and the Heavy Eyebrows were at the moment friends. He showed a letter which Bienville was sending to the governor of Santa Fe. He told the Little Ones that Bienville wished that they and the Padoucas and the Pawnees would make no more raids across the Sangre de Cristo Mountains to steal corn and horses and women from the Spaniards, since they were all allies now. But he had to have horses, in order to meet with his friends in the west and there make peace with the Pawnees and the Padoucas from strength. Therefore, since the Little Ones would not trade their horses, would the chieftain carry a message to his brothers, the Heavy Eyebrows traders in the village of the Missourias? He wrote a letter asking them for horses. He would pay cash for the horses and pay a bonus to any two traders who might accompany the savages with the horses, this bonus to amount to two hundred francs. A wonderful inducement to speed and good faith, since cash was scarce.

The shrewd chieftain of the Little Ones took the letter, perhaps happy to get away from the effervescing Heavy Eyebrows. He said that he and his gens could make the trip from the camp, one hundred miles, approximately, above the mouth of the Flat-Red-Waters, to the village of the Missourias on the Smoky Waters, in seven days.

The chieftain and the seventeen Little Ones rode off on Indian business and never came back. They probably warned the Mentos and the Pawnees about trading horses to the Heavy Eyebrows, since La Bruyère had sent some of his men to buy horses from the Mentos and they were not to be found. His disgruntled men had suggested that they obtain horses from the Pawnees, but apparently he was really afraid of them, since he wouldn't allow them to go to the Pawnees.

In despair, he left his men and set off for the French settlements on the Arkansas, near the mouth, but his men became discouraged and made their way to Santa Fe afoot, carrying what cargo they could so manage on their backs.

About this time in the early 1740's was perhaps the beginning of a situation among the tribes of the Missouri River—at least the lower Missouri—which has obtained to the present day, and has made of the phrase "the civilization of the American Indian" no more than a smug cliché implying inherent European virtues. This was the beginning in this region of the contact between the Little Ones, other Missouri tribes, and the immigrant gutter-sweepings of Europe. The Company of the Indies lasted longer than its founder in its colonial influence, but soon it had to let go, and this gave some liberty to the cutpurses, murderers, rapists, and human rats whom the company had brought over by the boatload to dump on the lower Mississippi. They cringed under control when there was sufficient power to keep them in control, but soon they sought freedom. Being the scum of the European gutters, they were not accustomed to the great forests and the loneliness of the prairie under the sky, and like dump rats, they had to seek refuge in human habitation. The greatest concentrations of humanity in those days were the French posts, where they dared not remain, and the Indian villages, where they came as Bohèmes and unlicensed *coureurs de bois.*

As their numbers grew, they became more assured and more vicious, and with their gutter-sharpened wits, began to demoralize the tribes with whom they lived. The Little Ones had a few of these, but only a few, at this time, since their reputation was well known and would have awed them as their betters often did. It was in the village of the adjustable Missourias where they became a menace, and Bienville had to order Benoit to send a detachment, an officer and six soldiers, from his garrison on the Illinois to restrain the low livers. Bienville courteously called them "traders." In referring to the policing detachment, he wrote, "Without that the traders would not fail to cause us some affairs with these Indians," and he ordered Benoit not to grant trading licenses for the lower Missouri River "except to men well known, wise, and under the condition that they will take the necessary things for the subsistence of this small garrison."

The French found it necessary to give a monopoly: "Therefore, in order to prevent such abuses from happening again which up to now have found their way among these nations, and in order that the trade of this country and that of Canada may not suffer from them, we have, with the consent of the King, granted to M. Deruisseau, Signeur en partie de L'isle Perrot, in Canada, whose ability and integrity are known to us, the exclusive trade of the entire Missouri River and all its tributary streams, etc, etc."

And here in the year 1745 was a European condition brought about by Europeans, and the first "No Trespassing" sign. "They," referring to the trading company of M. Deruisseau, "shall expressly forbid anyone to organize trade, or hunt along the entire river; those who violate the rule shall suffer confiscation of their belongings and goods, etc, etc."

This condition, characteristically European in all facets, finally necessitated a European defense, a fort. It is thought by some that the fort might have been built to protect French business from Frenchmen, under the aegis of French protection for natives, and some believe that it might have had as its reason for being trade with the Spaniards.

In any case the fort was built at the spot where the waters of the Konza (now the Kaw or Kansas River) debouche into the Smoky Waters (now the Missouri). This is the spot on which Kansas City, Missouri, now stands. The fort was built by M. Deruisseau and called Fort Cavagnolle, and was commanded by that Heavy Eyebrows the Little Ones had mentioned when parleying with La Bruyère on the Canadian: Chevalier de Villiers. At the spot where the fort was erected, there had been a Konza village, or was a Konza village at the time. There seems to be only a faint and doubtful tribal or gentile memory of this among the Little Ones and among the Konzas, now called Kaws.

But it could have served as a stepping stone for trading with the Spaniards, since parties could find their way from this spot across the prairie to the Arkansas, and eventually to Santa Fe. From here the French had made another treaty with the Padoucas and the Wichitas, the latter then called Jumanos.

About the time the French were experiencing a tension over the struggle with England for a continent, they were finally realizing their dreams of half a century or more. The gate was open along the Arkansas, and practically anyone who had something to sell could form a trading party and cross the Padouca country with impunity. Some of them even traded with the Padoucas themselves.

But the Little Ones became jealous of the trade with their enemies, the Padoucas and the Caddoan Wichitas, and stepped up their harassment of their allies, the Heavy Eyebrows behind the trade lines. There is no evidence that they made forays into the country of their enemies at this time, but killed and robbed the Heavy Eyebrows traders and trappers where they met them. They had been approached by the English along with French allies of the Algonkian tribes, the Illini, Peorias, and Cahokias. Governor Vaudreuil must have known something about this when in 1748 he wrote that the *voyageurs* were being attacked and killed by the Osages, "with whom, nevertheless, Louisiana has never been in open war."

23. *Wah'Kon* and George Washington

THE HEAVY EYEBROWS went to war again with the Long Knives, but this war was not the one for which both were consciously or unconsciously preparing; the one which would settle the matter as to which nation would control the North American continent east of the Mississippi. This was a balance-of-power war in Europe and was called the War of the Austrian Succession, lasting from 1744 to 1748.

There is much doubt that this balance-jiggling in far-away Europe affected the Little Ones in the least, even though it affected their Heavy Eyebrows allies at the mouth of the St. Lawrence. The French had put much hope in the fort on Cape Breton Island called Louisburg. While it was formidable, it was possibly more the bastion of symbolical dream strength and inspired hope and a feeling of well-being among the people of New France. This symbolical strength and determination of New France was much like the much later Maginot Line—one to awe and discourage the English colonies along the Atlantic Coast of the mid-eighteenth century as the other was to impress and discourage and even defeat the Germans between the great wars of the first half of the twentieth century.

This fort, which gave much comfort in its austerity and in the fact that it seemed to be watching the English colonies, fell to indignant Puritans in 1743. Its destruction was a disorganized, undisciplined Massachusetts Colony effort, conceived by their Governor Shirley, aided by four warships from England under Admiral Warren. But

220

what the besiegers lacked in discipline, they compensated for in a sort of religious ferocity, holy righteousness protecting them like the red fetish shield of the Little Ones. Fort Louisburg was to the Puritan fanatics a papal stronghold, "a Catholic center of the devil in the New World."

But it was the trade the English made with the French at the Treaty of Aix-la-Chapelle in 1748 which brought the Little Ones into the future conflict between European powers. They had once aided their allies the Heavy Eyebrows, to raise the English-Fox siege of Fort Detroit in 1712, and now they would be drawn into the military strategy of La Gallissonière.

At the Treaty of Aix-la-Chapelle, the French wanted their Cape Breton and the ashes of their fort back so badly that they traded Madras in India for it, and this annoyed the colonies in America as well as the people of England who had celebrated the fall of the French stronghold of France in America as a distinct victory over both the papacy and untrustworthy Latin France. The fall of the Louisburg Fort had been called the "darling conquest of the people."

This Treaty of Aix-la-Chapelle, which ended a war that had barely disturbed the Frenchmen and their allies the Little Ones far away on the Missouri and the Mississippi rivers, had greater after-effect on both the Little Ones and their allies the Heavy Eyebrows than the actual fighting. The French began to realize that some day they would be compelled to fight the English for the continent. This was borne out by the fact they began to build new forts and renovated old forts rather feverishly, and they began to harass the colonies by moving into the Ohio River drainage, back of the colonies and their allies, the Five Nations, the Iroquoian tribal league. "Allies" is perhaps rather too strong a term to use for a "friendship which was of a cautious and passive kind and would have stood no great strain." The French policy, besides penetrating into the headwaters of the Ohio, was to put strain on this English colonial Five Nations friendship.

This they did under La Gallissonière, and this made the English even more jealous and fearful of the satanic papists. The English colonist didn't think he might ever need land transmontane, covered with forests, but it would be very uncomfortable to know that the papists were bringing colonists to live at their backs across the mountains. This was of course part of the French plan.

Adventurers from the English colonies now felt less safe across the mountains than they had, since the bands of Iroquois seemed not to recognize their friends, and they often recognized the faces and the beards of Frenchmen among the Indians, dressed as Indians. Here and there they found leaden plates upon which was inscribed the French monarch's claim to the country. Here and there along the game trails they were startled by the exotic shields nailed to trees, conspicuously facing them as they followed the sharp turnings of the deer trails. Carved on these shields was the coat-of-arms of Louis XV.

And Gallissonière sent persuasive representatives down the Ohio and up the Mississippi to the Missouri, who thence made their way to the villages of the Missourias and the Osages and the Konzas. They sat in the villages and talked long about the fine things which the Long Knives had and how stupid they were, strung out like buffalo on a water trail, or like buffalo crowded and circling, facing the winter wolves. The promises of the Heavy Eyebrows were almost like things that you held in your hands; their effervescence and their own uninhibited joy in anticipation, and their boastings of the prowess of the Little Ones and the wisdom of their ancestors, made many of the chieftains of the Little Ones look at the hard floor of the lodge between their feet or shut their eyes so that the Heavy Eyebrows could not see the glory in their hearts. If the Heavy Eyebrows could see into their hearts, they might take away from the pile of promises.

This was in the early 1750's, and there is no reason to believe that the Little Ones had gone up the Ohio, after war came between the Heavy Eyebrows and the Long Knives, until 1755. In both the gentile and tribal memories, there is only one incident in which they might have figured, and this was the battle of Fort Duquesne, and is called "Braddock's Defeat."

Governor Dinwiddie of Virginia, who had sent young George Washington to build the fort at the forks of the Ohio, where Pittsburgh, Pennsylvania, now stands, seemed to have been a man who had some anxiety about the French activity on the other side of the Allegheny Mountains, an anxiety which, incidentally, was not shared

by all the colonial leaders, even after the French had run Washington
and his sappers away from their works and took over, renaming the
fort "Duquesne." Only after the defeat of Washington and his backwoods levies at Great Meadows in 1754 did Mother England listen
to her perturbed son, Dinwiddie, and others and send over General
Braddock.

The anxious Dinwiddie had co-operated with Governor Glen of
the Carolinas in the building of a fort in the Cherokee town of Keo-
wee, called Fort Prince George, but when Dinwiddie called upon
Governor Glen for the promised Cherokees to aid Washington and
Braddock, the Carolinian seems to have been in a pique with Dinwiddie and wouldn't send them. If he had, the Little Ones would
have met their Iroquoian enemies long before their wars of the nineteenth century. These Iroquoian Cherokees and others who did not
appear, plus the surly Pennsylvania farmers who refused to furnish
transportation for Braddock's army and the general indifference of
some of the colonists, were factors in Braddock's defeat. Benjamin
Franklin had to threaten and entreat with the farmers to obtain the
needed transportation, but the Little Ones say they saw no Indians
with the Long Knives. With the Heavy Eyebrows, there were *Nika-
Shu-Dse,* Red Men of many tribes, they said. Gentile memory has it
that they approached each other, reaching out their hands to feel of
the ornaments which the different tribesmen wore.

This esoteric fabric which is woven from gentile memory, or which
is, in fact, tongue-to-ear history, is not even a gentile symposium.
There can be no choice of one gentile memory over another, since
each memory represents only a few threads of woof or warp, and
these completely out of color or pictorial harmony with the weave,
even though they all have basis in fact.

In a European racial or national memory without the aid of the
written word, the things that Europeans were most interested in
would have been stressed. The Robin Hood story, the idea of retribution in the biblical story of the rich man and the camel passing
through the eye of the needle, the lamp of Aladdin, and Santa Claus
—all if not of European origin are Europeanesque. These are retributive dreams of the social, political, and economic underdogs,

strengthened as implements employed by the king and church. If the unlettered Frenchman had told the story of Braddock's defeat, without the aid of documents and without knowledge of the European backgrounds of the English and the French rivalry, there would be a much more intelligible story, even if he had attributed Washington's fortunate escape to a hovering angel. It would be intelligible to Europeans, because those practical things in which they would have been most interested would have been presented and stressed, and they would have only to supply the missing threads in the woof and the warp. The European would not have noticed this wilderness of bird song, for it was June; the mystery of the forests would not have impressed them. The constant listenings and the peerings and even starts of the Red Plainsmen they would not have experienced. The Woodland Indians were accustomed to the dark, dripping woods, but the Plains tribes were like deer feeding in a high wind. An eddied leaf could startle them.

There were 600 Indians from several tribes; there were Algonkians and Siouans represented by many tribes and 200 Heavy Eyebrows. They all fought like Algonkians, from behind the boles of trees and from behind windfalls and humps in the earth, in a spot which the Algonkians had chosen nine miles from Fort Duquesne which Braddock and Washington with 1,400 of the best trained troops had come to take.

The Plains Indians were not accustomed to fighting in this manner, and they found it difficult to remain behind their trees and their windfalls. Plains fighting was much more dramatic certainly, as compared with the panther-stealth and hunting-cat seriousness of the forest fighting. It was definitely histrionic. They of the Plains rode toward each other waving spears and standards and singing, and they stopped just out of range of fusil or bow, and there they challenged and finally skirmished, then rode away.

The *U-Dse-Ta,* the Down-Below People, the Little Osages, say that one of their chieftains became bored with the fighting from behind his windfall and arose, arranged his red fetish shield, flung the sacred bundle, the *wah-hopeh,* around his back, pranced like the bull wapiti back and forth, singing. The Little Ones say, he was the only

Indian the Long Knives saw, and their guns roared, and he fell, with his song fluttering in his throat.

The Long Knives acted exactly as the Heavy Eyebrows said they would act. They came like buffalo through the running oaks when the flies swarmed in summer. They cut the saplings so that they could get through, and some of them were dressed like *wah-shinkah zhu-dse,* the cardinal, and even had crests; and when they fell, they fell like the leaves of the sumac in autumn when the throat rattler (frost) comes.

When the Heavy Eyebrows and the Red Men fired from their trees and humps on the earth and from behind windfalls and rock, the Long Knives stood like buffalo before the winter wolves. Their chieftains rode among them and at times even hit them with their long knives, with the flat side. They rode toward the firing, waving their men on; but in the excitement, their horses held their heads high, slobbering and with rolling eyes, and took the balls and the arrows in the throat and head falling to writhe and groan, while the Long Knife chieftains crawled back on their bellies to the massed men.

This is the original weave of the tongue-to-ear history of the Little Ones in as many versions as there are gentes of the *Hunkah.* Here are the crazy threads of both woof and warp, with broken ones here and there and a hiatus here and there, and the separated threads that the batten has not yet pressed into the weave.

The Little Ones of 1755 had wondered at the amulets and fetishes and seashells of the woodland Algonkians, and had touched them and had handed the incident down to their sons and the sons of their sons. They had felt menace in the dark woods, where the tree boles could assume almost any shape the fancy urged, and the firelight was imprisoned not by outer darkness but by the leering trees, and shadows from the flame dance were not always shadows.

They wondered at the huddling Long Knives shooting at the trees instead of killing the Heavy Eyebrows and the Red Men, and their being packed like buffalo before the winter wolves, then running through the woods in panic, not like stampeding buffalo, but like striped-head the quail. But there was no incident worthy of gentile or tribal memory during the journey from the Place-of-the-Many-Swans to the fort at the forks of the Ohio River called Duquesne. It is likely they walked or came up the Ohio in dugouts with their French allies, possibly the river in dugouts, since the French used the rivers as their highways. There was no white wolf howling at their campfires at night, no death of a chieftain, no *we-lu-schka,* the "little people," causing death. There was no one struck by lightning, and there was nothing of religious significance; therefore, there was nothing to hand down about the journey until the Little Ones saw the strange Indians and the strange dark woods that dripped, and the Long Knives crowding upon each other like buffalo, firing at the trees. Of the 863 men killed and wounded and the 61 officers killed and wounded, many of the wounded were carried away with the mortally wounded Braddock; but there were many of the English dead on which to count coup, and from whom to rip scalps, since the Indians and the Heavy Eyebrows remained and did not pursue the enemy seriously. There were 600 Indians as against 200 Heavy Eyebrows, and the Indians were satisfied with victory. The Little Ones say that they did not come back with empty hands.

Questioning for twenty-five years the gentile leaders and the Little Old Men of the tribe about the details of the war movement against the Long Knives, far up the *Wah-Ba-She,* the Ohio, one comes rather unconsciously and suddenly into the era of recorded history appreciation; and the Eagle gens, out of gentile pride and boasting, supplied gossamer for the hiatus and the broken threads in the weaving. These threads, gossamer at first, through the years have become strengthened through the telling and perhaps colored to fit into the pattern of gentile and tribal tradition.

These threads of gentile identification with recorded history of the Europeans have to do with George Washington. There was a tall man, say the Little Ones, there at that battle with the Long Knives, riding toward guns and the arrows of the Heavy Eyebrows and the Indians, his horse naturally holding his head high, slobber-mouthed, with the whites of his eyes showing. He fell with bullets and arrows in the neck and head which might have killed the tall man, had he not been thus shielded. Then the tall man would ride forth on another horse, and this one would fall with bullets and arrows in his neck and head.

But the chieftain of the Eagle gens and his men were lying flat behind a great fallen tree, and to the side. They saw the tall man from the side as he rode toward the hidden Heavy Eyebrows and the Red Men. They say they shot at him with arrows, and for some reason the arrows seemed to miss him. Later they said that they curved around him. This was *Wah'Kon,* they said, Mystery. They became afraid of shooting at this tall, brave Long Knife, fearing the medicine that made the arrows curve around him.

This tall, brave man they say was George Washington, and he was spared to become the father of his country because of his strong medicine which the Eagle gens of the Little Ones respected. The glow of importance will come to the teller's face, and he might suddenly become as abrupt as very important men are supposed to be, as a gentile glory two hundred years old reflects upon him, creating an aura and giving outline and substance to a man lost and frustrated in his obscurity amid the miracles of a mechanical civilization.

But the Little Ones of the Eagle gens knew nothing of a colonial surveyor called George Washington, any more than did the French, or for that matter the English. The Little Ones would not know about him for many years, perhaps not until about the time of Thomas Jefferson, who impressed them by giving them medals. The French would not know him until the American Revolution, and the English would certainly know about him during the same war.

It is believed that the Little Ones might have taken part with the Heavy Eyebrows against the English in the battle near Niagara in 1759. This was a French defeat. It has been hinted that both the Little Ones and the Missourias were present, but there is nothing in the tribal or gentile traditions which might indicate their presence. If they did take part with the French, it is not likely that they stayed with the French the four years intervening between the defeat of Braddock and the battle near Niagara. The French were in control of the region of Illinois and the lower Missouri during the conflict, and must have been kept busy luring tribesmen of both the Siouans and the Algonkians with their histrionic promises. If the Eagle gens and others fought during Braddock's defeat, then other gentes must have been lured to the battle near Niagara, since they, the Eagle gens, did not come back with empty hands.

It is not likely that the Little Ones were much disturbed by the struggle for a continent, and the energies of the young men under their gentile chieftains were not absorbed. They continued their slave catching and their skirmishes with the Pawnees, the Wichitas, and the Sac and Foxes, and the Little Old Men were building a ceremony about the useful and therefore sacred *mo'n-ce,* the metal of the Heavy Eyebrows.

24.   The *I-Spa-Tho* Take Over

THE LITTLE ONES didn't know that after the Treaty of Paris in 1763, and because of a co-lateral understanding and agreement between Charles the Third of Spain and Louis the Fifteenth of France relating to a Family Compact between these two Bourbons, their allies the Heavy Eyebrows had given up dominion over them, such as it was, and that *Le Père Grande* was no more in Paris far across the great waters, but *El Padre Grande* in Madrid.

Late in the Seven Years War, called the French and Indian War in the colonies, about 1761, Louis XV, being beaten everywhere by the English, convinced his kinsman Bourbon, Charles III of Spain, that if France lost the war, the Spanish possessions would be in danger. This was not difficult since Spain had grievances against England. England had searched Spanish ships from the Americas, made settlements in Honduras, and had kept Spain from sharing in the Newfoundland fishing. Charles, represented by Grimaldi, and Louis, represented by Choiseul, got together there to renew the Family Compact; and Charles's representative got a promise from Louis's representative that in a peace with England there would be the consideration of Spanish grievances.

Spain was defeated in Cuba and in the Philippines, and France lost half a continent. In the treaty, Spain had to give up Florida for the return of Cuba and the Philippines and France had to give up New

France, and then in a secret agreement France ceded Louisiana to Spain to compensate for the loss of Florida.

It is not in the least surprising that the Little Ones would not feel the change in dominion when the Louisiana Frenchmen themselves barely felt it. The Little Ones saw the same Heavy Eyebrows traders, singing and sweating their way up the Smoky Waters with their pirogues filled with trade goods, and the Bohèmes continued to wander hairy and dirty up their river, finally to settle among them. The French officials and explorers continued to come up their river in their chipped-out, burnt-out trees with presents and effervescent friendliness when their numbers were few.

These were all well-known Heavy Eyebrows types, and the Little Ones saw no *I-Spa-Tho,* the Spaniards, for six or seven years after the Treaty of Paris, and then only when they became curious about the building of a *cabanage* on their side of the *Ni-U-Tonkah,* the Mississippi.

This new traders' settlement was established after the transfer of Louisiana to the Spaniards, but the Little Ones were never to know this, nor did the French seem to realize it.

When the Little Ones had a complaint to make to the commandant, they previously had to cross the river to Kaskaskia or to Chartres, but now the Long Knives had run the Heavy Eyebrows across the Big Waters, and about 1770 the commandant still spoke the language of the Heavy Eyebrows and lived at this place where they had once built a mission. This mission had lasted but a short time, since at that early period no establishment could last for long on the same side of the Big Waters with the Little Ones. This was the mission built at the mouth of the Des Pères River in 1700, where Father Cosmé had said mass, assisted by Henri de Tonti.

Now there was a traders' post, and it had been built by French traders under an exclusive license from D'Abbadie, the director-general of Louisiana.

When the Grand *Hunkah* asked some of the chieftains to go there and complain to the commandant about the traders' taking fusils up the Smoky Waters to the Padoucas and the Pawnees, and even to the Snow-Heads (Iowas), who were periodically allied with their other kinfolk, the Cut-Heads (the Sioux), their Heavy Eyebrows friend, a young man called Cadet Chouteau, went with them. He was a trader associated with the licensees Maxent, Laclede, and Dee in 1763, the exclusive privilege apparently granted by D'Abbadie the Frenchman to Frenchmen, the former still reporting to Paris rather than to Madrid.

This Cadet Chouteau had ascended the Mississippi as an assistant to Laclede. They had left New Orleans on August 3, 1763, and had selected this site for a *magasin* which would be more than a *magasin* and an entrepôt, rather a general headquarters for the Missouri fur trade as well as a refuge for the Frenchmen who found life east of the Mississippi intolerable with the suspicious, overweening English. Thus was the foundation laid for St. Louis on February 15, 1764, whose complexion would be French and not Spanish. Whether it was first called San Luis del Yllinois or St. Louis, it was named not for the current Louis XV but for the sainted Crusader of the eleventh century.

The privileges granted by D'Abbadie were revoked after his death and after Aubry came to the director's office, but whether or not granting trading licenses to anyone of good character who applied for them was the regulation after the revocation of the special privileges to Maxent, Laclede and Company, the latter carried on and aided the Spaniards in keeping the English from the Missouri River trade and from contact with the Missouri tribes, before whom the English could lay much better and cheaper merchandise than that offered by the French.

This was one of the reasons why the Little Ones came all the way from the Place-of-the-Many-Swans to the mouth of the Des Pères River to see the commandant of the new establishment, and they brought their friend Chouteau with them. He had been called a "boy" when he came up the river with Laclede, and now, about 1770, he was only seven years older and still a very young man. Therein may have resided his attraction for the Little Ones. His youthful enthusiasm for his romantic association with them all through the years and his pride when either they or the Europeans and Americans called upon him for aid was the pride more of the romantic than of the prosaic trader.

231

Also, all through their associations with the Europeans and the Amer-Europeans the Little Ones have put their faith in certain individuals, faith usually based on the individual's justness and conscientious "coming back" for his word after he had carried out his promises.

There is no doubt that Cadet Chouteau was very romantic as well as acquisitive, and the reflection from his intimate association along with his financial successes gave him confidence and a feeling of self-importance. There was romance in simply being in the wild land of America. The dragons of Europe had all been killed and chivalry was dead, and the privileged people around Louis XV and even the *bourgeoisie* in general left "an impression of vulgar decadence"; and the privileged ones, idle and debauched, laughed at romance and religion and vied with each other in creating obscene little *chansons*. They, for state and political reasons, even dragged their king, who naturally loved his hounds and his horses and his shooting, back to the lascivious little apartments to play with his mistresses.

Thus the first frontier histrionics in America west of the Mississippi might, as far as the young Frenchmen were concerned, have been the urge to express themselves romantically, assuming no ridiculous superiority. The showing off of the Bohèmes and Gasconaders was histrionics as well, but clownish and ingratiating.

Young Chouteau lived with the Little Ones with a species of joy of living and treated them with respect and kept his promises, and they trusted him. His personality was such that he could reconcile the exigencies of the fur trade with his romantic attachment to them without arousing their suspicion. And whatever the traders called their new settlment at the mouth of the Des Pères River—whether they called it *San Luis del Yllinois* or St. Louis de Illinois, it was known to the Little Ones as *Sho'to To-Wo'n*, Chouteau's Town.

By the time the Little Ones had come to lay their grievances before the commandant at the new St. Louis, Spain had sent Ulloa to take over the administration of the Louisiana Territory. The upper part, which included St. Louis and Ste Geneviève, was still referred to as Illinois. Aubry had much French enthusiasm about the possibilities of Louisiana, and tried to get Ulloa to accompany him on a tour of the country and visit the Indian tribes, but the gift from Louis XV to his kinsman Charles III of Spain had apparently been accepted with reluctance by the latter, and there was an atmosphere at this time of "let the French run it; they are accustomed." Ulloa, by his haughty attitude and restrictions on trade, caused an uprising among the habitants of New Orleans, and a man with the unlikely name of O'Reilly was sent from Havana by Spain to put down the revolt.

Also about this time Madame du Barry, who had the erstwhile man of the woods and horses and hounds, Louis XV, under her control, contrived the dismissal of Choiseul, and with his fall Spain lost French support. Before this she had been standing up to the English over the world, but now she seemed to be thinking of nothing except keeping the English out of Louisiana.

The commandant whom the Little Ones visited in St. Louis in order to tell of their troubles was St. Ange de Bellerive, who had been forced out of Chartres across the river, and his presence gave them confidence. Their troubles were caused by their own actions. They had been approached by people who had been sent from across the Mississippi by Pontiac, who had kept the English from taking over that which they had won, the old French territory just east of the Mississippi. The English were kept out by Pontiac's activities until 1765. He was an Ottawa chief, who had the idea that if the white man left—not necessarily killed, but driven out or kept out—the old ways would return.

The Little Ones believed this as well, possibly through oratory of the Pontiac messengers, and apparently they stepped up their activity against the traders who were still their old Heavy Eyebrows allies, but now under the Spanish governor-general at New Orleans, the brittle Ulloa. Apparently he must have decided to punish the Little Ones by cutting trade to them, as was certainly done later, with results that almost caused war.

The Little Ones had begun to rely heavily on this trade, and could scarcely do without it. The importance of *mo'n-ce,* metal, was so great that the Little Old Men were building a ceremony around it. Then there were such important things as gun flints. They could go to their Cretaceous limestone escarpments to the west and find plenty of flint as well as on their own Verdigris River, but the trade flints were much easier and much less trouble. The women had begun using flannel and Limbourg cloth, for wrap-around skirts. And, of course, along with the flints for their fusils there were powder and lead and more fusils. They now depended upon French knives and picks and hatchets and awls and blankets and kettles and brass wire, and gingham shirts and printed calico and glass beads and hawkbells for their dances.

There are many records of the conflicts between the brittle and haughty Spaniards and the red men of the Missouri, and especially are there many records of such conflicts between the Little Ones and the Spaniards. The French-spoiled, arrogant giants of the Place-of-the-Many-Swans of the plains and the woodlands, and the arrogant Spanish governors-general of New Orleans, were ever on the verge of conflict for twenty years after about 1770. The Spaniards, whose experience had been with the anchored Pueblo Indians of the headwaters of the Río Grande, who had been quite effectively contained behind the Sangre de Cristo Range by the Padoucas and the Apaches of the plains, had never had to attempt to control mobile cavaliers of the plains, whose villages were many leagues up sinuous rivers in the middle of the prairie-plains and who were not swayed by the Black Robes.

This was one of the periods when the Osages were at war with their close relatives and possible splinter, the Quapaws—a period just previous to 1777, since in that year the two tribes made peace, much to the disgust of the Spaniards, who were doing everything they could think of to build up buffers between the Osages and the Red River Caddoans and themselves. They had probably worked zealously to effect the strained relations and the skirmishes which took place, from which the weaker Quapaws always suffered.

But now in 1777, the *Pa'-I'n Ma-ha,* the Pawnee-*maha* from the Loup and Platte rivers, came down eight hundred warriors strong, ostensibly to fight their old enemy the Osages, but instead of attacking, they gave the Osage domain a wide skirting and approached the village of the Wichitas which straddled the Red River about where Jefferson County, Oklahoma, and Montague County, Texas, face each other across the river. They came to the Red River and down it and established themselves there with their kinsmen for the purpose of making war on the Osages.

This was obviously a Spanish-inspired maneuver, for the Spaniards were continually harassed by the Osage gentile war-movement activity, and had decided to organize the enemies of the Little Ones to move against them, feeling that the Caddoans with the strongest medicine, the Loups or Skidis, would give confidence to the Red River Caddoans.

As a matter of fact, on September 14, 1777, Athanase de Mézières, lieutenant governor of Natchitoches, presented to Governor-General Gálvez a plan for punishing the Little Ones. He proposed to enlist 1,270 warriors from ten tribes of Indians living within his jurisdiction. He said that "the Indians of this district who may be desired and regarded of service will come and enlist at the slightest suggestion, without asking for stipend, and solely to satisfy their hatred."

Mézières planned to leave Natchitoches in the spring of 1778 after organizing the Wichitas, the Red River Caddoans known as simply Caddos, the Natchitoches, Tonkawas, the Pawnee-*maha,* and the Padoucas. He would ascend the Red River in canoes to the Caddo villages, thence go overland to the villages of the Tawehash or Wichitas. These villages on each side of the Red River were to be the place of rendezvous; then the allies would march overland to the villages of the Little Ones, using canoes wherever possible. They had to go overland across the domain of the Padoucas since they didn't dare use the streams, which were Osage highways.

The attack was well planned. The horde of warriors were to move north across drainage, then attack from the west. Mézières' plan was that they would not attack the villages openly against the Osages' eight hundred warrior defenders, but slip up as close as possible and wait for the wind, then let fly incendiary arrows into the dried cattail walls and roofs. "This," he assured himself, "will deliver to the knife those who attempt to flee from the flames."

Whatever happened to this well-planned attack no one seems to know, not even Mézières himself, since one finds no record of it.

The modern hereditary chieftains, especially of the Bear, the Deer, and the Eagle gentes say only that the Padoucas would not enter their domain. When they wished to fight the Padoucas, they say, they had to go to the Padoucas, and they say further that of all these people only the Pawnee-*maha* had strong medicine away from their own earth. They might have tried to shoot flaming arrows at the lodges of the Little Ones, but no one "remembers" the burning of the lodges. They "remember," they say, only the backs of the Pawnees on their swift horses. The tongue-to-ear history of the Little Ones they speak of as "memory."

The next year Mézières was complaining again of "the large and indomitable tribe of Osagues," who were becoming more arrogant and more intolerable and notorious each day, "on account of their treachery and rapine," and in his last year as chief executive of affairs, he wrote to Gálvez that the Osages had weakened and almost destroyed the Caddo Nation by their continual warfare on them.

There is little doubt that most of these attacks were by the gentes of the *Hunkah* who had their semipermanent hunting and warrior camps near the Three Forks, the junction of the Verdigris and the Neosho with the Arkansas River.

This village was really occupied by one of the physical divisions of the Little Ones known as the *Co'n-Dse-U-Gthi'n* (now called *Sa'n Solé*) or those who stopped on the plateau to build their drying fires during the great flood, the Upland-Forest People.

They were led by *Gra-Mo'n,* Arrow-Going-Home, and *Wa-Tcha-Wa-Ha,* the latter known to the French as Jean Lafon. Apparently they were having much fun killing Caddos, and after the Caddos started moving from place to place to avoid them, they tried their luck with more and more important Frenchmen and Spaniards.

There were reports of a hunter's being killed on the Arkansas just below the mouth of the Poteau, and of four Frenchmen being killed on the same river. The Spaniards began to sweat again, since they had to remain on good terms with the Frenchmen at this time.

Wa-Tcha-Wa-Ha and Arrow-Going-Home were called to St. Louis, and on August 16, 1787, the officials demanded some of their chieftains as hostages to be delivered at New Orleans to guarantee their future tribal good behavior. The *Hunkah* and the *Tzi-Sho* at the Place-of-the-Many-Swans very likely knew nothing about the sporadic attacks of *Gra-Mo'n* and Lafon on Frenchmen.

Apparently the two made glib promises and did deliver up hostages supposed to be chieftains of the Arkansas Osages, but there is no reason to believe that the "chieftains" were really Osages. They could have been Padouca or Pawnee captives who had learned the Osage language and manners after some years with their captors.

The painted giants of the Arkansas River continued to ride over their earth, robbing trappers and hunters of their guns and horses and furs, and when led by the Bear or the Panther, would play with their frightened victims, who signed their own death warrants through their visible fright.

The Spaniards seemed to be more concerned with keeping the English from taking over the trade of Louisiana than in extending their own trade area; even a protective extension. They allowed such energetic and successful French traders as Maxent and Laclede and Chouteau to carry on, concerning themselves chiefly with fortification against the encroachments of the English. Thus did they extend their control little farther than the French, and the mouth of the Platte seems to be the farthest north point of their trade domain until after the American Revolution.

The English encroachments were a constant worry. The Englishmen came down from Prairie du Chien and the St. Peters River (the Minnesota), and the men from the Hudson's Bay Company and the North West Company were seeping in.

And in this circumstance, the Spaniards found themselves very much in the same position in which the French had found themselves when they feared both the English and the Spaniards and had to use the prairie-plains tribes as buffers, overlooking the joy-scalping by the Little Ones. They found themselves in a dilemma when they had to carry out their threat to the raiding Little Ones and forbid the traders to visit the Place-of-the-Many-Swans. The Little Ones had always considered the Caddoans their enemies, and their war with the Caddoan Pawnees was continual; they had resented the coming of the Comanches, and had always warred with the people they knew as Padoucas, and these two tribes remained their enemies. When the traders poled and paddled and cordelled themselves in their dugouts up the Smoky Waters, with their dugouts loaded with lead and powder and flints and fusils and hatchets and other merchandise for their enemies, the Little Ones swarmed out from the mouth of the Osage River and surrounded them, diverting their cargoes to the Place-of-the-Many Swans. They took the traders along with them, doing them no harm unless they resisted. However, there was little resistance, since serious traders ever have marketplace caution. When the Little Ones had taken what they wanted from the traders' stocks, which invariably meant the powder and lead and flints and fusils, they allowed the traders to float back down the Osage River and continue on up the Smoky Waters, and when they had sufficient pay load left to warrant the trip, they might then go all the way up to the mouth of the Konza River and up it to Buffalo-Dung-Waters, the Republican, or on up to the mouth of the Platte, the Waters-Flat-White.

The outraged traders, scratching their heads over their losses, would appear before the commandant at St. Louis, and he would write a letter to the governor-general in New Orleans, and back would come a crisp, indignant command that no more traders would be allowed to trade with the Great Osages.

Except for Chouteau's slipping up the Osage River for Laclede and Maxent or with his own limited merchandise, there would be no more full dugouts coming to the forks of the Osage.

After waiting some time, the Little Ones would sometimes go through the ceremony of the war movement. The *wah-hopeh* would be brought out and slipped head-first from its deerskin and reed shrine, and a war chieftain would be designated and he would go out to fast singing:

> *I go to learn if I shall go on*
> *To learn of Grandfather if I shall go on—*

Then when he returned, he would let the *wah-hopeh* fall, managing perhaps that it should fall with head to the west. Then there would

be great joy; the women would sing old songs of their gentile ancestors, and the warriors would rush to the dying redbud fires to
grab charcoal with which to paint their faces, and they would reach
into their quill- or bead-decorated buckskin bags to get their limonite,
and with this paint the lower parts of their faces black and orange,
the aboriginal earth signal of bluff and danger.

Part of the war party would depart afoot to the west, then turn
when out of sight of the village and get into their dugouts and float
down river to the mouth, where they would await the traders' cargo-
laden dugouts. When they came laboring into sight, the warriors
would push out from their ambush and, yelling, fire a few joy-shots
into the air. The old, accustomed Heavy Eyebrows simply waited for
them and demanded that unaccustomed ones leave their guns untouched. Those who had gone horseback would carry the plunder
from the dugouts not diverted up the river.

And during the years this went on; and at the last moment the
Spaniards would soften their commands or send Chouteau to the
Little Ones as a negotiator. The old relations would be resumed, and
broken again when the Little Ones believed that the traders were
taking guns and powder and lead to their enemies. There would be
little bands of Sac and Foxes and Kickapoos or Pawnees, and even
Konzas and Otoes and Iowas and Missourias, coming to St. Louis
to complain that the Osages had cut off the traders from coming to
them. They would wave their bows and their spears and their guns
when they talked about the Osages, and the commandant would be
compelled to appease them in some manner. Again there would be
letters to New Orleans and haughty, indignant, uncompromising re-
plies that were commands; and the same thing would happen over
again when the Spaniards found it to their advantage to avoid war
with the powerful giants.

But they had to keep the Missouri open. If their traders did not
supply the Pawnees of the Platte and the Republican, the Otoes and
the Iowas and the Konzas, then the English would supply them with
cheaper and better merchandise; certainly with more guns than the
Spaniards would allow them. This was protective. They must keep
Indian tribes contented, or the English would do so and thereby

239

attain control. On the Arkansas they could declare war on the Little Ones, not formally perhaps, but by bringing about confederation of the enemy tribes.

During the years between about 1770 and about 1790, when the Little Ones and the Spaniards were having the same troubles which the Little Ones and the French had before, the Spaniards had not extended their trade area, and kept on with the tribes with whom the French had traded: the Great and Little Osages, the Konzas, the Missourias, the Otoes and Iowas, the Republican and the Loup Pawness, and, of course, the Padoucas. After that time they began a protective extension which they had not dared to do before the probing English had been defeated by the colonists, who were now called Americans. But still their protective extension was to the north, and they finally reached the Arikaras and the Poncas near the mouth of the Niobrara, *Rivière qui Coeur* of the French and the *Río Escarnado* of the Spaniards. However, now with the wild Americans overrunning the Missouri, they considered the English, who were still a trade menace in the north and northwest, and the powerful Osages, who bullied Spanish-allied tribes, robbed traders, and scalped every adventurer, hunter, and potential settler who came into their domain, as really lesser evils.

In Governor-General Carondelet's instructions to Commandant Trudeau at St. Louis, he wrote: "You will try to restrain the Osages and protect the inhabitants against them and those of other savage nations, understanding that a fort is projected on the Arkansas River in order to restrain the Osages in that district, and make war upon them if they do not cease their incursions.

"You will exert yourself to maintain peace and good harmony with the English and Americans, but you must always bear in mind that the latter are much more terrible at present for the dominions of his Majesty than the English. In this concept, you will try to maintain in the mind of the savage the fear and mistrust which they have conceived of the Americans, and to live in harmony with the English without, however, permitting their traders in this part of the river."

Then amid all these troubles of the Spaniards, they thought they might checkmate the whimsical and dreaded giants with their wan-

dering Algonkian enemies north of the Missouri River, the Sac and
Foxes; but about this time, 1791, the Little Ones and the Sac and
Foxes buried the hatchet, and a large party of Sac and Fox hunters
were seen hunting on the Missouri with the Little Ones. This peace-
making might have been part of the strategy of the still persistent
English, even tied in with the defeat of St. Clair in this year. They,
of course, still claimed trapping and hunting grounds in the indefinite regions north and northwest of the Missouri, whatever right they
might have had to them. The feeble colonists were getting their
breath after the Revolution and could do little about the matter, and
the Spaniards could do little except worry. If the English could get
their strong ally, the Sac and Foxes, to make peace with the strongest
people on the lower Missouri, the Osages, then the Missouri might
be opened up to their Hudson's Bay and North West people.

The Little Ones and the Sac and Foxes were never quite the bitterest of enemies as were the Little Ones and the Caddoans. They
were much alike in many ways and even copied each other's dress—
later, certainly. The Little Ones had a deep respect for these Hard-to-
Kill People and there was even a physical resemblance, although one
was Algonkian and the other Siouan. It seems much more likely that
this peacemaking was accomplished by the English, since when a
group of Little Ones had made a pipe visit to the Sac and Foxes across
the Missouri River, their hosts had presented them with gifts which
represented trade merchandise which the Sac and Foxes had got from
the English.

But the war hatchets of the prairie-plains red men were buried in
shallow graves, and well marked. Certainly the buried hatchets between the Little Ones and their close kinsmen, the Konzas, Otoes,
Iowas, Quapaws, and Missourias, would lie long in their graves, but
never had there been more trouble among these kinsmen than in the
reign of the Spaniards in the Louisiana country. They all lived above
the Little Ones on the Missouri River or on streams feeding the Missouri, and naturally the amount of merchandise they got for their
deer, beaver, buffalo, and wapiti and wolf skins depended entirely
upon the needs or the whim of the Little Ones.

Auguste Chouteau spent the winter of 1790–91 with the Konzas on the Konza River, the modern Kaw, in order to protect the trade of Maxent and Laclede as well as his own and to trade for all the furs which the Konzas could obtain. But while he was wintering comfortably and perhaps domestically, several Sac and Foxes came with canoes filled with English merchandise and traded for most of the furs as Chouteau stood by helplessly. The Konzas got more and better merchandise for their hides and furs, as well as certain things which the French and Spaniards didn't have in their lists. On their way down the Missouri, the Sac and Foxes stopped by to smoke and feast with their friends of the moment, the Little Ones, and told them of the trading and of their friend the Heavy Eyebrows, Chouteau, in the village of the Konzas with his trade goods.

This angered the Little Ones. This was during one of the periods when the Spanish Governor-General Esteban Miró at New Orleans had instructed Commandant Pérez in St. Louis to stop all traders from going to the Place-of-the-Many-Swans to trade with the Great Osages. It seemed useless floating downriver to complain to Pérez, whom they didn't like, so they decided to go to the village of the Konzas to ask Chouteau about the reasons for Miró's actions, and also why he didn't come to them instead of to the Konzas.

They apparently did not prepare for the war movement, but kept the charcoal and the limonite in their deerskin pouches, hung from their belts or, as in times of no war danger, suspended from their left wrists. They carried their hatchets which the Heavy Eyebrows designed for them, ornate and pleasing. They carried their Osage-orange bows and dogwood and white-ash arrows, the latter now tipped with *mo'n-ce,* metal. Their quivers were made of buffalo-bull neck and swung over the left shoulder. Their shields were made of the tough neck hide of the buffalo bull, also. They even carried their round red fetish shields, and for those who were authorized to wear them, their women had placed just so the eagle feathers in the scalp-lock, the right side for *Hunkah* and the left for *Tzi-Sho.*

The Pawnees, as were the Nez Percé beyond the Continental Divide, horse-proud, and the Little Ones got many of their horses by capture from the Pawnees; therefore, they were fine ones, albeit it was said of the Little Ones that they rode or worked their mares too hard and they foaled seldom. They had saddles from the Spaniards now, but they also made their own. And they made their own shields for the breasts of their horses from buffalo hide, in imitation of the Spanish and Apache horsemen. Not all had horse shields and not all had saddles, but all reined their horses by a buckskin or wapiti-skin lariat or rawhide string looped about the horse's lower jaw. They might decorate the tails and the manes and forelocks of their horses, and they painted fetish designs on them, the significance seemingly lost through the years. Since about 1900 and the adoption of Peyotism, they wouldn't tell if they knew. These were the things which, among other things of the old religion, they had "thrown away."

They set out mounted and armed, but kept their war paint in their buckskin bags and carried the *wah-hopeh,* the sacred hawk skin. There were about one hundred of them, representing several gentes of the sub-*Hunkah* and the *Wah-Sha-She.* Some of them even led special war horses undecorated. They might have sung as they started up the well-known trail to the mouth of the Konza River, and if so, they would be singing the Wolf Songs and the Crow Songs. They would string out like buffalo going to water, and there would be as many chieftains as there were gentes represented, and the eagle feathers in their scalplocks would spin gently even in the slightest of prairie breezes. If the air was cold on this day in the latter part of February, 1791, they would have worn their buffalo robes well about their bodies and covering the backs of their heads.

The prairie over which they traveled was brown now, terra cotta after melted snow or after a rain. In this Light-of-Day-Returns-Moon, they could read the signs of earth preparing for spring. But the premature winds of Just-Doing-That Moon (March) might be blowing, and then their eagle feathers would bend over their heads like antennae and their robes flap about them, and the tails of their north-headed horses would be blown between their legs like the tails of humped-up horses in a blizzard.

The buffalo would stand or lie facing the wind or walk into it if there seemed to be no urgency, but if most of them were on the move, then the Little Ones would know that there might be a blizzard when the angry south wind stopped screaming like a crazy woman

243

in the tall prairie grasses. Buffalo walking steadily into the south wind, "drinking the wind," they would say, would mean that they would be out of the heart of the Arctic air when it came. This the buffalo would tell the Little Ones by such movements, and the Little Ones might ride faster to attain shelter under the limestone escarpments of one of the three forks of a tributary of the Osage River, the modern Grand River, where the Arctic winds would blow over them and the snow would not fly like smoke of the prairie fires, blinding them and stinging their faces. But by the speed of the buffalo and their urgency, they might judge the time when the Arctic air might come howling like a winter wolf over the prairie.

The coyotes told them little. When they hobbled their horses with rawhide thongs and were placing their fresh meat on sticks inclined to the fire just at sunset, *sho-mi-kase* would begin his chorus. But it told them little in this Light-of-Day-Returns Moon. The Osage scout with waving robe, or by riding his horse in a circle, by catching the sun with a thin piece of selenite or a piece of mica or quartz, or the smoke from buffalo chips, could tell them much, and his scouting aids would be the coyotes and the wolves and the buffalo and antelope. But when the scout would lay aside his selenite and his quartz and his waving robe and had put out his fire and come into the camp to stand in the spilled-ink moon shadows of the trees and played his sumac or red-cedar flute, he told the people on their robes only one thing and nothing more. This is all *sho-mi-kase,* during the Light-of-Day-Returns Moon, could tell the Little Ones. You saw them in threes and fours and fives now, following a female *sho-mi-kase,* and the males would not even see the Little Ones until the female stopped to gaze and interpret their intentions.

The trail over which they traveled was well worn, since it was the most direct trail to the river of the Konzas. It was so well chosen across the prairie that the modern Missouri Pacific railroad and Highway 71 run into the modern Kansas City on it or parallel to it, taking advantage of the same less difficult terrain. The land still has its lush beauty at all seasons, its hills and ridges and its streams like hairy fingers with their trees and undergrowth.

How fast the Little Ones traveled depended entirely upon the restiveness of the buffalo they had seen and whether a high wind blew from the south, and on their anger with Pérez and with their friend Chouteau.

They arrived in the Konza village on the first day of Just-Doing-That Moon (March), 1791. The Konza scouts would have seen them long before they came up river to the village, and already they would have interpreted their minds. It was too early for the summer hunt on the Republican and they were many, and some of them led war horses or buffalo horses, and they sent out no scouts but came strung out like buffalo up the river trail. These things to the Konza scouts could mean trouble, if their faces were unpainted.

They would have been sullen, and the chiefs would have waited dramatically before taking the proffered hand of the Konza chief; they would wait until he lowered it with hurt feelings, then they would have rushed at him one at a time with extended hand to throw him off poise. The Black Bear–Panther gentes were adept at this, since this was in imitation of the sudden bluff rush their symbol animals employed when the coyotes came too near their kills. They would have done the same to Chouteau, and there might have been *sotto voce* observations, such as *"o-ske-ka,"* which means "horse thief" and "liar," and many other things, since it is practically the only profanity known to the Little Ones besides *"pi-zhi,"* meaning simply "bad."

The Konza chiefs arranged for a council after feeding the Little Ones well, bringing out what they might have on hand from the autumn hunt. During this council they asked Chouteau why the traders came no more to the Place-of-the-Many-Swans, and he told them that it had been ordered by Miró from New Orleans; and the *I'n-Ta-Tse Shinkah*, of the *I-Spa-Tho*, far down the Big Water at New Orleans, had caused it to be done, because the Little Ones had gone to the Red Waters, the Arkansas River, and had killed every Heavy Eyebrows and *I-Spa-Tho* they had met. The French and Spanish traders and others since contact with the Little Ones tried to make them call the governor-general at New Orleans and the commandants at Cahokia and Chartres and later St. Louis "Father," and *I'n-Ta-Tse Shinkah* means "Little Father," to distinguish the

Governor-General Miró from his Catholic Majesty in Madrid, who would be the Great Father.

The Little Ones didn't take to this, since fire was really Father and the sun, Great Father or Grandfather. However, when they wished to gain a point, they used these terms. Certainly there had been nothing yet even in 1791 to indicate that either the Heavy Eyebrows or the *I-Spa-Tho* were superior to the self-important, arrogant Little Ones. The facts were that the Great Osages alone could have more than two thousand fighting men in the war movement within a few hours, while the best the French or the Spaniards could do was detachments of panoplied horsemen and armed detachments in pirogues, since they both during their occupations of Louisiana had to be on constant guard on the Mississippi. Their best chance was the recruitment of other tribes who had grudges against the Little Ones, offering them revenge. However, the Little Ones up to this time seemed able to cow the ambitious and revengeful enemy tribes who might join forces with the Europeans. This had happened in 1777 when the Spaniards tried to enlist the service of the tribes of the Red River, and again when the Spaniards got the Caddoans together.

So Chouteau, knowing them well and noting the fact that they had come one hundred strong for a friendly visit, realized that he couldn't scare them with Miró at New Orleans or with Pérez, the commandant at St. Louis. Also, he didn't know that the commandant of the Arkansas had already backed down over the Arkansas pillaging incidents.

When the news first came to them that no more traders would be allowed to come to the Place-of-the-Many-Swans to trade with the Great Osages, the wily *Hunkah* of that time had sent to the *Tzi-Sho* for a peace party to travel to the Arkansas Post to see the commandant. The party was led by a gentile chieftain of the *Tzi-Sho,* and they took along with them a wretched creature called *Pa-I'n,* the Pawnee. He was a captive, and on being brought in, he had been tied to the base of a tree by buckskin thong, his head fallen forward with eyes shut, as most prisoners sat, while thunder growled and lightning speared at the earth. The rain came, and soon the buckskin thong became slick and soapy and seemed to stretch in the captive's efforts, and he finally got his hands free and ran to the lodge of the *Tzi-Sho*. He entered dripping and stood in the east opening, the direction from which Grandfather came each clear morning. He was given sanctuary. He lived in the lodge of the *Tzi-Sho* for several years and learned the tongue of the Little Ones, but for some reason he had never been adopted by them.

Now, he would serve them. The party took him along to the Neosho, which runs into the Arkansas; thence they picked up the Quapaw trail to the post which Henri de Tonti had established near the mouth almost one hundred years before. They led the Pawnee before the commandant and said that it was he who had led the pillaging on the upper Arkansas.

Now the powerful Sac and Foxes were allied with the powerful Osages, and the English were sending their cheaper and better merchandise into the Missouri country, and the terrible, shouting Americans were crossing the river. This was no time to chase the Osages into the arms of the English. His Excellency, Miró, would approve, the commandant of the Arkansas knew quite well, since they all understood the danger which was embodied even in the wandering English and the Americans who were not traders but settlers.

Therefore the commandant made the chieftain of the Little Ones promise for the tribe that they would make no more forays on the Arkansas, killing subjects of his Catholic Majesty, the Great Father, and would allow the Quapaws to travel up the Red Waters to hunt buffalo, since the French had killed them out on the lower Red Waters.

After the facile promise, which had nothing to do with the sacred word, which one had to come back for, the commandant with his own hands stepped up to the captive Pawnee, declared to be the leader of the marauders of the Arkansas, and cut the captive strap which bound him. There was a feast, and the commandant loaded them down with merchandise and gave them Spanish flags. He also persuaded five of them to remain and go down with the next boat to New Orleans to receive medals from the Little Father, his Excellency Señor Esteban Miró.

These things they told Chouteau, and it was these things which had made the *Hunkah* sufficiently angry to send a party of some hundred men to ask Chouteau why there were yet no traders come to the Place-of-the-Many-Swans. They made fervent speeches and said that the commandant Pérez was at fault. They said that the commandant of the Arkansas and Miró at New Orleans were their friends, but that it was Pérez at St. Louis who kept the traders from the Place-of-the-Many-Swans. They told Chouteau to tell the *I-Spa-Tho* at Chouteau's Town that they would come there to take him.

This was strong talk for imitators of the black bear, the panther, and the golden eagle, who bluff to avoid fighting—that primitive balancing relationship between the species which the Europeans called diplomacy.

Chouteau might have recognized it for what it was, bluff, and must have indicated that he thought they were bluffing by an inflection or a mannerism, since they immediately assured him that they would kill Pérez and wipe out Chouteau's own town and that they would begin by taking what they wanted from his trade goods. He asked them to remember their friendship and the times he had come to the Place-of-the-Many-Swans to bring much needed merchandise to them when the *I-Spa-Tho* had kept traders from them. Their own oratory, as it so often did, created or revived the emotion which had inspired their coming north to the village of the Konzas, and the Konzas, seeing this, dared not interfere, and Chouteau was resigned to watching his trade goods being piled up for removal. Then apparently the chieftain of one of the gens of the *Tzi-Sho,* who had the honor of being leader of the whole party since this was not a war party, stepped forth, and the Konza chief and several chieftains joined him, and they persuaded the emotional young men to carry the things back to Chouteau's lodge.

When Chouteau got back to St. Louis, he reported to Manuel Pérez, the commandant, and the next month a letter was sent from Pérez to his superior, Governor-General Señor Don Esteban Miró at New Orleans, dated April 5, 1791.

The last paragraph of the letter, after recounting what Chouteau had told him of the visit of the Osages to the village of the Konzas, summed up the situation: "If what they have told Chouteau is true,

I do not doubt that they will come as they have asserted, and they will doubtless come in large number because of the war which they are having with the nations of the Mississippi. All I will be able to do is to receive them and placate them temporarily with something in order to prevent their doing greater damage to these districts which might be the result of my doing nothing, as they have strength enough to resist me if they are received badly." This strength on the part of the Little Ones called for diplomacy on the part of the Spaniards.

This matter was possibly settled by the liaison trader, Pierre Chouteau, some time later, but in November of 1791 the Grand *Tzi-Sho* sent four chieftains to St. Louis with thirty-two warriors to talk with Manuel Pérez.

The dilemma was growing. The English were wooing the Osages, and the Osages were intercepting trade cargoes going up the Missouri to supply the other Missouri River tribes again, which seems to point to another restriction of trade to the Little Ones after a series of scalpings of trespassers on their domain. They did no harm to the licensed traders; they took their cargoes or diverted them up the Osage River, or took what they wanted from the pirogues and carried the merchandise back to the Place-of-the-Many-Swans on their horses. But they took the hair of the Americans wherever they found them, molesting only those who came upriver past San Carlos, the modern St. Charles, Missouri, and the little log house on the north bank called Fort San Juan, and all those who came up the Arkansas past the Arkansas Post. They knew no friends among the Americans except those who were settled along the Mississippi and the Missouri anchoring themselves to their Spanish grants. The others, the hairy-faced trappers and hunters and refugees, they killed, their scalps having little meaning except in their great numbers, intrinsic war value, nothing.

Miró at New Orleans had cut off trade again and had instructed Pérez at St. Louis to demand hostages from the Osages to be taken to New Orleans, these hostages to be important men like chiefs or chieftains. This the Little Ones refused even to ask their principal chiefs about. They murmured, *"O-skee-ka,"* but remained calm. They demanded that the traders be allowed to come again to the Place-of-the-Many-Swans, but Pérez was firm.

When they prepared to leave, he had their movements watched closely by soldiers, who followed them overland to San Carlos del Missouri, just out of sight, fearing in their frustration they might fall upon a settlement. They watched them through San Carlos after they swam their horses across the river and struck the left-bank trail. They saw them past the log house called Fort San Juan del Missouri.

The grand chiefs were angry when they heard the report of the chieftain, and this time they sent two hundred warriors to the Smoky Waters to await the pirogues of the traders. They wore the black and orange bluff paint on their faces, and they were mounted and placed at several places along the right bank, each gens under their own chieftain. They needed only to ride to the edge of the war in full war paint, with their fusils across their horses' withers, and the traders, knowing that their lives were not in danger, moved over to them, protesting. They loaded the merchandise they wanted on their pack horses, and the traders followed behind protesting all the way to the Place-of-the-Many-Swans.

The traders even threatened, saying the Father at New Orleans would be angered when he heard of this. Both the *Hunkah* and the *Tzi-Sho* stood regally, keeping their tempers in the presence of the encircling "younger brothers" (young men) and the women who had come to see the hairy ones plead for their merchandise.

The chiefs answered the threat with speeches, both saying almost the same thing: that the traders' Father was not the father of the Children of the Middle Waters, and even though he was master in his town down the river, that meant nothing here where they were masters, and as far as their warriors could ride on their war horses in five days. There were limits recognized by the Illini on the east, the Sac and Foxes on the north, the Pawnees and the Plains tribes on the west, and the Arkansas River on the south, except that they had long before chased the Caddoans far south beyond the Red River.

They said that the traders might stay with them as long as they chose and leave when they chose, and if their hands were empty, the Little Ones would fill them, and they would give them horses to ride back to their pirogues, and instead of being unhappy, they should be very happy that they had their hair and that they still had some of their merchandise in their tree that floats.

And on November 8, 1791, Manuel Pérez, commandant at St. Louis, wrote to his superior, Governor-General Esteban Miró at New Orleans, concerning this last episode in the affairs of the lower Missouri: "This incident makes it clear that the Osages are determined not to let traders pass to the other nations as long as they are deprived of them, and it will not be possible to restrain them in any other way than by constructing a fort. . . . This is the means which I find the easiest. To deprive all the nations of the Missouri of traders does not seem to me to be a means sufficient to restrain the Osages for various reasons; first, because it would be a motive for the English merchants to succeed in attracting these nations, as they desire and search for all possible means to succeed in it; second, this same privation would perhaps be a cause for not only the Osages but also the other tribes to commit insults and robberies upon the hunters whom they might meet, and perhaps even [to attack] the small establishments away from St. Louis."

The English kept attempting to wean the Missouri red men away from Spain, and they kept urging the Illini and the Sac and Foxes and the other Algonkians who lived east of the Mississippi and north of the mouth of the Missouri to make friends with the Little Ones; and the Spaniards with their French traders and other Frenchmen who came over to live in Louisiana after the loss to the English of the true Illinois country were continually harried by the prospect of the Englishmen's getting control of the Missouri and the Americans' infiltration from across the river. These ingredients of acquisitiveness on the part of the English, perhaps with some idea of getting possession of the territory, and the overweaning, undisciplined restiveness on the part of the Americans whose government only just crystallized were already giving voice and action to freedom, were being kept yeasting by the Little Ones. The Europeans thought the Little Ones wanton and murderous and diabolical; as the French had said, *"méfiant,"* but they seemed less wanton during this period than they had when the French had used them as slavers and introduced them to

251

rum and brandy. Now their actions seemed to be in the style of the European struggle. The fusils and powder and shot and other merchandise which they seized on the Missouri would have been known in Europe as contraband. They had kept their domination over such strong tribes as the Pawnees and the Padoucas, and even had been able to keep the Sac and Foxes to the north bank of the Missouri through their position on the important Missouri and their primitive prowess. Both their position and their basic prowess got for them fusils from the French and horses from the Pawnees and Kiowas, and with these they had preserved their pre-eminent position. They must keep guns from the enemy, and any other merchandise that might aid him in the war movement. This balancing for the protection of their domain from the American, French, Spanish, and English trespassers would not have been called murder and pillaging and diabolical savagery had a European nation been doing it. This sort of activity would have been taken for granted by groups of grave men, snuff boxes beside them, counciling in ornate rooms with mirrors and crystal chandeliers, as representatives of several nations.

Later, in October 1792, it seemed that the hatchet which had been laid in the shallow grave was again dug up, and the Sac and Foxes and the Osages were at war again, but the Spaniards' dilemma improved not at all. Now they might be more severe with the Osages, although that meant even more trouble; but apparently by this time, Baron de Carondelet, the new governor-general at New Orleans, had advised Trudeau, the new commandant at St. Louis, that he was preparing to go to war with the Osages, and this good news was relayed to several representatives of tribes which the Osage had been bullying. Trudeau told these tribes that heretofore it had been an easy matter for the Osages to go to the Des Moines River to trade with the English if Spanish traders were not sent to the Place-of-the-Many-Swans, and the Father in New Orleans didn't want this; but now since the Osages were at war with the Sac and Foxes and with their own kinsmen the Iowas, they couldn't very well get to the Des Moines River to trade with the English. Therefore, war against the Osages would be better than withholding traders from them, since everyone could see the results of the latter. Each time it was done, the Osages became

angrier, and Trudeau thought they might even go further than intercepting traders on the Missouri, that they might attack Spanish villages and cause a migration which would leave a vacuum which the
Americans and even the English might fill. He had asked Carondelet
to allow him to send two years' supply of merchandise to the upriver
tribes, very secretly, by some other route than the river.

The tribes, more and more agitated by the infiltrations of the
Americans and English, the exigencies of the disturbed Spaniards,
and the activities of the angry giants of the Place-of-the-Many-Swans
and the Smoky Waters, became more and more petulant and vindictive in what might have appeared to be helpless rages. They came to
St. Louis to make speeches and wave their arms before the commandant Trudeau, complaining not so much about the Americans and
the English, but about the Osages. They not only complained about
the Great Osages of the Place-of-the-Many-Swans but about the Little
Osages on the Missouri River.

Not only were their supplies cut off by both the Little and the
Great Osages, but their hunters and their scouts were seized and be-
headed, and even their war parties were now attacked in the manner
of the Heavy Eyebrows—from ambush. The Osages, they said, had
learned the way of the Heavy Eyebrows and the Long Knives (referring to the venturing Americans), and no more came riding toward them, making finger signs of insult and trying only to count
coup and ride away untouched. This traditional manner of warfare
they understood, they complained, but now what did the Father in
New Orleans intend to do about the Osages' fighting like the Woodland people?

The Down-Below People, whom the French had called *Petit Wah-
Sha-She* and were now known as the Little Osages, were on their
way to becoming a separate tribe. They were not a gentile splinter
from the main tribe at the Place-of-the-Many-Swans, as were the
Omahas, the Konzas, the Poncas, and perhaps the Quapaws, but were
one of the five physical divisions resulting from the great flood in
Osage tradition. Not only did they not suffer from the Great Osage
activities in taking what they wanted from the traders of the Missouri, but actually aided them in this as they did in war. But they

253

seemed to have no permanent village. They lived for a time on the Missouri River proper just down from the Missourias and were closely associated with that tribe. They also lived in a village on the south fork of the Osage River just above the Great Osages, but of course *under* a ridge by a marsh.

About this time they had as their chief a man of the Bear gens, called *Mi-Tsu-Shee* (*shee* from *shinka,* meaning "little"), Little Bear. He had the same characteristics as his gentile symbol, the grizzly bear, and he kept the Little Osages in trouble.

He led some warriors on a venture down the Missouri and the Mississippi to the place where there was an island which was filled with wintering horses belonging to the settlement which the French had called Ste Geneviève, situated just south of St. Louis on the right bank of the river.

Little Bear was probably just wandering with members of his gens, with no intention of making a raid on such a well-behaved establishment as the village. Besides, the Spaniards had a garrison there and soldiers, but the inhabitants were mostly French and were treated with great solicitude by the Spaniards since they needed them. The village had grown just as St. Louis had grown after the Treaty of Paris in 1763, as people had crossed the river from the English dominions. Also, by this time, January, 1793, a few royalists were fleeing from the French Revolution and settling here among customs and religious observances which they knew. Long before, about 1715, the first lead mine had been opened, and later salt was refined and the rich, alluvial Mississippi made agriculture very important. It was populous and a Spanish outpost, and the inhabitants were not enemies of the Osages. Not caring to travel far to the southwest to the Great Salt Plains or even down the Neosho River to the salt deposits near the mouth, they came here to trade furs for salt and lead. Some of the inhabitants even dressed as Osages when they held their New Year's Eve festivities and sang old French songs, walking along the ways playing instruments.

The mouth-to-ear history of the Little Osages has it that Little Bear and his tribesmen stopped at the island to rest. They said they could hear singing across water in Ste Geneviève; however, the Twelfth

Night festivities were past, and this singing must have sprung from *joie de vivre,* even on a cold, late January night.

It was said that the wintering horses smelled the Little Ones and circled to snort at them in the dying light. Like the symbol of his gens, Little Bear must have playfully got down on his hands and knees in the twilight with a bear robe over him and watched the frightened horses circle wide and whistle through their noses in fear as he crawled toward them. Then, like the bear, he got an idea, and soon he stood upright, let the robe fall, and each man succeeded in catching a horse with his lariat and swam it across the intervening water to the shore; then they rode up the Meramec trail toward the Missouri drainage.

They took twenty horses, and the Little Osages say that each had a horse, so that if there were only twenty, it is certain that they rode fast to get away from the river, where there were many *I-Spa-Tho* and Heavy Eyebrows.

It is not known how many from the Spanish garrison trailed their horses to the Little Osage village, but the modern chief from tribal memory said there were many. This sounds reasonable, since later Little Bear sent fourteen of his people to St. Louis to talk to Trudeau and tell him why they could not return the horses. In his letter to Carondelet, Trudeau said that the Little Osages came "to St. Louis to weep, as is their custom and give up their medals and golas [a sort of gorget which the Spaniards gave to the red men as evidence of mutual confidence; a gift of silver, and the Osages wore them much as they wore their own gorgets made from the fresh-water mussel, symbolical of the sun]. They feigned the greatest sorrow about their being unable to stop the robbery and bring the horses without exposing themselves to losing their lives."

There was the old Spanish dilemma, and here were only fourteen Little Osages, and according to red man custom, Trudeau waited until the next day to give them an answer; and with the Spanish dilemma in his thoughts, he was undoubtedly wondering how to save the Spanish face when it was done for him, and he could write to Carondelet with great relief and with assurance of approval.

It so happened that one of the delegations of mixed tribes had come to St. Louis to wave their bows in the face of Trudeau, demanding war on the Osages. There were Sac and Foxes and Kickapoos and possibly other Algonkians and upriver Siouans, to the number of some two hundred, and they heard about the delegation of Little Osages. They surrounded the house where the Osages were quartered and began to shoot arrows into it and fire their flintlocks, making insults with their hands.

Trudeau came up at the head of a large guard, and they half circled him as he stood at the door of the house, like the people of Judea around Pontius Pilate. The house was joined by barracks, and there was a loft, so after standing guard inside the house with his soldiers until the tribesmen outside became more and more excited as the day closed, he had the Osages hide in the loft.

The next day he tried to make the tribesmen believe that the Osages had gone during the night, but they knew they were with the soldiers, and the red men became more and more angered with loss of sleep. Trudeau tried everything; he said the Osages had come to take the hand of the Father, and he had given his hand and had given his word, and what did people do about that? He would be compelled to fight and blood would run through the ways, and there were more people with guns in the village than even the Sac and Foxes had from the British.

There would be hours of quiet, when the red men lay here and there like lumps of earth under their robes and here and there fires flickered, and they ate in groups. Trudeau had flour and corn and squash brought to them and winter venison, and he fed the Osages in the loft of the house joining the barracks. He took time out to sleep, but for ten days got very little.

He sent messengers to bring the principal chiefs of the Kickapoos and the Sac and Foxes from the left bank of the river in pirogues, and they were met with a keg of *aguardiente* (brandy), and soon became amenable, he later feasting them so that they would not become maniacally drunk. Soon many of the two hundred assorted warriors wanted brandy, and they got it in return for a promise to come away from the house where the Osages were hidden. Soon there were only a few remaining in the village, since nearly all were around the keg just outside by the river. Those who refused to leave the environs of the house he got dead drunk, and on this tenth night of the siege he got the fourteen Osages out of the house and on their way. They were afraid of a trap, and warned him that if one of them should be killed, they with the Great Osages would never allow another trader to come up the Missouri; and in order to assure them that there was no trap, he with a small force of soldiers accompanied them for two and one-half miles out of the village, indicating to them the direction where there were no enemies.

It seems likely that the American Revolution had not affected the Little Ones directly, since the activities were centered east of the Mississippi, and even though Spain became an ally of the colonists, as did France, there was little to disturb the relationship between the Spaniards and the Little Ones west of the river, except perhaps the attack on St. Louis in 1780.

Spain joined the war in 1779, and the principal town of the upper part of the region was attacked on May 26, 1780. This attack on St. Louis was made by three hundred Englishmen and nine hundred Indians. These Indians were probably Iroquoians from Canada, with perhaps some renegade Frenchmen and Algonkians. They came down the Illinois River under the command of an English captain, one Emanuel Hesse. The British could control the Indians for some time through their lavish present-giving and by working up an emotional frenzy, but they could not control them as the French often did. Therefore, the attack on St. Louis was made in a mad dash; however, the coming of the English and the Indians was known in time for the lieutenant governor, one Fernando de Leyba, to scrape sufficient pesos together to build a tower on the west corner of the village. He had to sweat the money out of the citizens even though they were frightened, and he could only build one tower of the several planned. This one tower, however, was sufficient with its cannon to turn the English and their Indians back up the Mississippi.

The Americans aided, and later they sent Colonel Montgomery across the Mississippi with one hundred men and one hundred volunteers from the east side of the river, joining the French and Spanish, who had fifty Peorias with them, in a march up the Illinois to find the English. However, by this time the emotionalism had died in the hearts of the Indians, although the people of St. Louis lived in fear that a concentration of English and Potawatomis at Detroit might move on the village.

Montgomery and the commander of the St. Louisans, Cadet Beles-tre, left on the fourteenth of June to "chastise our common enemies." They found the nine hundred Indians evaporated and the English gone from their camp-village; and the St. Louisans and the Americans could do nothing more than vent their anger by burning their huts and destroying their corn and pumpkins, and they wrote out a long threat that they would come back with a much stronger army within a couple of months. This warning they placed in a bottle, which they suspended from the slave post (*poteau d'esclaves*).

The attack could have been disastrous, and one suspects that the frenzy of the Iroquois and Algonkians cooled after they had killed and mutilated many of the settlers just outside the protection of the village cannon. They found few, since the chasseurs and planters and wild-strawberry pickers had been called in, and they had been ordered to bring as much of their produce with them as they could in order to support the defenders, who apparently had been left on their own by the royal Spanish government. There would be little of matured produce in May, and the villagers suffered from hunger and from the fact that Leyba had bled them for his tower.

Strangely, the ancient ally of the English, the Sac and Foxes, re-mained loyal to the Spaniards, but the Pawnee-*maha* and the Konzas had a part in the attack on the side of the lavish present-giving English. According to the citizens' statement by letter to Governor-General Gálvez the next month, "exposing" to him their "disgraces and sad remains of a dilapidated fortune" in consequence of the preparations to receive the English attack, English flags were hoisted over the villages of the Missourias and the Sioux. Since they also stated that "the Sac and Fox nations are the only nations remaining faithful to us who can serve as a rampart against our enemies who surround us," this may mean that the English had placed a flag over the villages at the Place-of-the-Many-Swans as well, since certainly the Little Ones would have been important either as allies or enemies.

There is no tribal memory about being allied with the Long Knives, but it is not unlikely that, since they were not as closely allied with the Spaniards as they had been with the French, the bonds were very weak and the presents of the English were many and attractive. This attack on *Sho'to To-Wo'n* would not have seemed a good thing to all the gentes of the tribe, but certainly it would have harmonized with the spirit of the Bear–Panther gentes.

The Governor-General of Louisiana, Gálvez, took Florida, which Spain had lost to the English during the French and Indian War, and the colonists took the seaboard colonies and half a continent.

The effects would be that a new people would appear on the east bank of the great river, who were neither Long Knives nor *I-Spa-Tho* nor yet Heavy Eyebrows, and the Little Ones noted that there was a difference. They had seen very few Long Knife rangers, the trappers and hunters and spies who wore buckskin shirts and leggings and bear or coonskin caps, since they had dealt mostly with traders and agents of the big fur companies: the North West Company and the Hudson's Bay Company at the mouth of the Des Moines River, where the Little Ones had gone to trade their furs periodically to the anguish of the Spaniards.

These men who came to the left bank of the river were chopping trees and building and plowing and swearing, and they had hair on their faces like the black bear and like the *voyageurs* of the Heavy Eyebrows, and soon the Little Ones were calling them Heavy Eyebrows as well, but knowing them to be Long Knives.

The effect the Revolution had upon Spanish Louisiana should have been very important, since Spain had reconquered Florida and kept it, and the Spaniards might now feel that the menace of a powerful enemy, the English, was gone from the left bank of the river, and the Chickasaws would now be less inclined to make their raids from their bluffs on the east side of the river opposite the Arkansas. Also, the new American government was having difficulty being born and nurtured, and it would be a long time before it could menace the possessions of His Catholic Majesty, and it was very fortunate that the English had been so anxious to get the matter of the treaty over that they allowed the American claim to the land west from the

Appalachians to the Mississippi. They had only really been fighting for the seaboard. This might have caused Spain to believe that she had done much better than she expected when she allied herself with the colonists.

As a matter of fact, she got much out of the American Revolution, and France, which had actually saved the revolution for the colonists and had accomplished the most brilliant defeat she had ever inflicted upon her ancient cross-Channel enemy, got practically nothing.

Spain, on the other hand, had not only gained back what she had lost on the North American continent but was mistress again of the Gulf of Mexico, and she owned all the land west of the Mississippi to the Pacific and north to an indefinite line. The line was foggy, since knowledge of the land was still foggy. The line was supposed to run from west of Montreal up the St. Lawrence through the Great Lakes to the Lake of the Woods, and then westward from there it grew dim like the buffalo trails along the Mississippi, overgrown and lost. This vague boundary would cause much trouble later between English Canada and Spanish and American possessions.

His Catholic Majesty through his governor-general at New Orleans and the commandant at St. Louis could be more demanding of the Little Ones, and Spain seemed to take courage from renewed strength. They ventured farther up the Pacific Coast and had trouble with the Russians, who were feeling their way down the coast, and in 1789 they ran into the English at Nootka Sound on the west coast of Vancouver Island and had to withdraw their antennae.

Really, the character of one man, his Catholic Majesty in Madrid, indirectly affected the lives of the Little Ones more than did the French king. Spain was an absolute monarchy of the old regime, and in such cases much depended upon the character and the abilities of the monarch. If he was of strong character and yet of good will and interested in the happiness of his people, and he himself enlightened, then his nation became somewhat of a reflection of him; and when the governors-general of New Orleans stiffly sent up their orders to the commandant at St. Louis concerning the Little Ones, and until 1788 when Charles III of Spain died, there was still within these orders elements of reasonableness which could be expanded.

Charles III of Spain was one of the few Bourbons who was not mistress- or wife-ridden. He was a hunter and a man of character, the best of the Spanish Bourbons and the strongest of the Spanish kings since Phillip II. He spent his mornings working at his desk and in interviews on empire business, and afternoons with his hounds and his guns.

But just as Spain seemed to have in her possession the best of both North and South America, she began to fall back into the old state. Charles IV came to the throne in 1788, and his weakness became the weakness of Spain; and even though Louisiana would almost dissolve the Spanish dilemma by finally diverting the Little Ones' activities to the Arkansas, thus clearing the way to the upper Missouri, and would send explorers as far upriver as the Mandans on the Great Bend and regularize trade among the merchants of St. Louis, she would last only twelve years longer as mistress of Louisiana after the accession of Charles IV.

Spain's inability to hold the continent seems incredible. The American citizens she had invited to settle west of the Mississippi had little of the "Spirit of '76" and need not constitute infiltration. As a matter of fact, they seemed to be quickly disloyal to the government across the Alleghenies if their personal interests so dictated. Even several of the Revolutionary War heroes had been ready to turn over the trans-Allegheny region to the Spaniards. The governor of North Carolina's trans-montane cession to the Union, called the Independent State of Franklin, had a leader, one Colonel John "Nolichucky Jack" Sevier, who had written to the Spanish ambassador, Don Diego de Gardogui, proposing that Franklin come under Spanish protection.

General James Wilkinson, who would send Pike on his exploration in 1806, knew the attitude of the settlers west of the Alleghenies and connived with Esteban Miró, Spanish governor-general, to separate the West from the United States.

It could be that the United States, besides owing the Indian much for being Indians, later during the War of 1812–15 also owed Spain much for being Spain at a particular moment in history.

The colonial dilemma also became the dilemma of the merchants of St. Louis and Ste Geneviève, most of whom still bore French names. They were constantly writing their grievances to the governor-general at New Orleans, but they did recognize Louisiana's dilemma as being their own. It wouldn't have made so much difference to them where their goods were traded if they had received furs in compensation, and the furs of the Little Ones were good furs and plentiful, since they held a large domain upon which few cared to trespass, European or native. And they were important consumers of merchandise. This was indicated when the Governor-General divided the trade among the merchants of St. Louis and Ste Geneviève and there were twelve participants supplying the Osage trade, worth something like 12,000 pesos. There were four merchants for the Little Osages and four merchants designated to supply the Konzas, three to supply the Otoes, and three for the Omahas, and one each for the four Pawnee grand divisions.

But, of course, these merchants trading with the upriver tribes lost much of their merchandise to the Osages, or at least that part which the Little Ones wanted for themselves, and those articles which the Europeans in Europe would call contraband. The merchants lost not only their merchandise but their trade upriver and the friendship of the tribes.

And the merchants of St. Louis and Ste Geneviève knew what the Osages and the other red men knew: that the English merchandise was better and the red men could trade with the eager English with great advantage to themselves. The merchants and the commandant also knew that most of the merchants of Montreal had commissioner agents in England, and they in turn were funded by very rich men, who did not need an accounting every year and could wait several years for their huge profits. The merchants of Montreal received the merchandise from England on a deposit or on their own account, and from there, their merchandise was sent out to stations on the Great Lakes and beyond and exchanged for furs, and the payment was not made in England for several years.

The merchants of the lower Missouri sweated over the absence of every pirogue, turning from worried watching of the river to smiling ingratiatingly over their shoulders at their creditors.

Also, the price of English merchandise was fixed in London, and all the expenses of shipping to Canada and the shipping of furs from Canada was less since the insurance was less and England could employ fewer sailors.

Further, the English made merchandise especially for the red men, not only for the red men in general but to suit the needs of each tribe with whom they traded.

The Little Ones say that it was the Long Knives who introduced the square-framed mirrors, peeps-in-water, with handles, so that they could be carried during the dances and used in heliographic signaling. It was during the year of the great peace with the Sac and Foxes, 1791, when the Little Ones had gone to the Des Moines River and Prairie du Chien to trade with the Long Knives. There, they had a social dance not unlike the modern *i'n-lon-schkah* with the Iowas and perhaps the Winnebagoes and Omahas and other Siouans.

Before the dance they had dressed themselves and painted their own faces since they had no women with them. They had stuck the eagle feathers in their scalplocks, and in order to do all these things, they had to look into little pools of clear water. The next time they went to trade there, the Long Knives had little mirrors with handles in square frames decorated with carvings.

The boatmen who carried the merchandise from Montreal up the St. Lawrence and distributed it among the stations of the lakes and the north and west were controlled like soldiers, and were not the laughing, cursing, sweating *voyageurs* with *chansons* in rhythm with the stroke of the paddles of the French regime, nor were they the carefree *voyageurs* of the lower Missouri, although many of them were Frenchmen and did sing and laugh, and they might have called each other "citizen" and "comrade" in the vogue of the French Revolution, but they took off their stocking caps to, or saluted their English bourgeois. Now, the German order of the Hanoverians obtained there in the wilderness, and when the bugle was sounded at the stations, every man in the company's employ entered but remained standing until the important people were seated, and then he seated himself according to his category. He was hungry but ill at ease until he was freed from the atmosphere of dignity. When the cloth was removed from the table, only the bourgeois and his gentlemen remained seated to enjoy the wines and brandies. The *voyageurs,* long under a strain, left the dining hall with a great feeling of freedom, quickly going out into the free air, where they could smoke and laugh and mimic their superiors.

The English had sufficient natural advantage over the Spaniards without the Osage affair. They had to save their upriver trade from the English, but what could they do about the Osages who forced such difficult decisions on them? Perhaps war on them was the only answer, and the merchants of St. Louis and Ste Geneviève wrote to Baron de Carondelet at New Orleans, but were not quite definite about what they really wanted, weeping like frustrated Arab venders.

25. His Catholic Majesty Declares War on the Little Ones

THERE SEEMED TO BE no alternative; the obstacle to upper river trade must be removed. There was more than just losing the trade of the Siouans and the Pawnees upriver beyond the Little Ones; there was also a possibility of losing their territory to the English. So on the twelfth of June, 1793, his Catholic Majesty, Charles IV of Spain—whose domain reached from far into South America to a hazy line northwest of the Great Lakes in North America, and from the Pacific Ocean to the Mississippi River and across the Delta of the Mississippi to western Florida and the Florida peninsula, plus the Caribbean islands—declared war on the principal chiefs of the Great Osages and the chief of the Little Osages of the Place-of-the-Many-Swans near the forks of the Osage River in the Territory of Illinois.

In January of this year in far-away France, just outside of Paris proper, a mad yet nervous crowd waited in dead silence for the approach of their king. The clop, clop of the horse was drowned by the rumble-clatter of the tires on the cobblestones, which also drowned out the King's mumbling of the prayers for the dying read from the Book of Devotion. Any prideful chieftain of the Little Ones could have understood perfectly why the King later came to the edge of the scaffold to address words which he, the Divine Righter, believed would ring through the ages of history. "Frenchmen, I die innocent —I pardon my enemies. I desire that France—." At this moment General Santerre spurred his horse forward, and with uplifted hand

shouted, *"Tambours!"* and King Louis XVI was seized and guillo-
tined.

Although they could not have known it, this moment was important in the destiny of the Little Ones.

Spain, because of religious and national reasons, declared war on
the Revolution which was now France. The French were killing
each other and fighting to destroy the doctrine of kingship, and the
retrogressive Spanish monarch was defending the doctrine and up-
holding the Holy Catholic Church, which had been robbed of its
possessions by the civil constitution of the clergy of France.

In Louisiana, the Spanish must now pamper the tribes of the Mississippi, the natural enemies of the Little Ones. The tribe of the Des
Moines River whom the Little Ones called Snow-Heads and whom
the Europeans called Iowas or Ayoas, onetime English allies, came
to the Konzas of the Konza River to trade for horses, so that they
could trade them to the horseless tribes whom the Spaniards were
training to attack the Little Ones. They were promising all the enemies of the Little Ones, as well as many others of the Siouans and
the Algonkians, arms and horses and pirogues, and stuff for clothing,
as well as glittering trinkets for ornamentation and medals with the
profile of Charles IV.

However, the woodland-prairie Iowas had never seen such herds
of horses. They watched the beautiful pintos and coyote duns and
sacred white ones which the Konzas had collected, and which the
Iowas knew they would not trade, and they discussed the business
among themselves.

They had come in a large band, floating down the Mississippi and
paddling up the Missouri, stopping at San Carlos del Missouri for
their instructions from the Spaniards, where they were given more
merchandise to be traded.

Their sudden appearance at the Konza villages had surprised the
Konzas, and the time being Buffalo-Mating Moon, July, there was
little meat with which to feast the great number of Iowas, since the
buffalo hunters were not yet back from the summer hunt. But there
were always old bulls who had wandered away from the mating
excitement, standing like statues on the plains or standing under

some lone tree. These lonely bulls had been chased out of the herds by the younger bulls, and their fat had not been dissolved by the special madness of the season.

The Konza hunters who had stayed in the villages rode out now to kill some of the lone bulls to feast their kinsmen. When they were lost beyond the prairie swells, the Iowas stood watching the sleek, grass-fat horses and forgot the reasons for their coming. Emotion overwhelmed them, and they took the hobbles from the horses in the village and killed the people who tried to keep them from mounting, men and women alike. They rounded up the herd and drove them away, and drove them fast down the river, taking with them forty-eight women and children.

They soon left the well-worn river trail and, looking back over their shoulders, cut across the prairie and across drainage to the Des Moines River, and the Konzas were never able to overtake them.

The day after their arrival at the mouth of the Des Moines, they sent some of their men down with several of the captive children to make peace with Commandant Zenon Trudeau at St. Louis. Peaceful gestures on the part of any tribe that might be a potential enemy of the Little Ones were accepted now without questioning. One couldn't depend on the Konzas anyway when their parent tribe was involved, and, besides, the Iowas had brought back that which they had been sent to obtain—horses.

Trudeau wrote to Carondelet: "If Your Excellency can remit to me some medals with the duplicate of the commissions in blank, I will be very much pleased, since the present circumstances require that they be pampered more than is customary on account of the war with the Osages. Without that war Your Excellency might think by this time that it is my intention to create some new chief."

The Spaniards had a well-laid plan. They would wait until August, the month when the Little Ones would be coming back to the Place-of-the-Many-Swans in gentile groups, each under their chieftain, from the summer hunt. The several tribes could then attack a gens or several gentes at a time, and certainly kill the old men and young men left at the villages.

However, not all the tribes came at the same time to get their instructions and their arms and their presents, and no matter how the Spaniards might warn them that the striking time was to be in August and that they were to all strike at the same time, some warriors of the Miamis, the Sac and Foxes, the Potawatomis, the Quapaws, Pawnees, or Iowas would come to St. Louis and listen to the plans with their eyes shut, then load their presents and their merchandise and go back to their villages.

Some of them would send perhaps twenty-five or fifty of their warriors across Portage des Sioux, just above the mouth of the Missouri River, and they would ride up the trail on the north side of the river, then swim their horses across to the south side.

They would meet Osage hunters along the Gasconade or up the Osage River and if the group was small, they might bring back a few scalps and be met with songs at their villages. However, if they were unlucky enough to meet a gentile war party, they must flee back to the Missouri and cross it, perhaps leaving a few of their own scalps behind. If they took scalps of the Osages, they would float downriver in their pirogues and with great ceremony present them to the commandant at St. Louis, and demand more powder and lead and presents.

Some of the Algonkians from east of the Mississippi who had been defeated by the wandering Osage gentes would come back telling of victory and demand more presents and powder and lead and free merchandise, even expressing their anger and disappointment that the merchandise was not as good as that which they could get from the English.

They could pretend to the commandant of St. Louis that they had defeated the Osages, but they couldn't go back to their own villages with no evidence, especially since there might be several warriors missing from the party. And there was the matter of warrior vanity. A band of warriors might go far up the Osage River and actually meet some wandering Osages and skirmish with them, and they might come away without taking a single Osage scalp or counting coup, and possibly leave behind them the dripping heads of some of their companions on spikes which were stuck in the ground as a boast and as a warning to others from across the river. These war-

riors, especially if they were Sac and Foxes or Pawnees or Potawatomis, vainest of warriors, could not go back to their villages without
Osage hair, since they would have left them with great ceremony and
prayer-song and even with prayer-dancing.

When they were on their way back from the Osage country, defeated and pride-damaged, a lone tribesman from another nation or
a wandering black-haired European or a small settlement was in
great danger. Like the cougar who had gone back to its kill to find
a grizzly bear reared above it, and having circled several times growling, would finally leave, making catlike sounds of extreme rage, the
tribesmen would ride back or float back down the river in frothing
anger. And like the frustrated cougar, who would slap at a scurrying
pine squirrel, smashing and shredding it, and then toss it to one side,
the warriors might scalp the first person they met.

This had happened many times. Once when an Algonkian tribe
had sent warriors against the Great Osages and they had been defeated, they fled downriver and on their way home found two European bachelors living in a lonely cabin, not far from San Carlos del
Missouri. One was blond and the other black haired. They killed both
of them, but took only the hair of the dark one in order to save face
and make a triumph at their village.

All during the year 1793, no trader or trapper or hunter went up
the Missouri past the little cabin called "Fort" San Juan, and the
tribes came during the year to St. Louis to orate against the Little
Ones and to receive their arms and their presents and get their instructions for co-operative action.

But the Little Ones struck first. They could do this, although the
ceremonies for the war movement sometimes took ten days. If the
Sac and Foxes and the Spaniards and the Potawatomis had known
this, they might have made their surprise attack. Surely the French
voyageurs and the Pawnees must have known about these rites, and
known that the appointed leader of the war movement must go fasting and prayer-singing for seven days before the movement could
begin.

The ceremony for the war movement could be made quite simple,
since most of the ceremonies were just that: songs to be sung, recita-

tions, and involved symbolism, with which they could satisfy *Wah'-Kon-Tah* by simply making gestures if they were pressed. Also, the Little Ones had made the war movement adjustable to quick action, especially retaliatory. A single gens could form a war party, and several gentes from one of the grand divisions could form a war party, and the tribe could form a war party, and this current war was certainly a tribal affair.

Very likely word had got to the lagging summer hunters that the tribes of the Mississippi were planning an attack, and they came back to the Place-of-the-Many-Swans as fast as their burden of meat and hides would allow, since many of the warriors were needed to guard the travois and the pack horses and mules, and many were employed as paralleling scouts. These precautions were especially necessary if they had been hunting on the Buffalo-Dung Waters where the Pawness would undoubtedly be hunting.

Once they arrived at the village, they began their preparations for the war movement against the associated tribes and the Spaniards. Some of the gentes were told off to kill one of the lone buffalo bulls with the sacred arrow, kept in custody by the *Wah-Sha-She*. When the bull was down, they ceremonially made an incision on the hump or boss, exposing a thick layer of fat. The lone bulls, having been chased out of the herds and not allowed to participate in the rut, had nothing else to do except store up fat. They made the incision with a special knife which was used only for cutting the sacred willow. They ceremonially tasted of the fat.

Out of the skin of the left hind leg they cut the round piece which would become the sacred fetish shield for the breast, and from the skin of the left side of the body they cut the seven narrow straps which they would paint with blood-root juice. These latter were captive straps, and each warrior would carry several for the purpose of binding any enemy he might take captive. The round piece for the breast shield was also painted red since it symbolized Grandfather the Sun, and his power was in it.

All this was chiefly ceremonial, since it would take some time for the round green hide to dry after being stretched on its hickory frame, before it could be colored. And it would take some time to make

270

captive straps of the seven green strips of hide. There were piles of buffalo hides all over the villages, and the women were continually in the process of making the things from the hides which were needed both for war and for everyday practical use. Each warrior would have plenty of captive straps, and each would have his fetish shield as well as the practical shield which he wore on his arm.

The head of the *Wah-Sha-She Wa'no'n* gens would be called upon to lay the sacred pipe before the council. The council would select a man who would become *Do-Do'n Hunkah,* the Sacred-One-of-the-War-Movement. He would be the liaison between the people and *Wah'Kon-Tah.* When the pipe was given him, he turned the bowl down so that the dottle fell on a cut whisp of bluestem. The leaves of grass represented the animals they must eat to sustain themselves during the war movement, as well as the enemy they would kill, but this was really a prayer for the animals to be killed.

He took the sacred pipe and walked away to the west toward the prairie to pray and fast for seven days. He went up the river to the open prairie, rather than into the forests downriver, because the prairie-plains were in full view of *Wah'Kon-Tah* and there were no screens of trees.

The pipe was filled with ground sumac leaves and lit, and the smoke became the prayers of all the people as it ascended to the sky. He lifted it toward the sky to *Wah'Kon-Tah* and sang his prayers, crying to *Wah'Kon-Tah* to watch over the Little Ones who must go on the war movement. He prayed that he might find his answer during the seven days of fasting and vigil, since he knew that he would be held responsible for either victory or defeat.

He left the village when Grandfather was directly overhead, and he cast his eyes to him and sang his prayer:

> *I go to learn if I shall go on,*
> *To learn of Grandfather if I shall go on,*
> *To make the enemy lie reddened on the earth.*
> *To make the enemy lie blackened on the earth.*
> *To make the earth brown with the bodies of the enemy.*
> *To make the enemy lie scattered on the earth.*

271

THE OSAGES

To make their bones lie whitened on the earth.
To make their locks [scalplocks] to wave in the wind.

If he felt that his prayers were answered before the seven days were expired, and they often were in emergencies such as this one, he could come back to the village to keep vigil in the Lodge of Mystery. His hunger visions would be stronger as the days passed, but it was often a matter of vanity or honor to stay the full seven days. When Grandfather the Sun came up on the seventh day and he laid his last willow counting-stick with the others, he would sometimes wobble a little and his voice would be the voice of a pre-flight crow, as he made his morning chant to Grandfather.

In the meantime, the people had been prayer-singing, the *Hunkah* keeping the rhythm with their hands on their bare thighs and by clicking counting-sticks together. When they reached a certain stage in the songs of the sacred hawk, they then changed to the Song of the Rattle.

The rattle was a gourd, from which the tissue and the seeds had been taken, that was attached to a willow stick. Within the gourd were the teeth of a panther, taken from the right side of the lower jaw if the rattle were to be used by the *Hunkah,* and from the left side of the lower jaw if to be used by the *Tzi-Sho.* The gourd itself symbolized the head of a panther, which is round. In another aspect it symbolized the head of the gentle man of the *Tzi-Sho.*

This gourd rattle the singers shook in rhythm with their singing and as they danced. The handle represented the right arm of the dancer if used by the *Hunkah* and the left if used by the *Tzi-Sho.*

When the *Do-Do'n Hunkah* got back to the village and the people knew that *Wah'Kon-Tah* looked with favor on the war movement, the now very important *Do-Do'n Hunkah* would confirm the signs *Wah'Kon-Tah* had given him by taking the skin of the sacred hawk carefully from its shrine. He would take it out head first, as men are born, and then, with the others silent and eager about him, he would let it fall, and if it faced west, the sign would have been confirmed.

The symbolic man had been chosen, he who was chosen as the

symbol of the tribe at this time. They painted his face with dawn-washed red, and had him stand ceremonially facing east, the home of Grandfather and peace, the direction of the Light of Day. Then they would have him turn to the west, the direction of darkness and war, and there he stood facing west as the preparations progressed.

The women would place the blue clay of mourning on their heads —on their foreheads and on the tops of their heads. The people would choose eight officers, who would be in practical command of the war movement, the *Do-Do'n Hunkah* being the Sacred-One-of-the-War-Movement.

Four of these officers would be from the *Hunkah* and four from the *Tzi-Sho*. After resting and feasting, the *Do-Do'n Hunkah* was given a war club and a knife, a scalp, a bow and arrows, and the swan war standard. All these things were symbolical of the arms and amulets which the warriors would carry.

Sometimes they danced their prayers, but this might depend upon the exigencies of the moment. There always has been some confusion in the mind of the European about the difference between the war-dance prayers and the vindictive mourning dance when the Little Ones rode out afterwards to put in force the Mosaic law, of which they had never heard. They rode out to take a scalp to pay for a scalp which had been taken from one of their important men, an eye for an eye, and so on.

The Little Old Men said that there was dancing, but mostly there was prayerful ceremonial, mostly singing and fasting. The war party painted their horses, mostly with sacred symbols of their gentes, and in this tribal war movement, all the gentes of both *Hunkah* and *Tzi-Sho* were represented.

Early in the morning of the day the war movement was to begin, and just before Grandfather pushed back the darkness of night with his hand, two of the Little Old Men would have the two fires built of redbud and sing the ceremonial songs. At a gesture from them the warriors would rush to them to get their charcoal with which to paint their faces. They rushed to the fires, the embers dying now, and struggled with each other for the symbol of the living fire that overwhelms all things and gives no quarter; they thus captured the spirit of relentless fire in the charcoal which they would wear on their faces when they attacked the enemy.

At high noon they set out to the west, despite the fact that their enemy lay to the east, downriver. But soon they would turn abruptly and strike the old trail down the river. This could not deceive *Wah'-Kon-Tah*, but was a courtesy, this pretending that the enemy were to the west, the direction of war and death.

Their scouts, who had been sitting their horses on the high spots of the many hills, would come down, and others would take their places, and to these taking their places they would hand over their heliographic mirrors, their peeps-in-water.

Smoke signaling on the prairie-plains, where for many days the wind played with your moccasin strings, was not always successful, and at times could not be used at all, when the prairie grasses were dry from summer drought or when the buffalo chips were wet.

As they rode, under Grandfather immediately above them, with their horses trampling their own shadows, the leader would sing to Grandfather, and they could hear between the stanzas the women keening back at the villages, and they could hear the wolf-howling with the village dogs in accompaniment.

> *I go to learn if I shall go on,*
> *To learn of the sun if I shall go on . . . ,*

the leader sang, then after a while sang the ceremonial song:

> *Truly by the noon sun, I, as a man of mystery, go,*
> *To fall unaware upon the* Pa-I'n [*enemy*].
> *Truly by the noon sun, I, as a man of mystery, go*
> *To make the* Pa-I'n *to lie reddened on the earth. . . .*
> *To make the* Pa-I'n *lie blackened on the earth. . . .*
> *To make the earth brown with the bodies of the foe. . . .*
> *To make the foe lie scattered on the earth. . . .*
> *To make the bones of the foe to lie whitened on the earth. . . .*
> *To make the hair of the* Pa-I'n *to wave in the winds.*

274

From the Sun Songs the party would go to the Wolf Songs and then the Crow Songs, but they were uttering prayer-songs much of the time as they rode toward the settlements on the west bank of the Mississippi.

The *ca-xe,* the crows themselves, would appear over them; first one, then a flock scattered and talking to each other. When a scout *ca-xe* had seen the two hundred warriors set out from the villages, he had called to the others. They knew there would be men to "lie reddened on the earth," and there would be feasting.

And the wolves would trot at a distance from the flankers; first one would appear, then two, and soon there would be five or six. They knew, too, that there would be a feast if they followed the warriors. When the coyotes saw the crows and the wolves, they called to each other and came to watch and wait, keeping their distance from the wolves. When the warriors rested, the crows settled in the tops of the trees and remained silent with their faces to the wind, and the wolves lay in the tall grasses, twitching the vicious late summer flies from their ears. They had no need for absolute protective immobility.

The Little Ones were on the war movement, and they need fear no one. The wapiti would stand and watch them nervously, and the white-tail deer would jump high in their flight from the wolves, waving their flags of truce, but the wolves seemed not to see them.

On the river of the Little Ones that writhed like a snake, there were now no burned-out, chopped-out trees paddled by singing *voyageurs* and no canoes of birchbark bought by the *voyageurs* from the Winnebagoes and no bullboats made by themselves, and the swans could again fly low over the water. The campfires of the Heavy Eyebrows were dead and the ashes fingered by rains.

The *Do-Do'n Hunkah,* the Sacred-One-of-the-War-Movement, with responsibility heavy on him, would meditate while the others made the evening camp, then with his pipe he would vanish in the woods of the river bottom. He would search for a colony of black ants, so that he could pray to *Wah'Kon-Tah* through them. They were relentless and vicious fighters, and fought together.

He would come back to the campfires; then when darkness fell, he would go out alone again, after placing the dark earth on his forehead. He would find a spot, an opening in the trees of the river bottom, where *Wah'Kon-Tah* could see him, and there he would wait with animal patience.

Soon *wah-pokah,* the great gray owl, would call, or perhaps *ito'n,* the great horned owl, would give his hunting call, or perhaps a snake would splash in the water in his pursuit of a frog. These brothers could tell him much, as he sat there even with his belly full. He would interpret the splashing of the snake or the call of *wah-pokah* or *ito'n;* usually the first one he heard, as good omen, and he would make his way back to the campfires satisfied.

The war party left the Missouri bottoms and crossed over to the Meramec River drainage. The cabins of the settlers were abandoned, and with their closed doors they were like blind men. There were no children playing. The oxen and the cows were gone, and the corn leaves of the late summer rasped against each other sadly. There were no hoofprints of single horses leading toward St. Louis or Ste Geneviève, but the warriors saw the fresh trail of many oxen and horses and people, twenty and thirty in a group, and all leading toward river villages.

Now the Heavy Eyebrows and the *I-Spa-Tho* dared ride or walk only in groups, and their footprints always pointed east toward the river, and the Little Ones saw no Pawnees or Shawnees, the enemies who had run to the Heavy Eyebrows and the *I-Spa-Tho* of Ste Geneviève and asked that they punish the Little Ones. And they saw no Caddos from the Red River, who had wept before Baron de Carondelet at New Orleans, asking him to punish the Little Ones. There were no Shawnees crossing the Big Waters in their dugouts, and they saw no Pawnee-*maha* down from their villages on the Platte. They didn't expect to see Caddos coming up the *Camino Real* from the south to attack them. But where were their enemies? Were they across the river making medicine for the war movement?

Some say it was Yellow-Flower Moon (August) when the Little Ones rode down the river on the war movement, and some say it was Deer-Hiding Moon (September), and it has been said that the *Do-do'n Hunkah* was called *To-Wo'n Ga-Xe,* Town Maker, who was really *Gra-Mo'n* (or *Gle-Mo'n*), Arrow-Going-Home, since he was called by both names, but no one seems to know definitely.

The Heavy Eyebrows and the *I-Spa-Tho* and the American settlers were crowded in the little settlements, and they had left their corn patches and their squashes and their cabbages. They pitched horse-shoes with their guns leaning against the cabins or squatted in their shade, boasting and dramatically topping each other's stories of Osage outrages. Ordinarily when the settlers got together, shooting matches were the thing, and they took strutting pride in winning, and the winner boasted and "joshed" the defeated ones. But now they must save their powder and lead, so they pitched horseshoes and talked and drank.

They knew how the war should be carried on and what mistakes Trudeau at St. Louis had made in asking Carondelet to declare war because Don Luis Lorimier of Ste Geneviève had demanded it, and now was not financing it and of all things depending upon the tribal enemies of the Osages to carry it on.

But Trudeau had his opinion of the scoffers, and he wrote about them: "For obliged to unite in masses in the villages in order to be able to oppose and resist the raids and vexations of every kind com-mitted by those barbarians [Osages], there have been times when they did not dare go to their farms. That introduced among them a passive idleness which gave them over to the tasting of spirituous liquors and drunkenness, a taste fatal to all the villages, and which had caused the total ruin in these new settlements of the greater part of the best families, upon which was placed the hope of prosperity of this country."

The little village of Carondelet was not protected by the same towers which protected St. Louis, but Ste Geneviève had been par-tially inundated by the flood waters of the Mississippi in the year 1785, and part of it had moved to the higher ground, yet part re-mained on flood level and was vulnerable. And also St. Louis was "Chouteau's Town" *(Sho'to To-Wo'n)* to the Little Ones, and they had no desire to attack the village.

Here and there the Little Ones rode, in their charcoal and limonite, with their eagle feathers spinning above their roaches, attached to the only hair on their shaven heads, shaped like and symbolizing the tail of a bull buffalo and shaped like a scalplock, a perpetual challenge to their enemies.

When they let their robes slip to their waists in the heat of the day, their tattoos showed on their breasts like intricate geometrical patterns. In the early morning, as Grandfather the Sun peeped above the tall trees along the Mississippi, the frightened settlers collected in the area around a group of cabins could hear the primitive, soul-disturbing chant of the Little Ones. The warriors stood in gentile groups on high points, and as they were bathed in dawn red, they sang their prayers to Grandfather.

And here and there a band of Sac and Foxes or Pawnees or Shawnees or Potawatomis or Iowas or Quapaws or some tribe of the Illini confederation would cut off a small party of deer or wapiti hunters from the main body and there would be a skirmish, and some chieftain of the tribes might strut in front of the enemy, defying and boasting, trusting to a fetish, the bear-claw necklace he wore, or enveloped in some mystical, invisible protection. His scalp would be carried off by the enemy in triumph, and the skirmishers would melt away into the woodlands. But apparently the Little Ones met no cuirassed Spaniards, or French dressed in dirty Algonkian buckskin shirts, or Americans in leathern short pants and woolen stockings, wearing pigtails or shabby wigs. They insolently stopped to play with strange things—like churns and hurriedly abandoned, highly cherished spinning wheels—as bears might play with them, finally breaking them in bearish anger of frustration or casting them away before setting fire to the cabin.

Yellow-Flower Moon and Deer-Hiding Moon and Deer-Mating Moon (October) came and passed, and the Moon Woman grew cold in the sky, and the sugar maples and the pin oaks painted their leaves red, and the sycamores and hackberries became yellow, and the white ash turned as bronze-purple as the face of a spring warrior, and the sumac leaves dropped like red blood from a Pawnee's severed head.

There was no smoke from the chimneys of the lonely little cabins which had escaped burning through whim, and the heavy ears bore the dried cornstalks down, and the deer trampled the cabbage patches, and the abandoned tools of hope lay where they were left rusting among the wood chips.

Thus it was in the autumn of 1793, when the west winds carried the war songs of the Great Osages.

The war with Spain was a tribal war in which all the gentes took part under eight leaders, four from each grand division, but the tribal memory may have as many as twenty-two interpretations. One has heard several stories of the incidents of the war; from the Bear, Wapiti, Eagle, and Heavenly Bodies gentes and from two grand-flood physical divisions, the Little Osages and the Big Hills. While they all accord the ceremonial leadership to Town Maker or Arrow-Going-Home, each gens insists on giving special virtues to his own gens or division.

One can only deduce from the many gentile interpretations that there were skirmishes between the Little Ones and the Pawnees, the Little Ones and the Potawatomis and Sac and Foxes and Shawnees and Miamis and tribes of the Illini and Caddo on the Red River, but the Spaniards did not actually take part. The Eagle people said that their gens stood off on a hill above St. Louis and made insulting signs to the Spanish soldiery, indicating that they were women, but that they could not be induced to come out to battle. They said they took all the horses they could find and killed several lone Bohèmes, but only one of these killings and scalpings was recorded by the Spaniards through Trudeau's letters to his superior at New Orleans.

The Little Ones seemed to have a respect for *"Sho'to To-Wo'n"* as well as for the strength of the fortification, so they appeared before Ste Geneviève and threw the citizens into a panic. The fact is that there are no sanguinary attacks recorded by the Spaniards, and there is little in the tribal memory of the Little Ones to indicate that they did much more than ride over the land in black and orange bluff-paint singing their war songs. This to the Little Ones seemed to have constituted victory, since they were out primarily to keep the merchants of St. Louis and Ste Geneviève from sending their merchandise, especially powder and lead and fusils, to their enemies upriver. They apparently enjoyed the effectiveness of their bluffing, watching the settlers huddle in fear and the people of Ste Geneviève flee.

One morning in Single-Moon-by-Himself (January), in the year 1794, two hundred bluff-painted Great Osages rode singing to the village of Ste Geneviève, and the people fled to their shelters in panic. The warriors sat their horses and watched them with great satisfaction; then they saw a man running hard for the village, and they cut him off, chiefly to watch the fear come to his face and to hear his funny pleadings for his life.

They taunted him for some time, then a man of the Bear gens took his trade knife from his sheath and pretended to scalp him. The man screamed with terror, and the jocular Bear, suddenly and whimsically despising his cowardice, became angered and did kill him. He was left lying there, since no one wanted a coward's hair at the belt or tied to his horse's mane or dangling from his spear.

After the war party left, the citizens came to get the man's body, and with great French excitement and abuse of the Spanish government, they sent a delegation to Trudeau clamoring for peace at any price. This was a face-saver for almost everyone since no one wanted the war except the Mississippi tribes and Red River Caddos. Here was a very important village, Ste Geneviève, deeply concerned with the trade of the upper river, asking for peace at any price.

But there really had never been a war with the Little Ones as far as the Spaniards were concerned. It is true that on December 22, 1792, Carondelet had ordered all trade stopped with the Osages and all Spanish citizens "to kill any Osages encountered." He wanted the commandant of Arkansas Post to build a fort up the Arkansas, but was dissuaded by the commandant, who convinced him that the Arkansas that far up would be dry much of the time. This project was abandoned in 1793.

In May, 1793, Carondelet had ordered Trudeau to prepare for war, but after Trudeau sent a detachment to the mouth of the Des Moines River which found the English there on the west side of the Mississippi, he had to bring them to St. Louis under arrest. This was in October, 1793.

War was abandoned when France and Spain became involved in war and there was danger of being invaded by Americans in the west, and Carondelet turned the control of the tribe back to the traders.

It is not known whether Trudeau called Auguste Chouteau, or whether Chouteau knew the moment to be propitious. Anyway he was soon floating down the Mississippi among the ice cakes, that soon melted. He called upon the Governor-General, Baron de Carondelet, at New Orleans, and proposed to build a fort on the Osage River with his and his brother Pierre's own money, if the Governor-General would give to them the exclusive right to trade with the Great and Little Osages.

The Governor-General was happy to do this. If the Chouteaus could keep the Osages tranquil, supplying them with all they needed, then it might work out that the Osages would not be so sanguine about stopping traders to the upper river. The contract was signed and would run for six years, until 1800. The Osage trade was highly important, and there was much opposition to this contract among the other traders, but the people of St. Louis and Ste Geneviève wanted peace.

There was now formed a trading company called the Upper Missouri Traders, who were given exclusive trade with any tribe they might find above the Ponca near the mouth of the modern Niobrara, the Flat-Waters-That-Ripple, and called by the French La Rivière qui Court. They were later given exclusive trading rights with the Omahas, the Otoes, and the Poncas.

They, under the leadership of one Jean-Baptiste Truteau, went in a pirogue up the Missouri past the mouth of the Platte. The later pirogue voyages upriver and the travels of James Mackay explored many mysteries of the Missouri, up and beyond the Yellowstone, to the Mandan villages, and there got information about that which the Little Ones called the Waters-of-the-*Ka-Thu-Wah,* Borrow-from-Others-People (Kiowas).

Mackay found the same problems upriver as the independent traders had found downriver when the Little Ones decided to deflect the pirogues up their own river. On the upper river, just above the Waters-Flat-White, the modern Platte, lived the splinter of the Little

Ones called *U-Mo'n-Ha'n,* Dwellers-on-the-Bluff, the modern Oma-has. They wouldn't allow the trading pirogues to go into the country of their own splinter, the Poncas, or to trade with the Yankton Sioux, and this caused the Upper Missouri Traders much concern, and their leader, one Clamorgan, to be attacked for bad leadership and in-fidelity, like all intensely acquisitive people, they bemoaned their losses and must blame someone else for their failure. The shareholders immediately got rid of their shares, Clamorgan himself buying seven of them, leaving only himself and Joseph Robidou as shareholders.

This division and discontent affected the Chouteau-Osage contract and finally caused much trouble through the weeping letters from the traders to the Governor-General, especially through the discontent and jealousy and phenomenal activity of one Manuel Lisa. His one object in life at this moment was to get control of the important Osage trade.

26. Fort Carondelet

THE CHOUTEAU BROTHERS CHOSE A LIMESTONE BLUFF now called Haleys Bluff in Vernon County, Missouri, and their palisade was a real fortification with mounted swivels and a detachment of soldiers. It was on the south bank of the Osage River and was finished by August of 1795. Apparently they had no labor trouble—no paucity of laborers— since the fort was constructed by "90 of the best men of country" (the King's best men).

The Little Ones had not stayed to watch the wonderful activity of the building of the palisades, but during the construction, or most of the latter phases of it, were off on their summer hunt. Apparently the whole tribe had been organized for this hunt in the formal and traditional manner except for forty warriors under a gentile chieftain, and except for this gentile war movement, they arrived at their villages at the Place-of-the-Many-Swans, on the seventh of August, their Yellow-Flower Moon.

Warriors had pillaged hunters' camps on the Arkansas River and had taken horses and arms. The families of the people who had been pillaged seemed to be more upset over the fact that the Little Ones had left the bodies "blackening on the earth" than they were over the deaths, and Chouteau arranged to have the bodies buried. He also, for the sake of his own conscience, made the gentes return the horses and arms, and proclaimed, so that the settlers along the Arkansas should take note, that he would "place a price upon the head of the first partisan whose band would do evil." He knew he was powerless to stop the gentile raids, and, furthermore, Spain didn't have sufficient forces nor yet the inclination to do so as long as the Missouri was left open so that they could trade upriver and check the activities of the English. As a matter of fact, Trudeau implied as much in a letter to his superior, Carondelet, in New Orleans: "It is in this manner that Mr. Cadet Chouteau wishes to get rid of some evil subjects, upon whom devolve all the disorders that they attribute to the corps of the nation. . . ."

"Don Augusto" Chouteau, called Cadet, was possibly diverting the Little Ones in their war movements from the Missouri to the Arkansas, keeping the Missouri open according to agreement. He probably felt that their raids along the Arkansas did not disturb trade very importantly. And Trudeau could write to his superior that the situation was not at all bad anyway, since the Osages kept the marauding Konzas from the Arkansas River, "and certainly they would commit more acts of piracy and roguery than the latter [Osages]."

He assured his superior that "the Osages had been harmful in the River of the Arkansas, but I do not know whether it would be prudent to break with them at this point, in which they leave the important district of Illinois at peace, which is beginning to be settled by a large emigration of foreigners who can be attracted only by tranquility and quietness, which said settlement enjoys at the present time. It is, therefore, desirable that the governor-general regard and consider for a moment the prosperity of Illinois, and the slight evil suffered by the hunters and wanderers of the Arkansas River. That class of people is the scum of the posts. Let the governor attempt to restrain said Osages by way of gentleness and patience, until these settlements, having been assured by a numerous population, may themselves lend to the government aid and a strong hand to punish this tribe and any other which transgresses order."

The Little Ones felt the same about the hunters and trappers and vagabonds from the John Law settlements of the lower Mississippi who had in this time not yet had the gutters of Europe bred out of them. They were possibly the sons and grandsons of the worst of Law immigrants. The others of better breeding were gradually becoming the backbone of an important and gracious lower Louisiana culture.

The primitive Little Ones could classify Europeans quite accurately. They had ever placed the same value on the Bohème as did the French officials and trader-adventurers. The shifty eyes in the hairy face, effervescent friendliness, the eagerness to please which characterized the barbarians who came up the river from Arkansas Post and the lower Mississippi filled them with contempt, while men like Bourgmont, Esteban Miró, Spanish governor-general, Zenon Trudeau, commandant at St. Louis, and a man under incognito who called himself De Bon, and, of course, the Chouteaus, Auguste, Pierre, Edward, and all the others, were given great honor and respect.

Cadet Auguste Chouteau was pleased with his contract with the Spaniards giving him exclusive trade with the Osages and proud of his fort, which he called "Carondelet," honoring, of course, the Governor-General Baron de Carondelet. He and Pierre seem to have been very successful in carrying out their promises to the government of his Catholic Majesty, since they were not only very popular with the Little Ones but had married women of the tribe. Trudeau could write in 1798 that the Osages had been restrained, "because said Don Augusto Chouteau found means of diverting and dissuading them by good councils and by means of accredited ascendancy which he has among both tribes." The raids along the Arkansas were the safety valve for both the whimsical and the serious warrior energy of the Little Ones.

The Chouteaus had many characteristics which the Little Ones could appreciate, and despite the fact that they were acquisitive, they were interested and could understand their primitive minds. Also, they apparently wore no blinders of Christian liturgy, and had much respect for the God-concept of the Little Ones, without approving it.

Some time during the summer of 1795 when Fort Carondelet was being built, several gentes were camped somewhere on the Arkansas River, and having established a semipermanent hunting camp, they had built a Lodge of Mystery there, and the Little Old Men with them met and talked.

The first Arrow-Going-Home, the Grand *Hunkah,* who had supposedly led the Little Ones against the Spaniards earlier, was out on the plains with the main body of the tribe, but his wife's father was in the camp on the Arkansas as one of the Little Old Men. One night an unidentified tribe of the Natchitoches federation crept up the river and, singling out the skin-covered Lodge of Mystery, loosed flaming arrows into it and fled. In the lodge at the time was the father-in-law of Arrow-Going-Home and the *wah-hopeh* shrine, and both the old man and the Sacred One were destroyed.

The whole tribe was struck with fear, and they made ceremony for the war movement. Chouteau was responsible for their actions, and he tried to dissuade them from going on the war movement, since in their mood and not knowing what tribe had committed the sacrilege, they might attack whomever they would meet. When they explained to him, he understood, and he gave the hundred warriors who left the Place-of-the-Many-Swans, singing, his blessing, although he told Trudeau only that he "had employed every means to stop the vengeance," but that it had been "impossible to attain that goal, since the *loge*, considered as being destroyed, was a matter involving the courage of all the warriors of the village."

For the mysterious De Bon the Little Ones had a feeling rather of fellowship. He did not seek furs and hides, but happily wanted to become one of them; their stature and dignity and animal grace seem to have fascinated him.

Perhaps not as picaresque as St. Denis of the trans-drainage adventure to the Río Grande in the early years of the eighteenth century, this Frenchman De Bon made a deep impression on the Little Ones. He came as an inquisitive visitor to New Orleans about 1789, the year of the beginning of the French Revolution. He was very gracious to the Spanish governor-general and to some of the Spanish gentlemen, but he was aloof and stiff with all others.

After a stay at New Orleans, he finally decided he wanted to study the Great Osages and got permission to go up the Mississippi, up the Missouri, and thence up the Osage River to their village. The very fact of the Little Ones appealed to his sense of romance and adventure, and he seems not to have been disappointed when he arrived in their village at the Place-of-the-Many-Swans. He brought with him a trader with pirogues loaded with the choicest merchandise, and he made presents to them of every article. When he asked for no furs in return, they were astounded; and they believed he must be a great chief of the Heavy Eyebrows since their own chiefs held themselves above trading and only gave things away.

He rode with them and painted his face as they did and learned their songs and sang the morning prayer to Grandfather. He had his choice of the girls, was married by Osage formula, and left progeny in at least two gentes, one a "sumac" alliance.

It was said that he even tried to keep them from going on the war movement. When he left the Little Ones, the two chiefs, the *Hunkah* and the *Tzi-Sho,* fanned away evil from him with their eagle-wing fans, and many wept as they watched him float off downriver into the forests of the east. He would travel toward the light of day, toward the east, toward the coming of Grandfather, and that they knew to be good.

Some of the records have it that "the savages regarded him as a god," but this is of course a bit of French or Spanish romancing, since there would be no place for him in the religious organization of the Little Old Men. They might have made a song about him as they finally did for the very useful and wonderful *mo'n-ce,* but if so it has been lost.

After he left for somewhere, possibly not France, it was discovered that he was Prince Bourbon, son of Condé, and that he still owed merchants in New Orleans for the presents he had given the Little Ones.

Despite the Chouteau brothers, the Little Ones made the war movement not only to the Arkansas but to the settlements of the Mississippi, but apparently now they made raids on their Mississippi Algonkian enemies, since many of these tribes were trying to form a federation so that they could attack the Osages in strength.

In March of the year 1795 at least two gentes crossed the Mississippi; and, instead of attacking the assembly place of the federated tribes, if there was such a place at this time, the angered Bear gens attacked a white settlement at the place called Canteen Creek, only twelve miles above St. Louis. This was simply one of those results of Bear frustration rather than lethal jocularity. The accompanying gens might have been the Panther.

In March of 1800, the commandant of St. Louis had the militia made ready at San Carlos del Missouri, and under the command of Don Santiago de San Vrain, militia would be sent up the Mississippi to the mouth of the Des Moines to stop American traders. Also there was danger of conflict with England.

The Little Ones were deathly afraid of the *we-lu-schka,* the little bad things, which the white man carried in his semen and seemingly on his very finger tips, and certainly on his breath. In the troublesome year of 1800 for Spain, the Osage savages would be negligible—certainly after they had heard that the Iowas, the Snow-Heads, and the Omahas, the Dwellers-on-the-Cliff, and perhaps the Otoes, the Goes-Along People, had these *we-lu-schka* and were dying with great pustules on their faces.

The warring gentes rode fast to the Place-of-the-Many-Swans. When they reported what they had heard, the town crier walked about the villages howling the news like a winter wolf. The *Hunkah* sent the few traders not married to Osage women and the Bohèmes downriver without ceremony. These people liked wild garlic, and the Little Ones were not sure that the odor of their breaths carried no danger.

27.   The Americans

Now, HOWEVER, AT THE BEGINNING of the nineteenth century, there was less need to flee from the *we-lu-schka* of the Heavy Eyebrows and the Long Knives and the *I-Spa-Tho* than from the Americans, whom they were now calling both Heavy Eyebrows and Long Knives, undecided just what they were since they were neither.

The Spanish government had watched the Americans carefully as they cut the trees and plowed the land on the broad alluvial plains east of the Mississippi, and they had admired the manner in which they built their mills so that they would work efficiently. They used two stones, and this seemed to be a source of wonder to the Spaniards.

So the Spaniards invited some of the enterprising Americans over and gave them grants tax-free, and later even made no demands on them concerning the manner in which they worshiped God, although they still gave preference to Roman Catholics. They invited the slaveholders to come and live on the west side of the Mississippi—those who fled the Ohio country when the new nation called the United States prohibited slavery in the Northwest Territory by the Ordinance of 1789.

Spain still controlled the great water highway which was the Mississippi River, and the young country on the east side of the river had trouble with the Spaniards when they closed the highway. Some of the enterprising American traders moved to the west side of the river so that they might use the river for their trade without molestation.

289

Both Spain and England were reluctant to move from some of the forts and other strategic positions England had lost as a result of the Revolutionary War. The Spanish forts on the west side of the river and the city of New Orleans on the east side were Spain's to use as she chose, but the forts she had built on the east side of the river, such as the one on the Chickasaw Bluffs, were now in what had been English territory, and were American. Also the line between west and east Florida and the United States was like the line of demarcation of the north, foggy; however, Spain was claiming the thirty-first parallel as the dividing line. There had been an agreement about these things in 1795, and it had been conceded that New Orleans should become a port of deposit for the Americans.

Then there was trouble between the United States and France, and because Spain had some idea that she might gain much if France should win the contentions and the possible skirmishes, she became stubborn and would not free New Orleans for American boats according to the agreement, and kept putting the matter off until 1799.

After two American representatives extraordinary had been insulted by Talleyrand under the *Directoire,* through his agents' asking for a bribe from the Americans, war fever in America became white hot, and France didn't want American forts along the thirty-first parallel or the city of New Orleans used in any manner by the Americans.

Talleyrand didn't want the Americans to expand. In 1798, when Spain was still playing for time under American insistence on their treaty rights in New Orleans, he said in so many words that Spain was foolish to give up "posts essential to arrest the progress of the Americans in those countries." He was also made nervous and much impressed by the hairy-faced men spreading over the eastern half of the continent, whacking down trees, plowing, making "snake" and stake and rider fences, and building two stone mills—doing things much better and a little faster than the fur trappers and traders of France and Spain. He said that somebody had to shut them up "within the limits which nature seems to have traced out for them."

Talleyrand knew that Spain could never be able to keep the Americans within the space "nature seems to have traced out for them," since Spain was a reflection of the weak Charles IV in Madrid. So Talleyrand suggested that Spain cede Louisiana back to France, but she refused; then Talleyrand fell from power. However, on the rise of Napoleon to first consul, he was called back, and the first consul and Talleyrand decided that France must protect Louisiana from the American Federalists who they believed might bring the English back, and the English were their most powerful and hated enemy.

There was a secret treaty at San Ildefonso, October 1, 1800, wherein Louisiana was ceded back to France.

The result of this was that later Napoleon would be amassing his troops at Boulogne for an attack on England which never came off and would be in need of money, and the Americans would continue to demand access to the port, New Orleans. This was the chief outlet for the people in Kentucky and Tennessee, and they were vocal and loud, so that President Jefferson could hear them in Washington. He sent a commission to Paris to buy the city of New Orleans and part of Florida, but when they got there, they found that they could buy the whole of Louisiana for $15,000,000, and did so. War between England and France was now, in 1803, imminent, and Napoleon didn't want complications in America.

There was a great celebration in December, 1803, when the province of Louisiana was delivered to the United States.

The Little Ones knew nothing of what was going on during this struggle between European powers and between these powers and the Americans, but they would soon feel the results of this balancing; and it would affect them tremendously.

The American Heavy Eyebrows–Long Knives would swarm over their land. They would not sweat and sing up their river with pirogues filled with fascinating *wah-don-skas,* leaving nothing as they camped by the river on their way up or down except the ashes from their fires and the hooves and antlers of wapiti, deer, and buffalo, and the poles of their lean-tos. These new Heavy Eyebrows, the Americans, would stay where they built their fires and cut the timber and built their "half-faced camps," laughing and swearing and shooting at targets so that the old Ordovician bluffs of the lower river reverberated.

The "half-faced camp" was a shed with three sides made by tree trunks, the fourth side being left open, and the roof was made of saplings with bark covering. The settler would live in this shelter with his family. He usually set up his camp near a spring or a spring branch or on the edge of the river.

While living in the "half-faced camp," the settler cut down a sufficient number of trees for a cabin and called upon other settlers to help him build it. He made a clearing by grubbing up the undergrowth and cutting down the trees a foot in diameter and less, and girdling the others, cutting a gash completely around them to stop the sap. This opened up the area to sun and rain.

These spots were visible to the Little Ones, especially in summer when the browned treetops showed among the green ones or bare limbs were like skeletons. When these skeleton trees stood for several years, the Little Ones knew that the hairy one was a hunter, trapper, or a maker of *pe-tsa-ni*, firewater, or he did both. He would spend all his time making firewater or he would divide his time between hunting and firewater-making, killing deer, buffalo, and wapiti for the market. He would take sow bears from their sleep in caves, leaving the little ones to die. They felt that they must kill such men.

These new Heavy Eyebrow–Long Knives were, the Little Ones thought, like the Long Knives whom their old allies, the real Heavy Eyebrows, had told them about: the English of the coast who destroyed the timber and killed the game and made the woods acrid with slash-burning, while the Little Ones could still hunt game under the walls of the forts which the Heavy Eyebrows built.

These new people, called Americans, came up the rivers Gasconade, Osage, and Missouri and Arkansas, and had begun to settle on the Meramec, farther and farther away from the settlements along the right bank of the Mississippi and the settlements of the Missouri. They brought their oxen and their dogs and their children and their women, and they built their cabins; and the Little Ones knew that they must run them back across the Mississippi or into the little settlements where they belonged before they killed or frightened all the game away.

This was not the war movement now, when they must carry captive straps and must paint their faces according to the nature of their war movement. This was a defense of their domain, and when they had found Sac and Foxes and Pawnees and Potawatomis and Miamis or Red River Caddos on their domain, they had run them back across the recognized boundaries. But this thing was new and frustrating. Had these hairy ones ever heard of the powerful medicine of the Children of the Middle Waters?

Their villages were full of prayer-songs and dance-prayers now, and the Little Old Men sat long in the Lodge of Mystery, and when they sang their Rising Song, they felt that they had solved nothing.

There were few trails in the woods of the Ordovician hills, and the Little Ones knew them all; and now along these trails and along the banks of the rivers, they found these hairy ones leaning on axes, staring at them, the children peeping from behind their mothers' voluminous skirts. It was sometimes fun to watch the fear in the faces of all, but most of the time the Little Ones were too angry for amusement. They sat their horses and bluff-scowled, and the gens leader might dismount and walk toward the staring man, who would drop his axe and extend his arm with palm of his hand out, believing that "this yere wuz the way uh Injun made a peace sign."

This would often please the members of the gens and make them smile, but more often the leader would threaten and bluff and take his trade knife from its sheath, and point with it to the hair of a little girl. He would bluff thus, scowling all the time; then when he was satisfied with the fear he had inspired, he would mount and ride off, his followers following without signal or flourish, much like winter blackbirds following their leader.

Often the wretched people who had been thus visited by a gens of the Little Ones would hurry back down the river, but just as often they would stay. Those who left didn't have much to leave behind them, and those who went back down the river took with them little more than their hair, which the Little Ones at this time believed to be of little religious value. Didn't they have the scalplock of the Pawnee attached to their sacred hawk shrine? The Pawnees along with the Padouca enemies carried very strong medicine. Of what value was the hair of the Americans, the new Heavy Eyebrows?

293

The trouble lay in the fact that the seemingly isolated family was really a part of a group who were moving into the Osage domain for a common purpose, and after one or more families were bluffed-talked into retreating, they would come together with others and they would build a breastwork and clean their muskets, and the Little Ones would be compelled to destroy them.

There were parties of ragged hunters and trappers, many of them with the shifty eyes of a coyote. These they left where they killed them, the older warriors standing back to allow the young, unaccustomed ones to count coup and take their first scalps. The older warriors took the guns only.

There is little tribal or gentile memory about these things now—memories perhaps that the Little Old Men have conveniently forgotten. There is not a member of the Little Old Men in the whole tribe who won't evade the subject, become silent, or frown with displeasure when asked about the Americans who came into their domain a long time ago. These men were Americans, and it seems to them to have been a very bad thing to have killed Americans. They have said, a few of them, that the Little Ones never killed a white man, ever, and no doubt some of them really believe it. These things they have "thrown away," as they have "thrown away" the old religion organized by the Little Old Men through the centuries. The modern Little Ones will not talk about the *wah-hopeh,* the sacred hawk shrine, either, and still believe that if one without authority opens one, he will die.

When the American was a hairy-faced man building his "half-faced camp" long ago and shouting louder than the bird-with-the-long-bill, the pileated woodpecker, they had to kill him, but now they wish to forget those things. In a deer camp in the Rockies, *Tzi-Sho-Wah-Ki-Pa,* Meeting-of-the-Lodges, said that one ought not to bring such things to the attention of the men in Washington, since they might take the Osage oil away from them.

The Chouteaus' exclusive trade with the Little Ones would have come to an end in 1800, but the brothers had the agreement renewed for four years, though they asked for six. They had built their fort, and pursuant to agreement, they had induced settlers to come and live under its walls, and they also kept soldiers there.

The trade with the Osages was very important. For one thing they were not far from St. Louis, and the water haul was without portages. For another thing, the Osages were a people who in their pride demanded much, and who through their energy had otter, bear, wapiti, deer, beaver, wolf, panther, bobcat, buffalo, and fox hides, as well as both bear and buffalo tallow ready for trade at all times. To supply them with merchandise it took many pirogues, since their number was at this time about six thousand.

Considering this volume of trade, it was quite natural that there should be jealousy of the Chouteau brothers, but the policy of the Spanish government as well as that of the French after the re-cession of Louisiana in 1800 was control of the Osages, and the Chouteaus were able to do this, at least better than either of the governments had been able to do it. First the Spaniards and then the French had been much comforted by the arrangement with the Chouteaus.

Most of the jealousy and greed was given expression in the treacly letters to the governors-general, who for a time handled them with polite firmness, and the decisions were accepted by the disgruntled petitioners. However, there was one Spaniard who would not give up. He was constantly fired up by his acquisitiveness and his jealousy, and his energy was terrific. He would float down to New Orleans and there lay his story of injured innocence before the Governor-General, and then no matter what the complexion of the interview, he would with Latin verve come back to St. Louis and as he walked around the billiard tables, he would boast to the clicking of the balls that he and his partners would soon have the exclusive trade with the Grand Osages. He kept this up for several years never tiring, and through his magnificent energy, acquisitiveness, and wonderful persistence, he became very important in the story of the Little Ones. His name was Manuel Lisa.

He wrote long letters to Salcedo, governor-general, on behalf of his partners and himself, posing as the champion of the public welfare. He wrote that he was "impelled by the laudable intentions of obviating the repeated public wrongs occasioned to these representatives [his partners] and their fellow citizens by the exclusive privilege of fur trade granted to Don Augusto Chouteau, because of this individual alone reaping benefit from a branch of trade in the promotion of which all the inhabitants are interested for their subsistence."

He went on to write that the extinction of the Chouteau exclusive grant would restore the former liberty of the citizens. He was sure that his excellency would not take longer to act on the petition of himself and partners, well knowing his zeal for the public good and justice, and that a man so just as his excellency would not want to retard the matter of the resolution, since delays would harm the town, for which he and his partners had great love, as did his excellency. Obviously this was for the public good, and an altruistic action on the part of Lisa and his partners, this being granted the exclusive trade with the Grand and Little Osages.

He then suggested that the condition of one of his partners, one Don Gregorio Sarpy, could "only excite the sentiment of pity and justice of which Your Excellency has given unequivocal proofs from the first moment of his taking over the reign of his government." This was due to a fire which had destroyed Don Gregorio Sarpy's mill and a storehouse, 20,000 pesos thereby being lost. It is difficult to understand just what Chouteau's exclusive grant might have to do with this fire.

It was not in the mind of Lisa and his partners to "require from Your Excellency a favor which might be prejudicial or painful to the royal interests."

Lisa indicated that if the exclusive grants to trade with the Osages were not taken from the Chouteaus, agriculture would suffer. He, Lisa, and his partners would maintain the fort Carondelet on the Osage River which the Chouteaus had built, and they would revive agriculture by building a mill with two stones, and make flour as good as that made by the Americans, and also the people of St. Louis would not have to buy their flour from the Americans across the river, an intimation that there would be an end to the high prices asked by the Americans when the wheat and corn crops were bad on the western side of the river. He also indicated that the division among the partners would facilitate the control of the Osages, pointing out that the three partners—Sarpy, Don Carlos Sanguinet, and Don Francisco María Benoit—being related to almost everybody in St. Louis, and therefore having wide and natural solicitude for a great number of St. Louisans, would make every effort to protect them from the savage Osages, wherein the Chouteau family was not so large, since there were only two of them, and their sons, one of them the mixed-blood Anthony, dealing with the Osages exclusively. Could it have been that one had to have inspiration to protect the community commensurate only with the number of one's own family?

In any case, on June 12, 1802, Lisa got his exclusive rights to trade with the Grand and Little Osages, and the Chouteaus made protest, since their grant had actually been extended for four years from 1800. Their anger was so great that they immediately tried all their wiles on the Osages to get them to move away from their river and their old villages at the Place-of-the-Many-Swans. First they demanded compensation for stock they had at Carondelet and for their expenditures there.

28. European Economics

On their gentile wanderings, the Little Ones roamed from the Missouri to the Red River, and from the Mississippi to the red Permian cliffs of the front range of the Rockies, and since they had to be gone from the Place-of-the-Many-Swans for days and even months, they had established camping places all over their domain. One of the largest and a much favored one became a semipermanent village on the Gray-Green-Bark Waters, the modern Verdigris River and the Water-Like-a-Brown-Yellow-Body, the modern Neosho (Water-Like-the-Skin-of-a-Summer-Cow-Wapiti). The mouths of these two rivers are a very short distance apart where they join the Arkansas, and the area was later called the Three Forks.

Here, near a saline spring on the Verdigris, the wandering gentes had camped for years, and now at this time this camping place was made a base for operations by the Bear-Panther gentes. It was a base for their raids along the Arkansas, and to the Red River.

The hunting was excellent and the climate was more temperate than that of the Place-of-the-Many-Swans. The camp was at a spot which was ideal for the fur trade, since there was a heaving stratum of rock across the Arkansas River bed, and this made a natural terminal for navigation up the Arkansas. Here the furs and hides could be placed aboard pirogues and other types of boats and floated down the Arkansas to the Mississippi, thence to New Orleans; and the bringing of merchandise up the river was much easier and the route much shorter than the long way up the Mississippi, then up the Missouri, and up the Osage to the Place-of-the-Many-Swans. Ṣo, in 1802, Pierre Chouteau persuaded almost half of the Little Ones from the permanent villages on the Osage and the Missouri to move here.

The brothers had much trouble with the Grand *Hunkah* and the Grand *Tzi-Sho,* but they knew the psychology of the arrogant and vain gentile chieftains, and working on this vanity, when the Grand *Hunkah* and the Grand *Tzi-Sho* refused to move the village from the Place-of-the-Many-Swans, they chose the very susceptible chieftain of the Panther gens.

Ko-Zhi-Ci-Gthe, or *Ka-Zhi-Ci-Grah,* which means Makes-Tracks-Far-Away and refers to the wide wanderings of the tom panther in his hunting and especially during rut, was the•one they approached.

It is obvious that a single gentile chieftain like Makes-Tracks-Far-Away, even though he might influence his twin gens the Black Bear to follow him to his new home, could not have induced many more than the twin gentes to follow him, if *To-Wo'n Ga-Xe,* Town Maker, or under his formal name, *Gra-Mo'n* or *Ghleh-Mo'n* (the former meaning Arrow-Going-Home, and the latter meaning just Going), had not decided to come along, and bring with him many of the sub-*Hunkah* and *Wah-Sha-She.*

This man was known to the Chouteaus and other Frenchmen and Americans as Claremont and Claremore. His influence was much greater than the Chouteau creation, Makes-Tracks-Far-Away. It has been said that he was actually the hereditary Grand *Hunkah,* but that *Paw-Hiu-Skah,* White Hair, having been more amenable to Chouteau's designs, had through his influence been able to usurp the office of Grand *Tzi-Sho* during Arrow-Going-Home's boyhood. It is believed that the Chouteaus were able to persuade almost half of the tribe to come to the Three Forks, the Place-of-the-Oaks, due to the hereditary influence of Arrow-Going-Home.

Also it is likely that many of Makes-Tracks-Far-Away's people, the Panther and the Black Bear people, were already there, since they had used the Place-of-the-Oaks as a base for their raids. These people were called by the French, Osages des Chênes, Osages of the Oaks. They were also called Les Chêniers, They of the Oaks, which later, after the swarming of the Americans, was corrupted into "Cheneers" and even "Shainers." They would have a bloody reputation among the Americans and the Quapaws and the immigrant Cherokees. Their leader in one battle among the oaks would be called Le Chênier, the Oak, because he had stood behind an oak and routed his white enemies. Neither tribal nor gentile memory recalls the identity of their chieftain. The same chieftain or another of the Bear or the Panther gens was also known by the French as Le Peste, the Pest. This could have been Makes-Tracks-Far-Away or a Bear chieftain, or one from another of the gentes who came with Arrow-Going-Home.

The original tribesmen of the Little Ones who lived much of their time at the Three Forks or the Place-of-the-Oaks before Chouteau's removal were one of the physical divisions of the Little Ones, originated during the great flood, those who had fled to the upland forests and were called *Co'n-Dse-U-Gthi'n,* now *Sa'n Solé;* and this would indicate that they, like the Down-Below-People (the Little Osages), were beginning imperceptibly to splinter from the tribe.

The spot was perfect for brother Pierre's establishment, and he and Auguste had halfway defeated Lisa. The upland forest or forest or forest-plateau physical division of the Little Ones and the Bear–Panther gentes were certainly at home here and had been for some years. As a matter of fact, the Chouteaus had a trading post at the saline spring before 1802.

Here was the beginning of the disruption of the organization that the Little Old Men had labored to achieve through the centuries, so that the Little Ones could arrive at some mutual understanding with *Wah'Kon-Tah,* the Great Mysteries, and keep themselves strong and swift like the falcon, and through unity and prowess protect a domain large enough and fruitful enough to sustain them so that they could always "walk in the light of day." They might still attain old age if they could avoid the diseases of the Heavy Eyebrows, but gradually the robes of high honor which old age wore would become worn and mildewed, and the ambitions of the eager Nobodies would fit perfectly into the grasping hand of the acquisitive, often greedy Europeans.

Those things which the Little Old Men created through the centuries—the curlicues and iridescence of useless ornamentation in building their cage of understanding for *Wah'Kon,* the Mystery Force, would now be used as instruments for the Little One's destruction. The given word they had charged with sanctity, the latitude allowed the gentes in reflecting their symbol's characteristics and for independent action under their vain and ambitious leaders, who would give all for the burnishing of their self-esteem, would be a ready-fashioned tool in the hands of private traders, politicians, and commissioners and army officers of the new American government.

29.   Before the Invasion

Now just before the european-forced separation, just before the Little Ones were cut in half by the exigencies of European acquisitiveness, little had happened to their customs and manners and their tribal organization. The Black Robes up to this time had had practically no effect on their religious organization, and their social organization remained intact. The Jesuits might have been an important influence in the lives of the Little Ones if Charles III of Spain had not sent a decree to Louisiana and other Spanish colonies suppressing the Society. This decree was to be opened April 2, 1767, the same date as the Society was expelled from Spain. The Society had got into trouble in South America, where they became a trading firm, and had branches all over the world, which activity, of course, was in flagrant violation of the principles of the Society. Despite this fact, the Jesuits quite possibly represented the highest European culture with which the Little Ones had come in contact up to this time.

Only the economic organization of the Little Ones had been affected, and they had been given a new reason for the war movement in their slaving. They had strange and fascinating *wah-don-skas* from the traders which affected their economy and war movement. They had built a ceremony around *mo'n-ce,* metal, and it had become sacred for obvious reasons, and many of the *wah-don-skas* had become almost indispensable; there were beads and tattoo needles, and awls and French axes, and fusils and sewing needles and calico and blankets, and hawkbells, and that glory of vanity and of heliographical signaling and dance ornament, the highly decorated hand mirror which they called peeps-in-water.

Many of these *wah-don-skas* were labor-saving devices, and effort is seldom employed when it can be avoided, just as pain is avoided and called "danger." The making of the tattooing needles was not difficult, since they were made from the wing bone of the pelican or the eagle, but the steel needles of the traders arranged neatly in little packets were convenient. They got their sewing needles chiefly, at least for the finer work, from the splinter bone of the leg of walks-on-wings, the turkey, and this was, of course, not difficult, but the trade needles came in fascinating packets, all shiny. It was not difficult to flatten quills of the porcupine and color them for decoration of the tobacco bags and the charcoal and paint bags and parfleches, but the vari-colored trade beads were a delight.

The women had to bring only a few beaver skins or fox or wolf skins to the Heavy Eyebrows and exchange them for a packet of shiny needles or beads and store them away in their lodges. Then one day when the children were riding their *ka-wa shinkas,* their stick horses, or the boys playing rescue and the girls playing with their stuffed squirrel skins on their special little baby boards, the women would gather and each bring out her tanned deer or wapiti hides treated with gypsum, and gather her awls and her needles and paw-paw or linden thread about her. She might get up and go out to shut her eyes against the sun to get color pattern, then return and sit in the middle of her things, always with her feet straight out in front of her on the floor of the lodge. She could reach any article she might want, whether it be at her feet or at either side, or even behind her.

Sitting with the legs straight out in front of them with feet close together was the proper way for women to sit—in this manner, or with both legs drawn up alongside the thighs on one side. However, when they grew old or fat, they could only sit with legs straight out in front of them.

There was a practical reason for this posture just as there was for many of their customs. The reason in this case was the lizard. He stayed about the lodges and possibly lived on ants and crumbs and flies attracted by the domestic odors of the lodges, but into his long-held immobility and opaque stare, the women through the generations had read a sinister purpose, and they called him *uzi-wah-mo'in,* runner-up-womens'-legs. There, of course, could have been unpleasant experiences grooved in tribal memory.

The *wah-don-skas* of the Heavy Eyebrows were new and interesting, if not too greatly superior to the needles and awls made of wing bones and leg-bone splinters and quills. Nor was the trade blanket superior to the buffalo robe; as a matter of fact, it was inferior. Trade blankets came in bales enticingly thrown down in front of the traders hurriedly put-up lodge, and they saved long and weary days of labor and long, tedious processes for tanning. They were dyed so that the colors ran not transversely but vertically, like the sacred coloring of the finished buffalo robe. The English had first imitated the colored stripes of the buffalo robes, and the French had soon got the point, and were now bringing striped blankets as well as solid red and blue ones to be traded.

The French war axe was far superior to the migrated, glacier-rounded granite stone tied to an ash shaft with a wapiti rawhide, which the Little Ones used as a war club. Peeps-in-water, the mirror, was a sort of miracle.

Now, while the women were dressing him for the dance, the warrior could see his glorious image and give directions which the long-accustomed women didn't need and never heeded. The hawkbells tied around the dancer's legs just under the knees, had a wondrous metallic rhythm during the dance and swelled the heart of the warrior as he approached the dance ground. The terrapin shells filled with river pebbles were soon used no more for this purpose.

The Little Ones had begun to depend on these trade *wah-don-skas,* but the absence of these things would not have destroyed them if cholera or some chance of war or natural phenomena had wiped the European from the Mississippi Valley. They would not have perished as the *Ihalmiut* west of Hudson Bay did. These caribou hunters had killed off their caribou or changed their migration route by heavy slaughter and had trapped out their Arctic foxes on the demands of the traders, and they became so dependent on the traders' miracles that when from economic necessity, having to do with the price of furs, the traders left, the natives could not return to their old ways.

There was still a plentitude of game and fur-bearing animals in the domain of the Little Ones, but the periphery of the buffalo herds had already begun to shrink as a lake does when it becomes dry, dwindling to a mudhole in the center. The shrinking had already begun, and long before the century ended, the buffalo would make their last stand somewhere on or near the Buffalo-Dung Waters, the Republican River.

Also the wapiti were growing fewer, as were the white-tail deer and bear. Since the swarming Long Knives had to feed themselves and market anything they couldn't eat, if what they met with in the wild trans-Mississippi was edible or salable, then it was important. About this time they found that salted buffalo tongues were marketable as well as the hides and that the two ivory teeth of the wapiti were of value.

This beginning of scarcity is indicated by the fact that now the deer and bear hunters of the tribe were camping near the Three Forks, and the tribal buffalo hunters had to go farther west from their villages for their annual hunts. There were now buffalo camps on the Low-Forest-Water Salt Fork of the Arkansas, and instead of skirmishes with the Pawnees and the Kiowas, they tell of the short-legged, sun-darkened little men shooting from under the necks of their horses, and yipping like *sho-mi-kase,* the coyote. These were the [Lodges]-Make-Us-Stoop People, the Apaches, and the Wet Noses, the Padoucas.

And now the Little Ones had honey. They had ever been greedy for sweets and had traded buffalo robes and wapiti teeth for maple sugar or syrup with a people who lived on the lower Ohio River, whom they named *Sho-Ni,* Water-from-Tree People.

The Spaniards and the English colonists had imported the honey bee, perhaps from Italy, about the middle of the seventeenth century, and they had been brought west by the American settlers and up the river by the Spaniards and perhaps the French. They swarmed in the great hollows of the sycamores and post oaks when they left the settlements, and here the black bear found the combs and introduced honey to the Little Ones. They say that the grasshopper with flame-colored wings, who flies up from the grass to a height of perhaps three feet and hangs there like a hovering marsh hawk, but making a sound like electric sparks, was brought in by the white man.

The horse had given them mobility and that hauteur and sense of superiority and arrogance which horses have given all men through the ages, but stressed their original customs only, not shattering them. They need not make their buffalo surround in exactly the old manner, gourd-necking the buffalo over a cliff, but with horses they milled them like cowboys mill cattle when cutting. They now rode around them in the tribal hunts and set them to milling, then shot the fat cows and young bulls, charging quickly on their hunting race horses to come up with the ones that broke away. But there was a line marked by the crest of a visible plains swell, by a line of river cottonwoods or by any feature outstanding, beyond which no hunter was allowed by the special hunt officials to go, not even after a wounded buffalo. This boundary was called *wa-tha-da-bi,* and the reason for its establishment was obvious. Any Pawnee, Apache, Kiowa, or Padouca scout or hunting party knew what was happening out of sight beyond the plains swell when they saw the alkaline dust rise like pale smoke, and if the wind was right, they could hear the crack of rifles. Out of sight of the Osage hunters, they would hide in the crease of the plains or lie flat in the high grass of the prairie, then when the lone hunter came riding over the swell trying to close on his buffalo, the Pawnees or the Kiowas or the Apaches or the Padoucas would have one more highly cherished Osage scalp to boast over.

If the hunter did not run into an enemy ambush, when he returned to camp he was whipped by two men called the Whippers, who were chosen for the express purpose of whipping anyone who violated the laws of the hunt. The punishment was not individual, but was for tribal protection. If there were no designated visible boundaries, whole groups of highly emotionalized Little Ones could easily run into ambush. The Little Ones had a contempt for ambuscades; you might hunt as *i'n-gro-ḵah,* the panther, but you went into battle like the black ant and like a prairie fire, or came out of the sun like the golden eagle, or even broke your enemy as did the falcon.

306

The gun, on the other hand, was not really as important as one might have believed it to be. A warrior or a hunter had to carry shavings from arrow-shaft making for wadding, and bullets and powder, and he could fire only one shot before reloading. The fusil was long and difficult to handle from horseback, and the prairie winds often blew the powder from the priming pan. However, a war party riding across the plains with the sun glinting on their gun barrels had a tremendous psychological effect on the enemy, and the Little Ones according to their own tribal memory used this psychological bluff skillfully. But, whether on the war movement or hunting singly, in gentile groups or on the tribal hunt, they always carried their bows and arrows with them and used them much more than they used their guns.

It was the horse which was the most important factor in their lives, of all the things which the white man had brought to them up to the nineteenth century; but even he disturbed their organization little, chiefly stressing and extending the patterns of their tribal life and perhaps stressing the difference in classes, since he was private property.

Now, at the beginning of the nineteenth century, among the young men, and even among a few of the middle-aged men and women, there were faces like gypsum-rubbed deerskin rather than the bronze, and hair like the hair of the buffalo just after he had wallowed in an alkali spot, and sometimes the long hair of a young woman, rippled like the waters of the *Ni-O-Btha,* far north where the Poncas lived. And now there were pale people with eyes like the eyes of *sho-mi-kase,* the coyote, and eyes of staring gray flecked with brown. There were young pale-faced people now whose trail you would know from the many footprints, since toes of the left foot would not be pointed in the absolute direction in which the walker was traveling. And some of these pale men grew little charcoal marks of shiny black hair on their chests, and their arms became knotty like the roots of the wild grape vine, with hair like moss (black), and sometimes the eyebrows of the younger men and women were like the early phase of the Moon Woman painted with charcoal.

And a few of the white fathers or grandfathers of these youngish people would still live with the Little Ones, and tried to act and look more like the Little Ones than the Little Ones themselves, especially in the presence of Europeans. Some of them had lived with the Little Ones long enough to be honored with the name "grandfather," which meant that they had earned that name by having been formally married to their Osage wives by the tribal formula. Those who had taken widows to the sumac bushes or to the buck brush and became fathers and eventually grandfathers could never be honored by that name "grandfather," and would remain in the lower of the two social classes. This taboo applied to both the Osage men and women as well as to the white man.

When the traders and officials and the explorers and the royal adventurers lured women to their robes by presents, these women were chiefly widows whose chances of remarriage were not too bright, or girls of the second class whose immediate ancestors had mated in the sumac or the tall grasses under the Moon Woman, without benefit of formality. Those girls couldn't lose that which they didn't have, social standing, but they could gain a few baubles. Even so, most of the unmarried girls of the second class were looked after by their gens, and duennas were assigned to them as to all other girls when they reached the age of puberty, which was usually fifteen among the Little Ones. These older women carried flint or obsidian knives at first and later trade knives known as butcher's knives, not hunting knives.

There was an understanding between the amorous young man standing in the moon shadows outside the girl's lodge with his flute of sumac or cedar and the old duennas, or the group of young men who hid in the buck brush near where the duenna and her charges must pass to go to the bathing place. This bathing place for women was on one of the many loops of the river, under the ridge on whose crest the villages were situated and so chosen that the bathers could not be spied upon. But on the way the young men would aim the sun-reflected light from the mirror into a girl's eyes. She would duck her head into her robe giggling, while the old women would scold and with raised knives threaten the surrounding bushes.

The restrictions placed on pubescent girls seem ridiculous and even so mysterious that one might examine them for religious significance, but the formal marriage ceremony was not a religious ceremony, nor yet a political one. Mating among them was not for social status based on property or for political balance, without the least concern for eugenics as in Europe and England, where social ascendancy had to be maintained through the merging of property among the patricians, and international political balance had to be maintained through the royal matings. This system as often as not produced mentalities and bodies that were anything but royal. Political power and economic and social privileges were the objectives, while the objective of the Little Ones was warrior perfection and long life. Anything that detracted from those two objectives, was "thrown away" and was not allowed to weaken the medicine of the Little Ones.

The girls say the Little Old Men are like the Sacred One, the earth which Grandfather the Sun impregnates, and they are the carriers of the warriors of the future. The girls of the present had in their bodies the warriors yet in *Spiritland*. If like the woman *sho-mi-kase,* they ran over the prairie with all sorts of men coyotes and even some of the lazy, mangy camp dogs, which the village Dog Killer had overlooked with his powder from the mysterious weed, following her, then the Little Ones soon would no longer "walk in the light of day," and there would be no wrinkles of old age, and "no still traveling while old, like the flight of the pelican." Their medicine would grow weak, and soon the Caddoans would come back to claim their old home.

So they protected their girls for the strongest and bravest and handsomest warrior with the fierceness of the falcon, and when a girl's proud family gave their daughter to him, there was a formal ceremony.

The young men knew the taboos of the tribe, and they were also much afraid of the Whippers, so they only strutted in their finery or put their feet down hard as they walked to the dance ground, so that the bells would tinkle loudly. They began to play their flutes in the spring when the first little frogs sang and through the summer, until the excitement of the autumnal hunt or the excitement of the war movement stopped them and put glory in their minds.

309

It is true that the Little Old Men in their "ten commandments" omitted a penalty for rape, yet there was a penalty. The girls were so well guarded by the duennas that to seduce one of them must have meant that the old guard women were hoodwinked or injured or even killed. Here seemed to be the point: the old duennas embodied taboos, and ostracism or even death might have been the penalty for breaking them. Apparently they were respected and had been since the days of the organization of the tribe and the elimination of the influence of the Isolated Earth People.

But their taboo did not work when the Otoes, called Letchers by the Missourias and *Wa-Zho-Xtha* by the Little Ones, meaning "Goes Along." Their tendency was to "go along" with strange tribes. They were closely associated with the Missourias, and for a period with the strong medicine of the Pawnee-*maha*. They came down from their roaming north of the Missouri River to smoke the pipe with their kinsmen.

The Osage girls must have been pretty quite often, or else the givers of names in the child-naming ceremonies must have had a deep desire for them to be beautiful, just as a short-legged artist might give his subjects long legs, since there were many names among them which pertain to female beauty. They seemed to have been especially attractive to the visiting Otoes, and during these visits the duennas stood guard all night by the lodges where their charges slept. They squinted out into the night, holding their torches made of sycamore splinter soaked in bear tallow before them. They had a *pot de nuit* made of buffalo hide which had been dried in a rounded hole in the clay, lipped and brailed with hickory. The girls were not allowed to go out where the lecherous presence of the Otoe young men could be felt even in the darkness, and their urine was carried out in these pots by the duennas, after they threw the ashes of the willow, which was sacred, into them. This would nullify any love charm which the cat-prowling Letchers might throw over the urine, thus luring the girl to disgrace even against her will and the frantic determination of the old women.

There is nothing the Little Ones did that did not have its origin in the necessities of biology or in their imitations and their observations of nature about them. They knew well the eager trailing of the swollen-necked buck during Deer-Mating Moon, and his nosing one spot for some moments with all absorbing intensity, and they had seen him an hour later and several miles along the trail approach the waiting doe in regal pride, while she stood strangely submissive as if under a charm.

The duennas sat with small moccasined feet stretched out straight in front of them as they strung their beads against the buckskin bags of their men, in designs which Grandfather the Sun gave them when they turned tightly closed eyes directly to him. Or they got out their pressed hackberry leaves, the pressed leaves of the sugarberry, the post oak, the blackjack, and the black walnut, and got inspiration from their veining. They got ideas from the outline of the pin-oak leaf and from the cruciform post-oak leaf. They studied the designs *Wah'Kon-Tah* had placed on the cups of the acorns, the bur oak and overcup oak. These patterns were patterns from the woodlands. They got their geometrical patterns from the plains, and these patterns were evident in the conventionalized spiders tattooed on the backs of the hands of the women, the stylized sun rays, and the stylized eagles and other birds and animals done in beads on the tobacco pouches, and in the geometrical tattooing on the chests of the warriors who had earned that honor.

They sat and frightened the girls with old wives' tales about *mi-ah-luschkas,* the little people in human form, who were thoroughly wicked, playing all sorts of tricks on real people, and laughing at their discomfort, and even causing slow mysterious death, but who, when they crossed the trail of virgins, became serious and intent. And they must be careful with their robes and blankets, they warned, when passing young men. If the edge of a robe or a blanket flapped against a young man, the girl would have to marry him to save her honor, even if he was ugly or lame and had taken no scalps or never counted coup. Of course, as long as the Letchers were visiting, they were not even to be seen.

It was this protection of the girls that caused the medicine of the Little Ones to remain strong, and caused them to grow tall and lithe. A great young warrior with these attributes could have two, three, four, or even five wives.

30. Marriage of Bloody Hands and The Light

HE WAS CALLED *Sha-Wa-Bi'n* because he was even at twenty-one a famed warrior, and he belonged to the Eagle gens. He had an Eagle name, *Sha-Wa-Bi'n,* which means Bloody Hands or Bloody Talons of the eagle or the falcon. He might have been as much as six feet, three inches tall, and was allowed to wear the eagle feather in his roach: the stiff tail-feather of the golden eagle tinted with the red of the pokeberry juice on the white parts, so that they were no longer white but the dawn red of Grandfather the Sun. He had counted coup three times, twice on the dead bodies of the enemy. He had counted coup on an Apache and a Padouca, and had tapped the body of a very much alive Pawnee chieftain, and had ridden away untouched by Pawnee arrows.

His *o-do'n,* his war honors, were many and so outstanding that he became shy and looked straight ahead when he walked down the ways of the village. He didn't see the girls peeping over the edges of their robes as they passed with their duennas, nor did he seem to hear their giggles behind him as they passed. He carried his body straight with the thoughts of his *o-do'n* singing in his heart, and prayed to the red oak that stood downriver from the village. It had its head above the walnuts, the elms, the sycamores, the hackberrys, and chinquapin oaks. It was straight and young and beautiful, and yet had lived a long time and would live a long time after he himself would have passed on to Spiritland.

312

But *Wah'Kon-Tah* had given the red oak beauty and strength and long life, and he prayed through it for all these attributes. Now he could not wear his old buckskin leggings and his Otoe moccasins with the beads hanging, but must dress carefully in his gypsum-rubbed leggings, his honor eagle feather and his new moccasins, with his buffalo robe over his left shoulder, draped gracefully so that the stripes painted with the four sacred colors would make a pattern—that part over his shoulder horizontal and that part draped about him vertical.

The people, not only of the Eagle gens but of all the gentes, talked of him, and old women came up to touch him, and the old men were constantly giving him advice, but not so much assuming a prerogative of age as for the purpose of reflected importance. The little boys stopped in their games of shinny or popping ear-pops, oak galls, in each other's ears to gather around him and stand and stare as he passed. *"Tompah,"* they would say, "Bloody Hands is *Wah'Kon,* mystery medicine; the arrows of the Pawnees curve around him, and Heavy Eyebrows touch their foreheads when he passes." The little boys pretended they did this; this was dramatic and poetic.

The French made the sign of the cross periodically, when they passed the grave of a Frenchman and when they passed the pagan Lodge of Mystery, but only when the Little Old Men were in it, and especially when they sang their Rising Song. This last was protective; there was much of the devil in pagan ceremonial. When the lightning zigzagged and when the thunder roared, they made the sign of the cross. No greater homage to their hero, Bloody Hands, could the little boys give than when they pretended the Heavy Eyebrows touched their foreheads when he passed.

His parents had been married formally, as had his grandparents, and therefore his honors were not tarnished; and since his family had followed the traditions of the tribe, and since he could count many *o-do'n,* they began to look at the girls of other gentes, and they did this as though they were bestowing an honor on the girls and their families.

His uncle, *Sun-on-His-Wings,* referring to the glinting of sun on backs of the primary feathers of the soaring eagle, was called in by

313

his parents and was told to look for a girl. When the parents of eligible girls of the other gentes realized that Sun-on-His-Wings was seeking a wife for Bloody Hands, they went to their parfleches, or "trunks," and got out the beautiful buckskin garments made by the Otoe women which they had traded for during their periodic visits. The Otoe women were great artists with beadwork and porcupine-quill work and wapiti-teeth decorations on artistically cut buckskin. Soon the girls of the Bear, the Wapiti, the Panther, the Deer, the Cat-tail, the Crayfish, the Heavenly Bodies, the Thunder, and the other gentes were wearing their robes with conscious propriety as they walked with their duennas, so that their finery would be visible, and from them came the scent of *mo'n-pi-ha,* the seeds of the columbine (crushed).

The parents of the eligible girls could do nothing to influence the choice. They must wait in silence with their daughters. Only the Eagle girls were not excited, since they realized that Bloody Hands could not be married to one of his own gens.

One day Uncle Sun-on-His-Wings saw The Light, a strong, alert, quick-walking girl of the Bear gens. She was named for the light that shines in the eyes of the black bear. When the flaming sycamore splinter dipped in bear tallow was held by the hunters in the hiberna-tion caves and the sleeping bear was aroused, he opened his eyes, and they glowed in the light of the splinter torch. She also had the sacred spider tattooed on the backs of her hands, the beautiful convention-alized spider which was the symbol of the Grand *Hunkah* and which was a mark of honor.

When Sun-on-His-Wings came to the lodge of The Light's parents, he came at sundown. After he had eaten, he told them why he had come, as if they didn't know. "Ho," they said courteously, and they called the mother's brother; and when he appeared, they left the lodge, leaving the two uncles together. Standing Bear, uncle of The Light, said nothing when Sun-on-His-Wings told him the purpose of his visit. He pointed out a black bear skin as a bed for him, and he left. This was propitious.

The next morning Sun-on-His-Wings came back to the lodge of Bloody Hands' parents, and told them what he had done. They immediately, and with assurance, called in the family members and assigned duties to them, especially the women, who began at once to prepare a feast. They appointed *E-To-Pehs,* two members of the family being the head *E-To-Pehs.* These were the daughters and sons and granddaughters and grandsons, etc.

When the food for the feast was ready, it included all the good things which their rich domain nurtured: buffalo, deer, wapiti, turkey, fish, skunk, squash, lily fruits, wild potatoes, corn, ground chiefly, unless the wedding took place in the season of corn in the milk. These things the four designated women of the Eagle, headed by Bloody Hands' aunt, carried over to the lodge of The Light's parents. They walked in single file like buffalo going to water, and each woman had a vessel filled with food.

If the girl's lodge was in another village, the boy's parents and relatives camped close by, and sometimes the relatives of the girl built a camp, since there were so many gathered together. In the summer, when the weddings usually took place, they set up their lodges as they would during the tribal hunt, and they also made shelters with four, six, or eight straight poles made of hickory, oak, or ash saplings. Each pole was forked like the pincer of the crayfish, and the other poles were laid in the forks as beams, then they laid willow branches across the top for rafters and then made the roof of willow twigs and leaves. The summer winds of the prairie could have full play here and sweep the flies away.

The meat was cooked over hickory coals and draped over a conical framework of dogwood saplings, tied together with hickory bark at the ends, with the large ones stuck into the ground. This is much the same way they made the framework of their lodges.

After leaving the food, the four women of the Eagle came back to their lodges or their camp, and waited.

There were certain especially chosen relatives of The Light's parents, chosen in equal numbers from her mother's and father's families, and they had their places at the feast. The feast was spread on the ground on a bleached and pliable buffalo robe.

The fact that The Light's relatives ate the food signified acceptance of Bloody Hands, and when the feast was finished, the sisters and

315

cousins and Bear relatives of the bride, who were really "brides-maids," led by her mother's sister, washed the utensils in which the food was brought over. There were "kettles" made of buffalo paunch, dried and cured by placing it in a round hole in the clay, then filling it with melted buffalo or bear tallow. When the tallow hardened, the "kettle" was further dried and was used to cook food or carry food. There were bowls and plates made of the linden, ash, and from knots of the post oak, and now, after trade with the Heavy Eyebrows and *I-Spa-Tho* and Long Knives for many years, they had trade kettles and other wares. They still used the spoons made from the horn of the buffalo.

After washing the utensils, the women came in a line carrying them back to the camp and lodges of the boy's parents. When the waiting relatives of Bloody Hands saw the line of "bridesmaids" coming with the empty utensils, they knew that he had been accepted. The bridesmaids had very happy faces, and the parents of Bloody Hands smiled with their eyes as they awaited the maids. There was another feast for the Eagle relatives, and here the father announced that the boy had been accepted, and that all who wished might go over to the girl's camp and there meet their Bear relatives.

The next day the chosen relatives went over to the lodge of the girl's camp, and here Standing Bear and Sun-on-His-Wings directed the meetings, and there was a feast for the family of Bloody Hands, but they ate apart and talked among themselves about the marriage. Bloody Hands was not present, and The Light remained in her lodge with her attendants; as a matter of fact, they had never seen each other. She was bathed and powdered with a dark powder that came from a beanlike plant with leaves like an iris and an orchid-like flower, the powder coming from the seed pods. Her clothes were perfumed with chewed columbine seed.

She was nervous, and her hands played with the edge of her robe as the older women talked to her and fussed over her. Her meals were brought to her. They applied the dried pulp of pumpkin to her face to improve her complexion.

Bloody Hands sat in his parents' lodge, hidden from all eyes. He might sing the Crow Song or the Wolf Song to himself, beating the rhythm on his chest or by clicking counting-sticks together. Since his *o-do'n* were many, he might be privileged to shake the rhythm with the gourd rattle.

In the middle of this happiness among the Eagle and the Bear gentes, when all went about with lighted faces, some old woman might start keening, a sort of "joy crying," but with the rhythm of prayer-crying it seemed to inspire emotion, and this emotion grew and soon took control, and the crier, who had forgotten what originally inspired her weeping, suddenly realized that her father and her brother and her husband, and perhaps a son, had never returned from the Cliffs, the West, where the warriors died, and as her emotion built up, she was soon singing the Song of Death, and like dogs taking up the howl of one unhappy one to cry in chorus, the other women were soon keening dolorously.

There was no one who would stop them, but soon they stopped, turning their uplifted faces from the sky, and soon their faces resumed the light that was in the heart; and they felt again like ear-pop, the oak gall, as they say, light and careless which wind blows them.

They must all indicate happiness and they must all be courteous. The Bear relatives must be extremely pleasant to the visiting Eagle, and the Eagle must act as courteously as guests are supposed to act. The Bear relatives must donate food for the feasts, and the Eagle relatives must make their donations as well. This must be so, if they wanted the marriage to be a success. Quarreling, frowning, acting surly would not be propitious, and the young people might start out under a cloud.

The family and relatives of Bloody Hands did most of the cooking, and they not only wore smiles and bright faces, but they increased their activity in order to indicate to the Bear relatives that they were happy and alert people, and appreciated the joining of the gentes. They were up and had prepared the breakfast before sunup, and the women were standing outside the lodges of the Bear smiling broadly by the time for the morning prayer to Grandfather the Sun. Treated thus, the Bear relatives were inspired to become proud and dignified, subduing their inherent Bear antics.

By the time the four Bear "bridesmaids" were coming single file from the Bear camp to the Eagle camp carrying the washed utensils, the Eagle people had begun to prepare the dinner, but they stopped, and the women and men went to greet the women from the Bear with great smiles and laugh crinkles about their eyes.

The women in the lodges of the Bear had been making clothing to exchange on the wedding day, and the men in the lodges of the Eagle had been getting the horses together. Each relative must give a horse to the relatives of the Bear, and they chose their best horses. If a greedy, wretched Eagle relative came leading an inferior horse up to the place where the head Eagle men were accepting the gift horses, they would smile and graciously take the end of the flintlike, ugly rawhide rope, and the greedy one might become suspicious and leave, believing that he had overstepped himself after all. But when he had gone, the men would call *wah-tsde-pia'n,* the town crier, and have him lead the horse away, take off the old rawhide rope, tap him with it, and watch him run back to the lodge of the donor.

When the horses were collected, a donor, as if in afterthought, might bring forth a beautiful trade blanket and throw it on the horse's back, another would take off the old rawhide bridle and replace it with one made of horsehair or buffalo hair. Another might fasten little hawkbells to the headstall, and others fasten an eagle feather, not a sacred one, to the tail of his gift.

The Little Ones say that when the smoke from the camp fires rose high, like prayer-smoke, and the odors of cooking permeated the air, and the camp dogs replete with cuttings from the meat lay with their bellies distended and in fitful dreams, the horses seemed to be filled with pride. Ordinarily tranquil, these horses would sense something, and dance nervously at the hitching rail, rump-crowding each other, laying back their ears at each other, whinnying with excitement. Then when the wolflike cry of the *wah-tsde-pia'n,* the town crier, would come from the direction of the Bear encampment, they would raise their heads, distend their nostrils, and gaze all in that direction, with the prairie breeze playing with their manes. They would stand frozen as the cry of the town crier fell into diminuendo and he told the Bear relatives that the horses would now be led over to them as gifts from the happy Eagle relatives.

Albeit the town crier's instructions from the parents and relatives of Bloody Hands might have been imbued with family pride, since a great number and such beautiful horses would be given to the family and relatives of The Light, it was not the warriors who led the horses over, but nieces and nephews and cousins, some of the older boys leading as many as three. Here was a picture to swell the heart of both families: the horses wide-nostriled and high-headed, with dark sweat on their flanks, one line of people awaiting their gift, and the other line opposite them watching, filled with self-esteem.

Sometimes the horses were not accepted, and the donors must send over more, or refuse and thus end arrangements, but Bloody Hands was of great report, who killed as cleanly as the falcon, the sacred symbol of the tribe, and came home like the falcon swiftly and on sound wing. There might be a greedy relative who was not pleased with his horse, but the parents of the girl turned their ears from him or even compensated him with a horse of their own. Bloody Hands could have bought any girl of the Place-of-the-Many-Swans with no horses, if his parents and other relatives as well as the girl suddenly had no pride.

Ahead of the front horse, which was the best of the herd, walked the man who carried the Swan standard. Behind the horses would be the Eagle women carrying the dinner.

When they reached the line of Bear relatives, the horses were handed over to them and tied to a specially prepared hitching rail. The horses were tied with just ordinary rawhide lariats now. These replaced the precious, ceremonial eight-strand lariats made from the neck hair of the buffalo bull. They used the ceremonial lariats only to lead the horses to the Bear relatives and back to the Eagle with the bride, and for other ceremonials. They were very highly valued, since there were only a few men and women in the whole tribe who could make them.

The food was taken over by the "bridesmaids." Then they feasted, but both families ate separately.

Now the parents and relatives of Bloody Hands went back to their camp, and there they would await the single file of "bridesmaids" with the cleaned utensils, and from their actions get the decision about keeping the horses.

Back in the thicket of redbud there were five horses held in reserve, and when the Eagle camp saw the girls coming with the utensils, they guessed the decision; The Light was beautiful and strong and had two beautiful younger sisters. They guessed that soon they would see the horses being led back to their camp. They knew that of all the young men of the tribe, their son was the most worthy, but they were dealing with the Bear. The Bear would bluff and gamble, but the gamble was small, since the Bear also knew the Eagle; of all the birds he was the most dignified and the most majestic and proud, and they knew that the Eagle would send more horses, such was his pride.

The horses were led back, not so spirited now, since the excitement of the wolf-crying of the town crier had ceased and the tenseness evaporated. An hour later the horses were led back to the Bear, but this time with five additional ones from the redbud thicket, and this time they were accepted, and the Bear had shown the Eagle that they placed great value on their daughter The Light, and the Eagle had shown the Bear that they valued their own pride and The Light very highly.

The parents of The Light now called the names of their two head relatives, the father calling his two first; and they took their choice of the horses, each taking one; then they called the head men of the wife's family, and they took two horses. The names of the other relatives chosen for the wedding ceremonies were called, including the bridesmaids, and there was a horse for each one.

The parents and head men led by Sun-on-His-Wings came to thank the parents and relatives of The Light, and all knew that the wedding would take place the next day, the fourth day from the day the first food was carried over from the boy's relatives.

This was a dramatic moment, when the horses were accepted and the Eagle had come over to thank the Bear. And again the older women would start their "joy-crying," and soon it developed into a chorus of mourning, broken by sobs. Everyone waited patiently and with deep courtesy until the keening had ceased, then the family and relatives of The Light served a feast to the family and relatives of Bloody Hands.

The next day was the fourth and last day, the day of the wedding. The little nieces and cousins and nephews of the Bloody Hands family rose early and took presents to the bride—only these and no one else. There were three more horses led to the bride's lodge, and other gifts, chiefly rare traders' trinkets. Those who brought gifts on this last morning were feasted by the bride's family and were told to carry away all that was left over from the feast.

The sister of Bloody Hands was the counterpart to the aunt of The Light who was the head "bridesmaid," and the four counterparts of the four bridesmaids came over to the bride's lodge where she was being dressed, and as the sister exchanged clothes with The Light, the three others from the Eagle exchanged clothes with the three other "bridesmaids." By now the Bear had built a large lodge thirty by forty feet for the bride and her attendants.

The Light was then dressed meticulously, with all the love for such ceremony which the women always had left over from making dolls for their little girls and dressing their husbands and brothers for the dances. The finest of original and trade garments were placed upon her, and trade earrings were placed in her slit ears, and special Otoe moccasins placed on her feet.

The Light and her maids were dressed much alike now as they came out of the lodge and lined up with presents in front of them. These presents might be special cuts of buffalo or wapiti or deer, or trade gadgets, and they represented the prizes for the race from the Eagle camp to the Bear. The participants in the wedding on the Eagle side would line up for the race for the prizes. The brother of The Light fired a gun, and the race was on. The shot, or the signal before they had fusils, sent the young men and women fleeing across the space between the camps, the girls' hair flying with their buckskin skirts or their traders' shrouding bouncing from their knees. The young men laughed as though in jest and bantered each other in this puerile play, but at the same time running with their best speed. The jesting and bantering was a smoke screen for their manly pride, since they knew well that one or more of the girls could come in ahead of them at the finish line. Feigned merriment and lightheartedness made this possibility acceptable.

At the Bear camp there would be those designated to judge the race, and they would apportion the prizes according to value to the winner, and on down to the last one. There would be no argument, since the people in the Bear camp so designated made the irrevocable decision as to which runner was first, second, third, etc. The "brides-maids" went back to the Eagle camp with the runners, preceded by the Swan standard.

The Light was taken to the large lodge, and there in the center of it she was circled by her "bridesmaids" and their counterparts from the Eagle camp, and they exchanged clothing.

Soon the wedding feast was served by the "bridesmaids" and their counterparts, and a special buffalo robe was placed on the ground in the center of the large lodge and places prepared for The Light and her retinue and Bloody Hands and his retinue. When all was ready, the parents of Bloody Hands summoned *wah-tsde-pia'n* and instructed him to go along the ways of the camp and call their son in his loud, quavering, wolflike chant.

From the interior of his lodge, where he was waiting with shy solemnity, Bloody Hands heard his name come after the long wolf cry. His attendants, who were his brothers or cousins, lifted the buffalo-skin door and signaled for him to come. He deliberately threw his robe over his naked back, after rising with great solemnity. He had been dressed with great care by his mother or sister. He wore his special moccasins and the gypsum-whitened buckskin leggings, with the exaggerated fringes of the Eagle gens, which represented the tibia and tarsal feathers of the golden eagle. He wore all the things indicating his many *o-do'n,* his war honors. His roach quivered as he set off to the marriage lodge followed by his attendants.

When he arrived at the big lodge, his uncle pointed to a place by The Light. He took a sharp, coyote look at her, almost unnoticeable from the door of the lodge, then looked no more. This was the first time he had seen his bride. She sat with lowered head and only tasted of the food when her father's sister touched her on the shoulder. This was the signal for the feast to begin, but neither Bloody Hands nor The Light ate, but sat side by side in all their finery, and looked straight ahead of them at the floor beyond their food. But they were now man and wife.

After the feast the people struck their temporary lodges and went back to their homes, but Bloody Hands and The Light stayed longer. Then he went to his lodge, especially erected at his parents' camp for the occasion, and sat waiting. Soon his attendants came carrying The Light in a robe. They lifted the buffalo skin which was the door, and she entered. Later the two young people alone in a lodge, who had never seen each other before, began to steal glances at each other.

The next morning, there was a feast, during which the two uncles advised them about married life and its duties. This feast was given by the parents of The Light at the Bear camp. After the feast, The Light was dressed by the Eagle females, and they attempted to outdo the dressing for the wedding of yesterday. They put her on a horse covered with beaded robes, and she and Bloody Hands rode to the Bear camp followed by attendants on horseback. This time, when they arrived at the Bear camp and after another feast, they would be given a lodge, and this would be their permanent home, among The Light's people. However, Bloody Hands remained Eagle and The Light remained Bear, though their sons and daughters would be Eagle.

The parents of The Light had watched the alert, graceful son of the Eagle, and they had talked much with Uncle Standing Bear. The Light had two sisters, and they too were straight and tall and quick-walking. Would it be better to marry them with young men who were not heroes and were not as tall and handsome as Bloody Hands and had no *o-do'n?* How, they conjectured, could there be stronger and handsomer grandchildren than those that would come from the loins of Bloody Hands, and in whom would they have a better chance to live many moons after they, the grandparents, were in Spiritland than in the bodies and minds and souls of such grandchildren, and who could make the medicine of the Osages stronger than these many grandchildren who would come from their three daughters and Bloody Hands?

323

Standing Bear could bring to his mind no argument against such logic, though he sat for a long time with his eyes shut, thinking, while the parents waited.

The sisters had been present in their wedding finery, had eaten the feast, and had received as many gifts as The Light, including a fine horse each, so there was no problem.

The girls were summoned, and the older women of the relatives dressed them in their wedding finery, which was almost exactly like that of The Light; then they led them to the lodge of Bloody Hands and The Light. The clean killing and courage of the falcon and the beauty and strength of the Eagle and the courage of the Bear would be handed down by Bloody Hands and the Bear sisters, to make future warriors tall and handsome and courageous, and the medicine of the Little Ones would remain strong and they would attain old age.

One of the things necessary to symbolize honor among women the uncles had suggested to Bloody Hands during their advice-giving. He must supply his wife with a burden strap. He must do this ceremonially, so that there would be sanctity attached to it.

What the *wah-hopeh* was to the warrior, the *mo'n-sha-ko'n,* the burden strap was to the woman. This was a strap for carrying wood and impedimenta on the march, and could be used like a tumpline. It was a mark of the woman who lived in the traditional manner and symbolized the virtues and the prerogatives of the woman.

It was made from uncured buffalo, and was a strap, neatly wound about a core like a hank of yarn when not in use. Each woman who was highly respected had a ceremonial one, which her husband had made for her ceremonially, and this was never actually used, but as a symbol was hung by the side of the entrance to the lodge; on the left if her father was *Tzi-Sho,* and right if *Hunkah.* The ceremony of the strap was number three in the seven holy ceremonies.

But the burden strap was not sufficient to satisfy completely the warrior dignity of Bloody Hands; no matter how elaborate the ceremony of the cutting of the buffalo hide and the making of the burden strap, there was still the matter of the spider, the symbol of the Grand *Hunkah,* the original Isolated Earth People.

Only the eldest daughter of the first-class families might have the stylized spider tattooed on the back of each hand, as did The Light, since such tattooing was highly ceremonial and took many horses and perhaps robes or blankets to the specialist tattoo artist. He must have been a consummate artist, since his figures were perfect, and the handling of a wing-bone tattoo needle demanded the highest technique. But some of the first-class families who had many horses or many trade gadgets could afford to have the hands of the other daughters tattooed as well, if there were not too many.

Certainly the wives of a great warrior like Bloody Hands must be honored among the people. He talked with the parents of the girls, and soon the tattoo artist was called in to perform the ceremony.

He cleared the lodge of all the others except for the two women who were to be attendants and sponsors. The attendant women had to assure the artist that they were not in their periods, and they must leave their babies with relatives, since the nursing of a baby when the ceremony was in progress would not be propitious.

He placed charcoal from the sacred redbud on the back of the hand, then pricked out the geometrical conventionalized spider, and thus the charcoal was pushed into the epidermis where the prick was made, and this would last forever. After the spider was formed, the artist brushed the charcoal into his beaded buckskin bag, looking with frowns toward the buffalo-hide door of the lodge, to assure himself that there was nothing to mar the sanctity of the ceremony.

The second sister of The Light, White Feather, had flinched and cried out, but unfortunately not in the tone and the traditional expression allowed when the prick of the bone needle or the trader's steel needle caused pain. The cry conventionalized was *"a-tha-tha."* The artist and the two attendants looked at her intently, apparently believing that something might happen, and White Feather herself looked down frightened.

When the charcoal had been brushed back into the artist's bag and when he examined the punctures, there was a hiatus, where the punctures showed dimly.

And it was said that White Feather could never thereafter cook cornmeal without burning it. All of her life she had to leave her cooking of meal and say, "Sister, you must do this now, before it scorches."

It would seem strange that a daughter of the Bear should carry the name White Feather, if it were not well known that the swan, whose feathers are white, was the symbol of the sub-gens of the Black Bear.

Now the wives of the mighty Bloody Hands had their burden straps hanging on the inside of the lodge, to the right, which was the south side, the *Hunkah* side; and they now had the spider, the symbol of the Grand *Hunkah,* tattooed on the back of each hand, the mark of high honor; and especially did White Feather, the second daughter, walk proudly under the two honors, and was almost assured of domestic tranquility and of giving to the Little Ones warriors as swift and courageous as the falcon. Both the trumpeter swan and the black spider are effective guardians of their homes, the one with her punishing wings and her warning hisses and the other by smearing the faces of the most ferocious warriors and hunters with her web-house, because "where I build my lodge, all things came to it and broke their necks therein."

And thus the women with the spider on the back of their hands were holy guardians of the lodges and symbols of protective motherhood. Through them the Little Ones would attain old age and create warriors who would keep the medicine strong.

31. Little Stars from the Sky Lodge

THE BABIES WERE little stars from Spiritland, and as they grew older and when they became persons, they had to have names, but when they first came to earth (ontogeny recapitulates phylogeny), they were from the sky and they were even nameless and represented the old tribal *ga-ni-tha* before organization, even though their natal cries were not cries of fear of the tragedies and uncertainties of life but the prayer-crying to *Wah'Kon-Tah* in the tribal tradition. They had been taught this prayer before they came to earth. This was the infant chant to Grandfather the Sun—to his light; if a night birth, a cry to the Moon Woman. The Osages avoided night births if possible.

The expectant mother had a lodge to herself, and her mother and one other woman attended her. There was always moss that had been gathered from the sandstone, which had been left to dry as an absorbent, and there was the skin of certain ducks and Canada geese, as well as rabbit fur and several kinds of stimulants made from buds of the linden and the bark of the wild cherry. There was always hot water and two posts of willow to be grasped and a pit for the afterbirth.

But sometimes there was false presentation or prolonged labor, and the attendants called in the husband and the wife's family, since the wife and her husband were living in the village or the lodge-cluster of the wife's family, and after consultation the husband must go to the *Wah-Sha-She,* the Water People, if he happened to be *Tzi-Sho* or

327

sub-*Hunkah,* in order to obtain the otter medicine of that gens of the *Wah-Sha-She,* and lay before the man of that gens who claimed "otter medicine" acceptable gifts.

He was not exactly a medicine man, but of the Otter gens, and he claimed otter medicine, which meant that he could gain favors by praying to *Wah'Kon-Tah* through the otter, whose inane playfulness had inspired the medicine, just as his artful swimming had inspired prayer to him in time of spate on the Smoky Waters when the Little Ones found themselves on the north bank and possibly hard pressed by the Sac and Foxes.

The man with otter medicine would come dressed in clout of otter skin and with a long otter skin hanging down his back attached to his shoulders. He would carry a mysterious buckskin bag, highly decorated with trade beads or with flattened porcupine quills in his left hand and an eagle feather in his right hand.

He would walk with utmost dignity and seriousness, as men of mystery must do, then he would stop at the door of the lodge frowning and haughtily motion everyone to leave. He would enter and squat and wait for a spasm from the form on the bear hide. When the form began to writhe and sing a scarcely audible song of pain, he would rise and walk around her chanting to the otter, and when the writhing stopped, he would walk over into the farthest edge of the lodge and, sitting down, draw up his legs about his neck in the posture of a normal fetus, chanting all the time. Suddenly, with the grace of an otter, he would unwind and walk again around the form on the bearskin, then, with a feather, fan away the evil that possessed the poor woman. With another very quick and graceful otter movement, he would glide to the door with his head low and arms placed like those of a fetus, and bent as far forward as possible he would butt the buffalo-skin flap of the door with it and emerge. The lodge being the symbolical womb, once out of it he would cry like an infant with eye to Grandfather the Sun.

Here the man with the otter medicine had prayed for the aid of the otter who in its play makes slick slides down the banks of streams and glides down them into the water head first and with front legs tucked under him.

After the little star came to earth, he must be tended carefully, and cherished, since he must be made ready within the next few years for "personhood," when he would be recognized by *Wah'Kon-Tah* and given both a sky name and an earth name. His parents must have a board fashioned, with a hood of flint buffalo skin to protect his head from the wind. From this hood there must be little things that tinkled in the breeze, or downy feathers that moved with the air's slightest breath.

By the time Bloody Hands and The Light's first baby came, there might have been such *wah-don-skas* as trade sewing thimbles attached to the head of the baby board, and these would be considered wonderful objects of interest to the just focusing eyes of the baby, but, of course, there were the long, elegant tail-feathers of the scissortail flycatcher, the tail-feathers of the scarlet tanager or the cardinal, the latter two touched by *Wah'Kon-Tah*'s dawn.

But he would be an Eagle like his father, and his baby board could not be made of cedar or pine, even though cedar was a tribal symbol of long life and even though the black bear liked to walk in cedar groves. The cedar baby board could be used only by the *Tzi-Sho Wa'no'n,* the war gens of the Grand *Tzi-Sho,* because their symbol the thunder lived there, among the cedars. Bloody Hands and The Light must place their baby on a board made of poplar or birch, and though it would not have the sacredness of a cedar, the symbol of life everlasting, it would have the cross in the middle under the baby's sacrum, and would have the Eagle stylized symbols in beads or flattened quills. This cradleboard was called *o-lo-psha,* follow-trail-of-animals. The cradleboard was the beginning of the Road of Life, the true trail such as the animals make to water and food; for the animals have instinct and go straight to water and food.

On the top there would be a loop of wapiti hide, and the board could be either hung up in a tree while The Light was busy or carried on her back, the village world passing in view of the large, black eyes of the infant as the fields and the trees and the plowmen and the herds pass suddenly into view of the passenger on the back vestibule of a train.

The absorbent moss kept him comfortable until The Light could change it, and all day he looked upon a retreating world like a diurnal owl, neither crying nor whimpering; and when he was hungry The Light could feel his impatience and sling his board forward into her lap as she sat with back against a tree.

From the beginning he could cling to the two forefingers of Bloody Hands with owllike unconcern, but to toss him or hold him above the head or swing him was taboo, since he was an Eagle. The Little Old Men of the Eagle gens cannot give a reason for this, but it was a taboo of great importance and might possibly have had something to do with an experience with eaglets, since no other gens seemed to have this taboo.

About the time the baby stumbled about over the earth like a centuries-ago arboreal ancestor's first days on the ground, or like a veritable nestling eaglet fallen to the ground, Bloody Hands would pick him up every morning after the chant to Grandfather and carry him down to the river amid the running boys and adult men on their gleeful way in only their breechclouts. Here at the edge of the favorite swimming hole, he would let his breechclout fall and throw the naked little boy onto his back. There he would stand silently gazing across the water to the opposite bank, then with the quick movements of the otter he would dive, then come up quickly and look about. There a little way off would be either the brown bottom or the top of his son's shaven head, but no bubbles. He would rush to him and hold him out of the water, while the little one with flushed face would rub his eyes with his little fists. He might do this several times, or only once a morning for several mornings, then gradually build up until the little boy's face might light up with pleasure.

And since he would be an Eagle, his head would be shaved except for a fringe all around it, his head resembling that of a monk. This was the sign of the Eagle, and referred to a mottled eagle sitting on a round head-shaped rock in the marshes, which the Eagle gens referred to as the Little Rock. He possibly used it as a hunting station, and the shaven head of the little Eagle gens boys symbolized that rock, and the fringe of hair around the head symbolized the certain type of water weeds surrounding it.

He would wear his hair this way until he was about ten summers, then he could wear a roach like all adult Osages, and by that time he would have become a person; and before that he had been named so that *Wah'Kon-Tah* could take note of him. He and the two brothers following him and his first three sisters would receive formal names, two each, one for the sky and one for the earth. There would be common kinship names for the first three sons and first three daughters of the Eagle, but all others would be designated by the names given the third son and third daughter, which would be, respectively, "White Wing" for the son and "Eagle Woman" for the daughter. Thus all boys after the third would be called "White Wing" and all girls after the third "Eagle Woman" until named formally. But they would not go through the naming ceremony. After living during the time of his infancy with not even the status of a "person," and without a name except that given all the first sons or except one given to him by his playmates from some incident or characteristic, he might suddenly have three names: one for the sky, one for the earth, and one informal one. His sky name would be of the stars or pertaining to the heavens, his earth name since he was of the *Hunkah* Grand Division would be gentile and refer to some characteristic or habit or action of the golden eagle, but the informal one given from incident or characteristic might stay with him all of his life.

When Bloody Hands was ready for the naming of his first son, he sent for the *shoka,* the official messenger of his gens. The *shoka* was sent on errands and to deliver messages, and his status was not a high one but important enough. Each gens had one, and the Grand *Hunkah* and the Grand *Tzi-Sho* each had one. As a matter of fact, he might even be a Pawnee or a Padouca slave whom the *Ni-Wa-The,* Life-Giver of the Gentle *Tzi-Sho,* had saved from the keening, vindictive women or from trade with the Heavy Eyebrows.

When he arrived, Bloody Hands placed before him a robe and a pipe, and the latter would become his badge of office in the naming ceremony. He then ordered him to go bring the Little Old Men of the Eagle gens, those of the Star-That-Came-to-Earth gens of the *Wah-Sha-She* and those of the Gentle *Tzi-Sho.* It was from these two latter gentes that the Grand *Hunkah* and the Grand *Tzi-Sho* were chosen, and they had special honors, and here the two gentes would represent the sky and the earth. The Eagle gens of Bloody Hands guided the people to the earth from the Sky Lodge; the people had only to follow the golden eagle down to the red-oak tree of genesis. These two gentes—the Star-That-Came-to-Earth and the Gentle *Tzi-Sho*—were the peace gens representing the peace of the Sky Lodge.

The Little Old Men of these three gentes assembled at the lodge of Bloody Hands and The Light, and here Bloody Hands stood before these older men with diffidence. He was a great warrior, and there had even been songs made about his *o-do'n,* and even the Little Old Men respected him, but still he was abashed and uncertain in the presence of older men. He told them why he had called them, as if they didn't already know. When he had happily finished, the chieftains of these gentes turned to the *shoka* and told him to call the heads of the Panther, the Black Bear, and the Wapiti of the sub-*Hunkah;* the heads of the Fish People, the Deer People, and the Fresh-Water-Mussel gentes of the *Wah-Sha-She* divisions of the *Hunkah,* and the heads of the *Tzi-Sho Wa'no'n,* symbolizing the sun and called the Elder; the war gens of the *Tzi-Sho* Grand Division, the Carriers-of-the-Heavenly-Bodies, and the Buffalo gentes of the *Tzi-Sho.* The *shoka* then took his sacred pipe, the stem of which was made from a sapling of the sacred elder, and went to inform the Little Old Man of the Eagle gens who has been appointed by Bloody Hands to act as *xoka,* the "priest" or initiator and moderator of the ceremonies.

The Little Old Men of Bloody Hands' gens assembled at his lodge early the next morning, just before Grandfather rose to make the eastern horizon red, and the *xoka* began his almost endless song about the sacred articles with which he would be clothed. He would have his assistant paint the palms of his hands red, then he would step out and wait for the sun to paint the east. He would then smear his face with the red on his hands when he reached a certain line in his song, after he had raised his palms to the dawn, thus simulating the capture of the sacred red dawn and transferring it to his own face. When a certain line was reached in the song, the assistant took up a fluffy feather from under the tail of the eagle, and held it above the *xoka's* head, then he turned and placed the palm of his hands in a bowl made from white ash and smeared them with the buffalo fat therein,

332

and at certain lines in the song rubbed this melted tallow on the *xoka*'s head. As the *xoka* sang on, the assistant was ready with a string of beads made of crinoid stems with holes punched in them and supporting a pendant made from the fresh-water mussel shell. It was carved round and in its pearly whiteness represented the sun at midday, and was, of course, the symbol of the Mussel-Shell gens of the *Wah-Sha-She*. At the proper time in the song the assistant hung the string of crinoid stems with their pendant around the neck of *xoka*, and he wore it as a gorget.

All these things had great importance. First, the dawn red was sacred since it was a manifestation of Grandfather and hence of *Wah'Kon-Tah* and represented incidentally the Grand *Tzi-Sho* since the sun was the symbol of one of its gentes. The soft eagle feather from under the tail of the golden eagle, being soft and fluffy, represented peace, and was symbolical of the plume-shaped brightness that appears at the edge of the sun as it rises, and, of course, represented the gens of Bloody Hands and his son. The third, the tallow, was symbolical of a plentitude of good food since the tallow with which *xoka* was anointed must come from the young bull buffalo and was the fat taken from the muscle on the right (the *Hunkah* side) of the spine. The buffalo was *Tzi-Sho,* but one of the extra, very important gens, the universal giver of food and life. The last, the gorget made from the mussel shell, was symbolical of the sun and life everlasting.

Hence the dawn red, the plume-shaped light, the buffalo tallow, and the gorget represented the sun and the buffalo, without which there would be no Little Ones. Also, each division was represented: the Grand *Tzi-Sho* by the sun; sub-*Hunkah,* by the eagle plume; and the *Wah-Sha-She* by the mussel-shell gorget; the buffalo representing the Grand *Hunkah*. What could be more propitious for the little son of Bloody Hands?

Before leading the way to the Lodge of Mystery, the *xoka* wrapped a buffalo robe about himself with the hair out, and took along his pipe. There could be no successful ceremonial prayers without the pipe. On his way to the Lodge of Mystery he stopped to sing the Footstep Song, which has to do with his ceremonial approach.

The ceremonial was intricate and long lasting, since the Little Old

Men who created it wanted to be sure that the child about to become a person and brought to the attention of *Wah'Kon-Tah* was given every possible chance to attain old age. Each gens had a different pattern, but again, like all gentile variations from the tribal, they were fundamentally the same: some simpler than others, and some of labyrinthine intricacy.

In the Lodge of Mystery the gentile leaders were seated according to their divisions, the *Tzi-Sho* on the north or the left from orientation, and the *Hunkah* on the south or right. The gens to which Bloody Hands belonged, the Eagle, were seated in the east end of the Lodge with the *shoka* near them. Here were seated Bloody Hands and The Light.

The *xoka* called the *shoka* to him and, in order, sent a fee of a robe or a trade blanket to the head of each gens present. Along with the fee, he sent a plume to the Gentle *Tzi-Sho,* and corn to the Buffalo and cedar to the Star-That-Came-to-Earth, and a vessel of water to the Fish People. As each head received his fee, he recited his symbol's *wi-gi-e* or "recitation," and this seemed unending, but the ceremony must be meticulously carried through to obviate adversity in the later life of the little boy. The Little Old Men had covered every eventuality. *Wah'Kon-Tah* had many ways of showing his displeasure.

During the long, long recitation about each gens life symbol, the ones not reciting would lower their heads and shut their eyes, their inevitable posture of supreme animal patience. They were of the company but still alone, each an individual who must not move or talk for fear of sacrilege or breach of courtesy, but spiritually free to visit many fields of action, even to recall their own *o-do'n.* Each representative of the several gentes had his face painted with dawn red and he sat with legs crossed, with his feet drawn up under his thighs. The little boy, after watching solemnly the giant men decorated and painted and after hours of listening to the monotony of their soporific recitations, would drop his head into his mother's lap.

Finally the monotonous chant-droning would cease, and the *shoka* would lift the little boy into his arms and lay him in the arms of the leader of each gens. Some of them would anoint his forehead, body, arms, lips, and nose with water and rub over them cedar leaves; and

334

others, like the Buffalo, would touch his lips with ground corn as well as with water and cedar leaves, the water for cleanliness and for washing away disease and any evil that might interfere with the attainment of old age, the cedar symbolical of life everlasting, and the corn symbolical of a plentitude of food in his lodge all his life. Lastly he was blessed by the chieftain of his own gens, the Eagle, then taken back to The Light, and she placed the boy at her side as she chose between two willow sticks which the *xoḳa* held in front of her. These sticks each represented a name of the Eagle gens, and she must choose the one she wished for her son. This was an extremely important moment, and all eyes were on her, but she in her serious absorption, forgot her woman bashfulness. She looked at these sticks as if she might fathom every possibility of the good and evil influence of these Eagle names. One stick represented He-Who-Travels-Above, referring to the eagle in wide-foraging circles, far above the earth, and the other represented the name Holes-in-His-Wings. She wondered distressed in the deep silence of the lodge.

He-Who-Travels-Above was a glorious name—gliding in circles just under the eye of Grandfather, being envied by all earth-bound ones, then coming out of the eye of Grandfather to kill. But was this calling undue attention to a little boy who had no *o-do'n?* Would this name focus the attention of jealousy on her son? Would *Wah'-Kon-Tah* think him like one back from the war movement who boasts about *o-do'n* he doesn't have? What evil might come from such a name of glory, before her son could grow into a warrior and earn such a name?

Holes-in-His-Wings, on the other hand, was a humble name. With this name he would not be the focus of jealous eyes, and *Wah'Kon-Tah* might smile upon his humbleness and remember him. Maybe some day when he went on the war movement, a Pawnee might learn his name, and with great contempt look down upon him, and her son then, with the courage and the swiftness he would have, certainly could strike the unready, sneering Pawnee down, since he would expect little from such a name. It was not really a name of humility nor did it indicate an unbeautiful or crippled eagle; it related only to a missing primary feather which looked like a hole when the bird was circling high. He could still fly under the eye of Grandfather, but his humble name would not draw the jealousy of others and *Wah'Kon-Tah* might have pity on him.

She quickly touched the stick which represented the name Holes-in-His-Wings. Someday the name He-Who-Travels-Above might also be given her son as a special war name. She felt sure this would happen, and her face lighted.

The Light was back in the present now and she became very shy and uncertain, and as she walked behind the *shoka* to the place where the *xoka* sat awaiting her, she looked at her feet and the hard earth of the lodge floor.

When she came to the *xoka,* she spread her buffalo robe before him and sat on the opposite side from him. The head end of the robe she placed to the east and the tail to the west. Down the middle she had drawn a red line, and this was the path of Grandfather the Sun as he moved from east to west. In the middle of the robe and on the red path-line was a little red disk, and this represented Grandfather himself.

The leg skin, both front and rear, was still attached to the beautifully tanned robe, and each front leg skin and each rear leg skin was colored red, and the front one represented Grandfather dawn-red and the hind-ones his sunset-red.

She had worked hard on this robe in anticipation, and she had been very careful to make it perfect. She had decorated it with flattened porcupine quills, eschewing trade beads in case they might not be wholly pleasing to *Wah'Kon-Tah*. She had studied the web of the garden spider and acorn cups and veins of the leaves, and she had shut her eyes and turned them to Grandfather the Sun at midday, so that she might have some pattern for decoration suggested to her. Her decorations on the robe were pleasing and she was happy, but she kept her eyes on her lap as she listened to the *xoka* giving his advice.

She must ever keep the red line down the parting of her hair always fresh, he warned. This represented the path which Grandfather took each day across the heavens. She must cover herself and her son, who had just become a person, with the robe each night as a symbol of the buffalo who protects and makes possible the life of the Little Ones, who gave them the four colors of corn. She must cut a willow stick for support on the slimy lake bottom and wade into the waters at the Place-of-the-Many-Swans, and there take the roots of the sacred lotus and feed her boy so that he would grow strong. She must immediately on next Planting Moon plant seven sacred hills of corn, one grain in the first, two in the second, and three in the third, and so on until she had placed seven grains in the seventh hill. This would be sacred corn, and with this corn she must feast her gens along with squash, lotus root, and sacred humprib.

Every head was bowed and every eye shut with that animal patience that is almost like hibernation. There was no stir until the *xoka* said, "Hauh," and The Light went back to her robe seat, her heart singing. The members of the gentes arose and smiled toward Bloody Hands and The Light, and each one said something pleasant as he left.

There was obviously a practical reason why each child was not named with such ceremony, only six of them, the three first boys and the three first girls. Not only did Bloody Hands have to supply the fees for each gens represented, but he had to give a horse and other things to the *xoka,* and he had to give extra presents for the advice which the *xoka* gave The Light across the robe. There would be a matter of twelve horses and twelve trade blankets or robes for the *xokas* within a matter of a few years, not to mention the fees for the several gentes, which in some of the gentile ceremonials numbered three gens from each division of the tribe.

But now The Light had reached the pinnacle of respectability, with her tattooed spiders on her hands, the red line down the middle of her hair as a parting, and a husband who in passing drew the eyes of all like the smoke of the prairie fire. And her son named with a humble name. The second son or perhaps the first daughter would be White Feather's.

THE NEW LONG KNIVES

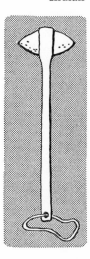

"To the white man, especially to the Anglo-American, the Indian was primarily a warrior, a fighting man, an implacable foe. The Indian's economy of life, his philosophy, his soul, were secondary and of little concern to the Anglo-American."—Walter Prescott Webb, *The Great Plains*.

32. Mauve Shadows

THE DISINTEGRATION OF THE TRIBE was in a seed within the tribal organization itself and the self-esteem of each individual. The urge to
attain glory as a warrior and to be noticed and honored, the intense
urge to be wise and pontifical and make statements of wisdom, and
the desire to be able to give generously made each man of little or no
standing in the tribe a perfect dupe and tool in the hands of the
shrewd European or American enterprisers.

There were twenty-four gentes, and each chieftain's dream was to
become a *Hunkah* or *Tzi-Sho* grand chief, and all the elements in
his makeup which had contributed toward becoming noticed as a
warrior or as an orator or a generous giver made of him a half-forged
tool for the trader, the United States commissioners, the military
leaders, the politicians. For a few brief hours of buzzy, personal glory
the chieftain might sell his whole tribe into bondage.

The Little Ones had been like a flock of birds or a herd of animals
in their simultaneous reaction to danger and in their cohesion in
attack or defense, yet the gentes enjoyed latitude and were protective
of their independence. Each gens had a special pride in its symbol
and a self-esteem that was almost a perpetual boast. And the seed of
disintegration that was in the tribe even before the European came
was certainly manifested by the separation from the Little Ones of
the Konzas and the Omahas and perhaps the Quapaws. According
to tribal memory, these separations were not due to economic neces-

sity in the lush woodland-prairie-plains as one might guess, but to gentile vanity and independence. The Down-Below-People, a physical division called the Little Osages, were already in the initial stages of separation, and already had their own principal chief, who might belong to any gens although the Eagle and the Bear seemed to have predominated, and the Osages-of-the-Oaks at the Three Forks, the physical division, called the Upland-Forest-People, who had a chief chosen for them and accepted him.

Without the inherent vanity and ambition and the gentile independence, not even a Chouteau could have effected the removal of half the tribe to the Verdigris River.

The creed of the Little Ones seemed to be Life, inasmuch as they were ever concerned as a tribe in prolonging it as a species of religious tenet. Old age was wisdom, and in their rituals everything had reference to the hope, the struggle, the necessity, the imperative urge to attain old age and thereby serve *Wah'Kon-Tah*'s purpose. In order to attain old age and carry out *Wah'Kon-Tah*'s law, they had to have valor, and this was an obsession. They were sometimes as afraid of lacking valor, as they were of having *Wah'Kon-Tah* "take away their remaining days," and from all the "little people" of the earth who had offered themselves to the Little Old Men, to serve as tribal symbols, they chose the hawk as the symbol of tribal valor, ruthlessness, swiftness in war, courage in attack, and artfulness in retreat, and the longevity which they believed he enjoyed.

In order for both the individual and the tribe to attain old age, the tribe must live and prevail, and there must be children, and old age wisdom. Therefore the hawk, children, and wise old men became sacred, and when there were children in every lodge and food in every lodge, and the wise old men in the long Lodge of Mystery, and the warriors came back wild-eyed and hoarse from singing of victory, the Little Ones "walked in the light of day."

Now there was the cloud that would dim the sacred light of day. It didn't come from the West, the Cliffs, whence came the storm clouds and the night which periodically and rhythmically devoured the light of day, the direction of "the enemy" and death, but from the east from across the Big Waters, the Mississippi.

342

Bearded men had already begun to make their "half-faced camps" in the domain of the Little Ones, far from the cabins and the forts and the missions of the Heavy Eyebrows and the *I-Spa-Tho*. They boasted of their freedom and they seemed to behave as if they had won part of the world from the King of England and bought the other half from Napoleon.

Most of these hairy men were then building their "half-faced camps" and their cabins along the Arkansas and the Three Forks, the Neosho and the Verdigris, and Makes-Tracks-Far-Away and Arrow-Going-Home, *Wa-Tcha-Wa-Ha* and son-in-law of Pawhuska leaders of the Little Ones now called Osages-of-the-Oaks, would take the horses and oxen of these people and burn their crops and their cabins and their stills and kill the men, taking the women and children captive.

Stern faced Long Knives would talk with the gentile leaders away from the Place-of-the-Many-Swans, and if their own party was a large one, warn them severely about things of which they knew nothing. They would tell them about people being killed on the Arkansas and near the Three Forks, and the chieftains would say, "Ho, ho that is bad, but we do not know about this thing." The new Long Knives would become very angry, and spit tobacco juice to one side, and swear that they would "git even," and " 'iffen they had their way there wouldn't be a goddam Injun lef in the country nohow."

And now the Americans were having their trouble with the Little Ones, just as the French and the Spaniards had before them. Tribes friendly to them were being attacked by the Little Ones, and Dr. John Sibley, agent for Indian affairs of the Territory of Orleans at Natchitoches was busy writing to General Henry Dearborn, secretary of war in Washington, from the time of the taking over of the Louisiana Purchase during several years, about "a Nation of Bad Indians (Ozages)."

The Caddoans came to him as they had come to the governors-general of both France and Spain to complain about the "Nation of Bad Indians," the Little Ones. Even the Pawnee-Piques of the Red

River and the Comanches called the Ietans on the far headwaters of the same river came to him to complain about them.

In his listing of the Indian tribes in the Territory of Orleans he wrote that "Caddoque or Caddo: their number of warriors about 100, and the remainder old men [this was only a small part of the Caddos, of course] and they live about 35 miles west of the main branch of the Bear River . . . near Natchitoches about 120 miles . . . they raise corn, beans and pumpkins . . . . Most of them have guns and some have rifles. They and all other nations we have heard of are at war with the Osages."

These people were at war with the Osages-of-the-Oaks, and very likely Makes-Tracks-Far-Away was not always personally involved, but was by now striking the posture of importance. He was probably in his village on the Verdigris some of the time making pontifical decisions and generously giving away Pawnee and Caddo horses to his people.

It has been said that *Ho'n-Mo'n-I'n* was the leader on most of the Red River forays. He would be of the Panther or Bear gens, and his name would mean Walks-in-the-Night, an obvious name of one of either gens.

When Sibley wrote of the Red River Pawnees, he informed Dearborn that they were about 800 miles above Natchitoches, and about 340 miles by land. There were about four hundred men in this division, and they lived on the south side of the Red River, and raised corn, beans, pumpkin, and tobacco for their own consumption. He wrote that they were at war with the Spaniards and friendly with the French and the Americans, but "They are at war likewise with the Osages as are every other nation."

In January of the year 1807, Walks-in-the-Night and his followers had gone down to the Red River to hunt bear. Sometimes in this climate the bear didn't hibernate until quite late, and sometimes not at all, and their hair was long and glossy just as if they were in their deep sleep farther north. They put on a special coat for winter, even if the winters were not the screaming crazy woman farther north.

A scout came in one day and reported that a large party of Caddos were coming down the river, loaded with buffalo robes and riding

and leading many beautiful Pawnee horses. These people went often
to trade with their linguistic kinsmen and the Pawnees.

The Little Ones knew that the Caddos and the Pawnees went to
Natchitoches often to try to get guns from the new Long Knives
there, and this was very bad; very bad for the Pawnees to have
many guns.

So Walks-in-the-Night sent some of the hunters to watch the Caddos and determine if there were Pawnees coming to Natchitoches
also. There were none, so the Little Ones painted their faces orange
and black, the colors of danger, some of them leaving the lower part
of the faces dawn red. They were all *Hunkah* and wore the stiff tail-
feather of the eagle on the right side of their heads.

They have said boastfully, and perhaps untruthfully, that they
didn't wait for dawn to attack the Caddos, but sent one of their
tallest men out in his full bluff-paint, and had him ride out on a high
place and sit there on his horse until the Caddo party came into view.
When he was sure that they had seen him, he got off his horse and
took his outlandishly decorated French hatchet from his belt and
began to dance wildly, raising the hatchet and letting it fall, while his
horse snorted and backed away, but he had a long rawhide rope
dragging.

This, say the Little Ones, threw the Caddos into a funk, and they
became excited.

Neolithic excitement was both destructive and ridiculous. There
was a definite animalistic terror in it, the terror that causes a horse to
run back into a burning barn, a herd of impala antelope of Africa to
jump high facing in every direction and landing in the same spot
when they are suddenly frightened by the lion's grunt, the terror that
causes female black bear to attack a man, or paralyzes a jackrabbit
when a golden eagle dives from the sky.

The Caddos had their women along with them, and the women
could induce excitement with their immediate and constant keening
when danger makes its appearance suddenly and unexpectedly. This
threw the men into confusion, and they even jumped from their
horses and fled, so say the Little Ones. One man, they said, ran about
in wide circles and shot his gun into the air.

345

It was easy to round up seventy-two of the finest Pawnee horses which the Caddos had just traded for and drive them off. The Little Ones touched not a Caddo scalp, and they threw the packs of hides down and left them. They rode off, leaving the Caddo two hundred miles from their villages, with all their robes and no horses.

The Caddo leader sent two men to the chief for horses, and two to Sibley at Natchitoches to inform him of another outrage by the painted giants from the Verdigris.

Later, however, Sibley could write to his superior, the Secretary of War in Washington, that there had been retribution in the form of the Creeks from across the Mississippi. He seemed to give Dearborn this information with some satisfaction.

On March 20 of the same year, he wrote: "Received information that a party of Alabamis and Appelaches were in the Prairie above the Caddo Village hunting buffalo & fell in with the same party of Ozages who Robed the Caddos of their horses. Attacked them in the night in their Camp killed five of them & defeated the whole party & retook most of the horses, there were more then twenty Ozages & only eight of the Other Partie who sustained no loss, the scalps of the five they killed had arrived at the Conchetta Village where all the Neighboring Tribes were collected to hold the War Dance; my informant was One of the Alabamis who belonged to the Party. The Ozage scalps were afterwards brought down and shown to me, they gave the Caddos Some of the horses again."

There were celebrations of this victory over the Little Ones. People from far away came to see the scalps and stood about and conjectured, and were vicariously heroic, like natives of the foothill provinces of India standing about a dead, man-eating tiger.

There was one Caddo who had taken part in the battle and who had taken an Osage scalp, either in this battle or another, who drew the eyes of all, and he was accorded great honor and given a hero's honorary name. He was given the name "Grand Ozages." He not only had a ball in his forehead from an Osage gun, but Sibley had sent him an officer's regimental coat, and he wore it with much more dignity than the fed-up officer who had to wear it in the hellish heat of a Red River summer.

346

The Creeks carried the Osage scalps with them and exhibited them frequently, especially when they wanted favors or trade guns from Sibley. How could they prove to the Americans better that they were their friends and bitter enemies of the "Bad Nation"?

Sibley soon "smelled a rat." The Spanish Governor Cordero of San Antonio was actually working on the Creeks to influence them to move over into Spanish territory. He was working on the Creeks and the Pawnees as well. His idea was to consolidate the tribes, the larger ones, in the Spanish territory so that they could be used in case of trouble with the Americans.

Sibley wrote to Dearborn that "a party . . . had lately arrived from San Antonio where they had been invited by Governor Cordero, they returned loaded with presents, dressed in Laced Cloathes, new Spanish Hats & every man in the Party had received a present of a Spanish Saddle & Two or Three Horses or Mules and the Gov. sent them Three Stands of Spanish Colors One for each Village."

The Pawnees of the Red River had urgent need for arms, even if they were not in conspiracy with Cordero in San Antonio; they never had sufficient arms for their wars with the Little Ones, although they told Sibley that "horses and mules were to them like grass, they had them in such plenty, they had likewise dressed Buffalo Skins & knew where there was Silver Ore plenty; but there was a Nation of Bad Indians (Ozages) who gave them much trouble and vexation, and they were more formidable to them On Account of that having Arms, etc, etc."

They arrived in large bands and often with the Hietans, perhaps the modern Comanches, and told Sibley that the Hietans had no guns at all.

The Red River Pawnees, called by Sibley *"Tawehash"* and by the Little Ones *Wi-Tsi-Ta,* Lodges-Far-Away People, were clever; they knew what the white man wanted most of all. He wanted horses and mules and dressed robes and silver. However, Sibley couldn't satisfy their desire for arms, even though he could give them some. There was also the possibility that Cordero was behind them and they were shrewdly playing Spaniard against American in order to get guns for the most important business in life, their traditional war with the Little Ones.

347

Besides the hairy ones who girdled trees and left their skeleton tops to whiten in the sun while they hunted for the market or distilled spirits, there were hairy ones who sweated and dreamed of two-story plank houses and of fields and horses and cattle. These latter hairy ones did not leave their girdled trees to stand until they fell through decay; but in the winters they had to kill the wapiti and the deer and the buffalo for their hides and tongues and leave the meat which they couldn't use to rot in the woods and on the prairie. These men believed in their own virtues as Christians and honest men, and they were sure of their superiority over the "Injuns." They were not too much interested in their government, and even suspected that their government might be in sympathy with the devil when they agreed to take over the salaries of the priests of the French and the Spanish regimes, so that the large left-over Catholic populations could have spiritual leadership. There were no taxes for such purposes, and the French and Spanish governments had supported the clergy.

And because of political and economic pressures caused by the activities of Napoleon, many Germans came to settle in the Louisiana country, many of them in the Osage domain, but they stayed closer to the Mississippi. They were prince-fearing and knew regimentation. All they wanted was land of their own and to be allowed to live in peace. When the hunters or diversion-seekers of the Bear or the Eagle or the Panther rode up to their clearings, they came forward without bluff-bravado or cautious too-glib friendliness because he and his men were mounted and imperious. The Germans called the leader "Herr," and worried about the frightened faces of their women and children, visible from around the corners of the cabins and from around trees left for shade and to hang things on. They had cut the trees around the clearing to a musket-shot distance from the cabin.

There were fugitives from the law east of the Mississippi, and hunters and trappers, and "walkers-on-the-earth," which the Little Ones had long ago called the French Bohèmes, dog-eyed men who came to live with them in their villages—men in reflected glory carrying water to the dancers on hot summer afternoons or helping the camp dog poisoner when the dogs became too many.

Besides the destructive seed of vanity in the Little Ones, there was

348

also a seed within the spirit of Christian virtues which these hairy men attributed to themselves—a seed in their dedication to the gaining of wealth or in their greed and their injured innocence when the Little Ones objected to their killing of game, razing their forests, and in general invading their domain, which would swell and burst and destroy the Little Ones.

It was they, the native invaders, both east of the Mississippi red men and the restless whites and the invaders from Europe, who would push the commissioners and the army officers and the politicians to nourish the seed of self-esteem in the gentile leaders and effect disintegration of the organization which the Little Old Men had built up over the centuries.

It was the natives and the Germans and later the Delawares and the Potawatomis and the Shawnees and the Wyandots, the Creeks and the Choctaws and the Chickasaws, the Seminoles and the Cherokees, chain-pressured from their old homes east of the Mississippi, who came like an invasion of alien species finally to defeat the imperious Little Ones. Not by their arms, not through their courage, not by their cunning except as cunning might be exemplified by the practices of a superior civilization if one considers agriculture as a higher cultural stage, but by their numbers. They came across the Mississippi like lemmings or grasshoppers, but stayed to develop the land, making geometrical patterns along the streams and later on the prairie.

The vast country across the Mississippi which the young United States had bought from France had to be filled up, and it had to be filled with people loyal to the new country. There must be a place to which the Indians east of the Mississippi could be removed so that they would cease being a nuisance to the Amer-Europeans who had taken over their best land.

This filling of the new land and the solving of the Indian problem east of the Mississippi became a Jeffersonian policy, along with exploration of the new land.

33. The New Long Knives Explorers

THOMAS JEFFERSON WAS POSSIBLY one of the most civilized men of his time, possibly of any time, and as the new White Father, was better educated and more civilized than any of the kings and emperors, a much greater humanitarian, the source of his humanitarianism not necessarily springing from the selfish concern for his own soul. However, as President, he could not come in direct contact with the Little Ones, and being chief executive of a democratic government must reflect the desires of the people, even though on the higher levels of diplomacy and of collective welfare he actually led them.

The invaders were afraid to go too far away from the Mississippi, the lower Missouri, the Gasconade, the Meramec, the lower Arkansas, and the Red rivers, since no one was quite sure just where the boundary between the United States and Spain ran. They settled about the nuclei formed by the villages along the rivers and at Chouteau's Three Forks settlement.

The mighty Missourias were no longer an obstacle. They had gone to join with the strong medicine of the Iowas and the Otoes, and later some of them would join the Little Osages. The Quapaws had become tamed and disease-decimated by long association with the French on the lower Arkansas River, and the domains of the Pawnee tribes, except those of the Pawnee-Piques (Picts) on the Red River, had not been seriously invaded by the agrarian culture from across the Mississippi. The Konzas still rode in their war paint over the prairies of the Kaw and the Republican rivers, from their village near the falls of the Smoky Hill River to the Blue Earth River and as far down the Missouri as the Little Ones would allow them. They were still periodically at war with the Little Ones.

The Sac and Foxes made their traditional forays across the Missouri from the north, but were now coming up the Gasconade, and not exposing themselves to the Little Ones hidden on the high limestone bluffs along the Osage River; they would come up the Gasconade, thence across country to the villages of the Little Ones or cross the Missouri north of them.

Other Algonkians, the Potawatomis and the Kickapoos, would cross the Mississippi or the Missouri and attack the Little Ones, but these were traditional skirmishes along the line dividing the range of two species in earth struggle. The Amer-Europeans and the Germans were not skirmishers but invaders, as would be the settlement of Algonkian and Iroquoian, Muskogean, and other eastern tribes when the policy of Mr. Jefferson would be carried out later by Andrew Jackson—invasions as the result of restlessness, expansion from economic and political and social pressure, executive order, and full-blooded self-importance and arrogant misguided expressions of freedom.

Even the Indian tribes resettled a little later would have edged into the agricultural stage of development, and the full force of the agrarian culture would meet the Neolithic Little Ones.

After the Americans took over the Louisiana country, they declared freedom of religion, and many of the rough settlers heard the call and became circuit riders. The Protestant circuit riders and the local priests seemed to be little interested immediately in collective heathen Indian souls. Here and there some individual of no gentile consequence would become fascinated by the settlements, and priest or circuit rider might employ the shepherd's crook.

The most important effect on the God concept of the Little Ones was through animal religious symbols which the invaders were destroying in order to maintain physical comfort either through their flesh or with their hides. These animals, upon which the Little Ones depended for symbolism in the rites of the *wah-hopeh,* were already at this time becoming fewer, and since the candidate for initiation into the war rites had been given seven years in which to secure them, with bow and arrow only, he found that he must go farther and farther away from the Place-of-the-Many-Swans and the Place-of-the-Oaks to secure them within the period of time allotted to him by the Little Old Men of the *Tzi-Sho Wa'no'n* gens of the *Tzi-Sho* and the *Wah-Sha-She Wa'no'n* gens of the *Hunkah,* the war gentes of the two grand divisions.

Besides the seven skins, he must have gifts for the *xoka,* the initiator, and the *shoka,* the messenger. He must within seven years obtain the skins of the following, shooting each one with bow and arrow, and was not allowed to take the black bear in his den during hibernation: He had to have the skin, shot by himself and without aid, of the lynx, the dark gray wolf (timber wolf), the male panther, the male black bear, the buffalo (taken on foot), the wapiti, and the white-tail deer. These were the tribal symbols sacred to war, as well as gentile symbols.

The Osages-of-the-Oaks had to go to the headwaters of the Salt Fork of the Arkansas to have a successful buffalo hunt now, and the shy panther was moving away from the guns and settlements of the invaders. The skin of the black bear and the wolf were salable and the tallow of the black bear almost priceless. There were still plenty of wapiti and deer, but they were being killed for their hides and for food.

The Little Old Men of the *Tzi-Sho Wa'no'n* and the *Wah-Sha-She Wa'no'n,* had to extend the period beyond seven years for the securing of the sacred animals, hides, and there was much hesitancy and unsolvable doubt by the candidates. They had not themselves made these regulations, but they had come down to them as the sacred laws. They did not think of them as having been made by the former Little Old Men, but given by *Wah'Kon-Tah,* as the Mosaic laws were given.

This was serious, and the most imaginative of the invaders could not associate the headless bodies of settlers or trappers or hunters or vagabonds, or the heap of ashes and black chips in the middle of a clearing, with their own bear traps, their pitfalls, their continual search for hibernating bears, their fear-shots during the night at the very devil himself, the panther who "screamed like a woman." They wouldn't have associated these atrocities with the piles of salted buffalo tongues or the swelling carcasses of hide-stripped deer and wapiti.

The Little Ones' manner of spiritual self-protection was practical, if not ultimately effective, albeit as effective as burning of witches.

Since the domains of the Little Ones and the Quapaws were closest to the west bank of the river, it was in these domains that the invaders began to attach themselves to bits of earth.

Not even Mr. Jefferson, the gentleman-thinker and president of the new country, knew where the extended borders of his country were, and the Spaniards didn't know either. There was delay and suspicion on both sides, and President Jefferson was impatient to determine the boundaries. He was anxious to make friends of the Indians in the new land, and confirm them in their claims to certain areas, but he thought the "bad Indians" of the Place-of-the-Many-Swans, the north fork of the Osage River called by the French the Marais des Cygnes (and Jefferson would have referred to it thus), might be persuaded to move down to the Three Forks, where the Neosho, the Verdigris, and the Arkansas rivers meet, to be reunited with the "bad Indians" there, thus leaving their ancient domain to be parceled out to immigrant "good Indians" from east of the Mississippi. Obviously they were all Indians; why should the *Wazazhes* not gladly move over and make room for their red brother?

This transplantation of good Indians and loyal, virtuous Christians could come later. For the present there were much more important matters than resettlement of eastern Indians and granting homesteads to loyal citizens. President Jefferson must first determine just what in the way of square miles he had bought from Napoleon. This vast area which was later called the Louisiana Purchase had been a dream of Mr. Jefferson's when he was secretary of state. He had sent a naturalist, one André Michaux, up the Missouri River with instructions to study weather, fauna, flora, geography, and native tribes, during the last decade of the eighteenth century.

This had upset the Spaniards, and now they were upset again when they heard that he was sending a Captain Meriwether Lewis up the Missouri to explore under the same instructions he had given Michaux: to send back specimens of animals, flowers, and birds, and study geography and weather and make friends with the Indians, as well as find a westerly running river which would debouch into the Pacific Ocean. This inspired many letters between the Spanish Commandant-General of the Provincias Internas of Chihuahua, one Don Nemesio de Salcedo, and the Spanish representative at St. Louis and New Orleans.

Rumors started. The Spaniards said that the Little Ones had made a raid into Mexico (perhaps only New Mexico) and had captured a pack train carrying silver, and, having no use for the silver, had hidden it. Now, averred the Spanish rumors, the Americans were making these and other Indians enemies of the Spaniards, and one Captain Stoddard and one Major Bruff were urging the Little Ones to go back to Mexico to get the silver. Spanish rumor had it that Captain "Merry Weather," sometimes just Captain "Merry," sometimes just Captain "Weather," and sometimes Captain "Wether," was to spy on them and that his expedition to the Pacific was only a smoke screen.

Captain Meriwether Lewis and Lieutenant Clark camped at the mouth of the Osage River June 1 and 2, 1804. They had one keelboat and two pirogues, and along the banks of the river some of the party walked and led two horses. The horses were used to pack the game they must live on along the way.

It had been raining and the light was cold and watery. During the rain of the thirty-first of May, a Frenchman floated downriver out of the mouth of the Osage with furs, and with him were an Osage man and a woman. The Frenchman had letters from the messenger Chouteau had sent to the Three Forks, with a letter to Makes-Tracks-Far-Away and Arrow-Going-Home, informing them that the Heavy Eyebrows were leaving, and now the new Long Knives, the Americans, would take over the land.

Makes-Tracks-Far-Away became angered and threw the talking paper into the fire. He and the others watched it burn and the charred bits lift and float away to the west on the slight east wind. The charred paper had gone to the west, and when it had completely disappeared, he felt that the Frenchmen, the original Heavy Eyebrows, would come back to the Place-of-the-Many-Swans and the Place-of-the-Oaks.

On June 7 the party passed the place where the Sac and Foxes sometimes crossed the Missouri to attack the Little Ones, and near where Chouteau's Fort Carondelet had stood, and in the language of the Little Ones it had now become a Place-of-the-Yellow-Flowers. Lieutenant (called Captain) Clark made note of the fact that the signs indicated that a party of Sac and Fox warriors were on their way to attack the Little Ones.

On September 19, 1806, on their return from the mouth of the Columbia River, they camped again on the spot at the mouth of the Osage River where they had camped in 1804. This was the only contact the Little Ones had with the famed expedition, but with Zebulon Montgomery Pike and his expedition up the Arkansas they would be intimately associated.

When the French and Spaniards wanted to bring their plans to a successful conclusion, whether it was trade or exploration, they first must feel out one or all three of the tribes who dominated the river highways, the Missouri, the Arkansas, and the Red. The first thing to do was to ingratiate one's self with the Little Ones, since they dominated the lower Missouri and the lower Arkansas and were feared on the middle Red. Then one would make overtures to the Pawnees, who dominated several areas along the feeder streams of the Missouri, Arkansas, and Red River highways, above the Little Ones. At the headwaters of these rivers, particularly the Arkansas and the Red, and even about the heads of the Republican and the Kaw were the people whom the French had called Padoucas, having Gallicized *Pa-Do'n-Ka,* the Little One's name for them.

Also, when the French or the Spaniards were making their plans to parley with one or all of these tribes, they expended great effort to find somewhere Osage, Pawnee, or Padouca captives with some other tribe so that they could buy them or bluff-free them or in some manner get them away from their captors, then they would restore them to their tribes with histrionics.

This was the plan which the United States followed when General James Wilkinson, American governor of Louisiana, commissioned Zebulon Pike to explore the Arkansas.

First, he must ingratiate himself with the Little Ones, who were harassed by and trying to hold back the hairy ones from across the Mississippi after 1803, and who hated the Americans because of this invasion. This, added to the fact that they had been taught to hate all Long Knives by the French, and even though they had begun to call the Americans "New Heavy Eyebrows," they thought of them as Long Knives and referred to Pierre Chouteau, their first agent, or in fact his office, as *Mo'n-I'n-Tonkah,* Big Long Knife, since he was now American.

Not only were they angry over the invasions of the Americans, remembering what they had been taught by the French, but Manuel Lisa, the energetic and powerful fur trader, was trying to effect an alliance between the Spaniards at Santa Fe and the four *"tribus indios poderoso,"* the Osages, the Pawnees, the Konzas, and the Comanches, so that he could monopolize the trade between Santa Fe and St. Louis through the four powers.

One could guess that the struggle among the Osages and the Pawnees and the Comanches would have few peace breaks, and one could never depend on the whimsies of the Osages and their splinter the Konzas. One day they might be allied against a common enemy and the next day they might be riding over the prairie in war paint hunting each other.

This was a difficult commission for the twenty-seven-year-old Pike and his handful of men, and he was certainly fortunate that General Wilkinson had found about forty-six women, young men, and children who had been captured by the Potawatomis, an Algonkian enemy of the Little Ones. The Potawatomis had waited for the men of a Little Osage hunting party to leave camp, then they charged the camp about ten o'clock in the morning and killed a third of the women and children and carried about sixty off to their villages, where the Potawatomi warriors were honored by their people. This had happened in 1803, and Wilkinson had succeeded in buying forty-six of the captives for Pike to escort to the Place-of-the-Many-Swans.

Not only this, but several leaders of the Osages and the Pawnees had been taken to Washington so that they might be duly impressed by the power of the Americans. This was an old strategy. The French had used it and the Spaniards had used it. The French had ordered Bourgmont to take the mixed delegation to Paris in 1725.

The delegation who were taken to Washington had not been presented jeweled snuffboxes and watches, but had been given presents and medals by President Jefferson. Traveling Rain, the chief of the Little Osages, had been given a large medal of Jefferson's head, and had been given an American flag and a stovepipe hat. *Paw-Hiu-Skah,* White Hair, the Grand *Tzi-Sho,* was given a general's tunic with epaulettes, a flag of the United States, and a stovepipe hat. Big Soldier had been given presents. The others, Beautiful Bird and Makes-Tracks-Far-Away had also received presents.

These leaders of the Little Ones were held in St. Louis until the forty-six captives were collected. At least those of the Place-of-the-Many-Swans, Traveling Rain, White Hair, Beautiful Bird, and Big Chief were detained in St. Louis until the others were ready, but Makes-Tracks-Far-Away and Arrow-Going-Home left for the Neosho and the Verdigris.

Now Pike would have four of the Osage leaders and the Pawnee chieftains, and this would assure him of a friendly reception at the Place-of-the-Many-Swans and in the Pawnee villages on the Republican River. He had only to ingratiate himself with the Padoucas, whom he called Comanches, and the Konzas.

Young Zebulon Pike's first duty was to restore the Osage captives to the Osage village at the Place-of-the-Many-Swans, and then make peace between the Osages and the Konzas, who were momentarily at war, and there seemed to be a lull in the continual warfare between the Pawnees and the Osages. This was fortunate. Then he must establish friendly relations with the powerful Padoucas, and "acquire knowledge of the Southwest."

His instructions from Wilkinson were terse and unimaginative and typically military, and little like the instructions which the highly cultured President had given Meriwether Lewis.

General Wilkinson had written to Lieutenant Pike several days before he set out from Wilkinson's new fort, Belle Fontaine on the lower Missouri River, and the letter was a trumpet's echo:

"My confidence in your caution and discretion has prevented my

357

urging you to be vigilant in guarding against the stratagems and treachery of the Indians, holding yourself above the alarm and surprise, the composition of your party, though it be small, will secure to you the respect of a host of untutored savages.

"You are to communicate from the Grand Osage . . . ."

The ransomed captive Little Ones seemed to be rather philosophical about the military discipline. They walked along the bank of the Missouri parallel with the boats being poled, and were under guard. When they got to St. Charles, they became quite worried, since in their party were only a few men and the chieftains, and they realized that St. Charles was on the north bank of the Missouri, the Sac and Fox side and the Sioux side. They knew what a temptation these unprotected women of the Little Ones would be. They seemed to think that Pike's handful of soldiers might not be equal to the fierce Sac and Foxes, or that they might actually join them. It had been rumored that there were five hundred Sac and Foxes and Iowas waiting for the Osages to come opposite a feeder called Big Manitou.

Lisa didn't like the idea of Pike's playing the theatrical benefactor to the Osages and the Pawnees, so he began to harass him. He had the interpreter, Vásquez ("Baroney"), arrested for debt, and had him brought back to St. Louis. However, he was later released.

On July 19, 1806, there was another rumor that spread among the Osages that there was a large party of Sac and Foxes waiting for them at the mouth of their river, the Osage. Someone had a plan to make the Pike expedition a failure.

To indicate how scarce game was becoming, comparatively, especially close to the settlements, of course, Lieutenant Wilkinson, son of the military governor of Louisiana, had to accompany the chieftains several days away from the river so that they could kill game, and finally had to purchase beeves for them, fearing that they would take beeves where they might find them. It wasn't until July 23 that Dr. Robinson of the expedition killed a deer, the first one, and they had been out since the fifteenth. Of course, it was July when deer and wapiti were quiescent, and the brush and foliage at climax.

On July 25, one of the Pawnee chieftains was missing, and the other said that he had seen an Otoe with the expedition and he believed the Otoe had killed him. As a matter of fact, the Pawnee had trailed a party of Potawatomis up the Gasconade River, and when he appeared to report this, the Osage women became frightened again.

Pike wrote in his diary: "Every morning we were awakened by the mourning of the savages, who commenced crying about daylight, and continued for the space of an hour. I made inquiry of my interpreter with respect to this, who informed me that this was a custom not only with those who had recently lost their relatives, but also with others who recalled to mind the loss of some friend, dead long since, and joined the other mourners purely from sympathy. They appeared extremely affected; tears ran down their cheeks, and they sobbed bitterly; but in a moment they dry their cheeks and cease their cries."

At the mouth of the Gasconade they "killed one bear, two deer, one otter, three turkeys, and one raccoon."

When they reached the Osage River, the Little Ones felt safer and some of their old arrogance returned, and there seemed to be some jealousy between two Osage chieftains, *No'n-Xu-Dse-Thi'n-Ge,* No-Ears, whom Pike called after the French, Sans Oreilles, and the natural leader of the group, *A'ki-Da Tonkah,* Big Soldier, of the Black Bear gens. There was a woman with the party who was hung with presents from the Potawatomis, and for some reason she had apparently been allowed to ride in one of the boats while the others walked along the bank. When they reached the Osage River and were a few miles up it, No-Ears came up with several young men, who had apparently heard the party discharging their guns in joy-shots or for the purpose of clearing their arms of damp powder when they came to the Osage River. The woman seemed to be the magnet which caused No-Ears to leave the others who were camped a few miles down river.

Big Soldier was an honor title given to an official of the tribal buffalo hunts and elected from the Bear gens. Naturally he became the leader, though Pike says he appointed him, but it is more probable that the others recognized his position. When he came up the next morning, he became very angry with No-Ears, and he said that hereafter no woman would be allowed to go in the boats. He had the authority as *A'ki-Da Tonkah,* Big Soldier, to flog transgressors, and

359

immediately flogged one of the young men, then turned to No-Ears, but it was soon settled.

Young Pike didn't seem to know exactly what to do about this, and was relieved when the head chief of the Little Osages made his appearance crossing the river on a raft. He was *Ta-Dse-K'o-E,* Soughing-of-the-Wind, but he has come down in history from Pike's journal as "Tuttasuggy." This chief with the poetical name gave Pike much needed confidence by his friendliness and his vicarious shame for the disorder caused by a woman. He said he "would throw them away," referring to a young man and his wife and baby, embroiled somehow in the trouble. Pike, however, persuaded him to allow him to take the woman and child in one of the boats.

There is some question whether Soughing-of-the-Wind was "head chief" of the Little Osages as Pike stated, or whether the principal chief of the Little Osages was *Ni-Zhiu-Mo'n-I'n,* Traveling Rain, or *Mi-Tzo-Shee,* Little Bear. According to the late chief of the Little Osages, who could trace his predecessors back six chieftainships, the principal chief of the Little Osages must have been one of these two. In Lieutenant Wilkinson's report about this meeting with the Little Osages at their village, he mentions that Soughing-of-the-Wind sent his younger brother to perform a service, and his name was *Ni-Zhiu-Mo'n-I'n,* Traveling Rain, but Wilkinson, who must have had trouble with Osage phonetics and very likely with his own spelling, referred to him as "Nezuma."

Ni-Zhiu-Mo'n-I'n, which name came to Pike's and Wilkinson's ears and off their tongues as "Nezuma," refers to the rain curtain which hangs on the plains and prairie horizons and can be seen traveling along a distant horizon.

There is no *Tzi-Sho* chief of the Grand Osages mentioned, only *Paw-Hiu-Skah,* White Hair, and he was definitely the Grand *Tzi-Sho* at this time.

One assumes that Pike could not have been mistaken in associating Soughing-of-the-Wind, "Tuttasuggy," with the chieftainship of the Little Osages.

Pike's mind was quite open, not crystallized by the military philosophy. He was so pleased with the number of deer some of the Osages brought in that he "gave them about one or two gills of whiskey, which intoxicated all of them." And, again, he manifested some species of humaneness, when "I passed over a remarkably large rattle-snake, as he lay curled up, and trod so near him as to touch him with my foot, he drawing himself up to make room for my heel. Dr. Robinson who followed me, was on the point of treading on him, but by a spring avoided it. I then turned round and touched him with my ramrod, but he showed no disposition to bite, and appeared quite peaceable. The gratitude which I felt toward him for not having bitten me induced me to save his life."

And this young man of twenty-seven could philosophize in speaking of his relations with the Indians: "If you have justice on your side, and do not enforce it, they universally despise you."

As he and his company worked their way up the river, news came to him that the Little Osages had made the war movement against the Konzas, "and the Grand Osages a party against our citizens on the Arkansas River." This was one of the gentile leaders again, possibly some one of the *Hunkah* gentes, either the restless, mischievous Bear, Panther, Eagle, or Wapiti gens.

Pike was much perturbed about this war movement to the Arkansas, and he wrote to his superior, General Wilkinson, about it. The news had been given him by three *"engagés"* who were on their way downriver. He had given them a drink, "poor fellows," after he had given them his letter to carry to St. Louis.

In referring to the gentile foray to the Arkansas, he assured his general that "This latter step [the war movement] the White Hair [*Paw-Hiu-Skah*] did everything in his power to prevent, but could not. If true, what are we to think of our bons amis, the Osage?"

A true Grand *Tzi-Sho* from the *Tzi-Sho Wa'no'n,* children of the Heavenly Bodies gens, might have been able to stop the gentile war movement, but apparently *Paw-Hiu-Skah* couldn't. Some times a Grand *Ki-He-Kah,* either the Grand *Tzi-Sho* or the Grand *Hunkah,* could stop such a movement, but pretended they couldn't. However, in the case of the supposed usurper White Hair, who was possibly of

361

the Buffalo gens, he could not stop this gentile war movement, or any other, and it is very likely that he would make every attempt to do so, since such things were bad for Chouteau's trade.

Pike suggested to his superior in his letter that Manuel Lisa was behind the Little Osages' attack on the Konzas. He wrote that he had even heard that Lisa wanted the Konza villages razed. He was very much worried, and he asked editorially in his letter, "What face will the Indians receive us with? . . . and to whom are we to ascribe their hostile disposition, unless the traitors of St. Louis?"

On August 17, Pike and his party came to the spot where Pierre Chouteau had built Fort Carondelet in the 1790's to keep the Osages from the war movement, particularly on the Missouri. This was just after he had passed Panther Creek, and on the south bank. There were ten French houses still in the environs, but Pike says that on the spot on which the fort had once stood, there was nothing to indicate that there had ever been a fort, except for the character and the greenness of the vegetation. The Osages had lugged the four brass cannon (swivels) to their village upriver.

After passing the Place-of-the-Many-Swans, which Pike referred to as the "second fork" of the river he was later stopped by a great drift and sent Baroney, his interpreter, to the village of the Grand Osages for horses, and later Lieutenant Wilkinson and Soughing-of-the-Wind came from the Little Osage village to which Wilkinson had been sent ahead to deliver the captives to their people. Wilkinson was full of the experience. He had already described to Pike the meeting of the long-separated relatives when they came forward to meet them down the river several days before. Then, he had said, wives had thrown themselves into the arms of their husbands, and children had cried and clung to their parents, brothers and sisters, putting away their traditional shyness (in each other's presence, which they had always felt after pubescence), met with arms around each other. They cried and prayed and turned their faces to *Wah'Kon-Tah,* and sang their prayers of gratitude. "In short," wrote Pike in his journal, "the *toute ensemble* was such as to make polished society blush, when compared with those savages, in whom the passions of the mind, whether joy, grief, fear, anger, or revenge, have their full scope. Why can we not correct the baneful passions, without weakening the good?"

And now Lieutenant Wilkinson described to his commander the meeting at the village as the relatives and the captives and Wilkinson and his men approached. Soughing-of-the-Wind had arranged the ceremony like a Frenchman. He placed Wilkinson between himself and a noted warrior, and he had the captives follow like a column of Spanish cavalry. When this queer procession was about half a mile from the village, 180 horsemen came galloping toward them, "painted and decorated in every fanciful manner." They were a guard of honor, and opened to the right and left as the column approached. A few yards to the right were 60 more horsemen, "painted with blue chalk."

This was when Soughing-of-the-Wind sent his younger brother Traveling Rain with a flag and a silk handkerchief as a prize for him who might win the race. The sixty horsemen "painted with blue chalk" lined up, and at a signal started, and ran their horses for perhaps a quarter of a mile, and there were two winners, and each got a prize.

As the strange column neared the village, the four cannon were fired as an honoring salute. Soughing-of-the-Wind had spent much time watching the manners of Fort Carondelet before it had been allowed to disintegrate by spiteful Lisa.

Wilkinson was taken ceremoniously to the lodge of one he calls "Soldier of the Oak," and there had a dinner consisting of green corn, buffalo (possibly hump ribs), and "water mellons about the size of a 24-pound shot, which though small, were highly flavored."

When the horses came from the Grand Osage village, Pike moved up to where Lisa had his establishment and camped at the edge of the prairie.

Pike had been working on the translation of the message which General Wilkinson had sent by him to *Paw-Hiu-Skah,* the Grand *Tzi-Sho.* He had to translate it into French, since the Osage of the interpreter seemed too restricted and couldn't be written. To give the precise "parole" of his superior, the General, he must give it in French, which many of the Osages could speak, but for those who couldn't speak French it could be translated into Osage by the interpreter.

While all seemed to be going very well, a messenger came from the Arkansas with word that some young men from the Osages-of-the-Oaks had fired on a boat coming up the Arkansas and had killed two white men, but it also happened that they were accompanied by the brother-in-law of *Paw-Hiu-Skah* and he also was killed, and soon the women were keening, the dogs howling and it may be supposed that the Little Old Men went to the Lodge of Mystery, and the long wolflike chant of the town crier must have added to the confusion.

Pike does not mention this, except to write that "this put the whole village in mourning." He had established his camp that day just below the mouth of the Marmiton River, and was very busy making an observatory from which he could take his bearings. This camp he named Camp Independence, and it was located between the two villages, and he was so busy this day that he couldn't hear what was going on in the village of the Grand Osages. There would be a mourning dance later, since the brother-in-law of White Hair would be important.

The next day, knowing nothing of Osage customs under such circumstances, he sent his interpreter Baroney to request White Hair to come to his camp for a meeting, and he sent a young man to the village of the Little Osages to request Soughing-of-the-Wind to come also. He informed the chiefs and their followers that he had called them in order to give them General Wilkinson's greeting. He hung a Jefferson medal around the neck of *Paw-Hiu-Skah*'s son. Also he had gifts for relatives of the Osages who had been killed by the Potawatomi raid, and then when he saw that *Paw-Hiu-Skah* had brought a retinue of 186, he wondered what to do, so he gave them something to drink, then they all rode to the village of the Grand Osages, where he was invited to eat at many lodges. He seemed to be most interested in pumping *Paw-Hiu-Skah* about the intentions of Lisa. He also took a "deposition" from Lisa's men, and since he did not have the men to take them to St. Louis as prisoners, he sent them alone downriver with a report to Joseph Brown, who had recently been appointed by

Jefferson as secretary of Louisiana Territory. He also forwarded his information to Dr. Brown.

The very fact that *Paw-Hiu-Skah* had come to his Camp Independence on request instead of demanding that he, Pike, with only a handful of followers, should come to his village, indicates deterioration of the tribal dignity and the compliant attitude of a Chouteau-made and controlled Grand *Tzi-Sho*. He himself seemed to have wished to make up for this traditionally undignified behavior by bringing the retinue of 186 men.

The next day he paid Pike a ceremonial visit, and brought corn, meat, and buffalo tallow, and Pike had to invite the large retinue to breakfast. During the afternoon Pike rode to the village of Soughing-of-the-Wind, and on the way back was caught in a terrific rainstorm accompanied by high winds. He almost lost his tents and did lose his observatory. He was experiencing the violent whims of *Wah'Kon-Tah.*

The next day was the day appointed for the grand council, at which time Pike would give his speech. There were little lenses of rain water shining in the sun like *mo'n-ce,* now sacred metal, or like the peeps-in-water the dancers carried. The unshod feet of the horses skidded and made ridges in the mud.

But while *Paw-Hiu-Skah* felt that he dared not use the traditional prerogative of the Grand *Tzi-Shos* by sending his *shoka* to say that he was ready to receive in his lodge, he managed to be late, sending his interpreter to Camp Independence pretending that naturally the Grand *Tzi-Sho* of the Grand Osages had thought the council would be held in his village. The pride saving was so obvious in the manner of the interpreter that Pike abetted the pretense.

However, later the Grand *Tzi-Sho* of the Grand Osages could answer the speech of Pike with only a few indulgent words, saying grandly that he would reply in full later, but after Soughing-of-the-Wind answered for the Little Osages, the *Tzi-Sho, Paw-Hiu-Skah,* White Hair or "Cheveux Blanche," as Pike called him, rose quickly from his buffalo robe on the ground, and allowing his hairless summer buffalo robe to fall from his right shoulder and tucking it under his arm and around his chest, he spoke like the thunder of *Wah'Kon-*

Tah. His six feet, seven or eight inches seemed to be even more. His eyes flashed, but he didn't point to Soughing-of-the-Wind. This would have meant the sign of death. He didn't even raise his voice, but as he talked, Soughing-of-the-Wind shut his eyes and lowered his head and seemed to grow smaller.

"Soughing-of-the-Wind," he said, "you have done a bad thing. You shouldn't have done this bad thing. You ought to know better, since you have been many times 'to the States.' You came with this army officer from Sho'to Town with these captives, and with these Pawnee chieftains, and you did not bring them first to my lodge. You took them to your village. That is not the way we do things. You know this thing."

He lowered his great height with dignity and grace, fanned himself with his eagle-tail fan. Soughing-of-the-Wind seemed to be asleep. Soon he rose in dignity, with not even a "haugh," and walked away.

In his speech Pike had asked for two or three Osages to accompany Lieutenant Wilkinson down the Arkansas, which he was to explore while Pike explored the Red. He wanted someone from the Grand Osages to accompany Wilkinson and his party down the Arkansas so that they might be well received in the villages of the Osages-of-the-Oaks. He would send a message from General Wilkinson, the Lieutenant's father to the Bear-Panther marauders, Makes-Tracks-Far-Away and Walks-in-the-Night, and unabashedly referred to one of them, perhaps he knew not which, as "Le Grand Peste" (The Great Plague), which was what the French called one of them; perhaps Makes-Tracks-Far-Away or Arrow-Going-Home or Walks-in-the-Night, who were the recognized chiefs of the Osages on the Arkansas River. He said oratorically, "The Grand Peste and his people are not Osage; if they are, why do they make war against the children of your great father?

"My Brothers: If the word that your great father in St. Louis sent by me for the Grand Peste, and for which I desire to be accompanied by some of your warriors, does not open his eyes your great father will abandon him, and will no longer wish that he and his nation be his subjects, but will suffer that his white and red warriors raise the tomahawk against him."

He wanted horses from them so that he could visit the Pawnees, and wanted several warriors to go along so that they could bring the horses back, and he wanted some of the warriors to accompany him "during all my trip."

He had no gifts for them, except small tobacco, mementoes, and bad spirits to accompany his bad French which was translated into Osage.

Chouteau would come up to the Place-of-the-Many-Swans soon and *Paw-Hiu-Skah* was not sure, but since Chouteau was now an American, he felt he ought to comply with Pike's wishes, but he had trouble collecting the warriors and the horses necessary. He came to Pike to tell him that his son would accompany him, as would his son-in-law, *Wa-Tcha-Wa-Ha,* called by the French, Jean Le Fou, John-the-Fool, originally, before the Americans tried to pronounce it, calling him not Jean Le Fou but Gene La Fou. There would be others he said and four horses.

Soughing-of-the-Wind sent his brother Traveling Rain and some young men and six horses. There were horses all around the villages, perhaps seven or eight hundred, Pike thought, and still he was offered only ten. He thought that White Hair had exerted all his influence, and therefore his influence even as Grand *Tzi-Sho* must be small. He also thought that Soughing-of-the-Wind had exerted all his influence.

It is easier to believe that *Paw-Hiu-Skah* might have been sincere in his attempts, since he was Chouteau's chief, and there is also reason to believe that he might be under the influence of Lisa. Certainly a Grand *Tzi-Sho* could have furnished more than four horses. He could have furnished many times more than that of his own alone.

Also Pike was having trouble obtaining the services of one Noel Maugraine, French-Osage interpreter. He refused to accompany Pike even after Pike had read Wilkinson's order to him. Pike was almost ready to "use military law."

John-the-Fool came to assure Pike that he would go along with him. He said that *Ki-He-Kah* (The Chief), his father-in-law, had called several meetings and the young men had refused to go and refused to lend their horses; not even the young men of the Buffalo gens would go along. He, Jean Le Fou, would go along, and this

367

meant much since he was a man of importance among the Grand Osages. Also the son of *Paw-Hiu-Skah, Paw-Hiu-Skah-E-Shinka,* came to Pike and said that the young men had turned their ears from the voice of his father, *Paw-Hiu-Skah,* and did not wish to go into the country of the Pawnees, and that in the country of the Konzas there would be only a few of them, and the Konzas would know this thing. But, said *Paw-Hiu-Skah* the Younger, "I shall go along with you taking two horses to carry provisions."

The interpreter, who was probably Jean Le Fou at this moment, said that the Grand *Ki-He-Kah, Paw-Hiu-Skah,* had been ashamed to send the answer to the captain of the new Long Knives, Pike, but that he would have the town crier call again tomorrow.

To these apologies Pike countered with the theme song of the European's relationship with the natives, which was comprehensive enough to cover both soul saving and fort building. This "for the good of the Indian" song was straight from the hypocrisy of gold-seekers and from the trickery of the marketplace. Pike wrote confidentially to General Wilkinson, "I had made the demand without explanation, merely to let the Osages act agreeably to their inclination, in order that we might see what disposition they would exhibit toward us: but why do I seek of their chiefs to follow me to the Pawnees? Is it for our good, or for their own? Is it not to make peace with the Kansa? To put the wives and children out of danger? As to their horses which they may furnish us with, I will pay them for their hire; but it is uncertain whether I can pay them here, or give them an order on the superintendent of Indian Affairs at St. Louis; but I do not wish them to be made acquainted with."

There were also other rumors of Potawatomi attack, and there was the stubborn refusal of Maugraine, the best interpreter to accompany the expedition, as well as the inability of *Paw-Hiu-Skah* to supply horses and men for the expedition, and there was a feeling that at St. Louis the atmosphere of the city and area was antagonistic to American activities. There is the sense that Americans were thoroughly disliked. This is found in many incidents and in Pike's letters to his General about his very efficient interpreter, one Baroney, who, he writes "appears to have renounced all his St. Louis connections, and is as firm an American as if born one; he of course is entirely discarded by the people of St. Louis; but I hope he will not suffer for his fidelity."

There was also the uncertainty of the *Ki-He-Kah,* the Grand *Tzi-Sho,* White Hair, and his troubles with the young men who left him to go to the Arkansas Osages. They seemed to feel that they owed him no traditional allegiance, since he was not of the *Tzi-Sho Wa'no'n,* the Heavenly Bodies gens, from which *Wah'Kon-Tah* (really the first generations of Little Old Men) had chosen his *Tzi-Sho Ki-He-Kah.* These young men had much more freedom with Makes-Tracks-Far-Away, Arrow-Going-Home, and Walks-in-the-Night, at the Three Forks. They had plenty of arms there, and there was no one to stop them when they went on the war movement to the west, and they committed depredation for which the whole tribe were blamed.

Paw-Hiu-Skah came to Pike about this, and requested that he inform General Wilkinson of the situation and ask him what he, *Paw-Hiu-Skah,* should do about an Osage who had killed a Frenchman on the Arkansas and the fact that this Osage was now in the Grand Village. How could he carry out the laws of the new Long Knives if they didn't make the Osages-of-the-Oaks behave? The Arkansas Osages would not allow him to send this Osage down the river for punishment, since he was a Bear. He didn't understand how he could carry out the laws of the new Long Knives, when the Osages-of-the-Oaks wouldn't help. He wanted Pike to ask General Wilkinson to support him, the Grand *Ki-He-Kah,* and he would then have little fear of the Arkansas Osages. Perhaps General Wilkinson would carry out the promises made in Washington that the government would bring back the Osages-of-the-Oaks to join those of the Place-of-the-Many-Swans.

The news of the death of *Paw-Hiu-Skah*'s son-in-law came to the village on August 19; and on the twenty-ninth of August, 1806, Pike saw one day of the mourning dance for this important man, but he referred to it as "the great medicine dance."

Pike and his party finally got away from Camp Independence and the villages of the Place-of-the-Many-Swans on September 1, after having trouble keeping the horses which some of the Osages had brought to him. Some would bring horses, then whimsically change their minds and come for them. They crossed the south fork of the Osage River and set out over one of the most beautiful prairies an artist could imagine, and Pike appreciated the fact, since he even mentioned its beauty in his prosiac chart Number 30: "Prairies boundless in view," and "Prairies which the eye assisted by the best glass could not compass." The Osages of his party knew more than this about this glorious prairie; they knew that the winds screamed there in the winter like a crazy woman and during Buffalo-Pawing-Earth-Moon, in June, when the bulls at midday were tired of their boasting, the winds talked there in whispers, and you could go there alone and sit on a little prairie swell and make a song.

But today the Little Ones were not happy; there were only a few of them, and one of them a woman. The Konzas knew that they had started, and their scouts had told them how many of the Little Ones and how many of the Pawnees there were. There were only three rather subdued Pawnees, four "chiefs" of the Grand Osages, and other reluctant people from the Grand Village, and of the Little Osages there was No-Ears with seven warriors. In all there were about thirty warriors and the one woman, whose name was *Goes-to-Meet-the-Men*. This might have no reference to coquetry or harlotry, but could refer to the fleet one who raced ahead to meet the warriors riding in from victory.

On the second day out, Pike got news that Chouteau was in the Grand Village, so he went back to meet him and receive the latest news. Then he rejoined his party.

Realizing their weakness, the Osages decided to skirt the area where the Konzas might be wandering, and thus took Pike south up Snake-with-Open-Mouth River, the Marmiton, then turned northwest at a spot about ten miles north of the modern Fort Scott, Kansas. They crossed the prairie divide between the Missouri and Arkansas River drainage, that looked like a long ocean wave frozen, to the Neosho, then back across to the Missouri drainage, and across the drainage of the Smoky Hill and the Solomon and north to the villages of the Pawnees.

The wariness of the few Osages remaining in the expedition after the Little Osages left him on the sixth of September under the leadership of No-Ears, and after *Paw-Hiu-Skah* the younger left with his hunter, all taking their horses with them, seemed to inspire Pike's contempt. Even at full strength, the Osage party was pitifully small, and after *Paw-Hiu-Skah* the younger left, there was none in authority, except perhaps the chieftain of the Eagle gens, Beautiful Bird.

One day as Pike called a halt near the divide between the Neosho and the Smoky Hill rivers at some convenient springs, the Osages noted the unusual nervousness of the buffalo during a time of normal atmospheric pressure. They had been running, and were still nervous, so the Osages knew that there was a Konza hunting party not far away, perhaps the very war party which they had been expecting to see.

When Pike paid no attention to the disturbed buffalo except to note their number and the possibility of securing some of them, the Osages became scornful, and warned him that they also might leave.

These defections along the way and the fear in which the Osages watched the horizons and the manner in which they watched the movement of game, and their constant sending of scouts to the highest points, to stand like statues, inspired contempt in Pike. When all was going well, he had praise for their bravery and their physical beauty, admitting that they were tall, erect, and dignified, but now when they were giving him trouble and had led him, according to his own reckonings, one hundred miles out of his way because, he said, they were afraid, and in many ways were wrecking his plans by leaving him singly and in groups and taking their horses, he became like any aggressive European suffused with a feeling of imposed-upon virtue.

Because they knew the Konzas were making the war movement and that a small party of Konza warriors of perhaps only twenty-five or thirty, ready and emotionalized, could wipe out Pike's twenty infantrymen and his small party of Pawnees and Osages and his few others in one dawn rush, the Little Ones were constantly on the alert and in fear.

After perhaps a dozen Osages had left his party with their horses and there were only a few left, "an Osage woman" informed him that two more of the Osages had planned to leave during the night and take some of the horses along with them. One of these men was the husband of the woman, and since only one woman had been mentioned as accompanying the party, this must have been Goes-to-Meet-the-Men, and since Pike had now engaged her as a spy, she may have been playing a Malinche role to Pike's Cortés.

"Thus," he writes in his journal, "we were obliged to keep ourselves on guard against our own companions and fellow-travellers—men of a nation highly favored by the United States, but whom I believe to be a faithless set of poltrons, incapable of a great and generous action. Among them, indeed, there may be some exceptions."

And after he arrived at the Pawnee village, he wrote to General Wilkinson of his troubles and of his suspicious reception at the Pawnee villages, adding that he had been led out of his course by the Osages, and "this was entirely owing to the pusillanimity of the Osage, who were more afraid of the Kans, than I could possibly have imagined."

There was another element in his injured innocence creating his bitter frustrations which he projected to the reluctant Osages. This was competitive jealousy of Meriwether Lewis, who was now floating down the Missouri on the way home.

But there was less gasconading than one might expect in a young man of twenty-seven with a tremendous responsibility, and this journal reveals him as much more than a military man doing his duty. However, there had been the sincere boast of youth in a previous letter to General Wilkinson, wherein he stated that he "would stand against odds" as the Greeks did at Thermopylae.

He also manifested his youthfulness one rainy day when the expedition was immobilized. He and his companions, grown tired of the Bible and Pope's essays, tattooed their arms with "some characters, which will frequently bring to mind our forlorn and dreary situation, as well as the happiest days of our life."

His humanity shows through not only in the incident of the rattlesnake but also after they reached the drainage of the Neosho, on the Cottonwood River of modern Kansas. It was the twelfth of September before they saw great herds of buffalo, wapiti, and pronghorn, which indicates that game was beginning to move away from the settlements to the east. Pike had stood on a high hill and had seen in one panorama, buffalo, wapiti, deer, pronghorn, and panthers. The expedition began to pass through great herds of buffalo, wapiti, and pronghorn, and his men, with that inscrutable urge to destruction the man escaped from the pressure of the social, political, and economic stratification of Europe seemed to have as unrestrained Americans, began slaughtering them. Instead of joining them, Pike ordered his men to shoot only as they needed meat. "I prevented the men shooting at the game, not merely because of the scarcity of ammunition, but, as I conceived, the laws of morality forbid it also."

The Pawnees of the Buffalo-Dung Waters, the Republican River, wanted to impress the Osages, and when they heard they were coming with Pike, they paid only formal attention to Pike, but received their enemy with much ceremony. They had made a small circular spot which they had cleared of grass, and there they requested the Beautiful Bird and four of the warriors to be seated, then they presented them with eight of their best horses. In the lineaments, in the high heads, flowing manes, and in the red or bay splashes on the ground white of these pintos, there were Pawnee boasts for these few Osages to take back to the Place-of-the-Many-Swans. The Pawnees were horse proud, and the Osages good horse takers but poor breeders.

These eight fine Pawnee horses represented generosity of an enemy with strong medicine as well, men whose bravery and dignity and strong medicine could well be represented by noble generosity.

Besides this, the Spaniard Malgares had set out from Santa Fe with 600 horses to visit the Pawnees of the Republican as well as the Pawnee-*maha,* and had just left the Pawnee villages when Pike arrived, leaving a broad, startling trail and a stand of colors and had decorated some of the leaders and had certainly impressed them with Spanish power. The comparison of Pike's handful with the Spanish cavalcade would have inspired respect for the medicine of the Spaniards against the weakness of the United States in the Indian mind. Also there was the energetic enterpriser Manuel Lisa and his grandiose plans, and his plans certainly did not conflict with the Spanish plan.

373

It is not unlikely that Lisa had with the aid of Malgares brought about the ephemeral peace between Pawnees and Osages; this was in his great scheme.

Malgares might have been instructed by clever, acquisitive Lisa or someone well acquainted with the psychology of the Plains Indian or someone who knew about the reverence among the Osages for old age, and knew about the same reverence in the Pawnees. So it might seem that when young Malgares had been chosen to lead the cavalry to the Pawnee villages on the Republican, he had been instructed to pose as just a young man deferring to the Pawnee chiefs. He rode over the prairie at the head of a proud troop mounted on white horses. On the ocean-waved prairie a flock of resting snow geese on their way to the Arctic Circle, would draw all eyes like a heliographic signal, and the Spanish horses were said to be six hundred. The Padoucas must have watched them crossing the plains with wonder and admiration, and certainly they sat happily in council with Malgares and his men when the Spaniards had gone down the Red River 420 miles for the express purpose of impressing them. The Malgares cavalcade then went north across drainage, across the Canadian and the Cimarron.

The scouts of Le Grand Peste must have watched them as they came to the big bend of the Arkansas, and the Konzas must have been awed by them, since they were eager to make peace when the next white men came along requesting it. And when the Pawnee scouts came racing into the villages of the Republican to tell their story, the Pawnee chiefs must have been half won over.

They were impressed by this grand parade of Spanish power, just as the Spaniards had planned, and they were impressed by the modest young leader Malgares, who, simpering, told them that he was too young to make binding agreements and that he had been sent to pay the great Pawnees a courtesy visit and distribute presents of mules, and medals and flags to flap over their villages. He gave them commissions written with flourishes.

Pike was upset by the magnificent display of the Spaniards and unhappy about his own motley handful, after the ceremonies of the

welcome and after he had pumped all the information he could obtain from the Pawnees about the Spaniards, who apparently were
looking for him and his party as a side line to their grand opera gesture. Pike and his superiors thought the whole expedition had set out
with capture of himself as their chief objective.

But as he sat in the Pawnee villages, he could now project the unacceptable, humiliating frustrations to the Spaniards, and give the
poor Osages a reprieve. He wrote Secretary of War Dearborn that he
knew now that the Spaniards had made this great, histrionic flourish
for the express purpose of frightening the Indians with a show of
Spanish power, and to create a combination of tribes to play against
the United States. Not only this, but they were making these maneuvers on the territory of the United States.

The odious comparison between the grand Spanish cavalcade with
its white horses and its fancy leader and the sweaty, tattered Pike
expedition was all in favor of Spain and Lisa, as was the comparison
between the young Malgares, vicariously powerful but modest before
old age, represented by the Pawnee leaders, and jealous, worried
young man Pike, projecting to the Osages and to Malgares the bitter
consciousness of disappointments and defeats which he would not
entertain as being only within his own ambitious mind, created from
his jealousy of Lewis.

The ceremony with which the Pawnees greeted their ancient enemy, the Osages, was impressive. The whole party were stopped about
three miles from the villages, and the Osages were asked to sit on the
cleared spot.

The Pawnees were showing off, too. They advanced within a mile
of the Pike party and halted and then divided into two parts, one
group coming to one side and one to the other side of the Pike men
and the Osages at full run, simulating a charge, yelling and pretending to fly their arrows, firing an occasional gun. Then they surrounded the little party, and the chief, whose name was translated as
Angry Chief, rode to the center of their circle and gave Pike his hand.

The Osages remained seated, but the Beautiful Bird, now recognized leader of the Osages since *Paw-Hiu-Skah* the younger had de-

375

parted, rose and walked to Angry Chief, the Pawnee, with a lighted pipe which he handed up to him. The Pawnee took a few mouthfuls of smoke, then handed the pipe back to Beautiful Bird.

The Chief motioned Pike on one side of himself and Lieutenant Wilkinson on the other, and thus they rode toward the villages, followed by the men and the baggage, and all flanked by the cavorting Pawnee horsemen. On a hill overlooking the villages, the column was stopped, and it was here that the Osages were given their horses as presents from their enemy-hosts.

Pike, during his stay at the Pawnee villages, did accomplish a peace between the Osages and the Konzas, despite the fact that the Little Osages had already left for the Place-of-the-Many-Swans, and after some effort persuaded the Pawnee chief to haul down the Spanish flag and hoist the United States flag in its place. Young Pike was not all brashness and of crystallized military mentality. After the Pawnees had hauled down the Spanish colors, with great reluctance, fearing the power on white horses, Pike could write in his journal:

"This probably was carrying the pride of nations a little too far, as there had so lately been a large force of Spanish cavalry at the village, which had made a great impression on the minds of the young men as to their power, consequence, etc., which my appearance with 20 infantry was by no means calculated to remove."

After the flag of the United States had been hoisted in front of the chief's door and after Pike had read in the faces of the council the fear and "sorrow," he took up the Spanish colors and told them "that as they had now shown themselves as dutiful children in acknowledging their great American father, I did not wish to embarrass them with the Spaniards for it was the wish of the Americans that their red brethren should remain peaceable round their own fires, and not embroil themselves in any disputes between the white people: and that for fear the Spaniards might return there in force again, I returned their flag, but with an injunction that it should never be hoisted during our stay."

Pike had a very difficult time, first because he had only a few men with him to back up his bravado, secondly because he was quite young and had received no diplomatically wise council from Jeffer-

son, Wilkinson, or Dearborn about the respect which youth, no matter what epaulets of rank he wore, owed to Indian old age.

There was no chance of approaching the Padoucas through the
Osages or the Pawnees since there was at the moment skirmish-war
between the Pawnees and the Padoucas, and Goes-to-Meet-the-Men
took this opportunity to run off with a slick Pawnee who had been
to "the States." The husband had been in the lodge of a chieftain of
the Pawnees, and the host Pawnee was insulted and proclaimed his
intention of killing "Frank" when he might come up with him.

The Pawnee leaders were so impressed by the power and glory of
the Spaniards under Malgares that Pike's plans to extend his explorations inspired fear and worry among them. They became gruff
and discourteous and told him that he was not to be permitted to go
any farther, since they had stopped Malgares of the Spaniards from
going farther, and he, the young man, learning the wishes of the older
Pawnees, had turned back. The trail which they had made on their
return to their home was plain with horse droppings and trampled
grass. They, the leaders, could show Pike that the Spaniards had gone
home.

Pike, however, insisted on going where he had been ordered, and
when he left the Pawnee villages on October 7, 1806, he followed the
broad trail of the Spanish cavalcade, and intended to keep it, realizing
that the Spaniards would know where to find wood and water.

The Pawnees in bluff-paint and gestures surrounded them and pretended attack, and Pike was worried and kept wondering what his
chances would be if the Pawnees really attacked. He decided to give
orders not to fire until the Indians had come within five or six paces,
and then to charge with bayonet and saber. He realized that his little
party would have been exterminated, but he could account for one
hundred of the Pawnees, he thought.

His party was really pitiful on the limitless prairie. There were
himself and Lieutenant Wilkinson, eighteen soldiers, one interpreter,
"Baroney" Vásquez, a sub-gentile chieftain of the Eagle, Beautiful
Bird, his hunter companion, another Osage man, and a woman. This
might have been the returned Goes-to-Meet-the-Men, or it may have
been another woman heretofore not mentioned. There had been only

one Osage woman with the expedition when they reached the Pawnee villages, according to Pike's journal.

Pike assured himself that his party consisted of twenty-five "warriors," represented by two officers, eighteen soldiers, one interpreter,
and four Osages.

As he followed the imposing trail of Malgares' cavalcade across the
Solomon, the Grand Saline, and the Smoky Hill rivers, Pawnee bluff-
riders would make simulated charges, circle, and make signs for him
to go home, and this display by a traditional enemy was too much for
Beautiful Bird and his soldier. They left the expedition at the Grand
Saline, saying that their enemies surrounded them and if they continued up the Arkansas instead of down it, their other enemies the
Padoucas would see them, and there would be only the weak medicine of Pike to protect them. There was no mistaking the Osages;
they always wore the quivering scalplock of perpetual challenge: even
the wolves, they boasted, recognized the deer-tail, gobbler "beard"
roach of the Osages. Their enemies were everywhere reaching out to
take them.

This left only the nameless man and the woman. When Pike's
party arrived at the Big Bend of the Arkansas, he and Lieutenant
Wilkinson parted, and the two Osages went down the river with
Wilkinson and five of the men. They spent some time at the Big
Bend making a dugout out of a cottonwood and a bullboat out of
four buffalo skins and two wapiti skins. Wilkinson, three of the men,
and the Osage woman seated themselves in the bullboat and a soldier
and the Osage man arranged themselves in the dugout with the baggage, while the sixth man walked along the shore.

Pike and Wilkinson held up their hands to each other and said,
"God bless you," as they parted, Wilkinson worried about how Le
Grand Peste down the Arkansas might receive him, or if a party of
Pawnees might appear at some point along the river. Pike with the
other members of the expedition would leave Malgares' trail here
and go up the Arkansas in search of the Red and become hopelessly
and miserably lost, but would have a peak of the Rockies named
for him.

It was October 27 when Pike and his Lieutenant Wilkinson wished

378

God's blessing on each other at a point in the vicinity of Great Bend, Kansas, and Wilkinson, annoyed with Pike for not allowing him sufficient equipage, wrote to his father about the manner in which Pike treated him. Actually Pike seemed to have been overgenerous with him to the sacrifice of his own equipment. They had been together a long time and were perhaps getting on each other's nerves, and the excitement had faded for Wilkinson. There were no more dramatic scenes of Osage captives meeting their relatives and friends and no more dazzling Pawnee histrionics. It had been hard work making a canoe out of a cottonwood and making a bullboat out of four buffalo hides and two elk skins.

He was a young man suddenly thrown on his own, and he was deeply worried about what he might find downriver. The Arkansas was more than a quill mark of cottonwoods and sand dunes and strings of water here at the Big Bend. The luxuriant growth of trees were menacing to one who had been days on the prairie-plains. "Their journey was a succession of discouraging difficulties and hardships, occasioned by the cold, rain, and snow, and frequent lack of food."

The Little Ones were on their autumnal hunt on the Salt Fork of the Arkansas, and Lieutenant Wilkinson was happy to hear that Soughing-of-the-Wind was in camp. Soughing-of-the-Wind appealed to him apparently, perhaps to his mind embodying romance and adventure. He was so enthusiastic that he ignored his condition and made his way across the thirty miles that separated the Salt Fork from its parent, the Arkansas, when Soughing-of-the-Wind had sent a messenger to say that he wanted to see his friend the messenger, saying also that Soughing-of-the-Wind was very ill in the hunting camp. This was November 30, 1806.

The young man was worried about the Pawnees' coming down to intercept him, and ahead of him was The Pest, one of the whimsical leaders of the Osages-of-the-Oaks, the Arkansas Osages. He had entrée to the camps of these Upland-Forest People called by the French, Osage des Chênes, but Wilkinson, like other Americans, might have called them "Shainers."

Just beyond the mouth of the Cimarron, he came to the camp of

Makes-Tracks-Far-Away. He was the chieftain whom Chouteau had made a chief when he removed part of the tribe to the Three Forks, and perhaps he was the one referred to by the French as "La Peste," and was certainly the one referred to as "Cashesegra" by the traders and writers of reports and by the travelers, which they translated as "Big Track."

On December 27, with his miserable party he passed the mouths of the Verdigris and the Neosho rivers and observed the luxuriant growth of cane which was almost impenetrable in the rich bottoms of the rivers. He noted that here among the mad Shainers a fort ought to be built.

Near the mouth of the Canadian they passed the falls which were nearly seven feet high and which are now a ripple and called Webbers Falls.

He must have been happy to arrive at Arkansas Post on January 9 and to arrive at New Orleans March 1 with only his original men, the Osages having gladly left him at one of the hunting camps or at the Three Forks.

Wilkinson was to command the military part of an expedition up the Arkansas, an imposing expedition of thirty-five, and Pike on his way down the Red River from his captivity among the Spaniards, was ordered by General Wilkinson to give the Arkansas expedition the benefit of his experience. This was May 20, 1807, but by July of that year the expedition "was suspended." This was due to the fact that General Wilkinson was under a cloud because of charges that he was associated with the activities of Aaron Burr.

The expedition had planned to stay with the Osages-of-the-Oaks near the Three Forks during the first winter.

34. The Little Ones Touch the Feather

To THE FRENCH, the Little Ones were *méfiant* when they interfered in any way with French plans for the conquest of their domain and their own subjection by the French. To the Spaniards, they were just plain *diablos* who walked in man's form, and for the simple reason that they were physically present and resistant. Baron de Carondelet, a governor-general of Louisiana during the 1790's, sent orders from New Orleans to the commandant at St. Louis that the Osages were to be shot by any citizen on sight.

However, the Latin nations were never quite strong enough on the lower Missouri River to do much about them, so they had to excuse their "depredations," or even pamper them, as the French did, and thereby save face as best they could. But that which the Latins had hoped for was now in the making with the swarms of Americans and their European immigrants and chain-pressured east-of-the-Mississippi Indians. They began to overrun the domain of the Little Ones, no matter how energetic the Arkansas Osages were in decapitating them, or how often the Little Ones of the Place-of-the-Many-Swans rode out in their bluff-paint.

And now the chain-pressured Potawatomis and Kickapoos of the Algonkians began to cross the Smoky Waters to attack their hunting camps when the hunters were absent and there were only old men and women and children there. The first Iroquoians they would meet in historical times, the Cherokees from Georgia and the Carolinas,

381

were seeping across the Mississippi into the Arkansas country, and of course their ancient enemies the Pawnee Caddoans and the Athapascan Apaches and the people called Padoucas were, as ever, pressing them along the struggle-line on the plains. But the struggles with the Pawnee and the Padoucas were range-boundary struggles as they had always been. They were still singing during their mourning dances, that "something must die in the west," despite the fact that the thing that would take away their "remaining days" was coming from the east, from across the Big Waters—the very direction from which Grandfather the Sun came. *Mo'n-Ha,* the Cliffs, the West, was still the direction of evil and of death, but something was wrong. What would the Little Old Men do about this medicine of the Heavy Eyebrows? They had accepted the power of his *mo'n-ce,* metal, and had availed themselves of its power through new ritual, but still the Heavy Eyebrows came onto their Sacred One and killed their "brothers," leaving them to lie and swell in the sun, and they could only sing and dance their traditional prayers and meticulously carry out every detail of the sacred war movement.

Would Wah'Kon-Tah tell them what to do through the Little Old Men? The Heavy Eyebrows were like the leaves from the oaks during Just-Doing-That Moon, March, when the mad winds carried leaves into the lodges, and eddied them into little piles. When the scolding women swept them out, the mad winds would blow them in again.

Behind the Jeffersonian policy was the hint that these "bad" Indians ought to be confirmed in their territorial claims, and they ought to make up their minds whether they wanted to live at Three Forks, the Place-of-the-Many-Swans, or at the Place-of-the-Oaks, the assumption being that they didn't need all the territory they had claimed for centuries and which had been necessary for their support as nomads and meat-eaters. Now they must give up some of their land to the Indians who had been driven from their ancient domains by the Europeans and other tribes using the guns of the Europeans. The ultimate result of this policy as the immigrants swarmed west would have been a final push into the Pacific Ocean, or a huddling of all the Indians of the continent, or at least that part of the continent controlled by the United States, on the deserts between the Rocky Mountains and the Sierra Nevadas, an enclave which would have been honored by the plowmen and the stockmen.

However, the new states in confederation couldn't quite understand their own destiny, their boasting notwithstanding. They were quite satisfied with their periodic "final settlements" of the Indians problem by relegating certain tribes to certain areas for as "long as the waters run." They smoked the "calumet" and shook hands all around, and the smug black-coated commissioners went back to Washington or to their political or military jobs.

Not so with the Indians. They had given their word over the pipe and believed that all the words given at the council were sacred. Sometimes soldiers of the Long Knives–Heavy Eyebrows were sent to aid them in carrying out the provisions of the treaties and in guarding their new borders, but it was like stopping a flood on the Smoky Waters.

The Anglo-Saxon invaders had a tribal memory as well as the Little Ones. It was a racial memory of British kings who could have you hanged from a cross-road gibbet if you killed a deer or a partridge in New Forest or any other royal or ducal preserve; and here in America they were expanding, as though through a safety valve, from the political, social, and economic pressures of the centuries. Not only did they have racial memories of suppression by princes and parliaments and hierarchies, but they might even have fresh memories of the class distinctions in the Thirteen Colonies. These free men were not scholars and gentlemen from the Atlantic Seaboard, but many of them, perhaps most of them, were refugees from the law and were men more savage than those whom they called "Injuns." It was these barbarians who shouted of their freedom from kings and strong governments and princes of both worlds, in the wilderness, and raped and murdered and stole horses and brought the *we-lu-schka,* "the little people," to the Little Ones and took away their "remaining days." Men, fugitives from justice, who would certainly have been hanged if they had not fled the areas where the law was not attenuated, but who when scalped by the Little Ones, became "American citizens." The "Flanders' knives" of the Little Ones was the only agency that could effect such a transformation.

383

It was these barbarians who were mobile and nomadic, and who were not satisfied to stay on their little bits of earth and dream of two-story houses and great barns and fields of cattle, but must steal horses from the Little Ones and hunt them when they had a rare chance, as they might hunt bear. It was they who cried to the authorities that the "goddam Injuns was a-settin' on land belongin' by rights to free Amuricans." The average free man expanding in the wilderness wanted only peace to realize his dreams, even extravagant dreams, in his racial memories of a prince's wealth and castle.

Before the Louisiana Purchase there were settlers from east of the Mississippi invited over by the Spaniards. The Spaniards had been selective and had granted lands only to the better class of American citizens. These grants were along the lower Missouri and the Meramec rivers and south, and both the French and the Spaniards had thought well of these men. In 1798, Zenon Trudeau, commandant of St. Louis, wrote to the Governor-General at New Orleans: "The few Americans who have immigrated to this district the last year have behaved well, for since they have found lands superior to those of the Ohio, they are earnestly beginning to improve them. Almost all of them desire good sites for mills. Those who have obtained them are earnestly increasing this industry; already they have constructed two small water-power mills (for flour) and one saw mill in distinct places where no one would have imagined even that could really work. Their houses are already better than those of the Creoles and Canadians who were settled in villages thirty years ago."

The new government of the United States had had its Constitution only a few years. It was a symposium of remarkably farseeing ideas contributed by native gentlemen and erstwhile Englishmen, but the very beautiful structure of government which they crystallized had no police arm long enough to reach across the Mississippi. The Latins, the French and the Spaniards, were much more able to control their subjects since they were fewer and still traditionally obedient, though their powers were also attenuated. Even after the French Revolution the French *citoyen* carried on much as he had done before.

The beautiful sense of justice embodied in beautiful words could not be applied west of the Mississippi during this period, because the

384

gentlemen and scholars and orators and jurists of the East had to depend upon rather frail agencies in the persons of pompous commissioners and acquisitive fur traders. These gentlemen almost believed that the words of the Constitution and of the Bill of Rights were sacred, as the Little Ones believed certain words to be sacred, with the exception that the Little Ones had the military power to back theirs.

However, it was surprising how many honorable men the new government had as agents and commissioners in the wild lands across the Mississippi, but even a William Clark, a Meriwether Lewis, or the Sibleys, father and son, could not stand against the swarming free men any better than the Little Ones could. The medicine of the new government on the Atlantic Seaboard was also weak.

On their return from the mouth of the Columbia River, Lewis and Clark coming down the Missouri River noted the high limestone bluff on the right bank which had deflected the current of the mad river for centuries, and here on this bluff, they believed, would be the perfect place for a fort.

They came into charge of the new country immediately upon their return. Lewis became governor and Clark became commander of the militia and the Indian agent of the Louisiana Territory.

They had very serious problems, and their problems were those of the French and, to a certain extent, those of the Spaniards. There was the encroachment of the English on the north, the activities of the Spaniards south of the Red River, who were, like the English of the north, attempting to organize the Indians against the new government and conniving with its more susceptible citizens. There was the fast-growing fur trade, and there was competition in this trade with the English on the north and the Spaniards to the south and west, and there was the immediate problem of the Little Ones, energetically defending their domain against the shouting free man.

The free men were not necessarily shouting for land, despite the fact that that was what one might suppose they wanted, because there was plenty of land to satisfy them in Kentucky and Ohio and Illinois. This was rather too obvious, so they wanted the government to do something about the "Injuns" who were occupying good farming land east of the Mississippi, since the sending of the east-of-the-Mississippi Indians to the west of the Mississippi was a Jeffersonian idea anyway.

Also there had been unrest in 1806 among the serious settlers east of the Mississippi because of the agricultural depression brought about by the Napoleonic wars.

Naturally the great expanse of the domain of the Little Ones, rich in soils and game and lead, came to the thoughts of those who advised the government on such matters. There would be plenty of room there for the unwanted east-of-the-Mississippi Indians. And anyway the Little Ones were classified as "bad Indians." The Indian problem could be solved by moving the Little Ones over several hundred miles to the west, and in so doing not even disturbing their villages on the south fork of their river called Osage.

The conscientious Meriwether Lewis, as governor, counciled with his old friend and employer, President Jefferson, and his old companion William Clark, and they got in touch with Pierre Chouteau, agent of the Little Ones, and ordered him to meet them on the Missouri River five miles above Fire Prairie, November 10, 1808. They would make a treaty with the Osages here.

However, difficulties arose almost immediately, when Pierre Chouteau and Noel Maugraine asked that there be incorporated in the treaty a transaction in which the Osages were supposed to have given land to them. This had been a request having to do with the tentative treaty, the one Clark had effected in September, 1808; but in the treaty which Lewis sent by Pierre Chouteau to the Osages to be confirmed by all the chiefs, and which he referred to as "number two treaty" in his letter to the President, Chouteau's claim to 30,000 arpents of land on the Mine River and Maugraine's claim to land on the Saline River, both within the territory to be ceded, were not considered; and Lewis tells his friend the President what he thinks of the claim. He thinks the claims invalid and deserving no consideration whatsoever. The honest Lewis would not say that either Chouteau or Maugraine used White Hair as a tool in the matter, but he hints a possibility. He assures the President that Paul Louis [Loise] the interpreter would be quite above misrepresentation in his translations.

Distortion of speeches was a practice among interpreters quite often.

His suspicions rested on rather solid ground, perhaps represented by the fact that after the Clark agreement of September, a delegation of Osages had come to St. Louis to say that they had been deceived and had been led to believe that they were ceding the large area included in the treaty to the Great White Father only for his children to hunt in. Lewis wrote to Jefferson that they might have been influenced to do this by someone, since he knew Clark well enough to know that he had taken meticulous steps to make the details clear to the Osages. Also there was the fact that Noel Maugraine had married a daughter of White Hair, and he himself was a mixed-blood, French-Osage. And, lastly, it was well known that White Hair, who claimed to be the Grand *Ki-He-Kah,* was really a creation of the Chouteaus'.

White Hair in a speech confirmed the claims of Chouteau and Maugraine, but this was not convincing to either Clark or Lewis. They might have been a little brittle in their attitude, and might have forgotten that they had suggested to the President the old strategy of cutting off supplies to the Little Ones, so that they might become submissive and sign the treaty which was being forced upon them by the broken, wandering tribes east of the Mississippi and the free men. Their cutting off of supplies to the Little Ones was much more effective than such attempts made many times by the French and the Spaniards, added to the possibility that the Little Ones might by this time have become almost completely dependent upon white man's *wah-don-skas,* with the decrease of game being a contributing factor.

The result was that the stiff honor of Clark came into direct conflict with the flexible fairness of the acquisitive Chouteau, and they were uncivil to each other and actually stopped speaking.

It might seem, however, that the imperious Little Ones, even in their dependence upon trade goods, might not have yielded to Lewis and Clark without the aid of Chouteau, if Sibley's impressions in his letter to his superiors later in 1812 is correct. He wrote that during the council between the Osages and the three commissioners of the government, Clark, Lewis, and Chouteau. Chouteau had spoken to the assembled Osages in substance: "You have heard this treaty explained to you. Those who now come forward and sign it shall be considered the friends of the United States and treated accordingly. Those who refuse to come forward and sign it shall be considered enemies of the United States and treated accordingly."

Then he wrote that the Osages replied in substance, ". . . that if the American father wanted a part of their land, he must have it, that he was strong and powerful and they were poor and pitiful. What could they do? He had demanded their land and had thought proper to offer them something in return for it. They had no choice. They must either sign the treaty or be declared the enemies of the United States."

This was neither the spirit of *Tzi-Sho Hunkah,* the Grand *Tzi-Sho* of the moment, nor the spirit of Arrow-Going-Home, the Grand *Hunkah* of the moment. The former is never mentioned, and the other was far away on the Verdigris and had refused to have anything to do with the treaty, representing at least half of the tribe. Nor, yet, was this humility the spirit of the tribesmen who were still at the Place-of-the-Many-Swans. This must have been the gist of the speech of White Hair, and because of its un-Osage-like humility and sweet reasonableness, it has been recorded by a really honest man who said he knew them well.

In article one, the United States government indicated that they were "anxious to promote peace, friendship, and intercourse with the Osage tribes, to afford them every assistance in their power, and to protect them from insults and injuries from other tribes of Indians situated near the settlements of the white people, [and] have thought proper to build a fort on the right bank of the Missouri, a few miles above the Fire Prairie, and agree to garrison the same with as many regular troops as the President of the United States may from time to time deem necessary for the protection of all orderly, friendly, and well-disposed Indians of the Great and Little Osages, who reside at this place and who do strictly conform to and pursue the councils or admonitions of the President of the United States through his subordinate officers."

The Secretary of War had been considering the old strategy of the Spaniards and the French, and had given consent to the organization of a large war party of Shawnees, Delawares, Potawatomis, and others to go against the Little Ones, when Governor Meriwether Lewis's plan of a treaty by which land would be ceded and the "lawless Osages" pushed farther west, and a fort to be built in their country, came to his attention. The organizing tribes were disappointed, and the Choctaws under their chief Push-ma-ta-hah had come all the way up to the mouth of the Verdigris in 1807 to attack the Little Ones there. The Quapaws, Choctaws, Chickasaws, and Shawnees had organized a war party of 800, and were intent on carrying out the Cherokee plan for taking the domain of the Little Ones as a home for the homeless ones east of the Mississippi.

The commissioners drew a line from the point of their meeting near Fire Prairie on the Missouri River straight south until the line touched the Arkansas River. This line would hereafter be the boundary between the domain of the Little Ones and the land of the settlers. The Little Ones agreed by the treaty to cede any claim to land east of this line. After the line touched the Arkansas River, it would run southeasterly with the river to its mouth on the Mississippi River, and therefore all lands north of the Arkansas River, east of the point where the north and south line touched, would be ceded to the United States. Also ceded were all lands "northwardly from the River Missouri."

The ceded land represented practically all of the modern state of Missouri, south of the Missouri River, and "northwardly from the River Missouri," and east of a line running from the modern Sibley, Missouri, and Fort Smith, Arkansas, and which also includes the modern state of Arkansas north of the Arkansas River, except for an ungenerous pie wedge represented by land lying between the north-south line between Sibley, Missouri, and Fort Smith, Arkansas, and the modern Oklahoma–Arkansas boundary. The only part of the modern state of Missouri not included in the ceded territory of the treaty of 1808 was a narrow planklike area between the old north-south line between Sibley and Fort Smith and the modern Oklahoma–Missouri boundary and the modern Kansas–Missouri boundary. An area, "almost equal to the state of Virginia, and much more fertile," Lewis informed Mr. Jefferson, referring to the ceded land.

The Little Ones also ceded a tract of land two leagues square, later

389

called "six miles," upon which to build the fort on the bluff overlooking the Missouri River, which site Lewis and Clark had chosen. This was at the point where the north-south boundary line had its beginning.

The United States on its part was to furnish the Little Ones with a blacksmith, tools to mend their arms, and utensils of husbandry. It pledged itself to build a large water mill, furnish plows, and build for the chief of the Grand Osages a block house and for the chief of the Little Osages a block house in the villages where they would establish their residences near the fort. However, the north-south line left the old villages at the Place-of-the-Many-Swans within the part of their old domain still belonging to them.

Article four of the treaty considered the best way "to quiet animosities which at present exist between the inhabitants of the Territory of Louisiana and the Osage Nations, in consequence of the lawless depredations of the latter, the United States do further agree to pay their own citizens the full value of such property as they can legally prove to have been stolen or destroyed by the said Osages since the acquisition of Louisiana by the United States, provided, the same does not exceed $5,000."

The United States through its commissioners also, "in consideration of the lands relinquished by the Great and Little Osages to the United States, promise to deliver at Fire Prairie, or at St. Louis, yearly to the Great Osage Nation, merchandise to the amount of value of $1,000 and to the Little Osage Nation, merchandise to the amount or value of $500.00." In addition, the United States would pay the Great Osages $800 and the Little Osages $400. They would be allowed to hunt as they had done formerly on "all that tract of country, west of the north and south boundary line, on which they, the said Great and Little Osage, have usually hunted or resided: *Provided,* The same be not the hunting grounds of any nation or tribe of Indians in amity with the United States; and on any other lands within the territory of Louisiana, without the limits of the white settlements, until the United States may think proper to assign the same as hunting grounds to other friendly Indians." No one would be allowed to cross the boundary into the Osage domain except the persons essential to the carrying out of the treaty provisions, or to cross the boundary line without special permit, and the Little Ones could arrest and deliver up trespassers or those doing mischief west of the north-south boundary and south of the Arkansas River. Stolen horses were to be delivered to the side of the boundary line from which they had been stolen, and the value of property taken by individual Osages was to be subtracted from the tribal annuities. Also, the Osages were not to supply arms to any tribe or nation not in amity with the United States, nor were they to be allowed to sell their lands to anyone except to the United States.

Several of the chieftains and warriors "touched the feather" for the first time that November day in 1808, making a cross with the quill, against which the clerk set down their names as Louis Paul gave them. The phonetics were bad, perhaps as bad as the half-hearted little speeches which Lewis later sent to Jefferson.

The names of the Grand and Little Osages, all of the Place-of-the-Many-Swans, who "touched the feather" are scarcely recognizable. There was "The Grand Chief of the Big Osage," spelled "Papuisea." This was undoubtedly *Paw-Hiu-Skah,* White Hair, who claimed to be the *Ki-He-Kah.* The original White Hair died sometime this year, and this might have been White Hair the younger. Then there was "Grand Chief of the Little Osages," spelled "Nichu Malli," who was at this time *Ni-Zhiu-Mo'n-I'n,* Traveling Rain. The "Second Chief of the Big Osages" was spelled "Voithe Voihe." This is impossible. One hopes he pleased both White Hair and himself with his speech, since he must remain obscure. "The second Chief of the Little Osages" was spelled "Voithe Chinga," which just possibly means "little" something. "Little Chief of the Big Osages" was spelled "Ta Voingare," from which one can only make *To-Wo'n-Ga-Xe,* which means Town Maker, and was Arrow-Going-Home's other name. He wasn't there. Then there was "Little Chief of the Little Osages," spelled "Osagahe," which could have been *O-Ca-Ki-E* of the *Tzi-Sho Wa'no'n* gens. There was another "Little Chief of the Big Osages," spelled "Voichinodhe," which should have been *Wa-Zhi'n-U-Tzi,* meaning Courageous. The last was "Little Chief of the Little Osages," spelled "Voi Nache," who might have been of the Eagle gens, but whose possible fame was destroyed by ignorance or care-lessness.

The Little Osages had once lived on the Missouri River in a valley on the right bank not far downriver from where the fort would be built. They had made their villages "down under" the cliffs in mem-ory of the position where they had built their drying fires and from which location they had received their name Down-Under-People, or Down-Below-People. This part of the Osage domain was familiar in gentile and tribal memory, and perhaps they had tribal memory of Sac and Fox canoes slipping up the Missouri in the darkness to attack them and destroy the villages of their allies the Missourias near them.

They came to live by the fort in accordance with the provisions of the treaty, but the Great Osage only came there for hunting supplies and provisions, and to be served by the blacksmith, before starting on their winter and summer hunts.

Governor Meriwether Lewis had written to the President that they had seemed contented with the treaty. They were perhaps wondering what had happened to their medicine, and there might have been in their minds the symbolism of being pushed toward *Mo'n-Ha,* the Cliffs, the West, and Spiritland.

35. Fort Osage and the War of 1812

THE UNITED STATES FIRST INFANTRY sent a force of eighty-one and the St. Charles mounted militia sent a force of eighty. These were the builders of the fort and served to garrison it.

Along with the regulars came the United States factor, Mr. George C. Sibley, with his trade goods in six keelboats; the militia, being mounted, took the old Osage trail.

Sibley was apparently a man of character, a surveyor and a dilettante scientist. The Little Ones were fortunate to have a man like him at this time to serve as their liaison with the Long Knife government.

He brought upriver with him traps, guns and ammunition, hatchets, knives, kettles, blankets, colored cloth, beads, silver ornaments, vermilion, and breechcloth, for which he would receive fox, beaver, wolf, bear, badger, and muskrat furs. He would also trade for buffalo robes and dressed and shaved deerskins.

Within a short time the factory was doing so well in functioning without loss that the private traders began to complain. It was the only factory operated by the government which was not showing a loss, but the disgruntled traders would add their voices to the cacophony, and in 1822 the government would abandon their profitable factory.

It was the Little Ones, of course, who made the factory a success. They were energetic hunters and trappers and were ever greedy for guns, so that they could remain powerful and continue to bluff their enemies, and their vanity and self-esteem were often amusing. They traded lavishly and improvidently with the French and then the Spaniards and now with the Americans, and to the government they were economically important.

It has been said that at times there were as many as 5,000 of them about the fort, sitting about fires that sent their strings of smoke above the trees when they came in the autumn to equip themselves for the autumnal buffalo hunts.

When they came in the summer or the spring, they stood about their smudge fires to take refuge from the mosquitoes that swarmed here among the trees where the breezes died. With their trade blankets half-blue and half-red or vertically striped, or their robes tied about their waists leaving their upper body bare, the men walked about with great dignity, like animated bronze statues. They might stand on the bluff by their fort and make obscene finger talk of contempt to the Iowas across the river.

They crowded into the factory, but were barred from the trade goods by a long counter, separating their long, exploring fingers from the fascinating merchandise. When they wished to discuss with each other a particular piece of merchandise or ask to examine some piece, they never pointed but pursed their lips at the piece. This was a gesture from the prairie and the woods used in the presence of game or when near the enemy. Protective immobility was sometimes tragically destroyed by the slightest movement of head or arm, or even finger, but one could purse the lips at an enemy crawling up a ravine, screened by bushes, or at a buck deer that was watching for slightest movement. Also, to point the finger was not only bad manners but a curse, and to the Bear gens lethal. If you put your index finger into your mouth and then pointed it at someone, he would die, they believed.

The clerks and the soldiers became accustomed to the pursed lips as an indicator, and both the clerks and the soldiers and Sibley had to know these things, not only for business reasons, but because the Bear people were like their life symbol, quick to become insensibly enraged, and now they carried butcher's knives with them.

But even the Bear were greedy for the *wah-don-skas* of the Long

Knives, and were therefore able to control their rages, and the clerks and the soldiers and Sibley were soon indicating with their pursed lips instead of with their index fingers.

The soldiers whistled often, but the Little Ones only quailed and feared, and left their presence as quickly as possible. It was better not only not to attract the attention of ghosts and *mi-ah-luschkas,* but to move away quickly fanning oneself with one's eagle-wing fan.

The fort was christened Fort Osage, but was often called Fort William Clark. It was a rough deltoid, high on its bluff of carboniferous limestone; there were four blockhouses or towers at the corners of the delta's base, and one main blockhouse or tower, all joined by palisades. There was an officers' quarters and a factory and barracks for the men, and a room for the blacksmith's shop and space for an artificer's house. These last were in the low houses which were a continuation of the barracks. Under the factory was a two-storied cellar, and on the first floor of the factory at the south end were Sibley's quarters, equipped with a fireplace.

The fort was completely surrounded by palisades, even on the river side. The river curved into the bluff from the north and when angry with snow waters in June, dashed at the foot of the bluff far down below the fort.

This was the first fort built by the United States government west of the Mississippi River, if one can except Wilkinson's Belle Fontaine near the mouth of the Missouri, and was rather in imitation of the British factory idea. It would not be the last fort built for the "benefit" of the Little Ones. There would be forts for the Arkansas Osages later.

The Little Ones, except for the interesting physical intrusion, allowed the new fort to have little effect on their *Tzi-Sho,* their Sky Lodge, or spiritual lives. They chanted each pre-dawn to the Morning Star and to Grandfather, and they held the mourning dance when one of their number died, almost under the palisades of the fort, but strangely enough not even Sibley seems to have made academic investigation of such traditional expressions. When visitors came down the river or up the river, they all stopped at the fort, and some of them fresh from Europe or England or from the Atlantic Seaboard were impressed according to their natures, and all asked questions of the courteous Sibley; but from the results of their writings later this information was meager, or else they believed the fumblings of the savages could have little interest for the readers of whom they seemed to be ever conscious.

A traveler from the East, one Henry Marie Brackenridge, visited the fort in the spring of 1811. He came up the river guarding a pipe which William Clark had asked him to present to No-Ears, who seemed to be sort of a regent for the little boy who would be chief and whose name was White Hair.

When the *shoka* ran to tell him that the boat had landed, No-Ears, expecting its arrival, was already dressed in his finest leggings and moccasins and had all the young men of his gens around him. He sat on a special mat in the middle of the lodge, periodically fumbling with his eagle feather stuck in his scalp roach.

Brackenridge when brought to him was very much impressed, and fell rather poetically under his spell until he learned that he was intriguing to become chief of the Little Osages, and that in his incredible vanity he refused to trade with the traders and gave away things to other people to make evident his generosity. This was new to Brackenridge, but was an old tradition among the chiefs. They held themselves above the trading and the ownership of things, though they kept their finery in a long parfleche and had herds of horses.

Every gesture No-Ears made was a grand one, even the motion to the *shoka* to bring the food, which was bowls of hominy. He was afflated with self-esteem.

The pipe was smoked, which is known among the Little Ones as the "chief's pipe," not calumet, and after the pipe, Brackenridge handed No-Ears the gift from Governor Clark.

The poet and the jurist in Brackenridge was rather startled and disillusioned by No-Ears' cunning in purchasing popularity by insane generosity and trying to imitate the office which he hoped to attain. He was only a chieftain at the time.

Brackenridge wrote later of No-Ears: "Such an ambition. Little know they of the state of society, who believe that it is free from jealousies, from envy, detection or guilty ambition. No demagogue, no Cataline ever used more arts and finesse, or displayed more policy than this cunning savage. The arts of flattery and bribery by which the unthinking multitude is seduced are the same everywhere and the passion for power and distinction seems inherent in human nature. It is not in the savage that we can expect to meet with liberty . . . ."

When he was awakened one morning by the chant to the Morning Star, he must have been afraid, but later he could write about it with smugness that one would not expect to find in a man of his attainments. He had been poetically excited about the clouds and the grass and the trees during that particular April of 1811, but thought the poignant weeping prayer by Neolithic man to his god "the most hideous howling I have ever heard." He had heard about the chant before and had possibly asked Sibley about it, but he had learned of "no satisfactory reason for it."

He thought, or someone had suggested to him, that it was "partly devotional and if it be true as supposed by some that they offer worship only to the evil spirit, the orison was certainly not unworthy of him."

What interested him much more were the seven Iowa scalps the Little Osage warriors brought to the village and danced over. They had worked themselves into such arrogance and high emotion that one of the warriors came to the gates of the fort and refused to halt at the command of the sentinel. The sentinel fired over his head, but he came on.

He had probably counted coup on two or perhaps three of the Iowa bodies and had perhaps killed the same ones, and their scalps had given him strong medicine, since one could have been a leader's scalp. Protected by this medicine and highly emotionalized, he came on in defiance of the sentinel.

The guard had to be called, and they seized him, but he only sneered and said that he would eat white man's bread in jail. He was defiant and the soldiers took him to the whipping post and applied the cat-o-nine-tails. This was the greatest insult you could offer a warrior; it amounted to many coups in one stroke.

He went to the village weeping and singing in disgrace, and when the others found out what had happened, they picked up their arms and marched on the fort. They could have taken it after setting it afire, and both sides knew this, but they finally dispersed when the cannons were swung on them from the towers.

This incident impressed Brackenridge, but he told of it in uninspired prose, and he was one with the nervous soldiery in his ignorance, since he had no idea of what was behind the warriors' actions.

The traveler, author, statesman, jurist, and poet Henry Marie Brackenridge left the fort disillusioned. His poetic soul had been ready to sing of the man in the "state of nature," but No-Ears' human frailties and the most "hideous howling" of the Little Ones to their god had shriveled it. It had been an eager soul on the way up the Missouri, and possibly he might have exhausted it through his appreciation of clouds and scenery, or on a demented white woman who ran wild in the woods just above the mouth of the Gasconade; his last stanza:

> *Alas poor hopeless frenzied maid,*
> *Who has thus sadly injured thee?*
> *Perhaps by falsehood's tongues betrayed.*
> *Or stung by viperous cruelty.*
> *Sad maniac of the wilderness,*
> *May heaven still in safety keep,*
> *And when thy darkened ray shall pass,*
> *The silent grove o'er thee shall weep.*

For the Little Ones he had one bit of praise. He wrote about them: "One good trait however deserves to be mentioned. They are rarely if ever been known to spill the blood of the white man." Unfortunately, this was untrue.

One of the visitors at the fort, John Bradbury, during the same period was more interested in botany and geology than Brackenridge had been, but even with his scientific propensities, he accepted the opinions of those whom he questioned quite often. He said that he had been informed that the reason the Osages cried and blackened their faces before attacking the whites (mourning dance songs and war movement prayer-songs) was that they felt sorry for those they were about to rob.

His boat had met a war party of Iowas, Potawatomis, and Yankton Sioux on the way up the river at Côte San Dessein, at the mouth of the Osage River, who were looking for Osages.

He very likely had not come up the river with the poetic eagerness and the illusions of Brackenridge, but he did seem disappointed when he saw a band of Little Osages walking along the bank parallel with the boats, and to him they were not the least romantic, and he seemed to be disillusioned when he had some of the conversation translated for him, especially the conversations of the women, which he called "obscene." He probably hadn't thought that there might be harlots among men "in the state of nature," and made much of the fact that a few widows and "sumac girls" made lewd finger signs to the boatmen. He watched long enough to convince himself that they had the success which women all over the world have who go to the docks to meet the men.

He wrote that the Little Osage village at the fort was made up of one hundred lodges made of "typha palustris," and he was intrigued by the persimmon cake mixed with pounded corn.

Dr. Murray at the fort had told him that the Indians "howled" every morning before dawn, and of course he was eager to hear them. He, being a scientist, was interested and waited for the mourning prayer. When it began, he arose and wrapped a blanket about him, tied a black handkerchief about his head, and stuck a "tomahawk" in his belt, then crept to the village and followed out of it a little way in the direction of the sound of chanting. It was moonlight, and he came near to a man who was "crying and howling," and he froze to watch him. Unfortunately the man saw him and stopped short, and would pray no more. He left and discovered another one with his back to a stump also "crying and howling," and this time he was not seen and had a good chance to watch the man. He got as little information about the "howling" as Brackenridge, and seemed to be contented with what Dr. Murray had told him; that they cried for the dead tribesmen as well as for favorite horses and dogs.

He saw some men helping the women and asked about them. His

informer said that these men were condemned to work with women because they had displayed cowardice in war. Quite often the homosexuals were cowardly in war, and did decorate themselves as women, and really enjoyed the company and conversation of women.

If the Little Ones had felt the terrifying shocks of the New Madrid earthquake in the years 1811–12, they would probably have had a very simple explanation for it—*Wah'Kon-Tah* showing his anger. This would not have seemed untimely either, since they had let the Heavy Eyebrows slaughter their "brothers," and had given up a great part of the Sacred One to the White Father. The shaking of the Sacred One, *Mo'n-Sho'n,* Mother Earth, would have been exactly what she and the Children of the Middle Waters deserved. Had they been in the center of it and had seen the trees topple into the Mississippi and great masses of earth and stone tumble into the river, they, like the mustang, would have given up.

Bradbury was in the center of the quaking area, and he was tossed about in his boats. He saw some frightened settlers on the bank, and he made his way to them and up to a house where several people of the area were assembled in fear. There was a Bible on the table. They had been praying.

They told him that most of the people had fled to the hills and that great crevasses had opened up. One of the frightened people was a man who seemed to know the cause of the quake. He said that the earth had got lodged between the horns of the comet that had been visible recently, and the rocking and jarring had been caused by the earth trying to get over one of the horns. If she made it, the settler thought, all would be well, but if she failed to get over the horn, all would be lost, the world and all in it.

The scientific man who had been identifying the plants and trees wrote, "Finding him confident in his hypothesis, and myself unable to refute him, I did not dispute the point."

Major Sibley placed the fort at latitude 39° 10′ 19″, longitude 93° 51′ 5″, and after satisfying himself of his exact position on earth, he set out in May, 1811, to visit the "Indian Country." This visit must be more than a social call or a get-acquainted visit, for rumors were that the British were organizing the red men, and by this time they had become more than rumors, and Sibley must assure himself and his government that the British were not drawing the Konzas and Pawnees into their alliance against the white settlers of the Lakes region and southward. He felt that he might still have control over the Little Ones.

The British had by now organized a confederacy among the red men, especially the Algonkians and perhaps some of the Siouan tribes, for the purpose of attacking the American settlements and for harassment of the United States government, whose people had begun not only to trespass on the natives' land but on territory claimed by the British. Also, perhaps, in the back of the British mind was the winning back of part or all the territory which they had lost in the Revolutionary War.

As a matter of fact, the War of 1812 was a-brewing, as a side issue and as a direct result of the Napoleonic wars in Europe.

Thus did Sibley set out in May, 1811, in order to ingratiate himself and his government with the Indians of the western drainage of the Missouri and along the Platte, especially the Pawnees. He had not gone prematurely, since in that same year the British agents had effected a strong confederation of the Indians of the Lakes region, with the Shawnee Tecumseh at their head, and on November 7 of that year, after Sibley's visit to the Konzas and the Pawnees, he, Tecumseh, and his Indians fought a European-type battle with American troops. This was on a tributary of the Wabash River, called Tippecanoe. They fought the battle by European rules, but, Indian-like, when they grew tired of the fight, they forgot their British training and retreated into Canada, thus making the battle really indecisive; and by thus leaving when they grew tired, they made William Henry Harrison, the governor of Indiana Territory, a national hero, and eventually a president of the United States.

Sibley's reading of the latitude and the longtitude told him exactly where he stood at the fort, but now he must know where he and America stood with "his" Indians, or would stand if the growing tension between England and the United States exploded into war.

He was impressed by the Kaw River drainage, and he wrote in his diary that it "abounds with game, deer, elk, some bears and sometimes buffalo." He kept reading the longitude and the latitude along his route. He had with him eleven Osages led by No-Ears, whom he called "Osage War Chief Sans Oreille." This might indicate that his companions were Little Osages, and this seems likely since they chose to move their village to the environs of the fort, taking advantage of the provisions of the treaty. Besides these, he had his personal servant and two interpreters—a party of fifteen.

He found the Konza village on the north bank of the Kaw River, one hundred miles by its course above its mouth at the Missouri, with the Republican River entering the Kaw "a few hundred paces" above the village. This should be about where the modern Fort Riley stands.

The British had apparently not yet come among the Konzas with their cajoleries, since there was an American flag plopping authoritatively above the chief's lodge. However, the Konza scouts certainly saw Sibley and his party coming a day or two before they arrived.

All right for the Konzas, but the British might conceivably draw into their confederation a strong tribe like the Pawnees. This might have seemed especially likely to an educated man, since it had been said that there were Pawnees with the British as well as their Iroquoian and Algonkian allies in the attack on St. Louis in 1780. The Little Ones with the aid of the Konzas had by this time driven the Pawnees from their villages on the Republican, and they had gone to join other divisions of their tribe on the Platte, settling about two hundred miles above its mouth. This might have aroused Sibley's suspicion, this concentration of the powerful Pawnees, and he seemed to want to believe the boast of the Konzas that they had driven them there "about two years ago." Otherwise, it would seem that four divisions of the Pawnees close together on the Platte might mean that they were concentrated for some special purpose. The divisions were quite close together, and the Pawnee-*maha,* or Loups, were only ten miles up the Platte from the others.

One of Sibley's commissions was to effect an amity among the tribes of the area and make of them a happy family of American allies in the face of British activity in the area covered by his authority as a factor.

He succeeded in patching up the differences among the Little Ones and the Konzas and the Pawnees. He left the Pawnee villages the fourth of June, and took a course sixteen degrees southeastward to the hunting camp of the Little Osages on the Arkansas, 175 miles away. He had parted with No-Ears some time earlier, and now he was to meet him at the Great Salt Plains in modern Oklahoma.

He was very curious about the salt deposit, and described it adequately in his diary. It is obvious that he wanted very much to come in contact with the people he called the Comanches, and whom the Little Ones called Padoucas, but since the Little Osages wore their paint, even though they were supposed to be hunting, he had little opportunity to meet with the Comanches or the Apaches. And this was fairly close to the skirmish line between the Osages and the Comanches; and the Osages, considering their numbers, were not anxious to meet a large party of either Comanches or Apaches.

It was time the new United States was making advances to the Osages, and all other tribes they might be able to reach. Not only did the Osages hate the American Long Knives, as did most of the other tribes of the area, but they had been taught by the French and by the Spaniards to hate the British Long Knives as well, and it might be difficult for the British to woo them. There was something in the British favor, however. Not only was the hate the Osages had for the Americans based on the urgings of their former allies the French and the Spaniards, but the Americans themselves were making the warnings of the French come true. The United States was the most unfortunate of the white-dominated nations in its association with the Osages and others because of the undisciplined and graceless invasions of the Indians' domain by the free men. The commissioners of the United States could no more hold their citizens to the provisions of the treaties they signed so solemnly than a usurping chieftain, bursting with *amour-propre,* was able to hold the tribe.

The "distracted" government was fortunate to have men like Sibley and Clark as its representatives, and especially its new citizens the Chouteaus, who were helpful in their commercial jealousy of the English. On the other hand, the Little Ones were fortunate to have them as liaison with European civilization, if only momentarily, even though, as great-hearted as he must have been, William Clark could not be considered to have had polish.

They could do little, however, to offset the greed and barbarism of the free men. It was the British maneuvers that sent most of the red men to ally themselves with the watchful enemies of the not yet fully crystalized United States government. The Creeks fled to the Spaniards, and were urged on to oppose the new government, not only by the Spaniards but by the English, and after being incited to rise against the United States by Tecumseh in 1813, were used by the British and were defeated by Andrew Jackson, and this made of him a hero.

The Algonkians and Siouans of the Lake regions were easily led into many battles of the War of 1812 with gifts and oratory, and remained allies of the British all through that very crucial period for the United States from 1793 to 1815, and were ready and poised when Madison declared war on Great Britain in 1812.

On June 1, 1812, the President of the United States sent a message to Congress advocating war on Great Britain because she "had urged the Indians to attack the whites, had ruined American trade by Orders in Council, had practically blockaded American ports and had impressed American seamen to serve in her own ships." The Congress acted, and on June 19, 1812, Madison declared that a state of war existed between Great Britain and the United States.

The Little Osages under No-Ears came to Sibley and offered their services against the English Long Knives, just two months before he was ordered to abandon Fort Osage. And he became angry with his government. The Little Osages could not in their numbers stand against the British allies and their old enemies, the Potawatomis, Iowas, Kickapoos, and Sac and Foxes, so they fled to the Verdigris, where their hereditary chief Traveling Rain took over.

Sibley wanted the government to build a factory at the Place-of-the-Many-Swans in order to hold the Osages together and thus make possible the use of their great strength, allowing them freedom to fight as they would. He wanted the government to send spies there so that the movements of the English could be watched. He was quite upset about their attitude of *laissez faire*.

The Eagle gens of the Little Ones may boast that they saved George Washington at the battle known as Braddock's Defeat, but they might have stronger grounds for their smug boasting if they declared that *Nika-Shu-Dse,* the red man, might have saved the United States from defeat simply because they had acted as Indians. Therefore, acting as Indians, they actually saved the United States. If they had not acted as Indians and had been capable of being trained in the European method of battle by Sieur Antoine de la Mothe Cadillac in the early eighteenth century, or being trained by British officers in the latter part of the eighteenth and the beginning of the nineteenth centuries, they might have changed history. If they had been susceptible of regimentation by La Mothe Cadillac and the British had been able to make quixotic European soldiers of them, it is reasonable to believe that the British might have won the War of 1812.

The primitive skirmish line vaguely separating ranges, the bluff skirmishes at salt deposits, and the sudden meetings of enemy buffalo hunters, and the Sac and Fox-like forays into another's domain were more like the conflicts of animals protecting a range necessary for their subsistence or like birds protecting their nesting areas.

Like the animals, the red man fought for his bit of earth from which he had been pushed, the Sacred One as the Little Ones called it. The Algonkians and Iroquoians by now had become men without a country; without a Sacred One, and away from their Sacred One, they were also away from their holy places, whence the souls of their ancestors had departed to Spiritland. Thus their urges and sometimes their fervency were still Neolithic, and they were guided by their traditions of borderline struggles, their tribal memories being deep within them.

Added to the fact that the war movement was semireligious, it must have taken a century of social and political pressure of the European kind to prepare the Little Ones and other natives for military regimentation.

The "distracted" government was also fortunate that Great Britain was almost completely occupied with Napoleon until the battle of Leipsig and unfortunate in that the free men of the west and north and the men of the south, more especially the free men "who intend to invade everything they see convenient to them," wanted Canada and Florida, and extremely unfortunate also in the disinterest of other citizens, especially the shipping and maritime people of New England, who didn't want to be disturbed in their prosperity by war.

The blockades by France and the Orders in Council by England against each other and the neutral world, and the United States' own Non-Importation Act of 1806, which was in force from 1807 to 1809, were ruinous to the new government. The agricultural depression caused by the blockades and the act filled the ranks and gave volume to the voice of the free men.

The "War Hawks" of the west, the free men who wanted war, were shouting for it, while the men of the east of the powerful commercial and shipping areas, even more seriously affected by England's and France's invasions of their maritime rights, were strenuously opposed to the war. They avoided the draft laws and traded secretly with the British, and the British, of course, were taking advantage of this attitude by graciousness in their relations with this section. These American citizens actually had a convention in Hartford, Connecticut, in October, 1814, and discussed a separate peace and even withdrawal from the Union.

Great Britain did revoke the Orders in Council just four days before the United States' declaration of war, and Mr. Jefferson, who had left the office of the Presidency in 1809, believed that the declaration was a very grave mistake, and could have been avoided if communications had reached the stage at that time which they attained later—perhaps a trans-Atlantic cable—but, "As the white frontiersman greed for land to the west pushed the Indian tribes into hopeless warfare, so this hunger for more land to the north and south was a large factor in producing the War of 1812."

During the War of 1812, from 1813 to 1815, the United States government had to abandon Fort Osage and lost to the English five northern factories. During this time the Little Ones were going to Prairie du Chien to receive their "presents" from the English; at least those of the Place-of-the-Many-Swans were making the trip to Prairie du Chien or receiving English gifts through the Sac and Foxes, their old enemies. During the last year of the war, the Sac and Foxes even came to the Osage villages, carrying a British flag that had been sent to the Little Ones by the British. The British-inspired armistice must have lasted even after the war, since the Osages, perhaps ten of them, visited at the villages of the Sac on the Illinois River, where Rock Island, Illinois, is now situated. This was also British arranged. The William Henry Harrison peace agreement between the Sac and Foxes and the Osages was only periodically effective.

It seemed quite proper that the United States government should arrange a council of the tribes as soon as possible after the War of 1812. The council was held on September 12, 1815, at Portage des Sioux, the old Siouan crossing of the Mississippi just above the mouth of the Missouri. It was "a Treaty of peace and friendship made and concluded between William Clark, Ninian Edwards and August Chouteau, Commissioners Plenipotentiary of the United States of America on the part of and behalf of the said States of the one part; and the undersigned King, Chiefs and Warriors of the Great and Little Osage Tribes or Nations, on the part and behalf of their said Tribes or Nations of the other part.

"The parties being desirous of re-establishing peace and friendship between the United States and Said Tribes or Nations . . . and in being placed in all things, and every respect, on the same footing upon which they stood before the war, have agreed, ..."

Article one agreed that all injuries or hostilities of either party against the other would be mutually forgiven, and Article two stated that there "shall be perpetual peace" between the United States and the Osages and that the parties were free to recognize the re-establishment of and the confirmation of all treaties between the United States and the Osage Nations.

This treaty was signed by William Clark, Ninian Edwards, and August Chouteau as commissioners, but Pierre Chouteau, agent to the Osages, and P. L. Chouteau, and John W. Johnson, United States factor and Indian agent, were present. The interpreter was the famed Noel Maugraine, mixed-blood.

There were ten of the Grand Osages who signed, among them being Bad-Temper-Chief, a man called "Gradamnsa," translated as "Iron Kite." It was also signed by No-Fear, and a man called phonetically "Hurate," translated as "Piper Bird," and Big Bear, Man-Whipper, Sun-Carrier, and for the Osages-of-the-Oaks, the Arkansas Osages, the chieftain of the Wapiti gens seemed to be the only signer. He was Against-the-Wind, which refers to the wapiti facing the wind as he walks. For the Little Osages, there were Big Chief, Traveling Rain, Does-Little, No-Ears, Big Soldier, He-Who-Arrives, and the Missourias, part of whom were now living with the Little Osages, there were Little Horn and The Cutter as signers.

After the treaty of 1808 with the Osages, the President had carried out his promise to the Cherokees and had safety-valved some pressure created by the free men, but this could not obtain for long. The Little Ones had resented the invasion of the Cherokees from the beginning, after the Muscle Shoals fight, and now they were face to face with them and fought them as they had fought any invader of their domain. After the treaty of 1808, the Cherokees came by the hundreds to occupy the rich ceded land of the Arkansas River east of the treaty's boundary line.

They were the first Iroquoian invaders of the Little One's range, and they were rather strange to them. They called them *Sah-La-Keh,* That-Thing-on-Its-Head, because they wore headbands of figured calico. The name would also include the recurved tail-plume of the snowy egret, which the Cherokees often wore, and which was held to their heads by the calico band or some other traders' cloth.

The safety valve which was the Osage treaty of 1808 was not long effective, and the chain-pressure began now on the west side of the Mississippi, and the free men began to crowd the Cherokees on the west side. These Iroquoians had reached the agricultural stage in development, and in the eyes of the government this seemed to imbue them with virtues which the Plains Indians didn't have, and land for the "good Indians" seemed to be the government's plan. However, in their virtuous and government-approved agricultural enterprises and their tribal organization, they were not only disturbed by the free men but also by the governing officials of the Missouri Territory, who obviously had their own opinions about Indians.

The Cherokees became so numerous in the Arkansas country and

408

the Little Ones kept trying to hold back the chain-pressured stream so vehemently that the government decided to send an agent to the Cherokees of the Arkansas.

He was William L. Lovely, and in his letter to William Clark of October 11, 1814, he seems to have been rather upset over his situation. He wrote that he was of the opinion that there should be two companies of troops "stationed here," and he begged that if they could possibly be spared, Clark might send two companies, "or one at least as there are some whites of the worst character in this country whose influence with the Indians is dangerous to the peace of the same."

When Clark answered favorably, he was almost gleeful, and suggested that the troops be stationed "as high up the Arkansas at least as this place. It would have a tendency to keep the Osages at Bay." He wrote from the old Cherokee agency, which was situated in what is now the modern Pope County, Arkansas.

In the same year of his arrival in the Cherokee Arkansas country, he wrote back to his superior, Colonel Meigs, agent of the eastern Cherokees in Tennessee, in August, 1813, giving a word picture of the country to which he had been sent. He wrote that he was "among the worst banditti; all the white folks, a few excepted, have made their escape to this Country guilty of the most horrid crimes and are now depredating on the Osages and other tribes, taking off 30 horses at a time, which will show the necessity of giving some protection to this place, the most valuable as to soil and valuable minerals that belong to the Purchase in all the country."

Lovely found the Osages and the Cherokees in constant struggle, but one day in 1813, the Grand *Hunkah* of the Little Ones, Arrow-Going-Home, came to him with warriors of several gentes and asked what he was doing there, and when he told them, they asked him to tell the Heavy Eyebrows–Long Knives that they, the Osages of the Place-of-the-Oaks, wanted an agent to aid them in the protection of their Mother, the Earth, from the Cherokees and the hairy ones, who killed their "brothers." Arrow-Going-Home said that he was the Grand *Hunkah,* and that he wanted nothing to do with White Hair or his Heavy Eyebrows–Long Knife chief, Pierre Chouteau, the Osage agent. He said in his vindictiveness that both White Hair and Chouteau were enemies of the American government.

And there was another thing he talked about: what about the furs of the Little Ones? Who would buy them? There were no Heavy Eyebrows with whom they had always traded. Now the Thing-on-Its-Head trade with the Long Knives across the river with the furs of the Little Ones. Now it would be good for the Little Ones to be friends to the Thing-on-Its-Head, since the Long Knives brought them here so that they too could trade their furs to the Long Knives with whom they trade, and from these Long Knives they could get more powder and lead. This would be the same thing, since the Long Knives got the furs belonging to the Osages.

Lovely was a sincere, quite naïve person, apparently, and did bring about a council between the Grand *Hunkah* of the Little Ones and the Cherokees at the mouth of the Verdigris in August, 1814. He impressed on the Grand *Hunkah* that if he wanted peace, the Osages must not kill and take the guns and traps of white hunters and trappers, even if they were trespassing, and that they must give up the killers of the recently slain white hunters, one Alexander McFarland, killed in 1812 on the Red River, and one R. Geterlin, killed on the Arkansas.

Arrow-Going-Home was very clever, vindictive, insolent, and filled with pride of position and tribal traditions. He probably was feeling the need for trade, since he was apparently cut off from trade across the Mississippi by the Cherokees, and possibly from British trade since the war. So, Indian-like, he would take this problem to Long Knife, this Big Long Knife who had come to live with the Cherokees. He possibly thought that, since the white men were swarming there in the lands north of the Arkansas and east of the line from Fort Osage to the Arkansas River and the numbers of the Cherokees were growing, it might be better if the Little Ones of the Place-of-the-Oaks had a Big Long Knife of their own at the Three Forks. Perhaps he could keep the Cherokees from hunting and trapping and trespassing in general west of that magic line and south of the River, which the Long Knives at Fire Prairie said remained for the use of the Little Ones. Also a Long Knife sent especially to them, the Little Ones of the Place-of-the-Oaks, might know how to keep the hairy ones, the *o-skee-kas* (liars, horse thieves, ambush-killers) out of their domain, since he would be a "brother" to these hairy ones.

In his formal speech to Lovely, he would not have used the undignified term "Long Knife," since the name was informal and was given because of characteristics, the sword worn by the formal British of the Des Moines River and Prairie du Chien. Likewise, when the chieftains or the grand chiefs of the Little Ones spoke formally to the French, they had not used the term "Heavy Eyebrows" for the same reasons, but instead referred to them as They-with-White-Skins. This was possibly a primitive courtesy quite beyond the understanding of the European, who referred to people of European and Indian blood as "halfbreeds" even formally and in official documents.

Now, however it was obvious that the people they had been calling Long Knives were not walking in dignity and speaking with dignity, as were the Long Knives of the Des Moines and Prairie du Chien; and also had such growths of hair on their faces that it almost hid their eyes like the first European people of the Place-of-the-Many-Swans had seen, and they were now beginning to call the hated free Americans "Heavy Eyebrows."

The council between the Cherokees and the Little Ones at the mouth of the Verdigris in August, 1814, came to nothing, and the pressured Cherokees and the white barbarians continued to cross the boundary to make raids, to ambush, and to hunt, and the Little Ones continued to hunt them and kill them where they could find them, not stopping at taking from them their guns and ammunition and traps and furs.

While the Little Ones of the Place-of-the-Many-Swans were momentarily at peace with their ancient enemies, the wandering, restless raiders, the Sac and Foxes, they had to fight the Potawatomis, the Miamis, and the Kickapoos who crossed the rivers in war parties with their trade guns. The Algonkians had been well armed by the British. The Little Ones of the Place-of-the-Oaks had to fight the Iroquoian immigrants, the Cherokees, and the free men, and of course their old enemies the Padoucas and the Caddos of Red River. Also, as a result of the breaking up of the tribal organizations of the Choctaws, the Chickasaws, the Miamis, the Delawares, the Shawnees, and the Peorias, displaced, disillusioned fragments of these strong tribes crossed the Mississippi ahead of their tribes who would be removed there later by the government. These fragments settled in Osage domain long before the treaty of 1808, but stayed close to the west bank settlements and there even pillaged the boats on the river.

There in the settlements they learned to drink spirits, and as they were pushed westward, became a drunken menace. "They are attached to liquor, seldom remain long at any place, many of them speak English, all understanding it and there are some who even read it."

However, since this harlequin fragment of displaced tribes from east of the Mississippi were not virtuous agriculturists, there was not much notice taken when the Little Ones met them and fought with them, defeated them or were defeated by them, since their number was imposing. There were said to be five hundred families of them, and since they had to feed themselves, they must have been a scourge, and too powerful for a single Osage chieftain and his gens warriors. They were ready to fight on either side—the immigrant Cherokees' side or on the side of the defensive Osages—and the Cherokees took advantage of this situation while the Osages were still fighting under the old traditions, alone and proud, attacking with the ferocity of the falcon and giving way with the cupidity of the panther.

An area which includes almost the whole state of modern Missouri south of the Missouri River and that part of modern Arkansas lying north of the Arkansas River and east of a line approximating the modern boundary between Oklahoma and Arkansas and Missouri and Kansas was not sufficient for the free men and displaced eastern tribes of the Missouri area and not sufficient for the free men and the immigrant Cherokees of the Arkansas area.

Fortescue Cumings said in his account of his travels, 1807–1809, that there was "a scarcity of population in Indiana and Illinois, and in Kentucky below Louisville"; and also called attention to "the restlessness of the population . . . the long journeys for trivial purposes, the abandoned settlements in Kentucky and Illinois."

The Cherokees were perhaps more intelligent than the Little Ones inherently, and they had been in rather intimate contact with the European and his ways for a long time in their homes in North Carolina, Tennessee, and Georgia, and they knew well how to employ the subtle chicanery of the European. Not only that, but their blood in many instances was well mixed with Scotsmen and English, some of the mixed-bloods becoming their aggressive leaders. They had even progressed in civilization to the stage where they in many instances owned African slaves.

The Little Ones, on the other hand, had been pampered by both the French and the Spaniards not from academic interest and humanitarianism but from stark necessity. The Americans had no such necessity with the opportunistic Cherokees and savage free men. The European-blood infusion of the Osages was chiefly French people who believed that *joi de vivre* was very important. They had few close contacts with Europeans other than with the energetic Chouteaus, the fur-trading Maugraine, Pryor, Revoir, and Roi. Also having been the successful and all-conquering Little Ones for centuries, they resisted the ways of the European. The Little Ones knew no English and refused to learn, feeling that one white man's language ought to be understood by all, but their French was often too much for the Americans. Their interpreters often had practically no synonyms in their earthy vocabularies, and being half-French often put "speeches in their mouth," when they spoke later in French or Osage.

While the free men poured across the magic line and crossed the Arkansas west of that line and the Cherokees, speaking English much better than the free men, posed as virtuous agriculturist Osage-harassed men of good will, their smart leaders were planning to divide among their tribal factions the Osage domain in what is now Arkansas south of the Arkansas River and modern eastern Oklahoma. They had a plan for taking the rich domain of the Little Ones for the Cherokees and the agriculturist tribes of the woodlands and pushing the plains nomads onto the semiarid plains. The organization, of course, would be under control of the Cherokee organization.

It is true, however, that the Cherokee people who were trying to make homes in the treaty lands were being harassed not only by the

413

free men but also by the local territorial government since 1812. There were veterans of the War of 1812 who had been given "Land Script," and, while some actually settled, others joined the free men, and still others, like the Revolutionary veterans, sold their rights to enterprising land speculators, who became a pressure group.

This is the year in which the old Louisiana Purchase above the thirty-third parallel became the Territory of Missouri, and the legislature of the new Missouri Territory, "ignoring the presence of the Indians," created in 1813 "the county of Arkansas" with the seat of government at the old Arkansas Post. This brought on more difficulties between the free men and the Cherokees, and added new pressure to force the Cherokees across the magic line into Osage domain, where gentile war parties, their faces bluff-painted, not only took their guns and furs and horses but killed them, and still believing in the bluff and warnings of the Neolithic world, hung their heads in trees so that they could be seen. The shocked Cherokee Iroquoians of a linguistic family who had burnt many a paleface alive on the Atlantic Seaboard cried "horror" in their adequate, agricultural, Christian English, and the harassed, benevolent, naïve Lovely echoed "horror" in his letter to Meigs; and wrote President Madison: "So may I say with propriety that I am entirely secluded from the land of the living, surrounded on all sides by Indians together with the Worst of White Settlers living just below me betwix them whom there are daily disturbances arising & against whom there are no possible means in my power of enforcing any laws."

The Little Ones were the law of natural balance, protecting their game and their *Mo'n-Sho'n,* Mother Earth. They found their buffalo of the woodland almost disappeared, but they came often on carcasses from which only the tallow had been taken, and the same with their bears. They found their deer and their wapiti stripped of their hides and bloated in the sun. They watched the turkey vultures circling and went there to confirm what they knew. They watched the wolves sitting on little hills, the breeze playing with their long hair, with eyes focused on a spot in a valley, and there, when they had crawled closer, they smelled the smoke of a Cherokee's or a white trapper's or a hunter's camp.

414

The actions of the free men represented no primitive unit or communal law, nor yet were they under European law as a result of the development of institutions there. They certainly were not even under the laws of the pack, the herd, the colony, or the flock. They seemed to be free from any restrictions except during certain periods of group defense which placed no obligation on the individual, if he could free himself from the difficulty, either by escape or through sacrificing the others.

These men had racial memories of debtors' prisons and of the gibbet, and a recent memory of superiors in satins and powdered wigs of the Atlantic Seaboard and New Orleans. They robbed and killed the conscientious white settlers as well as the Osages, Cherokees, and Caddoans. And made of the Constitution's fine words a hypocrisy.

Many of the Cherokees and other trans-Mississippi Indians were frustrated and vindictive, acting under the natural law which ordains that lack of security gives birth to irresponsibility and sometimes to wanton destruction.

But the Little Ones did not always wait for the Cherokees or the free-men hunters and trappers and horse thieves and murderers to come into the domain; they, as they had always done, went to the source of their trouble. They traveled to the White River east of the magic line and to the James River and to the Gasconade, all their former rivers where there were beaver not forbidden to them by the treaty of 1808, when they touched the feather near Fire Prairie. They raided John Wells' trapping camp and took all his bear and beaver traps as well as lead, and on the Gasconade they robbed Elijah and Abraham Eastwood of their horses, traps, lead, powder, and bullet molds. These men were lucky, perhaps because they were east of the magic line.

There was now the new element in the chaos of the ceded part of the old domain of the Little Ones. The Cherokees had been authorized by President Jefferson to remove to the Arkansas country, but the taking over by the legislature of the Missouri Territory had left them without title, and Lovely became even more perturbed and agreed that the Cherokee chief, *Tah-Lon-Tes-Kee* accompanied by a white member of the tribe should go to St. Louis to inform Governor

Clark of the situation now created in their country, which had "been swallowed up by the Missouri legislature." *Tah-Lon-Tes-Kee* said that the President had said there was plenty of game there, but he complained that the whites and others "do not destroy less than five thousand buffalos every summer for no other profit but for the tallow."

In November, 1815, Major Lovely talked with the Little Ones who came to talk with him. He reminded them that they had just killed two Cherokees and four white men. They must stop killing, he urged. In January of 1816 he met the Little Ones of the Place-of-the-Oaks at the mouth of the Verdigris to try to convince them that they must stop their killing of his virtuous Cherokees. He seemed to be little concerned about the "Worst of White Settlers" at the moment. However, before he could give them his usual lecture, the clever Arrow-Going-Home and the Buck-Making-Horns[1] (Tallai) laid their troubles on his lap, in harmony with the primitive philosophy which demands that, since They-with-White-Skins got them into trouble coming across the Mississippi in the first place and bringing their Cherokees into their domain in the second place, now they must do something about the matters of stoppage of presents from Prairie du Chien. And this thing too: on their last trip there, to trade with the Long Knives, they had received their presents at Prairie du Chien and were coming back when they were attacked by their "enemies," and lost ten of their warriors. Now they said they didn't want to go there again. What would the Big Long Knife of the Cherokees do about this? When White Hair made the war movement on the Arkansas and killed the new Heavy Eyebrows and the Cherokees, people said it was Arrow-Going-Home, the Grand *Hunkah*. White Hair was not a true *Ki-He-Kah* chosen from the *Tzi-Sho Wa-Shta-Ge;* his father had been Chouteau's *Ki-He-Kah*.

What would the Big Long Knife of the Cherokees do about this thing? Now Arrow-Going-Home and his people received no presents, since they dared not go among their "enemies." Arrow-Going-Home didn't identify the "enemies," but they were either Potawa-

[1] Buck-Making-Horns refers to the white-tail buck's scraping the "velvet" from his horns against saplings.

tomis, adequately armed by the expectant British during the war, or some other British-armed tribe of the Algonkians, perhaps Kickapoos.

The speech was given in French, and Lovely couldn't understand French, and obviously the interpreter "put words into his, Arrow-Going-Home's, mouth." Such Gallic treacle as, "We should be glad if you could appoint some person close to us that could see our conduct towards our brothers the Whites & and that could see our presents brought to our village," was a perfect giveaway.

A Little One, especially a Grand *Hunkah,* with *amour propre,* standing over six feet, with his robe over his left shoulder and with right shoulder and right arm bare, would have the dignity and majesty of a bull wapiti in full rut. The kindly Lovely came completely under his influence that day, and wrote to Governor William Clark that Arrow-Going-Home (he called him Clermont) was really a good man, but had many bad young men in his village.

Another delegation of Cherokees, this time headed not by the chief *Tah-Lon-Tes-Kee,* but by the white man, John D. Chisholm, went to St. Louis to complain to Governor Clark about the depredations of the Little Ones and gave him a letter from Major Lovely urging that a military post be established on the Arkansas "to maintain peace among the Indians." He said he would call a general council of the Osages, the Cherokees, and the Quapaws, and the Cherokee delegation was to inform Major Lovely that he had made application to the War Department to establish the military post on the Arkansas River.

Major Lovely was in a dilemma and, like all nonaggressive men, hated conflict, so he decided on a peaceful alternative to the obtaining of the peace by force represented by the military. The best plan, it seemed to him as it might to all kindly, peace-at-any-price men, was to yield to the conditions brought about by the increasing Cherokee immigrants, the marauding of the free men, and the action of the Missouri Territory legislature. He couldn't do anything about the legislature, the swarming free men, and the Cherokees, but he could satisfy the last by taking more land from the Osages.

He and Pierre Chouteau were to meet at Arrow-Going-Home's town. The Grand *Hunkah* had two names, *To-Wo'n Ga-Xe,* Town-Maker, and *Gra-Mo'n,* or *Ghleh-Mo'n,* which translated into Arrow-

Going-Home," or just "Going." The *Gra-Mo'n* or *Ghleh-Mo'n* suffered through French phonetics, and after going through several phases was at that time pronounced "Clermont," "Glamore," and later became "Claremore." He had his village up the Verdigris River in a wide valley-canyon cut by the river, close to the spot on which the modern town of Claremore, Oklahoma, was later built.

Chouteau failed to show up, so Lovely held the meeting at the mouth of the Verdigris instead. He presided over a meeting by the representatives of the Osages, the Cherokees, and the Quapaws.

The Major asked that the Little Ones cede a tract of land from their domain, bounded on the south by the Arkansas River, west of the line drawn by the treaty of 1808. The south boundary was to follow the Arkansas River to the mouth of the Verdigris where they sat that moment in council, and thence up the Verdigris to the falls four miles from the mouth, thence to a line running northeasterly to the Saline on the Neosho, about where Salina, Oklahoma, is now, which would represent the west and north boundary. From here the line representing definitely the north boundary would run straight east to the north and south boundary established in 1808; the land within these boundaries would be ceded.

Arrow-Going-Home and several chieftains of the different gentes agreed to this unauthorized cession of land in July, 1816. One will always wonder if the glib Cherokee leaders, the white Chisholm and the clever and able *Tah-Lon-Tes-Kee*, had talked to the Little Ones of the fort that would be built on the Arkansas and of the many Long Knives soldiers who would come to punish them if they did not cede that land. Surely the consideration for the cession was not a sufficient reason in the minds of the Little Ones. The consideration Major Lovely put before them was that the government would pay all claims against them by the Cherokees and the free men. Neither their fear of punishment nor their relief from a responsibility they could never have felt would have been sufficient reason for their calm acceptance of the proposal. It could have been part of the Cherokee grand plan for organization; they would have this land and much more to carry out their plan, but with what bluff or promise did they obtain the Little Ones' agreement? The last *Gra-Mo'n* (called Claremore) was asked about this in 1936, but his predecessors had told him little of the incident of the council, or else he had "lost" it or "thrown it away." He recalled the old days by bringing out a buckskin shirt profusely covered with Cherokee scalps, which had been handed down to him.

Major Lovely had no authority whatever to make this agreement with the Little Ones, and it was not binding on them certainly, and there was a letter from the Secretary of War to the Twentieth Congress concerning Lovely's Purchase. The kindly old man died in 1817, and perhaps never knew that his "Purchase" resolved nothing.

36.   Fort Smith

THE LITTLE ONES continued to paint their faces with bluff-paint and chant to *Wah'Kon-Tah,* "I go to learn if I shall go on to learn of Grandfather if I shall go on," and they did go on almost continually. They cried their prayers to the Morning Star and to the Sun every morning at dawn, then dried their tears, and each gens under their chieftain rode over their domain hunting for immigrant Cherokees, Choctaws, Chickasaws, Delawares, Shawnees, Miamis, and Peorias and the ubiquitous free men, and they could not see the invisible line running from Fort Osage on the Missouri River to the Arkansas at the mouth of the Poteau River, called Frog Bayou and Belle Pointe, any better than the Cherokees and free men hunters could see it.

The Cherokee organizers called a meeting in January, 1817, in Arkansas on the banks of the Arkansas River in Cherokee country, and they dispatched messages to their tribesmen of Tennessee, North Carolina, and Georgia urging them to come and join them in an all-out war on the savage buffalo Indians, the Osages. They planned to make an attack in May since the grass would then sustain their horses. There would be many horses and many men, and there would be glory and land for all. Many of the eastern Cherokees came on the call of their brothers, but the War Department got the information and ordered Colonel Meigs to stop the movement of the eastern Cherokees, but he was able only to stop the departure of some of the excitement-suffused warriors. They came by boats down the Tennessee to the Ohio, thence to the Mississippi and down it to the mouth of the Arkansas, thence up the Arkansas to the agency near the modern Russellville, Arkansas.

They must have swarmed there waiting for the members of the other tribes who were to join them, especially the harlequin fragments who would be ready for anything, especially a war on the mighty Osages. The attack failed to come off when scheduled. The tribes were ready apparently, but May happened to be the month when the Osages would be on their buffalo hunts on the high plains, and Grant Foreman suggests in *Indians and Pioneers* that "either from the influence of Colonel Meigs or from the fear of finding the Osage warriors at home, the campaign was delayed."

In July, *Tah-Lon-Tes-Kee* and another Cherokee chief, *Tak-Atoka*, sent word to the Governor of Missouri Territory that they would attack the Osages because they had stolen all their horses, and now the Cherokees, devoted to agriculture, had to work their land with only their hands, and, what's more, the Osages had only recently, "horrors," killed two young Cherokee warriors.

The War Department took this well-timed and well-worded threat seriously. Natives so dedicated to agriculture who could employ such dramatic phraseology should be encouraged and above all protected from the wild buffalo Indians. They decided to build a fort on the spot where the line drawn by the treaty of 1808 as the eastern boundary of the diminished Osage domain touched the Arkansas River.

On August 19, General Andrew Jackson communicated his orders to General Thomas A. Smith, commandant at Belle Fontaine on the Missouri, and the next month he ordered Major William Bradford and Major Stephen H. Long to descend the Mississippi to assume command of the detachment of eighty-two recruits who had taken boats at Pittsburgh on the Ohio River and were at the mouth of the Arkansas. Then they were to ascend to the point where the eastern boundary line of the Osages touched the river, and there build a fort. General Jackson then ordered, among other things, that Major Long was "to remove any portion or all of the intruders from the public lands in that section of the country, and . . . take suitable measures for its accomplishment."

On the high ground near where the Poteau flows into the Arkansas, called by the French "Belle Pointe," the United States government built Fort Smith. Major Bradford could not arrive at his command before Christmas Day of 1817, and before he could reach his command, the Cherokee leaders launched their war against the Grand *Hunkah* of the Little Ones, Arrow-Going-Home. They made for his village in the valley-canyon up the Verdigris. They had six hundred warriors and eleven free men.

They had got together the fragments of the Choctaws, Chickasaws, Shawnees, Peorias, the band of marauders of the right bank of the Mississippi, as well as recruits from the Koasatis, Tonkawas, and the Little Ones, old enemies the Padoucas who had no objective except to fight along with their allies the Caddoans. There was even a bona fide captain, one McLamore who had fought as a company commander of the Cherokees against the Creeks under General Jackson in the Creek War. He was now commander of the eastern Cherokee contingent.

If Mr. Foreman had been right in his suggestion that the May attack had been postponed because Arrow-Going-Home's warriors might have been in the village, the time chosen for the later attack might reveal much also. The time was October, and everyone knew the habits of the Plains hunters: that they had a summer hunt which ended in August, and an autumn hunt which ended in November or December; but there was always the likelihood that the hunters might find a canyon or a timbered bottom for protection against the Arctic winds of the plains and stay there all winter. Arrow-Going-Home and his warriors might have been at home during the Yellow-Flower Moon and the Deer-Hiding Moon, August and September, but during the Deer-Mating Moon, October, the month of the attack of the motley army, they were on the plains hunting buffalo.

The Cherokee leaders stopped their army on the Neosho at a saline springs called the Lick, then sent a letter to the village of the Grand *Hunkah* inviting him to send representatives to the Lick to talk about peace. The Cherokees wrote that only ten or fifteen of them had come all this way into the Osage country to make a treaty of peace.

Arrow-Going-Home had left the village in charge of an old chieftain, a leader of one of the gentes of the *Tzi-Sho* Division, the peaceful Sky People. Such a guardian was called *Ee-Eh-Keh* (Stays
Home). This old man received the message and set out alone to
meet the Cherokees to tell them that they must wait for the return
of the Grand *Hunkah* and the warriors. He could make no treaty
with them, since he was only a chieftain of a Sky Lodge gens. This
information was apparently what they had been waiting for. They
murdered him "in a species of barbarity and treachery unknown
among Indians of the most uncivilized kind; this also under the eye
of their chiefs Tulentuskey & Tuckatochee, the Black Fox and Bowls
. . . the latter gave him the first stroke, immediately aided by several
whites, Isaacs, the Chissoms and Williams. Isaacs and King, the
whites among them, is more savage than the Cherokees themselves.
The Choctaws and Chicasaws that is incorporated with the Cherokees together with the whites that live among them is a set of the
most abandoned characters ever disgraced a gallows."

This is part of what Major Bradford reported. Major Bradford had
only just arrived in the country. He was obviously shocked.

The able-bodied men had gone to the Salt Fork on the plains with
their Grand *Hunkah* for the autumn hunt, and there were only old
men, women, and children at the village. The attack was ferocious,
and no doubt the harlequin fragments of Choctaws, Chickasaws,
Peorias, Delawares, and Miamis were drunk, since that was their
normal state. The old men fought valiantly, singing their war songs
in their trembling voices, then fled toward the timbered mounds and
the high limestone escarpments and tried to hide in the V-shaped
canyons, but fourteen of them were killed. The women keened and
tried to herd the children to the mounds and the canyons, and sixty-
nine of the children and women were killed, and many wounded.
On one mound, several of the older boys were brutally emasculated,
and many died from the operation later.

The bloodthirsty army took 103 "or four" prisoners, mostly young
girls and boys who could be sold as slaves by the eastern Cherokees.
They set fire to the village and burned some of the wounded and the
old men and women who were unable to flee, and they burned the

corn and the squashes and the stored lotus roots, and took the smoked and jerked meat. They left nothing. They took the robes and the deerskins and the things which were useful to them and loaded the plunder on Osages horses, driving the others with them. They found twenty-five white scalps and a great number of Indian scalps in the village.

It has been said that the Verdigris turned red with the blood of women and children, and the mound to which many of them fled and on which the young boys were emasculated and the girls raped is called Claremore Mound, and the slaughter is called the "Battle of Claremore Mound."

The last week in September, 1959, a woman of the Eagle gens of the Little Osages, said in her beautiful, low voice, that no young man dares to climb Claremore Mound. "There is something there," she said sadly, "*mi-ah-luschkas,* I guess, but a young man going up there will lose his virility, or maybe, he will become —what you call homosexual."

The eastern Cherokees were paid off in children captives, and they traded them among themselves, and those who had not been lucky at capture bought them from those who had captured them. A horse was the equivalent of a captive.

In this attack on the Little Ones, the Cherokees had several men wounded, and one of the Delawares was killed, and this was a boast for years. Often when skirmishes or battles took place between the Little Ones and the Cherokees or even between the Little Ones and soldiers, the English-speaking people always had the advantage and did very well in their boasts until they inevitably overstepped themselves and gave a one-sided casualty list, such as putting the number of the Little Ones killed and wounded at perhaps one hundred to only five of themselves, and casualties perhaps amounting to fifty Little Ones and only one of their party wounded. But this time they could boast of a one-sided victory since the whole thing was verified by August Chouteau the younger.

When the news of the great victory reached the eastern Cherokees as early as November, they joy-danced around great crackling fires. Even Joseph McMinn, governor of Tennessee, wrote to George

Graham, then secretary of war, about the brilliant attack of the Cherokees on the savage Osage. They attacked, he wrote, "with brilliant success—scalps, prisoners, horses (and eight) baggage are the trophies of this victory . . . ." The news had been brought by a Cherokee runner. The Governor wrote, "Cherokee near to us have had several war dances in which there has been the strongest demonstrations of joy."

The participants were longer reaching their homes on their return, since they were now encumbered with stolen horses from the Osages, and many of them had to return by horseback. On November 15, 1817, a party of five missionaries came to the Caney Creek, south of the Tennessee River, and found it in spate. These men had been employed by the American Board of Commissioners for Foreign Missions "to visit several tribes of Indians residing in the southwestern parts of the United States." They were to council with the Indians and obtain their consent to establish schools "and other institutions" among them, the purpose being to instruct them "in Christianity, and the most useful arts of civilized life."

They tried to ford the swollen creek but failed. They were meek before the will of God and made the best of things, and as they were doing so, a party of Cherokees late in the afternoon came to the opposite bank of the creek from the west. They didn't hesitate, but swam their horses over to the east bank and made camp on a gentle rise, building a fire under a tall tree. The leader of the missionary group, one Reverend Elias Cornelius, bethought him of this mission, seeing the dozen Cherokees and realizing they must be from the Arkansas country, and went over to their camp to talk with them about a school and "other institutions in the Arkansas country."

He noted the things scattered about the campfire: the sacks of corn (from Osage fields), skins of deer and wapiti and bear on which they slept, and he noted their guns leaning against the trees and "tomahawks" and bunches of arrows with the dark stains of Osage blood still on them.

He noted these things, but his attention was drawn to a little girl about five years of age, and he asked the warriors about her. They said they had taken her in a great victory over the savage Osages, and when he asked where her parents were, one of the warriors went to his sack and took out two scalps, and holding them out toward the Reverend Cornelius, said in English, "Here they are."

The little girl could understand nothing of what went on around her. "The poor child gazed at them with an expression of mingled wonder and sorrow." The Reverend Cornelius thought she must have traveled five hundred miles with her captors without shelter from rain or cold for nearly a month. When he tried to take her in his arms, she began to cry, and the warriors smiled and said that her people hated the white people, and she was afraid of white people. He tried to make friends with her, and gave her a piece of cake "and a bright little cup," with which she seemed pleased, but apparently she didn't know what to do with the cake. "She was prettier than most children," thought Cornelius, and he immediately began to wonder how he could get her away from her captors.

The warrior who had taken her had sold her to another for a horse, and Cornelius tried to convince the owner that she ought to be sent to the Cherokee mission at Brainerd, assuring him that she would be clothed and instructed and the missionaries would bring her up as their own child, and payment to him would be arranged for her.

Cornelius noted that the warrior had an affection for the little girl and promised to send her to the school as soon as he reached home. In a letter to the superintendent of the mission at Brainerd, a Reverend Cyrus Kingsbury, he asked him to take the orphan and pay the $100 which the warrior asked for her and worried that $100 would be difficult for the mission to raise.

The next morning the waters of the Caney Creek subsided, the party rode across, and on the trail met several bands of Cherokees along the way with their Osage captives, but apparently they kept them hidden from the Reverend Cornelius and his party. When he reached Natchez, he was full of his story, and when a Mrs. Lydia Carter heard it, she offered to pay the $100 ransom, but there was more trouble about the little Osage captive. Her owner wanted to trade her for a Negro slave about her age, and, of course, the missionaries were horrified at this proposal, but they kept trying and

Cornelius even went to the lodge of the Cherokee who owned the little girl to see her. She seemed happy in her new environment.

The rumor sprang up that the President of the United States was demanding that all prisoners taken in the Cherokee-Osage wars must be returned to their respective tribes; however, this proved to be only a rumor, and the good Cornelius renewed his hope. Mrs. Carter's $100 was now at Brainerd ready to be turned over to the Cherokee warrior. The President of the United States ordered the Secretary of War to order Colonel Meigs, agent of the Cherokees, to place the little Osage captive in the school at Brainerd.

The missionaries searched for other captives and found the little girl's sister and a little boy, who had been sold to a white man. The little girl when placed in Brainerd was called Lydia Carter for the lady who put up the ransom money, and the little boy was called John Osage Ross because the Cherokee John Ross had found him.

Then there was a letter from William Clark stating that at a council with the Osages, a man had come forward to say that the little captive was his daughter. The conscientious William Clark had no proof that the man was not her father, but he thought the little girl ought to be brought back to her tribe and family. The story was likely, since the man who claimed to be her father was youngish and therefore would have been with the buffalo hunters on the plains at the time of the attack. Also, the little girl could remember the death of her mother. She told her foster parents that she and her mother were sitting in the bushes. Some men came and shot her mother in the breast, and the blood came out of it and dripped on the ground. The men then picked her up and put her on a horse, and she fell off the first time. Later she could stay on a horse even with the waters of the rivers about her as the horse swam.

William Clark said that the man who claimed the little girl as his daughter "seemed much flattered at the interest his child had excited." He had a right to be; he, and not the great men of the Osages, was discussed in the offices of the President of the United States, in the offices of the Secretary of War, and in the office of William Clark in St. Louis, and his heart could beat with self-esteem when Big Long Knives came to him and awaited eagerly his decisions.

Here in this concentrated interest of the President of the United States, the Secretary of War, and the Governor of the Missouri Territory, not to mention a Board of Commissioners for Foreign Missions, was revealed at this early date in the history of the United States a remarkable example of excitement over small things, wherein the big heart of humanitarianism can display its fervency. The tragedy of this little girl spoken of by the soft voices of the missionaries was heard in Washington, and the situation had interested the President of the United States, while the crying in the wilderness of Major Lovely for law and order had scarcely been noted—this urgent voice which wanted to stop murder and marauding, and which wanted the government to bring justice to the area, or at least to control the free men who "have made their escape to this country guilty of the most horrid crimes."

However, Fort Smith was established at the point where the line drawn straight south from Fort Osage intersected the Arkansas River, and although Major Lovely was now dead, his "Purchase" was ratified by the treaty of 1818. No matter if there was at this time plenty of land within the boundaries of the old cession of 1808 for people who desired to settle down and build homes and communities, there was not enough space for the activities of the free men and the schemes of the Cherokees.

The Cherokee plan must have been quite obvious, since the newcomer, Major Bradford, explained the situation quite clearly in a letter to General Jackson in 1818. He wrote that the Cherokees, looking for an excuse for the attack on Claremont's village the year before, dramatically shouted that the Osages had killed a Cherokee warrior called The Choctaw, shooting him from his horse's back, and this was the reason for their attack on Claremont's town.

Major Bradford wrote to Jackson that the facts he had uncovered were that a party of Cherokees had gone into the Osage land and had stolen some horses from the Osages, but were pursued by them, and in retaking their horses, they had shot The Choctaw from one of the stolen horses. He also saw through the Cherokee plan; he wrote that they would use any excuse to carry out their purpose to drive the Osages out and divide the country among themselves and their allies.

Tah-Lon-Tes-Kee had gone to see the Secretary of War about the matter. Bradford, being on the ground, they thought knew too much. This was in February, 1818. Governor Clark had been ordered to make peace between the tribes and had listened to the chief.

The Cherokees demanded what is now eastern Oklahoma for its wealth and as an outlet to the buffalo grounds, as had been promised by President Monroe, and Secretary Calhoun agreed.

Their clever leaders had much to do with the ratification of the agreement between Lovely and the Osages, which had not been authorized, until 1818.

The treaty was made September 25, 1818, in St. Louis, with William Clark, governor of the Missouri Territory, acting as representative of the United States.

Article one states that the Osage Nations had been embarrassed by the "frequent demands for property taken from citizens of the United States by war parties and other thoughtless men of their several bands [both before and since their war with the Cherokees] and their chiefs being ineffectual in recovering the property, conformably with the conditions of the 9th article of the Treaty of 1808 and deduction of annuities in conformity, would deprive them of any for several years."

So the Osages, in order "to do justice to the citizens of the United States and promote friendly intercourse, etc., etc.," ceded the "Lovely Purchase" to the United States legally this time. The north boundary was now designated as a line running easterly to the said Osage boundary line, at a point twenty leagues north from the Arkansas River, and with that line "to the place of the beginning."

Lovely was for paying the citizens who might have claims against the Osages as a consideration for the cession of the land, but the United States government put a limit on the amount for which they would be responsible. They would pay the citizens "the full value of such property as they can legally prove to have been stolen or destroyed by the Osages since 1814," provided the cost did not exceed $4,000.

The Sac and Foxes had remained allied with the Little Ones since the War of 1812, or perhaps unevenly so since the peace effected by William Henry Harrison in 1804, even though Manuel Lisa had tried to harass Pike by rumors of Sac and Fox attack. Just before the treaty of 1818, the making legal of the Lovely Purchase, the Cherokees, desiring a stronger argument for taking land from the Little Ones, got their rag-tag tribal fragments together and attacked them during the summer of 1818. They reported that the Osage party was larger than their attacking party, but since there was no claim of a victory and great numbers of slaughtered Osages, there was apparently no victory for the Cherokees.

The Osages recognized some of the Shawnee and Delaware fragments with the Cherokee party, and apparently for the first time called upon other tribes than their splinters, the Konzas and Quapaws, and their linguistic cousins the Missourias, who were now attaching themselves to the Little Osages, dividing themselves between the Little Osages and the Otoes. They became wise at last, and had begun to adjust their Neolithic, earth-struggle thinking to the Europeanized Cherokees' subtleties. They sent messages to the leaders of the Shawnee and Delaware fragments, knowing that they were always hungry, and especially almost horseless. They promised the leaders many horses and feasts if they would come to help them against the Cherokees. They sent messengers to the forks of the Kaw River to urge their Konza splinter to come to them holding the hatchet, and they sent for the disturbed Quapaws who had begun to wander toward the Red River to avoid the free men. They also appealed to the Creeks, who were still enemies of the Americans, and the Cherokees who had defeated them under General Jackson. These Muskogeans came with pleasure.

All these tribes were of the woods and rivers, dugout and trace people, with the exception of the chivalric Konzas, and any horse would please them, they having use for pack horses and mules, so that this bribe would leave a pile of rawhide hobbles or empty rawhide nooses at the village of Arrow-Going-Home on the Verdigris. The Konzas had little need for more horses as did the Place-of-the-Many-Swans people, who must have been called in to aid the Arkansas Osages.

Governor Clark had been ordered to make peace, and when he heard of the Osage preparations and the horses they were giving and the feasts and promises they were making to the Delawares and the Shawnee vagabonds, giving them permission to trap beaver on the Neosho, he decided to halt this strange war movement. They were supposed to have given away three hundred horses, one supposes of inferior quality, to their woodland guests. However, personal gifts from the Grand *Hunkah* would have been the best. Clark called the council for St. Louis in September, 1818.

After the treaty there were incidents. The Cherokees took twenty [forty] horses from one gens on White River as they returned from the treaty making in St. Louis. The trail from St. Louis to the Arkansas Cherokees crossed the White River about where Batesville, Arkansas, is today. And again the Osages prepared for an all-out war on the Cherokees. But this time Captain Nathaniel Pryor, trader, friend, and intermarried white citizen, counciled with them and asked them to wait until he returned from Fort Smith to talk with Major Bradford, and he urged the Major to visit the village of Arrow-Going-Home. He found the village full of Sac and Foxes, Iowas, Omahas, and Otoes, as well as Konzas and Quapaws—except for the Sac and Foxes, a Siouan family gathering, tense with Siouan preparation for the war movement. They sat about their separate fires eating the Little Ones' buffalo and deer and wapiti and skunk and passing the pipe which bound their agreements. There was Siouan emotion and Plains dignity. The Siouans were urging the Little Ones to attack immediately, their medicine made and all the rituals completed, and the modern Little Old Men say that only when it rained did the Sac and Foxes lose their war paint. Their muskets and vermilion and blankets and *wah-don-skas* hanging about their necks were British. These perennial raiders from north of the Missouri River were always ready for slashing and jumping back like the black wolf.

Major Bradford stopped this war movement with a promise that the Cherokees would return the Osage prisoners; and the next summer, in 1819, the Little Ones were informed that the Cherokees were ready to bring in the prisoners they had taken in the attack on Arrow-Going-Home's village (Claremore Mound) in 1817. Arrow-Going-Home himself, carrying the dignity of the Grand *Hunkah* to a meeting place where the undignified business was the reception of Osage prisoners, was objective. He rode to the meeting place at the mouth of the Verdigris in July, and there they awaited word from Bradford to appear at Fort Smith to receive their captive people. The morning chant to Grandfather turned into mourning, and tears ran down their cheeks when they thought of the prisoners.

The Cherokees had an agricultural excuse, which was readily understood by Secretary of War Calhoun as a virtuous excuse, and it was also understood by Bradford but with a different interpretation. Naturally all must wait until the civilization-eager and co-operating Cherokees could get their harvest in.

The meeting was postponed until September, the time when the agricultural Cherokees would have their harvest in and the Little Ones would be impatient to be away on their annual winter buffalo hunt on the Kaw, the Republican, and the Salt Fork of the Arkansas and the Cimarron. The Pawnees or the Comanches, seeing no lodges of the Little Ones on the headwaters of the Salt Fork and the Cimarron, might come there and kill buffalo.

Since the Cherokees had killed or taken captive nearly all the women and children left at the village, missing only those mature and strong enough to accompany the men on the hunt in 1817, each gens and perhaps each family of the physical division *Co'n-Dse-U-Gthi'n,* the Upland-Forest-People, who were now calling themselves simply *Sa'n Solé* and who were living at the village of the Grand *Hunkah,* Arrow-Going-Home, had lost members in the sanguine attack.

Arrow-Going-Home was short tempered and imperious, and hid his dignity in his robe again, and took many of his tribesmen to Fort Smith along with his counselor, *Ta-Heh-Ga-Xe* (Buck-Making-Horns), Tallai, and his son *Tse-To-Gah,* Bad-Tempered-Buffalo, and the white friend Captain Nathaniel Pryor.

The party rode to Fort Smith with anticipation, but though they were punctual, the Cherokees did not show up, but sent a message that the prisoners were mostly women and were married to Cherokee men and were very happy and did not wish to come back and live with savages. The post commander ordered them to produce the prisoners within a period of ten days, and then when they failed to show up, the commander, fearing the insulted dignity of Arrow-Going-Home, had them there by the following day, the twelfth from the day appointed for the meeting.

The English naturalist Thomas Nuttall who made it a point to be at Fort Smith during the council described the parting of one Osage woman from her captor husband, who wept and "pled with the chiefs to stay," but the Osages said that her mother and father cried each morning as the Morning Star rose, and that their heads were stained by the mud of mourning. The Little Ones went away angered since not all the prisoners had been returned, among them the little captive called Lydia Carter; and within twelve months this little Osage girl would become the concern of the President of the United States and the War Department and Governor William Clark again.

Nuttall had returned from the Salt Fork just in time for the council. He had suffered with what he called "intermittent fever" and had been under the care of the kindly French trader, M. Bougie, who had one of his trading posts at the mouth of the Verdigris.

Nuttall was ill, but he wanted to be present at the council at Fort Smith. This matter of the Cherokees' holding Osage captives had been dramatized by the story of little Lydia Carter.

People came to Fort Smith to gape at the renowned Arrow-Going-Home and the Bad-Tempered Buffalo, called Mad Buffalo, Nuttall was among them, taking in every detail.

He knew Arrow-Going-Home. There was dignity in the man, he thought, and perhaps "urbanity." He wore a hat ornamented with silver lace and a regimental coat. He was very proud, Nuttall thought, but he couldn't have guessed the profundity of that pride with all eyes upon him. He undoubtedly forgot in the warm suffusions of *amour-propre,* the former insults of the Cherokees in delaying the council and forcing him, the Grand *Hunkah,* to come in person to ask humbly for the Osage captives.

When Nuttall shook hands with him, and Arrow-Going-Home asked Nuttall if he had ever heard of him, he seemed pleased when Nuttall said he certainly had.

However, Nuttall was more impressed by Buck-Making-Horns, known as Tallai. He was chieftain of the Deer, and Nuttall seemed

433

to think he might be the power in the village on the Verdigris, though he was wrong in calling him the "hereditary chief." He wore no medals or other Heavy Eyebrows decorations. He told Nuttall that he needed no decoration. He was *Ta-Heh-Ga-Xe* (Tallai).

Nathaniel Pryor, their white friend and an intermarried trader, suggested that inasmuch as the Cherokees had not been strictly sincere about the Osage captives, the Osages ought to demand of the commandant at Fort Smith that they, the Osages, take the five Cherokees home as hostages. Bad-Tempered-Buffalo was opposed, saying that if they took the Cherokees as hostages, the women would see them and be reminded of the murdered loved ones or those held by the Cherokees. They would start weeping and keening, and soon the whole village might be incited to murder them.

The Poteau flows from the south-southwest into the Arkansas River near Fort Smith and was not within the area ceded in 1808 nor in that ceded by Lovely's Purchase ratified in 1818, but the Cherokees were coming across the boundaries to hunt and trap in accordance with agreements in the Lovely Purchase treaty, but they had not carried out their part of the agreement to return all the Osage prisoners. During the Light-of-Day-Returns Moon, February, Arrow-Going-Home's son, *Tse-To-Gah,* Bad-Tempered-Buffalo with his gens warriors went to the Poteau hunting bear. This was the moon when the bears' fur was at its best, and one could know the boars from the sows in the dark caves since the latter would have had their cubs during Baby-Bear Moon in December. They did not take the sows with cubs in the dens of hibernation. There were many caves in the Mississippi limestone and many writhing white roots of the sycamore trying to come out of the earth. Under these the boars liked to hibernate.

While they were inspecting the caves and probing under the roots of sycamores, they noted signs that the Cherokees were also hunting bears, but, like the new Heavy Eyebrows, they killed both sows with cubs as well as the boars. This angered Bad-Tempered-Buffalo and he set out to find the Cherokees, and did surprise them at their hunting, but his warriors were only able to kill three of them. They had short hair like the Heavy Eyebrows and wore bandeaus of trade

434

cloth. The Little Ones left a gens-marked arrow in the largest of the trees. The Cherokees would recognize this.

Bad-Tempered Buffalo and his gentile followers came along the southern bank of the Arkansas, which still belonged to them, and came to the mouth of the Verdigris and up it on the western bank, their side, until they came to the trading post of Nathaniel Pryor, one and one-half miles above its mouth. As they approached, they saw a large war party of Cherokees standing about the traders' store, but it was too late to turn back. They had only time to put on their bluff-paint and chant a prayer to *Wah'Kon-Tah* and take the *wah-hopeh* from its wrappings and hang it around Bad-Tempered-Buffalo's neck where it flapped on his back, as they put heels to their horses, but they now sang no songs as they rode boldly into the post.

Pryor noted the glee of the Cherokees when they saw that they greatly outnumbered the Bad-Tempered-Buffalo party, but he knew they would not attack them at the post; so he immediately had one of his men, David McGee, to call the leader of the Cherokees and his followers to the opposite side of the main building to show him some new shiny copper kettles which all tribes valued very highly for cooking their tremendous amounts of meats and vegetables.

While the Cherokees, who were somewhat Europeanized, wondered about the amount of beaver or bear hides it would take to own one kettle or how much of the precious bear or buffalo tallow they must bring to Pryor to trade for one, Bad-Tempered-Buffalo and his warriors fled on their strong Pawnee horses, and they soon left behind the badly mounted Cherokees, who tried to overtake them.

The Cherokees were angered, and they left the post scowling at Pryor, but they went only a short distance, then waited for darkness. They waited until the first barred owl boomed his before-dawn hunting call, then they slipped into the area around the post and very quietly broke into the store and stole 150 pounds of beaver fur.

These intelligent Iroquoians not only had many Scottish and English mixed-blood leaders and advisers, but even the common warriors and hunters, except those in the Smokies, had become partly civilized and knew all of the tricks of verbal evasion and could take refuge under the laws which they just as often flouted as cleverly as Euro-

435

peans. They were thoroughly versed in double-dealing through their association with white officials of their old home east of the Mississippi. Like white men, they didn't go to the trouble of denying the theft of Pryor's beaver, but under the aegis of the law, which recognized the fact that the Osages and the Cherokees were at war with each other and that this white man Pryor had not been neutral in the manner in which a citizen of the United States must be, but had aided the Osages. Pryor put in his claim to the War Department, asking for redress under the guarantee made when he was given a trader's license. The War Department agreed with the Cherokee contention. Under Secretary of War John C. Calhoun, the Department was interested, with General Jackson and Governor McMinn, in keeping the Cherokees well disposed toward full migration to Arkansas. Their lands were needed by the Amer-Europeans. The Secretary of War was typical of the period. He was an honest man. His rationalizations and his resulting firm stand on local matters, he could convince himself, were one with a patriotic stand on human rights.

The United States and Spain had finally settled on a boundary line running up the Sabine River to the Red, thence along the Red to the 100th degree of longitude and up this to the Arkansas, along this river, then north, in 1819, and in that year by an act of Congress on March 2, Arkansas Territory was established, and a man came from New Hampshire to govern it. His name was James Miller. The new territory embraced most of the modern states of Arkansas and Oklahoma, and most of the Little Ones, or perhaps half of them would be under Governor Miller, and his appointment was important to their interests.

About this time in the last month of 1819 the Cherokees were gathering their rag-tail fragments of Algonkian and Muskogean tribes again, to again attack the Little Ones, their slim excuse being the killing of the bear hunters trespassing on the Poteau. They had already collected the harlequins and had added to them the ever ready Caddos, who had fled south of the Red River some time before, as well as a harassed chief of the Quapaws and his half-hearted followers, searching for security in a chaotic world. The now Cherokee agent, Reuben Lewis, brother to Meriwether Lewis, dissuaded them, asking them to wait until the new governor of the new territory should arrive.

Miller was strange to the chaos of the area and believed, as Lovely had, that differences could be resolved by conference. Obviously the Cherokees were showing signs of civilization, and would be reasonable, they both assumed. Miller got four Cherokee leaders to go with him to the village of Arrow-Going-Home, and at Fort Smith picked up a sergeant and seven enlisted men, as well as a man called John McElmurray, trader and justice of the peace from the Missouri Territory, carrying twenty pounds of tobacco.

Miller reported that the Cherokees seemed to him little different from white people, and "considerably advanced" toward civilization. He had noted their settlements along the Arkansas with a feeling of respect for virtue. Their deportment was very good, he had noted, but to a man from New Hampshire it might have seemed a bit overdone, since it was an imitation of the white men of quite another part of the country, with a touch of obsequiousness in it that might have been suspect to a New Englander. He thought their country very rich and very beautiful.

When he arrived at the village of the Grand *Hunkah,* he counted the lodges carefully and found that there were 150, large enough to accommodate, as they varied in size, from ten to fifteen people to the lodge. And then he noted what all European visitors had especially noticed, the warriors' height and their bull-wapiti dignity, and the fact that they saw you without staring at you, and listened with their eyes shut while you talked, never interrupting. He reported that the men were in average height "more than six feet," and he concluded that "they were entirely in a state of nature," and it was evident to him that very few white people had been among them, and "they know nothing of the use of money, nor do they use any ardent spirits." He didn't know that they had been in touch with Europeans for perhaps 150 years. They were simply imperiously resistant.

The Cherokees wanted the Osages to give up to them the killers of the bear hunters and the Osages wanted the remainder of their people who had been taken prisoner in 1817. And here again the little Osage captive, Lydia Carter, and her brother, John Osage Ross, came into the consideration of this grave and tense council.

The Governor told the Cherokees that they must live up to their agreement and asked both tribes to meet him October 1, 1820; and between the meeting of August and the first of October, the Cherokees seem to have tried to carry out the behest of Governor Miller, since they took the little captives from the school at Brainerd and away from their foster parents, Mr. and Mrs. Chamberlain, the missionaries, who wept and prayed and asked prayers from others for the softening of President Monroe's heart. At least one captive Osage woman wept when she was forced to go back to her people, but Governor Miller of Arkansas Territory, like Governor Clark of Missouri Territory, seemed to have a high sense of justice, no matter what the game might have been in Tennessee, the Carolinas and Washington, D. C., and wanted peace among the tribes for the sake of peace and well-being of the tribes.

Neither one of them knew, possibly not even Governor Clark, that the Little Ones were not so much concerned about the land taken from them as they were angered by the fact that the land was given to their enemy. This was not explained to them; this matter of pushing them west so that the Cherokees could have land equal to that which they had owned in Tennessee, etc. It was not wholly the ceded land which disturbed them, but very much the destruction of their game; the swollen carcasses of the holy ones given them by *Wah'-Kon-Tah,* and through whom they prayed. These holy ones, the Big Animal, the buffalo, the Yellow Animal, the wapiti, and the Little Animal, the white-tailed deer, were given in trust to them by *Wah'-Kon-Tah.* And the holy ones, the beaver, the bear, the panther, the lynx, were being destroyed as well.

And it must have seemed to the Little Ones themselves that they were not now strong enough to protect these holy animals, and as a result were losing the favor of *Wah'Kon-Tah,* and the Holy Ones seemed no longer to want to lend the Little Ones their powers.

Both grand divisions, the *Tzi-Sho* and the *Hunkah,* had cried to the Morning Star and Grandfather every morning since the descent from the stars into the red oak tree, and had even appointed a special man in each physical division called *Wa-Si-Si-Kah,* who arose with the Morning Star, and called out, chanting as he walked through the ways, much as the muezzin of the Arabs called from the tower. He was instructed by the Little Old Men to allow none except the very ill or the very old to remain on their robes after he called, since the Little Ones must take no chances with *Wah'Kon-Tah*'s anger.

But now both grand divisions not only chanted and mourned at dawn, but the *Hunkah* began to chant to the setting sun, since the West, *Mo'n-ha,* the Cliffs, was the direction of war and death and all the things with which the *Hunkah* had to do, and the *Tzi-Sho* began to chant to the first stars to appear in the evening. Later Pierre Chouteau, their indulgent agent on the Neosho, had to write to William Clark at St. Louis about this fervent attempt not really understood by him of the mighty Osages to make up for their feeling of being in disfavor with *Wah'Kon-Tah.* He wrote, "There are innumerable objections to the present agency particularly on account of family inconvenience . . . every morning and evening we are distressed with the lamentations of the Indians for their lost relatives (Which you know is a religious Custom among them)."

They took great care now when they made medicine to go on the war movement, and they painted their faces meticulously and guarded their fetish shields, and the people in charge of the pipe— the Chief's Pipe, the Little Ones called it, not "calumet"—guarded it jealously. The Little Old Men made a ruling that all women at the very beginning of menstruation must be banished from the village, now, in these times of *ga-ni-tha* and have special lodges built by their relatives a little way from the center of the village.

After the Little Old Men had made a ritual around *mo'n-ce,* metal, they believed that they had gained some of the power of the Heavy Eyebrows, but now it seemed that they must add to it, and they made rituals to white metal and black metal and metal of other colors. There was more of a hint of *ga-ni-tha,* chaos, again, the ancient *ga-ni-tha* of the Isolated Earth People. They had begun to understand the manners and methods of the woodland Indians and the free men, when they were outnumbered and came fawning, but their earth-harmonized protective coloration and bluff and panther deceptions were inadequate against the agile chicanery of the Cherokees, which was beyond their mental grasp. It was like reaching out for something with only the hands *Wah'Kon-Tah* had given them; also, to whom could they pray for the lengthening of the outstretched arm and grasping hand of understanding of white-man subleties?

In trying to describe mental grasp of anything, in their efforts to talk of abstract things, they used symbolical physical actions. When an idea was unacceptable to them, they would cup both hands, then push them forward as if they were emptying them of water or dust, then hold up the right hand with fingers spread and palm outward, to defend further from the cast-off idea. When they wished to grasp an idea or explain the evasive abstraction, they would extend the hand with fingers open and the palm upward, then close the fingers into a fist and bring it back to the body in such manner that they actually seemed to be grasping that for which they had reached, only to find that they had not grasped anything when they opened their fingers.

This was the way they explained what was happening to them. The physical fact of the American invasion, the razing of their forests, the slaughter of their "brothers," the buffalo, bear, wapiti, and deer and beaver they understood, since it was simply an invasion which they tried to repel. But the European chicanery, the evasions and convenient interpretations of the Europeans' own Christian standards were much more subtle than those of the bear and the panther and the lynx, and therefore their own evasions and deceptions, and their extended grasping fists came back empty. They could understand nothing beyond the primitive earth-struggle of which they were a part, and that they might some day reduce *Wah'Kon-Tah* to earth-terms.

Much of the wire-tangle of their ritualism came now, in the attempts of the Little Old Men to reinforce and strengthen the cage in which they tried to hold the Great Mysteries, and they seemed to be mourning in their prayers to the Sun, the Morning Star, the first stars of evening, the descending sun, and Grandfather the Sun as he came immediately above them each day. All this because the bluff-paint, the Wolf Songs, the Crow Songs, the songs to *Wah'Kon-Tah* through the beaver, the deer, the wapiti, the panther, the bear, the buffalo, the otter, the red oak, the redbud charcoal, their seven days' fastings, and their hunger dreams, their fast and beautiful Pawnee horses, their dedication to the swiftness and ferocity of the falcon would no longer hold for them their *Mo'n-Sho'n* the Sacred One, Mother Earth. For the first time in their tribal memory, the Little Ones seemed to sense disaster, and in their frustrations, they were easily divided.

However, they remained resistant and stubbornly imperious, and the clever, adjustable Cherokees, and their Illini federation from across the Mississippi, and the Shawnees and the Delawares, as well as chain-pressured others—the Kickapoos, Miamis, Piankashaws, Weas, Peorias, Michigamans, and Wyandots, Ottawas, and Senecas—all under the process of Europeanization, wearing "citizens' clothes," thought the Little Ones were stupid, now, since the criteria for cleverness and ability had undergone a great change among the woodland red men. Stray members of these advanced tribes came to them now, and were fed and treated as guests under *Wah'Kon-Tah*'s laws. They wore "citizens' clothes," often long-tailed coats and stovepipe hats, lingering nostalgia represented by a flicker primary feather in the band or the bronze tail cover-feather of a wild turkey. They took these hats off and laid them carefully aside, then reached in the tails of their coats for their Bibles. Inherently Indian and filled with a desire to be important, which their tribal organization had denied them or no longer nurtured in deterioration, they stood with ears turned to them at last, often ears of distrust and curiosity, but with eyes closed and heads lowered in courteous silence; but this affected not the *amour-propre* of the new Christian. No white circuit rider could have been more dedicated to the Word, even though he might emotionalize himself into croaking hoarseness and a heavy sweat.

But these saved ones had no effect on the crystalline Little Ones, and they feasted and boasted in their villages, talked glibly, and were comfortable, then waited for the fourth day of the social dance when a horse might be "smoked" to one.

While the Little Old Men were creating more labyrinthine rituals in their urgency, several gentes of the Little Osages had moved down from Fort Osage to the Neosho, and there were about twenty families of Missouria with them. White Hair (the younger now) would come to the Neosho later with the *Wah-Ho-Ka-Li,* Thorny-Valley People, one of the physical divisions of the Little Ones. His village had about 400 people while the Little Osages could possibly count about 1,000. By this time Traveling Rain had become their chief. It would seem that there might have been three of the physical divisions, with all the gentes represented in each one, near the Three Forks. The Upland-Forest People had been on the Verdigris some time before Chouteau brought Makes-Tracks-Far-Away down, and now the Down-Below People and the Thorny-Valley People had moved there leaving only Sitters-on-the-Hilltops, and the Heart-Stays People at the Place-of-the-Many-Swans, both apparently in one village. Of these there were about 1,200. The Sitters-on-the-Hilltops were called by the French "Grosse Côte," and were already being called Big Hills in English, and their chief was *To-Wa-Ka-Heh.*

Thus because of many things—the disruption of the tribal organization, the invasions of the free men and the Cherokees, and the War of 1812—the tribe seemed to be gathering in one area again but the *Pa-Solé,* the Sitter-on-the-Hilltops, the Big Hills of perhaps 1,200 strong, and White Hair's 400 remained at the old villages at the Place-of-the-Many-Swans. There would be now, in 1820, about 4,500 of the Little Ones on the Verdigris and the Neosho rivers not far above the mouths of both rivers. The several villages of the Place-of-the-Oaks, called "Oua-Zha-Zhe des Chenes" by the French, and "Les Chenes," which Americanized became Chaneers and Shainers, were called by Sibley, in his report of 1820, "Chancers," who had been under Makes-Tracks-Far-Away, Walks-in-the-Night, and all under Grand *Hunkah* Arrow-Going-Home. The Little Osages were under their chief Traveling Rain, and the village of Great Osages under White Hair.

37. Rhythms of the Moon Woman

Even in this physical disruption of the organization, they clung to their old tradition just as they clung to *Wah'Kon-Tah*. During their time in the villages, the young men were not allowed to fall too much under the influence of the life symbols of their gentes in their idleness, the mischievous Bear especially, but their lives and traditions were still a part of the rhythmical earth, and they were ever in harmony. Also, during this time of constant gentile war movement, the energies of the young men were absorbed.

If there was jerked or smoked buffalo meat in the village and the pack rats had not found their way into the caches of corn and pumpkins and persimmon cakes and hackberry cakes, stored roots of the lotus and the poppy mallow and the blazing star, burr oak acorns, walnuts, and pecans and *do,* the wild potato, and the wild bean, and the white-tail deer were plentiful, which they were at that time near the Three Forks, there was little to do during Single-Moon-by-Himself, January. The bears were asleep, and this was the time of the year when the members of the Bear gens were supposed to be most tranquil. This was the time of year when the Little Old Men of the Bear taught the women and girls many of the things about the Great Mysteries that the women and girls of the other gentes were not allowed to know.

They taught them to wet the index finger of the right hand and point it at their enemies, saying "You will die," and the Bear women are not allowed to visit the sick. The Bear medicine is strong in the case of fainting spells, since the bear in hibernations "dies" and comes to life. However, like all "medicines," it must be used only by those who have the authority.

And this was the time for the grandmothers to gather the children around them and tell them stories, since the tale-bearing little people, the dragonfly, the swallow, and the snakes are not about to hear. The stories are endless, and one by one the children fall asleep, and the teller of stories knows that they are all asleep, and when there is not one voice responding, she stops her long, seemingly senseless tales, which are often the strange and very mystical experiences one may have in a dream. Some of these stories may have been the true dream of an ancestor of the teller, two hundred years before. The storyteller will stop in the telling suddenly and say, *"Hah'n,"* and the children will respond. She does this periodically, and each time there are fewer and fewer responsive *"hah'n"* from the children until finally there are none. The emotionless little owls have fallen against each other, and must be carried to their bear skins.

And this is a time when the duennas must keep careful watch on their charges, seeing that they do not crawl out under the edges of the lodges and creep closer and closer in the moonlight to the flute player hidden in the shadows. But everyone in the village listened with delight to the flutes of the lovers. This was the idle time when a woman or a girl walked from the village or camp alone, the women sitting together talking and making beadwork designs on their to-bacco pouches, parfleche moccasins, and trader's cloth, would say, "Ho, ho, where is she going?" There were white traders and trappers and others of the settlement of the Three Forks, and some of them had no women, but they had strange and fascinating presents to give.

The Grand *Hunkah* and the Grand *Tzi-Sho* would allow little idleness, and they had a ball made from buffalo hide and stuffed with the coarse hair of the bull buffalo's neck, and they had a ball made from the roots of the wild grape, and they would have the town crier go down the ways saying that they would play a game like hockey, but more like shinny. On one side would be the young men of the *Hunkah,* and on the other side the young men of the *Tzi-Sho.* The young women playing in another place would have the young women of the *Hunkah* on one side, and the young women of the *Tzi-Sho* on the other side. The *Tzi-Sho* to the left of Grandfather's daily path, and the *Hunkah* to the right.

Before the game started, everyone, even the oldest grandmother bent over her dogwood or hickory stick, would bet their most precious belongings. Horses and horsehair bridles, and even the four-strand buffalo-hair lariats, and special gypsum-rubbed skins, and soft buffalo robes. Piles of things piled up on the north of Grandfather's path, as well on the south side, the *Tzi-Sho* and *Hunkah* sides.

The players would line up on their respective sides, and the two sides would start a rhythmical chanting and counter chanting, and the game would begin.

After the game, even if the *Hunkah* side or the *Tzi-Sho* side had lost valuable property to the other, they would laugh and chaff each other and then sit down to a tremendous feast.

There were quieter games, nearly all of them gambling. Their daily lives were a gamble and so were their games, and their games were really training for their existence struggle. In the case of organized military training, which was for success in battle, the Little Ones were in constant struggle to attain old age, then enter Spiritland under the approval of *Wah'Kon-Tah*. The moccasin game was one of chance, of quick decision, upon which the warriors daily depended.

The players sat in two rows, and between them was spread a buffalo robe or a trade blanket. There were four moccasins. A stick or a buckeye nut (or perhaps by 1820 a hawkbell) was put into one of the moccasins secretly, then a rhythm was drummed and a chant begun, and the moccasins manipulated, then a player at a time was asked to guess where the stick or buckeye or bell was. This could go on for days, and a fevered gambler, losing steadily, would bet his most precious possession, but losing could rise to his feet, robeless and perhaps moccasinless, wrap his arms about him to protect himself from the sharp winds, and, singing to himself sadly, walk to his fireplace. There would be no woman there to scold him since she might be at the time in the same or another moccasin game or the hand game.

445

The hand game was similar to the moccasin game, but the buckeye was held in either the right or the left hand, and the hands held behind the back as the chanters chanted and the drum beat softly. A player on the opposite side would indicate with pursed lips the hand which he believed contained the nut and win the stakes.

When there was no war movement or no mourning dance at this time, and there was plenty of food and deer near for the taking, the people's energy was absorbed by such amusements, but in the next moon, The-Light-of-Day-Returns Moon [February] there was much to do. The black bear and the grizzly, for that matter, were some of the most important brothers which *Wah'Kon-Tah* had given the Little Ones. The bear's hide was used for bedding, and his tallow was used for many things, including torches. He had no sinews running down each side of his spine like the buffalo, but he furnished meat and tallow and hide and the sacred bear-claw necklace. And now, during The-Light-of-Day-Returns Moon, was the time for taking him in his den. This was not sport, as hunting him later in the woods might be, but this was the time when his hair was at its best and his claws at their longest and most attractive as ornaments. Later in the autumn they would hunt him for tallow, at which time his claws would be ugly and broomed and his hair brittle and broken, but his meat rich and less stringy.

They explored the caves and under the roots of great trees and windfalls. In the dark caves they dipped sycamore splinters in tallow and set them afire, the better to see the slumbering bear.

If their villages had consumed their corn and squashes and other things from their caches and their meat was growing small, parties of hunters must go for deer and wapiti. The bulls and bucks were beginning to lose their antlers now and were still emaciated and scarred from the last autumn's rut, so they must kill cows and does, and the foetus in either was a delicacy.

During this moon, the light of day was noticeably returning after the dark days of winter. It was quite apparent here, between the thirty-eighth and the thirty-seventh parallels, on the waters of the Neosho and the Verdigris. The frogs might sing tentatively, but *sho-*

446

mi-ḳase, the coyote, would drown out the flute players with his own love song.

And this was the time to take the beaver, because his fur was at its best. And now they had the traps of the Heavy Eyebrows, and they need not sit for hours waiting for the beaver to come out. The beaver had many traditional uses other than as food and fur, and he who had beaver medicine was very important. Sometimes even a woman of the Beaver gens of the *Wah-Sha-She* subdivision would have beaver medicine, and she would come to the newly put-up lodges in a new camp and walk around them four times singing. Thereafter they would be strong like the lodge of the beaver and no enemy could come into them or destroy them.

Then, when the next moon came, the little people, the frogs, would sing in full volume at the Three Forks, and the great horned owl would do silly things in his love-making, and the barred owl would frighten the little people of the grass roots and among the cane stems, and the children of the Little Ones would stop their play and come casually to their lodges. Only the screech owl was the embodiment of the evil spirit, the voice of the lost soul whose face had not been painted or had died in the war movement without the war paint, and had not been recognized in Spiritland. He wandered about during the autumn and winter moons, weeping softly, asking pity, but the bravest of the warriors didn't want to listen to him.

However, the children were afraid of *wah-poḳah,* the great gray owl of the Place-of-the-Many-Swans, because he was held up to them as an evil one who sat in the trees at night and listened to all the things they said and spied on them if they did not come to their lodges after nightfall. Here, near the Three Forks, the barred owl took his place and the children were afraid of him, and certainly his booming was much more dreadful than that of *wah-poḳah.*

When the little people, the frogs, sang strongly, the barred owl boomed and gurgled and talked and bowed in the moonlight, and the great horned owl also became drunk and silly with love. It was a witches' moon now, but the Little Ones called March Just-Doing-That-Moon. Walks-on-wings, the wild turkey, strutted, and the noise of their strutting sounded like far-away thunder, just as their mad gobbling sounded like Padouca warriors charging.

Now the hunters could sit at the heads of the ravines, where, putting their lips to the backs of their hands and sucking, they could make the gobblers come to them, and thereafter the women would be busy making awls from their wing bones and needles for the trader's cloth, and dusters from their tail-feathers, and with their wings they made brooms to keep the fireplaces clean. They used the hairs of the gobbler "beards," along with the tail hairs of the deer, to make the roaches which the dancers and the warriors wore. Also the wing bones of the walks-on-wings could be used for tweezers if split properly, to be used in pulling the scraggly face hairs of the warriors. Some liked them better for this purpose than the two halves of pecten shells.

The winds from the Gulf blew now, carrying the leaves far over the treetops and making little piles of them dance round and round the Osage fires like the dance of the Creeks. The limbs of neighboring elms and sycamores, scraping against each other, complained pettishly, and the squirrels rode the swaying limbs, hugging them tightly, and little boys tried to shoot them with their blunted dogwood arrows. This was a good time for the gentile war movement. The woodland Indians found it more difficult to ambush the Little Ones now, since the leaves had been blown from the oaks and the grasses and weeds and canes had been bent and broken. You could see the light of the Heavy Eyebrows' campfire a long way through the leafless trees, and you could come from the north and had to "drink" the high south winds of Just-Doing-That Moon, but even the scouts of the enemy couldn't hear you. Only *ca-xe,* the crow, might give you away when you came upon him down wind and he screamed murder and shouted, *"Nee-ḳah! nee-ḳah!"* "man, man!" Everyone listened to the alarm cry of *ca-xe,* even the stupid Heavy Eyebrows.

Then the first grass of spring came up in the bottoms and on the backbone of the ridges. The winter-starved horses of the enemy would have their "noses in the earth," eating greedily, and there would be no crazy lead mare to see or smell you and warn the guard boys. Just-Doing-That Moon referred to the whimsicalities of March, but the Little Ones might be just doing that as well, with time heavy on their hands. Only the women were busy, stretching the beaver hides to be traded to the Heavy Eyebrows, working the hides of the bears, rendering tallow, making needles and awls and magnificent roaches for the men, but there were always the games for all.

During the next appearance of Moon Woman, mad clouds would begin to race across the skies, as ragged as an old buffalo robe, and tassels would come to the oaks, and the elms would scatter their samara, which hid in the folds of your blanket and got into pots. Your horse might prick up his ears as if he saw deer, and sometimes snort when he came upon the dogwood or the plum, thinking them ghosts. Their white flowers startled even the warriors.

When these things happened and the chuck-will's-widow and the whippoorwill called monotonously from the dusky woods, it would be *Wah-Pi,* Planting Moon. April was the woman's moon. She planted the corn and the squash and the other things, but among all the things she planted the corn was the most sacred. It was the gift to the Little Ones by the most sacred of all the animals, the buffalo. He had given the yellow, the red, the blue, and the speckled corn just after they had descended from the red oak and had set out on their quest over the roads of the earth. Here was the female secret of life giving, the understanding among the three: *Mi-Ompah,* the Moon, *Mo'n-Sho'n,* the Earth, and *Wa-Cu,* the Woman.

For the corn, the woman made little hills far apart, after she had scraped away all the debris from the weeds and had cleaned the grass away. She did this with the shoulder blade of the wapiti attached to a handle of hickory or dogwood, but by this time she might be using a trade tool, if there was no taboo. This was a sacred procedure. No man was allowed about unless he was necessary to lift heavy things; then he must work only under instructions from the woman.

After she made the hills, she used a sharpened stick and poked a hole in the south or sunny side, or the Grandfather side, of the hill, then dropped from four to seven grains of corn into the hole. If she was *Tzi-Sho,* she covered the hole with her left foot, and if of the *Hunkah,* she covered it with the right foot, all the time singing and keeping the rhythm with her stick, as she looked at the sky.

She planted as many hills as she desired, taking the grains from a

449

woven sack flung on her back, woven of the nettle or buckbrush runners. She formerly, and at least ceremonially, painted her forehead
with one red and one blue line across the breadth, and one red and
one blue short line running vertically on each cheek.

Her song as she planted, beating the rhythm with her feet and the
planting stick, was the most beautiful of all the many songs of the
Little Ones.

> *I have made a footprint, a sacred one.*
> *I have made a footprint, through it the blades must push upward.*
> *I have made a footprint, through it the blades radiate.*
> *I have made a footprint, over it the blades float in the wind.*
> *I have made a footprint, over it the ears lean toward each other.*
> *I have made a footprint, over it I pluck the ears.*
> *I have made a footprint, over it I bend the stalks to pluck the ears.*
> *I have made a footprint, over it the tassels lie gray.*
> *I have made a footprint, smoke rises from my lodge.*
> *I have made a footprint, there is cheer in my lodge.*
> *I have made a footprint, I live in the light of day.*

In the villages at the Place-of-the-Many-Swans, where the Big
Hills remained and where all had lived up to the first decades of the
nineteenth century, the horses had sometimes to eat elm and cottonwood bark during very hard winters, but at the Place-of-the-Oaks,
there was always grass to be found under the weeds and the sere
grasses of the preceding season, and the horses were nearly always
ready for the spring buffalo hunt. While the women planted, the men
guarded their horses carefully and drove them to places where the
grass was advanced, and at night brought them close into the village.
To interfere with the buffalo hunts of the Little Ones was a part of
the strategy of the clever Cherokees, who, by stealing their best horses
just before the Little Ones set out for the Salt Fork and the Cimarron
and the upper Arkansas, might effect their own meat supply. Later
they would make bluff-invasion to keep the Little Ones from the
hunt. However, these activities were left mostly to the drifters and
vagabonds, since the Cherokees were true planters and this was the
time of year when they must be busy with their own plantings, upon

which they were much more dependent for corn and squash and other things than the Little Ones. Also the trespassing hunters and trappers were taking their furs to market during the season.

But this was the season of madness. The jungle moisture from the Gulf turned into ragged clouds, which sailed over from the south. When the cold air of the Arctic met them and caused swirling clouds to come out of the sky, the greening trees were shredded, and pulled up by the roots. Then the Little Ones would watch the tail of a tornado swing like a lariat to the earth, hissing loudly like a snake disturbed in spring, and they would run to the cane stems, the running oaks, or the sumac, to lie flat on their stomachs and hug tightly to Mother Earth. But they ran only if the swinging tail dropped southwest of them; otherwise they watched it until the hail came with the rain. Then they ran to their lodges or held flint buffalo hides over their heads. If the lightning came, they sang. It has been said that sometimes a few very frightened young warriors of the Thunder gens (the Mystery gens) would take their trade rifles to a high spot and there, throwing their robes off, challenge the lightning, singing their death songs, but no one remembers this now.

During May, the Little-Flower-Killer Moon, the women cultivated their plantings, then made ready to go with the hunters on the spring buffalo hunt. Little-Flower-Killer Moon was thus named because during this time the little earth-hugging flowers disappear, and the tall spiderworts and cone flowers and other tall flowers wave in the winds of the prairie.

The grass was greening the prairie now and the horses become fat and strong again, and each physical division organized its buffalo hunt with leaders and soldiers and whippers, and they set out for the plains. Along the trail to the plains they had special spots where they camped, each named for some incident, a tree, a large stone, a foot race or a horse race that might have occurred there, or a death, an accident, or for some topographic or geological feature; even for the prank of some young men. These places had been chosen carefully years before, and were chosen with water and fuel and grass and their enemies in mind. They didn't mind, they said, if their enemies knew about these traditional camps, since when they went to the plains for

451

buffalo, they traveled in physical division groups, or even in a tribal body.

The boys would play at buffalo hunting, pretending the camp dogs were buffalo, and they played "rescue" on their ponies. In the woods, when the streams stood in deep holes of water, they played "otter," slicking a slide, and no otter had more fun.

They might consume eight days, more or less, on their travels to the great herds. The final camp in several of the hunts of the Little Osages had the name, Bed of Big Lakes, evidently the environs of the Great Salt Plains. As a matter of fact, in 1811 George Sibley had gone there to meet Beautiful Bird of the Little Osages.

There was a camp at the spot where Coffeyville, Kansas, now stands, which was called Medicine-Man Creek, the first camping spot on the buffalo trail. The Little Ones found a strange Indian dead in a cave near there, and one of them with special power (medicine) fanned away evil. Beyond that was another camping place, where they camped the second night out, called Fire-Medicine Creek. Smoke was once seen rising from this creek and the horses were frightened. Far out on the headwaters of the Cimarron was a camp (the fifteenth from the Neosho) called *Mo'n-I'n-Ku-A-Ha,* where a man of the Buffalo gens died, and his importance called for a mourning dance. There was the camp on the creek called *Mi'n-Kshe-Ska,* which might have been the original of the modern Chikaskia. Another camp, called Waters-of-the-Cedars, might have been on the modern Cedar Creek, a branch of the Caney River. There was a camping place near the spot where the modern Elgin, Kansas, now stands. Here an important woman called Hawkwoman died. And a camp where the Little Ones had to dig a trench and put up breastworks against stampeding buffalo. This was the Place-Between-Two-Waters, and could have been the modern Arkansas City, Kansas, between the Arkansas River and the Walnut River, or a spot in the modern Oklahoma Panhandle on the Beaver River, between the Cimarron and the North Canadian. They had had to dig a trench around both spots at different times.

Then there was a camp where a visiting Konza won a race, named in his honor. And at the spot where the modern city of Bartlesville,

Oklahoma, now stands, the Little Ones had a buffalo-trail camp, and called not for a death, an incident, or creek, nor yet a topographic feature, but called *Ka-Wa-Skinkah,* which means "Little Horse" and refers to the stick horses which the children pulled up, a species of large cane which they rode about the camp playing Osage and Pawnee.

There was a camp, the sixth on the third trail, where a horse was castrated, which they called Pride-Taken, which was two camps westerly of the creek called Bear Creek, because there were always many bears there. However, both the sows and the boars might still be emaciated from their long hibernation, and their tallow not plentiful or good and their meat stringy and strong, but they might not have lost the sheen of their winter coats, even though they might have begun to shed their long silky winter hairs.

There was a Dog-Dies-of-Thirst camp, which implied some long-ago tragedy of Neolithic survival struggle with temperamental nature. There was the camp where the Papaws-Grow, and, far out on the plains, a camp which they reached in seventeen days, they called Door, because here there was a gap in the plains swells.

Each gens in the permanent camp had a Fire Lodge, where any member could go to get an ember, and this fire was supposed to be eternal, and there were especially appointed men to keep it going. When they reached their hunting camps, each gens established a Fire Lodge.

Each unit of hunters was organized according to the old tribal hunting organization of the Little Old Men, except in the physical division units, the chief of the divisions took the place of both the Grand *Hunkah* and the Grand *Tzi-Sho,* and if the hunting unit were gentile, of course, they were under their chieftain, but the organization of the hunt was the same.

Many of the hunters attached stag beetles to their shot and wadding pouches, since the stag beetle brought good luck. The children often took with them to the plains from the oak forests the insect called walking stick. When they reached the last camp and were settled for the hunt, the children would hold the walking stick up and squeeze it slightly, asking, "Where are the buffalo?" Under pressure, the insect would turn his head about and hold it in a certain direction.

And this was the time to gather the seeds of the *mo'n-pi-ha.* They would gather them before they left sometimes, and at other times they could find them on their way. They gathered the little black seeds and then chewed them. Then they blew them on their clothes, which they kept in the long, highly decorated bags called parfleches, possibly from the French *pour les fleches,* "for the arrows." They did make these bags for their extra arrows and especially for their sacred red and black ones. They picked the leaves of the *zho-hia* for scent, and ate the leaves of the sheep sorrel. They took along with them at all times the bark and twigs of the slippery elm, tied in little bunches, and when they killed fat buffalo, they could put this elm into the tallow and it would be preserved. They met with few bears on the plains, so they must carry bear tallow with them, into which they had put slippery elm as a preservative.

Sometimes they met grizzly bears on the headwaters of the Arkansas and even on the Walnut-Grove River, the North Canadian, and the Cut-Salt River, the Cimarron. They left the *wah-sabe,* the black bear, behind them in the woodlands, but *mi-tzo,* the grizzly, would come down the streams hunting the wapiti and the buffalo that had died the winter before in the screaming blizzards. He would stand and look at them, with dead flesh of the wapiti hanging from his closed mouth. If they didn't need his tallow or his great hide, they would go on about their business, but if they saw that his winter hair had not yet formed balls and tangles and he seemed fat, the hunters would lie in the grass and crawl toward him, moving the long bottom grasses; and he, in order to see better, would stand on his hind legs, then they would shoot him between the paws which were close together for balance over his heart.

But *mi-tzo* sometimes killed a hunter. If only wounded, he would scream and rush toward any movement, but before he could overtake the running hunter, another would wave his robe like a picador and the nearsighted one would go for the robe waver. Another would attract him by robe waving, and soon the wounded, bewildered beast would stand and give the hunters another chance; and arrows would fly from several directions, entering under the forelegs, crashing the shoulder, or seeking the jugular, but they never gut-shot *mi-tzo*. This would make a screaming maniac of him, so that he would not even stop to bite at the arrow.

They hunted *mi-tzo* afoot. Their horses were crazy with fear when they smelled him.

Some time after they arrived in camp, the Buffalo-Pawing-Earth Moon would make the lodges of the camp into spirit lodges, and the low trees bent by the winds and whipped by the sand along the strings of water in the sand-choked beds of the Salt Fork or the Cimarron were Shoshoni women, they said, looking for lizards. *Ca-xe,* the crow, was not there on the plains, since he did not dare follow the Little Ones so far away from the forests, but the vultures circled and *ca-xe-tonkah,* big crows, the ravens, came and angrily shouted, "Ku-wak, ku-wak," as they banked above the butchers of the buffalo.

The wolves and the coyotes sang seldom now, but the buffalo bulls had begun to paw the earth and roar. They became ill-tempered and stood looking at the Little Ones on foot away from the camp, as if they would challenge them.

The fires of the Little Ones must be made of cottonwood and elm and buffalo chips, unless for its merry crackling they had brought with them some mulberry wood, which they might save for some special occasion. The wind was ever present, and often even in Buffalo-Pawing-Earth Moon, it lifted the sand from the river beds and carried it like smoke from a prairie fire. Also the clouds with tails like the lariat would come, and the Little Ones must go to the thickets of the bottoms and cling to the stems of the bushes and resiliant trees, covering their heads with flint buffalo robes. And often now the Tree-Splitter, the lightning, would come, and they must ever be listening for the earth pounding of the stampeding buffalo. Always they dug trenches about their semipermanent hunting camps. When the Tree-Splitter came, they dared not use the wood of the tree he had touched.

When they came to the plains hunting each May and September, the Little Ones brought many of the things of the woodland which they might need on the plains. They brought squash and persimmon

455

cakes, yonkopin for food and medicine, but they didn't need the yonkopin for malaria out on the plains. They brought corn with them from their cache near their permanent village. They brought materials for dyes which they might need: the dodder (love vine), which they boiled for their much used yellow dye, and the bark of the maple for black dye. They had no need to bring walnut bark with them since they could go across drainage to Walnut-Grove Waters, the North Canadian River, to obtain it. They used the walnut bark for black-staining and also for a fish lure. On the plains there was little fishing to be had, but they sometimes fished on the way to the plains, in the feeder streams of the rivers. They made seines from buckbush runners and dragged the waters, first having baited the shoal end of holes of water with crushed leaves and stems of the black walnut. This, they say, lured the fish to a certain spot.

The hunting camp was ever busy. The women had brought dogwood limbs with them from the woodland, and with these they made conical structures, almost the shape of the frame of their lodges, but more conical and, of course, much smaller. These small limbs they bound together with sinew from the pawpaw, just as they did with the hickory of the lodges. They constructed these miniature lodges over foot-deep pits in the earth, in which they had built a fire of hickory. They had to carry the sinew and the hickory with them. They had many pack horses and mules now.

When the coals were ready, they placed the sheets of buffalo meat over the framework, exactly as if they were covering a lodge with skins. The meat had been sliced off the carcass in thin slices by the butchers, not in cuts. When the meat was sufficiently cooked, they took it off and laid it on a clean buffalo robe from which the hair had been taken, then they placed another robe exactly like the first one over the meat.

They danced on the covering robe and often became unbalanced on the uneven meat under the robe, but they laughed and made jokes and sang ridiculous songs to the rhythm of their handclaps. There was nothing sacred about this phase of food preparation.

When they had danced on it, they removed the top robe and put tallow over the meat, mixing it in well, then stored it in specially made parfleches.

The first thing to be done, even before the hunters came in with the buffalo meat and the hides, was to take care of the paunches and the heart sacs, which the little boy messengers called *xi-he-ki* brought up from the hunt. Little boys were eager unofficial messengers and ran here and there to deliver their messages.

The women filled the paunches with hot tallow and placed them in holes formed as perfectly as possible in the earth clay, then when the hunters came with the hides they staked them out, flesh side up, on the ground, and fleshed them.

While the women were doing this, the men cooked the ribs. The meat that was not to be preserved by smoking and cooking was cut into thin ribbons and hung on the drying racks. They could jerk much more meat on the semiarid plains than they could in the humidity of the Place-of-the-Oaks and the Place-of-the-Many-Swans. They often waited to tan the hides until they had arrived in the permanent villages again.

In the Buffalo-Pawing-Earth Moon they could harvest the roots of the plant which the French called *pomme blanche*. They could eat the roots raw or cook them, and they spent much time in their prairie camps collecting these roots and drying them for winter. There was also the prickly pear cactus, which was abundant on the plains and rather rare in the woodlands, and since it was very important, they gathered it during this moon especially for its peeled stem, which they used as sizing for their painted designs on robes. It was also very important for arrow wounds.

And there were the young sprouts and floral buds of the milkweed, which were delicious food. And if they stayed long enough, they could also have the matured fruit, which when boiled was delicious. It was like cabbage, they say. The stem of the young cattail they must also bring with them from the woodland. They boiled it.

The Little Ones were busy in their buffalo camps on the Cut-Salt Waters and the Low-Forest Waters and the Red Waters, and they must watch their horses carefully, and warn the boys who guarded

457

them in the daytime to remain in sight and watch the plains swells where the sentinels were. If they saw a sentinel running toward camp zigzagging like the Tree-Splitter, they would know that he had seen Pawnee or Padouca or Comanche scouts or hunters, and they must bunch the horses and run them into camp. Where the buffalo were, there the Little Ones would find their enemies, but these were chivalric enemies whom they understood, since they fought and hunted under a common code, and whose cleverness was the cleverness of the panther, the wolf, the bear, the coyote, the eagle, and the raccoon, and not the cleverness of the Iroquoian Cherokees, which was like lightning when there were no clouds, and like floods when there had been no rain, and was detached and strange to the animal world.

It was sportive to ride out under a gentile leader and appear on some plains swell so that a Pawnee hunting party might see you, then watch them to see what they might do; or if the party was small, engage them in a short skirmish and try to count coup on their leader, avoiding the giving of the death stroke with spear or hatchet, as well as avoiding his counter stroke, then ride off singing a song you had just made up for the occasion. And when your song was finished, your companions would say, "Ha-ha-ha-HEY," and purse their lips toward you and call you Saucy-Calf. Saucy or playful buffalo calves did not always escape from their merry adventures unsullied; they sometimes butted a skunk or a porcupine.

The sentinel and scouts were ever on the alert watching every movement through the plains heat dance. All things which moved on the plains now since the European had brought *mo'n-ce*, metal, were referred to by the Little Ones as *Si-Mo-I'n*, Walking-Glint. Now in the sun of the plains you could see the glint of metal for miles, even if it were only a *wah-don-ska* worn about the neck or a trade ear pendant, and certainly you could see the glint of a war hatchet and gun. It was for this reason that the Little Ones called all visitors either friends or enemies, *Si-Mo-I'n*. The least bit of metal worn by an approaching party would be as a heliographic signaling but talking like an idiot.

One of the first European metals the Little Ones saw were bullets brought up the river to the Place-of-the-Many-Swans by Heavy Eye-

458

brows during the seventeenth or eighteenth century, and they could think of only one thing which they resembled: in both shape and color they were like the nipples of a woman's breasts, which they called *mo'n-ce,* and thus did the first bullets become *mo'n-ce,* like-nipples-of-women's breasts, and later all metal was thus called, the word *mo'n* being the word for arrow. The bullet actually called *mo'n-ce-mo'n, mo'n-ce,* any metal, and *mo'n,* arrow, hence "metal arrow."

During the next moon, the Buffalo-Mating Moon, no sound could live where the buffalo gathered except the roaring of the bulls. They walked up and down challenging, they pawed the dust into pale smoke and wallowed like horses in special spots devoid of grass. Soon the Little Ones came upon solitary bulls standing in the shade of river bottom cottonwoods or standing with heads to the wind, as immobile as boulders, defeated and outcast from the herds.

By the time the herds had passed the headwaters of the Arkansas and the Cimarron and the Salt Fork, the Little Ones of the Place-of-the-Oaks were ready to move back to their permanent villages, and the Little Ones from the Place-of-the-Many-Swans were ready to leave the Republican and the Konza and the headwaters of the modern Marais des Cygnes and the Neosho to return to their corn and squash patches. This was the Yellow-Flower Moon now, August. The goldenrod had come and the compass weed, the broomweed and the partridge pea and the bluestem of the prairie was yellow-washed. The yellow butterflies floated over the tall bluestem of the prairie-plains, "just doing that," and the goldfinch bounced over the trees at the edge of the woodland, twittering, and there were the yellow-headed blackbirds beginning to flock.

For fifteen or sixteen days the Little Ones traveled along their well-known buffalo trails back to the villages, and along the way they gathered the fruits and the roots of plants which they used as food and medicine. Many of their plants grew on the prairie, and Yellow-Flower Moon was harvesting time for some of them, especially the seeds of the columbine, which were perfume for clothing when chewed and blown upon finery, as well as making a very good drink when powdered and dissolved in hot water. Young men prized it highly. They stole the powder from the women who were pounding

459

the seeds in an elm mortar, and secretly rubbing it on the palms of their hands, they tried to get the girl of their fancy to shake hands with them. If she did, they believed she would be bewitched and fall in love with them.

This was the Peacemaker Moon, as well as the Yellow-Flower Moon, the symbol of a sub-gens of the *Tzi-Sho*. The earth was full of the young of animals and birds and the four colors of corn were ripe, and their ears bent over the footprints of the women, the sacred gift of *tho-xe,* the bull buffalo. The pumpkins would soon turn and the squashes lay waiting. The cone flower was symbolical of the Peacemaker Moon, and nodded in the soft-talking winds to the Little Ones as they strung out across the prairie in a long line coming home, their parfleches full and the pack animals groaning under their loads of buffalo hides and heads and hooves.

But when they arrived at the villages the Peaceful Days did not enter with them, and they must look back over their shoulders to the prairie-plains, when they thought of the Peacemaker.

38. The Grizzly Bear Lunge

BUT EVEN THOUGH THERE WAS NO PEACE for people who controlled so desirable a domain, the peace of the plains they could understand. They could understand the border-line struggles and the chivalric invasions as they had always understood them, even though now the Pawnee-*maha* (Long-Hair [Lodges]-from-River-Bank) seemed to be coming down in great numbers especially to attack them. In April, 1818, sixty miles north of the Arkansas, on the buffalo plains, a party consisting of members of the Wapiti gens of the sub-*Hunkah* and the Spider gens of the Grand *Hunkah* were looking for Pawnee buffalo hunters in order to run them back toward their old hunting grounds on the Republican River. There were forty-eight warriors in the party, and they seemed to be an advance party scouting for the tribe before they moved out in May.

They saw several Pawnees sitting their horses on a plains swell, and they rode toward them. The Pawnees seemed to have great fear and would not wait for the Little Ones to approach, so they fled precipitately, lying along their horses' backs. The Little Ones, numbering forty-eight, felt secure and gave chase, but in their exultation they fell into a trap. There were four hundred Pawnees waiting for them just over a plains swell at the head of a gash canyon, and only one of the Little Ones rode back to the Place-of-the-Oaks. The Pawnees had forty-seven guns and forty-seven scalps. The Wapiti and Spider scouts were young men.

This, however, they understood: the Pawnees had ambushed them by decoys just as they had ambushed the Pawnees many times, but it changed nothing. The Pawnees went back to their villages on the Platte after hunting buffalo on the head of their river and on the Republican, and the women of the Wapiti and the Spider set the dogs to howling with their keening.

There was one mourning dance for all the slain warriors. The women put the blue clay of mourning on their heads, and the *Tzi-Sho* danced to the left and the *Hunkah* danced to the right, and they danced for four days, fasting. The Wapiti lifted their knees high as they raised their war hatchets and emotionalized themselves into a species of frenzy. They painted their faces yellow and black and blue, and the Spider painted their faces black with white and yellow lines here and there like the lines on some species of spider, although the symbol of their gens was in reality a black spider. The Spider dancers lifted both arms like the spider in defense-bluff as they danced.

On the fourth day the mourning party, starved and fervent, would ride out for Pawnee scalps, one for each scalp they had taken. This would take many days and there would be many mourning dances before they could take the forty-seven scalps to compensate for the scalps of the Little Ones, and some of the dead young warriors of the Wapiti and the Spider must wait for some time before they could enter Spiritland to be recognized by *Wah'Kon-Tah* as people of the Wapiti and the Spider of the sub-*Hunkah* and the Grand *Hunkah* of the Little Ones.

But warfare with the Cherokees and the free men was different. They would not go back to their villages across the Big Waters, the Mississippi, but wanted *Mo'n Sho'n,* the Mother of the Little Ones, for themselves. And this is why the Little Ones looked back over their shoulders to the prairie-plain for pleasant, peaceful thoughts and prepared their ears for more unpleasant things as they approached their village.

In this period of the early 1820's, the Cherokees seemed more and more intent on taking their land, and the Little Ones were still kept constantly busy taking horses and killing the hunters and trappers, both Cherokees and free men, when they trespassed on the land which Chouteau and Sibley and Lovely and Clark and Miller and Bradford had said would be theirs forever when they touched the feather.

They tried to understand why they must return horses which they had taken from the trespassers or pay with bodies of the killers of such trespassers, and whenever a *Mo'n-I'n-Tonkah,* a Heavy Eyebrows of importance, came along who would listen, they would ask the question. They had faith in Major Bradford of Fort Smith, and they had had some faith in Lovely, and part of the tribe had faith in Chouteau. Apparently both Bradford and Miller saw the justice in their position and even said so, and what Governor Miller saw, the new Protestant missionaries, who had just come up the Arkansas River to establish Union Mission on the Neosho and Harmony Mission on the Osage River after establishing Dwight Mission among the Cherokees, also saw and could write about in their journals.

In commenting on Governor Miller's attempts to bring about a lasting peace between the Cherokees and the Osages, the missionaries could employ with him the criteria of the European, which they thought of as Christian justice: "He [Miller] expects to hold a council with the Cherokees; designs if possible to induce them to comply to the terms of peace which the Osage propose, which are these: That the Osage do not deliver up the murderers, and that the Cherokees retain their captives. These terms will appear reasonable when we consider the fact that most if not all the Cherokees who have been killed, were killed in consequence of their encroaching on the Osage hunting ground, contrary to the former treaty."

The Little Ones naturally had no such criteria for Christian justice, but they were befuddled, and could not come out of the deep groove of natural-balance struggle and could not cope with the new force of reasoned aggressiveness and power and property greed of the European. The leaders of the Cherokees were for the most part mixed-bloods, of British and Scottish descent, and there was one leader, Tom Graves, who had not even one drop of Cherokee blood. These men were ambitious and much cleverer than the bearded barbarian, the free man in general, who had a racial memory of the gibbet and the debtor's prison. These mixed-blood men had a pur-

463

pose, and their objective was an empire in the beautiful and well-favored land of the Little Ones ruled by themselves, under special understanding with the United States, and living as an Indian nation in some category outside of territorial restrictions and statehood. They also had their racial memories of social stratification in England, and in racial memories they could feel the ingrained pressures. They would be as princes and dukes and knights in this new land.

They were relieved when they found that the just-arrived Protestant missionaries were not sent especially to make peace between the Cherokees and the Osages. They intended to get possession of the Osage land and, like canny Europeans, attacked from every angle.

They organized like Europeans and wrote letters to the President and to the Secretary of War, and they talked with those at the fort and at the missions, Dwight of the Cherokees and Union of the Osages, always putting themselves in the position of the innocent and demonstratively Christian agriculturists, who were being constantly harassed by the plains pagans and savages, "buffalo Indians" —a term of contempt. They drew to them with grand promises of land in the lush Osage domain the displaced Delawares, the Shawnees, the pressured Chickasaws, the Piankashaws, Peorias, Weas, Michigamans, Kickapoos, Senecas, and Oneidas, but all their advances across the boundary line were under the aegis of retaliation for some killing or horse-taking by the Little Ones. By 1821, Agent Graham was directed to locate fragments of the Kickapoos, Shawnees, Miamis, Piankashaws, and Weas as far west as possible, along the Osage line. The game had been killed off by the white men east of the Osage boundary, and these tribal fragments were starving.

The Little Ones, of course, were silent, inarticulate in their own defense. They knew nothing of justice or fairness; they knew only the primitive basis for all earth relationships. They could not put things like an eye for an eye and a tooth for a tooth into words, nor put into words the fact that might is right and weakness is wrong, or do unto others as you would have others do unto you.

These laws were the laws of the earth, and they felt them and were completely under their influence, or they never could have survived. The effects of the distortions of these primal laws by the

European for his own self-illusionment now faced them, and they were lost.

The Christian had really believed that he had invented the Golden Rule, when as a matter of fact he had only emasculated it and had said that "might does not make right," but he could never quite explain "right," even to himself. In force in the grass roots, on the desert, in the sea, in the forests, and on the plains where existed the perfect law in the balance of nature, it could be translated as do *not* do unto others that which others are equally able to do unto you.

Governor Miller tried energetically to bring about peace between the Cherokees and the Osages and the Algonkian fragments the former had inspired. He left his post at Arkansas Post and made difficult trips upriver to the Cherokee agency and on upriver to Fort Smith. He talked with the Osage chiefs and learned from Arrow-Going-Home that the Osages were tired of holding thumbs on the hammers of their rifles and wanted peace. Arrow-Going-Home told Miller he wanted to leave the old men and the older women and many of the younger children in the villages on the Verdigris when he took his people to the plains for buffalo hunting, and wanted his heart to swell as they came running to meet the hunters on their return in August and in December. Now he must take the whole village with him, and the Song of Death was sung many times before they returned. He told Major Bradford that his people did not ask for peace because their medicine was small. The Cherokees must be ignorant if they thought the medicine of the Little Ones small. He said he could send an army of fifteen hundred warriors to the Cherokee villages if they wanted to fight. But he did not want to fight, and the Cherokees would see no more moccasin prints of the Little Ones on their side of the magic line. When his warriors could come back to his village and say to him that they saw no footprints of the Cherokees on the Osages' side, then there would be peace.

During the spring and summer of 1821, there was tenseness, and everyone knew that the Cherokees intended to wait for a propitious moment to carry on with the war, and everyone knew that as long as the Osage warriors remained in the villages of the Place-of-the-Oaks, along the Verdigris and the Neosho, the Cherokees would not attack.

But they also knew that the Osages, fearing an attack by the Cherokees, would not go on their buffalo hunts, and this meant near starvation for the nomads.

The silence of the Little Ones and their Bear-Panther, Eagle gentes a-prowl from the Neosho to the Red River, taking arms and horses and scalps from the trespassers both Cherokee and Heavy Eyebrows, must have finally given Governor Miller a feeling of injured innocence, especially after a man who called himself Big Soldier, of White Hair's village at the Place-of-the-Many-Swans, had come to the Neosho and had lured young men from Arrow-Going-Home's village and from the village of the Big Hills on the Verdigris to follow him to the Red River looking for Heavy Eyebrows hunters. They found the trespassers and came back with five scalps.

Miller had exposed his health to the malaria and the storms and the hardships of the Arkansas, and in his "Well, my conscience is clear; I've done about all any human can do to reason with the Osages," he could actually find logic in the glib hypocrisies of the Cherokee chief *Tak-Atoka* and the mixed-blood and white leaders; and especially could he find reason in the great Cherokee scheme to obtain Osage land west of the Mississippi for the harlequins and the organization of Indian nations. To their voluble protestations of Christian virtues and agricultural innocence, he finally gave in. Naïve Lovely had salved his conscience by his famed purchase, but Miller threw up his hands and said go ahead. Trudeau back in 1793 in St. Louis, surrounded by the several tribesmen who would have the blood of the Little Osages and who had taken refuge in the barracks, reminded one of Pontius Pilate scornfully looking down upon the circling Judeans, but Miller was Pontius Pilate washing his hands. He left almost immediately for his home in New Hampshire on leave, but Major Bradford and Matthew Lyon, the factor at the Cherokee agency, induced the Cherokees to postpone their attack. This was not difficult since the disturbed Little Ones had not yet left for their spring buffalo hunt and the warriors were ready and riding up and down the boundary line. The Cherokees had been urgent in March of 1821 when they wrote to Major Bradford, warning him that "in a very short time" they expected to go to war with the Osages and stating that they certainly didn't want to do anything wrong concerning the white people living between themselves and the Osages. That would be wrong, and they wouldn't want to do anything wrong. ". . . there is a good many of you people in our way we do not wish to injure the persons or property of any Citizen of the United States and for that reason we wish them out of the way; you know very well that it is very hard to govern an army, there is wild young men among our people that is hard to govern which it is the case in all other armies . . . ."

Theoretically there were no white people on the Osage side of the magic boundary line, and except for those who had special permission, they had no right to be there. There was an agreement in the treaty of 1808 between the United States and the Osage tribe that the white trespassers on the Osage side of the boundary must be arrested by the Osages and turned over to the authorities, without harm to them. This didn't work, since the authorities could do nothing about the free men expressing their freedom, and they were back across the line as fast as the Little Ones could escort them out. Cutting off their heads or taking their scalps seemed to be much more effective.

So the Cherokees were warning the fort that the veterans of the War of 1812, who had been given grants in the Arkansas country, and the serious settlers, along with the wild, barbaric free men, must clear out, but Major Bradford seemed to be impressed only with the fact that the Cherokees were acting in a very civilized manner.

He made another attempt to discourage the Osages from killing free men and Cherokees, and the only answer he got from the savages was reports of gentile killing of citizens and Cherokees, and he too seemed to begin to forget his own words that many of these men "were a set of the most abandoned characters ever to disgrace a gallows." At least he might have remembered that they were slaughterers of the Osage game and wanton trespassers.

After warning Major Bradford, the Cherokees sent a delegation to Washington to lay before President Monroe the story of their abused innocence. The Little Ones were silent, and the Cherokees thought them uncivilized and obtuse. The Little Ones watched the faces of the new missionary neighbors on the Neosho and the face of Major

Bradford to find an indication of what might be wrong. Little-Flower-Killer Moon was approaching, and it was time for the spring buffalo hunt, but they remembered 1817, when Arrow-Going-Home's village had been burned and his old men and many of the women killed and taken prisoner. They had no idea whether it was fair or unfair for the Cherokees to attack their semideserted villages; their reason would tell them that such times when the warriors were gone would be the proper time for such attacks, but the Cherokees didn't go on buffalo hunts to the plains and the whole thing was out of rhythm. The Little Ones always left their villages and left their corn and squash growing in the fields and their caches full when they went on the winter hunt. They had put a flint buffalo skin over the doors of their lodges, so that the bears couldn't get in searching for prehibernation delicacies. The Pawnees and the Siouans would be hunting as well, and only the Potawatomis and the Sac and Foxes might, rarely, attack such a defenseless village, and the Caddoans never, since they were afraid of terrible retaliation.

So now Little-Flower-Killer Moon of 1821 was approaching, and the Little Ones had to have peace so that they could leave their villages. Either that or they must have war now and get it over before the Pawnees and the Padoucas scattered the buffalo on the headwaters of the Cut-Salt Waters, the Cimarron, and Red Waters, the Arkansas.

There is nothing to indicate that the Grand *Hunkah,* Arrow-Going-Home of the Verdigris, or the chieftain of the Little Osages, Traveling Rain or White Hair of the Place-of-the-Many-Swans, or any other of the Little Ones' leaders planned to frighten the Cherokees by an invasion of their country, but it was good strategy, since they must go on their annual spring hunt and they knew that the Cherokees were waiting for them to leave before they made an attack. The invasion of the Cherokee country by the Little Ones was the lunge of the grizzly to frighten away the prowling panther from his wapiti carcass, or the rush of the wolf with raised hackles and bared fangs at the coyotes sitting about waiting for him to quit the deer he had killed. If they made a bluff rush now, the Cherokees might not attack their villages when they were gone on the hunt; it might frighten them or throw them off balance.

Thus in April, 1821, the Little Ones of the Place-of-the-Oaks, four hundred strong, made a war movement. The *Do-Do'n-Hunkah* was appointed and the pipe was brought out by the proper gens of the *Wah-Sha-She* subdivision, and the *Do-Do'n-Hunkah* smoked the sacred pipe and went out to fast and pray, singing his prayers to Grandfather asking if he should go. The ceremony of the hawk, the *wah-hopeh,* was carried out, and when he was taken from his shrine and dropped, his head was toward the west, the direction of war and death, despite the fact that they must move easterly to attack the Thing-on-Its-Head People, the Cherokees, and all was propitious.

Bad-Tempered-Buffalo, the son of Arrow-Going-Home, was leader, and the young men set out for the mouth of the Neosho, where they hunted so that they would have plenty of meat, then they set off along the well-worn trail along the Arkansas River. When they had left, the clever Arrow-Going-Home rode to the Union Mission on the Neosho just twenty-eight miles east of his village on the Verdigris, and there pretended that the young men had escaped from his control and were on their way to attack the Cherokees in their own country. He warned the missionaries that they must keep their cattle and horses out of sight, since some of his young men might need them. He told them there were gentes from other villages and his control over them would not be strong; therefore, the missionaries must keep their livestock in. Otherwise, harm might come to them.

The wily *Ki-He-Kah Tonka* was interested in only one thing: getting away to the buffalo hunt. He wanted no trouble which might make necessary counciling with Major Bradford and others, thereby delaying his hunting. Bad-Tempered-Buffalo's thrust was the wolf lunge, the grizzly-bear charge, the closed-wing dive of the eagle, in order to have peace. He had no intention of attacking the Cherokees and he had no fear that the Cherokees would attack four hundred warriors of the Osages.

This was always happening since the people with That-Thing-on-Its-Head had come across the Big Waters. His young warriors would stop before reaching Fort Smith and apply their bluff-paint, then they would show themselves at the fort so that the Heavy Eyebrows there could see them and be impressed and tell the Thing-on-Its-Head People that many warriors of the Little Ones were on the war movement. There would be That-Thing-on-Its-Head People there at the fort also, and they would tell the chiefs.

When they arrived at the fort, they sat their horses across the Poteau River in their war paint, singing. It was Planting Moon, April, and the wind was chilly and they had their robes pulled well about their heads. Then Bad-Tempered-Buffalo and He-Sees-Far and Not-Afraid rode across the river to the fort. They said they wanted to hunt on the north side of the Arkansas, since the Cherokees came across to their side to hunt. This was denied them, but of course they had no desire to hunt and expected to be rebuffed. They asked if the others might cross over, but this would not be allowed by the nervous officers at the fort. The leaders had refused the outstretched hands of the officers and had refused to eat and would not take drink, but their faces were as pleasant as their bluff-paint would allow them to be. They examined everything and missed nothing with their black, darting eyes. The effects of their bluffing on the soldiers pleased them, and they could scarcely appear haughty and thunder-angry as they had intended.

The three Little Ones, He-Sees-Far and Not-Afraid under their leader Bad-Tempered-Buffalo, stalked about the fort, watching the faces of the officers. They pretended that they were seeking out the weaknesses of the defenses, although they certainly had no thought of attacking. There were miles of undefended stretches along the river, between the fort and the agency of the Cherokees. They were bluffing, so that the officers might tell the That-Thing-on-Its-Head People that the Osages were four hundred strong and were preparing to attack them.

When they left and recrossed the Poteau River to their own companions near its mouth, they made a great show of bringing timbers to the edge of the water, as though they would raft across to the foot of the fort. The officers in command at the time, one Lieutenant Martin Scott, immediately called their bluff and had two six-pounders brought into position. He had soldiers standing ready with lighted spills to discharge them, and the Little Ones could see all this quite well. They were very proud that the Heavy Eyebrows chief had been frightened.

They stayed along the Poteau and Lees Creek, and plundered the settlers along the Poteau, which was still Osage territory since the magic line of 1808 ran along the Arkansas. The settlers fled in panic across the river to the fort, and when the Little Ones came upon some subdued Quapaws trapping for a Heavy Eyebrows, one Étienne Vaugine, they killed three of the four and chased Vaugine across the river to the fort side. They even tried to intercept him as he paddled across looking back over his shoulder and shouting for Lieutenant Scott to fire.

They were probably emotionalized by this time and were really experiencing a grizzly-bluffed panther's angry frustrations. They came upon three Delaware hunters on Lees Creek and killed them.

It seems rather strange that, since the Poteau River was on the south side of the Arkansas River which divided the land ceded by the Little Ones both in 1808 and by Lovely's Purchase in 1818 and since this land south of the river was recognized as Osage domain, no one reporting to Secretary Calhoun and no mission journalists or letter writers in general seemed to remember this fact nor that the settlers whom the Little Ones plundered, as well as the trapper Vaugine and the Delawares, were trespassers. Even *Niles' Register* for June 30, 1821, and the *Arkansas Gazette* of May 12, 1821, stress only the claims filed with the government and name the claimants. Some of the claims were for horses taken, bacon, tools, corn, destruction of a salt works, pewter plates, and at least four stands of bees. It is not likely that Bad-Tempered-Buffalo and his warriors carried the bee stands very far, even though they loved honey as much as *wah-sabe,* the black bear.

Apparently the bluff, the grizzly-bear rush, was successful, and even though the Little Ones did little more than clear the Poteau of trespassers rather definitively in some incidents, their objective was bluff.

They must have been well pleased by the great excitement which

471

they created among the settlers both white and Cherokee above and below Fort Smith, without even crossing to the Cherokee side of the Arkansas. The rumors were dramatic, and people sought refuge in the fort or fled down the river, and like Chicken Little magnified the rumors, creating more dramatic ones. Rumor had it that there were eight hundred Osages, who were divided into eight groups; one group was coming down the river, another from the north out of the mountains, and a third was killing everyone they found in the more settled parts of the Cherokee country. It was rumored that they had broken into the garrison and plundered it.

Women and children were concentrated in a group of houses, and men had come to the factory for powder and lead. However, Matthew Lyon, the Cherokee factor, had loaded his 113 kegs of powder and 50 rifles on a boat and sent them down river.

Crittenden, who was acting governor, asked Calhoun, secretary of war, for "swords and pistols for two hundred troopers," who had not yet been raised.

But there seemed no good reason for killing Vaugine's humble Quapaws, since they were not actually trespassers, even though in the treaty of 1818 they had been pushed from their original domain, where they had lived by sufferance of the Little Ones. Later it was discovered, much to Arrow-Going-Home's chagrin, that his son, Bad-Tempered-Buffalo, had allowed a chieftain, *Mo'n-I'n-Pishche,* Does-Not-Walk, or Walks-Badly, referring to the eagle on the ground, to kill the three kinsmen Quapaws who might have been useful in war later. Some Cherokees had killed this young man's wife and child, and he said that he had mistaken the Quapaws for That-Thing-on-Its-Head People, since they had red trader's *wah-don-skas* on their heads, just like those of the Cherokees.

Apparently to soothe his might-be-useful-in-the-future kinsmen, Arrow-Going-Home made a great show of punishing the young man, possibly even handing him over to the Quapaws for punishment, but he fled the village, and could not be found.

How much the Little Ones had heard of the excitement they caused on the Cherokee side of the river is not clear, but if they had known of the dramatics and the fear they inspired without even crossing to

472

the Cherokee side, they would have been puffed with pride and very happy. And they apparently did think that their grizzly lunge was highly successful: Arrow-Going-Home with more confidence but with misgivings led his village to the hunting grounds on the upper waters of the Salt Fork and the Cimarron Rivers for the summer hunt in May of that year.

When Chapman of the Union Mission family on the Neosho rode the twenty-eight miles to the village of Arrow-Going-Home on the Verdigris to ask the Grand *Hunkah* if he might accompany the Little Ones on their summer hunt, he found the village deserted. He was a man of some culture, and like the early French missionary-explorers, he was trying to learn the Osage language. He followed their broad trail for some distance west of the Verdigris, then had to turn back. The trail led slightly south of west and would cross the Arkansas River just below the mouth of the Cimarron.

The Little Ones were perhaps fifty or sixty head of horses ahead of the Cherokees in the game of horse-taking, and these they, of course, took with them, although the Cherokee horses were not much at running buffalo.

When they were about twenty miles out from their villages, a white man came into their camp with upheld hand. He was unarmed and he went immediately to Arrow-Going-Home's lodge. After being fed, he said that he had come for his horses which the Cherokees had taken from him and which the Osages had taken from the Chero- kees. He pointed them out, and the young men helped him catch them and sent him on his way back to the Cherokee settlements.

But the wily Arrow-Going-Home would use him as a messenger, and he knew the grateful man would tell of the great chief's generos- ity in allowing him to have his horses. The Grand *Hunkah* was nervous and afraid that the Cherokees would come when he and his people were absent and destroy the villages on the Verdigris and burn the caches, and he knew that Bad-Tempered Buffalo's bluff would not stand long. He sent a message to the mixed-blood chief of one band of Cherokees who had been most dedicated to the hit-and-run war, one Walter Webber. He asked Webber for a three months' armi- stice, stating that three months would give the Cherokees time in which to make up their minds whether they wanted war with the Osages or peace. He implied that it would make little difference to him which they chose, but there must be peace or war; and if the Cherokees wanted war, the Osages would see that they got it. However, if the Cherokees wanted peace, they could send an agent to the hunting camp of the Osages, along with a chief who could carry with him his people's thoughts, and they would make a peace that would stand. He stated in the message that he could not talk for Traveling Rain of the Little Osages or for White Hair of the Thorny-Valley People, and not for *To-Wa-Ka-Heh* of the Big Hills, nor for the Heart-Stays People, but only for the Upland-Forest People. This is what had happened when the Heavy Eyebrows and the Cherokees had crossed the Big Waters, the Mississippi, and the Grand *Hunkah* could talk only for his villages.

This was only simple primitive cleverness. Three months would end during the Yellow-Flower Moon, August, when he and his people would be back from the summer hunt with their pack animals loaded with meat, and they would find their caches of corn and pumpkins and squash intact. Then on their return from the hunt he knew the Cherokees would not dare come on the war movement. Also, about the time the white messenger reached Union Mission, there was a strange rumor that the Little Ones were about to invade Cherokee country north of the Arkansas River, but no one seemed to know the source. Arrow-Going-Home had instructed his white messenger to stop at Union Mission and tell the people there about his proposal to Walter Webber, and perhaps might have implied that other physical divisions of the Little Ones, the Big Hills or the Thorny-Valley People, were preparing to invade the Cherokee country, especially the latter, since he disliked White Hair very much.

Since the Cherokees did not attack during the summer of 1821, this might indicate that the bluff was effective, and just as Arrow-Going-Home had thought, they would wait until a future absence to attack.

There were many interpretations of the actions of Bad-Tempered-Buffalo in not invading the Cherokee country the April before. One interpretation was that he or one of the chieftains under him had

had a dream which was unpropitious. This was probably put forth by the Union Mission or the Dwight Mission "family," since they were anxious to have the savages guided by spiritual power—Christian, of course. This could have been a legitimate reason for the turning back of the Little Ones, but it would have had to do only with their own concept: the voice of the early frogs in the bayou or the actions of a bear.

It was also said that the Little Ones lacked powder and ball, and that they were poor and miserable and sick of war. This was clever mixed-blood Cherokee propaganda to inspire their anchored agriculturists to action. No one except the Little Ones knew that it was a successful bluff which allowed them to leave for the plains on their summer hunt.

Webber did not accept the proposal by Arrow-Going-Home, but the results were the same as if he had. He made little forays into the Osage country and stole horses and plundered mixed-blood Osages and French intermarried citizens, and talked much about invasion. He and his band attacked the trading post of Chouteau and Revoir and killed the latter, causing his family to flee into the woods. Revoir was a very kindly man and was well thought of both by the Osages and the missionaries. He was in effect a member of the tribe, despite the fact that his mother had been a Pawnee. When the Cherokees arrived back at their agency lower on the Arkansas, they joy-danced around Revoir's scalp, while his family came from the woods to Union Mission, bringing along their pet wapiti calf.

However, quite seasonably a rumor was born to the effect that several hundred warriors from the Neosho, the Verdigris, and the Place-of-the-Many-Swans on the Osage River were on their way to invade the Cherokee country. This set the Cherokees to preparing fortifications. This was in July when Arrow-Going-Home and Traveling Rain and White Hair and *To-Wa-Ka-Heh* from the Place-of-the-Many-Swans were actually out on the plains in hunting camps with their people.

The Cherokees in their preparation to receive this attack got together the harlequin remnants of the Delawares and Shawnees as allies, and they came to camp near Dwight Mission at the Cherokee

475

agency, and blacksmith hammers rang on anvils making horseshoes for the war.

There is no reason to believe that the Little Ones had anything to do with the full blooming of these rumors, but they could have planted the seed of rumor as a protective psychology slightly elaborated over the trickery of coyotes.

The people of the three mission "families" of Dwight down the Arkansas River, Union on the Neosho, and Harmony of the North Fork of the Osage, now called Marais des Cygnes were dedicated humanitarians, a bit smug about their God-concept, and the very nature of their calling made them susceptible to and appreciative of dramatics. Arrow-Going-Home and perhaps the adjustable White Hair seemed to know this, and when they wished to plant a seed, they planted it at their missions, Union and Harmony, and they realized that the fullblood Cherokees were as cautious as they themselves were. However, the Cherokee mixed-blood and white leaders with titles of captain and major from Jacksonian wars against the Creeks and from the War of 1812, and with the white man's greed and dreams of power, they feared and could not understand. They used the people of the missions as liaison.

The military people like Major Bradford of Fort Smith and the factor Major Sibley of Fort Osage, Governor Miller of Arkansas and William Clark of Missouri, seemed to be dedicated to justice and fair play and had pride in their sense of justice, even if the Little Ones wore no shirts and sometimes ate with their fingers and yowled to the morning star and the rising sun. Miller traveled under all sorts of adverse conditions up and down the Arkansas from Arkansas Post, trying to settle the differences between the Cherokees and the Little Ones, so that there could be peace. But the constant stories of Osage atrocities, given him by the intelligent and glib Cherokees, and the taciturnity of the Osages and their imperious stubbornness and prideful unreason finally injured his vanity in being just, and he threw up his hands. He was like a devout woman filled with self-approval of her own Christianity, who made an appointment with God each day to pray for the safe return of her husband or son from the war and who, on receiving the telegram that he had not survived a battle, might raise her face to the sky and say, "I'll never pray again."

Major Bradford's report on the incident of the vicious Cherokee attack on Arrow-Going-Home's town in 1817 was probably the strongest indictment of barbarism that can be found in the documents of that period. He was profoundly moved to have used such bitter words, yet his tidy military mind could not comprehend the killings and the scalping of trespassers by the Little Ones, not so much to protect the Sacred One as to save the "brothers" *Wah'Kon-Tah* had given them, the wapiti, the deer, the buffalo, and the bear. Their existence depended on these "brothers," and they were fighting for existence, both spiritual (*Tzi-Sho*) and material (*Hunkah*).

Finally he, too, would find his vanity in his own military justness injured by the stupid reticences of the Osages and their "depredations" in the face of white-man logic.

While it might seem that Governor Miller might have had his change of heart through injured vanity, there is the possibility that Major Bradford's change was not wholly personal. He was an officer in the United States military service and Andrew Jackson was his superior, and Andrew Jackson's policy was to keep the Cherokees, Chickasaws, Choctaws, Creeks, and Seminoles flowing across the Mississippi to relieve the pressure in Tennessee and Georgia and North Carolina and make room for voters. The eastern Cherokees and the Creeks, Choctaws, and Chickasaws were afraid to come into the country of the mighty Osages, and the Osage power and activity were still playing their roles as deterrents to invaders as they had always done, though now the pressure was irresistible since it was created by transplanted Europeans on the move. This might be indicated through an incident of September, 1821, when the Little Ones had gone on their winter hunt.

During the summer of 1821, Bad-Tempered-Buffalo's grizzly lunge and his father's circling from the trail, up-winding the Cherokees, growling as he moved away like the bluffing grizzly, may have kept the Cherokees from attacking the villages in their absence.

39. Hunger Stalks the Little Ones

THERE WAS MUCH TALK and much counciling among the Cherokees during this summer, and Major Bradford, still trying to keep intact his fair-mindedness, went to the Cherokee country accompanied by the trader friend of the Little Ones, Captain Nathaniel Pryor, trying to dissuade them from renewing the war.

The two went to Arrow-Going-Home's camp when he returned in August from the plains. This was during the time when his people were harvesting their corn and squashes, and gathering lotus fruits and roots, the red, bitter wild plums, digging blazing star roots and *do,* the wild potato, and they decided that this would not be a propitious time for the council.

They returned in September just before the Little Ones would set out for the plains on their winter hunt, and they asked Arrow-Going-Home because he was the Grand *Hunkah* to restrain the gentes from his village and the gentes from the White Hair village and those from Traveling Rain's village from making the war movement.

The Little Ones, because of their stubborn and imperious reticence and their dogged scalping and plundering of trespassers, were thought to be primitive minded and even stupid, by both the Cherokees and the whites, but they could express themselves rather impressively and even with glory in war and in oratory, and in the latter art they were far superior to the Amer-European, who was redundant and flowery.

On this fifteenth of September, 1821, Arrow-Going-Home, in all

478

his Grand *Hunkah* dignity, stood up, and with his roach seemed taller than his six feet plus. Characteristically, he arranged his robe over his left shoulder in such a manner that his right shoulder and arm were bare.

He spoke much faster perhaps than a European could have spoken the same words, but he did not raise his voice, and his only gesture would be the raising of the hand, then letting it fall. In conversation the Little Ones often used descriptive gestures, but unless they were aroused and angered, their orations were in the manner of Cicero. He told Bradford and Pryor that he realized that his people had turned over *Mo'n Sho'n* (Earth) north of the Red Waters (the Arkansas River) to them, but they did not turn over their "brothers," the buffalo, the wapiti, the deer, and the bear. How could they give away those things which were not theirs to give away? These "brothers" did not belong to them, but were from *Wah'Kon-Tah.* He said that the Little Ones wanted these "brothers" for themselves, and the Cherokees had no right to come across the magic line and take them and leave their bodies for the vultures and the coyotes.

These "brothers" are our meat, he said, and we have not yet learned to raise hogs and cattle and do things as the That-Thing-on-Its-Head People do. If these people come across the magic line and kill the "brothers" of the Little Ones, then the women and the children of the Little Ones must go naked and hungry.

When *Mo'n-I'n-Tonkah Ki-He-Kah,* Long Knife chief in *Wah'-She-To'n* sent the That-Thing-on-Its-Head People across the Big Waters and gave them our Mother Earth, the Sacred One, he did not give them all the bears, the beavers, the buffalo, and the deer. There was nothing on the talking paper about this thing. Now we must have trouble and talk many times because these people come across the magic line to kill our "brothers" and steal our horses, and our young men must kill them.

We made peace with these people and now that peace has fallen to the earth and is broken. We made this peace at *Sho'to To-Wo'n,* St. Louis. We will say that it is all right if the Long Knife chief will kill all these things that have happened since we made that peace in *Sho'to To-Wo'n,* and make another peace between us and the That-

479

Thing-on-Its-Head People. We will not make the war movement on the That-Thing-on-Its-Head People if they do not make the war movement across the magic line. From this day until peace is made again, these people will not see the moccasin prints of the Little Ones on their earth across the magic line, if we do not see their footprints on our earth.

Major Bradford thought this a fair proposal and assured Arrow-Going-Home that their "Great Father" in Washington would hear of it, and he would further assure him that he would prevent the Cherokees from coming up the Arkansas to attack the Osages.

Their confidence restored by the assurances of Bradford, who sent the speech of Arrow-Going-Home and his proposal to Calhoun, the secretary of war, the Little Ones prepared to leave on their winter hunt on the plains. But this time they took their women and children and old men with them. They were late—it was September 20—and they feared that the Long-Hair [Lodges]-from-River-Bank People, Pawnee-*maha,* from the Platte or the *Ci-Ci-Ka A-Ki-Ci'n,* Republican Pawnees, might have run the buffalo from the environs of their old camping places. As a matter of fact, Arrow-Going-Home's scouts had reported that not only the Pawnees but the *Wi-Tsi-Ta,* Lodges-Far-Away Pawnees, the Wichitas, and the Borrows-from-Others People, the Kiowas, hearing mysteriously that the Little Ones were having trouble with the Cherokees, were running buffalo on the headwaters of the Cimarron and the Salt Fork.

At the crossing of the Arkansas just below the mouth of the Cimarron the Little Ones divided, the eager warriors going up the Arkansas to find the Pawnees, the Wichitas, and the Kiowas, and the others traveling along the old familiar hunting trails. When they reached the old camp near the mouth of the Little Arkansas River, the war party found that the report of the scouts had not underestimated the numbers of Pawnees, Wichitas, and Kiowas; and even though they were not hunting together, they sent messengers back to the main party, who had moved only one day's travel from the crossing, to have more warriors join them. This left old men, women, and children in the slow-moving hunting party, with only a few warriors to guard them.

Arrow-Going-Home was the supreme leader of the whole party, but the warriors who went to meet the Pawnees and others were under gentile leaders, whose names seemed to have been forgotten. Not even Bad-Tempered-Buffalo is mentioned in tribal memory, and the only information about this incident is gentile memory, and from a member of the *Tzi-Sho Wa'no'n* gens at that. Thunder Fear, the late *No-Pa-Wa-The* (Nopawalla), who was not even of the Plateau Forest physical division but of the Little Osages, could not recall the gentile leaders of the warriors, but thought that Traveling Cloud might have been one and Walks-in-the-Firelight another, and he thought that Standing-Brown might have been one of the gentile leaders who left the hunting party to bluff the Pawnees away from the herds. Traveling Cloud referred to the cumulous clouds floating swiftly over the prairie-plains, and Walks-in-the-Firelight referred to the deer who approach the campfires out of curiosity, and the last named, Standing-Brown, referred to the lone bull buffalo, standing on the plains facing the gentle winds and cutting the sky line. He was a glowing brown during the Buffalo-Breeding Moon, the July sun having bleached his hair.

The leaders readily left the camp of the hunters with the old men and women and children without much protection since they believed that Major Bradford would keep his word to them. Also, they were by now far away to the west from the Cherokee land, and they apparently knew where their plains enemies were.

The Little Ones had set out on their winter hunt immediately after Arrow-Going-Home's council with Major Bradford, some time in the latter part of Deer-Hiding Moon, September; and as soon as the Cherokees heard this, they gathered three hundred warriors together. They called the harlequin remnants of the Delawares, Creeks, and Choctaws: ten of the first, twelve of the second, and twelve of the third, and fifteen Shawnees, along with a number of free men.

They were not ready to ride until the Little One's Deer-Breeding Moon, October; and when Major Bradford heard that they were on the march, he went downriver to meet them in their camp about fourteen miles from Fort Smith, and there urged them to turn back and accept the armistice of the Little Ones. They said they had started

481

and they would go on and destroy the village of the Little Ones, but Major Bradford told them that this time Arrow-Going-Home had taken the women and children with him, and that White Hair and Traveling Rain would send delegates to meet in St. Louis with Richard Graham, Indian superintendent, for a peace treaty, while their people were on the winter hunt, and that they also had taken their women and children with them to the plains.

This seemed to anger the Cherokees, and the free men became too arrogant for Bradford's military concept of citizens' behavior, so he ordered them to return to the agency. However, he seemed unable to do anything about the Cherokees and one white leader, Tom Graves.

When the army of the Cherokees passed through Fort Smith, he not only seemed unable to stop them but seemed disinclined to do so. He had written to Calhoun of Arrow-Going-Home's logical proposal on October 1, and it wouldn't seem likely that he could have received orders so soon, but he did an inexplicable thing: he gave the Cherokees a barrel of gunpowder, according to Graham. It is true that Graham was deeply chagrined when he had to report to Calhoun that only delegates from the Osages had appeared in St. Louis to make peace, while the Cherokees had been contemptuous, and Bradford's allowing the Cherokee army to pass upriver through Fort Smith placed him in a very embarrassing position. How could a conscientious man trying to carry out instructions and do his duty know definitely what Calhoun and Jackson wanted?

The Cherokees were not only not stopped at Fort Smith on their way to make war on the Osages but were apparently encouraged, even to the extent that they didn't stop at the empty Osage villages but took the trail of the Little Ones when they found it where it crossed the Cimarron.

The signs were print highly illustrated to them. They saw the narrow hoofprints of the pack mules and the tracks of the dogs, and even the small moccasin prints of the women and boys, along the old hunting trail and read them perfectly.

And here at the crossing below the Cimarron the Cherokees also divided, and part of the warriors followed the hunting party and part followed the Osage warriors. The Cherokees who followed the hunting menage soon overtook them, and they saw from the hills that there were only twelve running horses in the remuda. It was Buck-Rattling-Horns Moon or Coon-Breeding Moon, the first of November, and the women were gathering cattail stems to make the bottom walls of the lodges or wading the shallow waters of river-abandoned lakes with their poles, feeling for lotus roots. It is said that the dogs didn't know they were near.

The Cherokees charged suddenly and began killing the old men and women and children. That night there was no sound of keening. The Cherokees had made their camp as far away as possible from the slaughter, and the women and children were hidden in the bushes, in the bottom of ravines, as silent as the grass roots after the owl's booming. The Cherokees baited and maltreated their thirty prisoners, who were salable boys, strong young women, and young girls; they killed and scalped the old men and the older women they had taken.

There were about one hundred Cherokees and their allies in this party, and they hurried back to their agency as fast as they could ride with their horses and their prisoners; and when they reached Fort Smith, they boasted that they had taken seventy horses, had killed forty Osages, and had thirty prisoners. As Major Bradford listened, he could see that the majority of the scalps were long haired, and not warriors' roaches. He immediately began to discover the facts while he awaited the larger party who had followed the trail of the Osage warriors.

When the two hundred more or less came onto the plains on the Osage warriors' trail, they became worried. They felt that even their thoughts might be seen where the horizon came down to meet the earth on all sides and one could see the white buttocks of the antelope for miles or the movement of the sound-screening ears of a rabbit a rifle-shot away. Woods-Indian-like, they found a feeder of the Arkansas, and screened by elms and cottonwoods and undergrowth, they prepared to make camp.

Being Iroquoian, the Cherokees were brave and effective warriors, but they now had assumed the caution of field-anchored people, and many had put their old religion behind them. There was no religious urgency to follow the warriors of the Little Ones onto the unfamiliar and fear-inspiring plains, and certainly the agriculturists among them must have had thoughts of their corn and hogs and their log cabins back in Arkansas Territory. It is likely that the barbarous free men and planning mixed-bloods urged them on. At least one white man was with them, the Osage-hating Graves. He might have slipped by Major Bradford at Fort Smith quite easily since he dressed as a Cherokee and spoke the language.

It would seem that the Little Ones had seen the Cherokees' woodland thoughts revealed here on the illimitable plains. They watched them make camp, and just when their horses were unsaddled and unburdened, and before they could place guards, they charged. The Cherokees stood and fought bravely, but they were no match for the fantastically painted giants, and darkness came as an ally.

When this badly defeated army came through Fort Smith on their shattered return, they could only boast vindictively that they had killed five Osages and exhibit several scalps, but only two of them were Osage roaches; the others were long haired and belonged to their own fallen. When accused of this, they couldn't very well deny it, since everyone knew that the Osage warriors wore roaches. They then said that they had scalped their own dead to keep the Osages from scalping them and carrying them back to their villages to dance the victory dance over them. Bradford believed that the Osages didn't need these few scalps since they had plenty of others from the battle. In his investigations to "arrive at the truth," he noted in his report to Calhoun that the Osages charged so ferociously and fought at such close quarters that many of the dead Cherokees were powder-burned.

This ruined the winter hunt of the Little Ones of the Verdigris for the year 1821, and during the winter 1821–22, they were hungry, and they visited often the villages of the Neosho and even the Place-of-the-Many-Swans. They visited their relatives of those villages in groups and stayed long and depleted the food of their relatives of these villages.

The Union Mission *Journal* in reporting the attack on the hunting camp said: "The very few who were at the Osage camp when it was attacked, kept the enemy at bay till the women and children could get off, but the resistance of 19 or 12 warriors against a large body of

Cherokees was small, and 100 of the Osage people are supposed to have been killed and taken prisoners. Several of the prisoners have returned, some have been killed, since they were taken. It may be a greater number are missing than they have yet known. How distressed their situation at present. They have returned with no provisions and are very poor. Their situation called for our prayers and for the prayers of all good people."

The writers in the Dwight Mission *Journal* at the Cherokee agency were not quite so moved by the plight of the Osages and assumed a matter-of-factness about the affair in a sort of news item: "The warriors of this nation [Cherokee] with a few allies have for about six weeks been in pursuit of the Osages. Today, a party of Cherokees returned from the campaign. When they separated from the main body of the Cherokees they were within one day's march of the main body of the Osages. This party consisting of about eighty fell in with a party of Osages about 75 in number all of whom were killed and taken prisoners without the loss of a single man on the part of the Cherokees."

This was the story of the triumphant party who attacked the defenseless hunting camp, and there was no comment on the disastrous defeat of the larger party.

However, later, when the people of Dwight Mission heard the details from Bradford and heard through a Mr. Scott of some of the atrocities committed by some of the free men, mixed-bloods, and full-blood Cherokees, Dwight Mission *Journal* carried the following: "They killed 29 women and children and took ninety odd prisoners chiefly old men women and children, three of whom a woman and her child and a young girl they most barbarously murdered after their arrival at their village . . . and threw their bodies to be devoured by the hogs which was seen by Mr. Scott on his way to this place . . . this murder was perpetrated by one Graves a white . . . ."

Why this Tom Graves was arrested and taken later to Little Rock, by this time the capital of the territory, is not quite clear, but the reasons for his acquittal were obviously three: first, the murders were committed on Indian land and the court had no jurisdiction, although actually, since the jury disagreed, it must have assumed jurisdiction;

secondly, Graves was a white man and was tried by his peers; and thirdly, the Little Ones were bad "Injuns."

Now, knowing the Osages, everyone began to fear the terrible retaliation. Mixed-blood settlers began to bring their children to the missions to be taught, chiefly because they would be an encumbrance to flight when the painted giants should appear. The mission "family" were given a feeling of success, but by the early part of January they had more children than they could accommodate.

These were Cherokee mixed-blood and fullblood children thrust by their parents upon the missions in their fright. The Osages took the view that the missions were bad medicine for their children, and the few who had been given into the care of the Union Mission "family" on the Neosho and Harmony Mission on the Osage River were called for by their bluff-frowning parents. The word of the Long Knives had fallen to the earth, and they said That-Thing-on-Its-Head's hogs were always hungry for Osage children.

Buck-Rattling-Horns or Raccoon-Breeding Moon, November, was cold and dreary for the Little Ones of the Verdigris. The women gathered the cattail stems for their lodges and hunted skunks and opossums, and the hunters could not supply the hungry camps where there was no buffalo meat.

While the women worked at sewing the cattail stems together, one would suddenly remember her child or the child of her sister or brother or all the children who had been murdered by Graves and his Cherokees, and who would be compelled to wander restlessly over the earth as lost souls, unrecognized by *Wah'Kon-Tah* because their faces had not been painted. She would let the stems fall to her lap and cast her eyes to *Tzi-Sho,* the Sky Lodge, and sing the Song of Death, another would join her, and then another, until the whole group would chant:

> *O-hoooooo, it is I who cause them to lie yellowing*
> > *on the earth.*
> *It is I who attack them thus.*
> *A-e the he, Ah-he the he*

Hunger Stalks the Little Ones

It is I who take from them their remaining
days,
Ah, hOOOooooooooooooooooooooooo.

Tears would stream down their faces as they mourned, and soon the village dogs would join them in long wolflike howls, but the babies on their boards hanging from tree limbs or on the ground by their mothers would stare complacently like little owls. The wailing would stop suddenly as if snapped, much like the barometric chorus of the coyote, and with it the howling of the dogs. The women would dry their tears, and pick up their dropped cattail stems and their needles of pecan wood.

And during this Bucks-Rattling-Antlers Moon of 1821, the women must save the roots of the cattails as they waded in the marshes to collect stems. They could make a sort of salad from them, or they were grated and then boiled and the starchy material was strained off, and they were then eaten as a vegetable.

They had elm bark left over from the spring for the making of their lodge coverings, and they must make many lodges for the winter. They first cut young hickory trees and trimmed them, then stuck butt-ends into the ground in an oval pattern of from thirty to forty or twenty to twenty-five. They used hickory saplings for the transverse parts, a foot or more apart. They then bent the hickory poles over until their little ends met, and they tied them together with hickory bark.

For the sides of the lodge they used the elm bark they had cut in the spring. The tree was cut and the bole cut to the desired length and split, and the bark taken off intact. This bark was fastened to the hickory-pole framework, running up to a certain height from the ground, then the cattails sewed together with the pecan wood needle about two feet long, carrying the thread made from the inner bark of the pawpaw. After taking this inner bark fiber, they boiled it, and transformed it into twine by rolling it on their naked thighs. They placed the big end of the cattail stem against the little end of another stem and sewed them together until they had a large piece of watertight matting. These pieces were attached to the sloping sides of the curving hickory framework beginning at the top of the elm bark, which stopped at the point where the poles began to curve. The cattail stems had the effect of shingling, since water would roll off them.

There were two fireplaces in each domestic lodge, one at each end, which was a depression dug to a depth of several inches and cemented with ashes and clay. For draught, a piece of wood was laid across the hole, then the other pieces laid at right angles to it, so that one end rested on the first log and the other end on the bottom of the hole. And there was a fire hole for each, covered by a buffalo hide. The door was always toward the east and Grandfather's coming each morning, and was covered by a buffalo hide stretched on a hickory frame, with a hole for the thumb or forefinger, and was pulled up and fell back into place as the person entered or left the lodge.

Usually they were on the plains hunting during this Bucks-Rattling-Antlers Moon, but during this one of 1821 they were busy in their struggle against starvation. The women gathered white oak and red oak acorns, and boiled the tannin out of them, then prepared them for food,[1] and they waded the marshes probing for lily roots with their poles. The wild grapes were gone by now, and they must hurry to beat the migrant robins, bluebirds, and flickers to the hackberries. They gathered pecans and black walnuts and red haws and, after the first frost, persimmons. The hackberries were mashed in a stone mortar, then as a pulp mixed with buffalo tallow, and thus could be preserved all winter.

The persimmons were gathered by the women and the boys and girls. If there were no great groves close to the villages, several women would take their children and go with their camp equipment perhaps thirty miles away to a large grove. They fashioned a flat piece of hickory or post oak. They spread buffalo tallow on the board, then placed a layer of seeded persimmons on it, spread tallow on this layer, then placed a second layer of seeded fruit on the first. This process was repeated until they had four layers on the board. The wood had been so designed that it had a handle, and one would hold the flat

[1] They put ashes into the boiling water and then cooked the boiled acorns until they could be eaten like crumbs of modern crackers.

wood over the coals until the first layer of persimmons was cooked, at which time the cake was removed and put away to cool. When it was thoroughly cooled, it was placed in a parfleche. When the parfleches were filled, they were put away for future use. This food would last all winter.

Sometimes the persimmons were seeded and placed on a rack made of buckbrush runners or of very young dogwood saplings and allowed to dry slowly. Dogwood resisted fire longer than many other saplings, and sticks of dogwood were used for roasting meat and about this time for baking dough. They stuck the meat on the sharpened end of a dogwood stick, then stuck the other end into the ground near the fire or coals, slanting it to the fire and turning it when necessary. When they first traded for flour, they made dough balls and stuck them on the sharpened dogwood sticks. This was their first attempt at making bread.

During this moon of 1821, the women and children gathered wild-rose fruits. The warriors made no raids on the Cherokee farmers for food. The latter had many hogs, and they ran semiwild, living on mast, but the Little Ones became nauseated when they smelled them, and they hated them. They called them *ni-da,* which name they gave to the bones of the mammoths which they found in the Cretaceous cut banks in the western part of their range.

There is little in tribal memory of this period, and therefore little of the Little Old Men's augmentation of ritualistic curlycues and ornamentations to counteract the misfortune which had befallen the Little Ones, but they must have spent many hours in the Lodge of Mystery talking about these things. Starvation was practically unknown among them, at least having its source in enemy actions. There had been hard winters and life-shriveling summers, but in their calendar there was no Hunger Moon. Single-Moon-by-Himself, January, was sometimes called Frost-on-Inside-of-Lodge Moon, but there apparently had been no period of starvation severe enough to warrant the naming of a certain moon for it.

40.   The Little Ones
Protect Their "Brothers"

AFTER THE WAR OF 1812 ended in 1815 with the famed Battle of New Orleans, there were jobless soldiers and restive people who really wanted to settle somewhere, and seemed especially bent on settling where they were not allowed to settle, on Indian land. Bearded men drove their wagons down the trail from Missouri or came overland from Tennessee and Kentucky or upriver in keelboats. Besides their wives and children, they had their cattle and their horses, and some had swine and chickens. Union Mission was on the Neosho, on the old Osage trail from their villages on the Osage River to the Three Forks, and since the mission was the only civilized spot in the wilderness, those from the north stopped there. Some of them wanted to trade for provisions or medicines or they simply asked for food and medicines or for the services of Dr. Marcus Palmer.

They went down the Neosho and picked up another Osage trail along the north bank of the Arkansas. This was the old Osage trail to the Quapaw villages near the mouth of the Arkansas. On this side of the Arkansas they were not trespassing on Osage domain, since the north bank was within the Lovely Purchase. They kept on this trail to Fort Smith, then they crossed the river, and seeing the bottom lands of the Poteau, the Blue, and the Washita rivers, they stopped, built their cabins, and put in crops, knowing quite well that this was and would remain Indian domain. They had heard about the imperious Osages, but they seemed to think that they were sufficiently far away from the "bad Injuns'" raiding.

The Blue River was noted for its beaver, the Poteau for its bears, and, of course, there were deer and wapiti almost everywhere. These rivers attracted trappers and hunters from downriver, and an outfitting establishment was set up at Arkansas Post.

These people knew they were trespassing, but there was no law enforcement, and they took advantage of this. Besides the trappers and hunters and settlers, those who might be called honest, there were the cutthroats and back-stabbers and rapists whose barbarism was incredible. Almost as shocked as Major Bradford and Agent Lovely had been at the vicious barbarism of the free men was the English botanist, Nuttall. He said: "These people, as well as the generality of those who, till lately, inhabited the banks of the Arkansas, bear the worst moral character imaginable, being many of them renegades from justice; when a further flight from justice becomes necessary, they passed over into the Spanish Territory toward San Antonio."

As they did on the Meramec in Missouri, many of these honest settlers set up stills in their houses and divided their time between distillation of spirits and killing buffalo for their tongues and hides and bears for their hides and tallow. But here in the Arkansas and Red River country the free men were preceded by the murderers, vagabonds, and cut-purses, brought over by John Law, and their descendants were still here in great numbers, as barbarous as their progenitors and no more civilized than when De Mézières, lieutenant-governor of Natchitoches during the Spanish authority, described them, a half century earlier: "[They] have committed robberies, rape, or homicide, that [the Arkansas] river thus being the asylum of the most wicked persons, without doubt, in all the Indies."

With these free men were fragments of the Cherokees, Delawares, Shawnees, Choctaws, Creeks, and Coschattahi, backed by the Caddos. These Governor Miller in his letter to the Secretary of War, June 30, 1820, had called a "banditti of outlaws" from whom he expected trouble. Not only this, but a chief of the Caddos actually held a commission as colonel from the Spaniards. It was believed that the pres-

491

ence and activity of these people, who always fled to the south of the Red River after their depredations, "was largely responsible for the incursions of the Osage with whom they were continually at war."

In the same year in which Cantonment Gibson was established on the Neosho, troops were removed from Natchitoches to the mouth of the Kiamichi, and Fort Towson was established.

From this fort the military attempted to enforce the laws about hunting on Indian land and to destroy the white trespasser's stills. They not only failed, but there was a citizen-military conflict, and in one instance the free men citizens congregated to attack the fort. This was February 2, 1825.

Commandant Cummings of Fort Towson gave United States district attorney of Arkansas the names of ten of the leaders of the white men hunting west of the Kiamichi River. The district attorney refused to prosecute, but instead would have Cummings and some of his staff indicted at Little Rock, and succeeded.

The facts that the Spaniards were undoubtedly encouraging the Red River harlequins, the United States Army was weak and challenged by the free men, and the Osages were protecting their "brothers" created a condition almost of chaos.

Both the Little Ones and Andrew Jackson, backed by the United States government, were trying to drive these people out, the Little Ones with much more enthusiasm than Jackson since their reasons were quite different. The Little Ones were protecting their "brothers," which *Wah'Kon-Tah* had given them, and Andrew Jackson wanted to remove the free men because he had a plan for removing the Cherokees, Choctaws, Chickasaws, and others from east of the Mississippi, where they were not wanted by the voters of the several established states, to this land west of the Mississippi.

As commanding officer of the Southern Division, he had given orders to Major Bradford of Fort Smith to remove all settlers whom he might find west of a line drawn from the source of the Kiamichi River to the Poteau—this, of course, after the ceding of this land by the Quapaws in 1818, who had held it by sufferance of the Little Ones. Actually, after this treaty with the Quapaws, the land was really public land but was blazed for Choctaw and Chickasaw occupancy, and those free men who settled on it after the treaty did have some logic in their contention that it was public land. Their stubbornness in settling on it was not totally unreasonable, just consciously unlawful.

Thomas Nuttall accompanied Bradford on the military junket. There were about two hundred families in their cabins, growing crops and attached to the land, whom he asked to leave; but he apparently did not come in contact with the trappers, hunters, and murderers, since they could easily avoid his dozen soldiers.

On the other hand, the Little Ones made it their business to find the killers of their "brothers," and apparently did not molest the settlers consistently. However, the gentile chieftains of the sub-*Hunkah* and the *Wa-Sha-She,* under direction no doubt of Arrow-Going-Home, the Grand *Hunkah* who remained in his villages on the Verdigris, rode often along the Poteau, the Blue, the Kiamichi, the Washita, the Red, and the Arkansas and the Canadian River looking for free men, Cherokees, and Caddos, and even Choctaws. When they found them, those who escaped told their story of the "massacre," and made it more dramatic and bloody at each telling, making of their own escape a heroism.

And during the hunger winter of 1821 and 1822, the Little Ones were hunting almost constantly. The winter was very cold, the snow beginning to fall as early as November 23, and scattered families of Little Ones would come to the Neosho and stand about the unfinished buildings of the mission, but the members of the mission, having only just begun their building at their location on the Neosho in February, 1821, had little to give them. The panthers had begun to find the mission pork much to their taste, and the wolves had a special fondness for shoats and pigs, and the prairie chickens were destroying their small grain.

When the new Long Knife chief came to Fort Smith, many of them went downriver to stand and watch from the south bank. In February when a gentile party of hunters went to the Poteau to hunt bears in their caves and under the roots of trees, they frightened the settlers on the north side of the river and the Cherokees became nervous.

493

The new chief at Fort Smith was Colonel Arbuckle. He had been ordered to the post by General Gaines, along with four companies of the Seventh Infantry to bring a stronger medicine to bear on the lawless situation and the war between the Little Ones and That-Thing-on-Its-Head People, the Cherokees.

Many of his soldiers died on the way up the Arkansas from the mosquito-infested swamps and marshes of the lower river. They had been delayed there by low water, and Colonel Arbuckle arrived at the post in February, 1822. He was depressed. The men at the post had malaria and many were chronically ill from the bad whisky which the white settlers near the fort made and sold to the soldiers. But he strengthened the fort by 250 men, and Arrow-Going-Home was one of the first to learn of this. The glib Cherokees were bringing their children to Dwight Mission now, saying they wanted them in a safe place when the soldiers and the Cherokees attacked the Osages and wiped them out. The Osages, on the other hand, came for their few children at Union Mission, saying that the hogs of That-Thing-on-Its-Head People must be hungry, so they would take their children home.

Major Bradford was relieved of his command and sent to Natchitoches.

Colonel Arbuckle apparently knew something of red man psychology, and he immediately set rumors going that there would now be peace between the Cherokees and the Osages, since there were many white soldiers who would see that this peace was made. Governor Miller came upriver again to meet with Colonel Arbuckle, and they planned to meet with the Osages and the Cherokees in January, 1822, and Nathaniel Philbrook, subagent, had been asked to go to the Osages to feel out the people at Arrow-Going-Home's village.

In their hunger the main village had been broken up into gentile villages, and each was maintaining themselves, and all had to move from the wind-screaming prairie to the sheltered bottoms of the river. They were difficult to find, but Philbrook had with him a young Osage, a boy who had been at the mission. He had been given the name of Phillip Milledolar by the missionaries, but his real name was *Mo'n Piche,* Bad Arrow (son of Tallai).

494

He could read the signs which the hunters and the warriors left in the trails. The hunters carried little sticks with them, perhaps willow, painted red and black, and on leaving the trail or at a turning they set one of these sticks in the ground, leaning to the direction they had taken, with the hickory bark stuck on the top end pointing in the direction the party had traveled. From this stick, Bad Arrow could know by the notches in it how many there were in the party—that is, if they were hunters or warriors; but if they were in family groups, they made little rings around the stick with pebbles, concentric little circles, with each circle representing a family, the circle of the pebbles representing the circle of the lodge.

The Little Ones marked their trails and their boundaries to warn invaders, and in the old balanced earth-struggle before the Heavy Eyebrows came, each tribe knew the markings of the others. They warned each other by leaving an arrow sticking in a buffalo carcass or by trimming trees near or on the periphery of their ranges. This was their way of warning possible invaders, and was much like the grizzly bear standing on his hind legs and scratching high up on a pine or a Douglas fir to mark his domain. The tom panther left a musk scent, then scratched the earth with his hind feet, and wolves and coyotes left musk messages on isolated rocks and trees, and mockingbirds and cardinals and thrushes and other birds sing for the same purpose.

Charlevoix wrote of *"les sauvage Osagien"* that "everyone is an enemy found in the warriors' path," and when Thomas Nuttall accompanied Major Bradford into the Red River drainage country to remove the settlers from lands meant for the Choctaws and Chickasaws, he wrote of the Osage domains and their trails: "These particular routes which they pursue are recognized by beacon, painted post and inscribed hieroglyphics near the boundaries of their range."

Tallai knew all about the Long Knife soldiers, and he was ready for a treaty with That-Thing-on-Its-Head People, before Little-Flower-Killer Moon if possible, so that they could go to the plains for hunting and fill their caches and parfleches again. He said he was tired of living with his thumb on the skunk leg of it-makes-things-cry-out.

495

Arrow-Going-Home was not interested, according to Philbrook, but he didn't like Philbrook and didn't want to listen to him. Later, he casually told the people at Union Mission that his people had made peace with the Sac and Foxes and the Kickapoos, and they were coming to help the Little Ones drive the Long Knives and the That-Thing-on-Its-Head away from their Mother Earth.

This inspired fear in the settlers and the Cherokees alike, and they began to prepare for an attack. The settlers came with their valuables to Dwight Mission for safekeeping, knowing that the Little Ones had never threatened any of the missions. After everybody was stirred up, it was reported that the Little Ones were planting and the men were getting their horses ready for the hunt the following month, and there were no Sac and Foxes or any other Algonkian tribesmen in the villages of the Osages. The Osages even proposed an armistice until after their hunt.

In Little-Flower-Killer Moon, Philbrook went to see them again. He urged them to make peace with the Cherokees. He said that war was bad for the Osages, since they had been cut off from trading for powder and the Cherokees had much powder. Also he said that it caused Governor Miller to have a heavy heart when he saw Osage women bringing water and wood to the cabins of the Cherokees. When the interpreter had finished, Philbrook was startled by the crying of a man. This man had just heard that his wife and children, taken prisoners, were still alive, and were carrying water and wood for That-Thing-on-Its-Head People. Philbrook, like many others, had believed that Indians never showed emotion.

When he arrived back at Union Mission, he said that the Osages had "nothing to eat besides a little corn" and they must go on their spring hunt, but "had waited in suspense in their villages" until they could make an agreement with the Cherokees. Philbrook, like everyone who listened to Osage oratory, was impressed, and he proposed to the commanding officer at the garrison that the Cherokees be stopped from "distressing these people any further."

An armistice was agreed upon, and Philbrook brought the written agreement up the Verdigris, and the Little Ones "touched the feather," and now they could make their hunt to the plains, feeling that

the armistice would be honored until the "big talk" with the Cherokees at Fort Smith July 30. If either party to the agreement violated
it, they agreed that that party should be punished by the Long Knife
soldiers.

One hundred and fifty of the Little Ones appeared at Fort Smith
July 30 to meet the Cherokees, and by August 9 the treaty of peace
was concluded and the Osage prisoners were returned to them.

Before this, on May 6, 1822, Congress had decided to discontinue
the factories. This was due to the jealousy of the traders; they objected very much to their government's being in business as rivals
to themselves.

The chieftains and the Grand *Hunkah* and the Grand *Tzi-Sho*
were called to the Place-of-the-Many-Swans to "touch the feather"
again on August 31, 1822. There were twenty-two marks made to the
treaty that day. *Paw-Hiu-Skah,* White Hair, was there and signed.
This was White Hair the younger, the young man who had volunteered to go with Zebulon Pike to the Pawnees in 1806, and who
after White Hair the original's death in 1808 had inherited the title
of Grand *Ki-He-Kah.*

For the sum of $2,329.40 paid to them in merchandise, the Little
Ones were to give up all claims on the United States concerning the
second article in the treaty of 1808, wherein the government was to
maintain all through the year a trading post or factory at Fort Osage,
where they could trade their hides and get supplies for the buffalo
hunts.

Now Colonel A. P. Chouteau and the other traders would have no
competition from the government, and almost immediately Chouteau persuaded White Hair to leave the Place-of-the-Many-Swans and
come to the Place-of-the-Oaks, bringing with him two physical divisions, the *Wah-Ho-Ka-Li,* the Thorny-Valley People and the Top-
of-the-Tree-Sitters, the *Pa-Solé,* called "Big Hills" by the English-
speaking people and "Gross Côte" by the French. These two divisions
would join the Upland-Forest People, the *Sa'n Solé,* who had established their villages there long before, and the *U-Dse-Ta,* the Down-
Below-People, the Little Osages, who had just preceded them and had
established their villages on the Neosho. Also part of the Big Hills

497

had migrated to the Neosho-Verdigris country previously. What happened to the fifth physical division, the *No'n-Dse-Waspi,* the Heart-Stays-People, no one seems to know.

Colonel A. P. and P. L. Chouteau opened up the old trading post which the former and Revoir had operated before the Cherokees had killed Revoir the year before. This was at the saline springs, and soon a boatload of merchandise from St. Louis came up the river to the trading post. A. P. Chouteau had come down to the Neosho with White Hair and a small party of his people to aid them in locating villages conveniently close to his trading post. This was in the autumn of 1822.

The soldiers at Fort Smith had been augmented by the Seventh Infantry and a commandant who apparently meant business and must carry out the urgent orders of his superior, Andrew Jackson. But so had the Little Ones been augmented by White Hair's removal to the Neosho. However, Colonel Arbuckle soon saw he had little to fear from the recent arrivals from the Place-of-the-Many-Swans. Not only was White Hair the Grand *Ki-He-Kah* but he was Chouteau's man, and peace was imposed upon him both by his being of the Sky Lodge and by the fact that Chouteau's boats from St. Louis must get through and he didn't want the Cherokees coming up the Neosho to burn his post and merchandise.

However, White Hair the younger was a usurper's heir and was not of the *Tzi-Sho Wa-Shta-Ge,* also called They-Who-Do-Not-Touch-Blood gens, the traditional gens from which the Grand *Tzi-Sho* must come; therefore, it is likely that he did not have the effective control over the Place-of-the-Many-Swans Osages that Arrow-Going-Home had over the Place-of-the-Oaks or Arkansas Osages. This was evident when some gentes of the Big Hills under their chief, *To-Wa-Ka-Heh,* said that they would not be bound by the treaty of August between the Cherokees and the Osages, since they were not a party to it. They said the new Heavy Eyebrows were killing their "brothers" on the Missouri and the Osage rivers, and they had come here to the Neosho and the Verdigris to get away from the killing there, and now they must protect their "brothers" here as well.

The treaty between the Osages and the Cherokees at Fort Smith in

August, 1822, stipulated that the Cherokees might cross the magic line and hunt in the Osage country if they did not establish commercial camps and hunt for the market, and the Osages could cross the line into the Cherokee country to hunt, and to them this meant protecting their "brothers" from commercial butchery. This was good, but the Little Ones asked that Tom Graves, the white man leader of certain bands of the Cherokees, should be punished for murdering the children and women of the Little Ones and feeding them to the hogs. He was very influential among the Cherokees of the west, and naturally they refused to turn him over to the Little Ones along with their Osage captives.

The Little Ones seemed to know Graves and his habits as well as his deeds and they had scouts watching his movements. They finally located his large hunting camp on the North Fork of the Canadian River, and the relatives of the people who had been murdered were called together. Under a leader they put on the charcoal and limonite, hung the *wah-hopeh* around the neck of the leader, and set out. Apparently they failed to surprise the camp since the wily Graves knew he must keep an alert guard in this territory, far across the boundary in Osage country. The emotionalized Little Ones ran the illegal hunters back across the line and managed to shoot a nephew of Graves called Red Hawk. They cut off his head and brought it back to the village in triumph. This paid for only one of the Osages who had been mutilated by the whites. Only one of those murdered could now enter Spiritland. The war was not over.

A bitter old chief of the Cherokees was *Tak-Atoka*. He decided to leave the Arkansas Cherokees, and with fifty or sixty warriors he went to settle in the Kiamichi Valley, and from there he would make forays against the hated Osages. He made an attack on a village on the Verdigris and took one hundred Osage horses, and then he made a woodland Indian ambush for the Osage warriors who followed his broad trail. The ensuing battle was a draw perhaps, but the dramatic Cherokees made a great thing of it, and they sent a number of warriors to the vindictive old chief's relief.

This was Yellow-Flower Moon of the Little Ones, August, and their attack on Tom Graves' hunting camp had been in Baby-Bear Moon, January, both in the year 1823.

499

This must have been quite disturbing to Arbuckle's military mind. He heard the very logical, very glib Cherokees out, and he was convinced that the Osages "are extremely ignorant and faithless; their chiefs are without authority, and their warriors are encouraged in dishonesty from their infancy." Then he would go to Arrow-Going-Home's village, and there listen to the tall, dignified, handsome man with his Ciceronian gestures explain in classical logic his position and his desire for peace. He would then come back believing with Major Bradford that the Cherokees were liars and with Governor Miller that they were keeping alive a "marauding, thieving, cowardly kind of warfare."

Also the Big Hills were active from their village above the villages of Arrow-Going-Home, but on the west side of the Verdigris River in the modern Nowata County, Oklahoma. White men were always coming by the mission on their way to this village to recover stolen horses. One of the gens of this Sitters-on-the-Hilltop physical division, the *Pa Solé*, now called Gross Côte and Big Hills, seemed to have been under a chieftain named *Shinkah Mo'in*, Little Walker, but it is more likely *Shonkah Mo'in*, Walking Dog, which really means "Walking Horse," since before the Little Ones had named the horse *ka-wa*, they had, along with most of the other Siouans, called him at times dog, perhaps *shonkah tonkah*, big dog. This writing of *Shinkah* for *Shonkah* was one of the very slightest mistakes in trader, soldier, and missionary phonetics.

But the Cherokees had convinced Arbuckle that *Tak-Atoka*'s attack on the Osage village was in revenge for a man of his band killed by the Osage the autumn before, a man who was making an innocent visit to the Three Forks, and Arbuckle's military sense of rightness finally had something it could grasp and hold on to. Something had to be done about this sort of thing. Here was a man, even though an Indian, who was killed when he was not hunting or trapping commercially on the Osage domain, and he was alone and not with a war party. Something had to be done.

The commandant sent the Osage subagent, Philbrook, to the Verdigris villages to get the murderer. This was in the Buffalo-Mating Moon and the man who was supposed to have done the killing was on the buffalo hunt on the plains, but the Little Ones in full council and after some moving oratory decided to give him up in accordance with the treaty terms.

In the meantime, the Little Ones didn't think their enemy *Tak-Atoka* ought to be living in their domain on the Kiamichi River, so they sent parties down to harass him, and finally after several attacks and counterattacks and much horse taking, he left and joined his people in the Arkansas country.

When the accused man got back from the buffalo hunt, two hundred Osages started with him to Fort Smith to carry out the provisions of the treaty by delivering him to the authorities. This was pure exhibitionism. When this party of two hundred were camped on Greenleaf Creek, their prisoner escaped.

There were rumors and excitement, and this upset the military mentality. Arbuckle, like all knowing ones, which did not include the missionaries, realized that one prisoner would not likely escape from an army of two hundred, so he hurried to Arrow-Going-Home's village accompanied by Walter Webber, Black Fox, and James Rogers of the Cherokees.

He and his companions stayed in the village three days, but he must have come away under the influence of Arrow-Going-Home's classical oratory and his personality, and at the mission where he stopped he said that they had accomplished nothing "as the Osage people complain of injuries from the Cherokees since the treaty was made." He said he would investigate their complaints.

The old Osage trace between their villages on the Osage River and the mouth of the Neosho and the old trace from the Osage River to St. Louis were filled with emigrants now. A man by the name of Austin was establishing a colony in Texas, and people were passing along the trace on their way there, and there were the usual restive free men and their families and their stock, and traders and military detachments and stray groups of Algonkians from east of the Mississippi, and they all stopped at Union Mission to rest or be treated by Dr. Marcus Palmer for "bilious fever" and "ague," "intermittent fever" and wounds by bear.

But the missionaries themselves were periodically sick from malaria and typhoid, as were the soldiers from Fort Smith. Colonel Arbuckle had sent to the mission for "Jesuite Bark," but they had used up their scant supply. One sister became demented.

For the Little Ones, 1823 was a good year. It was terrifically cold, according to the mission's thermometer reading, but there was plenty of game close to the villages; perhaps the unusually low temperatures had driven it there for shelter. There were buffalo during the winter of 1822-23 within fifteen miles of Fort Smith. The temperature reading by the mission thermometer was of December 1, 1822, "6 below cypher."

Game was so plentiful that year that some Delawares came to the Chouteau trading post to ask the Little Ones if they might trap and hunt on the Neosho, and the people of the mission knew later of a band of Kickapoos camped just fifteen miles from the mission. They kept themselves quiet and their camp well hidden, and they were off the well-worn trails of the Little Ones and not in the direction of their raids. Besides these, hundreds of whites and Cherokees were coming into the Osage domain, or at least that area which they had always claimed and dominated. By 1824, Colonel Arbuckle would state that there were two thousand French, American, Cherokee, and Delaware hunters between the Red and Arkansas rivers.

It would be only a matter of time until there would be battles between the Osages and the white hunters as there were between the Osages and the Cherokees.

There were two Frenchmen who lived at New Orleans who had had a thriving business during the War of 1812, but the war had ended unexpectedly and they were left with merchandise on their hands and no market. That is, there was no more lax, indifferent United States government represented by peculating buyers, so they moved their goods to Arkansas Post with the idea of trading with the trappers and hunters of the Indian country. They would be as careless as the government, and the Indians themselves even more so. These two men, Frederick Notrebe and Antoine Barraque, established an outfitting store at Arkansas Post.

Soon they wondered why they shouldn't get some of the profits which went to trappers and hunters by establishing their own hunting camp in the middle of the best beaver country. They got up a party of perhaps twenty-three or twenty-four which was led by Antoine Barraque.

The large party of commercial hunters and trappers found a spot on the Blue River, about thirty miles above the mouth, a spot which is in the modern Bryan County, Oklahoma. The party was composed of Americans and Frenchmen and mixed-blood Quapaws. They believed they were sufficiently far away from the Little Ones' warriors and hunters; and to make sure that they would not be attacked, even though trespassing, they hoisted the American flag, and they sounded the bugle every morning in simulation of military practice. When their trappers or their hunters set out, usually up the streams, one or more of the Quapaw mixed-bloods paralleled them on the ridges, constantly on the lookout for Osages.

There was an American army officer with them, who was either on leave and was having a little sport or sharing in the profits, or who was retired. Anyway, they were having wonderful luck on this great beaver river called by the French *De L'eau Bleu.*

Bad-Tempered-Buffalo, who had a reputation for his savage raids and his daring, was feared by all, and led several gentes on raids if he ordered them to follow. The gentile leaders were afraid of him as well, and he was called *Tse-To-Gah Wah-Shi'n-Pische,* which literally means Buffalo-with-Bad-Temper and refers to a buffalo bull in Buffalo-Mating Moon.

He and Walks-Badly of the Eagle had made a raid on the Pawnees sometime in October. They had been joined by a gens from White Hair's village, and they had come back with fifty horses. They said they killed nine Pawnees and lost only one warrior. This should have had much meaning to any enemy who noted the incident.

Bad-Tempered-Buffalo had apparently located the camp with the American flag, possibly astride a buffalo trail, since he was more angered than usual. There must have been the usual noise when white men got together: shooting matches, loud laughter, whistling and shouting to each other, and axe strokes and bawdy songs.

He got together two hundred warriors, since, when you went toward the Red River now, you might meet large numbers of Caddos and Cherokees and Choctaws, led by white men, and you could often bluff them back across the line with large numbers.

The large hunting party was camped where there were cane-brakes, and the Little Ones had chased the Caddos through these many times. They knew every twist of the river, where the buffalo and the wapiti trails crossed, and Bad-Tempered Buffalo and his scouts were highly pleased to find that the careless white men had established their camp in the cane-brakes. This was perfect for the Little Ones. They crept through them as quietly as the buck deer who lays his antlers on his back and with his nose straight out in front of him steals his way through the canes without even causing their tops to move.

There is no tribal or gentile memory of this battle with the white men, because, as one supposes, it was conveniently forgotten, and one is not sure whether *Mo'in Pische*, Walks-Badly, or Bad-Tempered-Buffalo led the attack, but whoever did lead it had bad luck, since of the five hunters killed, one was Major Curtis Welborn. The following took part in the battle: *We-Ts'a-She*, Little Rattle Snake; *Wa-Nah-Sha-She*, Little-Eagle-That-Gets-What-He-Wants; *Mi-Tsiu-Shi*, Little Grizzly; He-Who-Strikes-the-Padouca, *Heh-La-Shi-She*, Curved Antlers; *Nika-Bra'n*, Smells-Like-a-Man; *Xu-Tha-Shinkah*, Little Eagle. The others killed were just ordinary men from the military point of view, Americans and some of less importance, Frenchmen, and some of no importance, the Quapaw mixed-bloods, although it is doubtful if any of the last were killed. The Little Ones apparently killed four white men and one Negro slave belonging to Barraque and known as Ben, and the others scattered like the striped-headed one, the quail, in the cane-brakes, which favored the escape of the hunters as it had favored the attack of the Little Ones.

There might have been talk about Bad-Tempered-Buffalo's giving up the guilty ones, and several visits to the villages on the Verdigris by Colonel Arbuckle, and in general some military bluffing, but the savages had actually killed an officer of the American Army, and not only that, they cut off his head along with the heads of the others.

This attack occurred on November 17, 1823.

These men were not only trespassing but were violating the agreement their government had labored so long to obtain with the warring Cherokees and Osages, the agreement of August, 1822. Ordinarily, one supposes, not much would have been done about the matter, with the exception of visits by Colonel Arbuckle and Major Cummings to Colonel A. P. Chouteau and Arrow-Going-Home, if Major Welborn had not been killed and decapitated. The army became indignant and bloodily vindictive, and it might seem that this was more a manifestation of loyalty to an organization rather than loyalty to the white race and the championship of "citizens."

When the army became excited about the affair, the free men and the honest settlers soon took up the cry of "outrage," and great pressure was put on Colonel Arbuckle. Excited men, many of them attached to their little geometrical bits of earth in the Arkansas Territory, organized a cavalry troop in Crawford County, and another group organized in Miller County and there was a company of infantry organized.

There was plenty of ammunition for them at Little Rock. When Miller came to Arkansas Territory in October, 1819, to become the first governor, he had brought with him four hundred muskets, forty thousand rounds of ammunition, and "fifty horsemen pistols," and in 1820 the government sent two hundred cavalry sabers, "four hundred horsemen pistols," twelve drums, and twelve fifes.

The "citizens," both the honest settlers and the free men, were quite ready to "chase the Injuns clean outta the country" if the army gave the word.

Arbuckle sent Major Alexander Cummings to Colonel A. P. Chouteau to demand the surrender of the "murderers" by the "Shainers," and Arrow-Going-Home, Walks-Badly, and Bad-Tempered-Buffalo met him at the trading post with twenty-one horses they had taken from the hunters and later delivered the beaver skins they had taken and then five more of the horses.

The foxy Arrow-Going-Home made a few lame excuses for not having called a council as the military had suggested or, as a matter of fact, demanded. He said that the gentile leaders who attacked the hunters thought they were Cherokees violating the agreement of 1822, and when he saw in the manner of the Major and Chouteau that this was not adequate, he said that he had a "heavy heart" over the "mistake," but this seemed to affect the army officers very little also. Then he said that he couldn't very well discuss the matter with the gentes, since most of them were on the plains hunting.

He had heard that the Cherokees had volunteered their aid to the Heavy Eyebrows soldiers. (The Little Ones had dropped the term Long Knife for the Americans and were calling them Heavy Eyebrows.) Was this true?

The Cherokees had done just this, but had been turned down. The Major told the Grand *Hunkah* that the army would take care of the thing very well, and anyway the Cherokees had "their own axe to grind."

The visitors wondered about the many horses about the villages. Many of them acted strange, raising their heads suddenly and whinnying as horses in a strange place often do. Would these be the rest of the white hunters' horses? No, *Shonka Mo'in,* Walking-Dog, had taken them from the Cherokees and from the Pawnees on his recent raids.

The settlers and the free men and the Cherokees and the Choctaws kept shouting "outrage," and kept the pressure on Arbuckle. He wrote to his superiors that if the United States were considering war against the Osages, they must bring a great number of horses to the Verdigris, as well as ordnance and stores, and take the matter seriously, since the Osages were masters in warfare, the kind that would later be referred to as "guerrilla warfare."

In the Baby-Bear Moon, December of 1824, when all the gentes were in the villages, Captain Nathaniel Pryor, Tallai, and Arrow-Going-Home went to Fort Smith to talk with Colonel Arbuckle about this thing. Captain Pryor, a trader friend of the Osages, wanted the matter of the white hunters settled so that there would be peace, but possibly in the mind of the shrewd Arrow-Going-Home was the idea of determining the strength of the Heavy Eyebrows and evaluating their bluff.

During this visit he tried one more of his excuses, by saying that the gentile leaders of the attack on the Blue River tried to stop the young men but failed. Now, these headlong young men who could not be controlled by the gentile leaders ought to be punished. When he saw the disbelief in the eyes of Arbuckle, he then addressed himself to determining if, like the French and the Spaniards, the new Heavy Eyebrows, the Americans, would "assemble the Nations," to fight them. Besides the Miamis, the Potawatomis, the Kickapoos, the Delawares, the Caddos, and those chain-pressured Indians settled by Graham on their eastern border, there would now be the chain-pressured Cherokees and Choctaws, but the Osages would not give up the leaders of the attack. They would fight all these people as they had done before, since all of these people still fought like red men— all except perhaps the Cherokees, who fought in their own way, and this was not even the way of the Heavy Eyebrows nor yet the way of the plains.

But Arrow-Going-Home could see that since Colonel Arbuckle had turned down the Cherokees' offer of aid, he would not allow the others to fight, but the United States Army would fight the Little Ones. However, he also noticed that Colonel Arbuckle was not too abrupt or arrogant or demanding, and he sensed that they, the Americans, were not ready for war just yet.

Arbuckle, on his part, was afraid that in the meantime the Osages would attack; there were rumors of activity against the background of prayer-singing in the villages on the Verdigris.

Colonel Arbuckle had apparently conveyed his fears of an Osage attack to his superior, General Winfield Scott, in command of the Western Division at New Orleans. General Scott ordered him to remove five companies from Fort Smith to the mouth of the Verdigris River, but before he received this order, he was still trying to keep the Osages from attacking and had sent Nathaniel Philbrook to the falls of the Verdigris to meet with Major Cummings and the Little Ones. He wanted the talks to continue until the army could prepare itself for an attack and perhaps a long war. Philbrook never reached the falls of the Verdigris, but his horse was found at the mouth of the Neosho. It was supposed that he was drowned, but since his body was not found, Arbuckle was suspicious and perhaps was happy when orders were received to move his companies to the mouth of the Verdigris.[1]

[1] Philbrook's body was found later.

507

Major Cummings had given him an estimate of what might happen and an estimate of the strength of the Osages. He was sure that the Big Hills physical division would not come into the war and that the Grand *Ki-He-Kah,* White Hair, would not bring his people into war with the Americans. This, Cummings estimated, would leave the "Shainers," Arrow-Going-Home and his Arkansas Osages, with five hundred warriors.

When Colonel Arbuckle arrived with his force and selected a site on the east side of the Neosho, just three miles from the mouth, the Osages were impressed and completely bluffed. The women must have keened for days and must have fled from every messenger sent by Arbuckle.

Arbuckle's men had come by water and by land from Fort Smith, and they began to build their camps astride the old trail of the Little Ones where they had crossed for generations. The soldiers named their encampment "Grand River Arkansas," and this would later be called Fort Gibson, then Cantonment Gibson, but it would have been effective to bluff the Little Ones under any other name.

The site was selected April 20, 1824, and by June 7 of that year the Little Ones had delivered six men to Arbuckle as the leaders and perpetrators of the "massacre" of the white trespassers. The Little Ones had been urged to do so both by Nathaniel Pryor and by their new agent, David Barber. Thus, on June 7, they came to Cantonment Gibson. The bluff had worked beautifully. Five hundred of the Little Ones came to Cantonment Gibson. They came with the tamed spirit of the mustang; the wild, unconquerable spirit of the plains, which once captured, thrown, tied, and rope-burned, would after further handling be ready for the halter. The six men gentile leaders who had led the attack were ready for death by command of the Little Old Men and the Grand *Hunkah.*

There was *Tse-To-Gah,* Bad-Tempered-Buffalo, son of Arrow-Going-Home, possibly the leader of the Star-That-Came-to-Earth gens. There were *Wa-Na-Sha-Shi'n,* Little-Eagle-That-Gets-What-He-Wants, of the Eagle, and *Wa-Cabe Shinkah,* Little Bear, of the Bear, and Little Rattler (Snake), possibly of the one gens of *Hunkah*

Grand Division, and *Hi-Sha-Ki-Hi-Ri,* Caddo Killer, gens unknown, and the sixth very likely of the Panther, whose name was never recorded, since panther-like he escaped the first night after leaving for Little Rock.

Some of the missionaries paddled a canoe downriver, spending one night camped on its banks, in order to witness the surrender of the prisoners. Despite the fact that they attributed quixotic nobility to the incredible dignity of the prisoners, and to those who gave them over to be hanged, their description of the scene is interesting.

But there was poignant tragedy there that Tuesday afternoon on June 7, 1824, on the Waters-like-the-Summer-Cow, the Neosho, that neither the army people nor the Union Mission witnesses could possibly understand. It wasn't death of the prisoners that made the five hundred hearts cold and leaden within them. What was death to a warrior? It was always present; it came out of the sky, it peeped under the edges of the lodges, it howled over the white world of winter, it came as *we-lu-schkas* into the lungs with throat-rattler the frost, and came in the semen of the Heavy Eyebrows and from his breath. It lived in the heart of *mi-tzo* the grizzly, and on the points of the arrows of the Pawnees, the Padoucas, and the Sac and Foxes, and came with the *mo'n-ce* out of the guns of Heavy Eyebrows. It came from *shi-ku,* the snake, and it sometimes lived in the form of *we-lu-schkas* on the points of the claws of the panther and the black bear.

At death the spirit was released, and reached Spiritland, but the spirit of the man who was hanged by the Heavy Eyebrows could never escape. The rope that choked off his breath also closed the spirit's exit from the body.

The missionaries, in their report which appeared in the Union Mission *Journal,* seemed almost sorry that "It would exceed the usual limits of a Journal to notice in detail the interesting transaction." They were deeply impressed "to see six brave men come forward, and voluntarily submit to become prisoners; to be put in irons; and sent away to be tried for their lives; to see this done with firmness and decision, by the unanimous consent of the Nation, and without a single sigh from their affectionate wives . . . to see the sense of honor manifested on the part of the criminals, and the desire to do justice in the Nation, was indeed affecting to every spectator."

Colonel Arbuckle must have been nervous among this horde of Little Ones under such tense circumstances, and he delivered to them beef, pork, and flour.

The five remaining prisoners were delivered to Acting Governor Crittenden at Little Rock on June 25 under military guard. They were brought to trial in November in the Superior Court of the United States for the Territory of Arkansas, charged with the "murder" of Major Curtis Welborn, but only Bad-Tempered-Buffalo and Little-Eagle-That-Gets-What-He-Wants were sentenced to be hanged; the others were acquitted. The date for the hanging was December 21.

Colonel Arbuckle, whose sense of justice could now come into play, asked the War Department to "extend clemency," but Acting Governor Crittenden opposed this recommendation, albeit the date for execution was postponed to February 24. The War Department asked Crittenden to supply the Secretary of War the statement of evidence on which the two Osages had been convicted, and the date of execution was again postponed.

Then Alexander McNair, the new agent for the Little Ones, got busy and tried to get them to agree to move from the Verdigris and join the other members of the tribe on the Neosho, these villages being the Big Hills and Arrow-Going-Home's villages. He had been directed to effect this removal. Naturally they refused.

He felt deep sympathy for them, and this seems laudable in the former first governor of the new state of Missouri who had listened to the free men. He became quite active and wrote to President Monroe, informing him that "there was a very general sentiment among the army officers and the better class of white settlers that the two Osages should not be executed at all."

President Adams pardoned Bad-Tempered-Buffalo and Little Eagle on March 21, 1825.

The mere fact of being imprisoned was tragedy to the Little Ones, and they seemed dispirited and perhaps felt that their *amour-propre* was tarnished. Bad-Tempered-Buffalo had tried to commit suicide while in prison.

Literate people with an academic interest were on the side of General Bradford, McNair, and the officers and others, not so much through a sense of justice or a feeling of sympathy but from admiration. This attitude was expressed by *Niles' Register* of July 9, 1825: "Mad Buffalo and Little Eagle, the two Indians who were condemned to death for the murder of Major Wellborne and others in November 1823 have been pardoned by the President, and set at liberty. The magnanimity with which these Indians gave themselves up, to save their tribe, was not inferior to the famous self devotion of certain citizens of Calais, when that place capitulated to Edward the Third."

The excitement stirred up by the army over Major Welborn's "murder" and the dramatic unreason of the "better class of white settlers," along with hatred expressed by the free men and the Cherokees, was truly an American manifestation, as was the later evidence of sympathy for the convicted ones, even though Crittenden, the free men, and the Cherokees felt no reversal of feeling. What part conscience played in the attitude of the officers and "the better class of white settlers" can be found in the charge of "murder," perhaps.

There had been Fort d'Orléans on the Missouri, Fort Carondelet on the Osage, Fort Osage on the Missouri, Fort Smith on the Arkansas, and now Cantonment Gibson on the Neosho, all inspired by the activity of the Little Ones in protecting their "brothers" which *Wah'-Kon-Tah* had given them, so that they themselves might attain old age.

41. *Mo'n Sho'n* Becomes
a Shriveled Old Woman

DESPITE THE FACT THAT the Americans were not able to control the relations of their citizens west of the Mississippi with the Little Ones and the Cherokees under their beautiful Constitution and Bill of Rights, or even control their own military and the civil officials of Arkansas Territory, they characteristically tried to place the mantles of this highly civilized form of government called democracy onto the Neolithic Little Ones. The result was ridiculous.

The Arrow-Going-Home people called "Shainers" and Arkansas Osages were assembled at the Verdigris Falls to hear about a new thing which Colonel Arbuckle had to tell them. There might be more presents, also, but they felt they had better listen to the Heavy Eyebrows chief since his men were hammering and shouting and swearing three miles above the mouth of the Neosho, and there were log cabins and other buildings going up there, and it looked as if the Heavy Eyebrows warriors would stay there in the very heart of their country. So it was good if they listened to their agent, David Barber, and to Colonel Arbuckle.

When the Colonel asked if they approved of the thirteen men he had named to be national councilmen, they said it was good. Of course Arrow-Going-Home must become "president" and Tallai (Buck-Making-Horns), "vice-president." The council was to legislate on all important matters, and there were forty warriors appointed to carry out the laws of the council. On the council and the "national guard" there were a few obsequious Nobodies who had impressed both Barber and Arbuckle with their "spirit" of co-operation. Their strutting and the "government" lasted about as long as it took Barber and Arbuckle to arrive home.

About the time they were arranging the robes of democracy on the giant bodies of members of the new government, which they hoped would control the young warriors who kept worrying Colonel Arbuckle, he received a report from one of his lieutenants, one Richard Wash, concerning the situation on the Red River: ". . . the laws of the United States relative to the introduction of slaves and to trading with the Indians are set at perfect contempt and daily and extensively violated. In addition to this, a band of lawless marauders have established themselves on the Red River above our post and are in habits of committing the most outrageous acts of robbery, violence, and murder."

These were Governor Miller's "banditti of outlaws." The Little Ones had proved that they were quite capable of keeping the area stirred up in protecting their "brothers" and needed no further incentive to make incursions into this country, but they received this added encouragement in the horse stealings, rapings, and murderings by these people who continually made raids north of the Red River. Thus when General Winfield Scott ordered troops from Natchitoches to the mouth of the Kiamichi to protect the citizens and established Cantonment Towson, another fort had been built because of the activities of the Little Ones, albeit the primary reason being the protection of serious citizens and Indian land and game from tribal fragments and free white barbarisms.

The personnel of the fort seemed to be almost immediately occupied in trying to destroy the citizens' stills, so that they could keep their soldiers alert and sober. And within seven months after Barber and Arbuckle were presenting the Revolutionary gentlemen's creation in the form of a government to the Little Ones, the free men were organizing to attack new Cantonment Towson because it interfered with their distilling of spirits for the soldiers' consumption and with their hunting on Indian lands. Later they actually attacked the cantonment.

513

The Little Ones of the Place-of-the-Many-Swans had a very much better reputation than the Little Ones of the Place-of-the-Oaks. This was possibly due in part to the Chouteaus' control over White Hair and occasionally over the Big Hills, and partly due to the fact that the hairy ones of the lower Missouri and the Osage River were not burdened with Miller's "banditti of outlaws" and fragments of the Red River Cherokees, Choctaws, and rum and Spaniard-inspired Caddoans. The hairy ones of the Missouri, Meramec, and Osage and Gasconade rivers seemed to be more serious about settling and making homes, even though they were just as jealous of their fancied rights as free men and perhaps more land-greedy, since many of them were planters.

Further, the Missouri was the highway to Santa Fe and Taos, and the big fur companies helped keep it tidy. There was no need yet in the years between the end of the War of 1812, and 1815 and the closing of the American "factory" system in 1822 for the "Northern Osages" to cross the magic line extending from Fort Osage to Fort Smith, which represented their eastern boundary according to the treaty of 1808, in order to protect their "brothers." The hairy ones and the chain-pressured red men from the east had made this unnecessary; the "brothers" that had not been slaughtered had actually fled up the rivers to the contact line of prairie and woodland and were taking their refuge in the timbered bottoms and in the canyons of the prairie feeder streams of the Osage domain.

It was the eastern red man's pressure on the Little Ones with the pressure of the hairy ones, the same as it was on the Arkansas, that kept the Little Ones of the Place-of-the-Many-Swans agitated, as were the Little Ones of the Place-of-the-Oaks, and much of this activity was also inspired by the Cherokees. The Cherokee leaders were still dreaming of an Indian state, wherein the Cherokees would rule, but which would be made up of eastern tribes. There was not room in this state for the Little Ones, but their domain was a necessity and this kept the situation tense. Even when Indian agent Graham and William Clark and Colonel Arbuckle were listening to the Cherokee leaders telling of their plans for confederation, they were constantly agitating the Osages to another attack like that of Bad-Tempered-

Buffalo. Arbuckle, Clark, and Graham would, after listening to the voluble Cherokees, snap their mental fingers and say to themselves that the project was a perfect solution of the Indian problem. The Cherokee leaders would mention that all the eastern Indians and those south of the Great Lakes had been exchanging wampum and messengers about the confederation, and they would name to Clark the Shawnees, Delawares, Kickapoos, Piankashaws, Weas, and Peorias, the Miamis, Wyandots, Ottawas, Oneidas, and Potawatomis, but failed to mention that it would be necessary to drive the savage Osages from their ancient domain. Not even Clark seemed to be thinking of the "bad Indians" now. It was the creaking wheel again, and the need of axle grease.

Clark was impressed and immediately got in touch with Secretary Calhoun. Naturally the "object" met the approval of the government. But no one seemed to consider the Little Ones until Clark had heard a new chorus of "outrage" from the trespassers both red and white. And this only annoyed the government as represented by Missouri Senator Benton, and they began to wonder what they must do with the "buffalo Indians," the savage Osages.

The scarcity of game east of the magic line—the boundary of 1808 between the Little Ones and the hairy ones—became a national problem when the eastern Indians the government had collected through Graham east of the line upon this ceded Osage land began to starve, and the hungrier they became the more trespassing there was by their hunters on the Little Ones' side of the line, and the more "outrages" committed by the savages (the Osages).

The Osage domain had been patrolled by them like a great game refuge, and here the game was plentiful still, and the eastern red men on the boundary soon built up the same attitude of injured virtue as the free men had done. Earlier these displaced tribes had been ready to join the Cherokees to invade the domain of the Little Ones, but the government had stopped them. War was imminent for several years, and Agent Graham listed their potential in warriors available against the Little Ones. He figured that the Cherokee could put 600 warriors into the field; the Kickapoos, 400; Delawares, 600; and since the Potawatomis and Sac and Foxes had through the years depleted the people of the Illini confederation, the Weas, Michigamans, Piankashaws, and Peorias plus the Shawnees could field only 500. This would make a force of 2,100. He thought they might get the ancient enemy of the Little Ones, the Pawnees, to join them with perhaps 2,000 warriors. The Sac and Foxes would not take action against their old enemies.

Graham believed that the Osages could bring into the field about 1,250, with the Konzas. This would be only the Shainers, led by Arrow-Going-Home, if he had not by now grown too old, the Place-of-the-Many-Swans Osages remaining aloof because of the enmity between the Grand *Hunkah* and White Hair, called Great *Ki-He-Kah*.

William Henry Harrison, when he was governor of the Indiana Territory, made a treaty with the Sac and Foxes in 1804 in which they "promise and agree that they will put an end to the bloody war which has hitherto raged between their tribe and the Great and Little Osages."

According to the great warrior chief of the Sac and Foxes, Black Hawk, who gave his name to a war between the Americans and his tribe later, he himself had led his warriors across the Missouri to attack the Osages when he had only a handful of men and had attacked hundreds of Osages, of course defeating them, killing many and losing himself only a few men or none at all at times.

It was notable how the Algonkians and the Iroquoians exaggerated their own prowess in totting up the number of enemy they had killed and the number of their own losses; it was always so one-sided that it was incredible; but many of the chroniclers believed them, just as the impressionable magazine writers and travelers in the West of the 1860's and 1870's were impressed by the histrionics of professional buffalo hunters and American soldiers in their war with the Plains Indians. The Plains Indians themselves were either more chivalrous in their reports or the woodland Indians had been so long associated with the white men that they considered this exaggeration as quite natural. The Plains Indians, at least the Osages, seemed always to give their enemies full credit, being untrustworthy only when each gens talked of their own prowess.

The year 1822 was an important year in the history of the Little Ones. The Place-of-the-Oaks people had made a treaty with the Cherokees, which would not last, but at least it freed them to go on their necessary buffalo hunts to the headwaters of the Cimarron and the Salt Fork without fear of Cherokee warriors attacking their defenseless villages. Now if they saw the boot tracks of the Cherokees on their side of the magic line, they need not trail them if they were hunting only to fill their bellies and not hunting and trapping to sell the hides to the Heavy Eyebrows. However, they did trail them, and when they found bloated carcasses of deer, buffalo, or wapiti or bear, they tried to overtake the party before they got across the line. They could cross the line into the ceded land which now belonged to the Cherokees and the Shawnees and the Delawares, the last who sang their talk like *sho-mi-kase,* the coyote, but there was little game there, and they chose to stay on their own side most of the time in order to keep the Shawnees and Delawares from killing their "brothers." Lovely's Purchase line they almost never respected anyway.

A steamboat came to Fort Smith in the Planting Moon of that year, April, 1822, but there is no tribal memory of it, nor is there any tribal memory of the steamboat that passed the mouth of the Osage River, *The Yellowstone,* in 1819.

In this year (1822) they touched the feather again with the Heavy Eyebrows, and there would be no more *wah-don-skas* to be had from Fort Osage or from the "factory" established on their river just the year before. This was close to the meeting of the two forks, the Place-of-the-Many-Swans, in fact. It was just up the north fork which the French had called in near translation of Place-of-the-Many-Swans, Marais des Cygnes River. The little settlement of Papinville is all that is left of this "factory."

It was in the autumn of this year that White Hair moved from the ridge above the Place-of-the-Many-Swans with his villages, which probably included the People-of-the-Thorny-Valley, the Big Hills, at least part of whom also moved. However, they moved to the Verdigris above the villages of Arrow-Going-Home, and White Hair moved with his people to the Neosho above Union Mission.

The first European influence to divide the tribe was the rivalry of the fur traders Chouteau and Lisa. And now the move from the old village sites of the last of the Little Ones was occasioned by rivalry between the now powerful fur companies and the United States government, led by the powerful fur trader John Jacob Astor of the American Fur Company. He had lobbied in Washington against the "factory system," and Congress had acted. This left the private trading post at Côte sans Desein just below the mouth of the Osage River, as the place closest to the Missouri Osages where they might get *wah-don-skas* in trade for their furs. This was in the country ceded by the treaty of 1808, and the free men of Missouri often waited for a chance to kill and scalp a small number of Little Ones when they crossed the magic line. If they went in great numbers to trade with the friendly Frenchman, Baptiste Louis Roi, and his Osage wife, the free men would say that they were a war party and the troops might even be called out. There was nothing for them to do, they who by now must depend upon the trade goods of the Heavy Eyebrows since they had become accustomed to them.

Under the factory system, there was a superintendent of Indian trade with his headquarters in Georgetown, D. C., but after May 6, 1822, there was a superintendent of Indian affairs with headquarters in St. Louis. This office was given, quite properly, to General William Clark of the old Lewis and Clark adventure.

In 1825 when Bad-Tempered-Buffalo and Little-Eagle-That-Gets-What-He-Wants were pardoned by President Adams, there was much discussion about again moving the Little Ones farther west, and especially away from the areas of their ancient domain overrun by Cherokees and free men. The logic seemed to be that the east-of-the-Mississippi tribes had no homes, and since they were starving in southwestern Missouri and elsewhere because the free men had killed the game for the market, they ought to be moved into the Osage domain where there was still game to subsist them and where there were yet few free men to shout and disturb the government about the rights of free men. Also, to continue with the logic, since the Cherokees and the free men could not be kept out of the Osage domain and since by their invasions they disturbed the whole region, the government would punish the Osages by removing them.

A treaty was made at St. Louis, Missouri, June 2, 1825. William Clark, superintendent of Indian affairs, represented the United States, and it was signed by a long list of chiefs of the Great and Little Osages.

According to the government the treaty was made "In order more effectually to extend to said tribes that protection of the Government so much desired by them, it is agreed as follows": To cede all lands lying within the state of Missouri and Territory of Arkansas, and "all lands lying west of the said state of Missouri and Territory of Arkansas, north and west of the Red River, south of the Kansas (Konza or Kaw) River, and east of a line to be drawn from the head sources of the Kansas, southwardly through the Rock Saline, with such reservations, for such consideration, and upon such terms as are hereinafter specified, expressed, and provided for."

The second article assured the Little Ones that "within the limits of the country, above ceded and relinquished, there shall be reserved, to and for the Grand and Little Osages . . . as long as they may choose to occupy the same, the following tract: Beginning at a point due east of White Hair's village and twenty-five miles west of the western boundary of the State of Missouri fronting on a north and south line, so as to leave ten miles north and forty miles south of the point of said beginning, and extending west with the width of fifty miles to the western boundary of the lands hereby ceded and relinquished by said Tribes or Nations."

Teachers and persons attached to the Nation would be allowed to come into the reservation, and the United States reserved the right to navigate all waters on navigable streams. The United States were to pay annually for twenty years, in money, merchandise, or provisions, amounting to $7,000. They were to furnish 600 cattle, 600 hogs, 1,000 domestic fowls, 10 yoke of oxen, 6 carts, and farming tools. They were to furnish a blacksmith and advisers necessary to build "comfortable and commodious dwelling houses" for the four principal chiefs.

The United States would assume the debts to trading houses to the amount of $4,125.80 if the Osages would release them from the first, third, and fifth articles of the treaty in 1808, in which they, the United

States, had agreed to station troops in garrison at Fort Osage (referred to as Fort Clark) for their (the Osages') protection, furnishing a blacksmith and delivering merchandise at Fire Prairie.

The United States would take over the claims of the Delawares against the Osages to the amount of $1,000 as part consideration for the signing of the treaty.

In Article 9, the United States agreed to assume the responsibility toward its own citizens, in paying to them damages which they claimed were perpetrated by the Osages; "to quiet animosities, which at present exist between a portion of the citizens of Missouri and Arkansas and the Osages in consequence of lawless depredations of the latter, the United States do, furthermore, agree to pay, to their own citizens, the full value of such property as they can legally prove to have been stolen or destroyed . . . since the year 1808 which has not been paid under former treaties . . . the sum not to exceed $5,000."

Merchandise was to be delivered to the Osage villages to the amount of $4,000, and $2,000 was to be paid before the delegation departed from St. Louis, plus horses and equipage to the value of $2,600.

Lands in the just-ceded part of the old domain were to be given to mixed-blood children on the Neosho and on the Marais des Cygnes, and the United States paid A. P. Chouteau $1,000, Paul Ballio, $250, and William Shirley Williams, $250 in liquidation of debts of the Osages to these traders.

This treaty was signed by some sixty chiefs, chieftains, and warrior leaders of the Grand and Little Osages, some of them being, Arrow-Going-Home, White Hair, Big Bear, He-That-Sees-Far, Not-Afraid, Little Chief, Big Soldier, Traveling Rain, and Little Soldier.

By this treaty the Little Ones were pushed into a region which lies within the southern part of modern Kansas. This strip had its eastern boundary twenty-five miles west of the modern Kansas-Missouri boundary and was fifty miles wide. Its western boundary was the international boundary between the United States and Mexico.

Witnessing the treaty that second day of June, 1825, at St. Louis were Edward Coles, governor of Illinois; A. McNair; Osage agent Pierre Chouteau; W. B. Alexander, sub-Indian agent; and P. L. Chouteau, subagent.

For some reason this treaty of 1825 seemed to William Clark to be a farce, or perhaps the hypocrisy of which he had been a part as agent was just becoming clear to him. He had no way of realizing that a tribe of nomadic people could not long stand in the way of energetic European expansion, and that one day or another this resistant Neolithic people would be pushed farther and farther west, or destroyed completely. No one who had official or other relations with them realized that there was any law except that which had been handed down to the white man from Palestine through Rome and England. If they had known something of earth-struggle and the laws of biology, they might have felt no need to hide behind chicanery and lies which they turned into comfortable Christian truths, hypocritical or humanitarian urges to "protect" the Little Ones.

When Ethan Allen Hitchcock was traveling in the Indian country in 1842, he talked with Clark. Everybody came to see Clark, since he was considered a noble soul and a man of high standards and quite the best authority on Indians.

Hitchcock wrote: "I have heard General Clark say that he offered to take the conditions of the treaty himself, pay the money and own the country, and he said at the time it was the hardest treaty on the Indians he ever made and that if he was to be damned hereafter it would be for making that treaty. It really seemed to weigh upon his conscience."

The new state of Missouri (admitted in 1820) had come into rather difficult times. The depression which followed the Napoleonic wars had just reached Missouri about 1819, and a year after statehood the legislature had declared a moratorium on debts. This was in June, 1821. The people were barely saved from the barter system after the failure of the banks, and there was more restlessness than ever and more invasions of the domain of the Little Ones, which were very much like crossing into a game refuge by hungry men.

This constant struggle between the Little Ones and the free men and the suspicious and restless settlers would have been a sufficient reason for the treaty of June, 1825, but soon after the depression of the early 1820's, steamboats began to ply the Missouri, and the fur trade expanded and the western terminus of the trade was pushed upstream from Franklin to Independence. Then there was the road to Santa Fe over which the people of the United States traded with Mexico. This had to be kept open between Independence and Santa Fe, but the Little Ones and tribes west and southwest owned the land through which the trail ran, and there had to be another "touching of the feather" between the Little Ones and the United States government this same year of 1825.

There were some beautiful oaks on the upper waters of the Neosho River growing in a gash of the limestone of the high prairie, and the travelers from the "States" to Santa Fe made this beautiful spot a stopping place, since there was plenty of both water and shelter from the summer sun and the mad winter winds.

Here in this gash in the limestone prairie, a party of men met to make a treaty, so that the travelers to Santa Fe could have tranquility of mind as they traveled with their goods between the mouth of the Konza River almost to the Big Bend of the Arkansas. The new trail of Heavy Eyebrows commerce would run through the country which the Little Ones had controlled and which they claimed along with their splinter, the Konzas. This was the beautiful land which even inspired the military-minded Zebulon Pike to poetic expression, stiff though it was.

Here where the wind waved the tall bluestem and there was still the roar of the bulls in Buffalo-Mating Moon, and bull wapiti challenged on moonlit nights in Deer-Hiding Moon, where the Little Old Men say the Padoucas were afraid to come, and the Pawnee-*maha* came only in large numbers and on very fast horses. There were no free men here yet; they were too easily seen here on the high prairie, and the Cherokees dared not come here either.

During the Yellow-Flower Moon, August 10, 1825, perhaps sixteen chiefs and leaders of the Little Ones came with their old factor, Major George C. Sibley, Commissioners Benjamin H. Reeves and Thomas Mather, and William Shirley Williams, formerly of the Harmony Mission, as interpreter.

The Osages-of-the-Oaks were not present. White Hair led the delegation, and there were Beautiful Bird and No Ears and others of the Little Osages. They were mostly Little Osages.

522

The party sat under a large oak and agreed that since the Congress of the United States was anxious to promote a direct commercial and friendly intercourse between citizens of the United States and Mexico, the United States needed a road to connect the two countries.

The road would be free to citizens of the United States and the citizens of Mexico and the Osages must promise not to molest them as long as they kept to the road, and they even agreed to aid them. The road was to extend to a "reasonable distance on each side," so that travelers might leave the trail to find subsistence and proper camping places.

For permission to use this trail without molestation, the United States would pay to the Grand and Little Osages $5,000 in money or merchandise, "at such place as they may desire."

Naturally the commissioners had brought about $300 worth of presents to produce the right frame of mind for the signing. They seemed to think that chiefs and leaders representing only part of the tribe, would make the agreement legal.

Of course, the treaty makers had ever in their thoughts the Osage resistance to the government's plan to resettle the immigrant Indians on their old domain, where they would aid the free men in killing off the remainder of their "brothers." The government believed that they might create a buffer between the settlers of the state of Missouri and the Osages represented by a rectangular area fifty miles from north to south and running parallel to and twenty-five miles west of the western boundary of the state of Missouri. On the west it would be one with the eastern boundary of the reservation of the Osages. This buffer was to be called "neutral lands" and left without inhabitants white or red.

Consequently it was soon being settled by free men, and they were soon crying that the Osage devils were taking their horses and traps and guns. Later, just ten years later, in 1835, this Neutral Land became Cherokee Neutral Land, when the Cherokees had begun to demand more land west of the Mississippi, fearing that they might become crowded there. This land was sold to them, not given.

It was a perfectly naïve idea of the far-away government, since an old Osage man could walk across the twenty-five miles and back in a day, and he could ride it in much less time. Also, by this time the men in Washington must have known that they couldn't control the free men, whisky making, theft, and murder.

42.   The God of the Heavy Eyebrows

Harmony mission had been established on the Marais des Cygnes just above the spot where the "factory" would be established later, in 1821. It was the third of the string of missions established by the American Board of Commissioners for Foreign Missions under the Congressional act of March 3, 1819, which carried an appropriation of $10,000 a year for the purpose of teaching the Indian children agriculture, reading, writing, and arithmetic. The President, being empowered to select the agency for this purpose, chose this organization.

The "brothers" and "sisters" of these three missions—Dwight in what is now Pope County, Arkansas, established for the Cherokees; Union in the modern Mayes County, Oklahoma, just above (about five miles) the little town of Mazie; and Harmony on the Marais des Cygnes River in Bates County, Missouri—were stark enthusiasts. Their journals of that period are extremely interesting and quite revealing. They put down such details as the Little Ones' surrender of Bad-Tempered Buffalo and other little gleanings which light up the dark corners which were untouched by the military and official reports. Their entries are revelatory in that they bring out a severe humanitarianism along with a darkness of mind into which little light concerning the God-concept of the Little Ones could penetrate. They were interested in the manner in which the Little Ones cooked their food, and what they ate, and the manner in which they dressed and how the women set up the lodges, and they were swayed by the oratory of the tall, handsome men, but they seemed to have agreed, at least in attitude, with the Union Mission medical man, Dr. Marcus Palmer, when he was first introduced to Osage cooking just after their arrival on the Neosho in 1821: "It was so strange," he said, "as well as new, and withal they were so filthy, that I believe, if I were to live with them, I should have a dangerous seasoning."

The "sisters" apparently drew close their moral and Christian skirts when they came near them, but they would assist the doctor as he cauterized a bear-claw wound or probed for a bullet or an arrowhead, and they yearned to mold the thoughts of the children, few though they were, who were brought to them.

They married and had children, and their babies died, and they themselves suffered with malaria and typhoid, and yet they toiled under the illusion and the hope of saving the Little Ones from the clutches of the devil. They walked in the sight of God, and were brave and foolhardy, yet they toiled and suffered and were whipped and driven by a solemn religious intensity, but they wore the blind bridles of righteousness, and they were right and unyielding and cold, and, being so, lured few savage souls from *Wah'Kon-Tah*.

Harmony at the Place-of-the-Many-Swans had the advantage of having two very intelligent interpreters who were possessed of synonyms of cultured English and French, one a Frenchman part-time interpreter and one a Welshman permanently employed by them; and yet they, too, failed. Noel Mongrain was married to White Hair's daughter and was the man Pike had tried to coerce into accompanying him in 1806, and William Shirley Williams, the Welshman, was married to a Big Hill girl and had translated the Bible into Osage and made the *Washashe-Wageressa-Pahugreh-Tse* [the Osage First Book]. He had come to the Little Ones as a missionary and was living with them when the brothers of the mission first arrived and later became disappointed by their virtuous unreason and left them. He was accustomed to translate the sermon every Sunday at precisely the same time, snow or heat, rain or drought. The Little Ones sat in a half-moon group, and the brother who was to give the sermon would appear, stiffly and with great dignity, looking over the quiet people with the frown of an avenging angel, clutching his Bible in both hands in front of him. These were the days when Christian men said God was vengeful.

Standing by him, Williams would translate what he said. He read the sermon before it was given, and his advice at times about whether it would be understood by the Little Ones would be coldly brushed aside. Williams was devil-touched. Not only was he married to a Big Hill girl, but he got ecstatically drunk periodically. This might have been overlooked by the settlers on the old Spanish grants near St. Charles whence he had come, but his opinions about religion seemed a bit tarnished here at Harmony Mission.

One Sunday he objected to the subject for the sermon, the story of Jonah and the whale, saying that this story would destroy confidence among the listeners. His advice was brushed aside, and the sermon was given and Williams dutifully translated it. A chieftain of the Wapiti rose and said, "We know the Heavy Eyebrows will lie, but this is the biggest lie we ever heard," and with this he drew his robe about him and walked swiftly away. The others stayed with their eyes closed and made no move, but they stayed only from courtesy.

It is doubtful that these dedicated people would have gone in their fervor as far as the early Jesuits had in glorification through being burned alive by the Hurons, but they were martyrs in another way. They faced death in every form, from man and animal and insect and weather, and it is a pity that they could not understand the Little Ones' prayers to *Wah'Kon-Tah* at dawn and were convinced that the Little Ones had "no correct idea of the one superior God." It is a pity, on the other hand, that the Little Ones could not possibly understand that they were very brave men and women, for they might have attributed more importance to them because of this.

A Lazarist father came to the Little Ones of the Place-of-the-Many-Swans about 1819, and was with them periodically between that date and 1822, since he was roving missionary and was establishing a mission to be called Florissant, north of St. Louis. He was a man of culture and his name was De la Croix.

The Black Robes said that the Little Ones had sent for him or that they had made a special trip to St. Louis to ask that a Black Robe be sent among them. The people at Harmony Mission said that the Little Ones had requested their presence as well. In 1725, a French interpreter had translated a speech of a chieftain to the Frenchmen (at the time Bourgmont was preparing to take the intertribal group to Paris), and to please himself and the Frenchmen, he made the chieftain say, "We love the French and hate the English."

The Little Ones had a profound respect for men who claimed power from the Great Mysteries, and were animal-cautious about offending such men, fearing their "medicine." Since they were in a state of fear and agitation about the trespassers and the slaughtering of their "brothers," they might actually have been grasping at straws and willingly accepted the holy men of the Heavy Eyebrows, even requesting that they come to live among them, but not because the light of Christianity had crept into their hearts.

Father de la Croix perhaps had more luck with them than the Protestants, since the Frenchmen married to Osage wives were devout Catholics and the Father himself quite flexible and cheerful, eating their food with jollity and even showing respect for their Little Old Men and those who had "medicine."

The docile Osage women would go the way of their French husbands and Father de la Croix baptized their offspring, as well as themselves, and at least he could boast of a flock; and he rode up and down the river like a circuit rider from Florissant to Côte sans Desein, thence to Arrow Rock, and then to the "factory" at the Place-of-the-Many-Swans. He heard confessions and gave the sacrament and baptized the children and remarried the Frenchmen and the Osage wives by the formula of the Church.

It was about this time, according to the Buffalo gens of the Big Hills, that the Little Ones learned about the devil, and they somehow in their confusion believed him to be a rattlesnake, so they called him *shi-ku*. It was thought that they got the idea from a statuette which Father de la Croix showed them of the Virgin Mary holding the Infant and standing barefooted on a coiled snake. Father de la Croix might have told them through Maugraine (Mongrain) that this was the devil in the form of the snake being conquered by the Virgin.

It might seem to the Little Ones that since they were unable proper-ly to protect their "brothers" which *Wah'Kon-Tah* had given them, and since they had allowed *Mo'n-Sho'n,* Mother Earth, the Sacred One, to grow smaller like an old woman who is bound by the ash heaps circling the village, *Wah'Kon-Tah* threw his crooked lance of fire more frequently at them and sent the earth-shaking thunder more often, and the cloud that dropped its tail from the sky and took all loose things as well as men and women with it came now even in Buffalo-Mating Moon and in the Light-of-Day-Returns Moon, or even in Yellow-Flower Moon.

Wah'Kon-Tah's anger may have seemed more terrible and more frequent in their minds now because of their remissness, but still they belonged to him, and to him alone.

When the missionaries first came among the Little Ones, they agreed with everyone else who had seen them that they were tall, graceful, and quite handsome and behaved with a noble air. The Reverend Pixley said that one could not possibly believe in their sav-age ferocity and the obscenity of their ordinary conversation until one had lived with them for a while and learned their language. The interpreters, being half- or full-blood Frenchmen, chiefly failed to translate the conversations verbatim. The speeches were not thus burdened. However, it took less than ten years to convince the Rev-erend Pixley and others that they were not worth saving. Their re-sistance to the missionaries resulted not so much in bafflement among the missionaries as in some manner it seemed to damage their vanity.

Finally, the Reverend Pixley, a literate, facile writer and a man of high principles, after trying to win them to his concept of God, gave up. He had gone bear hunting with them once for the sake of cama-raderie and had nearly frozen, and was horrified when he saw the young men break the ice on the river in order to bathe.

He had sat with them at Harmony and Union missions and very carefully explained God to them, and had tried to answer their ques-tions. Some of them asked questions about the benevolent, omnipo-tent, vengeful God he presented to them: "Where is God; have you seen him?" And he wrote in his disillusionment to the corresponding secretary of the Board: "They speak of Him as hateful and bad instead of being amiable and good, saying they 'hate him; he is of bad temper; they would shoot him if they could see him.' "

Pixley was more disgusted with than horrified by this sacrilege. To the Little Ones the God of the Heavy Eyebrows seemed to be their enemy since everything had gone wrong with them since he came. He was an enemy God.

One day the Reverend Pixley was trying to explain to an Osage that the soul and the body had separate existence, and as he talked, he noted the Osage was intent on catching a fly. Finally, he managed to catch it, then he squashed it between his fingers, then placing it on the floor, he smashed it under his foot "until not a vestige of it remained," then he looked at Pixley and asked, "Where's the soul?"

When Dodge of Harmony questioned Sans Nerf about Osage religion, he said he knew about God from the Little Old Men. He knew nothing about sin. He was sure *Wah'Kon-Tah* hated him and the Osages since He did not help them keep the white men from killing their "brothers."

The Reverends Dodge, Pixley, Chapman, Montgomery, and others attempted to save the savages in the first years of the missions, and were filled with hope because of the nobility and bearing of the Little Ones, but now after seven years Pixley could only defend his failure and salve his hurt vanity, and the once noble, handsome "children of nature" had become thieves and liars, whose conversation was not to be translated for the ears of civilized men.

He had taken hope in the establishing of Hopefield in 1823–24, a branch mission four miles up the river, on the opposite bank from Union. Here the Little Ones who wished to come would be taught to grow their own food, and be taught weaving, and religion. At Hopefield, Chapman and Requa had small success. Some came there and actually planted and one *Paw-Hunkah* (spelled by the missionaries "Paw-hunk-shaw") was the very first of the Little Ones to go to market with produce. He and his family and others took their corn and vegetables to the garrison at Fort Smith.

The missionaries had gained some ground during an unidentified epidemic among the Little Ones. Dr. Palmer had succeeded in curing some of them, but failed in his attempts to save the life of the wife of

530

"Les-sa-mai-neh." After her death the missionaries began to plead that she should be buried according to the customs of Christians, and her husband and relatives "abstained from all the usual heathenish customs," except the painting of her face so that she would be identified in Spiritland.

Her face was carefully painted and she was placed in a coffin and taken to the grave on a bier, which was followed by all the people of the gens, and the missionaries and the Osages listened to the address at the graveside "with seriousness."

This was a victory for the missionaries, but it was a single one apparently as was the victory of *Paw-Hunkah* as a truck gardener. Pixley, who had been at Harmony Mission, was inspired by the success at Hopefield, and he and a Mr. Bright established a branch mission on the Neosho River ninety miles from Union and seventy miles from Harmony and called it Neosho.

About the time the civil government was being established for the village of Arrow-Going-Home, the missionaries got two young Osages to go to New England and finish their education at Foreign Missions School at Cornwall, Connecticut, and as was the custom among the missionaries, gave them the names of benefactors of the missions. One was called Stephen van Renssalear and the other Robert Monrau. This had been Tallai's influence, since one was his nephew and the other a relative. He had brought his son and another to Union when he was going on the buffalo hunt after the winter of the great hunger. He asked the missionaries not to make them "half white men," but to give them full dress of white man's clothes. "I want to see them dressed before I leave you so that I shall not weep when I am hunting."

But the Reverend Pixley got into trouble with the agent, which caused the abandonment of the branch station, Neosho, and it seemed that he thought the Osages were a complete failure.

When asked to write in full about these people whom he had admired in the first flush of his dreams, he could write nothing good of them. There was no single man who stood out as being worthy, and he seems to have forgotten his little successes during the years and his first enthusiasm.

531

He was disgusted with the women who cut their hair when they went into mourning, which ought to have been their "glory," and it reminded him of the Prophet's declaration, "Cut off their hair, oh, Jerusalem." As for the dawn-red paint and the charcoal-smeared faces of the warriors, they reminded him forcibly of those hypocrites of whom our Savior speaks "who disfigures their faces that they might appear unto men to be just." The Little Ones had been the failure, his vanity advised.

The corresponding secretary in 1828 had asked him to supply biographical sketches of Osages, and he had replied, "that in this regard" he knew of none that would be interesting "and deserves to be rescued from oblivion." He would, though, give a sort of biographical sketch and general chronology of an Osage man's existence.

"I would first present him to you bound to a board. I would next present him as a sturdy boy, almost without covering, ranging about with his bow and arrows in quest of birds, fishes and grasshoppers."

At length, he wrote, that same boy would begin to "put on the air of a man, and swell with self-importance. Today you may see him with blackened face and surly attitude, neither eating or drinking, but howling and crying in conformity to the manly custom, that he may find success in war."

After several days his fiendish image is "metamorphosed into a spritely, tripping dandy, most fantastically painted, his head glittering with tinsel and waving with plumes, stalking along with little bells tinkling at his feet, admiring himself and elated with the admiration he fancies himself to be receiving from others."

These could have been the words of a prideful man with damaged vanity, speaking of an imperiously resistant race, rather than a man of European culture conscious of his own superiority and righteousness, speaking of a "savage . . . a child of Nature."

In the next stage of Pixley's bio-chronology, the young Osage is ready for the war movement. He equips himself with a bow and arrows, "a little parched corn and a spare pair of moccasins" and rides or marches off to acquire that honor which comes to him for "stealing horses, killing men and murdering women and children." He writes that if the Osage falls in war, he will ever after be honored and will live in the memory of the tribe, "or if more fortunate he escapes the hatchet of his enemies and lights on a little child, he gives it a gentle rap, then hands it to another of his companions who does the same, to a third who cuts off its head, and thus by a singular refinement of policy, three braves are made by the killing of one person and that an infant."

Then he writes further that the young man becomes a brave and receives honors. Then he is ready for marriage, "and his bride takes him to the lodge of her parents, where he takes the command and ever afterwards holds the whole household in subjection to himself."

Then he grows old; as Pixley puts it in his letter, "It is not long before he begins to descend," and as he grows older, there is less and less respect for him until he is old; he "at last dies without virtue" and his burial "is like the burial of an animal."

His bitterness was so deep that he recalled even trivial incidents wherein the Osages would criticize members of their tribe who adopted white man's clothing and would drive them back to the robe through their scorn. He remembered the incident when Antler-Maker's favorite son, Bad Arrow, was brought to the mission branch called Neosho and was rechristened Phillip Milledoler for a Dr. Milledoler. He had given the boy a gray blanket which he had used in exchange for work he wanted him to do about the mission. The boy gave it back with shyness but with great determination. When questioned, his mother said the people at the village would laugh at him because the blanket was not blue, the color besides red they now approved of over the other trade blankets. Pixley also remembered that "such a thing as a basket, I never saw among them."

But even now it had never occurred to him or the other missionaries that Antler-Maker had not brought his son to the mission because he, Antler-Maker, was beginning to see the "Light." At the time, this had given them a feeling of triumph; however, Antler-Maker had brought him there because the attack of the Cherokees on the Osage hunting camp was still fresh in his and the people of Arrow-Going-Home's memory, and he knew that if That-Thing-on-Its-Head People attacked this time when the Little Ones were on the hunt, his boy would be safe. He would be with the missionaries, and not only

533

that, he would be dressed in the clothes of the Heavy Eyebrows. He wasn't sure that the people at the mission would keep their promise to make his son a "full white man and not a half white man," so he stayed to see him thus dressed, and went on the hunt with a heart like the oak gall.

The missionaries had missed a great opportunity with Bad-Tempered-Buffalo. He had sat in the Heavy Eyebrows prison with Little-Eagle-That-Gets-What-He-Wants and debated with himself whether it would be better to kill himself or be hanged by the rope of the Heavy Eyebrows. He thought long hours of his spirit which the rope would choke off and which would never gain its freedom to haunt the people of his father's village until they gave it a home. He knew that, if his spirit were free, on moonlight nights it would be a screech owl, and someone might recognize it and the gens would do something about it.

But there would never be a wandering spirit if the rope choked it off. He didn't know what might happen if he destroyed himself, but at least the spirit could escape. No Little One ever did this, but he finally came to the conclusion that it would be better, and he made the attempt.

Another thing he realized as he sat in the prison at Little Rock: there was no aid for him since there had been no dreams that could live in the morning light. He had beat the drum rhythm on the wooden *wah-don-skas* there in the prison, and had sung his prayers softly so that the jailers could not hear. But there were only rats there in that place, and there was no rat medicine. Not even Grandfather the Sun could see him there. He had a great respect for the medicine of the Heavy Eyebrows now, and he was ready to place himself under the authority of the Heavy Eyebrows' God. He had shown himself more powerful than *Wah'Kon-Tah*.

When he was pardoned by the President in 1825, he started home up the Arkansas. He was a lone, sick, chastened Osage now, and his hair had grown and the roach was almost "drowned" by it, so that the people whom he met on the trail could not know that this *wa-xpa-thi'n,* this poor man, was the great Bad-Tempered-Buffalo. The

Heavy Eyebrows gave him food and shelter. Now he was no menace to their security, and he had nothing they wanted.

The Little Ones were facile with the phrase, "Have pity on me," as they used it every rising of the Morning Star; and when they wished to deceive, the phrase became protective, like the coloration of the fur and feathers of animals and birds. It was perhaps more like the kildeer fluttering up from her nest to fall crying and with wings up and quivering like one in dying spasms, so that the disturber of the nest might think her crippled and run after her, while she kept just out of his reach and then finally flew off on sound wing.

But it was said that the once mighty Bad-Tempered-Buffalo sincerely asked for pity, as he rubbed his index finger on the back of his hand, which meant, "I am poor."

He came to the new mission, Hopefield, and brought his family and some relatives, and the people there were deeply pleased when he asked about the God of the Heavy Eyebrows. The missionaries were ready and joyous over this great man's seeking to learn of God. They sat long hours and attempted to explain to him about God's bounty and the hereafter, and perhaps about God's anger. But Bad-Tempered-Buffalo could only understand, he believed, if he went out and fasted in the old way.

He took off his clothing except his breechclout and his leggings and moccasins and went out onto the prairie hills and took only water for seven days. He watched the clouds and listened to the voices of the wind in the grasses and watched the winds of Just-Doing-That Moon pushing the clouds, and he saw Grandfather the Sun tint them before he went to rest.

The *sho-mi-kase* were still singing, and the wolves sang sometimes when he himself chanted to the Morning Star and asked for help to know about the strong God of the Heavy Eyebrows, but he received no message. Maybe it was because at this time, about 1830, there were few buffalo here in this place, and there was no message for one of the Buffalo gens. As he grew weaker from hunger, he had no dreams of significance; there were only the winds which *Wah'Kon-Tah* sent through the grasses, the excited talk of the flocking kildeer, and the love song of *sho-mi-kase,* the coyote.

The Moon Woman was sitting on the far horizon, and these were the voices and the things familiar to him from childhood; these were voices of *Wah'Kon-Tah,* and there was no sign from the God of the Heavy Eyebrows.

Emaciated and depressed, he went back to the mission and told the Reverend Montgomery that he couldn't find God out there; Had *he* seen him lately?

Montgomery wrote in a letter of March 7, 1832: "Mad Buffalo fasted seven days on the tops of hills and by the roots of trees. His ideas cannot reach beyond the visible evidence," and then he added: "He seems to meet a wall which he cannot penetrate against which his thoughts struck and often slipped aside." He used Osage imagery; this must have been the way Bad-Tempered-Buffalo expressed his frustration to the missionary. And again Montgomery wrote: "He wanted a new Bible to keep in his lodge, and leave to his children."

Bad-Tempered-Buffalo would take no chances. He had known the power of the God of the Heavy Eyebrows, and some day he would have the women make a shrine for the new Bible like the shrine of the sacred hawk, the *wah-hopeh.*

But one young lady of the mission had not given up. She was Cornelia Pelham, and she wrote faithfully to her cousins. She threw light into many a dark corner ignored by the reports of the missionaries, the military, the commissioners, the traders, and the agents.

She seemed to have two concerns: One was the discontinuance of the factories, and she didn't know why in the world the government wanted to abandon the factory at Fort Osage in 1822 and disrupt Harmony Mission school when the Osages of the Marais des Cygnes came to the Neosho. The other was the atmosphere of abandonment of the project to snatch the savage souls from the devil, and she was vehement in urging people in the East to send more money and more missionaries to obviate "the dreadful doom which awaits the impenitent Osages."

In one letter she wrote about a conversation she had with a young man called William. The young man had said that his little sister asked the same questions the Osages asked about God. She had asked this question of her mother: "Mother, can you see God?" and her mother had replied: "Ellen, can you see the wind?"

"No, mother, but I can feel it, and do look how it shakes the rose bushes and the tall trees."

William then said that their mother told them that they could feel the presence of God more powerfully than the wind, "if we kept him in our thoughts. She said to us, you may see him in those beautiful mountains that skirt the horizon, those floating clouds fringed with gold. You may see him in the sun, moon and stars and everything you see shows his goodness, wisdom and power. She talks to us about God and heaven and hell and Christ and salvation every day. I wish the Osages could hear her."

The Jesuits were active among the Little Ones of the Place-of-the-Many-Swans, since Bishop du Bourg had sent Father Charles de la Croix to them by their request. It is supposed that a party of Little Ones had gone to St. Louis to ask that Black Robes be sent among them. This delegation was supposed to have been led by an influential man, if not a chieftain, called by the French *Sans Nerf,* Without-Courage or Without-Nerve. He was spoken of by people around the mission as being of some importance in the tribe, it having been suggested that he was really the hereditary chief.

It is difficult to identify him, since the French had probably misinterpreted his name. About this time there lived a man whose son would become chief of the Little Osages later. His name was *No-Pa-Watha,* called later as *"No-Pa-Walla." No-Pa-Watha* means "Thunder-Fear," though it has nothing to do with fear of thunder, but rather means that the man might inspire the fear which thunder inspires, and therefore was named Thunder-Fear.

If he led the delegation to St. Louis and if he is identified as Thunder-Fear, the people he led would have been Little Osages from Fort Osage, and not Grand Osages from the Place-of-the-Many-Swans. Anyway, after Father de la Croix came to the Little Ones, Bishop du Bourg got the Jesuits again to take a deep interest in the Little Ones.

This was in 1820, and by 1823 Bishop du Bourg had gone to Washington to talk with President Monroe and Secretary Calhoun about establishing schools and missions among the Little Ones, and got the government to contribute $200 a year toward the support of the missionaries. He offered the Jesuits his farm near Florissant, Missouri, sixteen miles north of St. Louis, to be used as a novitiate and a mission post for the Indians. They accepted.

In 1827, Father Charles van Quickenbourne visited the Little Ones on the Neosho. He wrote: "From Harmony Mission I set off for the great villages situated on the banks of the Neosho two days journey from Harmony. About 100 Indians came out to meet the agent whose company I was. We put up at Mr. Chouteau's place. On the Feast of St. Louis, August 25th, I had the happiness of saying the first mass ever said in this country. I stayed with them ten weeks and baptized twenty-seven people."

Father Quickenbourne made another visit to the Little Ones and baptized seventeen people, but there is no record of this extant. On his third visit in 1830, he visited all the lodges, beginning at the village on the Marmiton near the modern Fort Scott, Kansas; then traveling southwest, he visited along the Neosho as far as the mouth of Saline Creek, north of Fort Gibson perhaps forty miles. He established missionary stations on Chouteau, Pryor, and Cabin creeks. This was the "earliest exercise of the Catholic ministry in that part of the Union."

On his visit to the Osages in 1834, Father Quickenbourne would select a site for the Osage mission, which would become famous in the lives of the Little Ones.

Before the Reverend Pixley abandoned his station to go to a white settlement in Missouri where he would get more gratifying response, he wrote to the corresponding secretary: "As if it were not enough to have to contend with the native prejudices of the Indians, strengthened by the uniform ill treatment which from the earliest times has characterized the conduct of the whites who have dealings with them, we have recently had a Jesuit Catholic Priest out here baptizing the half-breed children, giving out medals and telling the Osages that we do not teach the truth, and were not the true ministers of religion."

43. Little Chief and Hawk Woman Go to France

An osage along with missourias and others had gone to France in 1725 with Bourgmont, and the first White Hair had gone to Washington to see President Jefferson and then had gone on to New York City, where a Bible had been given him by the New York Missionary Society, and it is said that this Bible and a "tomahawk" were buried with him on a mound at the Place-of-the-Many-Swans in 1808. Traveling Rain and No Ears, Big Soldier and Makes-Tracks-Far-Away and possibly Thunder Fear had visited Washington just after the United States took over the Louisiana Purchase; and Mr. Jefferson had given them medals and military coats and other things and was very anxious that they have an understanding of the great power of the Americans.

Bourgmont had taken his Indians over to Paris in 1725 so that they could be awed by the power of France, and the Spaniards had done everything in their power to impress the strong tribes of the Missouri; but in 1827, a man by the name of David Delauney dressed himself in United States Army uniform to gain the confidence of the Osages so that he could carry out a promotion. He got the Frenchman interpreter for the Osages called Paul Loise to aid him. Loise spoke Osage, but he was later characterized by the United States consul to Paris, Barnet, as "illiterate, but as usual cupidity seems to be his ruling passion."

This is the same Paul Loise Governor Meriwether Lewis had ap-

539

pointed as official interpreter to the Osages in 1808 and whom he called Paul "Louis" and in whom he assured President Jefferson he had great confidence. He refused to believe that "Louis" would wantonly misinterpret.

Loise had been ordered off the reservation by the then Osage agent, I. F. Hamtranck. But urged by Delauney, he waited for the agent to leave for St. Louis, then slipped back onto the reservation and got twelve Osages together for a junket to France. This promotion had apparently been long in the making, if one is to believe the story of four years of hunting on the part of at least a group of Little Ones in preparation for the trip.

There were twelve Osages who had been persuaded by Delauney's grand paradings of officialdom in his impersonations of an officer of the United States Army and by Loise's blandishments. On their way down the Missouri with their harvest of furs to be sold in New Orleans or in France, their raft was wrecked near St. Louis and they lost everything, but fortunately all swam ashore. Here six of the party decided they had had enough and went back upriver at the first opportunity. The other six must have been well convinced by Delauney and Loise and one François Tesson. They decided to go on.

There were *Ki-He-Kah Shinkah,* Little Chief, who was thirty-six; and eighteen-year-old *Mi-Ho'n-Ga,* Sacred Sun; the latter's relative, *Gthe-Do'n-Wi'n,* Hawk Woman, who was nineteen and Little Chief's wife. Then there were *Washinka Sabe,* Black Bird, possibly husband of Sacred Sun; *Mo'n-Sho'n A-ki-Da Tonkah,* Great-Protector-of-the-Land, who apparently called himself Big Soldier and was called by the French, *l'Orateur.* Big Soldier was not a name but an honored office. There were three warriors chosen because of their many *o-do'n,* war honors, to head the ten hunters chosen from both *Tzi-Sho* and *Hunkah* to serve as officers of the buffalo hunts. One of these honored warriors was chosen from the Thunder gens of the *Tzi-Sho* and called Chief Soldier, one from the Deer gens, called Little Soldier, and one from the Bear-Panther gentes, called Big Soldier. The man who allowed himself to be called Big Soldier while on the Continent was possibly a Nobody strutting before Gallic enthusiasm. As a matter of fact, later, when Victor Tixier was traveling on the Osage prairies, Edward Chouteau told him that Big Soldier had been a town crier, whom the French would call Marmiton, meaning "scullion."

The sixth member of the gullibles was a man called *Minckchatahooh,* which is not translatable by the modern Little Ones.

These six people, the four men and two women, seemed to need some tribal or gentile distinction, since they were all quite young except the one who called himself Big Soldier, he being forty-five. The fact that he was not the leader, but was under the leadership of Little Chief, would indicate that he had no gentile or tribal standing, that what Chouteau had said about him was true.

When they arrived in New Orleans, much was made of them, and the men's hearts swelled.

They arrived at Havre on July 27, 1827, and *La Quotienne* of August 6 said that the Osages occupied the public attention all that week and that the streets were filled with people, even the masts of the ships in the harbor. They could scarcely leave the vessel to arrive at the Hôtel Hollande, and supplementary guards had to be employed when they started for the theater in a *calèche*. The hotel and the *calèche* were surrounded by the citizens.

Delauney had done his work well. Crowds at Rouen had awaited *"leurs majestés missouriennes,"* their Missourian Majesties, and when they arrived, ran alongside of the *calèche* to the Hôtel de Léon. The men were dressed in blue frockcoats and the two women wore red trade blankets. While the crowds milled in the streets before the hotel, four sentinels of the Royal Guard were stationed there. Upstairs the Osages played cards, a game new to them and which fascinated them.

At the theater they were seated in the governor's box with the Prince. He spoke to the jammed theater, and the Little Chief, who was called "Prince of the Missouri," answered: "My brothers, the good things done for us by the French people have entered through my eyes to my heart."

The opera was by Cherubini, and during the second act, the Osages took refreshments with the Prince and drank to the people. At the end of the opera the Prince said to the audience: "Never, perhaps did

541

our immense theater contain such a crowd . . . the strangers alone attract every eye."

The Osages liked fruits and drank only Madeira and water, and a great variety of gifts came to them, from fruit and wine to earrings, cigars, and cloth and trinkets. At the end of their stay they appeared upon the balcony and made their *adieus* to the people in the streets, who hailed them with scarcely more freedom than they might hail royalty. Their dignity inspired respect.

It was the same when they arrived in Paris and were driven to the Hôtel Terasse on the Rue de Rivoli. They came out on the balcony and received the salutations of the crowds that filled the street. Here one of the men appeared in a trade blanket, with his right arm bare, the blanket draped over the left shoulder and arm. The others were naked to the middle. On their arms they wore "large plates of silver," one between elbow and shoulder and the other as a bracelet. They wore several strands of pearls around the neck, with round plates of silver hanging from them like the mussel-shell gorgets. They wore un-Osage-like headdresses with snowy egret plumes colored and held in place not by beaver or otter bandeaus but by red trade goods. They held war hatchets, decorated.

The one woman who appeared had a "small stature" and her face was "full of sweetness." The observer noted her black hair parted down the center with the red line down the parting, representing the dawn road of Grandfather the Sun. She wore strands of pearls and a red blanket. She wore everything that had been given her.

They went to the home of M. le Baron de Damas, where they were the special guests at a breakfast for forty. The newspapers reported: "These foreigners were the object of the most delicate attention."

They were taken to Saint Cloud to meet the King, Charles X, and following their every movement, as were the journals of France, were the journals of New Orleans, which were taking a species of pride in their royal welcome and attention. The *Courier* of November 5, 1827, said that they were "making a considerable figure in Paris" and that they had been introduced at court, "caressed at diplomatic dinners, admired at the operas, and in short distinguished as the lions of the day. *Messieurs, les Sauvage éclipse Mi'lords les Anglais.*"

It was reported that at Saint Cloud Little Chief's face was painted with blue and red when they met the King, and after paying their respects to the Dauphin and the Dauphiness, they had breakfast with the Captain of the Guards. They were invited everywhere, and were taken to the theater so often that they became bored, even with all the glasses in the theater on them continually. They sat impassively, but because of their passivity, the audience thought they were bored. Certainly they would have given no sign of boredom. On the Neosho and formerly at the Place-of-the-Many-Swans, one had to sit for hours listening to the chieftain and the warriors of many *o-do'n,* and to the long medicine talk of the missioners, where one sat passively with closed eyes, behind which one could escape to thrilling personal experiences. Here at the theater in Paris it was not unlike the medicine talk of the Black Robes saying mass. They did not close their eyes.

One night Little Chief became angry, and the people could understand royal anger. He and his party had gone to the foyer for entr'acte relaxation, but the people left their seats to crowd them against the railings. He said that he would not come to the theater again, that he had escaped the anger of the sea, and he didn't want to be smothered here. Gendarmes and Delauney got them out into the Place de la Comédie.

The Frenchmen commented often on the fact that they were unusually continent as regards drinking of spirits and on the fact that they venerated old age. When they saw very old people as they were driven along, they even rose in their seats to raise their hands to them and say, "Haugh, my father [mother]," and when they left the Hôtel Dieu, where they visited, they commented to Loise that the woman who was the superior there must be very good since *Wah'Kon-Tah* had allowed her to become so old.

They didn't seem to know that Delauney was charging the public to see them, and that perhaps there was an agreement between Delauney and the theater owners. Delauney must have been dizzy with his success, and there was only one other attraction in all of Paris to give him competition: a giraffe had just been received at the Jardin du Roi.

The Court of Assizes members were fortunate in being able to see

543

the "Prince of the Missouri" and his entourage free when they were summoned there to appear as witnesses against a hotel servant who had stolen thirteen pieces of silver and some kashmir from them.

When interest began to wane, Delauney, who incidentally must have been a very able promoter and entrepreneur, arranged a *Fête Extraordinaire* and advertised that the Osages would take part. The entrance fee was five francs. They would dance the savage dances of the Missouri, he assured the public. Also there would be a balloon ascension, and Depuis, the balloonist, asked the Osages to watch from a special vantage point.

The newspapers reported that their "astonishment was complete," and that Little Chief had expressed a desire to fly and see the earth far down as the eagle could see it.

When Delauney learned about this, he must have been overcome with excitement, and he immediately asked if Little Chief would actually go up with Depuis. Strangely enough, he was the only one of the party who might dare to do this, since he would be under the protection of his life symbol, the symbol of the Eagle gens. He must have been impressed by the voyage across the sea, since he compared all dangers with it. He seemed to think that since he had conquered this great danger, he could conquer any danger.

Naturally the event of the "Prince of the Missouris'" ascension was widely and extravagantly advertised, and the crowd was enormous. Little Chief was very calm and dignified as he entered the basket, but, reported the journals, he uttered a "piercing and savage chant several times while in the air."

Actually, he had entered the basket thinking he might die, so the "piercing and savage chant" was merely a prayer-song, either to Grandfather the Sun or to the golden eagle, asking for the power to stay afloat.

Every maker of things in Paris embraced the opportunity. Vendors on the street were selling Indian dolls dressed in native costume, and shops were selling work bags with pictures of the six Osages embroidered or otherwise decorating them, as well as bronze groups of them which the students used as paperweights. Even the bakers seized the opportunity and sold Indian figures made of spiced bread. It can be assumed that Delauney sold the rights to all these opportunists.

Even the writers and would-be writers wrote articles and books, especially about the history and domestic and religious life of the Osages. Some of the naïve believed the fictions of both Loise and Delauney. Neither of these men could afford to answer that they didn't know anything about the Osages, but here they sensed the reflected glory that many a buckskin clad, long-haired histrionic strutter would feel later during the wars with the Plains Indians. They must have answers in order to remain with "their Missouri Majesties" in the camera lens of public attention.

French males were fascinated by the Osage women, even though one, *Mi-Ho'n-Ga,* Sacred Sun, wife of Black Bird, was obviously *enceinte,* and had begun to weep in her yearning for home where she might give birth to her baby in their own village. This weeping brought on the keening of Hawk Woman and distressed Delauney, who was now for some incredible reason going into debt.

The French women seemed to have been fascinated by the warriors, and Big Soldier said that he had been "married" three times while in France.

But the interest faded, and Gallic interest and emotionalism, the easiest to arouse, is also the quickest to fade. Soon the Osages were wandering with their guide here and there, and Delauney had begun to avoid creditors. He had borrowed some 9,000 francs from a M. Marcillac, and his widow was now suing him and had him arrested and incarcerated. In Ghent the Osages were called in as witnesses in a suit for libel by Delauney against a literary man because of an article in the *Sentinelle.* The trial was open to the public, and, as usual, there was a large crowd. The interpreter for the Osages was their old friend l'Abbé Charles de la Croix, who had come to the Place-of-the-Many-Swans in 1821 and who was the founder of Florissant just out of St. Louis.

The women wept and played cards and smoked the long black cigars, and the men were kept close to their quarters in the various hotels, since Delauney feared that they might try to find their way home. But now they were an unwanted responsibility, and he would soon forsake them, running from the responsibility of feeding them.

On February 10, 1828, at the Hôtel de la Pommelette, Liège, Belgium, Sacred Sun gave birth to twin daughters, and they were baptized in the church of St. Denis, sponsored by wealthy women in Brussels who stood as godmothers to them and saw them named with holy names. Maria Theresa Ludovica Clementina Black Bird was adopted by a very wealthy woman of Liège and died the next year, while Maria Elizabeth Josepha Julia Carola remained with her mother, Sacred Sun.

The unhappy Osages were seen at Amsterdam, Dresden, Frankfurt, and Berlin, perhaps fleeing with their guide and Loise, but not knowing why. The fee for looking at them had been reduced. Then one day there was an article in *Le Moniteur Universal,* January 12, 1829, which had been taken from a Munich journal: "The Osages abandoned at Fribourg, Breslau, by their conductor have been brought here by a friend of humanity; they find themselves in the greatest destitution, suffering from hunger. When did these savages, welcomed in the courts, applauded at theaters, become the concern of the public? Today, curiosity no longer attracts the crowds; at least charity should sympathize with these unfortunates who are without friends; without a country, abandoned in a land they do not know, isolated by the language and their habits . . . in civilized Europe."

Now came the flood of Gallic sympathy and humanity. Bishops, magistrates, and royalty were aroused and gave them presents again, and the great Lafayette gave them medals of his own image and collected money for them. They had to divide into two parties to get home. One party consisted of Black Bird, Minckchatahooh, and Sacred Sun. These were placed on a boat at Bordeaux in April, 1830. The other party, consisting of Little Chief, Hawk Woman, and Big Soldier, to whom Paul Loise and his son, also abandoned by Delauney, had attached themselves, were rescued by M. Du Bourg, bishop of Montauban. He had read of their plight, and he got them to come to Montauban and stay with him until he could raise funds for them. They told him their story, and he listened to them and gave them a feeling of security since he was the same Bishop Du Bourg who had sent Father de la Croix to them from St. Louis. This party, despite the fact that they were aided by United States Consul Barnet and the great Lafayette, were discovered by Delauney creditors as they were taking boat at Havre, and here their luggage and all their gifts and medals were seized.

They were landed at Norfolk, Virginia, and were held there by a determined patroness, one Rachel Henderson [Anderson] until the War Department could pay the bill.

Later, Lafayette recovered their gifts and other property which had been seized at Havre and had them sent on to Sacred Sun and Big Soldier, Black Bird and Minckchatahooh, having died of smallpox aboard ship.

The former *wah-tsde-pia'n,* the town crier, who called himself Big Soldier, walked in afflated glory for the rest of his long life. He wore the Lafayette medal constantly and seemed to be ever present when some traveler asked for information.

44. The "Buffalo Indians" and the Immigrants

ARROW-GOING-HOME DIED in 1828, and the people at Union Mission expressed great sorrow at his passing. The *Arkansas Gazette* eulogized him. He had made a great impression on whomever he met.

The Arkansas Osages still carried on with their attempts to protect their "brothers" between the Arkansas and the Red rivers and as far west as the 100th meridian at least. Here, however, on the plains they were simply carrying on their traditional range-line struggles with the Pawnees and the Comanches and the Apaches and now the Kiowas.

They were constantly in trouble through the decade of the 1830's, and had not moved with the others up the Neosho and Verdigris rivers into their reservation in the modern state of Kansas. These people of the Place-of-the-Oaks, the "Shainers," the Arkansas Osages, constituted more than one-third of the tribe. They didn't seem to realize that they had signed their Place-of-the-Oaks away just as the others had signed away the Place-of-the-Many-Swans by the treaty of June, 1825.

The "Claremore Band," as they were often called now, didn't seem to realize that their old domain had been given to the Cherokees by the provision of the Cherokee–United States treaty of 1828 and according to the laws of the Heavy Eyebrows they were now trespassing.

This old home of the Arkansas Osages had been given to the Cherokees in 1828 and much of the same land had been given also

548

to the Creeks, so that the two tribes had to settle the boundary in 1833. Arrow-Going-Home's old domain now belonged to the Creeks and Cherokees.

Even the buildings of the old A. P. Chouteau trading post on the east side and three miles above the mouth of the Verdigris were taken over by the Creeks, and by the 1828 treaty the Cherokees were removed from Arkansas to modern Oklahoma, taking over the land of the Osages they had always coveted—but not quite the way they had planned to take over. The President of the United States had his own plans.

Andrew Jackson was the hero of the white voters east of the Mississippi and the free men west of the Mississippi, since he was their champion. He had much the same attitude toward the Indian as most of his brass-lunged followers, whose reasoning was akin to the attitude of the early French *voyageurs* in living with Osage women: it couldn't very well be a sin to take the land of devils through trickery and bribing or even through murder.

Two-thirds of the Little Ones were now in their reservation in southern Kansas, but after the treaty of June, 1825, the other third were trespassing, but didn't seem to be aware of it.

In President Jackson's first message to Congress he demanded legislation which would authorize him to remove all the Indians east of the Mississippi to the west of the river, and a bill to this effect was passed and enacted into law June 30, 1830, after an extremely bitter debate.

Jackson had what he wanted, but he couldn't possibly have realized that he was forcing a species of invasion which was biologically artificial. His government had promised the Cherokees, Choctaws, Chickasaws, and Creeks land equal to that which they were forced to give up east of the Mississippi, and their lands were to extend to the 100th meridian on the Great Plains where the buffalo roamed. These people were agriculturists with the exception of a few, but even had they been buffalo Indians, the Apaches, Comanches, Kiowas, Pawnees, and Osages would have had much to say about their hunting there. The Plains tribes would be a menace to them even if they stayed in the woodlands. There was not a single problem of the

549

"Claremore Band" now, but a problem of "wild Indians" of the plains attacking the sedentary ones, even though the Shainer problem was still what it had always been, a pressing one.

Congress concerned itself about this problem and authorized a commission to investigate. In 1832, President Jackson appointed Governor Montford Stokes of North Carolina, chairman; and Henry L. Ellsworth of Hartford, Connecticut, and Rev. John F. Schermerhorn of Utica, New York, as members.

Naturally, ever since the Cherokees and the Creeks had come to claim their old domain, the Little Ones of the Arkansas stepped up their attacks on these two tribes. The kindly William Clark wrote to John H. Eaton, secretary of war, April 22, 1831—accompanied by correspondence between P. L. Chouteau, agent to the Osage, and Arbuckle, agent to the Cherokees, and Captain Pryor, subagent to the Osages of the Arkansas—"that the Osages late conduct toward the Creeks" made it necessary to move them to the Osage Reservation in Kansas allotted to them by the treaty of 1825.

In this year of 1831, the Little Ones who lived on the reservation on the Neosho in modern Kansas were baiting their agent, P. L. Chouteau, in many trivial ways. They also stole his chickens and killed his hogs and came to the agency to sit with him in large numbers, frequently straining his courtesy through his attempts to honor their own old tradition of feeding anyone who came to their lodges.

He wrote to Clark about it. He wrote that the agency was situated on a "Barren rocky Hill in a prairie about ¾ of a mile from the Neosho and ought to be moved for that reason alone, but there was another reason as well; the government had stupidly built the agency building over an Indian burial mound the reflection of which causes unpleasant feelings."

In February, 1833, Stokes and his commission counciled with the Osages of the Arkansas about moving to their reservation in Kansas according to the provisions of the treaty of 1825. Since they had heard about the Osages, the commissioners had a detachment of infantry marched up the river from Fort Gibson to Chouteau's home, which was located at the modern Salina, Oklahoma. The date was February 25, 1833, the weather was very cold, and the Little Ones seemed to be scantily clad and hungry. This may have been true, or they may have appeared in such a condition employing their old protective psychology, expressed by "Have pity on me."

Whatever the ruse or the facts, there were eight hundred of them, and this alone would indicate that they might have come for presents; certainly eight hundred were not necessary for making an agreement with the commission.

The commissioners did pity them, and they moved down to Fort Gibson where there was shelter and where rations were issued. In March, the negotiations were resumed, but after two weeks there was nothing settled, chiefly because the commissioners seemed to be interested in protecting the Cherokees and the Creeks from the Little Ones. This was an old story certainly, an attitude which the Little Ones had often seen in the long series of councils and treaties pertaining to Osage-Cherokee relations. They were rather astute in seeing or feeling this theme since, as a matter of fact, it stood out in all the treaties and councils, no matter what the officials, the army officers, or the commissioners might think privately, or how the matter struck their consciences or their sense of justice. Now there was much more power behind the idea that the immigrant Indians from east of the Mississippi must be protected from the "wild Indians" of the plains, since it was one of the President's chief concerns. Relieve the pressure west of the Mississippi by coming to terms with the "wild Indians" by agreement or force. The President didn't want the chain of pressure from the east of the Mississippi crinkled or pushed back upon itself, causing the links to become locked into a tangle.

Mr. Vaill of Union Mission wrote to the commissioners when they were counciling with the Osages in April attempting to convince them that they should move to their reservation. He wrote that there was no one to speak for the Osages, and he submitted a written argument against the efforts to remove them from their old home. He said that his argument was well received by the commissioners except. Rev. Schermerhorn, who was impatient with suggestions which might be in defense of the Indians. He wrote also that Rev. Schermerhorn had shown himself unsympathetic to Rev. S. A. Worcester and Rev. Elizus Butler, who went to prison in Georgia rather than compromise their principles in defending the Indians against illegal actions.

Arrow-Going-Home the second was now Grand *Hunkah,* but *Shonkah-Sabe,* Black Dog (really Black Horse), had become the chief of the Upland-Forest People, a physical division, and was a great influence. He was seven feet tall and weighed about 250 pounds, handsome, dignified, and blind in one eye. His descendants say that to see his face, one had to look up as one had to look up at the stars and at Grandfather the Sun.

Since there was no agreement with the commissioners, there were no signatures, and therefore one is not sure who the chief councilers were at Fort Gibson during March of 1833.

The Osages were to have met the Cherokees at Fort Gibson, May 1, 1833, to adjust "difficulties," but about this time the greatest flood of tribal memory made seas of the Neosho and Verdigris valleys and the Osages couldn't be present until five days later. The Cherokees were not there when they arrived, and after waiting a few days, they left; and the next day the Cherokees appeared and "pretended to be much dissatisfied that the Osages were not present."

The Osages in the mental groove of the Neolithic would continue to protect their "brothers," and it fitted the purpose of the Cherokees to keep them agitated. On their way down the Verdigris, the Cherokees met an Osage and killed and scalped him.

Colonel Arbuckle and Governor Stokes had a difficult time preventing an Osage-Cherokee war. The presence of the soldiers at Fort Gibson aided them.

If the government remembered that they had forced the treaty of 1825 on the Little Ones, "in order more effectually to extend to said tribes that protection of the government so much desired by them," they seemed to see no contradiction in the present counciling with the Little Ones through the Stokes Commission, which in effect had as its objective protection of the Cherokees and the Creeks from the Little Ones and other "wild Indians," not the protection of the Little Ones from the Cherokees and Creeks.

The Creeks stayed close to Fort Gibson and had to make their improvements close together along the bottoms of the Arkansas and the Verdigris rivers. This situation had to be relieved. There was little to be done about the Osages beyond the control of Fort Gibson. So General Leavenworth established a military post at the mouth of the Cimarron River. The Creeks could now move up the Arkansas with a feeling of being protected from the Osages.

If the plan to move all the Indians east of the Mississippi was to be carried out, something had to be done about the "wild Indians" of the plains, and since the bill had passed Congress in 1830 effecting this, the military had sent troops to the plains in 1832, but they did little. There was another expedition the next year, and it made its way to the mouth of the Washita River and had to return.

The Indians of the plains, the Kiowas, the Wichitas, Comanches, Apaches, and Cheyennes, were active; and now when the Little Ones went to the plains on their buffalo hunts, they seemed to meet their enemies more often, and they were now having border skirmishes with the *Ka-Thu-Wah,* Borrows-from-Others People, known as the Kiowas.

Perhaps the Arkansas Little Ones had been made surly by the long-drawn-out discussions with the Stokes Commission, since they lasted until almost Little-Flower-Killer Moon, the time when they must go to the plains for buffalo.

They, as a matter of fact, set out for the plains a little earlier than usual to escape more unpleasant talk about moving to Kansas and giving up their land to the Creeks and Cherokees.

They probably traveled in gentile groups and would get together later, and they traveled along their old trails and stopped at their traditional camping places. They were very resistant people, and their habits had changed little; only their clothing and their utensils had changed much, and even their clothing had changed only by the replacement of the buffalo robe with trader's blankets.

One gens or group strayed south of the Great Salt Plains and wandered down into the drainage of the Washita. Here the buffalo were plentiful, and they began to make meat. There were long green meadows, and here the buffalo were gathered fattening up for the rut. In one of these meadows, they found a spot where horses had been grazed, and there were signs of the herd boys as well, so they knew that they were not wild horses.

553

They soon found the place where there had been a large camp, and they knew by the moccasin prints and the cast-away things that the Borrows-from-Others People had camped here and had left only recently. They knew that next to the Pawnees these people called Kiowas kept some of the best horses on the plains, breeding their mares each spring to the wild stallions. These mares were easily taken when they were hobbled for their mating and were always taken out of sight of the camp so that the wild stallions would approach them without alarm. This was the time for the breeding, when the cotton from the cottonwoods was flying.

They looked for the mares, believing that they must be close since the signs of the encampment and the tracks leading away from the bottoms were fresh. The camp had been a very large one, and it had been situated in a beautiful meadow-like spot where a creek (the modern Rainy Mountain Creek) debouches into the Washita River, about where the little town of Mountain View, Oklahoma, is now located.

The Little Ones saw by the trail signs that they had frightened the Borrows-from-Others People, and this must have displeased them this time since they wanted Kiowa horses, and if the people fled, they would be on guard. They saw, also, that the trail which left the camp led to the south and was definite and easily followed, but it is said that they were about to turn back, believing the Kiowas were too many for them, when they noted that the trail split, but kept bearing south toward the Wichita Mountains. The Kiowas had hundreds of horses and the trail was very easy to follow. Soon the Little Ones saw that it had divided again, and this pleased them, since they followed the fork marked by the cut earth and that which had the most abundant droppings.

Soon they saw the trail fork again within the mountains, and they again followed the fork which gave evidence of the larger herd of horses.

This is the story of the Little Ones, and thus far it differs little from the story of the Kiowas. The Kiowas say that their buffalo hunters discovered the signs of the Osages north of the Washita, and not only did they find tracks but they found an Osage arrow stuck in a recently killed buffalo. They became worried and went back to their camp in the beautiful wild meadow at the mouth of Rainy Mountain Creek. They, like all tribes of the southwestern plains and the Mississippi River woodlands, knew the giant Osages and feared them. They immediately began to throw up earthworks of adobe. Then they waited for the Osages.

After several days, the Kiowas say, a large party of warriors left the camp to attack the Utes. The Utes were Rocky Mountain people and a war party must travel across the High Plains and cross the Sangre de Cristo Range to attack them. This seems odd. The Kiowas were worried sufficiently to throw up earthworks, knowing that the Osages had flintlocks against their arrows, and yet their warriors left the big camp when there were signs of the Osages all around them to make a quixotic attack across the front range of the Rockies.

The Osages say nothing of the war party leading to the west from the camp, saying only that the trail led off to the south to the Wichita Mountains, then divided. But they say that a party of two hundred Kiowas had gone on the war movement to the Verdigris to attack the Big Hills there, and they had been met by War Eagle and his warriors.

The skirmish was ended by a terrific rainstorm that made the bows of the Kiowas useless, and they fled on their horses while the dismounted Big Hills gave chase on foot. Even the fleet Osages could not keep up with Kiowa horses.

The Kiowa party with the most horses finally went through a gap in the Wichita Mountains and encamped at the head of a stream called Otter Creek. There they were supposed to await the return of the warriors, and there they began preparations for hobbling their mares in heat, so that they might mate with the very strong, wild mountain stallions.

The Kiowas say that one morning when the light was still dim, a boy went up a shallow canyon to take his family's horses for the day's grazing. Just over a great boulder he saw the quivering scalp-lock of an Osage. He ran back to the camp and gave the alarm, and the chief of the small subdivision shouted for the people to run to the rocks.

When the Little Ones went out to take horses, they always went on foot, and nearly everyone who has written of them say that the distance they could cover in a day was incredible. Some have it that they could walk sixty miles a day, and others said that they could walk thirty or forty miles a day. When they got near the herd, they stripped to their breechclouts, left them and their robes and encumbrances where they could pick them up later, and crept forward like panthers, with no shiny or noisy *mo'n-ce* on them. Taking advantage of the wind, they could creep among a herd of horses, sometimes without giving alarm. However, they say the best way was to rush them and stampede them. This threw the enemy off balance and frightened the horses so that they pulled up their own picket pins and ran off with them flying wildly.

Of all the animals that have come under the control of man, the horse never loses his alertness to danger. He is the first to see a distant object and the first to hear the faintest crackling of a twig or smell the midsummer musk of a grizzly bear. He knows the difference between the scent of his master and his people and other people, and when only his eyes tell him of danger and he can neither hear nor scent it, he stares at the blurry menace, perhaps the frozen figure of a strange man or a panther, and whistles through his nostrils. This whistling is so shrill and penetrating that it makes you sit up in your robes or reach for bow or flintlock.

The Little Ones on this occasion had walked to the camp of the Kiowas and were hidden among the rocks waiting for a moment to stampede the horses when the boy saw the roach of one of them and warned the camp. They could do one of two things: leave as stealthily as they had come or try to take the guarded horses.

For some reason the Osages attacked immediately after their discovery and cut the fleeing Kiowas down as they fled for the rocks. They must have become emotionalized, and kept killing people who apparently made no attempt to defend themselves, then cut off their heads. The Kiowas and all who write of this incident say that there were only old men and women and children in the camp on the west fork of Otter Creek.

The Osages cut off the heads of some of the dead and placed them in brass buckets which the Kiowas had got from the traders, and they set the brass buckets in neat rows in the center of the camp, took up the "medicine fetish" of the Kiowas called *Tai-me,* which in a way was as sacred to the Kiowas as the *Wah-hopeh* was to the Little Ones, and left with several captives. Some of the warriors had seen silver dollars scattered on the ground, and they took this *mo'n-ce skah,* white metal, with them. This money the Kiowas had taken from a pack train on the Santa Fe Trail.

There is little information from the Osages about this incident, and no modern gens or gentes seem inclined to claim the honor of having been the attackers. Perhaps they consider it not an honor now. It was a gens or gentes from Arrow-Going-Home's village or of Black Dog's, and the manner in which the attack was made and the apparent lack of reason for it would indicate the old partnership of Bear-Panther from some village on the Verdigris, since they took the silver dollars to Fort Gibson. The Bear in the excitement of having been discovered might well have whimsically attacked the camp, or the Panther in frustration might have massacred the Kiowas as their life-symbol squashed the pine squirrel.

The Kiowas were deeply disturbed, and they got in touch with the other southern plains tribes, the Comanches especially, and three of the bands north of the Red River collected at the east end of the Wichita Mountains waiting for the Little Ones to return.

On June 15, 1834, Colonel Henry Irving Dodge left Fort Gibson with nine companies of about five hundred men for the purpose of showing the power of the United States to the Comanches and the Pawnee Picts, or Wichitas, and urging the "wild Indians" of the southern plains to come to Fort Gibson to council about their harassment of the immigrant Cherokees, Creeks, Choctaws, and Chickasaws, Delaware, Shawnees, etc.

The Osages had delivered up to him at least one of the prisoners they had taken from the Kiowas the year before, as well as a Wichita captive, and he, like Bourgmont, who in 1724 delivered Padouca captives to their people, and like Pike, who in 1806 delivered captive Osages to their people, Colonel Dodge could now grandly deliver the captive Kiowa and the captive Wichita to their people.

557

He set out from Fort Gibson with his superior, General Leavenworth, and with two officers on his staff who would some day become famous. One was Lieutenant Jefferson Davis and the other Lieutenant Colonel Stephen W. Kearny.

He also took along several Indian scouts, Osages, Senecas, Delawares, and Cherokees, and had given permission to George Catlin, the noted painter, to accompany the dragoons. Washington Irving had gone along with an expedition of two years earlier which had the same purpose.

The Osages were *Ko-Ha-Tunk-a,* which Catlin translated as the Crow, but really should be spelled *Ca-xe Tonkah* and means Raven; *Na-Con-E-Shee, Mun-Ne-Pus-Kee,* and Man-Not-Afraid. There were also *Mo'n Pische,* Bad Arrow, and a Frenchman living with the Osages called Beatte, who had accompanied Washington Irving on his tour.

On the twenty-sixth of June the very impressive line of dragoons met an equally impressive and a much more dramatic line of Osage hunters under the command of *Shonkah-Sabe,* Black Dog, and they probably became a little excited.

The next day they saw a tremendous herd of buffalo, and fever-ridden General Leavenworth and Colonel Dodge decided to kill some of them, thus giving their horses a test, but General Leavenworth gave himself a test as well. In a race after a calf, which was an artful dodger, his horse stepped into a hole and the General fell to the earth. Catlin rushed to him and got him to his feet, but he fainted, and had to be taken on a stretcher.

This was a drought summer on the plains, and men sickened and died or had to be sent back. On July 1, forty-five men and three officers were sick, and on July 4, when the expedition had been ferried across the Washita River, they had to stop and reorganize. They had come only 180 miles in early July when the reorganization of the regiment became necessary. They had to leave 86 sick men at this place, with Lieutenant Kearny commanding 109 men to look after them, and General Leavenworth, who was this time very ill with fever, also had to remain here. Dodge took with him six companies composed of forty-two men each. He abandoned his baggage wagons here, and called the camp in honor of his General, Camp Leavenworth.

The dragoons saw large herds of buffalo and herds of wild horses, but the terrific heat was a deterrent inasmuch as horses and men were prostrated without such activity as running buffalo.

On the fourteenth of July, forty Comanches came to smoke and talk with Colonel Dodge, and he learned from them that the Comanches, Wichitas, and Kiowas were friends and allies and would, they boasted, defeat the Osages when they came back into their country.

The Comanches Colonel Dodge met seemed friendly enough, and he felt quite adequate there on the plains until his men began to drop out with heat prostration and malaria, and by July 19 the command had been reduced to 183 men. Not only had many sick been left behind, but there were desertions.

He visited the Comanche villages east of the Wichita Mountains, where they had encamped on Cache Creek to await the invasion of the Little Ones. When Dodge and his heat-stricken, hungry dragoons appeared, the camp was thrown into confusion, the warriors running for their horses and the women packing and keening. However, some of the wild-horse hunters came into camp to tell the people that they had met and talked with Dodge and that he had come all this way to shake the hands of the Comanches.

On July 21, 1834, Colonel Dodge and his hungry dragoons arrived at the Wichita village which was in the mouth of Devils Canyon northeast of the junction of Elk Creek and the north fork of the Red River, and south and east of the modern Quartz Mountain State Park of Oklahoma. The Wichitas had come to this isolated place because of the persecution of the Little Ones through the years, and there is some reason to believe that their long-ago ancestors had lived here in Devils Canyon. Here, in the year 1611, the Spanish explorers were supposed to have come under Fra de Salas in search of gold, and had established a mission here which was maintained until they were all killed by some tribe, perhaps the ancestors of the Wichitas, after ninety years.

The Wichitas, to whom Dodge referred as Pawnee Picts, from the French *Pani Piqué* (tattooed) and from the Osage *Pa-I'n,* Long Hair, which became "Pawnee," in English but to the Osages they were the Long Hair whom they then called *Wi-Tsi-Ta,* Lodges-Far-Away.

Colonel Dodge had been ready to fight or council, and when his weary, hungry dragoons were within five miles of the Wichita village, he halted them and had them fix bayonets. He had expected to see some sign of life, and since he had not, he thought the Wichitas might be waiting to ambush him. The next day, however, when they had proceeded a mile farther, they were met by sixty Wichitas who were greatly alarmed and begged Colonel Dodge not to fire upon them.

The village consisted of about two hundred grass lodges and was situated in a fertile bottom surrounded by "immense ledges of rock."

After his hungry dragoons had been fed with "corn and beans dressed with buffalo fat," and had dessert of watermelons and wild plums, Dodge held a grand council. He said what he had come to say, which was of course evasive since he had not been sent by the great white father all this way, making marches so fast that his men had not time to hunt, just to shake the hands of the Comanches and the Wichitas and to establish friendly relations. If the "wild Indians" had not been a menace to the pressured Indians from east of the Mississippi, the United States under their President Andrew Jackson probably would have ignored them for the time, since there were no free men shouting for their land. As a matter of fact, they were west of the line which had been drawn about this time which represented the "western Boundary of Habitable Land," and the domain of the Wichitas was within the boundaries of the land which would be allotted to the Choctaws. The possibility that the "wild Indians" might affect Jackson's plan for undisturbed resettlement of the tribes from east of the Mississippi was the chief reason for Dodge's presence at the Wichita village. However, there was one other reason. The United States had made a treaty with the Little Ones in 1825 which gave the United States permission to make a road so that trade with Mexico might be facilitated, and this road to Santa Fe was called the Santa Fe Trail. This agreement gave the United States right-of-way only to the Arkansas River, beyond which the Osages could not make their claims stick. This was the domain of the Comanches and the Kiowas, Cheyennes, and Pawnee-*maha,* and perhaps the Wichitas, who were also referred to as Pawnees.

There had been some trouble; these tribes had attacked the pack trains plodding along the trail, and there was sufficient evidence that the Kiowas were attacking trains through the silver dollars which the Osages had brought to Fort Gibson.

This interference with the trade with Santa Fe had to be stopped. Protection for both the pressured immigrant Indians and the Santa Fe trade was very important.

The first council, held July 22, did not go well. Perhaps the Osages were too conspicuous. They should have pulled their robes over their shaved heads and their quivering roaches.

So everyone in the great assemblage knew that the Osages were present and had come with Colonel Dodge, along with the Cherokees and Delawares and Senecas, as his scouts, hunters, and advisers. The people knew that the Cherokees and the Delawares at least were enemies of the Osages.

The Wichitas had come to this place to establish their village among the pink granite hills and boulders because of the Osages. The Osages had driven them from their homes farther down the Red River, and they had known no peace when the giants were a-prowl with their charcoal-blackened faces behind their fiendish-looking chieftain whose face was painted dawn red. These Wichitas were of the long-suffering Caddoans, and their tribal memory might have gone back to the time when the Siouans had driven them from their ancient homes. The people had begun to mumble, since Dodge was holding the captives which he had with him until he could get some information about a Judge Martin from Louisiana and his son. Some tribe of the southern plains had killed the Judge and his Negro slave while they were buffalo hunting north of the Red River. The Comanches had told Dodge that the Wichitas had killed the Judge and the slave and that they held the son captive.

When he asked them about the incident, they became sullen. But an Osage scout found the twelve-year-old boy hiding in a corn field, and during council the next day Dodge could say that he would exchange captives.

There were other things he wanted to know about, such as trade with the Mexicans from Santa Fe. He saw evidence of it and didn't like it, boasting to the Wichitas that the United States could trade with them more to their advantage.

The mumbling had been about the finding of the Martin boy by the Osages and about the presence of the Osages, and the conclusion seemed to be that the Osages were now allies of the whites and had come to destroy the Wichitas or lead them into a trap.

The speeches helped little. The speech of Dodge seemed to please the people. An old Waco chief said that they wanted to be at peace with the Osages: "We have been long at war with them. We wish to see the lands of the Creeks and the Cherokees; also to shake hands with them all."

Dutch, the very handsome and active Cherokee warrior leader, who elicited deep respect from the Osages because of his bravery, spoke, and assured Dodge that the Cherokees and the whites were friends and could visit each other without fear. He didn't seem to mention the Osages and the plainsmen. The Osages, Dodge knew, were the greatest menace to the pressured Indians from east of the Mississippi, since it was their old domain which was actually being invaded.

There were speeches by a Wichita chief, and the Frenchman with the Osage hunters and scouts, Beatte, made a flowery and ingratiating speech, calling Dodge "our father" repeatedly. *Mo'n Pische,* Bad Arrow, the mission-trained son of Antler-Maker, called Phillip Milledoler, also made a speech, saying little about the matter before the council. But seeming to assume a pontifical posture, he warned the people about the disappearance of the buffalo and said that all Indians must learn to raise stock and plant vegetables. The missionaries would have been proud of him.

However, the great event of the day was a Wagnerian opera flourish, without music. About thirty Kiowas dashed into the meeting and almost ran into Colonel Dodge's tent, "admirably equipped for fight or flight," as they fought the heads of their war horses and had their bows strung and their quivers filled.

The women began to keen and herd the children to the boulders, and the Wichita warriors ran for their horses, as did Dodge's dragoons. Obviously one shot from bow or flintlock would have precipitated a battle, in which Dodge and his men would have been destroyed.

Dodge got the warriors calmed by showing that he would give them back the young people the Osages had taken captive, and by saying that the Osages had promised to return to the man who had the authority the sacred *Tai-me* which they had taken at the place which would later be called Cut-Throat Gap.

This calming of highly emotionalized Plains Indians when they had been told that there were Osages in the Wichita village was somewhat a master stroke of diplomacy.

The captives were turned over to their Wichita and Kiowa relatives and then brought forth to sit among the chiefs, which was special honor, while two thousand armed and mounted Kiowa, Comanche, and Wichita warriors sat their horses in a circle around the counciling.

When the relatives had seen and then received the captives, there had been emotion, some of them coming up to cry and embrace Dodge, and this had much to do with making the situation more flexible. Dodge had been unable to carry presents, having left them when he had to divide his baggage and his men. After abandoning the wagons, he could allow only three pack horses to each company. The matter was not as serious as it could have been if he had not given the chiefs of the three tribes guns and pistols.

Fifteen Kiowas, including their chief, one Comanche, three Wichita chiefs, and the old Wacoan, *We-Ter-Ra-Shah-Ro,* finally consented to return with Colonel Dodge to Fort Gibson.

The Cherokee, Seneca, Delaware, and Osage scouts and the Kiowas, Wichitas, and the single Comanche and the Wacoan seemed to take some interest in each other, and apparently became friendly with each other as they sang together every night according to the journalist of Company One, who wrote: ". . . nightly they amuse us with their wild and unintelligible and unaccountable songs which are far from being displeasing as they all join in seemingly in endeavoring to exceed each other in noise, altogether creating a compound of the most unearthly discord."

At a camp on the Canadian, while resting the horses, attending the sick, burying the dead, and killing buffalo, Colonel Dodge received the news that General Leavenworth had died.

Obviously the Indians were supposed to go to Washington with Dodge to see the Great White Father, but apparently Dodge couldn't get them to travel farther than Fort Gibson, and here he held a council September 1, 1834, where there were representatives of the seven or eight tribes assembled and which lasted four days. The Cherokees, Senecas, Creeks, and Choctaws had been well instructed, and they spoke perhaps with some sincerity in trying to convince the "wild Indians" of the benefits of peace between the United States government and the pressured Indians and themselves. Arrow-Going-Home the younger spoke not of the peace between his people and the Cherokees and the United States, but of peace between his people and their pre-Columbian enemies, the Wichitas and the Wacos, and peace with all "within sound of my voice." One wonders what he had in mind?

Little or nothing was finally settled during the council at Fort Gibson, since Colonel Dodge was not authorized to make a treaty. Another council was planned for the next spring and was held at a spot just north of the modern Lexington, Oklahoma, in the buffalo country. Major Mason of Fort Gibson had to have a road constructed to the spot from Fort Gibson, and he had benches made and brush arbors built, and there was promise of many presents. The President was urgent.

The Kiowas were annoyed and wouldn't co-operate, and they didn't like Arrow-Going-Home's arrogant action when the Kiowa chief embraced him. This was to Arrow-Going-Home evidence of weak Kiowa medicine.

When the date arrived and Major Mason saw the great horde of Plains Indians coming to the council, he sent back to Fort Gibson for more soldiers, and Colonel Arbuckle sent two companies of the Seventh Infantry. By the early part of July, 1835, there were perhaps eight thousand Kiowas and Comanches, ready for presents, feasts, and talk.

The officers and soldiers and commissioners and others with a few exceptions had never seen anything so impressive. They had been accustomed to the harlequins and the other woodland Indians from east of the Mississippi, who raised hogs and planted squash and corn and watermelons and raised stock and chickens; bronze people who wore clothes of the white man, sometimes tattered, and wore shoes as well as moccasins, and nostalgically stuck flicker or turkey feathers in their bandeaus or into their slouch-hat bands. They had seen the chiefs wearing frockcoats and stovepipe hats, with wapiti teeth set in gold, or silver crosses hanging from their watch chains. Only the resistant Osages remained as they had always been, but these people had never seen them on the High Plains or on the war movement; they had seen them only in the woodlands, in gentile groups wary of ambuscade. But to this meeting they came out of the woodlands to impress their plains enemies. They came like plainsmen warriors, filled with pride and chivalric emotions.

The others of the woodland, the pressured immigrants, of much higher civilization, many of them Christians and agriculturists and speakers and writers of English, rode out with the commissioners, Governor Montford Stokes, and General Matthew Arbuckle. There were Creeks, Senecas, Quapaws, Choctaws, Cherokees, and Delawares, met by the eight thousand Plains warriors, who counted the eighty Osages carefully as they approached in their bluff-paint carrying their spears and shields, both fetish and practical, and Arrow-Going-Home and Black Dog each had a *wah-hopeh* hung around their necks. They carried the swan war standard and rode their best horses, but they had been requested by General Arbuckle to leave their enemy scalplocks at home.

It is quite easy to appreciate Major Mason's nervousness and his reason for sending back to Fort Gibson for reinforcements when the Plains warriors appeared in their splendor, their horses prancing and their feathers fluttering and their enemy scalplocks waving. The Comanches had even learned to swing their mounted warriors into a sort of brigade front, in imitation of the Spaniards.

There must have been an atmosphere of grand opera about the meeting, perhaps like Verdi's *Aïda,* or Boite's *Neroné.*

There were the soldiers' and the commissioners' tents, drab and utilitarian, and the grass lodges of the Wichitas, the rounded lodges of the Osages, the tipis of the Kiowas and the Comanches, and the brush arbors for the woodlanders. There were dancing and feasting and visiting and Plains strutting and boasting; and on August 24, the treaty was signed and the presents that had been promised were distributed.

The treaty was between the United States on the one hand and the Wichitas and the Comanches on the other, and between the Wichitas and the Comanches and the Choctaws, Creeks, Cherokees, Senecas, and Quapaws. The woodlanders could hunt and trap west of the Cross Timbers as far as the limits of the United States. The Comanches and Wichitas were to allow free passage to the citizens of the United States and Mexico in their trade intercourse along the Santa Fe Trail south and west of the Arkansas River.

Neither the Kiowas nor the Osages would sign this treaty, the former pulling their stakes and leaving before the council was finished. The Kiowas were not ready to take the hand of the Osages, and there had been too much urging of the Osages by the commissioners to comply with the terms of their treaty of 1825, which would send them to their Kansas reservation. They had become wary of touching the feather.

45. The "Little People" Attack the Little Ones

AND IN ORDER TO CARRY OUT the plan for removing the east-of-the-Mississippi River Indians to the west of the river in the Jacksonian manner, there had to be special laws enacted by a state and Jackson had to defy Chief Justice John Marshall and the Supreme Court. In order to take the homes and the land of the prosperous and cultured Cherokees and mixed-bloods, merciless pressure was employed, after bribery and cajolery and threat were used.

When these people, gentlemen and ladies from plantations and primitive hunters from the Great Smoky Mountains, were herded together at a rendezvous, they were floated down the Tennessee River to the Ohio and thence down the Ohio to the Mississippi and down it to the mouth of the Arkansas. Up the Arkansas the rain fell and there was a report that there was a terrifying epidemic of cholera on the Tennessee and the Ohio.

They were crowded together under decks, and soon measles broke out, and they stopped as often to bury the dead as they did to take on wood. The great number of shoals and snags or "sawyers" compelled them to travel only by daylight. They were slowed up by frequent repairs to paddle wheels, towing keelboats over the shoals, burying the dead, and taking on wood.

Finally, the towing of keelboats became so difficult that Lieutenant J. W. Harris ordered 102 of his party to go ashore at the mouth of Cadron Creek above Little Rock, Arkansas. Here among the cedars the people made camp awaiting wagons to haul their impedimenta. There were fullblooded Cherokees from the hills and the game trails, others of the fringes of civilization, some "agency" Indians, and families who had been associated with the highest culture in the United States of that period. These last had lived pleasantly on large plantations, with their slaves.

While they were washing and airing their clothing and bedding and allowing the air of spring to sweep away the odors of underdeck living, cholera came to them. Lieutenant Harris wrote, "At one time I saw stretched around me and within a few feet of each other, eight of these afflicted creatures dead or dying."

The settlers were afraid to come to the camp to give him aid in caring for the stricken, and he struggled along aiding the local doctor, Roberts, until the doctor died; then he himself was stricken, but recovered.

They had only opium and calomel to treat the disease, one-half of a grain of opium and from fifteen to forty grains of calomel. These two men, Lieutenant Harris from Portsmouth, New Hampshire, only a few years out of West Point, and the country doctor, Roberts, originally from Alabama, personified that nobility in man that seems sometimes to be only his own poetic assumption or just a chimera until it rises from and above greed, salacity, panic, fear, and ghoulish theft, as it did that April and May on Cadron Creek in 1834.

When the survivors of these people and others of the immigrants reached the rivers of the Little Ones, they separated to find their new homes, and soon soldiers at Fort Gibson, the missionaries and their families, and the Little Ones were dying like flies.

The missionaries lost Rev. Montgomery, and the Redfields lost all of their children, and many others died of the cholera. As if the cholera and the measles and the smallpox were not enough, this summer of 1834 was the summer of the great drought following the year of the greatest floods. The thermometer registered 100, 110, and 116 degrees at the fort.

The dragoons off on their expedition to the plains must have died from cholera as well as from heat and malaria.

The wife of Mr. Vaill of Union Mission became insane.

The "Little People" Attack the Little Ones

During the counciling at Fort Gibson in September of 1834, when Colonel Dodge and Major Armstrong were attempting to carry out orders from Washington to make some agreement with the Plains Indians and promote brotherly love among the Wichitas, Comanches, and Kiowas, on the one hand, and the Osages, on the other, and urging the Cherokees and Delawares and Choctaws and others of the immigrants to use honeyed words in their speeches, most of them were forgetting the object of the council and saying that they wanted peace with the Osages. To these speeches, Arrow-Going-Home the younger was saying: "You want to be friends with the Osages; but there are many more bands of Pawnees; some of them may not wish to be our friends; all the bands of the Pawnees are not here."

Each tribe was concerned about the attitude of their ancient enemies, not Plains brotherhood, and certainly they thought of the land over which they hunted and fought as their own, not knowing that the government would turn it over to the Choctaws and Creeks and Cherokees.

The Kiowas counted the Osages who had come to the council, and the spokesman for the Kiowas said that the Kiowas wanted peace and especially they wanted peace with the Osages, but where were the Osages? Why did not more of them come to the council if they wished to make peace? Beatte, the Frenchman, who had come with the Osages, informed the council that the Osages were dying by the hundreds from cholera.

Several of the Plains Indians died on the way back to their villages.

When the *we-lu-schka,* the "little people," came to the Osages, it was an attack like some extraneous evil. It had never occurred to them that malaria and typhoid had always come to them through the small "brother," who seemed to be going about his own business, just as *shi-ku,* the rattler, would do if you did not molest him.

The *we-lu-schka,* the "little people," had got through the armor of their medicine, and might be prayed into the cracks of their armor by an enemy. The cracks in one's armor might be caused by some remissness on his part in carrying out the rituals handed down by *Wah'Kon-Tah* through the generations of Little Old Men. There were many things now that might be causing the attack of the *we-*

569

lu-schka. There was first of all the very powerful god-medicine of the Heavy Eyebrows, then there was That-Thing-on-Its-Head People and the new people *Mo'n-Shko-Ge,* the Creeks, who were calling the Osages "troublesome intruders." These people could be praying that the "Little Ones must die."

When the Little Ones wished their sons to be straight and tall and graceful, they prayed to and through the red oak or the white ash, and when they wished their daughters to be beautiful and graceful, they prayed to and through the spiderwort, the primrose, or the wild rose. They prayed to and through the panther, the beaver, the otter, the hawk, the bear, the spider, the deer, the buffalo, and the wapiti, and many others when they needed those powers which *Wah'Kon-Tah* had given these "people" and had neglected to give to them.

So when they wished evil or death to come to someone of their enemies, they prayed to or through the accomplished fact, death itself. Or, like the Bear, they wetted their index fingers and pointed to one, saying, "You must die."

The Eagle, the Bear, and the Wapiti of the gentes and the Big Hills of the physical divisions have a story about a woman who wanted her son-in-law dead because he had his wife, her daughter, come to her lodge to get wood for their fire. This woman walked to the spring each day to get water. It was some distance from her lodge, and away from the trail a short distance there was the carcass of a buffalo. The wolves and the coyotes and the opossums had eaten the meat from the bones and there was nothing left but the skeleton and the hide shrunken down between the ribs, rain-dulled and flinty.

The mother-in-law became progressively more angry about the wood and the fact that her son-in-law sat in his lodge flaking flints over the fire which was made with her wood. One day she set her vessel down and turned aside from the trail and made her way to the carcass. There she stood looking down at it, and then she said, "Grandfather, I want this bad man to die."

Every day she came to the carcass and asked for the death of her son-in-law from death itself.

Then one day some boys saw her praying to the buffalo carcass and ran to tell their friend. The young son-in-law was their friend because he made arrows and bows for them; fire-blunted arrows sometimes split so that they caught little birds and lizards alive.

He went secretly to the carcass and dug a hole under it, then just before his mother-in-law came down the trail, he crawled into the hole and waited. When she came, she went through the ritual, "Grandfather, make that bad man die." From the carcass came a hollow, weary, but sepulchral, deep bass voice: "Go away—you die first."

The frightened woman ran back to the trail looking back over her shoulder, crying, "No, I don't want to die." When she got back to her lodge, she sent a boy to get an old man called Little Doctor, who claimed medicine from the pelican. He had made of himself a medicine man because he was scrofulous and pock marked and had a large nose like the *wah-don-ska* growing on the oak. He was important now.

He came to the woman's lodge and picked up the most beautiful pair of moccasins with trader's beads making the sacred hawk on the tops. They were very beautiful moccasins, but the woman was frightened and she pursed her lips to the moccasins and nodded her head.

The old man had her sit in the middle of the lodge with her hands in her lap, looking to the east, the home of Grandfather the Sun. Then he strode to the door of the lodge, which was to the east, and seemed to push something away with his eagle-wing fan; then he came to the woman, and standing before her fanned away the evil that might have clung to her, slowly, rhythmically, as he sang a song he had made for the occasion.

But for the *we-lu-schkas* that came that summer there was no defense. At first the Song of Death was heard at the rising of the Morning Star, at noon as Grandfather was immediately overhead and might carry the *we-lu-schkas* with him on his journey to the *Mo'n-ha,* the West, the direction of Death, the Red Cliff of the Rockies, but Grandfather seemed to have turned his ears away. The Little Ones then sang the Song of Death when the Evening Star came up, as well as before dawn and at midday:

THE OSAGES

A-he the he, Ah, the he.
It is I who cause them to lie blackening on the earth,
A-he the he, Ah, the he.
It is I who takes from them their remaining days.

Because of the confusion into which they had been thrown, the Little Ones had turned more and more to their Little Old Men, but they only made more rituals, and perhaps were almost ready to accept the Bible as a fetish, as the tragically confused Bad-Tempered-Buffalo had done. But a few of the clever ones could see that now when a man or a woman came to them weeping about the sick ones, they would give their most valuable possession to anyone who could give relief. Medicine men were many now since the Heavy Eyebrows, the That-Thing-on-Its-Head, and other Indians had invaded their domain and killed their "brothers," and the Little Old Men could only talk and sing and fear with the people.

And the recent years of confusion had been propitious for the No-bodies to claim importance as warriors and tell the strange Heavy Eyebrows that they were really chiefs, and this was the time for the chieftains to vie with each other and express that intense jealousy which inherent vanity and the urge to be important had bred into them through the centuries.

The traditional urgency, the necessity to achieve many *o-do'n,* war honors, seemed to have begun to deteriorate into a relentless urgency to satisfy self-esteem, no matter by what means.

And now the great sickness, the cholera, the *we-lu-schkas.* The large villages on the Verdigris and the Neosho split into gentile units or even family units. The great sickness seems to have struck the villages higher up on the Neosho, which ran through their reservation which they accepted by the treaty of 1825, as well as those on the Verdigris—the ones called Upper villages in modern Kansas and the villages of the "Clermont Band" and the "Black Dog Band" in modern Oklahoma.[1]

---

[1] The Little Ones called cholera *de-ko-ka,* which means cramps. They got some relief from swinging from two rawhide ropes. They hung two ropes from a tree and made loops in the end of each one. They then suspended them-

Arrow-Going-Home's village divided into at least six gentile units and fled to the prairie so that the winds that play there might sweep the sickness away. These gentile groups redivided into family units, and the Little Ones became scattered like striped-head, the quail, and there was no way to find them, even if there had been doctors who could leave their patients at the missions.

Soon the deaths were so many and so frequent that the spirit died, too, and there were no Songs of Death, and the dead were left where they died, their relatives fleeing from them across the prairie.

But *Mo'n Sho'n,* the Sacred One, was affected with the *we-lu-schkas,* too. The feeder streams that veined the prairie became dry, and their bottoms cracked. The grass became as the grass of Baby-Bear Moon and of the Buffalo-Mating Moon, and the leaves of the bottom trees, the elms and cottonwoods and sycamores and hackberries, fell crazily, zigzagging to the earth, and crackled when the Little Ones walked upon them. Clouds traveled fast across the prairies to escape the *we-lu-schkas,* and the Moon Woman seemed to be sick, and even Grandfather the Sun was pale when the smoke of the prairie fires hung in the air.

Those people of the villages of the Little Ones where the *we-lu-schkas* had attacked scattered far. The individuals of the family or the gens, when stricken, left the camp and staggered across the prairie to find some place to die, while the others sat bowed, fighting the scorching prairie winds for their blankets which they had thrown over their heads. The spirit of the mustang broken, they waited.

selves face down with arms in one loop and feet in the other. This allowed the abdomen to sag. This they say stopped the cramping.

46. The Little Ones
Ordered Off Their Old Domain

THE LITTLE ONES were now completely surrounded by free men, Creeks, Cherokees, and traders who had followed the Indians from the east. This on the lower Neosho and the Verdigris; the upper river people were not crowded, but they were having their troubles, even though pigeonholed by the government for the moment on the reservation.

The traders had followed the immigrant Indians, and other traders had come from New Orleans and other cities to bring their merchandise to the Indians since they had silver, paid to them by the government, and the currency of the states was now questionable because of the financial depression of 1837.

The more traders, the more Creeks, the more Cherokees, and the more Choctaws, the more game killed for hides and tongues, but the Creeks and the Cherokees became more vulnerable through their chattels. The pressure on the Creeks had been lessened by the establishment of the military post at the mouth of the Cimarron only in theory. The settlers of the state of Missouri were organizing against the incursions of the Little Ones of the upper river. The Little Ones were hungry again.

Their annuities were insufficient, their game had been killed off, and they had to go farther and farther to find buffalo among their Plains enemies. It was thought that perhaps as many as three hundred or even four hundred of them had died of cholera, and they were in consequence restive and surly, confused and afraid.

Even the chain of gentile and tribal memory seems to have missing links during this period, and there is little to learn from either. The Little Osages can name their chiefs for over two hundred years and this is the period when Thunder-Fear should have been their chief, yet the documents indicate that Beautiful Bird might have had some influence, though perhaps not in the Little Osage physical division. He was probably Beautiful Bird the younger since the first one had been killed some years previously.

And now in this period of depression, while the "Shainers" were helping themselves to the cattle of the Creeks in order to live and the officials were planning to hurry their departure from their old domain on the Verdigris, the Little Ones of the upper Neosho were forced to hunt again on their old domain now in the state of Missouri. The settlers and the free men and the fragments of eastern tribes had killed off much of the game of this region, and they had caused the game not slaughtered to migrate to the west onto the prairies. However, white men in the van of civilization were now trapping and hunting along the Konza and the headwaters of the Neosho and the Fall, the Elk, and the upper Verdigris. While this prairie-plains country wherein lay the reservation assigned to the Little Ones was still comparatively free from settlers and free men shouting for land, it was not free from the commercial hunter and trapper. The deer and the wapiti and the bear could conceal themselves in the woodlands of the Missouri country better than on the prairies of modern Kansas. The Little Ones went to hunt them where they found them, and this brought on trouble with the citizens of Missouri.

Now the tables were turned, and the citizens warned the Little Ones that they could not hunt "within their neighborhood," and they appointed a "Committee of Vigilance" and sent a message to the Little Ones that if they entered white settlements, "they would be flogged by the whites, their guns broken, and they, driven back, and that in case of refusal still to leave, severe measures would be resorted to."

The Little Ones replied that they had sold the land and not the

575

game, and they would come and take it as usual, and if "pushed out by the whites [with the hands of the Heavy Eyebrows] they would push with their knives."

Before this period of hunger they had protected their "brothers" to the best of their ability. Now they would kill no Heavy Eyebrows, but would take the "brothers" *Wah'Kon-Tah* had given them for food.

The above quotation was from a letter written by Issac McCoy to C. A. Harris, commissioner of Indian affairs. His reason for writing was fear that there might be a border war or that other tribes, sensing the tension and the suspicions, might take the opportunity to commit depredations and blame the Little Ones, which had ever been done, since the Little Ones had no friends.

The Heavy Eyebrows settlers could not afford fairness or justice and didn't have time from their existence struggle to indulge in humanitarianism, except toward the people around them within the same existence category as themselves. Their sympathy for each other and their aid to others in sickness or misfortune was on the soldierly basis as it obtains on the firing line. They felt close to each other, and they could become communally vindictive and unreasoning about the rumor of "Injuns," and were excited partisans in politics and haters of the Mormons, whom they believed to be in league with the devil.

When the hungry Little Ones of the upper Neosho crossed the neutral buffer strip, now called Cherokee Neutral Lands, they were not aware of the western boundary of the new state of Missouri, just twenty-five miles east of their own eastern boundary, represented by a plow furrow.

It is not known just how many of them crossed the boundary of Missouri, but the alarm cry of the settlers was probably out of proportion to the numbers of the Little Ones.

The Governor of Missouri was asked for protection, and 280 militia were raised by volunteer and draft, and were commanded by General Lucas of Jackson County, in which the hated Mormons had tried to settle.

Mr. McCoy's interest in the Little Ones was not that of the settlers in a more pitiable condition than the Osages—"within their own limits [the reservation in modern Kansas] there are not game and roots sufficient to keep them from actual starvation, and on every side they are repulsed, none, either red or white, being willing to have them nearer."

McCoy wrote that Lucas was quite active in removing Osages from the state. Several old men and women and children were moved across the boundary, and the military camped a short distance from a camp of Osage hunters, but there was no fighting, and when the military removed the hunters, there were no lives lost. McCoy believed that the whipping of Osages could have been rumor which under the circumstances would breed wildly.

However, Captain E. V. Sumner, in command of the dragoons which Colonel S. W. Kearny had sent down from Fort Leavenworth, wrote to his colonel that when he reached Harmony Mission in November, he was astonished to learn that a detachment of militia had taken five Osage women prisoners. These women had been married to Frenchmen fifteen or twenty years. The Captain with one of his two companies of First Dragoons overtook the guard of sixteen men, removing the weeping women, "marching in front and rear of these helpless and frightened women, and I had no hesitation in saying, that it was the most contemptible sight I ever saw, or ever expect to, in the course of my life."

He told the guard that he would be responsible to their General for the release of the women, then he rode back to the Marais des Cygnes to meet and talk with Lucas so that the women would not be retaken.

He posted guards at M. Giraud's house, and then met Lucas within a few miles of the mission; and as they rode stirrup to stirrup, he told him what he had done, assuming understanding between officers. Lucas seemed not to agree. He said that Governor Boggs had ordered him to remove *all* Osages from the state, and Sumner said that he had had the same orders from his colonel, but he didn't think this included the breaking up of mission families. It was, he suggested, a matter of discretion.

He told Lucas that he had placed guards around Giraud's house to discourage straggling militiamen. "My intention in saying this, and which must have been perfectly plain to him, was, that I did not think it necessary to protect a few helpless females against a General Officer."

Sumner then went on to one of the Osage villages on the upper Neosho to determine just what the situation was. There were rumors in Missouri that the Osages were planning an invasion in force. "Hostile" was the word when Indians took any action, defensive or offensive, and he had heard that the Osages were hostile. When he arrived at the village, he found that the Little Ones had gone on their autumnal buffalo hunt. He wrote that because of this absence of the hunters since perhaps September, "the assembling of the militia on the frontier was utterly unnecessary and highly improper."

Here at the village on the Neosho within their reservation, he saw no signs of the war movement in the hungry old men and women and children, and he didn't now, with McCoy, believe the rumors that the militia had flogged some of the Osages, since to touch an Osage was the highest insult.

The Captain sent twenty Osage men across the border, carrying out his orders, when he re-entered Missouri. He wrote, "The Indians undoubtedly commit many depredations upon the frontier inhabitants."

He was quite surprised that Lucas had made an attempt to take some of the women "that I had caused to be released." Apparently a militia colonel by the name of Wilson had come to the Giraud house in command of a group of men in "citizens' clothes" and gave the sergeant of the guard a written order, from Lucas, presumably from Sumner, to dissolve the guard. In his letter to his captain, the sergeant wrote that he had refused to do it and had told Wilson "that I could not obey and that I did not know General Lucas from the Devil." The guard and the rag-tag company in "citizens' clothes" almost opened fire on each other.

McCoy the humanitarian had pleaded with the United States government to send relief to "5,000 friendless human beings," and now on November 25, General Arbuckle wrote to Captain William Armstrong, acting superintendent of Indian affairs at Choctaw agency, that he believed the Osages would suffer if they did not obtain relief from the government. He wrote that he had urged the Osages to remain at peace and restrain their people from going to Missouri to hunt. He suggested that five of the principal chiefs should go to Washington to see "the great father in about two Moons and a half."

Armstrong wrote to C. A. Harris, commissioner of Indian affairs, in December of 1837 that the depredations committed in the state of Missouri were "doubtless confined to a few."

The next year during skirmishes between the Saints and the settlers, Governor Lilburn W. Boggs ordered the militia to exterminate the Mormons or drive them from the state of Missouri. They left in 1839.

In April, Governor Stokes wrote a letter to Poinsett about the condition of the Osages: "When you cast your eye over the map of the immensely extensive and valuable country obtained from this nation, for the accommodation of the Emigrants from East of the Mississippi and without which cession the Emigrants could not have been provided with a country, you will readily perceive that every principle of Justice and Equity demands from the Government of the United States, that this people should not be abandoned and driven to the conditions of robbers and perhaps shortly annihilated."

The government had been trying to effect the removal of the Verdigris Osages practically since the treaty of 1825, when the reservation was established, and it had been like pulling a wildcat out of a hole; but now they had the co-operation of hunger, and they began to set about making the most of the situation. Brigadier General Arbuckle wrote that he was not sure of the best method for giving relief to the hungry Creeks and Osages. "The sum appropriated in part for the benefit of these tribes will do much good if justly employed, and will assist the Osages [on Cherokee land] to remove to their own reserve, if it can be so used. The Osages referred to ought certainly to remove within the present year, from the Cherokee Country, and some means should be taken to pay for the property they have stolen from the Creeks, Cherokees and others during the last seven years."

Also the Creeks had warned the government that they would not appeal any more for relief from the predacious Osages but would take matters into their own hands, and in October, Arbuckle and Armstrong were ordered to hold a treaty conference with the Creeks to adjust claims for the great losses they had sustained in their forced removal from east of the Mississippi.

During this year of 1837, Arrow-Going-Home the younger died, and the people who knew the arrogant and vain man appreciated the power he held both in restraining his young warriors and in inciting his people to war. They were afraid not so much for the immigrant Indians, since they were clustered close to the forts and the growing population of traders and others. The Osages, they believed, in their distress might start a war with the Plains tribes. Even if of much less concern to the government than war with the immigrants, this possible Plains war must be obviated, since they might even federate and move against the hated intruders from east of the Mississippi, or stop international commerce over the Santa Fe Trail. There was a sense of urgency in the letters of Armstrong, Stokes, Arbuckle, and McCoy.

Finally, on January 11, 1839, at Fort Gibson, the Little Ones of the Verdigris—called Arkansas Osages, Osages of the Oaks, "Shainers," and Claremont's Band and/or Black Dog's Band, knowing themselves to be basically the *Sa'n-Solé*, or the People of the Upland-Forest, the people who built their drying fires on the plateau when the Little Ones fled from the traditional flood—agreed to do many things. This physical division of the Little Ones agreed by the provisions of a treaty signed that day that they would cede all title or interest in any reservation heretofore claimed by them within the limits of any other tribe. They agreed to relinquish all claims or interest under the treaties of 1808 and 1825, except the sixth article of the latter (sections sold for school purposes); and in consideration of such cessions and relinquishments they agreed to accept $20,000; $12,000 to be paid in money and $8,000 in goods, stock, and provisions. The government was to furnish a blacksmith for a term of twenty years, and was to furnish hogs, cows, gristmills, sawmills, hoes, and axes, and pay all claims against the Osages up to $30,000. The government had deducted $3,000 from the annuities to Arrow-Going-Home's people, and this amount was restored to them. These deductions were made by an agent of the government who seemed to be assuming too much authority. The government also agreed to build houses for the chiefs and give them wagons.

The provisions of this treaty of 1839, in which claims against the Osages were to be paid and the stock and provisions and the money as consideration for relinquishment of claims they might have in the territory of other Indians, might seem to be double consideration or supplemental to the considerations of the 1825 treaty until one realizes that during the same year Congress had to appropriate an additional $150,000 to feed the Creeks, Chickasaws, and Cherokees, as well as the Osages.

But still the Little Ones refused to leave their old home on the Verdigris, and General Arbuckle had to send Lieutenant Bowman with his company of dragoons to the old village of Arrow-Going-Home to warn them that they must leave the country at once. They had become wise in the ways of the government in their dealings with the agricultural Cherokees. The government believed any tale the Cherokees might present if it was based on the exigencies of agriculture. This excuse had been sufficient for ignoring dates for counciling and, especially, agreements with the Little Ones, keeping them waiting practically every time there was a date set for a meeting. On the ingratiating tongues of "buffalo Indians" this old excuse had no virtue, and Bowman had to tell them that they could not stay to plant their little orphan corn fields. Only those sick with smallpox would be permitted to remain.

The Osages of the Oaks moved up the river onto the prairie to their reservation to join the Place-of-the-Many-Swans people, who had left their home in 1825.

It would seem fitting that the story of the Little Ones should end here, in the year 1840. The God of the Heavy Eyebrows had proved Himself more powerful than *Wah'Kon-Tah,* and the "brothers" from whom and through whom the Little Ones had got the powers *Wah'Kon-Tah* had not given them were vanishing. They could now rub the forefinger of one hand on the back of the other and say, "Pity me; I am poor and humble" without hypocrisy. In their hearts they must have felt forsaken, with all hands turned against them, and *Wah'Kon-Tah* seemed to have forsaken them and turned his ears away from them, fearing the wrath of the God of the Heavy Eyebrows. The *we-lu-schkas,* the "little people," came more often now and took away their remaining days, and left them lying blackening on the earth. The ruthless, arrogant, warrior giants knew hunger now for the second time in their existence. Hunger does not allow warriors to grow into giants.

When Bad-Tempered-Buffalo "moved to a new country" on his own initiative and accepted the Bible from Mr. Montgomery of the mission, he cherished it as a fetish, as did White Hair the first when he instructed the man he selected to paint his face to place his gift Bible in the grave with him. Now, just as the Little Old Men had created a new ritual for the very useful and powerful *mo'n-ce,* metal, it would seem that they might create a ritual for the book to which the Heavy Eyebrows went to receive back the strong medicine with which they had charged it. But there is no tribal or gentile memory of this. Instead, it would seem that more and more of the Little Old Men, in the confusion of tribal frustration, had seen an opportunity to fire their own vanities and serve a growing greed not only for material things but for importance equal to that of the chiefs and the Heavy Eyebrows of the missions. As it had been through the ages among all peoples, the clever ones now began to use the gullible ones as an instrument for the creation of their own self-esteem, riches, and fame.

When the "brothers" had begun to diminish, the people turned their ears to medicine men who had collected powers into buckskin-wrapped *wah-don-skas,* such as the scrotum of black squirrel or the rattles of the rattlesnake. They chanted in words that had no meaning, and were jealous of the Heavy Eyebrows doctors and of each other.

The Little Ones were not only more frequently attacked by the "little people," the *we-lu-schkas,* but they saw more frequently the *mi-ah-luschkas,* the little people you could actually see, who dressed as they dressed. But they were sinister, these leprechauns of the Little Ones, and one not only fled from them but worried for days about seeing them.

The Little Ones had been in contact with the European since the latter part of the seventeenth century, 150 years and more, yet they would have nothing to do with his God, and they said that he himself was odorous because his body odors had no chance to escape past his collars and were also lodged in his boots, so they kept to their own moccasins, leggings, breechclouts, and robes. They learned to speak French because they liked their French allies; but when the new Heavy Eyebrows, the Americans, came, they could not understand French, and the Little Ones refused to learn their language because they didn't like them.

They should have been like the uncultured groups of the Cherokees, Creeks, Choctaws, Delawares, and Shawnees, with their flicker feathers in their hats, wearing their boots and trousers. They should have been loitering about the agencies or the forts, sitting in rows in the sun, detached from the world. Their Nobodies should have carried Bibles and become the afflated centers of attention of the Heavy Eyebrows and the Algonkian fragments. They should have sold their souls for the whisky and rum of the Heavy Eyebrows, and when sober and without furs, begged at the kitchen doors of the missions, the forts, and the traders' stores. They should have been living in little government-built log cabins, in the center of their little patches of corn and beans and squash, with their rooting hogs and their lazy dogs fighting fleas.

But in 1840, after more than 150 years in contact with European manners and mores and greed and fears, they were still the men preeminent. No one dared wear the clothing of the Heavy Eyebrows for fear of ridicule, and each morning when the morning star came up, men went to the high places to chant their prayers while the women stayed in their lodges or came out to stand in front of them facing east. Grandfather rose each morning bringing the light of day, in which they desired to live into old age, and *Wah'Kon-Tah*'s voice was still heard in the long prairie grasses, in the leaves of the oaks and the elms and the cottonwoods, in the patter of rain and the hissing of snow; and after fasting and prayer-singing with earth on their temples *Wah'Kon-Tah* would speak to them through the owl, the pelican, the curlew, the splash of a fish, the wind over the prairie, the clouds he had painted.

THE OSAGES

That is why the story of the Little Ones cannot end as it might with all other people. It is because they were resistant that they have a long story to tell.

ON THE PRAIRIE AND THE PLAINS

"Near by were a group of Osages; stately fellows; stern and
simple in garb and aspect. They wore no ornaments; their
dress consisted merely of blankets, leggings, and moccasins. Their
heads were bare; their hair was cropped close, excepting a bristling
ridge on top, like the crest of a helmet, with a long scalp lock hanging behind. They had fine Roman countenances, and broad deep
chests; and, as they generally wore their blankets wrapped around
their loins, so as to leave the bust and arms bare, they looked like so
many noble bronze figures. The Osages are the finest looking Indians
I have ever seen in the West."—Washington Irving, *A Tour on the
Prairies.*

47. On the Prairie

THE EARLY BOHÈMES, the illiterate *coureurs de bois,* the *voyageurs,* the Jesuits filled with their classical learning and their zeal and intelligent inquisitiveness, the traders of European culture, the harassed officials both French and Spanish, the young noblemen fleeing from the French Revolution seemed in their several obsessions to have seen in the Little Ones instruments for the working out of their designs or only a physical menace to their several objectives. Perhaps the Bohèmes and the *voyageurs* and trappers in their exuberant freedom from European restrictions might have seen them as human beings, since they lived with them and walked and gestured in the reflected glory of the Little Ones' prowess and therefore understood them better than any of the others, but unfortunately they couldn't write.

To the energetic Americans—traders, settlers, and free men—they were only physical obstacles; they blocked the way of the self-glorifying men who had defeated the King of England. To a literate missionary, with his facile plume, not one in the whole tribe "deserves to be rescued from oblivion."

But despite the lack of academic interest in the Little Ones, there were some men of conscience and humanity, even though without deep understanding, who were sent to them. They were fortunate in having among them men like Bourgmont, Trudeau, the Chouteaus, Bradford, Chapman, Vaill, De la Croix, Clark, Lewis, Sibley, Miller,

Lovely, Armstrong, McNair, Williams, Maugraine, Papin, Revoir, and McCoy, and others. These men had consciences and rather outstanding humanity. The attenuated French and Spanish powers knew their military power and psychology, and were busy saving face and checkmating. The missionaries theoretically elevated them to a plane of understanding upon which they themselves stood, and categorically declared that they knew not God, projecting to these close-to-the-earth men their own artificial fumblings and confusion.

The American military men were men who seemed to have assumed a species of chivalric honor without a very clear understanding of it. They assumed a saber-pride, but this didn't submerge a humanitarianism of the backwoods and a feeling for the underdog of their racial memories, their class memories. As fighting men, they admired other fighting men, and were as chivalrous and generous to the Little Ones as Andrew Jackson and later the agitations of the settlers would allow them to be.

To the American settlers, the early merchandisers, the town builders, the professional Christians and their emotionalized followers, the Little Ones were a menace to their comfort simply by their existence, and their wild hatred of the Little Ones was much like their hatred of the Mormons. The Little Ones killed their cattle, hunted game in their "neighborhood," and didn't work, and "howled" every dawn to some devil. The Mormons were better marketplace dealers than the average settlers and traded by barter agreement with the farmers of Jackson County, Missouri, and as if this was not sinful enough, they were also shameful and leagued with the devil.

Now in the decades of the 1830's and 1840's, cultured and academically interested travelers came among the Little Ones. Of course, these men were gentlemen from the East and from Europe. They weren't in struggle with the earth and the seasons and other men for their existence, and they naturally felt no urge to project the causes of their defeats and frustrations and their commercial and agricultural jealousies to the Little Ones. These men were approximately a quarter of a century advanced over the first travelers among the Little Ones, and the advance in the European culture of their respective nations had given to them a deeper understanding of themselves and the Little Ones. They had no religious, military, governmental, or commercial obsessions. Although some of them were a bit brittle and sometimes supercilious, they made every attempt to be honest.

The Missouri River had been the highway for scientific travelers and tourists, and most of the earlier travelers had met the Little Osages at Fort Osage, but now since the Little Ones had left the environs of the Missouri, the Santa Fe Trail became a highway, but still those who traveled the Santa Fe Trail did not pass through the reservation of the Little Ones in the southern part of modern Kansas.

The travelers now came to see the Little Ones; came to learn of their habits and their manners and hunt buffalo with them. They had been well advertised by the six who had traveled in Europe in the latter part of the 1820's, and apparently they had left a deep impression.

However, one of the parties of travelers of academic interest did not come expressly to visit them, but were inspired to come through their country through a chance meeting, and had the opportunity to go with the first troops sent out from Fort Gibson in 1832. Captain Jesse Bean's Rangers were setting out pursuant to the plan to come to some understanding with the "wild Indians of the Plains" whose land the government had given to the immigrant Indians from east of the Mississippi so that they could have outlets to the buffalo.

The chance meeting was between Washington Irving and Henry L. Ellsworth on a boat bound for Detroit. Ellsworth was a member of the Stokes Commission on his way to Fort Gibson, and he persuaded Irving and his traveling companions to come along with him "even to the buffalo range."

Irving's companions were Charles Joseph Latrobe and young Swiss Comte de Pourtales, about twenty-one years old, for whom Latrobe was companion and tutor.

They were an insouciant lot, Ellsworth and the tutor being a bit more formal and sedate than Irving and Pourtales, but they were highly civilized and intelligent, and they threw a few sidelights on the customs of the Little Ones that the traders had been too absorbed to notice.

They were too late to go on the buffalo hunt with the Little Ones, but they were in time to join Captain Jesse Bean's Rangers, sent out two years before Colonel Dodge's dragoons, which expedition was well described by Catlin and the Troop One's journalist, who were on a similar mission.

They left from Fort Gibson and followed the old Osage trail up the Arkansas past the old crossing just below the mouth of the Cimarron, then crossed and went up the Cimarron, left it and turned almost down to the South Canadian, then back to the fort.

On the Arkansas they met some Osages, old men and women and children who had been left in camp by the buffalo hunters. Ellsworth, remembering his mission of pacification, made a speech from the saddle to the old people, asking them to lay aside "all warlike and bloodthirsty notions," to which they gave their prayerful promise in the presence of these Heavy Eyebrows soldiers. Irving whimsically suggested that "indeed their age and sex gave some reason to trust that they would keep their word."

Some of them came to eat by Irving's fire, and after eating they lay side by side and began to sing softly, keeping the rhythm by thumping with their hands on their chests, ending each little song with an abrupt "Huh," which Irving thought sounded much like a hiccup. They had improvised little songs about these Heavy Eyebrows and apparently knew what they were doing here. The *joi de vivre* of the young comte seemed to appeal to them, and they made songs about him and the young girls.

Irving also noticed what the French explorers, traders, Spanish officials, and American settlers and hunters had not mentioned: that the white wolves on the plains and the prairie were more wary than the black and gray or yellow ones. They had to be; they had no protective coloration. Irving felt sure that the white wolf was "apparently less game" than the others.

Captain Bean's expedition was a failure from the point of view of carrying out the well-laid plans of the Stokes Commission, since they met only the village of old men, women, and children and a war party on the plains, to both of whom Ellsworth made speeches. About the first speech from the saddle to the half-frightened old men and women Irving made a quip; and from the one Ellsworth made to the

Osage war party he made a good story, which Ellsworth called "by way of addenda." He wrote that after Ellsworth's speech the Osages talked among themselves, and later Beatte, the interpreter, said that they had concluded that if the Great Father intended to put an end to Indian warfare, they must hurry and do that which they had set out to do.

Apparently Pourtales was twice disappointed: first, he failed to overtake the buffalo hunters, so that he could satisfy his compulsion to romance and excitement; and secondly, he failed to lure a "sumac girl" or a widow to his robes, despite his youth and dash.

Irving in his journals stated that White Hair the younger had died between April and mid-June of 1832 and that he had been "buried" in a cairn on a high hill. The cairn was surrounded by railings, and there were three poles from which scalps waved, accompanied by American flags. He did not mention that the flags were upside down, but this was the manner in which they were placed on the cairns of the chiefs. The scalps were of three Pawnees which *Paw-Hiu-Skah,* White Hair, had killed. Also there on the mound was a scalping knife, as if the chief might need it on his way to Spiritland. Nothing was said of the horse or the remains of the horse which must have been killed and placed on the cairn for the use of the chief on his last trip.

Irving noted the cairn and the scalps and the flags on the fourth of October, and White Hair had been "buried" sitting up and facing west dressed in all his finery sometime between April and June. The horse could have been eaten by wolves and coyotes, vultures and opossums during this period and the bones scattered. Irving did not mention that the sitting figure was facing west either, apparently feeling some hesitancy about approaching to have a look through the interstices of the stones since there was a mourner standing there like a statue.

He had met a mourner with the "earth on his face," and had learned to his satisfaction that the dead were "painted white and other colors" and that the mourners did not "eat until sunset." This was possibly trader information. No trader, trapper, missionary, military man, or commissioner who had been among the mighty warriors for some time would admit ignorance of the mores of the Little Ones.

Irving also mentioned in his journals that Sam Houston had come to live among the Cherokees of the lower Neosho, October 8, 1832.

The Frenchman Cortambert came to the Osages in 1835–36. He came as traveler, and his opportunities to study the Little Ones were better than Irving's, and as a matter of fact he was more interested in them. He wrote: "The appearance of these semi-nude men, with shaved head, warrior's face, the strange harmony of movement and the chants, makes pass in my soul a savage exultation."

He was the first among the Europeans or Americans to note that the Little Ones were really divided into five physical divisions and lived in separate villages in the locations that corresponded to terrain where long ago they had built their drying fires during the great flood.

He arrived at a village on the right bank of the Neosho in the modern state of Kansas, which he spelled in his phonetics "Manrin-habatso," which signified, he wrote, "more or less," that which touches the sky. The village was the trade center of the tribe, and here lived M. Melicourt Papin, representative of the American Fur Company, and the son of Noel Maugraine, Baptiste, who presented himself as "chief" of the village.

This village honored a chieftain whose name was *Mo'n-Xe-A-Gthe,* which means Reaches-the-Sky, and refers to the wind which blowing over the earth seems to reach the sky, where it also moves the clouds. His phonetics were not bad.

Heretofore this village had been mentioned as the Osage village, since here the furs were brought to be traded.

About five miles above this village was the village sometimes called White Hair's village because the old chief lived there, but it was called *No'n-Ni-O'n-Ba,* which means Peace Pipe. Above this village was the village of the Heart-Stays-People and the Little Osages. The chief of the Heart-Stays-People was *Mo'n-Sho'n-Shpshe-Mo'l'n* or *Mi-Tse-Moie,* Crawls-on-the-Ground. The Little Osage village was probably under *Mo'n-Sho'n Akita,* Protector-of-the-Earth.

Cortambert then located the villages of the other two physical divisions on the Verdigris where they were before the treaty of 1839.

These were the villages of Arrow-Going-Home of the Upland-Forest People and of *Tzi-Sho-Hunkah,* or "War Chief," or Big Chief of the Big Hills.

He was interested in everything which pertained to the habits and the manner of living of both the Amer-Europeans and the native Americans, the Osages. The term "gentleman" had a definite significance in Europe, and M. Cortambert was rather baffled by the transplanted Europeans' interpretation of the term. He wrote that they had pretentions *"au titre de* gentleman," but he couldn't understand their manner of drinking, eating, smoking, chewing tobacco, and spitting and their boisterous dancing.

Their questions were more than prying and were often personal insults. The officials at the boundary of the Osage reservation, where he showed his permit, went far beyond their official duties in asking him personal questions. They seemed to be rather fond of the Marquis de Lafayette, since they would ask, "Have you seen old Lafayette?"

Just as Cuming had noted in 1807–1809 among the people of the modern Illinois, Indiana, and Kentucky, "assumption of leadership on the part of the lawyers," M. Cortambert in 1835–36 noted in Missouri and Kansas that the profession of the preacher was the powerful profession, meaning influential rather than powerful, although preachers were certainly both.

He entered the village of the Osages which he called That-Which-Reaches-the-Sky probably profoundly intrigued as to the origin of the name, which he couldn't ascertain. He was not interested in the buffalo hides, the fox and beaver and wolf pelts, any more than Ellsworth, Pourtales, Latrobe, and Irving were, but he did not make shallow observations and indulge in whimsicalities and quips.

He wrote that as he approached the village That-Which-Reaches-the-Sky, he came to a "house of trade." This would be where Melicourt Papin lived and traded for the American Fur Company.

One thing which attracted his attention was the Feather Dance— the sort of thing which was always occurring in a large village, and about which the average traders, hunters, or trappers, or even more or less cultured travelers of two or three decades previous, might have

593

asked about casually, and have gone to look on with satisfying feeling of superiority.

Cortambert described the Feather Dance rather accurately, and undoubtedly asked the origin of it, but could get no satisfactory answer, apparently not even from Baptiste Maugraine.

His attempt to describe it was the first time that it had ever been noticed with such interest.

He wrote that his attention was drawn to the throbbing of drums. He was not actually so poetic; he wrote *"bruit,"* noise of the drums, and strange clamors. When he arrived at the dance, he called it a *"bal publique,"* public ball, which it was not. He saw several girls, dressed brilliantly, their hair disheveled, their eyes cast down, and a packet of plumes in each hand as they advanced in measure with sudden little jerks. Some men danced before them, periodically giving jerky cries. Two or three men beat the rhythm on the drum and were singing. The chant was aspirate and convulsive, nature unsubdued.

This is a most adequate description of the Dance of the Feathers by a Frenchman who couldn't even learn its significance.

The Dance of the Feathers was really a scalp dance. It was a greeting to the homecoming warriors, even if only part of them who left had returned. This dance was for the purpose of greeting them both in victory and in defeat. This dance would renew their spirits and, if need be, their courage. If they had brought no scalps this time, the dried scalps of another war movement waving above the dancing girls at the ends of poles would remind them that they were great warriors, and that their enemies were still riding over the plains.

And this dance was good for the spirit especially in defeat, when the women who had lost their men could be heard keening from the hills around the camp or the village. It was good to remember that the Little Ones were men pre-eminent.

The Dance of the Feathers or Scalp Dance was a girls' dance, the dance of the eldest unmarried girls. They carried feathers in each hand, and there was a scalp pole in the center of the circle which the dancers made; also in the center of the circle was the drum and the

594

singers. The girls danced in jerky steps, and they jerked their hands up and down in rhythm as they moved in the circle in pairs.

The dance was led by a warrior who sang the song of Red Shield or some other song of outstanding victory of the Little Ones over their enemies. The song of the warrior leader made the people have the feeling of victory, and the chant of the drummers, as Cortambert wrote long ago, was aspirate and convulsive, and this was the dance that inspired him to write, "This strange harmony of movements and the chants, makes pass in my soul a savage exultation."

He failed to note that the girls wore their buckskin skirts up to their knees and painted their legs yellow or white and wore by this time a trader's scarf of black across their breasts and tied it in the back with a large bow. They would have worn their very best beaded moccasins and would have painted their arms and shoulders and bare backs either yellow or white with the same clay they used on their legs. On the tops of their heads, whether their hair was disheveled as Cortambert saw it or braided in two braids or a single one, they were permitted to wear the warrior's scalplock of white-tail-deer hair and the "beard" of a turkey gobbler, the hair of the deer tail painted dawn red.

At first they held eagle feathers in each hand, and some of the modern people with tribal or gentile memory think they may have in the "old days" carried an eagle-wing fan in one hand and an eagle-tail fan in the other, but certainly they know that later they carried the dawn-tinted plumes of the snowy egret, which they got by trade from the Seminoles and perhaps the Creeks.

Around their waists the girls wore the inevitable belt of woven hair of buffalo calf. Later, however, they wore a trade belt of vari-colored yarn.

Like many travelers before him, Cortambert was awakened by the chant to the Morning Star and Grandfather the Sun, and he was intensely interested. He writes that "these lamentations are a hymn of grief addressed to 'Ouacanda' (master of life)."

Cortambert wrote that the buffalo had disappeared from his old habitat by 1835–36; that thirty years before that date they could be found in the environs of St. Louis, but that at the time of writing the Osages must travel two or three hundred leagues west of St. Louis to hunt them.

He wrote of some of the habits of the Osages and deplored some of them. The flattened head of the Osages caused by the baby boards interested him. He was deeply interested in phrenology apparently and wrote with relief that this practice did not modify the mentality of the Osages. This deformation did not mean that the mentality could "gain in one sense what it loses in another."

He would not have them changed: "I am an Osage. When I hear the chant of war of the Osages, I break the little bands by which civilization envelopes me like a mummy, and I range the prairie on a wild horse."

In 1839–40 another Frenchman came among the Little Ones, one Victor Tixier. He had studied medicine, but his interests were catholic, and he revealed much concerning the Little Ones and the Amer-Europeans which might have been lost forever if he had not come among them with no other interest than the academic. He was accompanied by three companions, but the editor of his *Voyage aux prairies osages, Louisiane et Missouri, 1839–40,* was able to identify only one of them with confidence, and that one might have been of special interest to some of the old men of the Little Ones, since he was the grandson of their friend Zenon Trudeau, lieutenant-governor of the Illinois country for the Spaniards from 1792 to 1799.

Tixier and James De Berty Trudeau had obviously met in Europe in medical school, and young Trudeau along with Major P. L. Chouteau, son of Pierre Chouteau, had deflected Tixier from a visit to Canada by making the Osages seem romantic, and Chouteau had said they might be in time to accompany the Osages on a buffalo hunt. Tixier wrote: "I accepted the Major's suggestion immediately; it allowed me to realize my greatest desire. I was going to live among the redskins in the manner of the redskins!"

He asked very intelligent questions and was quite observant, and did very well spelling Osage names and terms phonetically, despite the fact that his interpretations were sometimes wrong, as might be expected. Also, his informants, quite often Papin and Maugraine, had not been interested in the things which might interest a cultured man from France.

He referred to the Neosho as Nion-Chou, which is adequate, and he accepted Cortambert's commercial village, where Papin and Maugraine lived, "The-Village-Which-Scrapes-the-Sky," and the village of White Hair, "The-Village-of-the-Pipe." He referred to the two other villages farther up the Neosho. One he called "Maisons Cailles," which Cortambert did not name. He believed that the chief of this physical division was the "Great Chief" of the nation. He called this chief "Majakita," which was rather bad phonetics for *Mo'n-Sho'n Akita,* Guardian-of-the-Land. Tixier believed that "Majakita" meant Thick-Lips and called him "La Babine." This man may have had as his informal name one that indicated his big lips, but this would have been *Ha-Kshe-Tonkah,* which sounds not at all like "Majakita."

The fourth village he noted would be the Heart-Stays physical division, whose chief he calls "Man-Chap-Che-Mani," The-One-Who-Crawls-on-the-Ground. This is quite close to the Osage *Mo'n-Sho'n-Shpshe-Mo'I'n,* which means Crawls-on-the-Ground.

The fifth village he believed to be a "small independent republic." The Little Osages, a physical division, had been gradually separating from the tribe as were the Upland-Forest People, under Arrow-Going-Home and Black Dog, since 1802. However, the Little Osages were much more advanced toward independence. The chief of this village was, according to Tixier, Beautiful Bird, whom he refers to as Handsome Bird, and gives his Osage name as *Wah-Shinkah Lagri,* spelling it of course, "Ouachinka Lagri." His phonetics are perfect here, but *Wah-Shinkah Lagri* was often confused in the minds of travelers and commissioners and perhaps traders with *Shinka-Wah-Sa,* which is the real name of Black Dog and has nothing to do with either black or dog but means Dark-Eagle or Sacred-Little-One. He was the head of that part of the Upland-Forest People who were called Black Dog's Band and were forced to move to the reservation in southern Kansas from the modern Oklahoma in 1839, along with the people called Claremore's Band. He even appears as a signer of the treaty of June, 1825, as "Chinkawas sa or Handsome Bird" and as signer of the treaty of August, 1825, as "Shin-ga-wassa (Handsome Bird), Chief of the Great Osages."

He was of the Eagle gens, and how he came by the name Black Dog no one of the Eagle gens seems to know—perhaps through an incident which had to do with a black dog or black wolf. His original informal name, if that was what it was, could have been translated *Shonka Sabe,* which means Black Dog, but might also mean Black Horse, since the horse was once called "big dog" by the Little Ones.

One is in complete confusion concerning the identification of the villages on the Neosho within the limits of the reservation in the years 1839–40, and to a certain extent uncertain about the identity of their chiefs. One knows that the chief Tixier called "Majakita" must have been *Mo'n-Sho'n Akita,* Guardian-of-the-Land. If, as he writes, he was a son of White Hair and married a Little Osage girl, he might have been chief of the Little Osages at this time.

The *Paw-Hiu-Skah,* White Hair, mentioned by Tixier as being eighty years of age and walking with a stick, might have been no kin to the White Hair who died in 1832 and whose cairn with scalps and flags waving over it Washington Irving had seen. *Paw-Hiu-Skah,* White Hair, was a very popular name with the Deer and Bald Eagle gentes of the *Wah-Sha-She* subdivision of *Hunkah* as well as with the *Tzi-Sho Wa-Shta-Ge,* the Gentle *Tzi-Sho* gens. Analyzed, *Pa* or *Paw* could mean "head," *Hiu,* "eagle," and *Skah,* "white," therefore Head-Eagle-White; and this eagle of the white head, the bald eagle, was the symbol of the sub-gens of the Star-That-Came-to-Earth, the gens from which the Grand *Hunkah* was chosen.

There is white under the head of the white-tail deer which terminates at his throat, and a member of the Deer gens might be named White Hair. Examined closely, the white feathers on the head of the bald eagle are almost hairlike. When this eagle turns his head rather abruptly, the silky feathers adjust much as disturbed hair adjusts itself.

M. Tixier was clever with his interpretations when one takes into consideration the mélange of the traders' and the mixed-bloods' prideful and face-saving misinformation, with the Osages themselves attempting to give him, out of courtesy, the answers which they believed he wanted.

He describes the village and the lodges; and apparently the Little Ones, the resistant ones, had not changed the manner of erecting their lodges and the materials used; cattail stems, bark, and hides covering the hickory ribs and cross ribs. He wrote: "We were walking through the village between groups of men nonchalantly lying on thin blankets spread on the ground; not one look, not a sign of surprise on these impassive faces. The children went on playing without turning their heads in our direction. The women, although as much the daughters of Eve as white girls, did not come out of their lodges to watch us as we passed."

As he suggests, he was "far from imitating this indifferent attitude of the savages," and he seems to have missed nothing. He would never know, however, that the "indifferent" savages knew every detail of his Heavy Eyebrows dress and every characteristic of his face, and the manner in which he moved, and his attitude, and perhaps had come to some conclusion about what he might do under a variety of circumstances.

He noted the fact that the Osages knew about vaccination and had been vaccinated for some time. He was deeply impressed by their courtesy in council. "There are in the brilliant society of the most civilized cities in Europe, in the most learned societies, in the most eminent diplomatic bodies, many men who, like me, might be given a lesson at this Osage Council on how to discuss matters. The chiefs spoke in turn after taking time for reflection; they paused as often and as long as they wished, sure that no voice would be raised before they had concluded their speech with 'I have spoken' or its equivalent. They know how to listen without showing impatience at the objections presented to them; later I realized that they took the trouble of pondering over them before answering them or presenting any themselves. I have never heard two speakers at the same time around the warriors' fire."

M. Tixier went on a buffalo hunt with the Osages, and his cultured interest has thrown many little lights into the dark corners of their Neolithic customs. He noted that in the hunting camps at night there was complete silence, except for the sudden chorus of the wolfish dogs and the distant howls of the wolves and the yapping of the coyotes. It was a camp of the dead, except for the periodic howling of the wolves, dogs, and coyotes and periodic nostril flutterings of the horses. There was no sound from the lodges. His bed was hard and he was awake one night and his thoughts centered upon the fact that in all the encampment, there was no sound of snoring. He confirmed this by listening intently for several nights, and thought it quite odd, but he was led to the conclusion that this was protective, either conscious or unconscious. They, the Little Ones could not afford to reveal their presence at any time. "Is it not conceivable," he believed, "that the will might exercise its influence while all the other faculties are practically non-existent?"

He described the buffalo hunt and the strict organization of the hunt. He described the *Danse du Charbon,* the Charcoal Dance, wherein the warriors about to make the war movement prepare for it. He also mentioned the Scalp Dance of the girls. Unfortunately, someone told him the *Ni-Shu-Dse,* Red Waters, the Arkansas River, meant "The Caldron of Water." He described a night in the hunters' camp when he couldn't sleep because of his hard bed. The dogs were silent and moving like shadows behind the lodges searching for food, and there were no wolf or coyote choruses.

"I found my bed rather hard and was not able to go to sleep immediately. I watched the lodges illuminated by the flickering light of dying fires, the marauding dogs passing like furtive shadows, or, rather, skeletons, and young warriors looking for some sentimental adventure."

The next morning before daylight he was awakened by the prayer-song of the Little Ones to Grandfather the Sun. "This supplication," he wrote, "was accompanied by abundant tears."

The Little Ones were still making their gentile war movements as they had always done, but they now refrained from killing the Heavy Eyebrows. They had met a party of Pawnees on the Arkansas in 1838 and had taken eleven Pawnee scalps. They had taken horses from their Plains enemies as they had always done, and the removal in 1839 of the Big Hills and the Upland-Forest People from the Verdigris to their reservation in southern Kansas changed their traditional manner very little.

The Cherokees, as they had done previously in attempting to get the Shawnees, Delawares, Weas, Kickapoos, Peorias, and others to join them not only for defense against the Little Ones and other "wild Indians" but for the purpose of taking over the Osage domain, were still trying to confederate the immigrant tribes, and now they had the co-operation of the Creeks and Choctaws. They stated that they wanted the "establishment of intercourse regulations among the tribes by which peace and harmony might be maintained, and prosperity insured."

They erected a large council house for the purpose at Takatoka on the Illinois River, and there held council September 15, 1838. General Arbuckle and Governor Stokes were present. The Osages and other Plains tribes against whom they were presumably protecting themselves through their "intercourse regulations" were not invited; and Governor Stokes felt that this omission "indicates feelings of unkindness."

In May, 1842, the Creeks called a council to be assembled on a spot near the modern town of Eufaula, Oklahoma, the environs of which had enchanted La Harpe in 1819. The Little Ones were invited by the Creeks, as were the Wichitas and the Pawnees. Naturally the Shawnees, Delawares, Senecas, and other immigrant tribes were invited, since this council was for their benefit, as were the others. They were all officially represented except the Cherokees, whose official absence may have indicated jealousy.

The great General Zachary Taylor was to be present, and in some manner the messenger from the Creeks to the Osages must have stressed the fact, since the Osages made their appearance at the council driving a herd of stolen horses. From their manner it was quite obvious that they expected horses stolen from them in exchange. This was possibly more embarrassing for the "intelligence and virtue of the Choctaws, Cherokees and Creeks," which intelligence and virtue, according to Stokes, were to be "a sure guarantee of their disapprobation of such nefarious practices." It was such naïveté as this, combined with the illogical resistance to any changes in the tribal organization set up by *Wah'Kon-Tah* through the Little Old Men, which convinced the Europeanized immigrant tribes that the Osages were stupid.

This council gave the Creeks' chief a position of mentor to the Quapaws and Caddos and perhaps the Comanches, who had begun relatively uninterrupted trade with the immigrants. The Creeks were Indians, but they wore the clothing of the white man and lived as he lived and talked his language as well or better than he did. They seemed to have his power, but still were Indians, and therefore the Plains Indians trusted them.

Instead of receiving their horses stolen from them at the council, the Little Ones had been given in exchange for delivering up their stolen horses grave warnings that they must change their ways or be punished for the next offense.

Perhaps on their summer buffalo hunt, for which they left almost immediately after the council, the giant, the famous horse taker, who always crept into the lodges as stealthily as a panther to hit a chieftain with his coup stick, or who took a herd while the enemy slept, did at this time take thirty mules from the Kiowas and Wichitas, who then ran breathlessly to the Creek Chief Roley McIntosh. All the Plains tribes knew this giant horse taker, since he always announced himself by his song, which could be heard above the thudding hooves of the horses. "This is *Shinka-Wa-Sa* (Black Dog)," he sang back over his shoulder, and it was said that even the camp dogs of the enemy could not drown his words.

When Chief McIntosh sent Creek messengers along with a delegation of Kiowas to ask for the return of the mules, the giant looked down upon them and with grand gestures returned the mules. He had been present at the council, and he might have felt pride-injury when he brought his stolen horses to the council. Beneath the surface at the great council there must have been indulgent amusement, and certainly above the surface there was sanctimony.

It has been said that the band known as Black Dog's had pack mules that were so many that they reached from valley to valley on the way to and from the buffalo hunts.

The worries of the immigrant Indians over attacks from the "wild

Indians" from the plains, and over their "intercourse regulations among the tribes," the worries of the United States government over protecting the Indian immigrant and the commerce of the Santa Fe Trail, was now added to by the worry over Mexico. The Comanches spoke Spanish, and now this powerful tribe and the powerful Osages were seen hunting together. The Texans had forced the Comanches to trade north and east of their border, and the Osages had the things which they needed. This business needed watching.

There was another council, this time called by Cherokee Chief John Ross, of eighteen western tribes. It began in Tahlequah in June, 1843, and General Taylor was again present, as were nine Osages, under Black Dog and Beautiful Bird, both of whom and two others "held the feather" for the Osages, along with two other leaders. In the delegation was Big Soldier, an old man now but still parading as a man of importance, with his Lafayette medal. When it was learned that he had been one of the six Osages who had visited Paris in 1827, he was one of the councilors who had the honor of having his picture painted by John Mix Stanley, the famed artist.

Major Ethan Allen Hitchcock, who had been assigned from his special duties in the War Department to visit the Indian Territory to make a report on the charges of fraud against Indian agents and contractors, attended the great council, as everyone else did if possible. It was a tremendous spectacle, representing every stage in the development of Europeanism among the Indians of that area, in both dress and attitude.

The Iowas attached little bells to their costumes and walked about tinkling merrily; the Cherokees and other immigrant Indians were dressed in what were known as "citizens' clothes." Some were shabbily dressed and some dressed elegantly in top hats, black morning coats, with stocks and diamond stickpins, and twenty-dollar gold pieces rimmed and chained and hung from their waistcoat fronts. The Plains Indians came in their buckskin leggings, moccasins, robes, and paint, carrying fancy trade hatchets.

As for the Little Ones, the military man, Major Hitchcock, described them: "Some half a dozen Osage Indians made their appearance last evening at the council ground. Their heads were shaved and ornamented with feathers, and they wore blankets in primitive style. The Cherokees gathered around them and gazed at them with as much curiosity as if they had never seen an Indian. The Osages would hardly have attracted more curiosity in the City of New York. The Osage tribe is out of favor with all their neighbors. They are thieves to a man, wild, ignorant and barbarous."

48.   On the Plains

THERE WAS PERHAPS symbolism in the fact that the Little Ones were gradually driven from their mountain forest–prairie–plains domain, from the east, the direction of *Wah'Kon-Tah* and life, to the *Mo'n-ha*, the West, the Red Cliffs, the direction of death. There is nothing to indicate that the Little Old Men were aware of this symbolism, but they probably were, since they were certainly aware of the fact that now *Mo'n-Sho'n*, Mother Earth, the Sacred One, was only a shriveled old woman. Their reserve was only fifty miles from north to south, and not far north around the mouth of the Konza River were the reservations of their old enemies; not only their traditional ones like the Sac and Foxes, but the invaders from east of the Mississippi. They were placed on little reservations west of Missouri's west boundary, and along its southern borders of the reserve of the Osages. North of the border of their reservation was one tribe which they seemed to tolerate as they came into the Osage's domain to hunt, since their reservation, along with that of the Shawnees, was on the river highways where the great trails of the Heavy Eyebrows would fork, one to Santa Fe and one to Oregon.

These men who talked, the Little Ones say, like coyotes, singing their words, they called *Wa-Ba-Nika,* Men-Calling (-to-Us) or Men-Inviting. These were the Lenapes or Delawares. They seemed to have no fear of the Little Ones and came into their reserve in small groups to hunt, and they invited the Little Ones to feasts and at times sided with them against their own close allies, the Shawnees, when the latter were too much influenced by the Cherokees and the Creeks and Choctaws.

So now, it seemed that the Little Ones turned to the west, where they found people with customs and mores like their own. They knew what the pale Walkers-on-the-Earth, who were now great horsemen, the Cheyennes, would do under most circumstances, and they knew what the Big-Noses, the Arapahoes, would do, and the [Lodges]-from-River-Bank, the Pawnee-*maha,* were thinking most of the time.

And now since the separation of Texas from Mexico, the Comanches had come to them with outstretched hands and finally the Comanches' allies, and the once bitter enemies of the Little Ones, the Borrows-from-Others People, the Kiowas, had come along with their old friends the Comanches with their hands outstretched. They rode together now trying to find the Cheyennes, the Arapahoes, and the Pawnee-*maha,* so that they could fight the chivalric fight of the plains. They could use their coup sticks, and here on the shimmering plains, their fetish shirts and their red shields and the sacred hawk would protect them, and here on the plains when the fight was over, they could watch the Cheyenne and Arapaho warriors melt into their own white dust as they left the battle undecided to go back to their villages. And there would be another day.

And there were many days of fighting here on the plains, where there were no plowed furrows and blaizes on trees and piled stones to restrict their activity like the old bounds set by the Chief Soldier during the buffalo hunts. Their reservation opened up on the plains, and here were no magic lines, and here the Heavy Eyebrow soldiers and the free men and the immigrant Indians had not come.

Their new allies, the Kiowas, Comanches, and Apaches, were in constant struggle with the Cheyennes and the Arapahoes before 1840, and gentile parties of the Little Ones would come out to join them. In 1838, there was a battle on Wolf Creek, close to the 100th meridian, in the northwest corner of the modern Oklahoma. This was a long and bloody battle between the Cheyennes and Arapahoes on one side and the Comanches, Kiowas, and Apaches on the other. They had fought along Wolf Creek and Beaver Creek, counting coup on each other and killing off the leading men in each tribe, "and there was fighting about the village [Kiowa–Comanche] until the sun was low in the west, but at last the older people began to call out that they should stop fighting; that the southern Arapahoes were going to make peace" as the Cheyennes and Arapahoes set out for their camp on Beaver Creek about thirty miles distant, "the Kiowas all mounted and rode up on a ridge and watched them from a distance."

Two days later, warriors of the Wapiti gens of the Little Ones came up the Wolf Creek trail to the villages of their trade friends the Comanches and their friends the Kiowas and the Apaches and tried to convince them that they ought now to follow the Cheyennes to their villages on Beaver Creek and attack them there, but their spokesman said, "No, they are gone; let them go."

This was the spirit of plains warfare, and yet there is evidence that the Little Ones had learned something from their long struggle with the Heavy Eyebrows military men and commissioners and the Europeanized Cherokees, Creeks, Choctaws, and Shawnees. There is a hint that there might have been some grounds for the fear expressed by the government commissioners and the military men that the Osages might attempt to form a confederation of the great fighting tribes of the plains, to whom they were closer in culture and understanding. But again, the Neolithic warrior was just that, a Neolithic warrior, and could never be regimented. Even if the Osages had succeeded in forming a confederation of the mighty Plains warriors and had attacked the immigrants at the mouth of the Konza River, on the lower Missouri, the lower Arkansas, the lower Neosho, and the Verdigris rivers, they could have defeated them easily, and perhaps overcome the malarial garrisons at Forts Gibson and Smith and Towson. There would have been no war, only a battle; each Cheyenne, Arapaho, Comanche, Kiowa, Apache, and Osage emotionalized with self-esteem over the coup he had counted on the officers and on the Cherokees and Creeks and Choctaws wearing frockcoats and top hats, as well as excited over the number of scalps waving from his lance.

The Pawnees were as much a part of the prairie-plains as the Osages and the Missouri Sac and Foxes were not immigrant Indians in the sense that those from east of the Mississippi were, but the Osages included them in this category since they came onto the plains to hunt and fight—chiefly the Osages. The fact that the Plains tribes did band together to fight these ancient enemies of the Osages might indicate Osage influence and vindictiveness. The allies had only to move eastward down the Arkansas and the Red and the North Canadian rivers to the cabins and the corn fields and the hog pens of the immigrant. They had perfect targets in the new manorial houses built by the cultured planters of these tribes, who were trying to recreate the plantations of the Old South.

Farther west and near the edge of the plains were the immigrant Indians who had obtained permission from the Chickasaws and Choctaws to live on the Canadian and Washita rivers, and the plainsmen would have come to them first. They were great warriors, but were now anchored to kitchen gardens and peach and apple orchards, although the women did most of the work in the Indian tradition. These were respected immigrant enemies, perhaps not as cultured as the Cherokees and Creeks and Choctaws and Chickasaws, but they were still warriors and had guns. These were the Shawnees who drifted to the southwest after the death of Tecumseh, who had separated from the others of their tribe located on the Missouri and Konza rivers. Here also by permission were the Kickapoos and the Delawares, with their cabins and orchards, who had drifted from their reservations on the Missouri to the Washita.

The Little Ones say that when some gentile war party appeared suddenly near the fields and orchards, in their bluff-paint, the Shawnee women in their ground-scraping mission frocks got tangled and fell weeping. They said the Cheyenne women would gather their long hair in front of them clutched over their breasts, and, with faces upturned like the Pawnee-*maha,* could outrun many a young Osage warrior. Their buckskin frocks came only to their knees.

The Pawnees seemed to be on friendly terms with the Shawnees, Delawares, and the Potawatomis, and the other Plains Indians often saw them among the Pawnee hunting parties with their slouch European hats with turkey feathers stuck in the bands. They therefore associated the Pawnees with the immigrants, and there was evidence that the other Plains Indians had begun to ally themselves against this invasion of immigrants under Pawnee protection.

While the Pawnees were on their summer hunt in 1852, they were attacked by Cheyennes, Arapahoes, Kiowas, a physical division of the Sioux, the Comanches, and the Osages. This was on the Republican River, and the battle lasted for several days, the fighting ceasing on the whim of some leader on either side, to be continued the next afternoon. Finally Alights-on-Cloud, the well-loved and famous chief of the Cheyennes, was killed, and after the Pawnees retreated, the Cheyennes then gathered up the fragments of the dead warriors whom the Pawnees had hacked to fragments, laid them all in a ravine, and retreated weeping to their villages. They cut themselves with their knives and cut off their hair and cut their horses' tails.

There is little in tribal or gentile memory concerning this fight, when the Little Ones seemed to be allied with their old enemies, the Sioux and the Cheyennes, against the Pawnees and their immigrant allies. They apparently didn't want the Pawnees to know who they were, and perhaps did not wear their great deer-tail–gobbler "beard" roaches but covered their natural roaches with their robes, as there is only one mention of them and their other allies, the Comanches, in the reports of either the Cheyennes or the Pawnees, and then it was only an assumption on the part of the Pawnees. They thought they were attacked on one of the days by Sioux, but later assumed that they were Comanches since among the fallen they found an Osage identified by his roach.

The Europeanized Shawnees, Delawares, and Potawatomis were not very romantic figures in their trapper's buckskins and their white man's hats, but the Potawatomis especially were deadly with the flint-lock. They carried long sticks with which they formed forks for rests as the early French *voyageurs* did, and were cool and deliberate, not wolf-quick and rash like the Plains Indians. Their leaders for several generations had been trained by the British; instead of firing *par hasard* like the Plains Indians, they formed rank, fired a volley with deadly aim, then stepped back to reload while the next file stepped up to fire. They didn't circle the enemy, riding on the sides of their horses and firing from under their necks, but trained their horses to stand perfectly still while they fired, when they remained mounted.

The last fight between the Cheyennes and the Kiowa-Comanche combination was the one fought on Wolf Creek. Two years later, a peace was established between them, and this 1840 peace was lasting. Thus the Osages if they wished to continue with their Kiowa-Comanche allies must now be on friendly terms with the Cheyennes and the Arapahoes and the Apaches and even some groups of the Sioux.

It is not clear what part they might have had in the plans of the Kiowas and Comanches to federate the Plains Indians for the purpose of driving the whisky peddlers and shifty white traders from the plains in 1847.

The Sioux were apparently interested since the first emigrants were using the Platte as a highway, but this did not affect the Osages, and it is likely when the Kiowas and Comanches came with their pipe, the Little Ones gave them a feast but refused to smoke. They had had much experience with the Heavy Eyebrows over many generations and they knew the power of his God.

The plan came to nothing anyway. Some of the Cheyennes and Arapahoes had smoked with the Kiowas and Comanches, but the military had heard about it and Lieutenant Colonel Gilpin led two troops of cavalry out to camp in the middle of the Cheyenne villages.

However, when the Kiowas came again to offer the pipe to the Osages, they took it and smoked. This time the Kiowa-Comanche-Cheyenne-Arapahoe plan was to drive the immigrant Indian back across the Mississippi. This was exactly what the Little Ones would desire. It is not known in what tribe of the Plains Indians the idea was conceived in this year of 1854, but the Osages were much more concerned than any of the others, since not only had their domain been given to the immigrants but they were actually occupying it, and they could have been the instigators. Part of the domains of the Apaches, the Comanches, and the Kiowas had also been given to the immigrants, but it had not yet been occupied, and it is doubtful that any of the plainsmen besides the Little Ones would know the difference between the Algonkian, the Iroquoian, and the Muskhogean. They called all Indian immigrants "Shawnee."

The activities of the Little Ones had aroused the suspicions of the commissioners and the military men, who appreciated their power and their vindictiveness. This passing of the pipe in 1854 could have been their plan, since several Plains tribes accepted the pipe—six besides the tribe which had the honor of offering it.

The seven tribes gathered in council where the Santa Fe Trail crossed Pawnee Fork. The entire tribe of the Kiowas and two bands of the Comanches. There were two bands of Cheyennes and one band of the Arapahoes, and the Little Ones were represented by a part of the Big Hills.

The Big Hills had brought along their guns, and among them there were at least two gentile leaders with the *wah-hopeh* hanging on their backs.

The lodges were all Plains tipis, which could be quickly struck by the women when the intertribal war party was formed. There were the yellow tipis of the Cheyennes and the tipis of the Kiowas and Comanches with pictorial stories on them. It would seem that the Cheyenne and the Kiowa speeches had great influence, or perhaps their influence was due to their numbers. They had been defeated by the Pawnees the year before, and their urgency seemed to be in their hearts rather than in their heads. Attacking the immigrants far away in the wooded valleys of the Red and Arkansas and Canadian rivers and in the forests of the Ozark and Ouachita Mountains was almost academic to them when they knew that their old enemies would be hunting on the Konza. They were either going on the war movement to attack the Pawnees or those immigrants who actually came to the Plains to hunt: the Potawatomis, the Delawares, the Shawnees, and Kickapoos.

If the Little Ones held out for descending the rivers to wipe out their old Cherokee enemies, as well as the Creeks and the Choctaws, they were overspoken, and the large war party moved out northward and not eastward.

They found the Sac and Foxes and the Potawatomis near the Konza River, and there they attacked. Both tribes had British guns, as their fathers before them had had, and there was still some trade in such guns since the Oregon question had only recently been settled and the frenzied controversy over slavery was at its height and the Mexican War scarcely over. The free men had shouted hoarsely for war with England during the Oregon dispute.

Both the Sac and Foxes and the Potawatomis got off their horses and leveled their guns, and as the plainsmen came on singing their war songs in Siouan, Shoshonean, Kiowan, Algonkian, and Athapascan, the Europeanized Algonkians remained silent and fired at both horses and men. The Sac and Foxes knew how to fire by volleys also, and only the Little Ones of the plainsmen had guns; the others shot their arrows, both the sacred ones and the others, and sang their songs and had great faith in their fetishes, but the cool firing of the Potawatomis was too much for them and they had to retire, leaving several horses and several Kiowas and Comanches who lay within the range of the deadly guns of the Potawatomis. They left one Apache and two of the Little Ones, but the guns of the Little Ones were the best that could be obtained and they killed five of the Sac and Foxes and wounded four others.

Both the Sac and Foxes and the Potawatomis recognized the quivering scalplocks and the war paint of the Little Ones, and they knew that their warriors had been killed by the bullets of the Osage guns, since their own ordered firing had kept themselves out of range of the arrows of the Plains allies.

They watched the plainsmen retreat and were afraid to follow them, but they could wreak their vengeance on the dead enemy, especially the two of the Little Ones who lay dead. These Algonkians, who had long been allies of the British in their fight for a continent, and of whom the latter had tried to make European soldiers, ceremonially cut the breasts of the Little Ones, took out their hearts, and put them into their bullet pouches, then smeared their faces with the blood. The hearts of the Little Ones rubbed on their bullets would make them true and deadly. They would seek vengeance against the Little Ones later.

It would seem to the Little Ones that their old enemies, the free men, now after the Mexican War, had followed them to the plains. There were more and more Heavy Eyebrows on the plains and more wagon and pack trains along the Santa Fe Trail, and one came upon market hunters in their camps along the stream with the lobo wolves sitting waiting for the carcasses of buffalo from which the hunters had taken only the tongues and the hides. There is no doubt that they treated these hunters as they had treated the other hunters in the woodlands on the lower Arkansas, Red, Canadian and Kiamichi rivers. Here on the plains there were no Cherokees or Creeks or Heavy Eyebrows to run to Forts Gibson and Smith or to the Chouteaus to tell of the "depredations" of the savages. Here on the plains there were only the ravens and the wolves and the coyotes to read the moccasin prints of the Little Ones or know their identification arrows sticking in the Heavy Eyebrows hunter who was supposed to be the leader. Or he might only be the largest one. These "brothers," the ravens and the lobos, took the places of the crows and the timber wolves on the far away Osage and Missouri rivers, who used to wait for the war movement of the Little Ones.

The Little Ones who came to the plains had become angry giants and kept the war paint fresh on their faces, and their voices became cracked from singing their war songs. But why didn't they do more than attack the wagon trains of the Santa Fe Trail; why didn't they lead their powerful Plains allies to the settlements of the immigrant Indians and wipe them out? From the very beginning one of the most important projects of the French, then the Spaniards, the independent fur traders, and lastly the United States through Zebulon Pike, was the forming of an alliance among the powerful tribes of the Missouri and the Southern Plains. They each in turn had tried to make allies of the powerful Padoucas and the Osages and the Pawnees so that they could ally the three tribes with themselves. They had failed. But now the powerful Comanches needed the Little Ones for trade, and with them they had brought the equally powerful Kiowas and Apaches, and these two had made a treaty with the powerful Cheyennes and the Arapahoes. And for an attack on the Wichitas, the Little Ones had been allied with the other power of the plains, the Pawnees. This confederation, if it may be called that, was not brought about by Heavy Eyebrows maneuvering, but through Neolithic necessity as a result of the Mexican War. Texas had become a state in the Union, and New Mexico, which had been part of the

Republic of Mexico, where the Comanches had raided, was now a territory within the Union. The Little Ones, with the eastern boundary of their reserve twenty-five miles from the western boundary of Missouri, still had access to the trading posts of their old domain on the lower Neosho and the Verdigris besides their own trading post in the village called Reaches-the-Sky. They could bring the Plains Indians those things they needed, which included powder and rifles and lead and stuffs, and they could bring back horses and mules stolen from the Mexicans as well as Mexican captives of the Comanches whom they sold to the settlers of their old domain. They were slavers again, but this time they did not make the war movement; they brought their merchandise which they had got on credit from the eager traders of the Neosho and the Verdigris and the Arkansas to the Comanches and others on the plains, and there they received the Mexican captives and horses and mules in exchange.

And now that which Bourgmont and Malgares and Lisa and Pike had tried to bring about was accomplished, even in regard to the Pawnees, if the Little Ones had taken the leadership as the government officials assumed they had the power to do, or at least inspire the plainsmen to action against the government. Major Armstrong, superintendent of Indian affairs of the Western Territory, had reported some years before that "the wild Indians look upon the Osages as the most formidable of tribes."

The activity on the plains after the Mexican War and the greater movement along the Santa Fe Trail and the beginning of the professional buffalo hunting were not sufficient, but far out on the American River in California a contractor for Captain Sutter, one James Marshall, while standing wondering what to do about the mud and gravel which had been deposited in the water ditch of the waterwheel sawmill he was constructing for his employer, saw the glitter of gold. This was in January, 1848, and by November news of the strike had reached the Eastern states. During the year 1849 an old Spanish trail was used along the right bank of the South Canadian River from Fort Smith to Santa Fe across the plains, through the domain of the Southern Plains Indians. Men left their jobs in the East and their homesteads in the Middle West and along the Arkansas and the Missouri to take the trails to the gold fields. Soldiers deserted from the forts. They came like a great string of ants across the plains. If some romantic took a shot at a Comanche, perhaps an old man or old woman, then the Comanches would take a shot at the next white man they saw in retaliation; and if an Osage mourning party took the scalp of a bearded barbarian who was lagging behind his party, then the party in retaliation would take a shot at a Cheyenne chief.

The Little Ones, instead of using their power to inspire the Plains tribes to concerted action, attacked the wagon trains of goldseekers, especially on the Santa Fe Trail, in their panther frustration, and the Comanches and Kiowas aided them. They knew nothing of gold, but all this eager activity meant something else to them, that which the Mexicans had told them during and after the war. The Mexicans in the 1840's, like the French and the Spaniards and the British of the seventeenth and eighteenth centuries, had tried to lure the power tribes to their side; and among the many stories they told was the one that the United States would build a large town at the crossing of the Arkansas and another at the crossing of the Canadian for the express purpose of killing off the buffalo and starving the Comanches. This chicanery turned out to be a prophecy. Certainly the military officers of the United States later condoned the barbaric slaughter of buffalo as strategy in their war with the Plains Indians.

The Big Hills of the Little Ones believed this, and the story has been handed down, and there are some who still believe that the Heavy Eyebrows did do just this.

During the summer, the Little Ones, knowing no bounds to their reserve to the west, became disturbed about their "brothers" of the plains, the buffalo. They could see that soon they would go with the wapiti and the bears and the buffalo of the Neosho and the Verdigris.

The Comanches and the Kiowas were attacking the wagon trains of the goldseekers and the Santa Fe Trail, and in the summer of 1854 the Little Ones joined them, though they attacked independently. In some manner the attacks of the Comanches and the Kiowas were not as serious as those of the Little Ones. The Comanches and the Kiowas were probably doing no more than taking toll for the passage through

615

their domain. This was not the Osage domain; this territory south of the upper Arkansas River had never been within the domain of the Little Ones, but their "brothers" again were their chief concern and *Wah'Kon-Tah* had not restricted their movements to any one area. They attacked both above and below the Arkansas.

Perhaps because of their terrifying bluff-painting and their great size, or perhaps because they seemed to be intent not on levying toll but on taking scalps, their activities were immediately proclaimed to be "intolerable," and it was thought that "emigrants and freighters will scarcely be permitted to pass the road next season." It is quite possible that they were often mistaken for the Pawnee-*maha,* since they also shaved their heads leaving only a scalplock.

There were only the First and Second Dragoons and the mounted riflemen, three mounted regiments scattered through the frontier posts from the Mississippi River to the Pacific Ocean. On March 3, 1855, the Congress authorized the creation of two regiments of cavalry for the purpose of fighting the Plains Indians.

Colonel Pitcairn Morrison left Fort Gibson with a detachment to travel along the Santa Fe Trail as a bluff-march and to select a site for a fort far up the Arkansas River. This site was on a bluff about one and one-half miles above "Bents Fort," which was a private trading post. At the post he held a council with Cheyenne, Apache, and Arapahoe Indians; only the Kiowas, Comanches and the Little Ones felt guilty, and were not present.

It is difficult to ascertain just how many of the gentes of the Little Ones were active on the plains most of the seasons, while the others came out from their villages only in Little-Flower-Killer Moon and Deer-Hiding Moon each year on their buffalo hunts. Perhaps there were not a sufficient number to inspire the Plains tribes to war against the immigrants, especially the Cherokees. There may have been only some gentes from the Big Hills and perhaps from the Upland-Forest People. Also, after the establishment of Fort Arbuckle up the Canadian about 1851, the Chickasaws, their old enemies from across the Mississippi, with whom their splinter the Quapaws had fought and against whom they had played the buffer in the early days, were now not afraid to leave the protection of the Choctaws in order to build their cabins and plant their land on the edge of the plains. The fifth tribe of the Five Civilized Tribes, the Seminoles, had moved from Florida onto their lands in the old Osage domain.

Thus was a powerful alliance of Plains tribes ineffective through inertia, and the Little Ones, it seems, could have been the natural leaders, but for some reason they took no grand action. They only allied themselves with the Pawnee-*maha* for a brief period to almost annihilate the Wichitas, October 3, 1846. Also there was a tribe of wandering Indians who ate anything they could catch and kill during the disturbed conditions during and after the Mexican War. They came wandering up into the Chickasaw country from Texas. The Little Ones knew about them, but had never bothered to do anything about them until they came aimlessly into the region over which, while not considered a part of their old domain, they had exercised war influence. Now it was Chickasaw country, and they heard that The Swallowers had come there. They were disturbed. These people they called The Swallowers were cannibals, and were called Tonkawas.

The Little Ones went to the people who independently had been attacking the immigrants around Fort Washita and whom they, the Little Ones, had persecuted for generations, the Lodges-Far-Away People, the Pawnee Piqué, or Wichitas. Both the Wichitas and another Caddoan tribe, the Kichai, accepted the pipe. These Caddoans knew about The Swallowers, and knew their habits and their moccasin prints. They built no houses, only bark lean-tos and other primitive shelters, and their fires were built with large poles which could be pushed into the fire as they burned.

These miserable people had eaten members of the Wichita and the Kichai tribes, and they were afraid of them. They did not eat the dead bodies of enemies whom they had killed or found dead for the transmutation of great courage which the enemies might have, but because they were hungry.

The Little Ones knew that their dead must be painted for identification and placed in cairns on high hills where *Wah'Kon-Tah* could see them. Also the gasses of the body must be lost into the atmosphere. If they were eaten, their spirits would wander over the earth or plead with the voice of the screech owl like one who had not been painted for recognition in Spiritland. They must kill them, and leave none. They did not succeed in total destruction of them, for some of The Swallowers got away and hid, and there were no warrior decorations to reveal them. They were like lizards on rocks.

49. *Nika-Sabe,* the Black Man

On the reserve the three physical divisions, the Thorny-Valley People, the Heart-Stays People, the Little Osages, and part of the Big Hills had had comparative peace for thirty-nine years, ever since they signed the treaty of 1825. The Upland-Forest People and a part of the Big Hills had only been forced onto the reserve in 1839, and had only fifteen years of comparative peace.

There had been whisky peddlers and trappers and hunters who trespassed on the reserve, and the Potawatomis and the Shawnees and the Kickapoos and Delawares had crossed the northern border, but they had only hunted and not settled, fragments of them settling on the Canadian and Washita rivers in modern Oklahoma, by sufferance of the Choctaws and Chickasaws, where they were welcomed as buffers.

This relative peace was shattered in the year 1854 through an incredible madness that had come among the Heavy Eyebrows. They came up the Arkansas and thence up the Neosho and the Verdigris, then spread out over the land to create little communities. They came up the Missouri and the Konza, and they came overland from the Missouri towns. They carried their jugs, and they quarreled among themselves, goaded the Little Ones, stole their horses, and shot individual men and women whom they met on the prairie.

Wagon trains rolled up the Konza and the feeder streams. The Heavy Eyebrows settled at Fort Scott, which had been established in

1842 on the river which the Little Ones had called Snake-with-Open-Mouth Waters and the French had named Marmiton. They came where the government said they would not be allowed to come, into the Cherokee Neutral Land, which was the twenty-five-mile-wide buffer between the Missouri settlers and the Little Ones.

This madness of the nation seemed to have little to do with land greed. Some of the more serious settlers were sponsored by the New England Emigrant Aid Company, but many of the others on both sides seemed to be lustful, and spent much time talking, drinking, and quarreling, gun-proud and fanatical. The latter were the ones the Little Ones saw, since they settled on the Neutral Lands, which as a buffer was supposed to be free of settlers.

The Little Ones had seen *Nika-Sabe,* the Black Man, whom the Cherokees and the Creeks had brought with them from their homes across the Big Waters, the Mississippi, and they had seen the slaves of the Chouteaus and of Melicourt Papin at the village called Reaches-the-Sky, as well as the slaves of other traders. They knew well the dandified black body servant of Edward Chouteau who wore a "Prince Albert" in imitation of the Prince Consort of Queen Victoria of England. They must have been impressed by black men or some incident associated with them, since, when they anthropomorphized the *we-lu-schka,* it was often a black man who disappeared under water.

However, they had named a creek which flows into the Konza River about forty-two miles up the river from its mouth *We-Lu-Schka* because there they had seen "water dogs" disporting themselves in the water as they came to cross. Their horses snorted and wheeled, and the "water dogs" barked at them and disappeared.

During the beginning of this period of the Heavy Eyebrows' madness, some men came to this place, *We-Lu-Schka,* led, so the Little Ones believe, by a man with red hair. The Heavy Eyebrows built a village here, and in trying to pronounce the Osage word *we-lu-schka,* which was the name of the creek, they called it "Wakarusa." The Little Ones immediately gave the little community the name *Pa-Hiu-Schutze* for the redheaded man who seemed to be the leader, although the Heavy Eyebrows called their community "Lawrence."

Up the river (about thirty miles) other men came to the place where the Papin brothers and their Konza wives had a trading post. Near here the *Shonka Nunka Ga-Xa,* Running-Wolf Waters, ran into the Konza River. This was the place where the Little Ones and the Konzas came to dig potatoes, and they called it *Do-Pegeh,* Dig-Potato-Place. The Heavy Eyebrows who came there to make a village, called the creek "Shunganunga" and the town which they built "Topeka."

These people who settled along the Konza River were busy, and the Little Ones came here to watch them. They were like *sho-mi-kase,* the coyote, these Heavy Eyebrows, they said; they laughed and talked and they could hear them from their place of concealment.

Some years earlier, they had been afraid of the Heavy Eyebrows who came up the Missouri and the Missouri Konza, and had traveled up the north fork of the trail they had made from the mouth of the Konza River. They had brought the great "cramps" to the people at the mouth of the Konza, just as the That-Things-on-Its-Head People had brought the "great cramps" to them when they lived on the Verdigris. The Little Ones had fled back to their reservation and stayed there for a long time, going only to the west to hunt buffalo.

The Heavy Eyebrows swarming along the trails and in the little communities near the mouth of the Konza had fascinated the Little Ones, and often gentile parties would stay out for a week watching every detail of the activity, listening to their loud swearing and their laughter, and even their talk floated up to them where they would conceal themselves.

One day some young men of a *Tzi-Sho* gens were on a hill above their old river, the north fork of the Place-of-the-Many-Swans, which the French had called "Marais des Cygnes" and the Americans were calling "Merry Deseen." Their old trail was used by the Heavy Eyebrows now.

As the young men watched some covered wagons, they stopped and the oxen were outspanned by a creek which ran into the Marais des Cygnes. Soon a group of women came through the tall bottom weeds holding their skirts close to their legs. They looked around at the trees and bushes as they chattered, then one of them climbed through the weeds to a little eminence and sat on a log, which was on the trail they had taken from the wagons. The others took off their clothes and had a much-needed bath.

There was nothing very strange about women bathing to the young men, who were still under twenty perhaps, since they often spied on the young girls of their villages, sometimes even shining peeps-in-water, the trader's mirrors, into their eyes, so that they would giggle, and the old duennas would come searching for them with their butcher's knives calling them many things.

But they had never seen the Heavy Eyebrows women out of their voluminous clothing, and this was a unique incident, perhaps even a thrilling one. They talked about it much and told others, and soon the little stream where the women were bathing was called *Uzi-Hu-Walli(a) Ga-Xa,* White-Women-Genitals Creek.

Later, when the excited Heavy Eyebrows came, they tried to pronounce the name, but could get no closer than "Osawatomie," and here they built one of their little communities and called it by that name.

The Little Ones could know nothing of the men who called themselves Free-Staters or Free-Soilers, Abolitionists, "Anti-Nebraska" men, Pro-Slavery men. If they had been told what madness had come into the hearts of the Heavy Eyebrows, they wouldn't have believed it. They would have put a hand over the mouth in surprise, and wondered why there were not a sufficient number of *Nika-Sabe* for all the Heavy Eyebrows, and why these men killed each other over the *Nika-Sabe* when there were practically no black men on the prairie to fight over. They naturally had known nothing of the Missouri Compromise of 1820 which allowed their old domain to be incorporated as a part of the state of Missouri. After they had ceded the northern part of the modern Arkansas and the southern half of modern Missouri in 1808, there had been a line drawn along 36 degrees and 30 minutes of latitude, which became the boundary between the two territories. Before the Free-Staters would allow Missouri to become a state, there had to be a compromise between the Free States and the Slave States. The compromise was this, that the line along the latitude 36 degrees, 30 minutes, extended, would represent the boundary between the Slave States and the Free States.

After the Mexican War a tremendous territory was added to the Union, and the territory would be divided into smaller divisions which would one day become states of the Union. And California, in the excitement of gold and population flooding, forced itself into statehood and joined the Free States. This caused an unbalance of sixteen Free to fifteen Slave, and the controversy became bitter again.

Then a short man, rather square and high-domed, with tremendous energy and an all-absorbing ambition to be President of the United States, obtained as a steppingstone the office of senator from Illinois. This man, through his brash energy and his oratorical ability, put through the Congress a bill which repealed the rather sanctified Missouri Compromise. His bill was later called the Kansas-Nebraska Bill, because the territories of Nebraska and Kansas were created out of the country referred to as the "Platte country," which had been thought of as an area to which all the Indians could be removed. The Little Ones, the Delawares, the Sac and Foxes, Wyandots, Shawnees, Potawatomis, and Kickapoos and others had already been removed to the southern area of the "Platte country," which would be given the name of the Little Ones' splinter, the Konza, and called for them "Kansas," which was the name by which the Americans were now calling the tribe.

This brash little man through his influence effected this legislation which no Southern gentleman would have dared suggest, and the Southerners were jubilant, because the bill provided that even though the "Platte country" lay above 36 degrees, 30 minutes latitude, the states to be created out of it could decide the question of slavery themselves, and he grandly called the principle "popular sovereignty," which his opponents soon turned into "squatter sovereignty."

But there were only about 1,500 Heavy Eyebrows in this land, half of them attached to Indian agencies and to missions. There were the Little Ones and fragments of the east-of-the-Mississippi Algonkians and Iroquois, the Konzas, and a few Cheyennes and Arapahoes and Pawnee-*maha* in the western part; these and scattered traders and people of the missions and people attached in a variety of capacities to the Indian agencies, as well as the inevitable trespassing hunters and trappers and whisky peddlers. Before you can have "squatter sovereignty," you must have squatters, and this mad rush into Kansas of the rabid partisans must have surprised even the brash little high-domed man, Stephen A. Douglas of Illinois.

With the Little Ones one might wonder about this epidemic of madness. It might appear that there was no pragmatic reason for the coming of these intense partisans carrying tools and guns and Bibles.

There certainly seemed to be a hint of religious fanaticism in their barbarities.

It had been explained to the Little Ones in some manner that the Heavy Eyebrows were fighting over *Nika-Sabe,* but there were so few of *Nika-Sabe* there on the prairie to fight over. The abstractions were too much for the Little Ones, and they couldn't see any rea-son for these wild, unthinking men murdering each other, burning houses and whole communities, and shouting themselves into uncon-trollable emotionalism.

The people from Massachusetts sponsored by the New England Emigrant Aid Company were themselves not materially affected by the fact that certain people in the South owned slaves. They came to establish "squatter sovereignty" and keep Kansas a free state, despite the fact that many of them had never seen a Negro. Some of them had read the pamphlets of William Lloyd Garrison and Harriet Beecher Stowe's drippy fiction called *Uncle Tom's Cabin,* but since these Amer-Europeans of New England never had both feet off the earth at the same time, the real reason for their consenting to come to Kansas, the real lure, might have been the propaganda of the militant idealists who sponsored the New England Emigrant Aid Company's promise of land and material aid.

However, when they arrived in Kansas, they had to fight against the proslavery people who burned their cabins and murdered their neighbors, and it might be understood that they themselves became holy killers and could condone the murders of John Brown.

The proslavery people countered the New England Emigrant Aid Company with organizations called Blue Lodge and Sons of the

South, and they lured conscientious settlers to Kansas with the same promises, who when they arrived found that they must protect themselves, and in order to do so, must league themselves with free men and free-lance haters, who had run out of Indians and game, and to whom killing Free-Staters from ambush was a thrilling novelty.

Most of these emigrants sponsored by the organizations had economic reasons rather than ideological ones for coming to Kansas. They had been poor whites in the Old South, where slavery had imposed upon them conditions of poverty and economic insecurity. They came to Kansas to be free, but remained sympathetic to slavery.

Despite the pamphlets and the novels and the poetry and bitter sentimentality, these unconscious tools of politics and emotionalism did have practical reasons for their migrations, as did the people from New England. They came not only from New England and the South, but from many other states. The year 1857 was a depression year.

The Little Ones might have understood John Brown of their *We-lu-schka* Waters, now called Wakarusa, and of their *Uzi-Hu-Walli* Waters, now called Osawatomie. They might have understood that after reading his Bible—even without fasting—he might go forth to call his enemies of Potawatomi Creek from their robes to shoot them down or split them with cutlasses.

The Little Ones had no Lord's Day, but they could have understood that Sunday before dawn would have been propitious for the murder of defenseless slaveocrats by Brown and his sons and other followers. The list of his victims in his pocket they could not have understood, since they seldom singled out individuals of their enemies when they sneaked into their lodges to count coup. John Brown sitting apart from his followers with his back to a tree, awaiting the early morning moment for his massacre, singing hymns softly to himself, they could have understood.

They might have wondered why, since his party outnumbered his sleeping victims, he didn't grasp the greater honor by tapping them with his coup stick, shouting his name, and riding off in the moonlight. But perhaps this was like their Mourning Dance, when one took the Sacred Hawk skin from the shrine and dropped it to note if it faced west; then, if it did, jubilantly singing, "Something must die in the west." Something he found in the black book of mystery of the Heavy Eyebrows had been favorable to his war movement, and naturally he would shout something must die.

This is conjecture. No tribal or gentile memory recalls the bearded madman, but his actions would have made sense, even though they could not have understood wild mouthing about slavery.

The Osage mission on the Neosho had been established, and Jesuit Father Schoenmakers came there in 1847. The mission was located just six miles above White Hair's village, which seemed to be the largest and the center of the activity of the Little Ones. The Little Osages had a village about where the town of Chanute, Kansas, now stands, and were under their chief Striking Ax (1853), and it would seem that the man who might have pretensions to chieftainship of the physical divisions called Little Osages, one Little Bear had drawn the Bear gens of that division away from the village and had established himself on the Neosho near the mouth of Elm Creek (1855).

The other divisions were on the Neosho, but there is no way of determining the exact locations, since most of the villages moved from place to place, the only exceptions being those where some trader had set up his log cabin. These communities became more or less permanent.

The Little Ones were moving frequently now, during the year of the beginning of the Heavy Eyebrows madness and those years that followed. The Song of Death was heard often now, and a whole village might vanish overnight, leaving their dead for the wolves and the vultures. Again, as in the time of the great "cramps" in 1833 and 1834, many Little Ones died; in January of the year 1852, White Hair died, and by May of that year several hundred of his people had died of measles. In the struggle for "squatter sovereignty," the Heavy Eyebrows were bringing the Little Ones their diseases, for which they had built up no immunity.

In the summer of 1855 the grasshoppers came and ate the missionaries' corn and vegetables, and the same year the *we-lu-schkas* came again, this time the *ge-ta-zhe,* things-on-your-face, smallpox. Father Schoenmakers of the mission wrote, "Upward of 400 Osages have died since last winter of smallpox and other contagious diseases."

The Osage mission run by the Jesuits was well established, and both Father Schoenmakers and Father Felix Ponziglione were ardent and highly respected by the Little Ones, and especially by the mixed-bloods, and they treated the people from the outside who stopped there periodically with their accustomed courtesy, whether they were proslavery, called slaveocrats, or Free-Staters. They even treated some Texas Rangers who had been sent to Fort Scott to "rout Old John Brown" with meticulous courtesy.

Down the river there was a high bluff, and close to this bluff a stream ran into the Neosho from the northwest. This had been a favored spot for the Little Ones, and here they had a village which they called *No'n-Nu-Ba-Shi,* which means Little Pipe.

The stream that ran into the river from the northwest was forbidden waters, just as the waters which the Americans called Wakarusa were forbidden and for the same reason, but the *we-lu-schka* they saw here were not "water dogs," but something else. *We-lu-schkas* could be "little people" who were invisible or they could be unknown bugs or chimeras.

A gens were moving their village site one day, and as they approached this creek, the women were walking ahead. The word for bridge in Osage is also the word for a tree fallen across a creek, and they looked for such trees. However, if they could not find one lying just right for a bridge, they would cut one so that it fell across the water.

This day there was a log lying in the water, with each end touching a bank, and the first woman stepped on it, and with spread arms started across. When she had taken only a few steps, the log rolled a little, then "swam" away downstream.

The terrified woman splashed to the shore, and the others fled with her to tell the people that they had seen a *we-lu-schka.* Thereafter this creek was called *We-Lu-Schka Ga-Xa,* Mystery-Thing Creek. When August Chouteau later established a small post there, he translated *We-Lu-Schka Ga-Xa* into *Rivière de la Bête,* which became simply *La Bête,* The Beast.

About 1841, Chouteau sold his post to John Mathews, a Virginian

627

by way of Kentucky. He owned trading posts at Fort Gibson and one at the Osage mission, and he established the third one here in 1849, and established his home here on the river's bluff. He built a large house with two chimneys, one at each end, and built a race track and had 140 acres of land cultivated. He was called *Mo'n-ce-Gaxe,* Metal Maker, and his community was called Metal-Makers-Town. At each one of his trading posts, he had blacksmith shops and metal and the things made from metal, and the power of metal had impressed the Little Ones from the time they saw the metal fleshers and awls the French *voyageurs* had given their Missouria women in the seventeenth century.

Later, the village which grew up about the trading post and was inhabited chiefly by the Little Osages was called Little Town.

Then one night in 1856 free men who happened to be in the pay of the Free-Staters burned one of his barns, and Mathews was awakened by the squealing of horses. He immediately formed a company of proslavery men and set out to run the settlers out of the buffer strip called now the Cherokee Neutral Lands. While the Missourians who lived on the east side of the twenty-five-mile strip were proslavery, the Free-Staters were settling families loyal to them on the forbidden buffer lands.

When at his trading post at the Osage mission, he noted that the Jesuits were favoring the Free-Staters and had begun to persuade the Osages to their side. He couldn't let this happen. He had great influence with the Osages, as traders often had, but besides this he was married to Sarah Williams, daughter of William Shirley Williams, who had been missionary and interpreter at the old Harmony Mission, and a Big Hill woman. When the Big Hills came to Little Town, they came to his house without invitation, and courtesy dictated that he must feed them as long as they wished to stay.

He influenced *Tzi-Sho Hunkah,* chief of the Big Hills, and his people, as well as the highly intelligent *To-Wa'n-She-Heh,* Tall Chief, gentile chief of the Buffalo-Face gens, to come over to the proslavery partisans, and he got *Shonka-Sabe,* Black Dog, to come over with his band.

The Black Dog of late 1850's was not the giant horse taker, but his heir along with *Sho-Mi-Kase,* The Wolf. The giant horse taker had died in 1848.

He worked on the Little Osages under Striking Ax and those gentes who lived at Little Town, but they would not follow him. Father Schoenmakers had talked to them first. This angered John Mathews.

Father Schoenmakers was a Jesuit and his Society of Jesus had been persecuted by kings and governments periodically for centuries, and here in the Protestant United States they were wary, even though the President and the majority of the Senate had been elected by Democrats. There was a difference between Free-Soilers and Free-Staters on the one hand and Abolitionists on the other. The Free-Soilers and the Free-Staters wanted to keep the new territories which might become states above the latitude of 36 degrees, 30 minutes free, while the Abolitionists wanted the slaves freed even where slavery had become an institution. Being a learned and civilized man, a Jesuit, it may be assumed that Father Schoenmakers was an Abolitionist.

It seemed not enough that hundreds of the Little Ones would die with the measles and the smallpox and the free men on both sides should steal their horses and use their old men and old women for target practice, but they must now be confused by the opposing interest of Metal Maker, the trader, and the Black Robe, the man of mystery. They had great respect for both. The things which the trader brought to them were like gifts to them, and the generous giver was ever honored among them. They did not ever consider the great value of the furs and hides which they traded to him for the *wah-don-skas* they cherished. They knew nothing of his magnificent profits. For the Black Robes they had great respect. They had seen the great power of the God of the Heavy Eyebrows, and these men of mystery, the men of *Wah'Kon* could do them great harm through the many sacred things they had, and when they could, they tried to protect themselves with the Black Robes' medicine. Many of them wore crucifixes around their necks just below the mussel-shell gorget which symbolized the Sun, god of day.

John Mathews, with his great house and his long table covered with antelope, deer, buffalo, corn, squash, and fruits in season from his own trees, and John Mathews, with his store full of many *wah-don-skas,* whose blacksmith shod their horses for an insignificant beaver skin or buffalo robe, did not have the strong medicine of the Heavy Eyebrows God on his side.

However, Black Dog and his people and *Tzi-Sho Hunkah* and part of the Big Hills stayed with him, and they came to his house at Little Town often to talk about the things they didn't quite understand and to reassure themselves and to feast at his table.

Now the Little Ones, after generations of playing as the balance of power between Spain and France, Spain and England, and France and England, between Chouteaus and Lisa, which they could understand, at least partially, were now asked to play that role between abstract ideologies which they could never hope to understand, which had something to do with *Nika-Sabe,* the Black Man.

But each Little-Flower-Killer Moon and every Deer-Hiding Moon the Little Ones went to the plains to hunt, leaving their pitiful little corn patches and their squashes and melons. But now many of them kept cattle, and when they went to the plains, they would drive their stock across the Neutral Lands and across the Missouri state boundary and there have the proslavery settlers take care of them while they were gone. Whether the settlers took one or two cows from each Osage, or whether they thought their caretaking was worth much more, is not known, but one assumes that this depended on the attitude or the interest of the agent at the time. It was better than having the cattle stolen or butchered by the Free-Staters and the free men.

They chanted each dawn to Grandfather, and they arranged the marriages of their young men and women, and they held the nuptials as they had always done, except that now they dressed the bride in a general's dress tunic and a top hat with a tinted snowy egret feather in it. When White Hair and Traveling Rain and others had gone to Washington to see President Jefferson, he had paid special attention to them, showing them the power of the New Heavy Eyebrows or Long Knives. He was very anxious to impress these "bad Indians" from the Missouri. Among other things, which included medals bearing his image, he gave them general's dress tunics and flags and hats. When they arrived back at the Place-of-the-Many-Swans and the Place-of-the-Oaks, they each put the medals away in their parfleches, over which their women stood guardian. The flags, they ordered, must be placed on their graves, upside down.

When they gave their nieces away, they dressed them in the general's tunics and hats. The tunics were worn over their other, traditional nuptial dress, and after the wedding, the tunics were put away in parfleches very carefully. At first only the chiefs and chieftains were entitled to flags over their cairns, but later almost every man who died whose family wished to walk in reflected glory had the United States flag plopping over his cairn, until the crazy winds that whipped the hilltop shredded it. And soon every girl was married in the general's tunic. When the original ones wore out, they made new ones from trader's stuffs, and they kept the board epaulettes with their golden encrustations from generation to generation.

On the high hills of the prairie, the flags attracted the attention of the free men, and it soon became known among them that the chieftains and the chiefs were dressed in their finery, and given their best bow and arrows, along with food sufficient for their journey to Spiritland; then they were flexed into a sitting position and the cairn built over them.

The scalplocks and the painted robes and the buckskin leggings and moccasins and the trader's silver bracelets and arm bands had much value. The free men would come there to these cairns, and drag to one side the dead horse, whose spirit was to carry the noted one to Spiritland, and throw the stones to one side, topple the dead warrior, and take his finery, leaving him there for the wolves and the vultures and the opossums. Even the flag had value if it was not tattered by the prairie winds.

The traders and the missionaries and the agent warned the Little Ones to do nothing about this insult, but often when fasting warriors came back from their mourning movement after the Mourning Dance, the scalps waving from their spears or coup sticks were not always black and long, but only the ones with long, black hair, or the roaches of the Pawnee-*maha*. The hair taken from the tribes with strong medicine was attached to the scalp pole during the Feather Dance.

Apparently their medicine was still strong and respected by the Plains Indians, despite the statement of Father Schoenmakers in 1856 that "ten years ago the Osages numbered 5,000 souls, but presently they hardly exceed 3,500."

Despite the epidemics of measles and smallpox and the encroachment of the free men, and the slaughter of their "brothers," all of which ought to have been overwhelming evidence that they were being defeated by the great mysteries of the Heavy Eyebrows, they remained as resistant as ever. They wore their traditional clothing except for the trade blanket and the trader's *wah-don-skas* they hung from their slit ears, and the silver bands and the crucifix. They chanted their prayers and danced their ceremonial dances and painted the faces of their dead so that they would be recognized in Spiritland. The strong medicine of the God of the Heavy Eyebrows was tragically disturbing, but the Little Ones were still the men pre-eminent.

During the year of the great drought, from September 1, 1859, to October, 1860, when scarcely an inch of rain fell all year and there was not a single snowflake during the winter months, and the following summer the thermometer reached 132 degrees Fahrenheit, tempers were short, and prayer meetings long and frequent. Relations between the trader John Mathews and the Jesuit Father Schoenmakers became very bad, beyond repair. It seemed that the Little Ones, while not resolving their doubts, would follow the trader. Perhaps they could appease the anger of *Wah'Kon-Tah,* if he was angry, and the drought along with other things might indicate that he was at least displeased. He had devoured the lakes and the marshes and bared the lotus bulbs to the sun, and some of their horses had died. Perhaps by fighting with the trader and the Heavy Eyebrows led by him, the Metal Maker, they might have the benefit of the medicine of the Heavy Eyebrows as well as their own.

John Mathews recruited Cherokees and Creeks from his trading post at Fort Gibson, and he got the Big Hills young men to go with him to drive the Free-Staters out of the Neutral Lands. After the Civil War began, he became more and more active, and the breach between him and Father Schoenmakers became a chasm, and he finally drove Father Schoenmakers, the loyalist, from the mission, in June, 1861.

On August 9, 1861, he and his mixed company drove sixty trespassing Union families from the Neutral Lands, and they fled to Humboldt and other Union communities, and Father Schoenmakers fled to St. Marys, Kansas.

The Confederacy seemed to be in control of southeastern Kansas, and they were now making plans to make treaties with the Indians. They inspired an attack on Humboldt, September 12, 1861, and the Union loyalists accused John Mathews, calling him a "notorious scoundrel" and his followers "a band of desperadoes" in their newspapers. This was only a few of the names the slaveocrats and the Free-Staters were calling each other. When there was a clash between two parties, one proslavery and one free-stater, the Unionist papers indicated that the Free-State men were not just killed in the fight but "murdered." The *Emporia News,* of a settlement high up on the Neosho north of the reserve of the Little Ones, informed its readers that of the settlers who were squatting on the Neutral Lands, the sixteen who were killed in the fight with the Mathews party "had been brutally murdered," and that Mathews and his party were "devils in human shape." The same bitter language would be employed in the press of the Confederacy in Missouri to express their hatred of the Union. On the other hand, Confederacy men were not "killed" in their border struggles but "murdered."

When General James H. Lane of the Union took his troops into Missouri to burn towns such as Osceola and Warsaw on the Osage River, a company of Confederate border men sacked Humboldt in Kansas. The *Kansas State Journal* of Lawrence declared that "the party consisted of 125 men, a part of them white and part Indians, but the whites were disguised as Indians."

The *Fort Scott News* asserted that "the notorious Mathews came up the Humboldt with about 150 of his gang, and plundered several stores, besides carrying off a number of negroes."

In September, 1861, Lieutenant Colonel James G. Blunt, stationed at Fort Scott and commanding the Sixth Kansas Cavalry, defeated

Mathews' company and overtook Mathews just above the south boundary of the Osage Reserve when he was on his way to his post at Fort Gibson.

They took from the Mathews trading post six bearskins and five hundred buffalo robes and over fifty horses from his stables; and these Blunt divided among his men as payment. He had Mathews' buildings burned, and arrested all the white people of the village of Chetopa, south of Little Town. Mathews had been killed in this area close to the boundary line, and the community was under suspicion. The people were brought to Little Town and court-martialed, September 18, 1861, but were freed. It was known that the agent for the Osages was a Southern sympathizer, and Dr. George Lisle had served as a clerk under Dorn to make payment to the Osages from their funds according to the provisions of the treaties with the government. Dr. Lisle had been Mathews' friend, and he lived in Chetopa, having named the village for the chieftain *Tzi-Topa.*

Tzi-Topa, Four Lodges, did not indicate ownership of four lodges, but the name had been given to him as an honor, since he had taken four lodges of the Pawnee-*maha,* during his gens' attack on a Pawnee village.

The *Emporia News* of September 28, 1861, after Mathews' death, assured its readers that "his death puts an end to all danger from that quarter, and for the present at least, we look for peace and quiet in that part of the State."

The Confederates thought that this might happen as well, and both the Confederacy and the Osages were now without a leader in that essential area. As the *Emporia News* had stated in its relief over the death of John Mathews: "He was possessed of great influence with the Osage Indians."

The agent of Richmond, Albert Pike, a very able and intense Southerner, now became active on the Confederacy's behalf, to fill the vacuum in southeastern Kansas. He had met a gens of the Osages near the Red River in 1832, when he made an exploring trip to Santa Fe. When his men were sick and hungry, the gens chieftain had asked them to come to his camp, and there he feasted them.

The idea of luring the Indians to the Confederacy was not of the moment. As early as May, 1861, Brigadier General Pierce of Arkansas had written to Jefferson Davis that his state had appointed him to command the western frontier with headquarters at Osage Mills in Benton County. He asked Jefferson Davis to send to him Hardee's *Tactics,* since they had no *Tactics* in Arkansas, and he and Captain Pike were anxious to secure immediately the co-operation of the Indians.

Albert Pike got in touch with the confused Little Ones immediately and held council at Park Hill, and there got the whole tribe with the exception of the Little Osages to sign a treaty with the Confederacy.

Park Hill is in the Cherokee country, eighteen miles east of Fort Gibson and on the east side of the Illinois River, near the mouth of Barren Fork. It was established in 1829 by a few highly cultured immigrant Cherokees, and later, in 1839, a mission was established there and the printing press made it a center of culture.

The reason for the meeting here was John Ross, chief of the Cherokees and a man of advanced European culture, with some influence over the tribal fragments which the Confederacy must have as well as the Osages. He got in touch with them at the request of Albert Pike.

The council was held as soon after John Mathews' death as possible, October 2, 1861. The chieftains of the Little Osages, *Tzi-Topa* (Four Lodges), Little Bear, and Striking Ax, the latter the physical division chief, would have nothing to do with the Pike convention; however, he got the Big Hills, the Upland-Forest, and the Thorny-Valley divisions to sign a treaty with the Confederacy of forty-four articles. *Paw-Hiu-Skah,* White Hair, "held the feather" for the Thorny-Valley People, and *Ki-He-Kah Tonkah,* Big Chief, held it for the Upland-Forest People, and the old friend of Mathews, *Tzi-Sho-Hunkah,* Sacred Sky, or Sky and Earth, chief of the Big Hills, held the feather, as did *Shonka-Sabe,* chieftain of the Black Dog Band, and *Shaba Shinkah,* Little Beaver, chieftain of the Beaver gens. The chieftain of the Buffalo-Face gens of the Big Hills also signed. He was *To-Wa'n-She-Heh,* Tall Chief, a very influential councilor. Signing for the Upland-Forest, called Claremore's or Claremont's

635

Band, was a leader who stamped his moccasined feet on the ground when he became excited during his own oratory. This great warrior was *Wah-Ti-An-Kah*.

The Little Ones were confused. They had not known just what they ought to do when Metal Maker and the Black Robe talked to them, and now with the Black Robe gone and Metal Maker killed by Heavy Eyebrows soldiers, they were more confused, and they "held the feather" because this man Pike and the Cherokee John Ross persuaded them to do so.

Also, they were always happy to attend councils. There were always feasting and dancing, and there just might be presents. There is no definite memory of their having received anything, if much, but the records show that the Cherokees received $150,000 in Confederate notes and $70,000 in gold. Of course, they had a treasurer and a government.

The Little Ones always painted themselves in their friendly dance paint when they were near the council grounds, and at some stopping place got out their dance clothing and their paints, and with their peeps-in-water dressed and painted their faces and tied on their high, quivering roaches. When they appeared, just as had happened at the Tahlequah council in 1843, they were gaped at and followed, and people instinctively made room for them on the benches or in the circle on the ground. There was only one other thing that would swell an Osage warrior's heart more than this attention that had both fear and admiration in it, and that was to hear a song made about his *o-do'n*, his war honors, by those who had seen his feats of daring and skill.

Inspired by their own importance, indicated by the attention they received, they signed the treaty with Albert Pike, representative of the Confederacy, and there were so many ordinary warriors who "held the feather" that day besides the chiefs and chieftains that there might have been much more than mere deference to suffuse them with self-esteem.

The treaty was the usual thing, except that the Confederates promised to do that which the United States government had promised to do and couldn't. They would protect the Little Ones against their enemies whether nations or individuals and secure them in their present reserve against all trespassers, and promised them that their reserve would never be included within the bounds of any state or territory, and they used the same old clichés in assuring the Little Ones that they would "have exclusive and undisturbed possession during all time, as long as the grass shall grow and water run."

The Confederacy would ask only that they be allowed a "tract one mile square" for each military post they would establish within the reserve, and stipulated that they would use the waterways. They would allow the Little Ones to hunt in all the unoccupied country west of the possessions of the Cherokees, Seminoles, Choctaws, and Chickasaws without molestation from any quarter, "while engaged therein under the protection of the Confederate States." They had been hunting there for generations.

The Little Ones went home up the Neosho, and here on their reserve there was no Confederate leader to point out to them whom they should fight. The "border ruffians" were of no aid, since they took their horses when they needed them and tried to get them drunk so that they could steal their robes and furs and rape their women.

Only the Black Dog and Arrow-Going-Home people of the Upland-Forest remained loyal to the treaty. Big Chief led the Arrow-Going-Home band, and Black Dog the younger led his own people, and they wandered about during the war enjoying freedom they had not enjoyed since the dragoons had driven them from the Place-of-the-Oaks on the Verdigris in 1839. They met the Big Hills and the Thorny-Valley People and the Little Osages and the Heart-Stays People on the plains, but they only ventured back periodically to the Kansas reserve with them, usually staying among the Creeks and the Cherokees; and when the Creeks, their hosts, were misused by both the Union and the Confederacy, they brought them up into Kansas to live with them.

Little Bear of the Little Osages led his gens to join the Ninth Kansas Infantry, which was both infantry and cavalry, and White Hair allied his people with the Union troops at Fort Scott. White Hair's loyalty was perhaps more protective than active, and he furnished few soldiers for the Union Army, while Little Bear's people actually tried to become soldiers in the European manner; but although the Americans on each side were not trained to statuesque regimentation of the European, even the slouchy formality and military restrictions and drills were too much for the young warriors of the Bear. They might imitate their life symbol in many of his characteristics, but the Himalayan bear's subjection to the organ grinder or the circus men they knew nothing about.

Neither side could very well claim dominance over the reserve of the Little Ones and the Neutral Lands, but both the Union and the Confederate scouts rode across them, spying out the forces and the loyalties of the other. The Union would send scouts from Fort Scott and Humboldt, and Stand Watie, the great Cherokee general, loyal to the Confederacy, would make attacks across the boundary and attack Humboldt, but this struggle in the southeastern part of Kansas was only a sideshow. The scouts, either Confederate or Union, would dress in each other's clothing quite often, and often tried to disguise themselves as Indians. This confused the Little Ones more, and those who stayed on the reserve and remained loyal to the Union were comparatively inactive and inconspicuous and quite decorous when in their villages in southern and southeastern Kansas, only acting with their traditional imperialism when on the plains.

But most of their confusion was due to the "insatiable land hunger of the politicians, speculators, and would-be captains of industry, who were, more often than not, rogues in the disguise of public benefactors." They came with those who would establish "squatter sovereignty," and had been trying to cause cession of the Osage Reserve since 1854.

During May, 1863, Confederate General Kirby-Smith, commanding at Little Rock, Arkansas, felt that something ought to be done about the static situation in Kansas. He conceived the idea that the Indians of the plains and the Southwest generally might be a tremendous power which was not utilized, so he sent twenty-two officers up the Arkansas and up the Verdigris and into the Reserve of the Little Ones, whence they would go to the plains, divide up, and try to influence the various tribes to come into the war with the Confederacy.

The Little Ones were preparing to leave for their summer buffalo hunt on the plains. Their absence would increase the Union's Major Doudna's responsibility for the area, of which their reserve was part. The Confederates would soon know, especially now when they needed new strength, of the Little Ones' traditional absences on the plains. This their scouts would know about, and they might even invade the area.

Major Doudna was in command of the southernmost post of the Federals, which was Humboldt, and he had told the Little Ones to bring trespassers to Humboldt, thinking of the Confederates, of course. He was not interested in the depredations of the free men if they could claim Union allegiance.

On a May day, the sixteenth, in 1863, Colonel Charles Harrison and Colonel Warner Lewis led their fellow Confederate officers sent by General Kirby-Smith on a special and secret mission up the Verdigris. They seemed to have ridden rather boldly across the reserve in daylight, believing perhaps that the Little Ones had gone on their hunt. Their campfire, or the charred sticks, and the droppings of their horses which had been tied close by, and the fact of their neatly shod hooves, gave the party of ten Big Hills all the evidence they needed.

The party under their leader followed the trail, and soon came upon the officers, numbering twenty-two. They, the Big Hills, numbered only ten. They recognized none of the faces of the officers. One of the things Major Doudna had done to make sure of the safety of his scouts was to bring them to the villages and let the Little Ones see them, so that they could know them when they met them on the prairie. These horsemen were strangers, but they said that they were of the Humboldt command. They were disguised well, but still the leaders of the party insisted that they accompany them to Major Doudna.

They started to ride off, telling the Little Ones that all was well, but the leader of the Big Hills tried to stop them, and an officer pulled his pistol and shot one of the party, then rather haughtily rode on. The Little Ones picked up their dead warrior and raced back to the village, the dead man's horse following with head high and to one side, dragging his rope rein.

When the women saw the limp form over the withers of one of the warrior's horses, they began to keen, and the men asked the town crier to announce the news.

Soon there was a force of perhaps two hundred warriors gathering. *We-He-Sa-Ki,* Hard Rope, chieftain of the Heart-Stays People, and *Shaba Shinka,* Little Beaver, chieftain of the Beaver, were in command. It has been said that Little Bear was also of the party.

They rode fast and overtook the Confederate officers, who seemed sure that their long-range rifles would keep them at a distance, but the Little Ones flanked them on each side, as they did buffalo when they wished them to go in a certain direction. Staying out of range of the officers' rifles, they could still control their direction. Only one warrior fell from his horse dead near Lightning Creek, and they managed to knock two of the officers from their horses, neither party paying any attention at the moment to their fallen. They carried on with their running battle, and soon the officers were in the trap. They had been forced into a patch of timber which hid a high bank of the Verdigris River. Here there was a sandbar under the river bank, and the river ran deep and swift against another high bank on the opposite side. The officers were unable to escape except by way of the river, but they had to leave their horses on the bank.

The Heavy Eyebrows fought bravely, and when they were on the sandbar, they ran out of ammunition, and they came at the Little Ones with pistols and clubbed rifles, and the Little Ones counted coup on them, everyone trying to be first to count coup on Colonel Harrison, who seemed to be the "chief." But he had no scalplock; his head was shiny bald, but he had a magnificent fan-shaped beard, and one of the warriors took this.

The officers lay on the sandbar, headless, and the Little Ones fastened their scalps to their coup sticks and rode away singing. On their way to the village they picked up their dead warrior and took him along.

Soon the odor of blood brought the blowflies, and a scout vulture saw the conformations of death from his height, and soon the others that had seen his actions joined him, and they circled and circled like aerial skaters.

Hard Rope was a very able warrior and a grave and wise counselor of caution. He fingered the bloody papers they had taken from the officers, but he couldn't read them, nor could anyone else in the village, so he sent a messenger to the mission to get a mission-trained man, called poetically by the Heavy Eyebrows Big Joe. Not until the "talk" of the papers was known could they be sure about the officers they had killed. If they were Union officers, they would be in trouble. Maybe they wouldn't have killed them if they had not resisted and shot the warrior.

The more the leaders talked about the matter, the more they were convinced that they ought to inform Major Doudna. Finally they sent two messengers to Humboldt to tell him that they had fought with the Heavy Eyebrows and that the Heavy Eyebrows were dead, because they wouldn't come to Humboldt to be recognized.

Doudna with half his force left immediately for the Big Hills village and arrived before midnight, and even above the howling of the dogs when they heard him coming, he could hear the keening of the women. When he came into camp he saw the two dead warriors already painted for burial, flexed in a sitting position, but still tied with their backs to trees. In front of each one of them was a woman with hair cascading to the ground, hiding her face as she sat chanting the Song of Death. On the right side of their heads was the blue earth of mourning; they were *Hunkah* women.

The Little Ones didn't expect Doudna so soon, so they were silent, and as they feasted him and his troops, they were nervous. Big Joe had not arrived from the mission to tell them what the bloody papers "talked."

Doudna saw their nervousness and knew the source of it, but he felt quite sure after hearing about the reluctance of the officers to come to Humboldt that they were Confederate. He was brisk and military, and insisted on going to the scene of battle the next morning early.

They came to the two officers who had been killed in the running battle and buried them where they had fallen. One had been eaten by the wolves and there were only bones, but the wolves seemed to have found the other one not to their taste, as they had left him intact, but

641

the soldiers who dug the grave rolled him into it with their gun barrels and held their noses.

They came to the loop of the Verdigris with its patch of timber toward which the Little Ones had flanked the fleeing officers. The gorged vultures rose heavily, and one too gorged to lift himself from the sandbar walked away looking back. The four dead horses lay swollen and untouched.

The soldiers tied sponges filled with assafoetida over their noses and mouths, then cut sticks just below the forking of two branches from the bushes and trees, cutting one of the branches close so as to form a hook, and waited upwind until the trench diggers were finished, then they came forward with the heads they had collected and threw them into the trench, then with hooked sticks rolled the bodies into it. The soldiers became nauseated.

Doudna and his men could definitely know from the clothing, which was not well disguised, and by the equipment that the officers were Confederate. They found eighteen bodies on the sandbar, and these with the two killed in the running fight, amounted to twenty, while the papers later indicated that there were twenty-two. When the Little Ones were sure that they had not killed Union officers and there was no danger of reprisals, they became excited and sang their war songs again.

There were boot tracks discovered some distance up the river from the bodies, well traced in the sand, where the officers had first found themselves trapped by the river and the high bank on the other side. However, when the tracks led away from the sandbar and into the weeds and grasses, they became difficult to follow. They were the tracks of two officers walking close together, one apparently supporting the other. The Union soldiers wanted to follow them, but they couldn't, and they couldn't possibly interest the Little Ones in a couple of wounded soldiers, in their excitement.

They had told Major Doudna at first that they had thrown the papers into the river, since they were blood-stained, but when they found that the soldiers were not Union, they readily handed the "talking papers" over to him when they reached the village. He, in turn, allowed them to keep the excellent Confederate horses, as well as the pistols and guns and saddles and sabers. They said that the horses were very good ones, and they were very sorry that four of them had been killed in the battle.

Little Beaver was an old man and Hard Rope was dignified, but some of the gentile leaders who had counted first coup on the fallen officers, especially on the "chief," Harrison, mounted their warriors and, in imitation of the Heavy Eyebrows cavalry, drew them up in line "and their front exceeded the front of two troops of cavalry."

That night the troops saw the Scalp Dance and other dances, with seventeen scalps and a great beard waving from the scalp poles.

The Little Ones felt like the men pre-eminent again, and were ready for the traditional war movement, and their agent, Peter Percival Elder, was jubilant. He had been influential in bringing the Little Ones back to the Union, and now he wished to have an Osage company formed which would be commanded by Major Doudna or some other officer. He wrote to General Blount at Leavenworth, Kansas, about the Little Ones: "They are in high glee, and have been furnished with ammunition. They are anxious to be thus organized and act for their mutual protection."

There is no doubt that they sensed that their old prowess had come back to them, but Elder had misinterpreted the courteous answer to his direct questioning about becoming soldiers.

This enthusiasm about the loyalty of the Little Ones was also expressed by W. S. Coffin, United States superintendent of Indian affairs, in his annual report from Leavenworth, August 20, 1863: "... in view of the important geographical position occupied by these Indians [Osages] between the white settlements in southern Kansas and those within the rebel States no effort on my part has been spared to counteract the machinations of the enemy and to hold them in loyalty to the U.S. Government in which I have been ably assisted by Father Schoenmakers and his associates at the Osage Catholic Mission."

In order to hold the loyalty of the other divisions and gentes, he permitted "quite a number" of Black Dog's people to come back to the reservation. This was in September, 1864. Father Schoenmakers had returned from his refuge at St. Marys, Kansas, in March, 1862.

So pleased were the military men and the citizens of Kansas, and especially Colonel William C. Coffin, superintendent of Indian affairs, southern superintendency, that they were inclined to exaggerate the importance of the Little Ones' defeat of the officers of the Confederacy. Coffin became almost dramatic in a letter to Commissioner of Indian Affairs William P. Dole. On June 10, 1863, he wrote in reference to the running fight wherein the officers were destroyed: "I have no doubt that this will afford more protection to the frontiers of Kansas than anything else that has yet been done and from the frequency and boldness of the raids recently, something of the kind was very much needed."

He thought that medals given to the leaders in the fight would be a very good idea, as appreciation "for important service rendered and promotive of good." This after he had written to Commissioner Dole the details of the fight, informing him that the Osages had "murderously attacked a group of Confederate recruiting officers." Despite the fact that the Rebels were always "murderers," whether in defensive or offensive action, they were still white men.

He also wrote that the Osages might sell twenty-five miles by fifty miles off the "east end" of their reserve, and twenty miles wide off the north side, "but I will write more fully of this in a day or two."

There were so many speculators and local politicians during this chaotic period of border history maneuvering for control of the Osage Reserve that they frustrated each other. When the speculators might succeed in getting a resolution before the Congress, the Commissioner of Indian Affairs would report adversely on it and often kill it; and on the other hand, when the Commissioner himself tried to influence the Osages to sell parts of their reserve, he was frustrated by the Congress through the activities of local politicians. Both sides always presented their arguments in the spirit of humanity and Christianity and as protectors of their red brothers.

When Commissioner Dole made one of his attempts to get a part of the reserve, he was frustrated for the moment by Quantrill's attack on Lawrence and by the Delawares. He had arranged to meet at the Sac and Fox agency with the Osages (carefully selected leaders and ambitious Nobodies) for the purpose of making a treaty wherein he and his associates would obtain a part of the reserve.

After his delay, he found the Osages had gone back to their villages, and he followed them there and talked with them for two days. He finally concluded that he could get all the Osage land he wanted for twenty-five cents an acre, but doubted if the Senate would ratify the agreement, and, anyway, he wrote, "I have some doubt succeeding in a treaty since the Indians do not understand parting with their land in trust."

These men far away from the constant sounds of cannon and rifle were trying to get control of the Osage Reserve one way or another. They had been trying since 1854, the year of the beginning of the "squatter sovereignty" struggle, and would continue during and after the war, finally running the Osages south of Latitude 37, which became the southern boundary of Kansas.

And during this time there was a great variety of tricks and political maneuvers, none of them very clever or original, each acquisitive man or group frustrated by another acquisitive man or group.

Commissioner Dole checked James H. Lane's Senate Resolution of 1862, which proposed the extension of the southern boundary of Kansas to the northern boundary of Texas, on the grounds that the Indian country should be left to the Indians. He also checked Pomeroy's attempts to have the Neutral Lands confiscated, possibly basing his argument on some universally recognized Christian principle which men wouldn't dare deny.

Superintendent Coffin had discredited one Dr. J. B. Chapman, who had made a rather successful try for the confidence of the Osages. Coffin and Agent Elder were jealous of each other and watched for surreptitious approaches by each other to Osage confidence.

There seemed to be implanted in the minds of all the interested ones that if they remained modest in their greed and tried for only a part of the reserve, then the deal might not attract so much attention. They named the eastern part or the northeastern part. Here free men had been sent to trespass by some of the enterprisers, believing that they might have an argument on the basis of "squatter sovereignty." They hoped that the Senate, in considering this basis, might be more prone to approve their agreements with the Osages. There might even be a bit of patriotism here as well, when they pointed out to the Senate that these free men whom they had encouraged to "squat" were American citizens seeking homes. To strengthen their arguments, they could drop the fact that Black Dog and the Claremore Band had joined the "secesh." These were Osages; more'n half of the tribe, they might exaggerate.

They could think of nothing more clever to present to the Osages in the form of arguments than the worn-out phraseology that after the sale of part of their reserve, the remainder would remain their sacred reserve, undisturbed by white men and protected by the government forever.

The politician- and speculator-backed free men trespassing on the reserve did little to convince anyone that they were humble homeseekers; they, instead, became characteristically overbearing and recalcitrant. The military and the government were merely menaces to their independence. Their racial memories of kings and princes and landlords, pest-hole prisons and the gibbet, were still strong, because they were as old as European civilization.

The United States Senate seemed to have been the only friend of the Little Ones during this period. Apparently even their agent and superintendent and commissioner were interested in their land, despite the fact that they praised their action in destroying the Confederate officers and wanted to give them medals. The military men were only interested in them as a buffer, since they were not of the least importance to them as soldiers.

Colonel William A. Phillips, commander of the Union Brigade, the three regiments of Indian Home Guards, was irked during the severe winter of 1862–63 because the weather made campaigning with Indians impracticable. The first regiment was made up of Creeks, very intelligent and very good soldiers. The second regiment, after getting rid of its "unmanageable elements, mostly Osages and Quapaws," became a Cherokee regiment, and the third regiment was composed of Cherokees. These were civilized Indians.

Thus it was that the Little Ones, at least four out of the five of their physical divisions, remained loyal to the Union. Once, with the Padoucas and the Pawnees, they had represented the balance of power between France and Spain, later between Spain and England and France and England, in the New World. After the United States government bought the Louisiana Territory, Zebulon Pike was sent to ask the Little Ones and the Padoucas and the Pawnees to be on their side, and to persuade them not to join the Spaniards or the English; and just before the War of 1812, George Sibley was sent to do the same thing.

Now, between North and South in the War of Rebellion, they were simply a buffer. They were a harassed, uncertain, tranquil buffer, renewing their traditional imperialism only on the plains. In their confusion, they became almost submissive in the prairie-woodlands. Except for the destruction of the Confederate officers, and *Tzi-Topa*'s war movement, their mourning dances, and their before-the-dawn chanting to Grandfather, and other ceremonials, it might have been assumed that the enemy God had conquered. Only in some of the individuals was the mustang spirit broken, not in the tribe. Their quiescence was animal caution.

There had been intertribal clashes, but these incidents were of little importance to the military or to the representatives of the national government as long as they didn't affect the larger conflict or the tranquility of the settlers. However, *Tzi-Topa*'s war movement brought a company of Heavy Eyebrows Union soldiers out onto the prairie.

Tzi-Topa, Four Lodges, was called "Chetopa" by the Heavy Eyebrows. He was a chieftain of the Little Osages. He was a very proud man, and when he was accused by the Delawares of taking horses from the Heavy Eyebrows, he with great dignity said that he had not taken the horses but that warriors from south of the boundary had taken them. He knew by their paint that they were of Black Dog's band. He said that he would go to the Cherokee Nation and recover the horses if the Delawares would deliver up the horses they had taken from his people.

The fact that this savage Plains chieftain knew about the horses which they had taken from his people frightened the Delawares, and they went to Agent E. H. Carruth, and he, believing that the mighty Osages might go on the war movement, called on Captain Insley to send a company of soldiers.

When Carruth and the soldiers arrived at the Delaware village, they found these civilized Indians painted for war, and Carruth tried to discourage them. With a few counselors and the soldiers he set out for Four Lodges' village.

As they rode along, they heard singing from behind a prairie swell. It was an Osage war song punctuated by rifle fire. As the war-painted giants came over the swell, Carruth could hear the drum which beat the rhythm of the song, and he heard an Osage flute. This was unusual and must have been an imitation of the army bugle, though the young warrior who played it was not sounding a charge.

The Osages were in full war paint. They were Little Osages and were led by Four Lodges. Carruth and Lieutenant Watson went forward to talk with them, but the warriors pretended that they didn't see them, and the song was unbroken.

The two Heavy Eyebrows stopped at about 150 yards distance and called to Four Lodges, but it was as if they, the Heavy Eyebrows, were not there on the prairie. They dared not approach closer. They went a little way off the Osage trail and made camp and appointed guards. Before dawn, some of the Delaware guards slipped across the prairie to the Osage village and took several horses and came back to their guard duty, filled with glee.

When Carruth and the soldiers discovered the Osages' horses, they made the Delawares drive them back, and the whole party followed to Four Lodges' village. They found the warriors, and when asked about their war movement of the day before, they said they had no intention of making the war movement against Those-Who-Call-Us, the Delawares, nor against the Heavy Eyebrows. They said they were on the war movement against the Kickapoos. The Kickapoos, they said, would often go to the headwaters of the Cut-Salt-Waters and the Low-Forest Land Waters before them and scatter the buffalo, because they were woodland people and they didn't know how to hunt buffalo.

This incident was of September, 1862, and it was during this month,

Deer-Hiding Moon, when the Little Ones went on their winter hunt. This movement of Four Lodges was not a war movement, but a bluff-movement against the Kickapoos, so that they would be frightened and would stay and guard their villages while the Little Ones moved to the plains. This was the bluff-lunge of the grizzly bear again.

At war's end the Little Ones were lucky that they had suffered nothing more than smallpox, measles, and constant harassment during this barbaric period in American history.

50. Between the Heavy Eyebrows
and the Arapahoes

THE RELATIONS BETWEEN the Little Ones and the Europeans and later with the people called Americans depended upon many things, which usually had to do with the Europeans' economic needs and their numbers on the new continent.

The Little Ones had the position of geography when the French first came up the Missouri and the Osage rivers, and being a powerful tribe of both the plains and the woodlands, became a perfect buffer between the competitive Europeans; and the attenuated powers of the French and then the Spaniards had made the mobility and the power of the Osages important. These Europeans stated in their letters and reports their problem in not being able to do anything about the Osages, and in these letters one finds them looking forward to the time when by their very numbers they could overwhelm them. Thus the Little Ones remained important because of their geographical position and their prowess until the Americans swarmed across the Mississippi and President Jackson demanded that the east-of-the-Mississippi Indians be given homes on their domain, and until the numbers of the settlers grew and the free men became more active and recalcitrant, and the United States began to take pieces of their domain and shove them farther and farther west toward the semi-arid plains. They in effect were moved ahead of white settlement, until in 1854 they became surrounded, an enclave, and there was an impasse. A commissioner of Indian affairs, D. N. Cooley, thought

650

that since the Osages were nomadic and in constant struggle with the whites who were trespassing on their reserve, they ought to be moved to the prairie-plains part of their reserve, so that they might be nearer the buffalo, which he called "nature's commissary." Nearly everyone now believed they ought to be removed to the Indian Territory after the war.

From the time of the first missionaries, the first trappers, hunters, fur traders, French, Spaniards, and American officials, there had been no time for academic thinking about the Little Ones, and now during land speculation, inventions, railroad building, gold in the Rockies, and Northern former soldiers swarming from across the Mississippi, they didn't have the importance of buffalo. They couldn't be eaten.

Kansas had become a state on January 29, 1861, but the Osages and others were expressly excluded from any control or jurisdiction of the state, although Kansas officials and settlers did eventually control the situation by refusing to aid the federal government in keeping their citizens from trespassing and in keeping the Osages in a constant state of defense. As a matter of fact, they at times encouraged trespassing. The Amer-European had finally attained numerical superiority over the Little Ones, and he became more and more arrogant. The mighty warrior inspired fear no longer; he was only in the way, and Amer-Europeans became contemptuous of him in the communities where he outnumbered the painted warriors, but when they were few out on the prairie or plains trails the free men and the trappers almost groveled and called him "Mr. Injun."

The Amer-European, with his European racial memories of the economic, social, and political underdogism, was ever eager to promulgate laws for the protection of and for justice to the image of himself in racial memory, but as soon as the laws were promulgated and administered by the government, the government became the overlord, the prince, or the noble of the deer forest; and here in free America and as a citizen of the free United States, he must manifest some disdain of government as the embodiment of this racial-memory prince and overlord. When the free man trespassed on the reserve, he was expressing his independence. The underdog of racial memory was expressing his freedom from centuries-old overlordism. The local laws he was a part of, but federal interference he resented.

The Amer-European could have rounded up the Osages as he rounded up coyotes and jackrabbits later, but he couldn't flout the law which was the symbol of his own protection from the overlord of racial memory, and in dealing with the Indian he had to make gestures to the law both civil and Christian, pretending that his actions were actually for protection of the Osages and for their welfare. He felt quite self-righteous and comfortable with his hypocrisy.

He had the power now to do just as he wished with the Little Ones. If he had taken the reserve in the same manner in which he did take it, but without the mealy-mouthed hypocrisy, the end would have been the same. However, the ingrained conscience urgings of his underdog racial memories demanded compensation to the Little Ones. These common men who swarmed the continent, even though they slaughtered the game and frightened the wilderness with their shouting and their boasting and their swearing, were perhaps manifesting a nascent soul rather unique in men of power up to this time, simply because they had for centuries been the underdog and their racial memories were deep.

Biology was on their side. They, even they, hairy and blatant, had passed the Neolithic stage two thousand years before Christ. There was no place now for the Little Ones in the struggle; and since their power had been overwhelmed, they couldn't possibly retain the respect they had always inspired. They couldn't stay in their enclave after the buffalo disappeared, roaming over a rich reserve that the white man needed for his plow; but what could be done about them? And anyway, without the buffalo they would become hungry. Could they be removed to some still primordial mountain park and there fenced in and allowed to live as they would until the Amer-European himself reached that stage in civilization when he could recognize the tremendously interesting *Wah'Kon-Tah* and study the spring sources of Neolithic culture? The Amer-European would have known much more about himself and his own development if he had done this, but how could he have done it, even if he had had the culture himself to desire to do it?

Of course, paying for the land taken from the Little Ones could have been more practical than feeding them if the Americans had taken their land without payment, since they must remove them to a smaller reserve, where the free men would come to slaughter their game as before. If they wanted to get rid of them, they could have had no more propitious time than now, after the war, when the freed Negro was being enfranchised. The philanthropist demanding enfranchisement as an act of justice, the North vindictive and establishing Reconstruction in the South as a punishment for secession, and the party politicians busy over the same matter, the Northern politicians suffused with victory like warriors with scalps "waving in the wind," going so far as trying to impeach their Union-Democrat President. It isn't likely that much attention would have been paid to a handful of Osages who had become an obstacle to a virtuous Union state if the federal government wished to take their reserve instead of buying it.

They might well have done this in the period after the Civil War when federal morals were at a very low ebb. The sentimentalists seemed to have been at this time absorbed by the "act of justice" in seeing to it that the Negro got the vote. The Little Ones had always been a favored people, and their luck was holding. The Heavy Eyebrows who demanded that they leave Kansas, and finally effected their removal from Kansas to the Indian Territory, were acting in a natural manner and were quite in harmony with the struggle of the earth which the Little Ones knew so well. It is a shame that the federal commissioners and local politicians had to play the Christian humanitarian hypocrite and lie to themselves about the obvious, practical, biological reasons for removal.

The commissioners of the federal government, the agents and the superintendents and the people of Kansas and their politicians had to search rather diligently to find reasons for the removal of the Little Ones upon which their self-righteousness could stand with confidence without breaking through. The signing of the treaty of loyalty with the Confederates would have been all they needed, but there was the Big Hills destruction of the Confederate officers and Little Bear's soldiers, and Black Dog and his band, who were chivalrously and

653

periodically active south of the border, and then only between the semiannual hunts on the plains, which could be a feeble excuse. The Rebel loyalty among the Cherokees, Creeks, and Choctaws was all the government needed south of the border in Indian Territory, and this was the basis for punitive negotiations after the war, wherein the government attained land upon which to colonize other Indian tribes.

In the matter of Osage removal, they didn't have this fate-created boon, and yet humanitarian reasons were not absolutely necessary in this period of federal moral ebb and the Kansans' eagerness to get on with the progression toward some vague civic glory and prosperity. This attitude of the Kansas settlers, wherein there was no academic or humanitarian interest in the Little Ones, has constantly been referred to by writers. Its virtue, however, was double-edged: not only was it an honest attitude but it was a perfectly natural and practical one. This complete honesty was evinced by the *Lawrence Tribune* in reference to one of the attempts to obtain the Osage Reserve between 1865 and 1870 by a railroad. In writing of the attempt, the *Tribune,* indignant with the maneuvers of the railroad, stated: "This is unreasonable and unjust, not particularly to the Indians [Osages], for we do not go much on Mr. 'Lo' but to the hard working honest settlers of Kansas."

Legal authority over the reserve was vested in the federal government, and the proposal for the removal of the Osages from Kansas had to have more lip service to humanitarianism, since one couldn't face Congress with such phrases as "for we do not go much on Mr. 'Lo'."

Senator James Henry Lane from Kansas had introduced a bill in the Senate as early as December, 1862, which provided for the extinguishment of Indian land titles in Kansas and for the removal of the Indians from the state. In his introduction he had to employ the trite phraseology that had been used since 1808. Removal of the Osages would be a characteristically humanitarian act of the white man, since their reserve was in the middle of white settlements and the whites were pressing in on them from all sides and destroying them. He mentioned the fact that the treaties with the Indians in Indian Territory were voidable now, since the Cherokees, Creeks, and others had given their loyalty to the South, and the Osages could be given part of their land there. The idea was that since the Osages could not be protected within their own reserve, which the U.S. government had assured them would be inviolable, now the government owed them protection only through removal.

But the Senator was not compelled to rely completely on trite phraseology. He didn't weaken his argument by declaring baldly that there was plenty of land at this time, but he presented an item of economic interest when he argued that when the whites improved the land adjoining the borders of the reserve, this automatically raised the value of the land of the Osages, which the settlers hoped to purchase later.

It is likely that his humanitarianism and his concern about land values were effective, but his best argument was in the category of defense in this year when the Union was not performing with its later brilliance against the Rebels. The Osage Reserve stretched from the Neutral Lands to the plains west, and this formed a rectangle in which was included almost the whole of southern Kansas. This was supposed to be a buffer strip between the Unionists and the Confederates, and the Osages were supposed to act as scouts, but they were not minute men.

Lane suggested that this reserve was actually an avenue of invasion for the Confederates south of the border, and the Osages' occupation of it only facilitated the movements and the scouting of the Confederates. The assumption was that with the removal of the Osages, it could be populated by loyal settlers and a brigade or two might be stationed within the boundaries of the vacated reserve.

Lane had conducted emigrants to Kansas in 1855, his neighbors sent him to the United States Senate in 1861, and Lincoln appointed him brigadier general of Volunteers. He was a man of ability, and in the introduction of his bill in 1862, he was not only carrying out the desires of his fellow Kansans to effect the removal of the Osages, but his own wishes, since he was an expansionist and a supporter of the homestead policy.

He perhaps didn't know, however, that the best of his arguments for his bill was the vulnerability of the Union through the Osage

Reserve. None, be they Cherokee, or white horse thieves and cattle rustlers, could ride across the reserve without some gens of the Little Ones knowing about it. They saw every broken twig, every horse-nipped tussock of bluestem; also, horses long ridden and with bits in their mouths slobbered on the grass, and there was grain in the droppings of the Heavy Eyebrows horses. No group of Confederate scouts dressed as Cherokees or Creeks could deceive them.

The Cherokees and the Creeks were not plainsmen, but had their way of riding, which the Little Ones had noted many times. The Heavy Eyebrows had this way of riding, and seemed always to have some *mo'n-ce wah-don-ska,* metal thing, on himself or his horse which "talked crazy" in the sun.

And sometimes the Heavy Eyebrows from the South, dressed as Cherokees, and especially if they attempted to dress as Osages, were very funny; and sometimes a gens of the Little Ones would follow them all day, watching them, lying on their bellies on some ridge top when they stopped to rest or drink or make a small fire in the bottom of a ravine. They would look so funny with wild turkey feathers stuck in headbands of red figured calico, like That-Thing-on-Its-Head People, the Cherokees, and their Heavy Eyebrows movements looked so funny that the Little Ones would expect actions even funnier yet to come, so they would follow them, periodically putting their hands over their mouths in surprise of some funny action, as when disguised as Osages they fumbled with their breechclouts or tied their moccasin strings on the inside instead of the outside.

Members of the Bear-Panther gentes, led by a young leader, might follow the party of Southern scouts for a day or two, finally turning back when the amusement palled and the Heavy Eyebrows did nothing spectacular. This group of Heavy Eyebrows might have been a spying party or a liaison party making contact with Southern spies in the North. This would mean little to the Little Ones even if they happened to think about it in their delight in watching them. When they grew tired, they would do nothing, even if they suspected they ought to tell the chief of the soldiers at Humboldt. They would put their horses into a lope to their villages to fill their empty stomachs.

But the fate of such scouting parties might depend on the characteristics of the life symbol of the gens who discovered them. They would be fortunate if the Thunder or the Deer or the Buffalo-Face discovered them, as they might watch them for a while then allow them to go on their way, according to their mood; but the Bear-Panther, the Wolf, or the Eagle might become capricious and surround them and take their horses or bluff them out of gifts or take them, as they had been requested, to Humboldt, and turn them over to the Union officer in charge.

One day some Eagle young men saw a group of Heavy Eyebrows horsemen coming across the prairie. It was a terrifically hot day, but the young men followed them. They were soldiers, but they weren't sure whether they were from Humboldt or south of the border. Sometimes the soldiers from the South dressed in the uniforms of the soldiers of Humboldt.

They didn't care this hot day. It was the kind of hot day which made you want to kill Heavy Eyebrows like these riding so boldly across the reserve. But there were too many Heavy Eyebrows now, so they didn't dare.

There was a drought, and the ravines were dry, with cracked mud in their bottoms, and already the leaves of *ba'k'a-hi,* the sacred tree, the cottonwood, were dry and falling, and the grass was like the grass of Baby-Bear Moon. The wind was hot on their backs as the Eagle Little Ones watched the Heavy Eyebrows "dance" in the heat.

They were angry with the heat and with the Heavy Eyebrows, but soon they knew where they were headed; they were headed for *Ni-Hni-Tonkah,* the big spring on the Verdigris close to where the Fall River runs into it. "Ho," said the leader, "it is hot. We are thirsty." The others looked at him and knew that something was up.

They rode fast and arrived at the spring where the shade was cool and wasps came to get mud for their lodges. There were deer tracks there, and the tracks of the coon and the wolf and walks-on-wings, the turkey. The young men lay on their stomachs and drank long, each saying "haugh" as he arose.

They were well ahead of the Heavy Eyebrows, so they lay on their backs, and one began to beat a rhythm on his chest, and they sang softly as the hot winds played in the tops of the trees and the cicadas also sang.

657

"We shouldn't let them drink," said one of the young men.

"They have guns," said another.

"And they have long knives."

One of the young men sprang to his feet, and with wolfish movements pulled off his breechclout and defiled the water. They laughed and went to their horses, and they were still laughing when they climbed out of the bottom onto the prairie. They didn't wait to watch the thirsty Heavy Eyebrows, but rode away happy. Soon one of them pursed his lips to the man who had committed the nuisance and said "Ho, ho *Ni-O-Shey,*" and the others laughed and pursed their lips at him and said, *"Ni-O-Shey,"* Spoils-the-Spring. That became the young man's informal name as well as the name of the place.

After the war, of course, it was obvious that something must be done about the Little Ones. They were disturbing the trespassers on their reserve, especially the eastern and northeastern part, and there were more and more frequent conflicts. As the numbers of white settlers grew and the trespassers became more recalcitrant, the greater number of incidents, and it behooved the government to protect the Little Ones again. The trespassers became bolder and more confident when the Little Ones became aware that retaliation in the prairie-woodland part of their reserve might cause some of the young men to be hanged by the neck. They were not quite so reticent and within the deep groove of animal reaction as they had been in the Cherokee wars, when the government had to protect them by allowing the Cherokees to have their lands, but they seemed more malleable and their Nobodies seemed to have increased in numbers.

The treaty they signed with the United States government, September 29, 1865, at Canville Trading Post, included no original reason for the cession of part of their reserve. Article one stated that "having now more lands than are necessary for their occupation, and all payments from the Government to them from former treaties having ceased, leaving them greatly impoverished," they were apparently "desirous" of disposing of their surplus lands. Such lands to be ceded were represented by thirty miles off the eastern part of their reserve. This plank-shaped cession was thirty miles from east to west and fifty miles from south to north, and included their segment of the Neosho River. This pushed them thirty miles closer to *Mo'n-Ha*, the Cliffs, the West.

In Article two of the treaty of 1865, the Little Ones also ceded to the United States a tract of land twenty miles in width from north to south "off the north side of the remainder of their present reservation" (after the cession of land in Article one). This land would be held in trust for them and surveyed and sold for their benefit under direction of the commissioner of the General Land Office. The proceeds, after deducting expenses, were to be placed in the United States Treasury to their credit, the interest to be 5 per cent, this being used annually for the building of houses, purchasing agricultural equipment and stock animals, and the employment of physicians and mechanics; and provisions were made for the boarding and clothing and education of the children, and land for Father Schoenmakers' Osage mission or Osage Manual Labor School.

Within six months after the ratification of the treaty, the Little Ones were to move away from their villages on the Neosho to the Verdigris and its tributaries. The southeast corner of their diminished reservation was a point one mile east of where the Verdigris crosses the Kansas south boundary.

Most of the stipulations and provisions of the Lane Bill of 1863 were incorporated in this treaty of 1865, but the latter went further and definitely provided for the eventual removal of the Little Ones from Kansas.

The cession of part of their reserve only moved the settlers closer, and the situation became worse, since the Little Ones had no refuge. The Commissioner of Indian Affairs first tried to carry out the provisions of the federal legislations of 1863 which authorized the removal of Indians from Kansas. He appointed a commission and gave them the reasons for their appointment. "My object is now to make a treaty with all these tribes and get them out of the State." Nothing came of this, but in 1867 the Superintendent of Indian Affairs at Atchison, Kansas, wrote to the acting Commissioner of Indian Affairs that the welfare of the Little Ones "demanded" that a new treaty be made, "because the Osage Reservation was being intruded upon to the extent of four or five miles beyond the line of white settlers ... and they [the settlers] paid no attention to what the officials of the Indian Office said and that nothing less than a military force would suffice to keep them off the Osage Reserve." He also wrote that "the Adjutant General of Kansas had sent arms and ammunition to the settlers in order that they might sustain themselves on the Osage land."

Removal seemed to be both a solution of a bad situation and a ladder for politicians, as well as a boon to the free men and the settlers. The representatives of the Secretary of the Interior seemed to have been a bit more affected by the mania of railroad building and town building and land speculation which blinded them to their responsibilities than those agents and superintendents of the plains.

However, in the plains the Indian agents and superintendents had to fight only the military men and whisky peddlers, and they were federal military men far from home, and not wholly of militia made up from the settlers of whose interests they were a part.

The atmosphere of the whole nation was lusty, and morals had become rather a nuisance, and the moral relaxation seemed to have colored the activities of the nation, having come from laxity in administration in Washington. Andrew Johnson was honest but vulgar, and without the support of the South had little defense against the vindictive North, and an "ominous spirit had been rising in the North."

General Grant was honest, but his military and Presidential glory seemed to have drowned whatever astuteness he had enjoyed, and it was particularly under his administration that the acquisitive ones of the nation really created the atmosphere of lust for titles, power, riches, and pre-eminence.

It was difficult for an Indian agent or a superintendent, a beneficiary of the spoils system, with no goad of public moral or administrative opinion to keep him on his salaried way of honor. When get-rich-quick land speculators looked over the emerald bluestem waving over the prairie in May and June and saw the swells veined with watercourses feeding the rivers, they became excited with anticipation, and they then had only to see the right men and they could work out an argument for cession based on the usual humanitarian treacle to satisfy moral hypocrisy.

There was something in the transplanted European which had been suppressed for centuries in England and on the Continent, something more than his vindictive enjoyment of his misguided freedom and his urge to be important in the wilderness of the new continent. It was another urge born of his racial memories. He, the common man, had pretended to despise the titles and royal privileges under which he had developed through the centuries, but this also was only one of his self-illusionments, a part of his inherent hypocrisy. Cortambert had said that American tugboat men wore tall hats and frockcoats and that when you wished to attract the attention of an American on the street of the town, he would probably not heed you if you called him "Mister," but if you called him "Captain" or "Major" or "Colonel," he stopped to hear your question and was quite affable.

This self-illusionment was nascent before the war, but after the rebellion, when there was money and new inventions and land craze and gold in the mountains and railroad speculation to make you rich in a hurry, it developed to rather a fantastic degree. A trader on the Platte or the Kaw, along the stage-freight and Oregon Trail routes, would open his store to supply everything from wagon repairs, calico, and horseshoeing to whisky to the emigrants and trail drivers and perhaps neighboring soldiers from the forts. He would look at his establishment from a distance with pride, and soon he would buy a big hat and let his hair grow and call himself "Colonel."

Impressionable newspapermen and magazine writers had begun to come to the romantic plains, and for a nation in postwar prosperity eager for romance, they would write fantastic stories. Of captive white women, fearless white men six feet, six inches tall and handsome, with their long hair streaming in the plains wind. Of the Indians, and only the old trappers and traders seemed to know one tribe from the other. The tribes wandering over the plains of Kansas became at once "devils in human form," and because of their dignity, their general physical makeup, their chivalric freedom, and their fighting ability, became also the mirror before which histrionic men paraded.

661

These men were at once "slayers of the savage" and his diligent imitator, even going so far as scalping. They allowed their hair to grow, had fantastic buckskin pants and shirts made for themselves with buckskin fringes, and they wore gauntlets that could have been a menace either in hunting or in fighting Indians, with whom, according to their stories, they were always engaged.

It seems incredible that the same Amer-Europeans who could become murderously fanatical over the servitude of the African, could become sentimental over James Fenimore Cooper's fantasies, could also read in their journals with vindictive interest if not with pleasure about an eleven-year-old boy by the name of Bill Cody who was supposed to have killed his first Indian when he appeared within range of his Yaeger muzzle-loader. This was rather a heroic thing to do obviously, and he became known as "the youngest Indian slayer of the plains." This was like a modern boy attaining national honor as a Boy Scout or in Four-H Club endeavor.

This boy was on his first trip to the plains as a messenger with a wagon train and had lagged behind. There was no Indian attack and no alarm. A lone inquisitive Indian appeared, and the boy shot him. Of course, the boy or those who told about him had a vivid imagination, but the point was that, truth or dramatics, the spirit was praiseworthy even in that period before the climax of frontier histrionics.

Still more interesting, in order to get his messenger's job, he had to sign the following pledge: "While I am in the employ of Mr. A. Majors, I agree not to use profane language, not to get drunk, not to gamble, not to treat animals cruelly, and not to do anything else that is incompatible with the conduct of a gentleman. And I agree, if I violate any of the above conditions, to accept my discharge without any pay for my services."

General Phil Sheridan, commanding the Department of Missouri, which included western Kansas, eastern Colorado, Oklahoma, and New Mexico, in his attempt to patrol 150,000 square miles with 2,600 poorly disciplined, inadequately paid rabble, became annoyed with both the Indian agents who accused him of desiring to exterminate the Indians and the so-called Indian scouts about whom he wrote:

"Indian scouts whose common boast was of having slain scores of redskins, but the real scout—that is, a guide and trailer knowing the habits of the Indians—was very scarce, and it was hard to find anybody familiar with the country south of the Arkansas, where the campaign was to be made." He wrote to agent Tappan: "When we come to fight Indians, I will take my code from soldiers and not from citizens."

But it was only in the plains part of their domain that the Little Ones came in contact with frontier histrionics. However, when they went there to hunt, they found the carcasses the buffalo hunters had abandoned, but refused the pipe brought to them by the Cheyennes, the Sioux and the Arapahoes. These people were in trouble with the Heavy Eyebrow soldiers, and they wanted the Little Ones to go on the war movement along the Waters-Flat-White, the Platte, and the Buffalo-Dung Waters, the Republican.

It became more and more difficult for the Little Ones to find the buffalo, and to make matters worse, it was about this time that they became enemies of the Cheyennes and the Arapahoes, and these were the tribes with whom they shared their segment of the plains. Now, when they went to the plains on their semiannual hunts, they had to keep their young men on the plains swells as they traveled, and their scouts must stay up all night lying on the crest of the swells watching. Now they must examine carefully the moccasin prints in the sandy places, the moccasin prints with the straight soles, which made a straight line on the inside. These would be the moccasin prints of the Big Nose, the Arapahoes, and the Walkers-on-the-Prairie, the Cheyennes.

It was the Big Nose who became their enemy, but Walkers-on-the-Prairie and Cut-Throat, the Sioux, were friends of the Big Nose, and they fought the Heavy Eyebrows together, and now they would fight the Little Ones together.

It was all the fault of the red shield. There was a young Arapahoe, whose real name the Little Ones couldn't recall. His father and his uncle had told him the story of the red fetish shield of the Little Ones and how years ago when they fought with the Little Ones, they

663

couldn't kill those who wore the red shield around their necks if nothing had happened to kill the medicine of the shield and if it hung properly on the breast of the warrior.

The more the young Arapahoe thought of the strong medicine of the red shield worn by the warriors of the Little Ones, the more eager he became to own one. His people and the Osages were friends, and he couldn't take one from a dead warrior, and there was no horse among the Cheyennes that could be traded for one of the shields which had not lost its medicine; they would trade only those which had lost their medicine, he believed.

The red shield was the descending sun after a prairie fire, sometimes in the early morning the sun was a red shield, so there must be strong medicine in it. He became possessed by the idea of obtaining a fetish from the Osages.

One October, when his people were camped on the very headwaters of the Smoky Hill River, the scouts talked of a hunting camp of the Osages, farther south on the Cimarron. The young man listened intently to the location, and then persuaded some of the young men to accompany him. Young men of the Plains Indians were ever ready for some sort of adventure.

They rode down to the Cimarron and there located the hunting camp of the Big Hills. When they had come in sight of the camp, one of the young men got off his horse and waved his robe three times, the old signal of the plains for "I am friend," which seems to have originated with the Padoucas.

In camp the young men looked around and ate at several lodges until they were uncomfortable, but all the time they were thinking of the red shield. These fetish shields were never allowed to rest on the ground or on the floor of the lodge, but must be hung from a pole; and when a woman or girl of the lodge was menstruating, the pole with the pendant shield must be taken outside the lodge and so placed that one could not pass between it and the sun.

There was such a one, but the young Arapahoes pretended they didn't see it. When they saw a dog, they came close to him so that he could smell them and know them later, but the dogs raised their hackles and circled them, snarling.

The young man wouldn't have had time to fast and make medicine to counteract the medicine of the red shield in case the medicine was aggressive and not defensive only, so he came at midnight, wriggling in the sand and among the sage. The wind was high on the plains, and he came upwind, and there was no sound of the dogs. His heart must have thumped during the dramatic moment of taking the shield, since he must gamble his life.

When he returned to the camp of his people, he took the shield and went out to fast, and very likely the hunger thoughts created the image of the red shield when he closed his eyes, and there was perhaps a voice saying that he must call himself Red Shield to get the full benefit of the fetish. This he did when he came back to the camp. He told everyone that he was now to be called Red Shield.[1]

The first time he tried the power of the shield he took ten Pawnee horses, and the next time the bullets of the soldiers went around him. Then for several years he could not be hit when in battle, and no one could catch him when he crept into lodges of his enemies to count coup. However, the Big Hills saw him with the shield, and twice he had come into the camps of other physical divisions of the Little Ones to count coup and once he stole horses from under the noses of the guards. They saw nothing of him but could hear him singing his song and crying out, "It is I, Red Shield."

The Big Hills took the pipe to the Little Osages and to the Heart-Stays People and to the Thorny-Valley People, but they refused to smoke. The shield had lost its medicine now on the chest of the Big Nose, they said. But the Big Hills thought of it as an insult, so they waited for the proper time, and when their scouts told them that Red Shield was in a small hunting party, they descended upon them and killed them all, taking the scalps back to their camp, singing. They raised the scalp of Red Shield on a pole, and the girls danced the Feather Dance, and a warrior was chosen to sing the Feather Dance song. The young men of the Big Hills, belonging to several gentes, who had taken part in the killing of the Arapahoes, formed a club or a band, and they called themselves "Red Shield."

[1] After peace was effected between the Osages and the Arapahoes, the Osages gave the red shield to Left-Hand, brother of the Arapahoe who had called himself "Red Shield."

But they had started a war with the Arapahoes and the Cheyennes and their allies the Sioux, these very powerful tribes who were actually defeating the United States soldiers, attacking the railroad workmen, and had cowed 1,000 workers in Fort Harker, who were afraid to come out of the community to work on the railroad. These allies were co-operating with each other in their fights with all their enemies, and the Little Ones had to go to the plains in tribal force. They were kept from peaceful hunting by these tribes, and their defeats before they had got their supply of buffalo had the effect of causing near starvation. This was the greatest possible boon to those who had been trying to have them removed from Kansas. They made much of one particular defeat of the Little Ones by the allies. The Neosho agent, G. C. Snow, wrote to Superintendent Thomas Murphy, January 13, 1868: "I find that most of the Little Osages and many of White Hair's town are *very destitute*. They are near suffering for provisions. Thirty-nine lodges lost all they had. From a full count, since all got in, we find the number of horses lost by the Osage Indians on the plains to be 328. These they think the Arapahoes got. *Something must be done for these people at once."*

Destitute though they might have been—and there is some likelihood that the allied tribes on the plains were keeping them from full hunts—they couldn't be persuaded to make a treaty to cede the now diminished reservation to the United States, and Agent Snow had been told so repeatedly by them; but he was persistent and wrote to Superintendent Murphy, February 25, 1868, that the various divisions and gentes were not in accord, and this prevented the selecting of a delegation to go to Washington to come to some agreement about selling their land in Kansas. He was constantly trying to bring about council so that the delegation might be chosen, and his eagerness and his persistence were not apparently being inspired by Washington. He wrote that White Hair, when he went to his village to persuade him to call a council or meet in council, had said to him that he would not be dragged down to the Big Hills village to a council, since he had no land to sell.

Snow was not in the least deterred, and he wrote: "I staid there until noon the 21st, hired a team, and got most of White Hair's leading men to go down. After councilling two days and one night, they decided not to send a delegation to Washington."

Superintendent Murphy transmitted Agent Snow's report to the Commissioner of Indian Affairs in February, but in March put quite a different light on the subject when he wrote to Secretary of the Interior Browning. He reported that the reason the Osages had declined to send a delegation to Washington to consider the sale of their lands was that they were at war with the Cheyennes and Arapahoes, but that they actually wanted to sell their diminished reservation to the government. When the Secretary of the Interior wrote to the President about the matter, he said that negotiations were begun by the superintendent of the Central Superintendency, Mr. Thomas Murphy, Senator Ross of Kansas, and others.

In April, President Johnson appointed commissioners to negotiate with the Great and Little Osages. He appointed Nathaniel C. Taylor, commissioner of Indian affairs, Thomas Murphy, superintendent of Indian affairs, Albert G. Boone, special Indian commissioner, and Agent George C. Snow.

When the commission was appointed, the Commissioner of Indian Affairs, in anticipation of the government's obligation to select another reserve for the Osages, had written to the Cherokee delegation in Washington at this time.

The Commissioner chose a spot for the counciling near the mouth of Drum Creek, called Drum Creek Springs, which here ran into the Verdigris. Taylor, who had been chosen president, and one A. N. Blackledge, the chosen secretary, and the others arrived at the spot accompanied by thirty soldiers of the Seventh Cavalry, under Captain George W. Yates.

They were eager. This eagerness oozes from the old records and the attitude of the commissioners, especially that of Taylor. William Sturges, president of the Leavenworth, Lawrence and Galveston Railway, was present, and the morning meetings were secret, and, as the Osages delayed committing themselves, the negotiations became progressively more interesting to the settlers of Kansas and their representatives and spokesmen. Also for the second meeting of the council, May 15, Colonel C. W. Blair, president of the Missouri, Fort

Scott, and Santa Fe Railroad Company appeared and asked that his company be allowed to purchase one-third of the Osage Reserve at the same price and on the same conditions agreed upon with the Sturges railroad company.

The eagerness of the negotiators and the unusual interest of the Department of the Interior agents in the welfare of their charges, the Osages, and the presence of Sturges not only brought competing railroad officials to the meeting, but began to arouse suspicions among the settlers and their leaders.

Colonel Blair even tendered his good offices in attempting to get the Osages to sign the treaty, if he were allowed to have that part of the reserve which he wanted. The alternative to his trying to influence the Osages to sign a treaty, if he were not promised his third, would be his working against such agreement. The commissioners filed this offer with the threat, one supposes, for future consideration.

Taylor made a long speech to the Osages on the eighteenth, an introduction to the proposed treaty, giving a summary of it; and naturally, as was the custom among eager negotiators with the Little Ones, he warned them that their game was disappearing and that they must settle down and go to work, and he wished to settle the difficulties the Osages were having in Kansas and on the plains by seeing them removed to the Indian Territory, where the white man would bother them no more.

Two days later he was obviously becoming a little impatient with the Little Ones, and he then told Colonel Blair that he had been "instructed" to inform him that neither of his propositions was acceptable. The next day, the twenty-first, apparently the welfare of Kansas, the public interest of the United States, and the interests of the Osages directed the commission to permit the Leavenworth, Lawrence and Galveston Railroad to buy the Osage Reserve for $1,600,000, this amount being $400,000 less than that which was offered by Colonel Blair's railroad.

The negotiators had lured all the Osages they could possibly lure to the council grounds by promises of feasts every day of the council and by the promise of presents, and they had delayed bringing the provisions owed to the Osages provided for by the treaty of 1865, so that they could make a great show of bringing them to the council grounds at the propitious moment.

The Little Ones came to the camp, some said, five hundred strong, and if they did come in this number, the agent's concern about their being *very destitute* after their conflicts with the allies of the plains might have some basis.

There had been secret meetings among the commissioners, and the plans had perhaps been well laid for the taking over of the diminished reservation and the trust lands by the Leavenworth, Lawrence and Galveston Railroad, so that by the twenty-third, when the Osages made their inevitable speeches, everything had been settled.

Apparently it was not quite clear to the Little Ones why they had been urged to come, or they might have understood well enough but were animal-protective and took refuge in the dappled shadows of complaint. The Heavy Eyebrows had come onto their Sacred One, destroyed their "brothers," harassing them and even putting thoughts in their minds about the power of *Wah'Kon-Tah.* They had to look up to *Tzi-Sho,* the Sky Lodge, more often now to see his order in the seven stars of the Great Dipper and the perfect order of the coming of Grandfather and the Morning Star.

So after the feasting they talked, not like the Judeans half circling a Roman procurator, strident and gesticulating, but each one got up with dignity, draped his robe over his left shoulder, allowing the right arm and shoulder freedom, and became pontifical, as the others of the tribe listened in traditional courtesy. All the while the commissioners passed whispered new thoughts to each other.

Among the speakers for the Little Ones was *Tzi-Topa,* Four Lodges of the Little Osages, and *We-He-Sa-Ki,* Hard Rope of the Heart-Stays People, who were now under *Paw-Hiu-Skah,* White Hair. There were *No-Pa-Wathe,* called Nopawalla, also of the Little Osages, and *Ox'po'n Tonkah,* Big Elk, *Wah-Ti-An-Ka,* the celebrated warrior and orator, Forked Horn, and White Hair and others, but only a few of them touched on the treaty under discussion; all except one of them as a matter of fact dwelled on unfulfilled promises made in all the other treaties and most recently in the treaty of 1865 at Canville Trading Post. Before touching the feather again, they demanded that their annuities be paid. Obviously, they had come to the encampment to feast and demand fulfillment of previous treaty promises.

The commissioners and Sturges must have been almost out of patience. This was an opportunity which must be grasped immediately since the Congress was jealous of the Indian treaty-making power of the Executive, especially through commissioners; and here were 8,000,000 acres of prairie, most of which was ready for the plow, and they knew that since there were only the signatures of the chiefs and chieftains of the Little Ones between them and this incredible windfall, they must conceal their impatience.

The Commissioner of Indian Affairs, Taylor, president of the council, was especially eager and in a hurry to turn this land over to the railroad. Not only would he and the railroad people have to face Congress, but there were many settlers and others who came to stand about and listen to the proceedings of the council. These people had few amusements in their grubby lives, and they would be keenly listening, and it would soon dawn upon them that this land would be turned over to the railroad company, and they might have to pay dearly for their claims.

When Taylor spoke, he agreed with the Little Ones about the lack of faith displayed by the former treaty makers, but the only way to make up for this was to make another treaty. He also said that the Great Father in Washington "would be sad" if they did not sign the treaty; and if they did not sign, he would think that the "Osages could get along without him."

This was a threat that the "childlike" Little Ones could understand very well. The Great Father would send no more supplies, and they, the Osages, would have to stand alone against the intruders on their reservation and the Arapahoes and Cheyennes on the plains. He said this thing must be done immediately so that the Osages would have their choice of lands for a home in the Cherokee country of the Indian Territory before other tribes took the best land.

Superintendent Murphy told them in his speech that if they would sign the treaty, the commissioners would go at once and make peace between the Osages and the Plains Indians. It seemed to make no

670

difference to him that the commissioners were limited to making a treaty with the Osages for cession of their diminished reservation and trust lands.

Another member of the commission, one Colonel Boone, told them that they had the choice between going to a rich land in the Indian Territory and fighting the Plains Indians.

The next day, after considering the proposition, the Little Ones turned it down. Now something had to be done.

Congress had already heard speeches by Congressman G. W. Julian of Indiana, an intense former "Free-Soiler," and Congressman William Lawrence from Ohio. The attitude in Congress and the voice from the Kansans which would grow in volume must not be encouraged by long deliberations. Time was important, and here they were, Sturges and Taylor and Murphy and the others, held up by a few orating savages. There were too many of them, and all speaking against the treaty. Why not persuade them that the best way was to place the rejection or acceptance of the treaty on the laps of a few, say, twelve, councilors and warriors instead of the chiefs. One could make gifts to lesser leaders and Nobodies, and they would be much more appreciated; and above all, one could elevate some of the members of this "Committe of Twelve" to offices in the tribe to satisfy their self-esteem.

However, these twelve warriors and leaders could not defy their chiefs and chieftains, in their presence at least, so they suggested the compromise that had worked when employed by the government previously: they agreed to sell a strip of their already diminished reservation. The commissioners again explained the treaty and pictured all the dire consequences if it were not signed; and if the commissioners knew the nature of the twelve warriors they had chosen, they must certainly have fired their vanity, since the twelve away from their chieftains and chiefs, in the tent of Taylor, drowned in their own self-appreciation, agreed to sign the treaty as proposed. Since they had been elevated to the importance of chiefs, they could be traditionally generous also.

One of these twelve was a Big Hill warrior of renown called *Pa-I'n-No-Pa-She,* Not-Afraid-of-Longhairs, and another was *No-Pa-Wathe,*

Thunder Fear of the Little Osages. These men were not Nobodies, but warriors of great ability, and Not-Afraid-of-Longhairs had been taught by Father Schoenmakers and his staff of the Osage mission and Father Ponziglione had said that he had a bright mind. Thunder Fear was probably the chieftain of the Thunder gens of the Little Osages. Taylor needed some ability in his leaders of the "Committee of Twelve," so he chose Not-Afraid-of-Longhairs because of his better understanding of those things which might happen to the Little Ones, even the hint that if the treaty was not signed, the soldiers might be sent to drive the Osages out of Kansas. A bright, mission-trained mind could understand this.

This was the twenty-fourth of May, 1868, and the commissioners were probably congratulating themselves on their success, but on the following day, the day on which the treaty was to be signed by the Committee of Twelve, the intelligent, mission-trained Big Hill known as Not-Afraid-of-Longhairs rose and arranged his robe, then with the quiet inflections of classic oratory, told all present that he was opposed to selling more land to the Great Father. He said that listening to the Great Father had cost the Osages much of their Sacred One, and had brought upon them the conditions which all could see, and about which they had come to talk in this place. He said that the other treaties had promised that the Osages would be protected by the Great Father and could live as they had always done. He said that the Osages had held the feather before, and the Great Father had said that he would keep the Heavy Eyebrows from coming on their land and killing their "brothers." Now these Heavy Eyebrows had come, and they had said to the Osages, you will be unprotected, and instead of removing the settlers, they have come for more land.

Certainly it wasn't logic that would decide the matter, since the matter had been decided, but now the commissioners must get the marks of the Osages on a treaty. There were more and more curious settlers standing about the encampment watching and listening, and on the day, May 25, Colonel Blair of the Missouri, Fort Scott and Santa Fe Railroad Company came back and renewed his offer to pay the Osages $2,000,000 for the diminished reservation and the trust lands and requested that he be allowed to present this proposition to the Osages themselves, thus breaking down the privacy of the treaty negotiations. The Leavenworth, Lawrence and Galveston Railroad had offered only $1,600,000.

This would be embarrassing, and Taylor wrote a note in which he informed Colonel Blair that he couldn't transfer the authority which the President had vested in him and his commissioners, and, further, he pointedly said that the "present indications are entirely favorable to a successful termination of our labors."

What might have happened to the so-called "Sturges Treaty" of May 27, 1868, no one could know, with the Osages adamant and the settlers of Kansas waking up to the spirit of the later cry of one of their journals: "The white man first; the Indian next; monopolies never." But there was the incident of the scalps.

This incident was one of the long list of incidents which sometimes deflect the current of history even in the sluggish currents of the backwaters. This was the Little-Flower-Killer Moon, and while the people were being detained by the council on Drum Creek, others, perhaps five hundred of them, set out for the plains, either to hunt, since this was the time for the beginning of the summer hunt, or on the war movement against the Cheyenne-Arapahoes. It was said that they were painted with bluff-paint and that might indicate that they were making the grizzly bear lunge at their plains enemies before the others of the tribe arrived in order to frighten them away from the buffalo herds of western Kansas. The bluff-paint and the fact that some of the warriors came back to the council grounds at Drum Creek with scalps and erected their scalp poles apart from the camp and began their dances might make this more than an assumption.

If this be true, then it must be known that the settlers crowding about the council, the detachment of the Seventh Cavalry, and the commissioners must have experienced a back-of-the-neck tingling fear. The trespassers might either stay close to the soldiers and federal authority or melt into the prairie. One who had never seen painted giants in only breechclout and moccasins, with a trade hatchet in one hand and an eagle-tail fan in the other—the moccasined feet actually sprung back from the sentient earth in rhythm to the drums and the exuberant singing, while the head jerks and the turkey-beard–deer-tail roach quivers, cannot possibly appreciate the reactions in the white people who watched. As the emotion seemed to mount in the dancers and the singing grew frenzied, the veneer of European centuries seemed to fade and there was a species of primordial exultation which turned into animal uneasiness later.

This must have been the state of the Amer-Europeans when the dances were ended, this feeling of animal uneasiness. This must have been the state among the soldiers and the commissioners and the trespassers when the two white men came among them weeping. Their horses must have been lathered, with bellies like bellows.

All the eyewitnesses say that one at least was crying, and all agree about the story they told. The one who was crying said that one of the scalps which the Osages had was that of his brother. They were hunting on the Walnut River, which was of course within the Osage Reservation.

The Osages were of only one gens or the whole party, no one knows, and may have been camped in their usual place, which they called *Ni-Cko'n-Cka,* Between-the-Rivers, the spot where Arkansas City, Kansas, now stands. No one knows whether the white hunters fired on the Osages, which is quite likely in their arrogance inspired by their numbers now in the reservation and for the purpose of boasting; or whether the Osages, feeling that they were near the plains, became angered at what they might have found in the way of carcasses near or upon their traditional camping place between the Walnut and the Arkansas rivers. There is only the story of the weeping white men. The Osages have no gentile or tribal memory of the incident, or they have "thrown it away."

The teller of one story concerning effects of the incident said that the white people at the council camp in their fear shouted, "Kill 'em, kill the dogs!" and the Commissioner of Indian Affairs in his fear put the councilors and the chiefs and chieftains under arrest, and had the soldiers restore order.

When order was restored, he must have realized his advantage. He called the chiefs and chieftains and the councilors before him and suggested that they had seen the excitement of the people, and he pointed to the detachment of soldiers, saying that they could see that there were not enough soldiers to keep order; and if something happened, the Osages would be killed by the soldiers who would come later or chased from their reservation. Some of their people had taken the scalp of the white man, and this was a very great crime, and because of this they would lose their land. But if they delivered up the murderer and signed the treaty, the crime would be forgotten and the Great Father would forget what they had done, and they would be allowed compensation for their reservation and the Great Father would give them another one.

The Osages delivered up two men as hostages, and they were put in irons and later taken to Lawrence, Kansas, and thrown into prison.

Father Ponziglione of the Osage mission, mentioning only one hostage or prisoner, later wrote that he was taken to the spot on the Walnut River, despite his protestation of innocence, where he was supposed to have committed the crime, and while the people were gathering material for the gallows, he escaped from a shanty where he was held. They searched for two days, then left, disappointed.

The fresh scalps were in evidence, but whether the scalp in question was Arapahoe or trespassing white hunter, or whether the incident was arranged as the last hope of Sturges and Taylor, is not known. Whether the signing of the treaty by the Osages, some 108 of them, May 27, 1868, was due to Taylor's bluffing of the Osages or whether due to the influence of more gifts and the handing of a paper signed by Taylor to Not-Afraid-of-Longhairs, making him "Governor of all the Osages," and a paper signed by Taylor and handed to Thunder Fear, making him chief of the Little Osages. This last was signed by N. G. Taylor, commissioner of Indian affairs, May 26, 1868, appointing *"Num-pa-wala"* (*No-Pa-Watha*) "head chief of the Little Osage Indians," to hold office "during good behavior."

The current *Paw-Hiu-Skah,* White Hair, was a strong character, and everyone knew or believed him to be the chief of all the Osages, and he and his family were referred to in Washington as "royal," so that when the treaty was signed, Taylor, depending on the ignorance of the people in Washington and not being able to get White Hair's

675

signature, had Not-Afraid-of-Longhairs' name placed first of the signers, as "Joseph Paw-ne-no-pashe or White Hair, his X mark, Principal Chief." There is some doubt that a man who had been trained at the mission and could sign his name with a Spencerian flourish would be contented to make his mark only.

It is likely that the real chief of the Little Osages at this time might have been *Wah-Hopeh-She* (Son-of-the-Falcon or Sacred Son or even Little Eagle), *No-Pa-Wathe,* Thunder Fear, being only a gentile chieftain.

It took Congress almost two years to consider this treaty before Grant withdrew it. Even the "Free-Soiler" G. W. Julian from Indiana and the congressman from Ohio, William Lawrence, one of the early opponents of the system of Indian treaties for the acquisition of land rather than by act of Congress, fought it implacably. These two and others opposed its ratification, as did Governor S. G. Crawford of Kansas and other Kansans.

During this time the voice of the Kansas settlers and trespassers and their newspapers and leaders were crying "monopoly" and defending the "poor settlers" and the trespassers on the diminished reservation, who were becoming bolder and defied authority. They would have assumed that they would eventually take over the reservation of the Osages even if there had been no Sturges Treaty before the Congress; such was the arrogance of free men. But now with the Sturges Treaty before the Congress, and the journals and the politicians talking about it and the shame of it, they felt that they would do well to become established before the opening of the reserve.

The Congress was apparently not interested in the rights of the Osages but in the rights of Congress; and the Kansans, as they had frankly declared, were not interested in the rights of the Osages but in the virtues and rights of their citizens. It was sometimes quite useful in order to "secure to Settlers all their Rights" to name the Osages when the opponents of the Sturges Treaty needed just one more tiny weight to add to the scales of justice. This implied virtue and humanitarianism to put against the devilish machinations of the monopolists.

The treaty was finally withdrawn from Senate consideration because the Indian treaty-sale system was opposed by those who believed in Congressional control of the public domain and because of competition among several railroad companies and groups, and because there had been no provision in the treaty for the reservation of sections 16 and 36 for educational purposes. There was a very strong sentiment for these reservations in Kansas, and the Congress had pledged themselves to aid the citizens of Kansas in their demand. There were, even within Kansas, monopolists arrayed against antimonopolists, and there were the settlers fighting the railroads and there were the vehement trespassers who sincerely believed that the land belonged to them because they were American citizens.

The last would bring about military activity and come close to bringing on war with the Osages before the government finally bought the diminished reserve and the trust lands.

Governor Samuel G. Crawford of Kansas was drawn into the fight against the Sturges Treaty by Colonel Blair, who became intensely vindictive, but before the matter was settled, Crawford became interested in the activities of the Cheyenne-Arapahoes in western Kansas.

He had been present at the Medicine Lodge Creek council of October, 1867, where the Medicine Lodge Treaty was made with the Plains tribes. Here he had known the Commissioner of Indian Affairs, N. G. Taylor.

Exploitation of minerals and the search for gold among the whites and the spirit of frontier histrionics working in the militiamen and other soldiers as well as in their commanders had stirred up the Cheyennes, Arapahoes, Sioux, and Kiowas and Comanches, and the Cheyennes especially were derailing trains, shooting at them, trying to rope them; attacking wagon trains along the South Platte and burning "ranches" and stage stations.

Many of these attacks were made in western Kansas, so Governor Crawford decided to aid Generals Sherman and Sheridan in their plan to "punish" the Indians. He raised the Nineteenth Kansas Cavalry, resigned his governorship to command it, and urged General Sheridan to employ Osage scouts. These people knew every red canyon and every selenite mountain of the Southern Plains; and not only that, they were at war with the Cheyenne-Arapahoes. Judging from Sherman's opinion of the barroom "Injun slayers" strutting about

677

Hays City, Kansas, in fringed buckskin and flowing locks, he must have accepted Crawford's suggestion readily.

The Civil War generals who were sent west after the war to deal with the Plains Indians knew nothing of Indian character and were map and woodland fighters. Here on the plains there were no maps, and the Indians were not animated quixotic chessmen. They were often considered cowardly because they might disengage in the heat of the battle because the war chief's medicine might have suddenly gone bad, or simply on the war chief's whim, just when one had one's troops in beautiful deployment. To follow them after they disengaged thus was like trying to find the mountain stream you have been following when it reaches the desert, where it fingers out and is then completely lost. The trail of a thousand Plains Indians, clear and broad and marked with horse droppings, would soon finger out, and suddenly there was no main trail at all, only trails of parties of twos or threes curving out to right and left.

However, General Sherman did find a weakness. In the summer when the Indian horses were strong and there was not the need for shelter, it was impossible to "punish" Indians; but in the winter when their horses were gaunted and weak and the plainsmen had to seek the few river bottoms for shelter and firewood, and had to put up their tipis for shelter and remain for some time, then was the time for the army and the militia to attack them on grain-fed horses.

The General learned another thing about Indians, that they were divided into tribes, as different from each other quite often as the people who were coming to New York City from Europe. He also learned that they were not all "hostiles" and that some were "friendlies," but when he sent his officers out on their punishing expeditions, they seemed to be confused concerning the difference.

This is what happened when Sheridan sent Colonel Custer out from Fort Supply. He chose the right season, the proper time, the late autumn of 1868, and fortunately the proper weather. There was a terrific snowstorm, and Governor Crawford failed to make rendezvous with the national troop.

However, the Osage scouts arrived wrapped in their buffalo robes with the hair on the inside and with beaver bandeaus, to which they had attached the otter crowns. Naturally they couldn't wear their turkey-gobbler roaches under these crowns. Hard Rope and Little Beaver were in charge of the scouts, and with them were Big Lynx, Eagle Feather, Wolf, and *Ce-Ce-Mo'n-I'n,* Trots-as-He-Travels, referring to the trotting buffalo. He was known simply as Trotter.

The stories of the scouts differ little, each story revealing their constant uneasiness about the Heavy Eyebrows soldiers. There was no action on the part of the soldiers to indicate that they were not trustworthy, but the Little Ones were suspicious of them.

The Custer command set out in a snowstorm on this twenty-third of November. The snow came horizontally and wiped out the landmarks. The command went up Wolf Creek for about eight miles, and here the most stupid of the woodland militiamen could have found the trail of the Cheyennes in the snow until the plains wind had covered it. They crossed the creek and went south, and one band crossed the South Canadian near the Antelope Hills and the other band went down the river. The scouts followed the trail that led to the south, believing that the Cheyennes would attempt to make the Washita River bottoms for shelter.

But there were eighteen inches of snow and the trail almost vanished, but when the sun finally came out, they could see the little humps in the snow which indicated the trail. Hard Rope and Wolf had to walk ahead on foot to trace the trail, but Hard Rope said that he knew what he would have done, and that was what the Cheyenne leader, Crows Neck, did.

The buffalo were disturbed and were pawing the snow and grazing after the storm, and you could see the steam rise from their bodies. It was very cold on the South Canadian River.

When night came, a crust formed on the snow, and the hocks of the cavalry horses bled and the cracking of the crust made loud sounds, but Custer would not stop.

After several days, they came near the Washita. Custer made his men whisper their conversations. The noise of broken snow crust could mean many things to the Cheyennes: it could be caused by wild horses or restless buffalo in the cold, moonlit night, but words and the clank of sabers could come only from an enemy, so Custer also made his men take off their sabers.

The rounded little red hills threw black moon shadows, and the temperature the soldiers said was below zero, and when the soldiers stopped, Hard Rope crept to the first escarpment of the Washita River valley and looked for a long time. Soon he smelled charred wood, and since there was no wind, he knew it must be close, so he went back to tell Custer. The Long Knife chief came with some officers, crawling along with Hard Rope on their bellies to the escarpment. Once he stopped and pointed to their spurs glinting in the moonlight, but the officer paid no attention to him. When they came to the escarpment, they wrinkled their noses like rabbits and later said that there was no fire. He told them that the fire was dead and that it had been the fire built by the boys who guarded the horses. Then Wolf heard a dog howl down in the river bottom. There were no wolves howling, and the camp dogs would not leave their beds on such a cold night. The dogs might have heard the horses in their nervousness crackling the snow crust, or they might have smelled the very strong scent of the Heavy Eyebrows. They must wait for the "Indians' hour" just before dawn, then attack.

They could light no fires and they must not talk to each other and they must not stamp their feet to keep warm. It was as if all life had left the earth in the white silence.

As the night wore on, the Little Ones became nervous. They knew that the Cheyennes were great fighters, and there might be many of them there along the dark line that was the growths of the river bottom. They wondered if the soldiers would turn them, the Little Ones, over to the Cheyennes if they were losing. They huddled together and they communicated mostly in the sign language, and they decided that they would stay close to the standard bearer, so that they could judge for themselves how the fight was going; they would retreat with the colors and, taking the best horses, flee to the north.

Before dawn the moon went down, and they felt the tenseness in the darkness. All were eager and watchful. A soldier pointed to the east, and they all looked and on the horizon there was a fire, but soon the Morning Star came up over a red plains swell. The Little Ones chanted under their breaths.

Then there was activity, and the Little Ones moved over to be near the standard bearer as the soldiers moved over the escarpment. Soon the band played "Garry Owen," and the soldiers began to yell and charged the Cheyenne camp. The people were asleep, and they came out of their tipis and scattered, and soon there was silence again except for distant shots, and there were bodies of men and women and children lying about, Chief Black Kettle and his wife lying close together. There were villages downstream, and many Comanches and Apaches, Cheyennes and Arapahoes and Kiowas, and Custer was afraid to go down there to attack. He burned the tipis and robes and the horses he didn't need, he ordered shot, then with his prisoners started back toward Hays City, Kansas. The Little Ones were happy about this, since they knew that the Cheyennes and Arapahoes downriver would have killed all Custer's men, and they themselves would have been a great prize for the Arapahoes. The time was right according to Sherman's reckoning. Custer's command had left in a snowstorm, and they had struck the Cheyennes on a below-zero morning, but had destroyed Black Kettle and his band, who were more than a "friendly" band; Black Kettle had been trying to bring about peace between the Indians and the whites.

Trots-as-He-Travels, called Trotter, remained with Custer as a scout, and that morning on the Washita he learned much. He remembered the nervousness of the Little Ones and the way they kept fingering their bandeaus; nervous about their tell-tale scalplocks, their natural hair like a buffalo's tail left after shaving their heads and to which they attached the turkey-beard–deer-tail scalplock. They were afraid their bandeaus would slip off and the Cheyennes would identify them by their shaven heads. On the plains and on the prairie these were a challenge to their enemies, but here, with only a few of them alone with Heavy Eyebrows soldiers whom they mistrusted, they must keep their identity hidden.

Later when Trotter was scouting for Custer on the Little Big Horn, he had let his hair grow and kept it piled up under his bandeau or hat. He suggested to Curley, the Pawnee scout, that he do the same, and at the Battle of the Little Big Horn, when Custer and his command were wiped out, Trotter and Curley simply took off their bandeaus and let their long hair fall, losing themselves in the swarm of emotionalized Siouan warriors.

681

51. The Friends

FLOWERS ARE OFTEN found growing in the decaying walls of a temple in the jungle. The founders of the democracy on the new continent dreamed of a temple for a new world and had actually laid the foundations, but the walls remained unfinished and neglected and now seemed to be falling into decay. In the *laissez faire* atmosphere of the U. S. Grant administration and the greedy fever which it inspired in a nation, there was a spiritual light which became effective since it was integrated with the national government and therefore had the government's power behind it, but was not tarnished.

The Jesuits had worked, often with government subsidies, among the natives but without the power of the government behind them as had the Franciscans and others. The Presbyterians and the Baptists and the Methodist had worked with governmental subsidies but without the power against prejudices and the cynical influence of those who considered the Indians a vested interest. But now the Friends became a part of the government, as far as the Little Ones were concerned. They were hard, intolerant men, and they, too, lifted the Neolithic man to the stage of European civilization which they themselves represented and expected him to attain in a few years that which had taken them almost four thousand years to attain.

But though they were hard and implacable in their convictions, they were just as implacable in their honesty, which like their convictions was not just self-satisfying and passive, and yet not really aggressive, but was something like a benign wall which one finally must learn could not be dented.

They recognized the situation in the relationship between the government and the Indians, but like the North after the war were too absorbed to do much about it. An Episcopalian bishop, Henry M. Whipple of Minnesota, started writing letters to President Lincoln in 1859, and from those letters and the sentiment which he expressed, "Every [Indian] employee ought to be a man of purity, temperance, industry, and unquestioned integrity," a philosophy developed embracing this attitude and was eventually adopted by the government.

Later, the army officers and some of the newspapers of the West liked to say that the sentimentalists of the East, who had never seen an Indian, were partially responsible for the "atrocities" committed by the Plains Indians against the virtuous whites, but strangely enough the sentimentalists of the East and North had their sentiments well absorbed by the question of enfranchisement of the Negro. Some of them with income and leisure which might allow them to be academic were worried by the petroleum discovered on Oil Creek in Pennsylvania, in fear that it might displace whale oil. They also seemed to have expended much of their vindictive sentimentality on the slavery question before the war and were now affected by the new atmosphere.

At this time, it is obvious that Congress was not being urged by the sentimentalist or anyone else to solve the problem created by the invading buffalo slaughterers, the long-haired "Injun fighters," gold-seekers, trespassers in general, and men who, finding themselves formed into militia companies, felt compelled to kill some redskins.

Thus it was the people who had migrated from the East and had come in contact with the Indians, the more civilized settlers, who saw the conflict between the swarming whites and the tenacious Indians, who decided that something ought to be done about it. It was these who brought about the "Peace Policy" of the Grant administration.

This policy was conceived and nurtured by the Episcopalians and the Friends, who got the military man Grant to adopt it, which in itself was very important, since Grant in a speech in 1868 said that "the settlers and emigrants must be protected, even if the extermination of every Indian tribe was necessary to secure such a result." The problem was rather simple, since there was a practical solution to the conflicts, and the military mind couldn't allow justice and morality or civilized academic interest to complicate such clear thinking.

After Grant had been elected President, the Society of Friends met in Baltimore and there prepared a memorial, based upon all the honest evidence they could gather, which showed that military supervision of the Indian was not the answer. The Friends brought their memorial to Washington and got an audience with the President January 25, 1869, and the next day there was a visit from another group of Friends.

In February, Grant's aide-de-camp, Brevet Brigadier General E. S. Parker, who was a Seneca Indian, asked the Friends by letter to submit names of persons whom they would endorse as qualified candidates for the office of Indian agent. They were also assured that the President would give all the encouragement and protection that the laws of the United States warranted.

This was more than the Friends expected, but Benjamin Hallowell was worried that degenerate influences might affect the Friends if they had no safeguards. It was a wide gap between the President of the United States and an agent far out on the reservation. He went to Washington and asked the President to allow the Society to appoint the whole superintendency—appoint all the employees from superintendent down, subject to approval by the President and the Senate.

The Friends did not win all they wanted from the military minds. The Indians must be placed on reservations, and when on their reservations they "are under the exclusive control and jurisdiction of their agents. They will not be interfered with in any manner by military authority, except upon requisition of the special agent resident with them, his superintendent, or the Bureau of Indian Affairs in Washington. Outside the well-defined limits of their reservations they are under the original and exclusive jurisdiction of the military authorities." The military would treat all Indians who did not now go immediately to the reservations and stay there, as "hostiles," when they found them, and "particularly if they are near settlements or the great lines of communications." This would place conflicts between the

684

troops and Indians off the reservations in the category of disciplinary action rather than war, and naturally this was a great boon to the Indian fighters and the free men. They could now enjoy target practice with impunity and add to the collection of their "sculps."

E. S. Parker, the Seneca, became the first commissioner of Indian affairs under the new Peace Policy plan, but felt with his President that one ought not entrust the supervision of the Indian entirely to the civilians, and he and Grant insisted on taking care of some of the left-without-jobs officers. There were perhaps some 216 of these, and the President and his Commissioner of Indian Affairs attached 60 of these to the Bureau of Indian Affairs.

This was a boon, in this period of national moral ebb, to the Little Ones to have strictly honest officials supervising them, even though they could not now go beyond the reservation boundaries to the west on their hunts without permission and without some Heavy Eyebrows to see that they did not attack the Cheyenne-Arapahoes and the Pawnees.

However, their problem remained as it had always been; it wasn't a matter of their leaving the reservation to harass buffalo hunters and loiter near the lines of communication, but what to do when they came back from their buffalo hunts to find their villages taken over by Heavy Eyebrows trespassers. Retaliation meant that some of their young men would be hanged and their spirits would never escape the body. This was much more serious than simply being shot without the paint. There would be more screech owls to haunt them from the trees above the lodges and more *mi-ah-luschkas* along the deer trails.

The Little Ones went on their buffalo hunt in Deer-Hiding Moon of 1869, and did very well apparently, but when they arrived home to the reservation during Single-Moon-by-Himself, January, 1870, they found that one whole village had been destroyed, caches rifled, and graves robbed. They also found their first Friends agent, one Isaac T. Gibson. He had received his commission from President Grant on December 21, 1869, but had taken charge of the Neosho Agency on October 1 of the same year.

This invasion of the reservation by trespassers was the most serious yet, since there were not only more of the trespassers, but they were more arrogant and cynical, and even dared the Little Ones to remove them. They even made complaint about the Little Ones to their state and national senators, which included rather humorous complaints against the Little Ones on whose reservation they were trespassing.

One said that when the Osages came back from the hunt in January, 1870, they weren't as pleasant as they had been before, and they began to burn crops and cabins and demand exorbitant payments. Another good reason why the Osages should be removed, he believed, was that the women folk were afraid of them.

Father Ponziglione said that almost every day the Osages were seen in groups ordering the trespassers off the land, and those who had put in crops and couldn't leave them were made to pay for the privilege of remaining until they could harvest, and those who would not pay received Indian vengeance, but he didn't give the nature of the "vengeance."

Some of the trespassers were frightened and left, but others formed small patrol squads and kept lookouts on the prairie swells. He says that when the Osages learned of this brazen action, they began to burn the wheat crops almost ready for harvest, destroy the cabins, kill the hated hogs, and steal the horses.

Agent Gibson believed that war was imminent. He first went about over the reserve trying to reason with the trespassers, then he would call the Osages together and try to reason with them. At one meeting with the settlers he described them as "a crowd of angry wicked men. . . . Many or most of them wanting to take my life."

Finally the proud man, who wanted so much to be effective both for his personal satisfaction and so that his actions would reflect on the Society, had to send for the troops. He did this after Hard Rope and Four Lodges had ordered all white settlers to leave the diminished reservation. Because of this order, war, he thought, between the Little Ones and the white trespassers was more imminent "than with the Kiowas and the Arapahos." Now, he believed, was the time for the President to do something about removing the white intruders, and he got in touch with Superintendent Hoag, who got in touch with Commissioner Parker, who in turn relayed the request to Secretary of the Interior Cox, and he talked with the Secretary of War.

These were peaceful Friends who had inspired Grant's Peace Policy asking in their distress for military intervention. After the troops arrived, there was a despairing entry in Gibson's diary: "I must use the troops to remove those settlers tomorrow. . . . Go forward or resign . . . ."

A calling together of the trespassers and the Little Ones in one grand council and then four days of Mourning Dances by the Little Ones, as the soldiers stood by, would have given relief for some time, but the removal of the trespassers or the Osages was inevitable. In this biological situation the invading species were numerically stronger than the indigenous species, and the Little Ones must go. In order to "protect" the Little Ones, the government must move them again.

Gibson and Captain Upham and his company might have been more effective in protecting the reservation against trespassers if Parker, the commissioner of Indian affairs, had not informed Gibson that the settlers were not to be removed, the troops having been sent to preserve the peace and protect the Osages in their occupancy. The offenders were to be arrested and turned over to the civil authorities.

On July 15, 1870, legislation was passed which provided for the removal of the Osages from Kansas, but the troops remained until October of that year, after the Little Ones had gone on their winter hunt and the danger of war was not so great.

Before the Little Ones left for their summer hunt and during their absence, their superintendent, Enoch Hoag, and the agent, Isaac T. Gibson, now knowing that their removal was inevitable, fought for their interests in Washington. Hoag sent Gibson there to talk with congressmen about the price to be paid for the diminished reservation. He had the offer from the Atchison, Topeka and Santa Fe Railroad to which to attract the attention of Congress. This was an offer made by the former superintendent of the Central Superintendency, Colonel Thomas Murphy, on behalf of the railroad company, offering the Little Ones $2,560,000 for their lands in Kansas. Under the former superintendent's influence, the railroad officials had made the offer very attractive, offering to buy the new home in the Indian Territory with $200,000, and offering $50,000 for subsistence of the tribe for a year, and $50,000 for erecting the necessary agency buildings, the remainder of the money, $2,200,000, to be invested in 5 per cent government bonds.

The people of the Bureau of Indian Affairs were concerned over the possibility of Congress' passing a bill to buy the Osage lands at a lower figure. A senator from Kansas actually wanted the price for the Osage lands to be that which they had agreed to accept under the Drum Creek Treaty with the railroad, and the other senator from Kansas wanted to sell the lands to a group of railroads.

Agent Gibson had support from Senator Lot M. Morrill of Maine, who opposed the Senate Bill No. 529, which would authorize the sale of the Osage lands. He pointed to Article two of the Canville Trading Post treaty of 1865, which provided for sale of the Osage lands at $1.25 an acre, whereas this Bill No. 529 authorized only eighteen cents an acre.

Senator Morrill was apparently of the prewar school of the upholders of the honor and dignity of the United States, and it was clear that the United States had given their word to the Osage Indians. Now it could do nothing less than stand by it, and the argument that the Osages must be removed from their own land to prevent war was shallow and not worthy of consideration. He argued that the United States had pledged to keep the white people off the Osage reservation and that the very presence of the white people on the reservation had violated that pledge. The public domain could not be opened for settlement except by authority of law, and therefore there was no excuse whatever for the trespassing of the whites on Osage land. The way to evade war was simply for the United States government to live up to its pledge, he argued.

The people of Kansas were becoming impatient with Congress. They wanted the Osages removed so that the land could be sold to actual settlers, and some of them assembled at Winfield and resolved that the Osage title be extinguished and the land sold to the settlers at $1.25 an acre. This was helpful to Agent Gibson and Superintendent Hoag.

When the legislation passed on the last day of the session, July 15, which authorized the sale of the Osage lands in Kansas at $1.25 an acre and the removal of the Osages to the Indian Territory, Agent

Gibson made a gleeful entry in his diary: ". . . passed both houses about as Senate & myself wanted it—Such tumult & Bedlam I never saw before—adjd Sine die at 5 P.M."

Now their charges would be removed from the atmosphere of lawlessness and war, and the Friends were happy. They had only now to go through the farce of having the Little Ones approve the legislation, which in their tidy, righteous minds was no farce at all. For this purpose a committee of the President's Board of Indian Commissioners came to council with the Little Ones.

The first meeting was scheduled for August 20, 1870, but when the Little Ones had not shown up yet from their buffalo hunt on the plains, they reset the date to August 29. Gibson had sent runners to advise the chieftains that the committee had arrived. They had first chosen a council ground about twelve miles below the junction of Big and Little Caney, and about one mile west of the 96th meridian, which was to be the eastern boundary of the Little Ones' reservation in IndianTerritory, but now they decided to hold the council on Drum Creek in Kansas near the agency. While waiting for the Little Ones, the committee and the agent held religious meetings and visited the proposed new reservation in the Indian Territory, and they had the 96th meridian surveyed.

The Little Ones did not appear on the twenty-ninth of August. This was a very late date for their return from the summer hunt, and their relationships with the Plains Indians began to haunt Gibson's thoughts. He remembered how disturbed Four Lodges and Hard Rope were by the trespassers, and there had been rumors that they might join the Plains Indians in their struggle on the plains and bring their allies back with them to settle the problem of the trespassers on the prairie part of their own reservation.

This was more than a rumor. Hard Rope and the other leaders had talked much of making one last stand against the Heavy Eyebrows and fighting without surrender, all dying with their songs on their tongues. They talked of dying on the war movement either independently or with the Kiowas and Comanches and Apaches and even the Cheyenne-Arapahoes as allies.

On the thirtieth of August, Gibson wrote in his diary: ". . . nothing done . . . ½ breeds come in . . . but no wild Osages . . . discouraging . . . ."

The next day, however, Not-Afraid-of-Longhairs came in from the plains with the Big Hills. He was their recognized leader now, and was called "Governor Joe," and later, on September 2, Black Dog and Claremore (perhaps Arrow-Going-Home the third) came in with the Upland-Forest-People. Thunder-Fear and Four Lodges brought the Little Osages in from the plains on the eighth of September. When Claremore and *Ta-He-Gaxe* (perhaps the second counselor known as Tallai), Antler-Maker, came to the council, Gibson could write in his diary: "Now we will go ahead . . . ."

He was quite pleased to see the Little Ones, since he knew much about their attitude toward the trespassers and about the rumor of the war movement with the Plains Indians. The committeemen with no suspicions were rather short-tempered and impatient with the Little Ones, having had to wait for them since the thirtieth of August.

The trespassers stood about as they had done during the counciling about the Sturges Treaty. They were intensely interested and wanted nothing to occur which might have a tendency to anger the "big chiefs" and cause them to refuse to approve of the legislation. They were friendly now, almost solicitous.

Obviously the Little Ones were not in a good humor, but only Gibson sensed this, as expressed by entries in his diary. The members of the committee were unaware of the atmosphere, and were impatient. They were sincerely interested in the welfare of the Little Ones, but it never seemed to occur to anyone that these "wild Osages," as even the kindly Gibson called them, were really without guidance and counsel. The Friends, like all other Amer-Europeans, had elevated them over nearly four thousand years of development, and although they didn't employ chicanery to gain their ends, they recognized the Little Ones' equality with themselves only in such councils and as bearers of souls; otherwise, they would say that they "were like children," with all that might imply.

The committee finally got them to hold the feather, and one member of the impatient committee had already left when *Wah-Ti-Anka,* chief councilor of the Upland-Forest People, arrived late on the twelfth, after Vincent Colyer, chairman of the committee, had made his farewell speech on the previous Saturday. He spoke for the Black Dog and the Claremore bands. He and the two bands knew that the council was in progress, but they preferred to sulk in their lodges, appearing the day Colyer was to leave. This was the spirit of the Judeans before the Roman procurator again.

It was said that *Wah-Ti-Anka* always wore his bluff-paint when he talked to white men in council, holding on to a necessity of the animal world. He stood, and with right arm free of his robe, said that the people shouldn't have signed the paper until he arrived, and he demanded that the new reservation extend to the Great Salt Plains.

Colyer had to catch a train, and he asked the two bands to sign the bill immediately, and *Wah-Ti-Anka* replied that he thought it was to be a long council and that it was too bad that Colyer couldn't stay. Colyer lost his temper and suggested that the two bands could stay as long as they wished, but the committee must leave; and he suggested further that it would make no difference whether the bands signed or didn't sign, that there were sufficient signatures to constitute approval by the tribe.

Wah-Ti-Anka replied that he must wait until he asked his people some questions, then he, Colyer, could travel all night, "go to the ocean," if he liked.

The Neolithic bluff-paint didn't work, and the bands signed.

Typically, after signing the bill, Not-Afraid-of-Longhairs came up with a talking paper which he wanted the committee to approve.

The Little Ones did this often in their negotiations with the Heavy Eyebrows. After signing a treaty or an agreement, they would bring up matters which they wanted included, in the spirit of having made a gift to the Heavy Eyebrows; having done that which the Heavy Eyebrows wanted, they now expected a gift in return.

This time in dealing with Friends they did get the treaty modified through recommendations by Parker, the Seneca commissioner of Indian affairs. He suggested approval of some of the modifying requests to the Secretary of the Interior, who approved and handed them on to the Congress.

Not-Afraid-of-Longhairs had counseled with his people for several days, and the results were requests for modifications of the bill: (1) The Osages wanted more land; (2) They wanted assurance from the United States that they would be protected from trespassers in the new reservation, in the form of a formal treaty; (3) They wanted the control of part of their funds by the chieftains; (4) They wanted to hold their land in community until they should request a change; (5) They wanted acreage equal to the number of acres which the state of Kansas had held for school purposes, and they asked the United States to buy this acreage for them; (6) They wanted the right to hunt buffalo on the plains beyond the western limits of their reservation; and (7) They wanted permission to send delegates to Washington to talk in their own behalf.

The Commissioner of Indian Affairs approved the request to hunt buffalo on the plains and the request that they be permitted to send delegations to Washington when they had the funds. He thought that the request that they be compensated for the sections 16 and 36 which they turned over to Kansas for school purposes should be granted. The most important request of all was number 4, which was granted, this having to do with holding of their land in community until they might request a change. Not-Afraid-of-Longhairs stood up in council under an elm on Drum Creek in September, 1870, and spoke for his people for the signing of a paper which the government wanted signed, a paper which the impatient committee under orders must urge them to sign; and with the expectant trespassers waiting in a circle about the council, they turned over to the government their lands in Kansas. Now they would ask a gift in exchange. They did not want their new reservation owned in severalty; they wanted to own it in common. Surrounded by Heavy Eyebrows, they, like their Sacred One, grew smaller, and they must stay together.

Apparently they needed no Heavy Eyebrows advisers. Holding their land in common would later make their name known all over North America.

After the signing of the paper, the women sobbed their mourning songs every morning for days. They must leave the graves of their fathers and their children for the third time.

52. Blackjacks and Prairie

ABOUT FORTY TRESPASSER FAMILIES had decided to build a town near the agency on the Verdigris as early as 1869, a year before the reservation was sold by the Osages to the United States government. They found so few trees with which to build their houses that they were compelled to thatch their roofs with bluestem and other grasses. The Little Ones had called this village Hay-House-Town. These people had organized a county and called it Montgomery, with an attitude of vain impudence. They were very eager about the Little Ones' approving the removal legislation, and before the legislation was approved, they became genial, as the intruders did all over the diminished reservation during this time of uncertainty. However, as soon as the Little Ones signed the bill, many of them returned to their old attitude of belligerence and arrogance.

It was different with these people who built lodges with grass, say the Little Osages who had their village just north of Hay-House-Town. While like all the others they had little time in their struggle with the prairie during the establishment of homes to have an academic interest in the Little Ones, especially since the very existence of the Little Ones was an obstacle, there must have been some sort of *rapprochement* with some of the Osage bands. A week after the removal bill had been signed and before the Little Ones went on their winter buffalo hunt, never to return to Kansas to live, fifty warriors went to Hay-House-Town, and in the very middle of the little village began to change to their dance clothing and to paint their faces.

They danced. Possibly one of the social dances, apparently as a gesture of farewell. As the people of the town watched, they must have begun already to have a feeling of nostalgia which couldn't possibly have a logical basis. Possibly in their great relief in the knowledge that they would never see the Little Ones again, they might have been filled with well-being and generosity.

This was much the way Agent Gibson felt after the Little Ones had left Kansas on their winter hunt after the signing of the removal bill. His feeling of relief would have a different basis, however. He would have a clean slate, upon which the Friends would help the Little Ones write their future history. His first report to Superintendent Enoch Hoag, October 1, 1870, was very long, and he wrote with *élan*. The staid, conservative, practical Friend became almost poetic, and because he was so intent on the welfare of his Osages and so hopeful for them he did in several paragraphs in the report allow the mustang of fancy to get the bit in his teeth.

He wanted to be sure that Superintendent Hoag really appreciated the Osages. "Physically," he wrote, "the Osages are strong in constitution. The men are large and erect, the women strong and healthy, the children bright and active."

He wrote that there were about 250 mixed-bloods. He had learned courtesy from his charges and now did not refer to mixed-bloods as "half-breeds." He said the full-blood Osages were divided into seven bands. This was sufficient evidence that the old organization of the Little Old Men was breaking up. Of the original five physical divisions originating in the great flood—the Big Hills, the Upland-Forest, the Thorny-Valley, the Down-Below People (the Little Osages), and the Heart-Stays People—the Upland-Forest People had been split at the death of *Gra-Mo'n*, Arrow-Going-Home, and there was now a Black Dog band and a Claremore band of the Upland-Forest, and Gibson had unofficially added, for convenience in signing the bill, an apocryphal band, the mixed-bloods, but here he was still calling them the "Half-Breed band." He mentioned the Beaver gens of the Thorny-Valley People as "the Beaver band."

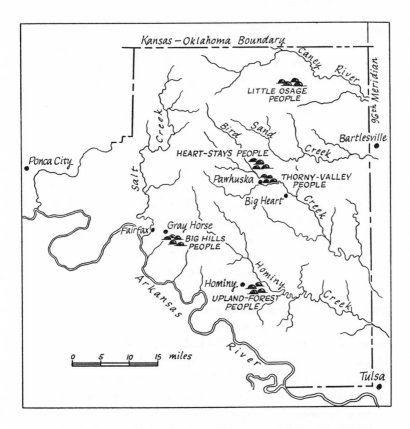

LAST OSAGE RESERVATION, NOW OSAGE COUNTY, OKLAHOMA

In his report he described the lodges, and they seem to have changed very little in three hundred years. He wrote that the frame was still of poles and that they used buffalo robes and "matting made of flags," which was the original cattail. All that had been added were puncheons. Possibly these were used at the bottom of the lodges.

He was heartsick over the thought of the manual labor the Osages performed in preparing for their hunts and in their preparation of hides and the making of horn spoons and bows and arrows and the repeated labor of moving camp four times a year: from the prairie-woodlands to the plains twice and from the plains to the prairie-woodlands twice. Even their planting was laborious, he believed. If only, he thought, they could divert this labor to agriculture, it would place them in "affluent circumstances."

He wrote that he would be glad with the Osages to be free from the whites of the diminished reservation—their killing each other over claims they had no right to, their searching for treasures in the graves of the Osages, and their purposeful agitation of his charges. He wrote at length of the conflict between the whites and the Osages for a decade or more: "The question will suggest itself; which of these people are the savages?" When he wrote of the new reservation in the Indian Territory, he seemed to have renewed confidence in the government. He wrote that while the removal legislation was being considered, "Several hundred professional squatters have anticipated this and taken claims on this new home, but from the noise made by the demagogues, I apprehend the troops sent by the government to eject them, are doing their duty."

As he was writing his long report to Superintendent Hoag, he must have been arrested in his enthusiasm and have wondered if he were being just to the settlers of Kansas, and he must have suddenly thought of the many people who had come to the diminished reservation sincerely believing it to be free for the taking, as the land speculators and the politicians had assured them. There had been Union soldiers from across the Mississippi coming to claim their government homesteads, many of whom listened to the speculators and the politicians and the free men, and settled or tried to settle on the Osage Reservation. He might have remembered the immigrants of his own faith who settled on the reserve of the Little Ones, and caused some embarrassment.

Desiring to be just, he wrote: "Right here before noticing the present and moral condition of this people, I wish to remark that whatever strictures I have made or may make upon the white intruders upon Indian reservations are intended solely for that class. The term squatter, settlers, etc., is necessarily used but it is by no means intended to include that grand army of pioneers who respecting law and the rights of others have with industry, energy and courage worthy of all commendation, made the wilderness to bloom as the rose."

He also mentioned in his first report that the Osages had made peace with the Plains Indians, but shut his eyes to the facts, pretending to himself that they made peace because they were inherently peaceful. He suspected that they had taken the pipe to the Cheyenne and Arapahoe tipis for the purpose of confederation against the wagon trains and the gold-seekers, the buffalo hunters, and the trespassers of the plains in general as well as against the trespassers on the Osage diminished reservation.

He might have washed the thoughts about their peacemaking and their unusually long stay on the plains during the summer of 1870 from his mind with the following encomium: "This tribe of Indians are richly endowed by nature, physically and morally. A finer looking body of men with more grace and dignity or better intellectual development could hardly be found on the globe. In judging of their moral character some facts in their history must be remembered. They were once the most numerous and warlike nation on this Continent, with a domain extending from the Gulf to the Missouri River, from the Mississippi to the Rocky Mountains, but they have been shorn of their territory piece by piece, until at last they have not a settled and unquestioned claim to a single foot of earth. Their numbers have been wasted by war and famine. This little remnant is all that remains of a heroic race that once had undisputed ownership over all this region. It is almost without precedent, yet strictly true. One great cause of their decline had been fidelity to their pledges."

One of the facts that did not escape him was that they had seldom had the opportunity to know representatives of the more advanced stages of European civilization, and that the essential factor in their civilization would be contact with higher stages of this civilization in the persons of agency employees and the licensed traders. This would be his objective.

The Little Ones came directly from their winter hunt to the new reservation among the blackjacks and prairie in January of 1871. The agency had been established at Silver Lake, but later had to be removed to the west, since this spot was found to be east of the 96th meridian.

By 1872, the five physical divisions had established their villages on terrain which resembled that to which each group had fled during the great flood far away in dim tribal memory. There was the new magic line, and again east of the magic line were the That-Thing-on-Its-Head People, the Cherokees. This magic line was the 96th meridian, that section running from the Arkansas River to the Kansas state line on the north.

When the chiefs of the five physical divisions sought terrain which harmonized with their traditions, the Thorny-Valley People had chosen the bottomlands around Silver Lake, and because *Paw-Hiu-Skah,* White Hair the last, came there, and because the name White Hair was ever associated in the minds of the officials with the grand chieftainship, here they located the agency in 1871. The agency had to be moved later to the center of the new reservation to another thorny valley, called *Ni-A-Xe-Ye-Shku-Be,* Deep Ford, on *Wa-Shinka Ga-Xa,* Bird Creek.

The Upland-Forest-People under Claremore and Black Dog settled their people on a wooded plateau to the south drained by *Ho'n-Mo'n-I'n Ga-Xa,* Walks-in-the-Night Creek, named for Walks-in-the-Night, and Not-Afraid-of-Longhairs (Governor Joe), now called by the Heavy Eyebrows "Big Hill Joe" and with the chief counselors *Shonkah Mo'in,* Walking Dog (horse) and *Ta-Wa'n-She-Heh,* Tall Chief, settled their people among the buttelike and rounded hills in the southwest part of the reservation, near *Ni-Chiu-E Ga-Xa,* Salt Creek, and their village was called *Ka-Wa-Xo-Dse,* Gray Horse. In the lenticular bottoms of Bird Creek north of the Thorny-Valley village was the village of the Heart-Stays People under Saucy Chief, and *Shinka-Wa-Sa* and Hard Rope, and down Bird Creek in another bottom was settled *No'n-Ce-Tonka,* Big Heart.

The Little Osages under Four Lodges, Thunder-Fear, and Striking Ax came to a creek in the northeastern part of the reservation called *Mo'n-Co-Tse Ga-Xa,* Whistle Creek, because here the little boys found reeds from which they made whistles, very numerous. They settled here and on *Pa-I'n Ga-Xa,* Longhair Creek so named because they had killed a Pawnee here. The Heavy Eyebrows would call these creeks Mission and Pond respectively, and the creek which drained

OSAGE VILLAGE AREA, INCLUDING THREE FORKS AND THE OSAGE RIVER

the plateau where the Upland-Forest People settled under Black Dog
and Claremore they would call Hominy for *Ho'n-Mo'n-I'n.*

Wah-Na-Sha-She, Little-Eagle-That-Gets-What-He-Wants, was
born on the Verdigris River just above where the Heavy Eyebrows
would build their lodges of grass. He was born "during-time-when-
we-gather-cattails," November, in Deer-Break-Their-Horns Moon,[1]
during the time when the Heavy Eyebrows were making the war
movement against each other, sometime between 1861 and 1865.

But he had only heard of the Heavy Eyebrows until they came
[1] Also called Coon-Breeding Moon.

699

there to make their town out of grass, and he was afraid of them. When he was much younger, his grandmother had told about *wah-pokah,* the great gray owl who came to sit above the lodges in the moonlight, listening for lies. She had told him of the *mi-ah-luschkas,* who came along the deer trail in the moonlight, dressed quite often in their war clothes and sometimes only in their breechclouts and moccasins, and danced around a miniature drum. If one saw them or heard them, one must run home and pray. She told him of the Heavy Eyebrows with hair like the black bear on their arms and hands and faces and on their chests, who would come and carry little boys away if they didn't do all the things they must do.

He was afraid of the great gray owl, the screech owl, the little people who danced in the moonlight, and the hairy ones. But when he heard that they had come to the river and were making their lodges of grass, he wanted to go down to see them, but he was afraid. Then one day one came up the river to talk with his father, Eagle-That-Dreams, his uncle *Wah-Hopeh-She* (Sacred Sun), and Thunder-Fear, the chief.

He wore a black coat and a tall hat and sat in his saddle with his legs straight out toward the nose of his horse. Eagle-That-Gets-What-He-Wants ran with the other little boys and hid in the tall grass of the bottoms, then they came back like antelope to see what would happen.

They waited until the talk was over, and when the Heavy Eyebrows came out of the lodge of Thunder Fear, they didn't run but stood in a row and watched. There was a mixed-blood with the Heavy Eyebrows called Bayett who talked for him in the language of the Little Ones.

The strange Heavy Eyebrows had hair on his chin like the hair of the lynx. As he stood and talked with Thunder Fear and Striking Ax and other leaders of the Little Osages, the little boys stood like deer watching *i'n-gro'n-kah,* the panther. They watched him when he rode away as far as they could see him, and they had just begun to talk about him when Little-Eagle-That-Gets-What-He-Wants' grandmother called him. She was busy with the black trader's kettle over the firehole, and talked to him "through her back." She said that warriors never stood and stared at people. She asked him what happened when he stared at deer or a bobcat, and he looked at the toes of his moccasins. She said that "people" didn't like to be stared at; sometimes when they wouldn't run away like the deer or slink away like the bobcat, they might become very angry. This incident would come up to embarrass him the rest of his life, and he would refer to it quite often for the purpose, it seemed, of clearing his mind for pleasanter memories.

The Heavy Eyebrows was Isaac T. Gibson, the new agent.

Soon after this the lodges were struck by women, and the pack horses were brought in by the boys who had been guarding them. There were plenty of horses for everyone. The Heavy Eyebrows of the Grass-House-Town were not horse-takers.

Their saddles for packing were the same as those used for riding. They were made of elm, and fresh buffalo hide was stretched over the saddle tree and allowed to dry. The saddle was complete, except for other hides they might wish to throw over it. The women collected the buffalo-horn spoons and the spoons made of hickory, the dishes made from the knotty growths of the post oak, and dishes carved from the linden, and put them in large bags made of buffalo hide, which they tied to the saddles. The parfleches they tied across the saddle.

The always hungry dogs knew about the movements of the villages, and they gathered expectantly. There were always bits of food left after the packing or thrown away.

Finally the Little Osages, the Down-Below People, began to move across the prairie to the southwest. They had to cross the Water where Fork-Tailed-Hawk-Was-Killed (Elk River) in bullboats. These were hairless buffalo hides that had been shaped and dried in a square with upturned corners, and in them the old people and children were placed, seated on piles of things which might get wet if the horses had to swim. Usually the old people and the children were carried across on the horses with their arms locked tightly about the elder boys or the warriors, and the yellow water of spate would tear at them, and sometimes the old people would sing their death songs and weep.

When there were only impedimenta and food in the bullboats, they attached buckskin thongs to two corners and two men would take the other ends of the strings in their mouths and swim across, pulling the boat. Two women would swim behind the boat, pushing, holding in their mouths large trader's knives. If the boat shipped water, they would reach under and slash the bottom, therefore saving though wetting the contents.

They strung out across the prairie to the southwest, and came to one of their old camping places on one of the buffalo trails to the plains. Here was a very beautiful spring and a good place to camp. When the rains came, the water did not run off quickly but stayed shining in the sun, and the people on their way to the plains had called this place *Ni-O-Ta-Tse,* which means Beautiful Water.

This had been one of Chief Little Bear's favorite camping places, but he was not with them now. He had died in 1869 in his camp where the Fall River and the Verdigris came together, at the place where the young warriors had defiled the spring.

They continued southwest until they reached the place which was called Hawk Woman on the Caney River. This also was a traditional camping place on one of the buffalo trails.

Little-Eagle-That-Gets-What-He-Wants would lag behind the long strings of travelers, and his grandmother became worried about him. Each day when he was not visible near the head of the long line, she would send a messenger back to find him, and the messenger always found him walking at the end of the line with several of the other small boys.

There was a great storyteller, whose "eyes laughed" continually. His name was Walking Buffalo, and the little boys would be lured back to the end of the line where he walked. As he told his fascinating stories, he would also talk with his long copper-colored fingers, and he often placed his hand on the heads or the shoulders of the boys. He was fascinating. He wore no eagle feathers of honor, and no scalplock with the deer-tail hairs tinted red and the turkey gobbler "beard" quivering, and the paint on his face was neither the paint of the war movement, bluff-paint, nor yet mourning. It was like the smearings which the little boys employed when they played warrior and played "rescue" on their horses.

One day when the messenger came to get Little-Eagle-That-Gets-What-He-Wants and he had loped to the place in the long line where his grandmother was, she called him to her and told him that this Walking Buffalo was an evil man, and that he must not go back there at the end of the line.

When they left the camp on the Caney called Where-Hawk-Woman-Died, they came to Whistle Creek, and here some of the gentes stayed. Some of them went on to Pawnee Creek. The Little Osages in 1871 didn't go to the agency at Silver Lake, as did some of the others, but were scattered in gentile groups over the northeastern part of the new reservation.

Thunder-Fear was the recognized chief of the Little Osages at this time. There were also Four Lodges and Striking Ax and Sacred Sun and Eagle-That-Dreams, the last two being sons of Thunder-Fear.

So difficult had the procuring of the animal skins necessary for the seven rites become that men sometimes reached an advanced age or even old age before they could qualify for the rites. There were still panthers in the new reservation and other animals necessary, but the buffalo had become so wary with hunting that if you proposed to take one afoot with bow and arrow, you might not have the chance for years unless you lay in wait at the water holes on the plains, and by this time the Heavy Eyebrows hunters were following the trails to the water holes and waiting there with their long Sharps rifles.

However, Four Lodges had finally become qualified for the one of the seven rites he had not yet taken, and the Little Osages gathered on a creek in their part of the new reservation, and there the ceremony was held. This creek ran into the Caney River, and thereafter they called it *Tzi-Topa-Ba-Wa'tho'n Ga-Xa,* Waters-Where-Four-Lodges-Sang.

He felt happy now, a sort of completeness, and he would be ready now to travel to Spiritland. He had a tendency to be esoteric. He said that when he went out under the night sky to talk with the Moon Woman, after fasting for seven days, she told him much. He always fasted for seven days in July and in January, and then, when he looked at the sun, the sun gave him a message. If there was a small circle around the sun, he, Four Lodges, would kill an enemy, but

703

if there was a large circle around the sun, he knew that he would only take his enemy's horses.

And he knew that the buffalo would soon be gone forever through a message he received while fasting one Buffalo-Mating Moon on the plains, through the song of a light-yellow buffalo calf, whose mother he had just shot to appease his great hunger. He heard the calf singing, "I can't find my mother, except her head." This was symbolical. You saw few buffalo on the plains now, but everywhere you saw the heads with black holes for eyes.

He was ready for Spiritland except for one matter. There was a gens of the Little Osages living away from the others, and he had not seen them for several years, and they had perhaps forgotten him. This worried him. He could only be remembered by the future generations through the tongue-to-ear method of tribal history, and if there were Little Osages who had forgotten him, his moccasin prints would be washed away by the sheet water of oblivion.

He worried about this for several moons, then one day he had his two best horses brought in. When he was ready, he had his wives bring the parfleche with his war clothes in it and the little buckskin bag filled with his paints, which he tied to his saddle; then, leading his best buffalo horse, he rode off alone.

On the way out to the village he experimented with the making of a song. He would raise his voice in a falsetto and his horse would lay his ears back. At night he listened to the coyotes and the wolves and the chorus from the grass roots, and finally he had a song, and kept singing it to himself as he beat the rhythm on his chest.

When he came near the village where the Little Osages lived, he dismounted in the shade of a lone elm, and his saddle horse dozed, resting on three legs, while the led one, filled with energy, blew at an ant hill. Four Lodges spread his robes and painted his face as if he were on the war movement. He held the peeps-in-water, the trader's mirror, and he applied the paint carefully, then he dressed in his war clothes: his buckskin leggings, moccasins, and shield. He attached his scalplock to his "buffalo tail" scalplock, his natural hair remnant on his shaven head.

This took some time. When he was ready, the buffalo horse shied and snorted as he approached. After saddling him, he took some Pawnee scalps from a buckskin bag and tied them to the horse's mane, then he mounted and rode toward the village, allowing the saddle horse to follow. The fresh horse, used to hunting buffalo, held his head high and his ears forward, but Four Lodges kept him quiet until he came to the village, then he moved his own body as if he saw buffalo and the horse began to prance sideways, his tail elevated and his mane flowing in the plains breeze.

At the edge of the village he began to sing the song he had just made. He sang that here riding among the lodges was the great *Tzi-Topah,* Four Lodges, and that all should come out and see him.

The little boys stopped their playing and came to watch him, and the little girls dropped their terrapin shells and stuffed squirrel playthings, and stood watching. The women dropped their work about the fires or let their hands fall from their mat making, or rose from their positions over the buffalo hides pegged to the earth, twisted strands of cascading hair around their index fingers, lodging it behind their ears in one swift, graceful movement; allowing the fleshing tool to hang from their hands as they watched. The warriors watched from their robes.

All watched and listened as the resplendent Four Lodges rode up and down the ways singing, and the town crier watched with them since he was not needed.

When Four Lodges rode back to Waters-Where-Four-Lodges-Sang in the new reservation, he was happy in the assurance that long after he had passed on to Spiritland, the people would know who he was. The little boys and the little girls who had stood like surprised deer would tell their children, and as long as the Little Osages had tongues and their children had ears to listen, he would live in tribal memory.

The new reservation was a southerly and southwesterly extension of the diminished reserve in Kansas, of limestone prairie and waving bluestem, with drainage veins and arteries flowing into the Arkansas and Verdigris rivers. It was geologically the same with the sandstone ridges of the Carboniferous in Kansas, but more hairy with blackjacks and post oaks, and the western part was prairie-plains, extending even to the plains redbeds of the Permian.

Wah-Ti-An-Ka, who had urged the Little Ones to remove here rather than allow themselves to be pushed farther west, had said that the Heavy Eyebrows would never come here because "he couldn't put the iron thing in the ground here," and Agent Gibson said that it was "poorly adapted for civilizing purposes."

The streams cut deeply into the sandstone hills and found the limestone, and there they formed little lenticular flood plains, but there were not enough of these little valleys to subsist the tribe if they did turn to agriculture. After the mistake in locating the 96th meridian was discovered and the agency was moved to the geographical center of the reservation, the Osages received more land by Congressional act of June 5, 1872, which carried the proviso that they allow the Konzas, now called Kansas or Kaws, to settle on a tract in the western part of their lands. This left them almost a million and a half acres of poetically beautiful country of blackjack hills and prairie.

Agent Gibson now meticulously counted them by bands, and gave the Big Hills, 936; Claremore's band, 239; Big Chief (*Tzi-Sho Hun-kah*) band, 698; Beaver's (*Sha-Ba*) band, 237; the Little Osages, 696; Black Dog's, 511; White Hair's, 362; and the Mixed-Bloods "band," 277; making a total of 3,956.

The Little Ones came to the new reservation with twelve thousand horses. They had their interest of $15,000 annually from $300,000 paid in cash, and interest on $69,120, amounting to $3,456, which amount was used for educational purposes, the principal representing moneys from the treaties of 1825, 1838, and 1865. The Secretary of the Interior held in trust for them United States and state stocks to the amount of $41,000, the interest on which amounted to $2,120, and was also used for educational purposes.

They could finance education, one of the essentials in the Friends' plan for their civilization, but Agent Gibson worried about the lack of agricultural lands, and there was ever present in his mind the experiences with trespassers in Kansas, and he thought the Indian Territory ought to be divided into judicial districts and that United States commissioners ought to appoint "a corp of marshals selected with reference to their moral fitness as well as animal courage."

The agent and his staff moved from Silver Lake to Deep Ford, where the Thorny-Valley People settled about May 15, 1872, and he started having buildings of logs built for the agent's offices, a commissary, and houses for the physician and the blacksmith. Here was a large valley, and he induced both White Hair and Beaver to start planting immediately, since they had been able to bring little with them from Kansas, and he gave wagons and harness to Four Lodges, Thunder-Fear, Striking Ax, and *Weh-Ho-Ka* of the Little Osages on Whistle Creek (Mission Creek). He tried to keep the others from going to the plains for the hunt, but he was practical and realized that they must have meat and robes, and must take their chances with "Injun" slayers with long-range rifles who would use them for target practice when they found several separated from the band. The buffalo were scattered, and there were bands of Cheyenne-Arapahoes wandering over the plains, and the inevitable free men.

The Osages wandered in bands, but they brought back only small amounts of meat and robes, and "one of the wilder bands" took "toll" from the Texas cattle along the trail near where it crossed the Salt Fork. They had met the Cheyennes and had fought with the buffalo hunters.

Gibson was almost happy when their meat supply of that year was exhausted and some of the people had to come to be fed by White Hair and Beaver people of the Thorny-Valley and trade for corn.

They seemed to be interested in planting, but their interest was really in the worm or stake and rider fences Gibson had built to protect their planting. They were interested because they had always had trouble with their horses. They often when on the war movement picketed them, hobbled them, or tied their favorites to a foot as they slept. When stampeded by Cheyennes or Arapahoes, their horses would often jerk up their picket pins, and if frightened could jump away in great leaps with their hobbles on. Many had been jerked out of a sound sleep and dragged from their robes by the snorting horse they had tied to a foot. Now they could build these *wah-don-skas* of the Heavy Eyebrows. These fences would be a good thing at their permanent villages.

They had made a ritual around *mo'n-ce,* metal, when the French had first brought it to them, and now they had learned that *mo'n-ce-*

ska, white metal, the silver dollar, would buy many things. They often made holes in silver dollars and hung them from their necks. Agent Gibson, seeing their deep respect for silver dollars and their interest in worm fences, urged them to make rails and build fences. He offered them $2.50 a hundred to make fences around their lodges and their corn and squash patches. Fifty-eight of them remained to create the novelty in Deer-Hiding Moon, September, of 1873, but the others left for the plains in full tribal strength. However, this seemed to have no significance for him.

They said that the Cheyennes saw them camped on the Antelope Flats between the *Ni-Ckiu-E Tonkah,* Salt Fork, and *Ni-Ckiu-E Ga-Shki-Bi,* Cutting Rock Salt Waters, the Cimarron. They rode away, and perhaps the buffalo hunters saw the smoke of their many lodges, and they could hunt in peace after allowing the Cheyenne-Arapahoes and the Heavy Eyebrows hunters to see them in tribal strength, then break up into bands or even gentile groups, if they were to be successful.

Now there was more for the agent to worry about than the Cheyennes and the free men; there were the would-be settlers of the western part of their ceded diminished reserve. Since they could settle legally now, the settlers seemed to be half-hearted. The year 1873 was a depression year, and the winds had begun to tear at their fields. Many of them left their dugouts and shacks and began to wander over the plains hunting and stealing for a living. Many had been intent settlers, but without food they became one with the free men of the border, and it was they who finally precipitated the conflict which Gibson feared.

During the summer hunt of 1873 (or 1874), during Buffalo-Mating Moon (July) and Yellow-Flower Moon (August), when the Little Ones would be coming back to Deep Ford with their robes and meat, Gibson heard strong rumors that the Plains Indians were preparing to attack the whites of western Kansas and in what is now western Oklahoma, the hunting grounds of the Little Ones. He immediately sent out runners to call the bands in.

These rumors came to him through the Little Ones themselves and were verified by the always dramatic settlers of the border. The Little

Ones had friendly contacts on the plains not only with their friends there but even with their enemies the Cheyenne-Arapahoes. They learned from the Comanches especially that the buffalo slaughterers, the hide hunters, were crossing the Arkansas River, since the buffalo had become less plentiful north of the river. The hide hunters were indignant about the competition created by the train passengers, shooting buffalo from the windows and vestibules.

They began crossing the river from Fort Dodge into Indian country, despite the military patrol and the provisions of the Medicine Lodge Treaty of 1867. The government had promised the Plains tribes through this treaty that white hunters would not be allowed south of the Arkansas.

The Comanches had brought the pipe to the Little Ones at their hunting camp on the Cimarron, and told them that since the government would not honor their talking paper, the Plains tribes would drive the white hunters out. The Little Ones had refused the pipe and told their agent the plans of the Plains tribes.

This summer the Little Ones were scattered because the herds of buffalo were scattered, and some of them were in gentile groups. Big Wild Cat and his people were coming home from the Cimarron headwaters where they had very bad hunting. When this happened, they would wander up to the Salt Fork or the Medicine Lodge Creek within the boundaries of their recent diminished reservation, where they were free to hunt as long as it remained unsettled. They understood this, but Gibson had asked them to stay out of Kansas.

The scouts found a herd of buffalo near Cedar Springs eighteen miles southeast of the modern Medicine Lodge, and they made camp there. There were only twenty-nine of them, including ten women and children, and they intended to stay only long enough to make meat; the robes were not the best this time of year. They were preparing to start home when they noticed a party of Heavy Eyebrows coming toward them. They thought they might be soldiers, but then they stopped, and they saw that their horses were of many colors and shapes, some of them like the horses used to haul a plow. They also noted that they were dressed in all sorts of clothing of the border, and that they had shotguns and rifles and some had only revolvers.

The women were frightened and started to herd the children to the brush. The motley group of Heavy Eyebrows stopped and waited, then formed a square with one side open. Big Wild Cat sent two men to ask them what they wanted, and when they arrived the leader shook hands with them in a very friendly manner, then suddenly disarmed them. Two more came up to see what was wrong, and after them two more, until there were eight. The others couldn't see from the distance that the first ones had been disarmed and detained.

The border men seemed to be waiting for more of the Little Ones to approach them, and they became wary. They were outnumbered, and they had their women and children with them. They had only four muzzle-loading guns and two revolvers, and most of these had been taken from the men who had been sent to determine what the Heavy Eyebrows wanted.

Big Wild Cat said that he was like the rabbit sitting moving his ears wondering which way to run, when the firing began. The border men were shooting the men he had sent to talk with them. Then he said he knew what to do. He had as many of the horses caught as possible, and this was also difficult since the horses sensed the excitement and those who were ordinarily gentle, snorted and with manes flying ran away.

The members of the party got together south of the border, like scattered quail, and they made camp with what they had. They had left their parfleches, buffalo-hide sacks, kettles, saddles, lodge coverings, and their meat and fresh hides. They made camp, and the women had nothing to do since they had none of their familiar things around them.

Soon a straggler came into camp, and as they recognized him as one of the men sent by Big Wild Cat to talk with the Heavy Eyebrows, they wept, thinking of the others. Finally four of the original eight came in, and so miraculous had been their escape from the border men that they were confused as to which fetish had saved them. The people who fled with the women and children were untouched by the bullets of the border men also, who they said followed them for two or three miles firing at them.

That night some of the hunters went back across the border to the place where the Heavy Eyebrows had attacked, and they found all their equipment and their meat and robes and kettles gone. Fifty-four horses, mules, and colts had been driven away, but they found three of the bodies of those who had been shot, and two of them had been scalped and all of them hacked. They could not find the fourth man.

The bodies were hacked so that parts fell away when they tried to place them on mules, and finding no stones there for the cairns, they laid them at the bottom of a cut bank, and stamping and digging at the top caused them to be buried by the crumbling soil.

The dogs came in one by one, having fled before the people and having waited until they heard the old familiar sound of keening. When the men who had buried the hunters came back at dawn and the women saw that they carried no bodies, they wept and mourned.

When a runner reached the agency with the news, Agent Gibson sent two large wagons out to meet them. They had gone five days without food, and some of them were almost naked. When they saw the wagons, the women wept quietly to themselves, mumbling their praises of Gibson.

The situation was tense in the valley under the post oaks, where Gibson built his log buildings and the traders had built their stores and palisades. Just as Gibson had the people convinced that they must not retaliate, a group from another part of the reservation would ride into the valley and start mourning, then the others would take it up, and some chieftain quaking with anger would rise and urge the people to put on the paint and chase the Heavy Eyebrows back across the border.

To make matters worse, 1874 was a grasshopper year. They came in swarms that were like a cloud curtain and ate every green thing, and the settlers in the plains part of the ceded diminished reservation of the Little Ones left their dramatically lonely claims and wandered here and there. Some took up whisky peddling, and some formed patrols under some foxy leader and shot at every lone Indian they saw, below or north of the border, provoking skirmishes so that they could be mustered in as militiamen and be fed by the state. The Governor of Kansas had mustered the border men who had killed the Osage hunters into the militia, dating the papers back so as to legalize the killing of the Osage hunters. When Gibson's investigating committee arrived at the cedar palisades which was then Medicine Lodge, they found the men quite military with breech-loading carbines and under the command of one Captain Riker and Lieutenant Moseley, the latter wearing the fringed buckskin shirt and guns at each hip. The "youngest Indian slayer of the Plains," little Billy Cody, was now a self-glorifying Indian scout and had been lionized in the East, and everybody knew about him, and fringed buckskin shirts, gauntlets, long hair, and revolvers on the hip became a vogue on the plains.

When Gibson's commissioners got no satisfaction from the some sixty border men of the cedar palisades, they went on to see the Governor of Kansas and got little satisfaction from him.

The situation became worse. The border men forced from their claims by grasshoppers and drought had to be subsisted, and the best way they knew was to wander along the border shooting at stray Osages in order to keep up the fiction that the Osages were about to invade Kansas. Thus they received rations.

Obviously the situation at Deep Ford was very tense since the agent couldn't give the Osages any answer to their questions about what the Heavy Eyebrows would do about the Cedar Creek killings. The border men who had to have rations kept the other settlers along the border frightened, and when Gibson asked them to send a committee down to Deep Ford to see for themselves that the Osages were not preparing to attack them, since they would see the white employees going about the agency business with no sign of arms or fear, they refused to come, and the tense situation continued. Gibson in his report wrote: "It can not be denied that the menacing attitude of the border at this time when the Osages are smarting under their recent wrongs requires vigilance and constant effort to counteract."

The buildings in the valley of the post oaks were now being replaced by buildings of the local sandstone. The agent's house on the hill and the dormitories raised their heads above the blackjacks and the post oaks. In the valley were the agent's office, the doctor's house, and the blacksmith's house, and a council house all in stone. There were frame houses for the employees and traders and three traders' stores, with palisades.

Of the Amer-Europeans who came among the Osages, the most important and the most influential with them were the traders. The fact that they brought miracles in the form of *wah-don-skas* to them ingratiated them, and their merchandise was practically considered as gifts, and therefore inspired a feeling of gratitude among the Little Ones. They valued their robes and furs very little because they had always been easy to attain until recently, and the trading activities were more like friendly counciling and the trade merchandise became as handsome gifts.

Gibson realized this, and he would license only those traders who could prove that they were "moral, temperate and regular attendants of religious services and Sabbath school at home." He fixed prices and had credit cards printed with limits for credit for each family.

The employees had to be men and women "of ability, of pure life and conversation, overflowing with love for their kind, magnetism, patient and hopeful." With such people around him an agent "can accomplish all that can reasonably be expected of him."

The Osages made peace with the Pawnees during the winter of 1873–74 and had a fight with the Cheyennes, and were becoming angered by the hide hunters who were coming south of the Arkansas River.

Their traditional enemies had been the Pawnees, and when the mourning parties went out, they tried to take the scalp of a Pawnee, since the Pawnee medicine was always strong. Later, mourners took scalps of the Cheyennes and Arapahoes and Wichitas, but now since the Comanches had come to them with the pipe, urging them to join them and the other Plains Indians to drive the Heavy Eyebrows back across the Arkansas, and since now when they went to the headwaters of the Cimarron and the Salt Fork, they could see from miles away the slow circling of the turkey vultures on the edge of the woodlands, and the ravens flying to a certain place as if they had seen a signal on the plains. Sometimes when they rode over a plains swell and came in view of a valley, there would be hundreds of wolves, snapping and dashing at the impatient ravens. If the stench was not too great, they would examine the carcasses of the buffalo. Only the hide and the tongues had been taken.

Thus it was that now their mourning parties were angered, and revengeful and would sometimes bring back the scalp of a Heavy Eyebrows. When these mourning parties went out on the Black Dog Trail, they usually met no enemy until they came to the place where the trail crossed the Salt Fork. A Heavy Eyebrows had come there in 1870 and established a trading post and way-station for trail drivers. The trail of the Little Ones was about a mile south of this man's stockade. This man's name was Eli Sewell, and the Little Ones seemed to have no grudge against him, possibly because he was a trader; but now, angered by hide hunters and border barbarians, their mourning parties took several scalps from the Heavy Eyebrows along the cattle and freighters' trails. Near the old Pond Creek Stage Station, they took the scalp of a man named Tom Best and another named Chambers; and Ed Finney, trail trader for Dunlap and Florer, traders of Deep Ford and scout for Agent Gibson, thought that a mourning party of Osages might have taken the scalp of Patrick Hennessey, a freighter on the Chisholm Trail. Eli Sewell believed the Cheyennes had done this.

Finney had spent the winter with Bone Heart, brother of *Pa'I'n-No-Pa-She* and a leader of the Big Hills hunting camp near Antelope Flats between the Cimarron and the Salt Fork.

The Friends believed that if they sent trail agents out with the Osages, they might be restrained, and Finney was acting in that capacity in this winter hunting camp of 1874, as well as camp trader for Dunlap and Florer. He had taken twenty-five wagons heavily loaded with supplies of flour, bacon, coffee, trade blankets, trade hatchets, strouding, calico, arrowheads, etc., and "all kinds of trinkets" to be traded for buffalo robes, wolf skins, etc. He and his "brave" had unloaded the wagons and placed the merchandise in one half of the large lodge built by the brave, Big Hill Charley, and his wife. In the other half Finney slept with Big Hill Charley and his family.

The herds were large since they seemed to be flowing before large parties of Cheyennes. Everywhere were the signs of the Cheyennes, but since the Osages numbered four hundred, there was little danger.

When the scouts of each tribe saw each other at a distance, they stopped and studied each other; the Little Ones wore no war paint and they could see that the Cheyennes wore no war paint, and there was between them the understanding of the grass roots and the woodlands and the plains that were a part of the great balance pattern.

It was Light-of-Day-Returns Moon, February, and the Moon Woman was happy, and she had forgotten to send the screaming winds with flakes of snow that passed you like birds. At night you could hear the mothers crooning to their babies in earth rhythm, and far off in the large camp there would be a drum throbbing, and perhaps singing. Sometimes the wolves would howl and the coyotes would talk and laugh like *Wa-Ba-Mi-Ki,* the Delawares.

The Chief Soldier and Big Soldier and Little Soldier, the officials of the hunt, had to tell the hunters that they must stop killing buffalo for a few days and give the skinners and the women time to prepare the hides and the meat, and Finney was able to get his hides baled, and Big Hill Charley was constantly busy trading.

Little Coon's lodge was close to the trader's lodge, and one night from the darkness came the notes of a flute. The women were always moved when they heard the lovers' flute, and Charley's wife straightened up from her hide-baling and, twisting her hair behind her ear, listened. It was not a plains sound, but a voice from the prairie-woodlands. Finney stepped out of the lodge and listened, then when he came in, Charley said, "Yellow Horse." This was all that was necessary in the way of explanation since they knew Yellow Horse wanted to marry Little Coon's daughter, but he had no horses, and he could only talk with his heart there on the dark plains.

Yellow Horse's uncle would not tarnish his dignity by going to the girl's uncle, since he had nothing to offer, not even a tall warrior with *o-do'n,* war honors. Yellow Horse was unprepossessing, and therefore was conspicuous among the handsome warriors of the Little Ones. He wore a very large tail-feather of the golden eagle in his scalplock, but had let his hair grow long like that of the plainsmen and wore trader's gadgets fastened to his trader's vest, which was his only garment above his waist when he tied his blanket around his middle. He was very proud of a revolver which he carried constantly.

715

His mouth turned down in a sort of perennial sulk, and his trap-
pings seemed to have been worn to compensate for his unhandsome
face.

After several nights the people in the trader's lodge heard his flute
no more, for Yellow Horse and several young men of his gens had
left the camp. The women were caught up with their work and Finney's hides and skins were baled, and the hunters went out again, but
Yellow Horse and his young men did not come in.

The leaders became restive. If the young men had gone out for a
skirmish with scouts of the Cheyennes, they would have been back
within a week. But now when they didn't appear after a week, the
leaders knew that they had gone to a Cheyenne camp to take horses,
and would not by their trail lead the Cheyennes to the Osage camp,
but would make a circuitous trail to Deep Ford. This was very bad.
The Cheyennes in searching for their horses would come to the camp
of the Little Ones, and knowing the strength of the camp, they would
come in great numbers, and the Little Ones, with their women and
children and their great stores of meat and robes and their hundreds
of horses, did not want to fight.

They packed up and left, and since Finney had no wagons to haul
his merchandise, they urged him to leave it. All their pack horses
were loaded and they had none to spare. He said he would stay with
his merchandise and his bales of hides, but asked that a runner be
sent to old Eli Sewell's stockade to intercept returning freighters with
empty wagons and ask them to come to him.

The Little Ones came back to Deep Ford with great loads of meat
and tallow and 10,800 robes in this drought and grasshopper year,
and Gibson was so happy that they had not fought the Cheyennes
that he wrote in his report of that year: "Most of three bands are
almost civilized and some of the other bands are civilizing."

He was constantly afraid that the mourning parties would get the
tribe into difficulties, especially since they were incensed over the hide
hunters coming across the Arkansas, and now they had begun to
take white men's scalps as their principal enemies. They had to pay
the Wichitas in money, blankets, guns, and horses to the amount of
$1,500 for a Wichita chief whom they had scalped after a mourning

dance, and now Gibson had his employees over the reservation listen for the mourning drums and the chants, and observe them "in forming of these parties which require several days to effect." Thus they, the employees, would have ample time to send to the agency for him. Also, the Cheyennes came to get their horses which Yellow Horse and his young men had taken. Since his relatives had already given them to Little Coon for his daughter, the tribe paid the Cheyennes with money.

Also in the summer of 1874, the United States Army was wandering on the plains south of the Arkansas. The soldiers had not come explicitly to protect the hairy ones who took only the hides and the tongues and sometimes the hump ribs of the buffalo, although later they believed that the complete destruction of the buffalo, "nature's commissary," would be a good idea. The Indian would be compelled to stay on his reservation if there were no more buffalo.

This land over which the Southern Plains Indians were roaming on the buffalo hunts was not the picture-book land of the woodland prairie or the prairie-plains, but the land of "cows and sky" of the Spaniards, and both were still ample, and that is why the hairy ones greedy for more hides had come south of the Arkansas, where the treaty of Medicine Lodge promised the tribes they would not be allowed to come. When the Plains Indians saw the hairy ones and came upon the carcasses of buffalo and saw no soldiers herding them back across the Arkansas, they became angered and frightened, and that is why the Comanches had brought the pipe to the Little Ones in their hunting camp and why they had taken the pipe to the Kiowas and the Cheyennes and the Arapahoes and Apaches. The others had accepted.

Perhaps if the Little Ones could have seen Coyote Droppings, the Comanche medicine man–prophet sitting his pure white horse on a hill with his naked body painted yellow, while the warriors of the Kiowas, Comanches, Cheyennes, and Arapahoes attacked a base camp of hide hunters called Adobe Walls, they might have been emotionalized to the point of joining the attack, but they were not there. Gibson had called them into the reservation with their 10,800 robes and their abundant tallow.

717

The Comanches, having no ritual appropriate to the occasion, had made the Sun Dance, in imitation of the Cheyennes and Arapahoes and Kiowas, but with modifications, just before the attack on Adobe Walls. Several were killed on each side, but the medicine of Coyote Droppings failed when the plainsmen fell before the long-range rifles of the hide hunters, and the Indian allies drew off. He was supposed to have given the others the same immunity to bullets which he enjoyed, but a Cheyenne killed a skunk, and this killed his medicine.

The allies were now raiding all over the southern plains, even above the Arkansas on Smoky Hill River, by the autumn of 1874. The army had the consent of Washington to attack the Indians in their own country and "punish" them for attempting to save the very basis of their existence, the buffalo.

The soldiers under General Miles came south from Camp Supply, and Major William Price moved east from Fort Union, and Lieutenant Colonel J. W. Davidson operated from the west from Fort Sill. Colonel McKenzie came up from Fort Concho and Colonel G. P. Buell came up the Red River.

Agent Gibson knew that the Osages were conspicuous with their shaven heads and their tall scalplocks, and once off their reservation they might be "punished" with the long-haired plainsmen. They had authority from the government to hunt on their own hunting grounds, but here the soldiers would only know that they were Indians and that they were off their reservation.

He had also been annoyed by two Cherokees, C. N. Vann and W. P. Adair, who came to Deep Ford to collect $330,000 which they said the Osages owed them for effecting the defeat of the treaty of 1868 with the railroad. He wrote that they had threatened him. They eventually asked for $230,000, and when they failed to collect that amount, they finally settled for $50,000.

Agent Gibson spent much time with the leaders of the Little Ones trying to divert their minds from the Medicine Lodge incident, and as one of his civilizing projects was an attempt to get them to labor for rations which were bought with their own money, he tried to force the families to send their children to the handsome new sandstone boarding school on the hill. He had his traders of good morals

718

and his employees of pure minds, but there was not sufficient arable land for agriculture and the parents would not send their girls to the school; they would bring their boys reluctantly. His conscience was heavy since he could not make his promise good about the Medicine Lodge killings, and in his worry he reported in 1875 to Edward P. Smith, the new commissioner of Indian affairs, that "revenge will be taken sooner or later on some innocent person is not questioned by those acquainted with the religious customs of the Osages in the unjustifiable killing of their people."

The department asked Congress to make some provisions for the orphans of those killed.

Isaac T. Gibson left the agency in 1876, and Cyrus Beede took over. He wrote to the Superintendent of Indian Affairs at Lawrence, one William Nicholson, that "the Osages as yet are most of them wild, blanket, scalping Indians, far from civilized, many of them hardly ready to give up the war dance and the scalping knife."

The grasshopper-ruined settlers of the ceded diminished reserve asked for an extension for paying of their installments, which was granted, and this threw the Osages into debt, and in August they had just returned from the plains with little meat and no robes, which was almost disastrous for them since they must forego their interest on the settlers' payment. As if this were not enough, floods had come in July and washed away their corn and the squashes, their intriguing worm fences, and some of their government-built cabins.

Added to this, Heavy Eyebrows came across the border to steal their horses, and there was a detachment of cavalry still at the agency "to keep the peace."

By 1877, the border Kansans were over their fear of Osage invasion and were inviting them to come trade with them, and Beede especially praised the people of Chautauqua County, Kansas, but deplored the fact that their friendliness to the Little Ones was offset by the whisky peddler and the horse thieves.

The disastrous hunt of 1876 was almost the last buffalo hunt of the Little Ones, as their next agent, L. J. Miles, wrote, they had "almost given up the hunt," but tradition still held them. They planted in the Planting Moon, April, but even if they didn't go on the buffalo hunts, they did not cultivate their crops.

Rations were stopped since they refused them, saying that "they were fed like dogs." Miles, being a Friend, believed that the keystone to civilization for the Osages was agriculture and education, and he worked hard to get the parents to send their girls to the sandstone buildings on the hill. But he was so sincere about the matter that he must surely in his dedication have transgressed some of his own principles. He got the Osage Council to pass a compulsory education law, wherein annuities were withheld from parents who refused to send their children to school.

He developed water in the valley, and had great stone towers built on the hill, which supported 500-barrel tanks, and with a system of pipes he furnished water to every building. He had a steam pump to lift the water to the tanks at the tops of the stone towers on the hill.

They made leases to cattlemen so that the bluestem could be utilized, and suddenly the people who had their eyes on the last reservation of the Little Ones began to deplore the prospect that soon the poor Osages' horses would be crowded off their own grass by the cattle of the cattlemen, and starve.

Major Miles decided that one deterrent to the progress of the Little Ones was their organization which the Little Old Men had developed through the centuries. He strangely enough did not interfere with their religion, stating only once in his reports to the Commissioner of Indian Affairs that the Friends were doing missionary work among them. His report for September, 1882, included a statement that Jonathon Osburn and wife, members of the Society of Friends, held meetings regularly at the agency and that during the summer "a Sabbath-school has been kept up Bird Creek, 25 miles south of the agency." He believed that much more ought to be done "to instruct these Indians in the right way, and induce them to give up their superstitions, to which they cling tenaciously."

He seemed more interested in education, perhaps as a preparation for Christianity, and he had the Osage National Council pass a law which would force the Osage parents to send their children to school, the penalty being that the children, and therefore the parents, would be deprived of their annuities. The National Council under his direction passed a law January 12, 1884, that children above the age of seven and under the age of fourteen who have not been in school four months out of the six months preceding the annuity payments should be enrolled in school and their payments withheld, unless sick, as certified by the government doctor. In case children ran away from school or their parents took them away, if they were brought back within five days after leaving school, "absence shall not be counted."

The Little Ones created a constitution based on the constitution of the Cherokees, December 31, 1881, at the Osage Agency, which was being called "Pawhuska" for *Paw-Hiu-Skah,* White Hair. The Great Osages and the Little Osages became one and would henceforth be called the "Osage Nation." The government would be divided into the executive, judicial, and legislative. The legislative was represented by the National Council of fifteen members, three from each of the five districts, and would be elected every two years, the council meeting annually on the first Monday in November.

The executive was represented by a "Principal Chief of the Osage Nation" and an assistant chief; and the judicial was represented by "Supreme Court Judges" elected by the council.

There were four sheriffs and police officers appointed by the chief and approved by the council. There was an "Osage National Prison," which was a small house with barred windows, which the mixed-bloods and the traders and employees called the "calaboose."

This government under his direction pleased Major Miles, and he believed that white man's government would break up the gentile organization and the units which he called bands; and since the religion was based on this organization, which itself was part of the religious organization, the religion would go.

In his eagerness to guide the Little Ones toward Christian and labor-conquers-all Utopia, the Major was a bit naïve. The Chouteaus had tried to break up the organization of the Little Old Men in 1802, and had succeeded in doing so through the use of the chief frailty of the tribal organization, the compulsion to distinction in the warrior which was translated into European processes. Again Murphy and the railroad's Sturges had done it in 1868, without any desire to disturb the religious organization.

721

The new Osage Nation and its government would work well enough to attain the Amer-European approval through their agents and the Commissioner of Indian Affairs, since Agent Gibson's seventh "band," the mixed-bloods, were strong enough to make it work; but behind the structure, the religion of *Wah'Kon-Tah,* the organization of the Little Old Men, still survived, even though it was becoming more and more obvious that *ga-ni-tha,* disorder, had come into Grandfather's world.

The new council could fine or even jail people who refused to work on the roads of the Nation two days of each year, and they established a whipping post, and one would be fined or imprisoned if he set fire to the prairie in any month except May, June, and July.

Quapaws with their white man's hats and shabby clothing came into the reservation of the Little Ones as a refuge, and a few ragged people of the Potawatomis came, and the Little Ones hired them to cut stakes and rails for their fences and log cabins, which the government insisted they build, while they themselves danced and feasted under the shade of the post oaks and elms of Bird Creek, Hominy, Salt Creek, and the Caney River. They danced and feasted and told stories of their former greatness.

A few of the Little Ones let their hair grow long now like the plainsmen, and some of them replaced their beaver or otter bandeaus with the cool calico of the traders, and they wore trader's blankets and occasionally black hats, but this was the only change in their clothing.

Major Miles could hear through his long, narrow south windows in the sandstone residence on the hill the indescribably moving pre-dawn chant to Grandfather the Sun, coming from the Bird Creek bottoms or from the blackjack hills beyond Mud Creek. He would rise before his set time, with the self-accusation expressed in the Amer-European motto, "It's later than you think."

He must distribute more wagons and more implements, and build more houses and force more children to go to Carlisle in Pennsylvania or to the Osage mission in the ceded reserve in Kansas or to Haskell at Lawrence, Kansas, and other places, as well as to their own stone buildings on the hill.

In his later-than-you-think-inspired activity in sending children to

722

school and building houses and urging plantings, wondering what he ought to do about polygamy, all was stopped about July 8, 1882, when smallpox was reported from Black Dog's village on the Arkansas River. The virus he sent for was spoiled by the heat before he could get it to the agency. He sent his wife and children away and placed saucers of carbolic acid in the windows, since they must be raised during the heat of the summer.

"The Major made trips—pleading with the people to bury their dead underground; using every argument in his power to make them see that burial in cairns would only help spread the disease, but they would not see this. They could not bury an Indian in the ground where he would be lost; where it would be difficult for *Wah'Kon-Tah* to see him. *Wah'Kon-Tah* could see stone cairns on the hilltops. This Great Sickness of the white man did not devour the spirits of those who died, they said, that they should be buried in ground like white men.

"Like the wounded buffalo which leaves the herd to die in some wash on the plains, and like the sick wolf which leaves the pack to crawl out on some naked rock to end his days in solitude, the people of the Reservation followed the law that the herd or band must not be impeded. They crawled away from the camps into the woods and the high grasses, and there died alone.

"In beautiful valleys stood the hickory framework of lodges, where little breezes played with the gray ashes in the fire holes and the stridulations of the insects and the chirruping of the crickets became dirges, and hungry, half-wild dogs slunk away, looking back over their shoulders.

"When the Major drove up to deserted camps and called familiar names, his voice seemed to die in the heated air."

The Little Ones were at about the same stage in development as the Germans Tacitus wrote about, eight or nine hundred years ago, perhaps moving only to that stage in progression since the French brought metal to them. The agents and the commissioners of Indian affairs and others might have learned much about their own history if they had properly interpreted the extreme and sometimes incredulous ineptitude of the Little Ones face to face with the simplest of mechanisms. In the great sandstone building which was the school dormitory even the stairway was a mystery to the little girls, and when they wished to ascend, they crawled up, and when they descended, they bounced down on their bottoms. It wasn't fear so much as ineptitude, unbelievable to matrons and other employees three thousand years ahead of them in development.

There was many a runaway Indian team when the driver could not fathom the brake on his light wagon, until he learned about brakes and how to use them. They came rattling down the clayey, twisting roads from the hills into the valleys, women weeping and children falling out with the kettles and lodge poles, forcing the horses to spread and break the traces, to end up shivering with fear and hopelessly entangled, with perhaps the wagon overturned with a wheel still spinning. The occupants usually were thrown out or jumped before the bottom of the hill was reached.

A door knob was at first a mystery. One cold winter's night, the lodges of the Buffalo gens of the Big Hills blew down, and sleet began to slant against them. Their camp was on the hill near the great stone buildings of the agency. Near by was the house of a mixed-blood, who was of their gens and their physical division, and they came to him for shelter. They brought their robes and bears' skins with them, and soon they were lying on the floor in the kitchen.

The host knew the traditions, and he made preparations to keep his guests as long as they wished to stay, and the greater part of hospitality and traditional courtesy being represented by abundance of food, he got the girl of all work up before dawn to start the fire in the cookstove. She was a daughter of a white settler north of the border in Kansas and had been brought in by permit by her employer, and was frightened of "Injuns."

Finally she was urged to enter the kitchen where the Little Ones lay hidden under their robes in a circle close to the walls.

She shoved the wood into the stove, looking back over her shoulder at the humps, then quaking in her fear, she forgot to open the damper and the smoke came from every stove lid and crack. A man raised his head, and smelling and seeing smoke, jumped up hissing, and the others came out of their robes, and all rushed for the door which led to the outside, but they couldn't get it open. It was not locked, but the mechanics of turning a knob they could not understand. They had begun to break out through the windows when their host came in and turned the knob. Later the food had to be carried out to them in the entry-way of the barn.

After Miles left the agency at the end of his first term, a Captain Carrell H. Potter of the Eighteenth Infantry came as acting agent.

He seemed to be surprised that the Osages had unlimited credit with the traders, and always paid. He failed to mention it, but they carried little sticks which they notched each time they owed a dollar, and when their annuities were paid, they came with their sticks, and they matched well with the credit card kept by the trader and with his books as well.

The military man thought they spent too much time dancing, and he knew they were indolent, and he wondered why young men returning from Carlisle, Pennsylvania, went back to the blanket. He thought them obedient, and that their chief sin was one of omission. When there was horse stealing from across the border or murder, or there were white men taking refuge from the law in their camps, they refused to inform the agent.

The military man thought that United States troops ought to be stationed on the reservation to protect the Osages from invasions of criminals from Kansas and the Cherokee borders.

The annuities were growing larger fortunately now as their hunting was practically over, and there had been no hiatus between furs and dollars in their economic importance to the Heavy Eyebrows.

"Major" Laban J. Miles returned to the agency in 1889, and was almost discouraged. Since the Osages seemed to have progressed little in education and in agriculture, their comparative riches meant little to him, even though their increasing wealth was the direct cause of his unhappiness since white men were coming into the reservation to sell whisky, steal horses, take refuge from the law, and marry the Indian women. The mixed-bloods were increasing and were almost equal in number to the fullbloods, and when the Cherokee Allotment Commission arrived in June, 1893, and urged the Osages to take allotments and sell their surplus lands as the other tribes would do, they refused, solely on account of the fact that the fullbloods still out-numbered the mixed-bloods, who were almost unanimously for allot-ment. The fullbloods stayed true to the attitude they took in 1870, when they asked that their land be held in community.

Their agent at this time was Captain C. A. Dempsey of the Second Infantry, acting U. S. agent, and he advised them to allot, believing that it was a "step toward civilization." The military man following him had a most tidy military mind. He was Lieutenant Colonel Free-man of the Fifth Infantry. He was a severe man, who had been a prisoner in Libby Prison during the Civil War, and had been one of the party of prisoners who had dug a tunnel and escaped. Later he had been in command of a Negro regiment.

The comparative riches of the Little Ones now lured free men in great numbers, and the opening of the Cherokee Outlet west of the last reservation of the Little Ones had brought more trouble, and the little towns along the border were worse than the Kansas border towns had been.

There were twenty-one licensed traders now, and the Little Ones were ever in debt to them. If the traders refused to sell them mer-chandise beyond their credit limits, they went to the little towns on either border, where the merchants were eager to allow all the credit they desired, knowing that the federal government would make the debts good.

Colonel Freeman had a mind which seemed to be periodically policed by a fatigue detail, so that not a scrap of a useless thought could be noted. He felt, naturally, that the Little Ones danced too often and feasted too long. The dances which they created through the centuries, one might hope could gradually be abandoned as they became Christianized, especially the troublesome Mourning Dance which terminated with the taking of an enemy scalp. But instead of diminishing the number of their dances, they added one about 1885, which they got from their once-removed splinter, the Poncas. This was a social dance wherein they danced for four days, and on the fourth day members of the tribe who desired self-aggrandizement gave away valuable presents to visitors from other Siouan tribes. The man or woman who wished to appear as important as the chiefs must practice generosity, and in so doing, made a great show of giving.

One would go to the singers seated around the drum and promise them a beef or flour and coffee, or all three, and the singers knew that this meant they were to sing the song of this person's ancestors at a certain time. The one who was to parade his generosity and therefore add to his importance would have the things which he intended to give away readied, and he himself would sit apart so that all could see the great man.

The singers would beat the drum in a rhythm, and this was like the heart beats of *Mo'n-Sho'n,* Mother Earth. Then the leader would start the song, usually in a falsetto, as in the first note of the coyote chorus, then in diminuendo the others came in, and the generous one would rise with concentrated gravity and dance about the drum. Soon others of his family or gens would join him. When the song ended, he would have the *shoka* or some boy of his family carry the robe, or *mo'n-ce skah,* white metal (silver dollars), to the one designated to receive the gift. If he gave food, he would have the town crier announce the fact that he was giving food to a certain person. Or if the gift was a horse, the animal would be led onto the dance ground and its halter handed to the one who was to receive it. The horse would snort at the swarming color under the willow-branch covering of the open structure which shaded the dance ground, and his flanks would twitch.

When the Little Ones first received this dance, they carried a pipe from the giver to the recipient and each smoked; later they discarded the pipe, but still the fourth day of the dances was called the day when the Little Ones "smoked" gifts to their guests.

Sometimes a man who had little to give would become intoxicated with the image of himself as a generous giver, and filled with illusions of grandeur, he would trade all for the few moments when all eyes were on him and his song was being sung.

This dance was called *I'n-Lon-Schka,* the Playground-of-the-First-Son. Colonel Freeman became almost as worried about it as he did about the Mourning Dance. When the rich Little Ones held the *I'n-*

Lon-Schka, their Siouan kin came from the Dakotas, from the Salt Fork of the Arkansas, to dance and feast and play the moccasin game. Many of them were poor now, since they had been forced to stay on their reservations and some of them forced to accept allotment, and they loaded their ponies with gifts as they set out on the return trip to their villages. The poorer the recipient of some Nobody's generosity, the greater the "ho-o-o-o-o-o-os" of praise and gratitude, and the more concentrated the attention drawn to the giver, and the greater the welling of self-esteem within him.

Colonel Freeman in his report to the Commissioner of Indian Affairs indicated that this business was too much for his tidy mind. "As the one who gives most is regarded as the greatest, the hosts frequently strip themselves of all movable property."

He was annoyed by the white horse thieves and whisky peddlers crossing the border into the reservation, and one feels that he would have liked to charge all along the border with drawn saber. These people had only one means of sustenance: horse stealing and whisky peddling. He was disgusted with the pretense of law enforcement along the border and with the Little Ones for refusing to testify against the intruders, even when they shot at them for sport. Freeman thought there ought to be a garrison of United States troops or a police force properly mounted, so that the Little Ones could receive protection.

He wrote: "The country is overrun with U. S. [deputy] marshals. One cannot ride ten miles from the agency without meeting them but their efforts seem confined to arresting Indians who may at some time have had a bottle of whiskey. I did not know of a single instance of a white man arrested by them for theft and very few in whiskey cases, while the arrests of the Indians will I am sure amount to upward of a thousand."

Colonel Freeman was agent to the Little Ones from 1894 to 1898, and they won his military heart completely. He saw that the mixed-bloods were increasing and the fullbloods diminishing, and that citizenship in the tribe was quite often being purchased, and white men were eager to marry Osage women. There were in 1897, according to his calculations, only 900 fullbloods and 829 mixed-bloods, and their per capita income was now $214.

He with the council had given a lease to E. D. Foster of Rhode Island for mining purposes. This was on unoccupied land, and was to run for ten years.

To the correct, irascible, military Freeman nothing went as it should have gone during his four years as Osage agent. Some of the mixed-blood citizens of the Osage Nation and the white men from Kansas and the Cherokee Outlet were stealing walnut timber from the reservation and selling it. There were whisky peddlers and horse thieves and wife hunters and people buying their enrollment as citizens of the Osage Nation, guardians stealing their protégés' money; and Colonel Freeman wrote to the Commissioner of Indian Affairs in 1896, "I most heartily thank you for your assistance in the Indian Office generally for the support given me in this the most difficult position in which I have ever been placed."

Do what he might, he seemed to be frustrated in bringing a sort of terse military order to the reservation of the Osages. The intruding white people were enough to cause apoplexy, but the Osages themselves danced, talked, and rested, continually visiting each other. They wore their moccasins in the wet snows of winter and caught pneumonia, and while they sought no whisky, with few exceptions, when it was brought to them, they greedily drank all available in order to remain in the strange, exotic world of fantasy and escape, into which the few first swallows had transported them. In this world each Nobody was a happy warrior, detached from the restrictive world of the Heavy Eyebrows.

The Colonel would train the minds of the children through education as one would train troops for success in battle, and when the girls over seven and under fourteen were held in their villages by their reluctant parents or when they would find loose pickets in the tall picket fence that surrounded the grounds of the great sandstone school building and escape, he would send the Indian police for them.

There were some men of character and standing among the Indian police, such as young Thunder-Fear and Gray Bird, but there were others who became suffused with their importance, and when the girls resisted, they would hold their arms behind their backs and load them in the wagon, tying them to the bow slots. When after reaching the agency some of them jumped from the wagon and ran, the police overtook them on their horses, and roping them, they would drag them up the dusty hill to the school buildings.

These were the older girls, who fought like brought-to-bay bobcats. They would fall as they struggled against the ropes, and their long black hair would make traces in the deep dust of the road, and their clothing was rent, but unlike the brought-to-bay bobcat, they made no sound and there were no tears; only silence and sweat that muddied the dust of their faces.

The boys were like the mustang, and finally gave up. They climbed onto the lower or middle rib of the tall picket fence in their part of the grounds, and stood in rows looking over the pickets far across the hills.

When Colonel Freeman made his report in 1897, the word "Pawhuska" appeared for the first time along with Osage Agency. He assured the Commissioner that the Osages were still going visiting and dancing and feasting and wouldn't stay on their farms with their neat little log houses and their worm fences. "The old men sit and talk of the past." He was contemptuous of the white people who had brought suits against him, depending on their peers to render judgments in their favor. He had won them all.

But he wrote, "I have been more or less intimately acquainted with Indians and Indian affairs for upward of thirty years and know that the administration of their affairs has constantly improved while personal experience has taught me that St. Peter himself could not manage an agency to the satisfaction of everybody, especially if he sought to enforce the law and protect the Indian."

William J. Pollack was the agent to the Little Ones the last two years of the century, from 1898 to 1900. He wore a monk's skullcap to hide his bald spot. An agent had great power and was a very important man among the blackjacks and on the prairie, and must guard his dignity, being careful of his actions and his manners. Only the mixed-bloods and the employees reflected this importance, but that was sufficient since the fullbloods didn't count. The mixed-bloods often named their children for the agent's wife or children or himself; the ancient attitude of respect of the *coureur de bois* for his bourgeois dying hard within them.

This pleased men like Pollack, so he wore his skullcap and enjoyed his position, seemingly. He seemed to be efficient and did his job well. He observed the Osage: "He loves to sing, to dance, and to rest." Then in his after-dinner ease in the great sandstone residence, he seemed to reflect, "He is human."

The Little Ones had his respect, too, since they were wealthy, but he seemed to be a bit disturbed by this fact. He wrote, "They are aristocrats and like all wealthy people, they don't care for manual labor." There seemed to exist a delicate understanding here between a man who respected people who were not compelled for economic reasons to come far out into the savage blackjacks and prairie-plains and the "wealthiest people per capita on earth," who owned those same blackjacks and prairie-plains.

He counted 886 fullbloods and 879 mixed-bloods, and he reported that the fullbloods still clung to their ancient dress and shaved their heads, leaving a "crest." He reported that they were very quiet and peaceful and liked to gather where they could recount their feats of former times.

He noted that the annuities were $200 per capita, and paid in quarterly payments "by a paternal and benevolent government." This was a jealous distortion rather than a careless one.

He saw no future for them and gave a statistical table covering twenty years of their history, which he said would "illustrate the natural tendency of their exit from earth and that will soon 'be as much forgot as the Indians canoe across the bosom of the lonely lake a thousand years ago.'"

PEYOTE AND OIL

"They have adopted the Man on the Cross, because they understand Him. He is both *Tzi-Sho* and *Hunkah*. His footprints are on the Peyote altars, and they are deep like the footprints of one who has jumped. No bird they know can launch itself into the sky, without first jumping."—John Joseph Mathews, *Talking to the Moon.*

53. Disintegration and Confusion

AGENT POLLACK SAW ONLY the surface when he said of the Osage, "He loves to sing, to dance and to rest." Behind their singing and dancing and resting now there was a fear that haunted them. Their "brothers" the buffalo were gone, as were the wapiti and the antelope, and since they had not been able to protect these "brothers," *Wah'Kon-Tah* had forsaken them, or at least the God of the Heavy Eyebrows, the enemy god, had confused them.

The buffalo was more than just a "brother"; he was the giver of the varicolored corn, and had been a part of their existence, perhaps the very basis of their existence. In their organization of the gentes, the Little Old Men had deferred to him and had shown him courtesy, and the gentes themselves hesitated to choose him as a life symbol; finally one of the gentes employed only a phase, the Buffalo Face, and even then, the Little Old Men out of respect gave this gens no onerous mundane activity in the gentile organization. The organization was complete when the jealous buffalo, finding that he had not been chosen as a life symbol of one of the gentes, came roaring up to the council lodge of the Little Old Men with tail of anger raised and pawing the earth, demanding that he be made a symbol, and he did along with jealous thunder become the symbols of "those who came late."

Now the buffalo had vanished and with him the paternal protection of *Wah'Kon-Tah,* and now they elected their "principal chief,"

735

"assistant chief," and fifteen councilmen, and the *a'ki-da*, soldiers, were appointed by the "Supreme Court of the Osage Nation," and were called Indian police. The Little Old Men now had no power, and the gentile leaders were not recognized by the Heavy Eyebrows Long Knives (the agents). They were not even known; but the physical division leaders were recognized, because they lived with their people in widely separated places over the reservation. They were not recognized as the *Sa'n Solé*, the Upland-Forest People, but Claremore's band and Black Dog's band. The *Pa Solé*, the Big Hills, were now Big Hill Joe's band or Tall Chief's band, and the *Wah-Ho-Ka-Li*, the Thorny-Valley People were recognized as White Hair's or Beaver's band, and the Down-Below People, the Little Osages, were often referred to as Striking Ax's band, while the Heart-Stays People seemed to have been forgotten.

The prestige of the Little Old Men and the gentile leaders was now faded, and some of them tried to clutch to themselves, and hold up for all to see, their traditional importance. Some of the Little Old Men, especially as they grew older and there were no ears turned to them, assumed esoteric powers, and even presumed to cure diseases by magic. They became medicine men to retain their self-esteem and their traditional importance.

The Osages experienced *ga-ni-tha*, chaos, again, and the people were easy victims of the medicine men, who became a nuisance to both the Friends and the military agents, especially when they claimed "medicine" for the cure of wounds, blindness, and disease. The gullible people gave them valuable presents for a few fannings from an eagle-wing fan and mumblings which could not be understood. The agents could do nothing about this situation, but it was finally partially saved by a doctor named Dobson, in whom the people had faith. He spoke the language well, and had a deep feeling for them.

However, during this period an energetic medicine man need not become celebrated in his own tribe only, but might have attained the stature of an all-Indian prophet.

The tribes of the plains were also thrown into confusion, and had finally succumbed to the enemy gods; being resistant and vindictive but without arms and buffalo, they were ready for a prophet.

The Amer-European, with only his burden of religion and property, could lose both in the manner in which all things become unattached and one became separated from them. He was still a unit in himself and part of a collective voice. His religion had not come out of the earth which now nourished him, but from far away in a country of arid harshness, and it had been modified by the culture of Rome and later Europe and England. The asceticism of the desert had been metamorphosed by the marshes and the meadows and the rivers and the forests of Europe and England, and in America had become ramified and seemed rather a philosophy instead of life itself. He, in the place of the Indian, could have adjusted himself to the new conditions, assuming a new concept of God, and acquired more property in the manner of his conquerors to revive his prestige.

The religion of the tribes had come out of the earth where they lived except in the cases where they were removed to far-away reservations, and it was a part of their existence, not a thing-apart philosophy, hence their bewilderment when the alien enemy gods weakened the medicine of their own.

Had it not been for this, one might now have expected the Osages to live in their log cabins, with their garden patches enclosed within worm fences, and expected them to seek the churches scattered here and there in order to get some relief for their confusion. Since they had not put away their concept of God and their blankets and moccasins and their leggings and their scalplocks and their predawn chants in 1825 when they turned over their land to the immigrant Indians and were assigned to a reserve, one might expect them to do so now since their buffalo were gone and they had a larger communal income than the Heavy Eyebrows surrounding them. Now perhaps one might expect them to cast away their blankets and their moccasins and their bear-claw necklaces and their mussel-shell gorgets and their quivering scalplocks of turkey "beard" and deer tail. Instead of their otter and beaver bandeaus, one might expect them to wear floppy black hats with greasy bands and shabby "citizens'" clothes. It was the logical time for those who must have prestige to fill the vacuum created by the disintegration of the old tribal organization wherein they were important, by carrying Bibles about and preaching in a language they understood not too well, about an enemy God of a bewildering number of facets.

They remained resistant. They chanted each morning to the Morning Star, and they fasted and they held the mourning dances with no change except where individuals might evince anxiety and make slight changes of adjustment. There was an unsureness about their religious ceremonies, and the once formal Ceremony of the Dove became more popular, and unscrupulous medicine men used it for profit and self-aggrandizement, but this was the beginning of deterioration rather than adjustments inspired by anxiety and doubt.

The Little Ones had always believed that the dead should not start on the journey to Spiritland until Grandfather was immediately above them at noon. Then the "door was open," and the spirit of the dead one could travel home with Grandfather. But now the man whom the relatives summoned to paint the face of the dead one so that he might be recognized in Spiritland would have him laid on his back outside the lodge according to tradition, then paint his face with the symbols of the gens and the division on a ground of red. He painted the back of the neck as well, just a little, so that he could be identified from both directions. The Christians buried their dead facing east, and apparently they traveled east to Spiritland, and the relatives didn't want to take chances. The painter of the face now talked to the spirit of the dead man and asked him to go where the other spirits were, and reveal to them the identity of the man who had painted him and sent him there as being the grandson of one who was already there. After assuring himself that the messages concerning the goodness of his deed would be heralded in Spiritland, he asked the spirit of the dead one to be sure to inform those in Spiritland that the Little Ones were true to their ancient customs.

The man who had been summoned to put on the moccasins for the last journey of the dead one also asked the spirit of the dead man to say that the Little Ones were keeping the old customs, but then told the spirit that it was not to go to the West but to the East. This was a gesture on the side of safety. The dead man was painted correctly and could not possibly become lost, so what matter if he went to the East instead of the West? This might, after all, be the right direction, since the Heavy Eyebrows spirits traveled to the East, the direction whence their *Wah'Kon-Tah E Shinkah,* their Son of God, would appear when he came again.

When the face painter and the moccasin man had finished with their work and had finished instructing the spirit of the dead man, they stood and mourned in the old manner.

But there was no change in the burial. He was taken to a high hill, and there was flexed into a sitting position dressed in his finery, and stones were piled about him. Then the United States flag was set in the stones, and his favorite horse choked and dragged to the cairn, lying half upon it.

The mourners went down the hill, to where the feast was prepared. Each one held his hand over a fire of cedar and laved his hands in the smoke to drive away any evil that might be present. If he were an important man, the Mourning Dance would start, and after four days, the mourning party would set out for a scalp.

The advice to the spirit by the face painter and moccasin man who were worried evinced fear of the enemy God, but the mourning party's refraining from taking an enemy scalp was due to Heavy Eyebrows power. They sometimes did so even near the turn of the century, but the Heavy Eyebrows Long Knives had finally convinced them that would bring trouble to all of the agency if they did not adjust to the times. Sometimes they would hire a Pawnee. They would cross the Arkansas River to the Pawnee Reservation just across from the Big Hills and give a horse and other presents to some long-haired Pawnee to play the game. He would lose himself in the hills and the mourning party had to track him down and pretend to take his scalp by simply cutting off his long hair. It was a delicate business. The mourning party were short-tempered with hunger and emotionalized.

Also there was a Heavy Eyebrows woman who lived just across the border in Kansas. She allowed her yellow hair to grow to her knees and would sell a strand to each mourning party. She also sold whisky and love.

739

54. Moonhead

Land and communal wealth did not compensate for the disruption of the tribal organization and the god-concept that was part of every man, woman and child. *Wah'Kon-Tah* was not detachable from the men pre-eminent, the Little Ones. There must be tribal adjustment, already indicated by the individual adjustments, to the teachings of *Wah'Kon-Tah E Shinkah,* the Son of God of the Heavy Eyebrows. There must be a leader who would regulate the unrestrained medicine men and give the people faith again, a leader who was wise enough to understand that the old ways had gone with the buffalo and could give them a god-concept they could understand under the changed conditions. The concept of the Heavy Eyebrows must be modified to harmonize with their own concept, which was in everything they did and felt. Because He was an abstract philosophy of the Heavy Eyebrows, their God was beyond the understanding of the Little Ones, nor could they understand those who talked about him. The hope, as it always had, lay in *Wah'Kon-Tah E Shinkah,* the Son of God, the Heavy Eyebrows' Christ.

As a man they could understand Him, because He had come from the stars as they themselves had, and He had come down to earth by the command of his father, as any young man among them must have done, showing obedience to and respect for age. He was both *Tzi-Sho,* of the Sky Lodge, and *Hunkah,* of the Earth, and now in their own unsureness and anxiety, they became more interested in

740

what the Heavy Eyebrows said about Him, and suddenly they were identifying themselves with Him.

The Heavy Eyebrows had killed their "brothers" and brought other tribes and Heavy Eyebrows to occupy their ancient lands and chase them away from the cairns of their grandfathers, and they had killed *Wah'Kon-Tah E Shinkah* by nailing Him to a cross. It has been said that some of the *Tzi-Sho* gentes, the peaceful Sky People, had begun to include Him in their predawn chants to the Morning Star. Like the instructions of the face painters to the spirit of the dead one, this was only an individual adjustment inspired by anxiety given birth through and freedom from the traditions of the Little Old Men, through the confusion of tribal disintegration.

A prophet was due, but he would not come from within the Little Ones. Their leaders were complacent and suffused with their own importance, and the fifteen councilmen were satisfied with their self-esteem. They were not hungry, vindictive, burning with ambition to be all-conquering. Some of the gentile leaders, while ignored by the agents and the mixed-bloods and the employees, were recognized by the people, and when they became candidates for the Osage National Council from their district, they were usually elected if there were not many mixed-bloods.

The leaders of the Little Ones lived in *Hunkah* comfort, with their *Tzi-Sho ga-ni-tha* (spiritual confusion) haunting their dreams, and attributing greater menace to lightning, *we-lu-shkas,* and the voices of the screech owls.

Leaders with glory-hunger, with bloodless vindictiveness, expressing the proper humility of a people gunless and buffaloless on reservations scattered over the plains, came from the *Pai-Utes* and the Caddos.

Wovoka, a *Pai-Ute* of Nevada, prosaically known as Jack Wilson, had a dream while in a faint, and when he awoke, he was an Indian Messiah; and the gunless, caged men of the plains, still vindictive, believed him when he said that the buffalo and all the warriors who had been killed would come from the West, swarming over the land again and driving the Amer-Europeans back into the East, and the tribes of America would live happily again. The point seemed to be that a gunless but vindictive Indian needed no gun, since he would accomplish the vanishment of the Amer-European and the bringing back of the buffalo simply by praying and dancing. There would be no soldiers who didn't know "friendly" from "hostile," or men from women and children, since they would be powerless against the prayers. The Son of God would not help since the Heavy Eyebrows had nailed Him to a cross, and now in this second coming he was an Indian, a *Pai-Ute* known as Wovoka.

Pai-Ute, or whatever, the Siouans were ready for him, and they were excited. A great leader among the *Hunk-Pa-Pa* Sioux, who was known all over the world as Sitting Bull, came to the agency of the Cheyenne-Arapahoes at Darlington, in modern Oklahoma, in the autumn of 1890, and gave instructions in the prayer-dancing connected with Wovoka's vision, which was called Ghost Dance by the Amer-Europeans because many of the dancers wore white flour sacks as fetish shirts. The shirts, to be effective against the almost certain bullets of the soldiery even though the prayer-dancers carried no arms, must be white and have the sun, the moon, the morning star, turtle, crow, and eagle painted on them.

A Caddo medicine man, *Ni-Shu-Kun-Tu,* or John Wilson, came to this Cheyenne-Arapahoe prayer-dance to get the word from the great Sitting Bull. He was a man of consequence among the Caddos, but he was very small there by the great Sitting Bull, and there was no chance for his histrionics, so he must content himself with bringing this prayer-dance to his people, the Caddos.

The credo of Wovoka, the Indian "Messiah," appealed to the subdued Caddos as well as to the Little Ones, now feeling for solid spiritual ground. It was said that Sitting Bull on his way back to the prayer-dancing of his own people stopped by to visit with the Big Hills and told them of the dance, even instructing them, as some will have it.

They established a camp at the headwaters of Sycamore Creek in the Big Hills country, and there danced in a circle holding hands, moving from the left to the right, wearing their fetish shirts, chiefly made of a gypsum-rubbed doeskin.

They were ready for the credo and perhaps believed in the medicine of the shirts, but they were only tepidly vindictive and were not hungry. They had no need to place lookouts on the hills to watch for the soldiers, and the traders sent wagons loaded with supplies to be unloaded some distance from the dance grounds, the drivers, not allowed to approach closer and not caring to, since by this time the Amer-Europeans were becoming dramatically excited about the Ghost Dance and newspaper correspondents and magazine writers were swarming to the Sioux country, standing in line at the telegraph office, each awaiting his turn to imply a bloody and imminent war.

The credo of the Indian "Messiah"—Do not harm anyone; do always right; do not fight; and when your friends die, do not cry—was acceptable to the Little Ones if they could get their warriors and their "brothers" back, but they soon became disinterested. They were supposed to dance four nights in succession at intervals of six weeks. They danced four nights and then abandoned the idea.

The prophet of the Caddos did not give up. He found a chance to express mysticism and create importance for himself. He was not satisfied with the rather subdued, rather prayerful dancing in a circle with joined hands; he must be conspicuous, like the white religious fanatic who in his emotion climbed the center pole of the camp-meeting tent. Wilson would leave the circle or, breaking through it, would dance on one foot with eyes closed, pointing the forefinger of his right hand upward. During the four days of dancing Wilson would cry out periodically like a lost soul, and could be heard all over the camp day and night.

He used the Ghost Dance to promote his importance; then after the massacre at Wounded Knee, when the Ghost Dance began to wane, he became a medicine man. But this was not an adequate glory.

One day he loaded his wagon, took several sacks of peyote buttons, and he and his wife went to a secluded spot where there was some fresh water. He stayed several weeks and ate all his peyote; seven and eight and finally fifteen buttons for each journey to the moon. He followed the "road" which Jesus had traveled from his grave to the moon. He called this "dying," and he remained "dead" for four days each time.

While under the influence of the peyote, he had auditory hallucinations as well as visual, and experienced schizophrenia, and "heard" songs which he later sang. His guide was "Father Peyote," who showed him how to construct the altar for his Peyote church. He told Victor Griffin, his principal disciple among the Quapaws and Osages, about his "visits" to the moon: "I saw another world, saw a world you never did see before, never saw anything over there, no animals, birds, people, anything, just saw that world. To start with going there, a person came after me and was taking me. At this time this person showed me, showed me there was a grave, an empty grave, told me that is bad. There was a Great Man came to this world, born and raised same as you or anybody else, born in this world. A great man sent by the Creator, and the peoples killed this Great Man. Killed Him but He didn't die and stay here like other peoples did; they buried this Great Man with the earth here but He came alive and was gone. He went back to your Father."

Then Griffin, the disciple, went on to explain Wilson's impression of the Person he couldn't see. He could only hear his voice. Griffin said: "He is a great Ruler but he has got rulers here; the sun, moon, stars, lightning, thunder, they worship his work. They worship this Ruler and ever'thing God made they worship it. Daytime, big ruler comes along is the sun, night time the moon. They tell God they give him the messages, they tell the Creator (same time God knows himself but anyway that is their work) that is their work, that is what they have to do all the time. What went on through that night and day, next day at noon hour they report. If no moon, stars report, if night black, stormy, thunder and lightning report."

This is the way Victor Griffin the Quapaw explained the peyote dreams of John Wilson to *Shonka-Sabe,* Black Dog, and *Gra-Mo'n,* now called Claremore, of the Upland-Forest People of the Osages, now called Hominy People from *Ho'n-Mo'n-I'n,* Walks-in-the-Night. He told them how he had been instructed to build fireplaces which were called "Moons," which would symbolize the grave of Christ.

This was the sort of thing they could believe, and they would not find it too difficult to relegate the Moon Woman to a messenger's role under the Creator who was still *Wah'Kon-Tah.* Grandfather the Sun must now be a messenger of the Ruler also, and the Morning Star degraded, but still the lightning and the thunder could be messengers and manifestations as they had always been. All this had been indicated to them through the later years, and now this Caddo had discovered to them what had happened through peyote.

Victor Griffin went down to the Caddo country to get Wilson to come to the Quapaws and the Osages. Wilson was not prepossessing, and Agent Pollack had him run off the reservation several times, but finally he got permission to come to the Upland-Forest People at Hominy and build two fireplaces, two moon altars. He cultivated his moustache so that it curved like an inverted crescent moon, and his hair fell upon each shoulder. He looked more like a French mountebank than a Caddo, and in fact he was one-fourth French, one-fourth Delaware, and half Caddo. The Osages called him *Mi-Ompah-We-Li,* Moonhead, because of his obsession with the moon.

Victor Griffin, the Quapaw, his Boswell, had a compartment in his memory which he kept sacred and dedicated to Moonhead. He recalled: ". . . one nice morning he wanted to take a walk, told him alright. We was in house where I lived. On a hill there nice trees, no grass or nothing, horses had been rolling around. 'Nephew [courtesy from older man to younger],' he said, 'this is sure good place to have a meeting here, good place for fireplace.' Just listened to him. Never thought anything about it. I just listened. Sure enough two or three days after that some of the old chiefs came over, he said, 'You chiefs, my nephew has found good ground up here, take you up there.' We all went up there and he said, 'Sure good place to have meeting.' They didn't know what he meant. None knew what up to, but he knew what we are to do. 'What do you say, lets fix a place here.' He laid down, hands out like that [extending the arms], said: 'Make mark where hands extended, and head here, now, nephew make marks there.' In two, three days we had meeting there."

Moonhead had placed his body so that, lying on his back, he faced west, and with his outstretched arms his body modestly formed the cross. The altar built at the spot was in the form of a grave, the grave of Christ and Moonhead's own.

When he went over to the Upland-Forest People at Hominy to build an altar for Black Dog and one for Claremore, he came face to face with Osage resistance. No matter what the invisible Person had

745

instructed him, Black Dog would not have his altar facing east. This was the Heavy Eyebrows way; all Osages knew that one traveled to Spiritland with Grandfather the Sun, starting at noon, therefore the altar must face west. Two hundred dollars and some very fine horses and other gifts from Black Dog and Claremore submerged whatever scruples Moonhead might have had about west-facing altars, but he told Victor Griffin later: " 'But this here what you see, this does not belong here. This belongs another place, another country. Now I am going to tell you. God didn't authorize me to build this. Christ didn't authorize me to do this. None of the employees of God. I done this of my own free will, done it to get through, to get by. When build four, ready, I am going home.' " He seemed to have built four "West Moon" altars: one for Griffin, one for a man called Frank Williams in the Caddo country, and one for Black Dog and one for Claremore.

There is no doubt that Moonhead modified the image of the Moon Altar given him by the Person who guided him on the road which Christ took from the grave to the moon when he came face to face with Osage self-assurance and convictions, and with their deer-skin tobacco pouches now used for carrying *mo'n-ce-ska,* white metal (silver dollars).

Both the West Moon and the East Moon altars were symbolical of the grave of *Wah'Kon-Tah E Shinkah,* Christ. The "grave" of the East Moon was more casket-shaped than grave-shaped, and there was a depression, on each side of which were aprons, all made of cement. In the East Moon there was a line running from the door which was on the east or foot up through the middle to the west or top. This was the "road" which Moonhead had traveled when transported by Father Peyote, and it pierced three cement hearts: the "heart of goodness," the "heart of the world," and the "heart of Jesus," reading from west to east. Around the "heart of Jesus" was a circle representing the sun. The "road" was crossed near the top with another line representing "the road across the world," and with this crossing, the Cross came into being. There was an inner apron and an outer apron, the former without lines and the outer one with seven lines representing the old magic seven from the star groups, and below, five others, which added to the seven represented the twelve appearances of the moon. At the west end of the cement casket, the Road Man sat.

The West Moon altar was not much like the East Moon. There was more than the difference in the directions which each faced. The East Moon was plains-geometrical and the West Moon was woodland-curvilinear, and this would seem quite in harmony with the Osage traditions, since they were of both cultures; however, their pictorial religious expressions seemed to be more geometrical than otherwise, as in the stylized spider and the tattooing in general.

The cement depression of the West Moon which symbolized the grave of Christ was much more grave-shaped than that of the East Moon, and all the lines except the one representing the "road" which Jesus took in ascending from his grave and the north-south "road across the world," which intersects the former and forms the arms of the Cross, were flowing ones. The actual depression which represented the grave, with its top to the east, was slender-ovoid, with the lower end, the western end, open, which might suggest uterine characteristics and symbolism. Where the two "roads" crossed was the "heart of the world," and the "heart of goodness" of the East Moon now became in the West Moon the heart-shaped boss where Father Peyote rested during the ceremony. On the single apron of the West Moon, there were jagged lines representing lightning, and this was possibly a protective gesture of Moonhead's after lightning struck a Peyote meeting. Lightning was possibly jealous and wanted to be represented, like the buffalo bull who disrupted the meeting of the Little Old Men in ancient times.

On the lower part of the "road" was the Morning Star. The Road Man sat on a spot at the top or east end of the outside ovoid figure facing west. The dedicated disciple of Moonhead, Victor Griffin of the Quapaws, could not give empirical explanations or interpretations since he was befogged by the esoteric. Why destroy the gossamer weave of man's urge to understand God, or hammer at his own self-importance with logic?

The footprints of Christ were on the lightning line at the top, and placed on each side of the heart where Father Peyote rested. These footprints, incidentally, from the Road Man's position at the top altar in both moons, were W's and from the Fire Man's point of view, M's; one the first letter of "Wilson" and the other the first letter of "Moonhead," all depending on the point of view.

There were the hearts in cement, probably suggested to Moonhead by the Sacred Heart of an early Catholic training, and the footprints of Jesus, who left the impressions by first jumping to become launched into the sky, as birds must do from the ground (except those who launch themselves by running along the ground or on the water), and a confessional, but there was no Bible among the essential sacred paraphernalia. Moonhead had learned this from Wovoka, who believed that Bible reading was a species of penance which the white men must pay for their crucifixion of Jesus, and that the Indian could talk directly to God. However, only the idea was borrowed by Moonhead, and here again his own Catholic training was evinced through making the peyote button the parallel of the wafer, but he attributed to it an identity of its own, not as symbolical of the body of Christ, and called it Father Peyote. The Osages in the Peyote meeting talked through the peyote button to *Wah'Kon-Tah,* their petitions carrying the theme, "Have pity on me." They called it Chief Peyote. This would seem strange to the Heavy Eyebrows with his detachable religious philosophy, who envied the Osages for an economic independence which quite often was the Heavy Eyebrows' sole objective. Why should a man of property ask with deep sincerity to be pitied? If he were still young and not old and afraid? He could make donations to his church, build a church even, and buy memorial stained-glass windows, buy a car for his pastor, or contribute to the missionary fund.

The Osages had always been wealthy in domain and in the numbers of their "brothers," and their prowess had made them arrogant and imperious. They had only called themselves the Little Ones to obviate the jealousy of *Wah'Kon-Tah.* They called themselves the Little Ones aloud and repeatedly in all their ceremonies, but there was the feeling always that they may have been like the converted playboy who, in confessing to his pastor the sinfulness of his amorous experiences, gives the impression of boasting.

But now this spiritual *ga-ni-tha* they were experiencing was deep and quite pathological. The *Tzi-Sho* self was confused and afraid; therefore the tribal body which was both *Tzi-Sho* and *Hunkah,* spiritual and material, was sick, even though the *Hunkah* had no fear of hunger or disease, and enjoyed its traditional position which demanded respect. Their former prowess as warriors and their former influence from geographical situation and rich domain were now translated into dollars. But because of the *Tzi-Sho ga-ni-tha,* they must plead with *Wah'Kon-Tah* sincerely through Chief Peyote, praying, "Have pity on me."

The Osages went into peyotism with eagerness. They built sweat lodges due east of their churches. The churches were permanent and built on the sponsor's own land. They were octagonal, with diameter of about thirty feet, and were surmounted by the white cross, but the buildings were red.

The Osages have always believed that they were constantly being frustrated by animate and inanimate things, not so much evil as mischievous; however, the evil nature of the things which persisted in frustrating them was such that they grew more menacing and important during the progress of the Osages' struggle with the Heavy Eyebrows, and seemed to be tending toward integration and development into a devil similar to the Christian's devil, but not apparently anthropomorphic. Certainly by 1930 there were evil spirits which loitered about their Peyote meetings, but remained in the darkness, afraid to approach the altars.

These mischievous things of evil intent which persistently frustrated the Little Ones during the pre-Peyote days, they could then not cope with, it seems. When the warrior went out to fast and make medicine or receive some indication from *Wah'Kon-Tah* through his life symbol or through some other agency, some trivial thing would appear to smash the message and the warrior would go back to the village in despair. The thing was no *weh-lu-schka* nor a *mi-ah-luschka,* but might be both visible and normal. It might be in the form of a dung beetle struggling in the grass roots or a terrapin staring at the faster with outstretched neck. It might be a voice—the sudden croaking of a cuckoo which the faster had not seen or heard

749

previously; or it might have been the sudden song of the cicada at midday when he was not supposed to sing.

Now, through Chief Peyote, a less harsh *Wah'Kon-Tah* would hear them if they also called him Creator. However, if they would present themselves before Chief Peyote, they must rid themselves of all evil, the mischievous, evil things which attacked their bodies and their minds. They must first rid themselves of evil through sweating.

On Thursday afternoon just at sunset, the sponsor of the meeting, who was usually the Road Man for that particular altar, had a shallow pit dug, and a lodge was built over it with a flap door to the east. He went himself to get limestone rocks, since they hold heat well. He brought them to a firehole outside the lodge, and therein laid logs as supports, then laid logs on them forming a sort of platform within the firehole. He then put the rocks on this platform and piled wood around them, and left them until the next morning, Friday, at sunup.

At sunup he lighted the fire with a flint, and as the rocks heated, the worshipers arrived, naked except for their breechclouts. They entered the sweat lodge, and then the heated rocks were brought in and placed in the pit within the lodge. There were three buckets, one containing warm water and one containing cold water and one empty. When all were in sitting in a circle about the pit, the water was poured over the rocks and soon the lodge was filled with steam.

The Road Man at the top of the circle, facing the east and the door, then took up a cornhusk and rolled it with tobacco, lighted it, and prayed to *Wah'Kon-Tah,* the prayer visibly rising with the smoke. Cedar was thrown on a few coals, and the incense filled the lodge.

Buckeye root was then placed in a container, and hot water was poured over it to make a tea. It was passed around clockwise, starting with the man on the end of the circle just to the left of the door as one entered. After each one drank of the buckeye tea, the Road Man passed water to each one. Buckeye root is an emetic, and soon one would lift the side of the lodge in the rear and pass out to vomit. He carried the primary feather of the crow with him to induce vomiting. Each one should vomit four times if he could possibly do so in order to conform to the tradition associated with the magic four, but they could not always do this.

When they came out of the lodge shiny with sweat, they looked at the sun, then went to the creek to bathe, no matter what season. If there was ice, they broke it. Now, however, they have showers.

During the remainder of Friday and on Saturday, they cleaned the church in preparation for the meeting and went for groceries, and the women and girls pounded the peyote buttons, which are dry, in a section of a post-oak bole, stopped at the bottom. They used a pestle of the same wood, and when the buttons were well smashed, they poured water over them to make the peyote for the meeting. It now had the consistency of dough.

Saturday night the Road Man painted his face with his special "Peyote paint," which might be horizontal or vertical jagged marks like lightning on each cheek, usually red on one side and blue on the other or alternating blue and red on each cheek. He made the red mark along the parting of his long hair, which represented the road of Grandfather the Sun and therefore also represented the straight road which all must travel. The peyotist allowed the hair to grow long, and some braided it with colored threads or ribbons and allowed it to fall over their shoulders and hang in front. When they accepted Peyote, they "threw away" the shaven heads and the majestic roaches, as they did the *wa-hopeh* bundles and tattooing, and they refused to talk about the old things and tried to pretend that they were not a part of their history.

The Road Man appointed two men to sit at the ends of the "road of the world" which formed the crossbar of the Cross, and then indicated the places where the others were to sit on the apron on each side of the casket-like altar. The men at each end of the "road across the world," or the arm of the Cross, aided the Road Man, and were usually visiting Road Men from other altars.

To the right of the Road Man was the Drummer, and down from him the man called by Moonhead the Cedar Man; however, the Osages of the East Moon have no Cedar Man, but one who prepares the cigarettes for those who later wish to employ prayer-smoke. The Drummer had the crock or kettle, made into a water drum by stretching buckskin over the lip and fastening it around the edges by sinew wound about seven marble bosses. Before the buckskin was stretched, water was put into the crock or kettle, just the right amount to attain the right tone. The sinew was fastened about the marbles in such a manner that they were made to form seven crescent moons, and the seven marbles symbolized the magic seven of the stars, and the four mescal beans in the drum had significance, the magic four. The drum-stick was decorated with beadwork and had a buckskin thong hanging from the handle.

The gourd rattle was now filled with gravel or beads, and though it still had the shape of the panther's head, the jaw teeth of the panther were never used. They were of the ancient religion and a part of that which has been "thrown away." The handle was beaded.

Besides the Drum Man and the Cedar Man, there were three Fire Men. The head Fire Man was very important and knew the liturgy as well as the Road Man; he sat by the door to the right as one entered. The other two were just wood gatherers and ash arrangers.

The Road Man from his place at the top or western end of the altar facing the east, told the people what the meeting was about, which was ritualistic, then he told the Fire Men to get the water.

When the water was brought, the Road Man rolled a cigarette with a cornhusk, and lighting it, prayed. The prayer was one which came to him on the moment. He then passed the sage around, which the worshipers waved before their noses, and touched their persons with it, one side then the other. This was sent around clockwise as well.

The Drum Man rolled the doughy peyote into little balls about the size of a golf ball, from which the eaters made four little balls. It was passed clockwise, each worshiper taking a bit with his fingers and eating it. The Fire Man was then ordered to make the fire on the "heart of the world" at the point where the "road across the world" crossed the "road." He scraped the ashes, dividing them, and built up small sticks of wood in the form of the corner of a worm fence or wedge, with the pointed part of the fence span or wedge pointing to the Road Man.

The Road Man then began singing, and then sent the arrow around clockwise, handed to each man until it got to the first man to the left of the door as one entered. The arrow symbolized the necessity of food in order to live, inasmuch as it had ever been the weapon with which the Osages obtained their food, and now nothing was said about its association with war. War is one of the things "thrown away." The arrow was grooved and painted, and the feathered end was decorated with soft feathers, feathers that would actually impede true flight. There was another tuft of feathers hanging from this end, like the feathers that hang from the scalplock of *Tzi-Sho*. Then there was an otter skin hanging from the proximal or feathered end of the arrow, and also an opossum skin. The arrow was held vertically with the head down, and there was a special slot for it in the cement in front of the Road Man when it was not being handed around to the singers, and it was not allowed to lie flat.

When the arrow reached the first man on the other's side of the doorway, the head Fire Man was instructed to get the drum, and he went around the worshipers clockwise, beating the drum for each man who wished to sing. Each singer usually had his own rattle, but if he had not, one was brought to him. When the Fire Man had made the round of the worshipers and reached the original place of the drum, the second Fire Man took the drum and the head Fire Man went out to get wood.

The wood for the fire was red oak, and might or might not be a left-over from the ritualism of the Little Old Men. (Some of the modern Road Men seem to have forgotten the significance of the red oak in the history of their tribe, and say that red oak burns well, doesn't pop and crackle, but gives off heat in winter. In the summer they use hackberry and redbud.) When the Fire Man returned with wood, he put all the ashes together and then spread them out and divided them in the middle with a forked stick about three feet long, and this dividing of the ashes symbolized the opening up of Mother Earth to receive the bodies of men. The worshipers each took a pinch of the ashes and rubbed it on themselves.

The Road Man sang the four starting songs which Moonhead received during his auditory hallucinations, and there were many other songs, sung by the others. "We have some big songs alright, that has big meaning; but we . . . they sing them sometimes, after midnight . . . toward morning" said a Road Man.

These songs, big though the Peyotists believe them to be, vibrate no long-dormant, primitive chord in man's soul; there is no nascent exultation and vague animal uneasiness in the listener. They are not from the pulse of the earth or from the elements or from earth-struggle like the bugle of the wapiti on a moonlit night, the call of the caribou, or the wolf song in midwinter. They are nervous songs with quick tempo directed through Chief Peyote to a Creator who seems to be busy with the petitions of the Heavy Eyebrows. They are prayer-songs that pluck at the sleeve of the Creator, not the ancient prayer-songs of men pre-eminent, upon whom *Wah'Kon-Tah* focused his attention as they hunted and fought and mated and danced and fasted.

At midnight, the "door is open" to Spiritland. The singing ceased, and the drum was brought back to its place with the Drum Man and the arrow was stuck in its slot. The Road Man rolled a cornhusk cigarette and prayed. The new days coming and the future were mentioned in the prayer, and the old desire for long life was expressed.

Any time during the night, after the Road Man and the men at each end of the Cross or the "road across the world" and the Fire Man had prayer-smoked, anyone in the meeting might then offer prayer-smoke to the Creator. The head Fire Man came up to the man on the Road Man's left and took the cornhusk and the tobacco to whoever had requested it. This man rolled the cigarette and gave the tobacco back to the Fire Man, then went up to the fire on the "heart of the world," and faced the Road Man. He then told the people why he wanted to make this prayer and took his cigarette to the Road Man and stood directly in front of him. He lighted the cigarette and put it into the Road Man's mouth, then laid his hands on the head of the Road Man, then on his shoulders, and then on his chest. The cigarette was lighted, and the petitioner sat down after the Road Man had placed his hands on his head. The Road Man prayed for him, then the petitioner came back and confessed his misdeeds and bad thoughts, and as he did this, he cried, and tears streamed down his cheeks. He must cry thus so that the Grandfather the Sun and Father Fire and Mother Earth will really see that the confession comes from his heart. If he were not sincere, they wouldn't help him, and sincerity is in his tears that wash the evil away.

The sincere one was now absolved of evil, through the emetic (the buckeye root) and the sweat of his body and the cleansing of his thoughts through confession. He was then asked by the Road Man to stand at the fireplace, and the others "fanned him off," fanned the evil away.

After midnight the Road Man started the arrow and the drum around again, and the singing and the eating of peyote continued. By this time the people were being affected in various ways according to their constitutions by the peyote. Sometimes they experience nausea, which passes, and they have colored pictorial hallucinations, the dominant colors being red and yellows. Sometimes songs come to them through auditory hallucinations, and they feel an urge to make a song, but all remains quite tranquil and prayerful.

If one must leave the church for relief, he went out into the darkness holding the tail-feather of the golden eagle. Out there in the darkness were the evil and mischievous things of the old religion, but now assuming, if not the form, the characteristics of the Heavy Eyebrows' devil. He dares not come near the church, but a lone person must protect himself by carrying the eagle feather, and even then he might get some of the evil of the devil on him; and when he returned, he touched with the feather the peyote button on the altar which symbolized the Chief Peyote, and the Fire Man fanned the evil away from him with the eagle-wing fan.

When dawn came, the drum and the arrow were brought back to the Road Man, who placed the arrow, head downward, in the slot in front of him. If there was someone who had serious trouble or who had been sick, the Road Man had him stand in front of the fireplace, and the others rose and fanned the evil away with their eagle-wing fans or with the fan made of scissortail flycatcher's tail-feathers.

Just as Grandfather the Sun peeped over the eastern horizon, the people followed the Road Man out of the church and stood facing the east to greet the Grandfather. The Road Man, facing the sun, held up the arrow and the gourd rattle to him, and then the Drum Man held the drum with Chief Peyote resting on the head. As the people came by the Road Man, each one fanned the evil from him. They all stood praying to the sun; however, it was not the old chant but a plea to the sun as a messenger, not in the role of the Grand-father of the ancient religion. They did not sing but prayed, using the word *wah-piah,* assuring the sun they were humble, repeating, "I am a pitiful man," and asked him for help. After this they followed the Road Man back into the church. He placed the arrow in its slot, and the Chief Peyote was put in its place between the arrow and the fire.

The worshipers were then ready for the wild honey, which was brought in by the women folk of the Road Man, and each worshiper took of the honey. Recently, however, candy and cookies are served instead of honey.

After the honey, the Road Man waited for someone who might want to rise and say something "good"; recite some pleasant experi-ence while transported by Chief Peyote. Sometimes one sees ridicu-lously cavorting animals who act "crazy," and he can scarcely sup-press laughter which would not be seemly, therefore he remains silent. Others may talk of beautiful experiences in strange lands by strange rivers, where they might have heard exotic birds, and they may have an urge to sing the song of some bird of that strange land.

If there were no talks of experiences, they began again the same routine of the Fire Man with the drum, of the passing the arrow, the rattle, singing, and taking peyote. At noon on Sunday, the Road Man sang the four Rising Songs, and the meeting was over, and all went to partake of the feast of soup, pork, beef, chicken, corn, squash, costue (fried bread), lotus roots when they can get them, watermelon, and cake. After this feast some of the older people went to sleep in the dappled summer shade, but some had no feeling of fatigue what-ever and could not go to sleep until midnight.

In this compromise between the Neolithic gods and the concept upon which European civilization had been built, called Peyote, the Osages clung to the idea that if one were to reach Spiritland, his face must be painted for identification there, and he must be ready to fol-low Grandfather the Sun to the west, so they continued to face their dead to the west. They bury their dead in the graves of the Heavy Eyebrows now and not in cairns.

When a member of the Peyote church dies, his family calls upon a Road Man to paint his face and "lay him away." The Road Man appears just at sunup and meticulously paints the jagged lines on each side of the face of the one who is going away. These symbols had been given to him who is going to Spiritland by one who had the authority to give them and they belonged to him alone. They were his personal identification and had nothing to do with the ancient gentile, physical division or tribal identifications, since these, too, had been "thrown away." The identifying lines were of red and blue, and then a red line was painted down the parting of the hair.

The body lies in an expensive casket facing west, with candles burning at the head. The relatives and friends come up in line facing the one who has passed, and each one touches his forehead, his hand, and his chest, then touches himself in the same spots and passes on. There might be a little controlled sobbing in the room, and some old person might break into the old mourning chant, about to ask in the old way why *Wah'Kon-Tah* "had taken away his remaining days," but there would be no others to take up the chant, and it would die abruptly and there might be an embarrassed silence.

The candles would indicate that the one who had passed on might be a Catholic, and if so, he would be taken to the church for the funeral Mass at ten o'clock, then taken to the cemetery or to some high sandstone hill in time to go with Grandfather. There at the grave the man chosen by the family to say good-bye, stands at the foot of the grave, facing the man who is going away and the east. He shoves a cedar stick about three feet long, and of four sides, into the ground and looks into the grave, saying that here Mother Earth is open to receive back their brother; then looking up at the sun immediately overhead at noon, he asks Grandfather to take their brother with him. A long-fingered, bronzed hand places a laborer's lunch box on the foot of the casket, filled with the same food those left behind will partake of later, so that the brother will have food on the long journey to Spiritland.

The Osage words die in the heat of high noon, or the sharp winds of winter will clutch at the speaker's blanket and tear the words from his lips. As he steps aside, the priest in his black cassock prays in Latin for the soul of the departed, as he shakes the aspergillum over the casket.

All the people leave to partake of the feast, after laving their hands over the cedar smoke.

But the acceptance of the compromise between the old religion of the Little Old Men and Christianity which is Peyotism was not only a recognition of the power of the enemy God and the necessity to make some compromise with this powerful God of the Heavy Eyebrows for tribal comfort and spiritual safety, but Peyotism is also vindictiveness in identifying themselves with the Great Man, Christ, whom the Heavy Eyebrows also mistreated. They won through defeat and saved their self-esteem. They were also like an obscure boy who, burning with vindictiveness, might take up scholarship or the ministry and receive much of his contentment and satisfaction through sneering at the gaucherie or the sinfulness of the millionaire, but covering well his own deeply hidden respect and admiration for him.

55. The Mourning Dance

PRANCING HORSE LOST HIS SON. Peyotism, the new religion, had not yet reached the Thorny-Valley People, though Moonhead had made "Moon Altars" among the Upland-Forest People and one on Bird Creek fifteen miles below the agency at the edge of one of the lenticular valleys of the reservation, where Red Eagle and Brave lived with their followers. The church was on the left bank of the creek near the modern low-water bridge north of the modern town of Barnsdall, Oklahoma.

The mourning over the son of Prancing Horse was not the last mourning dance of the Osages, but the last among the Thorny-Valley People. Prancing Horse, aided by his relatives, especially *Wa-I'n-Na-Sha*, Stands-Up-with-Something, who contributed food from the trader's stores.

Prancing Horse chose the eight men necessary for the ceremony: four from the *Tzi-Sho* grand division and four from the *Hunkah*, and they assembled at the village, which was just east and a little north of the agency.

From the *Tzi-Sho*, who would take their traditional place on the north, he chose *Mo'n-O-Zhu*, which means Quiver (William Pryor), *No'n-Ce-Tonkah* (Big Heart), *Konza Hunkah* (Kaw Eagle), and himself. For the *Hunkah*, who would take their traditional place on the south, he chose Pressing-Him-Down (Embry Gibson), *Hi-Si'n-Moi'n*, Yellow-Calf-Walking, or a buffalo that Appears-to-Be-Yellow,

Hunkah Hopi (can't translate), and *Ka-Wa-Heh-Tze,* Roan Horse. Each one of the eight wore leggings and moccasins except Prancing Horse and Pressing-Him-Down, who wore breechclouts. Each one painted his face with gentile and tribal symbols of identification, but all had the chin and lower part of the face painted black.

The spot for the dance was just west of the village. They put up the lodges, many of which were now walled tents, and there were two men to act as guards; the one to the northwest was *Tzi-Pah-Kah-Keh,* and the one to the southwest *Wah-Eh-Kah-Ha.* Both carried new trader's hatchets.

The two leaders or head warriors were Prancing Horse and Pressing-Him-Down. The dancers chosen by Prancing Horse painted their chins and lower face black with redbud charcoal, but the leaders who wore only their breechclouts were painted black with the charcoal all over their bodies. On their heads quivered the scalplock. Pressing-Him-Down, the *Hunkah,* set out dancing to the right, and Prancing Horse, the *Tzi-Sho,* danced to the left, each dancing around the village, and everyone was very careful not to cross their circular paths.

Each man carried a gourd in the right hand and a swan standard in the left, and each wore the fetish shield, and they cried *"Ah da ha in'n nika wassa"* at intervals, the last note drawn out like the winter howl of *shonkah,* the wolf. Freely translated, they were crying, "Something must die in the west."

There had been two lodges (really tents) erected for the leader-warriors about fifty yards apart in a north-south line, one to the south and one to the north. The one to the south was for Pressing-Him-Down and the one to the north for Prancing Horse. In front of these tents were four mourners walking back and forth. This was more or less a lowly office. Each mourner was wrapped in a dull gray issue blanket, the more tattered the better. When the leader-warriors moved from their tents to make the circuit of the village, the mourners followed them, each carrying a forked stick about four feet long on which they would support themselves at intervals, and they also carried U. S. flags upside down. They were not permitted to sit down or rest from sunup to sunset. Hanging from their backs were pipes and tobacco pouches, hanging by a thong from their shoulders.

When the two *Sha-Peh-Wa-She-Walla*, the leader-warriors, halted in their circular dance, the mourners halted. When the leader-warriors had made the half-circuit and met, they danced about each other, then continued on until they came back to their tents.

Occupying the space in front of the leader-warriors' tents were two very important men. On the north or *Tzi-Sho* side was *O-Paw-Ha-Moi'n*, Puts-Something-On, and on the *Hunkah* side to the south was *Weh-Gla-I'n-Ki-A*, No-Scent. This refers to game which is upwind from the hunter and therefore unable to scent him.

These men were naked except for their breechclouts and were painted on the chest with large circular spots in black, from which extended two black parallel black jagged lines which terminated on the shoulders. They also carried tobacco pouches and pipes suspended from their shoulders.

In the *Tzi-Sho* and *Hunkah*, the north and south tents respectively, there was a fire built, and here the drums were warmed for the dance. There were two town criers especially selected for the occasion, mounted on piebald horses which were called "paints" or "pintos" from the Spanish *pintado*. The horsemen cried out in long wolflike howls that all should come to the place of the dance. Pintos were usually complacent and lacking in spirit, but if one happened to be unaccustomed to the color and the singing and dancing and painted giants, he might become excited. One day during the Mourning Dance, one became nervous and, walking sideways and chewing his bit, finally got it between his teeth and ran away with his rider, scattering the women and causing great excitement among the dogs. These things were of course *pische,* bad.

The drum began in the *Tzi-Sho* tent, and Quiver stepped out and began dancing between the tents, carrying the swan standard and a rattle. His body was painted black only above his breechclout now, and down his legs were two parallel zigzag lines in black. He danced bending low, then straightened up and shook his head like a carrion-eating eagle shaking off flies. He would bend low again and look from side to side as if he were following tracks of the enemy.

The drum sounded from the *Hunkah* tent, and *Hi-Si'n-Moi'n,* Yellow-Calf-Walking, came out to dance between the tents, and he carried the swan standard and the rattle and was painted like Quiver, and he went through much the same maneuvering. They were very serious, and with their faces painted were like evil people from another world. Their feet seemed to spring back from Mother Earth, giving the impression that they might be afraid of offending her, giving the impression that their feet had scarcely touched her. It was a gracefulness that is seen only in a stalking panther or a trotting doe.

The other dancers appeared now, and they seemed to have forgotten the pride they showed in the *I'n-Lon-Schka,* the social dance. They seemed fierce and yet humble. The four mourners began a circuit of the village, going first to the south, then to the east, and returning from the north. They were now followed by Quiver and Yellow-Calf-Walking, and they in turn by the drummers and the singers. As they made the circuit of the village, they stopped periodically, and all danced and sang except the mourners and the leader-warriors, who now carried only their swan standards while the others had the shields hanging on their backs.

When they arrived back at the starting point, they all rested except the leader-warriors, the guards, and the mourners, who cannot sit when the sun is visible, from sunrise to sunset.

In the first circuit the drummers and singers and dancers had started from the *Tzi-Sho* tent, the north tent; now they made another circuit of the village from the *Hunkah* or south tent, and this time they went to the north then to the east and came back from the south.

The feast came at about 2:00 P.M., prepared by the women and brought in by the eager boys, and the drummers and those who danced voluntarily were asked to eat first. Small amounts of food were placed in the mouths of the mourners, and then the leader-warriors and other warriors ate.

In the afternoon the leader-warriors and the volunteer dancers again painted their faces as they had done for the morning dancing, and they repeated their morning circuits around the village. The drummers and singers of the two grand divisions, the *Tzi-Sho* and the *Hunkah,* took up positions to the west and between the two tents, and the dancers of the two grand divisions danced in circles in opposite directions but did not unite, and there was an opening in the circle so that at one time the *Hunkah* going to the right and the *Tzi-Sho* dancing to the left would change places in respect to the periphery of the circle. The *Hunkah* would dance on the outside, and then the *Tzi-Sho,* each division led by a man carrying a swan standard, the *Tzi-Sho* standard having been stuck in the ground west of the north tent and the *Hunkah* standard having been stuck in the ground east of the south tent most of the day.

There would be a rest period during which one of the warriors would rise and facing west recite his *o-do'n,* and when he had finished, the drums sounded approval. In such recitations the warrior had to tell the truth, or he would be held in contempt for the rest of his life and his infamy even handed down to his children.

There would be several of these rest periods during the long afternoon, and at each rest a warrior would rise to recite his *o-do'n,* and the drums sounded approval and the others sang out "ho-o-o-o-o-o-o-ah," then the dances and songs again until sunset; and just at sunset, the eight warriors formed a crescent facing west, with the end of each horn of the moon a warrior holding up a swan standard. In front of them were the four mourners, the two leader-warriors, and guards, all looking at Grandfather as he left. When he had left, the mourners and the leader-warriors might sit for the first time since they appeared in the morning.

The song and the drum began again in a different tempo, and the head man of the *Hunkah* dancers stood up and danced to the other end of the line, then when he had regained his seat, the head dancer of the *Tzi-Sho* danced to the end of the line; and after he had sat down, the next *Hunkah* danced, and then after him the next *Tzi-Sho,* until all had danced, *Hunkah* and *Tzi-Sho* alternating.

Grandfather had gone, and food was brought by the boys, and blankets for the naked leader-warriors and the two head warriors, and small canvas shelters provided for the four mourners, with an entrance to the east so that they might not miss Grandfather when he first appeared the next morning, when the village would wake to chant to him.

763

When not performing, Quiver and Yellow-Calf-Walking, the leader-warriors, did not leave their tents and food was brought to them. The others sat in a semicircle in the evening and sang of their *o-do'n* (their honors) in the war movement, and they sang also of those honors they dreamed of attaining when the time for the *do-ta'n,* going-for-the-scalp, comes at the end of the fourth day. These songs are traditional and serve now only to quicken and make dearer the tribal memories. The *do-ta'n,* going-for-the-scalp, would in 1902 be empty and ceremonial only, but they pretended that they would come back with Pawnee, Padouca, or Cheyenne scalps. But they must have seen for themselves that this could not be. About the village they saw the children from the sandstone school buildings high on the sandstone hills of the agency, who had been turned out to see the "war dance" of their people after promising their matrons and disciplinarians to speak only in English. There were also the curious employees of the agency and a few visiting friends of the traders and a few of the traders themselves, and at this dance was an anthropologist present, one G. A. Dorsey.

However, when one sang and danced in the evenings there were no Heavy Eyebrows staring at them and there seemed to be no Heavy Eyebrows encircling them. In the evenings when they danced the *wah-sho-she-tse,* the ordinary dances, they sat and sang, and each one rose and danced individually as the drum beat the pulse rhythm of the earth.

There was no whinneying of the carriage horses of the Heavy Eyebrows answering the excited horses of the town criers, and all the visitors had gone and the children collected by the matrons, who were like turkey hens calling and rounding up their poults. The *o-do'n* which they dreamed of seemed actually possible.

The second day was much like the first, and the third like the second, except that on the third day Pressing-Him-Down and Prancing Horse carried swan standards which seemed to take precedence over the ones carried the two days before.

Now came the day of *do-ta'n,* going-for-scalp, the fourth day. The *wah-hopehs* were brought early in the morning of the fourth day. The participants were freshly painted and the guards formed in line and then behind them the mourners in their shabby issue blankets. Then came the warriors, the drummers, the leader-warriors, and the dancers, and they all moved to the west for about two hundred yards, where they stopped and made a temporary camp, and the drum began its earth rhythm, and the dancers danced then circled the warriors who were "going-for-the-scalp."

The old ceremony of opening the *wah-hopeh* shrine was performed. The falcons were drawn from their buckskin and reed and buffalo-hide wrappings and were hung about the necks of the warriors. The warriors jumped on their horses and rode away in a lope to the west complete with their shields and bows and arrows and guns, with the lower part of their faces blackened with the sacred charcoal of the redbud, and each had the identification paint of gens and tribe on his cheeks.

Instead of riding over the limitless plains watching for Pawnees or Wichitas or Cheyennes, the mourning party split up, one part rode up Bird Creek to find a deer, and one part to the cabin of a yellow-haired woman to buy hair. There were two yellow-haired women, apparently, who sold strands of hair; the one who lived just over the border in Kansas and one who obviously had a permit to live on the reservation and lived not far from the village and had only hair to sell.

When the mourning party arrived back at the village, they cut the head from the body of the deer they had killed and staked it to the earth with the four swan standards, then they took the carcass to the camp of the mourners and feasted. The strands of the yellow hair they divided among the mourners, who, when each received his strand, murmured, "This is what I want; I am glad I have it," and each mourner dropped a few strands of his portion over the grave of the son of Prancing Horse and tied another strand to a *wa-hopeh* bundle that had been carried on the *do-ta'n,* and attached another strand to the stem of the pipe he had carried during the ceremony.

The falcons had been rewrapped in their coverings after the party returned from "going-for-the-scalp," but the next morning the bundles were opened and prayed to in the spirit of thanksgiving, and thanked for the benefits given the tribe by the falcon, which were counted by willow sticks; a willow stick laid at the side of the *wa-*

hopeh when the specific benefit or blessing was mentioned, then the falcon was reconditioned and wrapped up again.

The mourning party had sung on their return, "We have killed enemy; the spirit of our friend can enter Spiritland," but in the deer thrown over the withers of the leader's horse and the strand of yellow hair on the end of his bow there was only pretense, and they must have ridden, singing, back to the village like actors who could still recite their lines perfectly but had forgotten the meaning. All, except *No'n-Ce-Tonkah*, who would wear his scalplock on his shaven head almost into the jet age.

56. The Crow Dancers

LITTLE-EAGLE-THAT-GETS-WHAT-HE-WANTS, of the Eagle, married Sacred-Arrow-Shaft, of the Bear, who lived with the family of Quiver (William Pryor). They tried to live as the Heavy Eyebrows lived, because Eagle-That-Dreams, Little-Eagle-That-Gets-What-He-Wants' father, had said that he had been teaching his son the wrong things in preparing him for the old life, and also because he would one day be chief of the Little Osages. He had taken him into the agency as a little boy so that he could go with Thick Hand, Major Miles, the agent, and with others to Carlisle in Pennsylvania. During vacations from Carlisle he was sent to live with very thrifty German farmers, where he worked for his board and learned how to farm. He remembered how considerate they were of his shyness and his reticences.

When he came back and the chieftainship came to him through the deaths of Four Lodges and Thunder Fear, he went to live on his farm on Bird Creek, which had looped itself a little to the east and north a few miles from the agency. He plowed, walking behind his mule and his oxen, with his trade blanket tied around his waist. His long, tapered bronze fingers were always getting in the way of the simple mechanisms of the day, and he had difficulty getting the pin holding the doubletree of his wagon to fit.

His wife, who had been known as Julia Pryor, was really a descendant of Baptiste Maugraine, but had little French blood. She and her sister had worn the prissy clothes of the Heavy Eyebrows of the day, but one night at a dance the Heavy Eyebrows men were drinking, in which circumstances they were almost always quarrelsome. Eventually during the dance, the men pulled their revolvers and started shooting at each other, and one was killed. Later, Julia and her sister Rosie put away their corsets and their bustles and their laces and assumed the old shrouding and leggings and moccasins and colored shirts of their people. They had had enough of civilization.

So when Striking Ax came to the Pryors' to ask for Julia as a wife for Little-Eagle-That-Gets-What-He-Wants, she was ready to be married in the old manner.

But now it was Little-Eagle-That-Gets-What-He-Wants, the full-blood Osage who had listened to his father and remembered the pleasant Heavy Eyebrows of Pennsylvania, who wanted to be a good example to his people, the Little Osages; show them the new way of the Heavy Eyebrows.

But something was wrong; his children died one after the other. The twin brother of his little son, Sun-on-His-Wings, died, and then finally his favorite daughter, *Mi-Tse-Ge*. He sat on the floor at her feet. She lay still on the pallet with eyes made large by the *weh-lu-schkas,* and as he mourned under his breath, he watched the spirit preparing to leave her body, but she was not afraid. There were murmurs in the room; the women were mourning under their breaths, and there was a hum from the back of the room where the White Chests, the nuns, were praying.

With her large feverish eyes on her father's face, she said: "When my brother and grandmother died, you mourned and did not eat and did not drink until sunset. You wore old clothes. You did all the old things which you have left behind. The Saviour doesn't mean that. Enjoy yourself and wear good clothes. You will mourn and you will not forget me, but you must be happy. I go to a good place. I can see Jesus reaching out his hand to me, but when you mourn in the old way, he takes his hand back."

According to the Heavy Eyebrows the spirit now left the body. The White Chests came to kneel at the pallet and pray, and the women in the room began the Song of Death, but courteously subdued, so as not to disturb the presence of *Wah'Kon-Tah E Shinkah,* the Son of God.

After the burial, Little-Eagle-That-Gets-What-He-Wants and his wife gave away all their clothing except the very poorest clothes in their parfleches and their Heavy Eyebrows trunks. They gave away everything in the farmhouse on Bird Creek, and cried each predawn and at the leaving of Grandfather each day. They put on the blue earth of mourning and wandered down the creek, fasting and mourning. They hired a Delaware girl to take care of the two little daughters, and had their two sons taken care of.

Wah'Kon-Tah was not listening to their mourning nor was the God of the Heavy Eyebrows, both taking away the remaining days of their children.

They wandered down the creek and found themselves sitting under an elm tree near the house of *Tzi-Sho-Shinkah,* who was called Red Eagle, the *Tzi-Sho* eagle tinted by the dawn-red of Grandfather as he flies. One or the other would break into mourning at intervals, but there were no more tears, it seemed.

As they sat there, a man of the Deer came up on horseback. He was of *Wah-Ti-Ank-Ah*'s band, and they called him Deer Legs. He was of the Upland-Forest People where Moonhead built his altars, and when he saw them there crying, "Have pity on me," he got off his horse and began to talk to them about Peyote. They went to the house of Red Eagle, and he and his wife also told them of Peyote, and they made a sweat lodge near the house and got some buckeye root. But the religion of the Little Old Men was very powerful and harsh, and evil must be driven out in the old way as well, to be quite sure.

The wife of Red Eagle sent for four men who could do the Crow Dance, and they came and built a fire and warmed their drum, then painted their faces with redbud charcoal. They painted down the sides of the faces like the sideburns of the Heavy Eyebrows, and they took off their clothes excepting their breechclouts, then fastened a "crow belt" around their waists, so that crow feathers hung behind perhaps to their knees. These feathers were lashed together in such a manner that they became a garment open in front.

While one of the four beat the drum, one of the others would rise from a squatting position and dance around the fire, making a sound like the wild gobbler in Just-Doing-That Moon, March. He acted like a crow, yet he gobbled and kicked his foot out in a ridiculous manner. When he finished on the dying beat of the drum, another rose from his squatting position and began to dance as the first dancer came and squatted among the others. When they were not dancing, they didn't sit or stand but squatted, and only one danced at a time. The people who have seen the dancers or heard of them say that they "danced crazy."

This dance was obviously for the purpose of driving sorrow and perhaps even evil away with silly antics, so that sorrow and evil would no longer molest Little-Eagle-That-Gets-What-He-Wants and his wife. The crow songs are serious, but one knows that there are amusing facets to the crow, and this dance may pertain to them. He does do silly things. He picks up bright things and hides them, and he makes silly talk which has nothing to do with his defensive or offensive flock vocabulary. It would seem that if the Osages wished to drive away or avert serious things like sorrow and evil with ridiculous antics, then they might have chosen for this symbolism their old friend and "brother," the otter, or the black bear, or even the yellow-breasted chat.

Later, when Little-Eagle-That-Gets-What-He-Wants went back to his farm on Bird Creek, he had Victor Griffin, the Quapaw, disciple of Moonhead, to come to his place and build a Peyote church. *Wah'-Kon-Tah* and the Heavy Eyebrows God were no longer enemies, and you could talk to both of them through Chief Peyote. Little-Eagle-That-Gets-What-He-Wants became a Road Man, and his children grew to be men and women.

57. The Great Frenzy

THE HEAVY EYEBROWS had come from Kansas and Indian Territory and elsewhere to marry the Osage women when the Osages became rather outstanding as men of property in this temperamental land where men fought grasshoppers and drought. They had paid seventy cents an acre to the Cherokees for their 1,470,559 acres. This land had been taken from them by the treaties of 1825 and 1839 for the Cherokees, and now in 1870 they bought it back.

From the sale of their land in Kansas after they had paid the Cherokees, they had $8,500,000 in the United States Treasury at 5 per cent interest, and their per capita income at the turn of the century was about $200. This represented riches not only to the elements and land-fighting settlers, whisky peddlers, and horse thieves, but even to an agent to the Osages of the period.

The result was that the mixed-bloods would soon come to out-number the fullbloods, and some of the Amer-Europeans who had bought and bribed their inclusion on the tribal rolls had managed to have their names remain after the purging of the rolls in 1893.

On account of conflict between the mixed-bloods and the fullbloods on the council, the "national" government of the Osage Nation was abolished by the Secretary of the Interior in 1900. It was extremely fortunate for the tribe that the Cherokee Commission for allotment had visited them in the early 1890's and the so-called Osage Commission had urged them to allot in 1894 while the fullbloods were still

771

in the majority. They had refused to allot as the tribes around them had done, and they issued an ultimatum to the commissioners that they would never allow their lands to be allotted, but would hold them in community in the traditional manner.

Many of the mixed-bloods were descendants of the jolly, *laissez faire coureurs de bois* and the *voyageurs* and traders. They not only retained their ancient respect for the bourgeois and the official, but they liked to walk in reflected glory of great enterprises like the railroad-building frenzies of the last half of the nineteenth century and the first decade of the twentieth. They glowed with reflected glory of the hopeful activity associated with the first producing oil well on the Edwin B. Foster blanket lease, October 28, 1897, from which oil was not run until May, 1900. This was in the far eastern part of the reservation, but they drove in their single buggies and their wagons and went horseback to see it and glow in the promise it gave them of a brilliant future of riches and importance, vague though it might be.

While the French mixed-bloods were satisfied with vague dreams of future glory and shook hands with, and sometimes with Latin courtesy took off their hats to, the visiting commissioners, eager to acquiesce in their plans for allotment of the tribal lands, the Anglo-Americans who were lured to the reservation by Osage "riches" entertained dreams of throbbing cities and factories and farmsteads.

To the mixed-bloods and the other non-fullbloods who became members of the tribe, the fullbloods appeared as stupid, stubborn "blanket Indians." They were "uncivilized" and had "no git up and go." This attitude of contempt did not escape the full-blood leaders, and they followed Big Heart (Peter) in demanding that the hydrocarbons be held in community, even though in 1906 the mixed-bloods, now in majority, got their railroads and their five townsites within the reservation.

The act of June 28, 1906, was called an "allotment act," but was not in the sense that other acts individualizing tribal property were allotment acts. The other tribes, many of them more civilized and less obtuse than the Osages, certainly tired, disillusioned, and less resistant, accepted individual allotment of 160 acres each, on the urgings of the commissioners, who could hear the politicians and the ever present Heavy Eyebrows shouting for more land. The Osages, on the other hand, by the act would hold their land intact but not communally as they held their hydrocarbons. The land was allotted in severalty to the 2,229 members of the tribe, each member receiving a tract of 160 acres tax free and approximately 498 acres "surplus," which would total for each member of the tribe approximately 658 acres. The Osages described their allotments by using the phrase they used in referring to the limits prescribed by the officials in the buffalo hunt. They called their allotments *wah-tha-do-bi,* "can't-go-beyond." There would be no "land run" into the Osage Reservation, but there would later be an "oil run."

The tribal trust funds would be divided, and the pro rata share of each member of the tribe would be credited to his account in the United States Treasury, and the interest and the royalties from the exploitation of hydrocarbons would be distributed per capita to the members of the tribe quarterly, after the agency operating expenses were set aside. Before allotting the lands to the individuals, certain tracts would be set aside as communal property: 160 acres for the Upland-Forest People of Hominy Trading Post, 160 acres for the Thorny-Valley People, the Little Osages, and the Heart-Stays People near the agency at Pawhuska; and at Grayhorse Trading Post among the Big Hills, 157.5 acres were set aside for the same purpose. These reservations from per capita allotment were for the people of these places who wished to continue the traditional village life, and there were the Agency Reserve at Pawhuska of 88 acres, the Reservoir Reserve of about 17 acres on a sandstone hill west of the agency, and 20 acres deeded back to the tribe by a member, which is located near the city of Sand Springs.

This act of 1906 also established an Osage Council composed of an elected principal chief, an assistant chief, and eight councilmen to be elected biennially. The council was authorized to execute mineral leases subject to the approval of the Secretary of the Interior.

The authority allowed the Osage Council by the Secretary of the Interior may be symbolized by a lariat rope dropped carelessly upon the ground. If the secretary is only a political appointee, he may have as his commissioner of Indian affairs one whose mediocre abilities or energy may give him a sense of importance in the great organization of administrative department of government; then the Osage Council and the tribe in general must depend upon the Congress for protection of their very important and desirable properties. The lariat rope of authority has then a wide loop, with the knot end dropped.

If the secretary has definite opinions about Indians, his commissioner is apt to have the same opinions, and the knot end may be held tightly while the loop becomes small, embracing only the delegated authority to the council to execute mineral leases and nothing more. However, if the secretary has a sincere humanitarian interest in Indians and their rights, his commissioner will certainly have the same interest with much more time to evince it; then the size of the loop might well depend on the abilities and sense of tribal service of the chiefs and the councilmen.

Always in the background is the Congress, which almost always affords the protection necessary.

On November 16, 1907, the Osage Nation became a part of the state of Oklahoma, and the reservation became Osage County. Town lots were sold in old Hominy Post among the Upland-Forest People, and at Fairfax near the Grayhorse Trading Post among the Big Hills and the new town was called Fairfax. Lots were sold at the agency and the town called Pawhuska, and there were town lots sold on the high prairie near the head of Bird Creek and called Foraker, and near the homes of Red Eagle and Brave, Big Heart and Big Horse near the old Peyote church and called Big Heart.

Oil had come to Osage land, and the mixed-bloods felt the buzz of glory. Then the railroad had come through the reservation, and they had waved their hats with one hand and whooped, managing their frantic, slobbering teams as well as they might with the other. Lightning had struck a gas well, "the terrific ground-shivering roar and the light that spread over the whole valley; the light that made the blackjacks on the hills look like ghost trees, appeared to the mixed bloods standing there as a symbol of that indefinite glory that was coming. That light that you could see as far away as Cherokee country, and that roar that drowned all other sounds, gave them a feeling of vague greatness and importance in the universe."

The light that could be seen in the Cherokee country was a sort of retribution, they believed.

On November 16, 1907, when Oklahoma became a state, the bell in the old sandstone council house went crazy with ecstacy, and rifles and shotguns were fired into the air. The Osage Reservation was now Osage County, and Pawhuska a county seat, no less.

The oil flowed and wagon roads wriggled up the sandstone hills, but led no more to a lone log cabin or a house and corrals. They led to a derrick, with a steam engine and a great creaking bullwheel. There was the hissing of steam among the blackjacks like the hissing and whistling of the geysers among the lodge-pole pines of the Yellowstone, and night and day there was the clank, clunk of the drilling tools.

Soon Dodge roadsters labored over the sandy trails and over the prairie, and bronzed young geologists were everywhere. People came from everywhere, and here and there over the old reservation were dance halls and mysterious places with signs reading "Quick Eats" and "U-No" chalked on the windows.

A chart of the oil royalties to the Osage—the old reservation was often called "the Osage" now with the same implications of "the Comstock [Lode]" or "Tonopah" during the years between 1916 and 1932—resembled a cross-section of the Sierra Nevadas from Death Valley to the San Joaquin Valley, with the chart line falling precipitately from the peak in 1925, represented by royalties per capita of $13,000, to $712 in 1932—Death Valley.

The climb from royalties in 1916 to royalties in 1925, from the San Joaquin Valley to the crest, was more precipitate than the actual cross-section would indicate.

The frenzy was far reaching and affected the Heavy Eyebrows in every field, all actually not benefiting directly by the dollars of the Osages or by association with the oil companies or through shops and services, but many others could parade in the very glory of them; the sentimental writers, taking the opportunity to be vindictive and the magazine writers and Sunday supplement writers enjoying the bizarre impact of wealth on the Neolithic men, with the usual smugness and wisdom of the unlearned.

THE OSAGES

The sentimentalist often passed up the impoverished Cherokee fullblood of the hills, the Sac and Foxes, and the Potawatomi, the Ponca, and Otoe-Missouria who had been allotted in severalty to write of the defenseless Osage who had been driven from the graves of his fathers to be finally corraled in the rocky waste which was his last reservation, a land which no white man would have. But what retribution when oil was found on his reservation. The writers often experienced *élan* in their sense of reflected glory of the Osages' dollars and felt that their essays were vindication for culture and Christianity.

It was odd that the Amer-European should have in his illusions about himself created standards of Christian ethics which he couldn't possibly live up to and yet be natural and sincere. His created criteria for ethical actions and relationships among men made of him a hypocrite. There was no reason whatever why any acquisitive Amer-Europeans who had little of the wealth of the country shouldn't follow the exploiters of oil into the Osage, to take advantage of the Osage's Olympian attitude toward money and devise schemes to share in the royalties. They were in the position of the English and the French along the St. Lawrence River and the Great Lakes and the headwaters of the Ohio River in the early days, who in competition could not stop to consider rum as a debaser of the natives. Each had to trade whisky for furs to compete with the other. They had come, like Cortés, to get rich.

The acquisitive followers of the oil exploitation were quite natural, and their transgressions were transgressions only through their own illusions about themselves as Christians following Christian principles. The Osages had no standards against which to judge them, and therefore the Heavy Eyebrows judged themselves against their own standards, and if finding themselves transgressing their own moral laws, they could hide their transgressions from their Christian God with words implying their humanitarianism in which they could make themselves believe. They used words in the preambles of all their treaties with the Osages to make their God believe that they were honorable men and only interested in protecting the Osages. The Little Old Men had used words, too, not to hide their transgressions from *Wah'Kon-Tah* but for mysticism, and the word became sacred and not a screen; but the Heavy Eyebrows believed in his screen as much as the Osage believed in the mystic sacredness of his words.

In the old days when the valley of the agency was tranquil and dusty under its post oaks and its sandstone council house, its agency offices, the doctor's house, and the blacksmith's house, and the plank houses of its traders and mixed-bloods, the people came from all over the reservation to receive the per capita share of the tribal income. The fullbloods camped on the hill back of the great sandstone school buildings and down in the bottoms by the mill; the Big Hills from Grayhorse, and the Upland-Forest People from Hominy chiefly, since the Little Osages and the Heart-Stays People now lived with the Thorny-Valley People in the village near the agency.

They came every March, June, September, and December. The town crier, *Ho-La-Go-Ni,* would walk up and down the area in front of the council house crying the "payment." He circled the community with his long-drawn-out cry, which was sustained for a long time, then ended abruptly.

The payment was at first made from a window on the west side of the council house, each head of family stepping up to get his money as the town crier called his name. Later the payments were made from a kiosk in the middle of the area.

The people paid their debts to the traders and visited with them, since the traders then were more than traders; they were friends, and they were casual in their relationship with the Osages because they were sincere and felt no necessity for marketplace friendliness. The tall Osage pulled from the folds of his blanket his willow sticks and laid them on the counter and the trader consulted his credit card and then the books, and the sticks and the card and the books usually were in harmony.

The first traders were licensed by the first Friends agents during the period of Grant's "Peace Policy," and were men of honor. They were often men who had been lured into Indian trade through a species of Victorian romanticism, and they learned their language well and could exchange ideas with them.

Some of the old traders or clerks who replaced them were still among the Osages when the frenzy began, and when the agency became a center of chaotic activity and the main street and *Ki-He-Kah* avenue had been paved, the Osages tied their horses off the pavement since their horses were afraid of it and often in their fear slipped on it. They came to the stores of the old traders and stood about as though they were seeking security, and there they sat and talked with the trader while he attended to the demands of the new Heavy Eyebrows.

When an Osage walked into a store, the old traders might greet him and continue to serve a customer, and the Osage would stand about and wait, but the new businessmen with their new gadgets would leave a customer to serve the aristocrat of the community, with bows and pidgin English. But even the old traders continued to give the "blanket Indian" the preference. There would be no haggling, but talk and mention of humorous incidents, and both would stand and laugh as the trader measured his bolt of calico or red or blue silk for shirts, which they now wore, on the brass-headed tacks stuck along the edge of the counter, each tack one yard from the other.

Later, the Osages would drive their cars into the towns of the new county and take refuge in one of the trader's stores which still held the strange tropical odors of spice, dried apples, maple sugar, and cigar smoke. Sometimes the odor mélange would have as its theme-scent the delightful odor of leather from saddles and harness.

When the first automobile appeared in the agency, it was driven naturally to the village of the *Wah-Ho-Ka-Li,* the Thorny-Valley People. The hundreds of dogs came out with hackles raised and fangs bared, barking in a hundred keys, and the children left their play to run to the lodges, where the women peeked secretly from the door flaps. The stately men brought their robes up above their heads and pretended not to see.

The town crier's activities were restricted to the *I'n-Lon-Schka* dances. But in the frenzy, the amount of the royalty payments were headlined in the state newspapers, and this drew some prostitutes and petty thieves and murderers to the agency, and things happened. One night the house of Saucy Calf (called Sassy Calf) in the village was robbed and was set afire, and he was burned with the evidence.

In 1932 the frenzy ended. The Osages had been recognized as citizens of the United States in 1921 and they had learned to drive their cars, but most of them hired chauffeurs, and there were many Peyote churches over the reservation, but now for the first time in the centuries of their imperialism their individual self-esteem seemed to dim as the royalties grew small. The compliant Heavy Eyebrows in some cases had experienced a rise in his fortunes, and he now drove expensive cars as well, and the Osage became just an Indian standing to be served and waiting his turn, or even ignored. This hurt his vanity deeply. For the first time in his history, he himself was the Nobody at whom he had always sneered. Even when the White Father, Andrew Jackson, was pushing him off his land, giving it to the eastern tribes, and the free men and the Cherokees were slaughtering his "brothers" and the Cherokees were killing his women and children in the hunter-deserted villages, he might have had periods of hunger, but he was still respected by all, and he was still the man pre-eminent. He could see the respect in the eyes of the Heavy Eyebrows, in the faces of the captive Pawnees and the proud Kiowas. He had seen it in the faces of Lovely and Bradford and Arbuckle, the Union officers, and in the faces and attitudes of the intruding Kansans. All this he had known in tribal memory.

A few of the leaders were still heralded, but only a few of the leaders, and the Heavy Eyebrows came from all over the area to say good-bye to Star-That-Travels. He had two names, one formal, the other gentile. The first name referred to the falling star and the second to the fat that lies under the skin of the black bear, which in the form of tallow was very valuable in the lives of the Osages as well as in the lives of the early settlers. Through a misinterpretation he was universally known as Bacon Rind.

He was much over six feet tall and very handsome, embodying all the physical attributes that calendar artists had conceived. Like most of the fullbloods, he wore his traditional buckskin leggings and moccasins and his otter bandeau with an eagle feather stuck between it and his Peyote long hair. He wore beautiful blankets and colored silk shirts. He wore the *wah-sha-she-skah,* the disk gorget carved from the fresh-water mussel, representing Grandfather the Sun, and he wore

779

a large crucifix hung about his neck. He walked each day in the eyes of Grandfather, but also in the eyes of the impressionable journalists and magazine writers. He was of the Bear-Panther gentes, and no one carried the spirit of gentile life symbol better than he.

The people who put him away directed the hearse up the high sandstone hill east and north of the agency. There was only one steep, wriggling road to the top of the hill, and at noon, when Grandfather was immediately overhead, he followed Grandfather to Spiritland, while the journalists, the tourists, the inquisitive people who had seen his picture and the story of his passing in the state papers, and Pawnee Bill, who had once been a partner of Buffalo Bill, all sat in their stalled cars, which in a line reached from the crest of the hill to the valley bumper-to-bumper like some segmented worm.

But only a few walked in the light of publicity; the tribe as a whole and some of its more important chiefs and chieftains were ignored. Red Eagle was buried on his ranch about this time, in the beginning of the 1930's, with only a few mourners outside of his gens. And in the Big Hills cemetery in 1939 *Tzi-Sho-Wah-Ki-Pa,* Meeting-of-the-Lodges, was buried and attracted no tourists. But not even Star-That-Travels, the man with his profile on coins and letterheads and brochures, received the publicity given to *Ho-To-Mo-I'n,* Roars-as-He-Walks. He had had scrofula in his youth and his people believed he carried the evil spirit, so that he went to live by himself. In the pre-frenzy days he roamed with his many waif dogs about the hills of the agency, pulling his blanket over his head and piling the leaves over himself in winter as he lay down for the night. Later, when he became important as an annuitant member of the tribe, he had a guardian, who built a log house for him on the hill south of the agency. Later the country club was established near him and the golf course hacked out of the blackjacks. He was seen watching the golfers hunting in the rough for their balls with an indulgent smile of amusement. His passing was mentioned in *Time* magazine.

Many of the mixed-bloods and the fullbloods who were competent and had received certificates of competency had sold their land, and being untrained in the professions or in skilled labor, were in a bad way; but the incompetent fullbloods, who had no certificates of competency and by the act of March 3, 1921, were limited to $1,000 a quarter from their accumulated incomes, were financially secure. However, it was not the mixed-bloods, who as white men might have felt degraded by their change of fortune, who might have lost prestige in their own eyes, but the fullbloods who were still receiving more than $4,000 a year, almost the salary of the governor of the state. It was a hurt tribal vanity, the self-questioning of the man pre-eminent concerning his own pre-eminence.

They invited the impoverished Kaws and Poncas and Otoes and Missourias and Quapaws, those whose 160-acre allotments produced no oil or zinc, to their *I'n-Lon-Schka* dances. They invited the lean, hard-living Sioux from South Dakota to their dances, and they all came in their old Fords and even in wagons and camped in the village by the dance grounds. They hired singers from the Poncas and the Otoes.

They themselves sat in their comfortable houses or under striped canvasses while their women dressed them in their finery; in their gypsum-rubbed leggings, their moccasins, silken shirts, wide beaded belts, wampum necklaces, and silver arm bands, and otter-tail pieces, and silken scarves knotted about their necks carelessly. They placed the traditional scalplocks on their heads in the traditional manner, but their hair was long now. *Wah'Kon-Tah E Shinkah,* the Son of God, had long hair.

They used to carry hatchets when they danced; now they carry beaded quirts or coup sticks, and as they approach the dance grounds, the hawkbells fixed below their knees like Elizabethan garters sound rhythmically.

The *I'n-Lon-Schka* was originally a Siouan dance, and came to the Osages through the Kaws and the Poncas. Since it means the *Playground-of-the-First-Son,* the drum is handed around from boy to boy in the tribe, and for one to "have the drum" and the honor which goes with it, his parents or sponsor must bear the expense of the annual dances, which are organized.

There are eight headmen, *ta'n-ha'n,* who are in authority. There is the Keeper of the Drum, and four *si'n-ce,* or Tail Dancers, two *wa-no-sha,* the Whippers, and two water boys, and in the center of the dance ground the singers sit around a large kettledrum. The dancers come jingling onto the dance ground, which is covered by a roof on pole supports, and around it are benches. Each dancer puts his folded blanket down for a cushion, then settles himself with great dignity. The little boy who has the drum is also dressed like the adult dancers.

The drum goes from boy to boy each year, and the selection is made by the headmen, who give each of several willow sticks the name of an eligible boy, then place them on the ground and choose one.

The dances begin each afternoon and last for several hours, and after a feast, each group to his own tent, they dance again at night.

The *I'n-Lon-Schka* is held in the Buffalo-Pawing-Earth Moon, June, and may among the Sioux have some ancient significance. With the Osages it is now a social dance or a "Give-Away Dance," which was once referred to as the "Smoke Dance," since the pipe was smoked by the giver of gifts.

On the fourth day, the Osages make their valuable gifts to their visitors: a beef, a horse, blankets, silver dollars, and always groceries. Not only are they for a few hours the men pre-eminent again, the Great Osages, but the songs sung by the singers inspire tribal and gentile memories. When a gentile family song is sung, the members present arise and dance around the drum, both men and women. The women must wear a blanket, and they usually bring one with them on the hottest day for such an eventuality.

After the gentile or family song is sung, one which may have been handed down for hundreds of years or more, and the dancers move to their benches, the individual whose song has been sung arises and, going to the one whom he has chosen to receive his gifts, hands them to him.

The singers are never forgotten; the crier may rise and announce that a certain person wishes to give a beef to the singers, or the person may go to the singers and hand them silver dollars. Now, in mid-century, some girl or woman, her hair beautifully coiffed, her expensive skirts about her knees, a diamond sparkling in a sunbeam coming through a crack in the roof, her small feet in shoes, with a stilletto heel that stabs the earth of the dance ground, will drape her blanket meticulously about her, obscuring her pearls, and walk to the singers after they have sung the song of her gens or family and which she has just danced with sedate woman rhythm with others, and hand them money.

The men dance with great dignity, as they did hundreds of years ago. When the singers join the drum rhythm, the dancers rise from their benches, adjust the long otter-skin tail-piece, then move out and dance toward the drum and circle it. After they return to their seats, the drums start again, but this time only the Tail Dancers dance, and the drumbeats cease sometimes even before they reach the center of the dance ground, and an uplifted foot may stop in midair with the beat.

No matter how fantastically their guests, the Poncas and Otoes and Missourias may whirl and gyrate in their buttocks-decoration of pheasant tail-feathers going through their Lindy Hop or Black Bottom adaptations, the Osages never lose their incredible dignity and air of dedication. The Otoe and the Ponca dancers have become nationally famous, going from place to place like the rodeo performers, and they have found such modifications of their own dancers inspires hand-clapping. There is no applause at the Osage *I'n-Lon-Schka*.

Self-esteem comes to the man pre-eminent again when he can give expensive presents on the fourth day of the dances, and a heroic tribal or gentile memory comes when his song is sung, but with the euphoria may come the memory of past glory of his ancestors, and if he happens to be one of the "agency Indians" who tries to triumph over prosaic life by drinking too much, he will weep as he dances, unabashed and apparently unnoticed.

The dancer may have these moments of chiefly generosity and euphoria and sadness, but there is another moment which comes when he may lose a feather or hawkbell from his dance finery. Someone will pick up the feather or the garter bell, and take it to a Whipper. When the drum ceases and the Tail Dancers are back on their benches, the Whipper holds up the feather or the bell and begins to recite the *o-do'n* of the ancestors of the man who has lost it. After every incident, there is a flurry on the drum, and the women, chiefly the Siouan women present, make the tremolo.

For a few minutes the tribe and the gentile brothers of the man are suffused with their ancient glories.

58. The Old Eagle Goes to Spiritland

It was mid-century and the Yellow-Flower Moon, August. The Chief of all the Osages lay on his bed in his house at the village. The Peyote fan of scissortail flycatcher tail-feathers hung from the back of his bed on one side and on the other side a crucifix. He had lost so much weight that his profile as he lay there was startlingly like that of the head and beak of his life symbol, the golden eagle.

He had no remaining days, but he smiled at the ceiling. "There's a fly there," he said. "Soon he will fly away, and then he will come back with many other flies. He will tell them: there lies the chief of the Osages—he has no more power to kill us."

We stood atop the high sandstone hill on his ranch. It was isolated from the blackjack ridges and seemed purposeful, as if *Wah'Kon-Tah* had placed it there with some plan in mind. There was the Assistant Commissioner of Indian Affairs, William Zimmerman, Jr., who had flown in from Washington. There was Pat Patterson, curator of the Woolaroc Museum, and there were several people of the Field Service of the Department of the Interior. There were members of the Eagle gens, the family, and others.

Little-Eagle-That-Gets-What-He-Wants had been painted that morning with his individual Peyote symbols by Victor Griffin, the disciple of Moonhead, and that morning the funeral Mass was held; and now as Grandfather came overhead, the Road Man was talking to Mother Earth and to Grandfather the Sun.

A pack rat gnawed at something under the sandstone rocks and this seemed a sacrilege, and just as the Road Man finished his prayer, a smoky-bellied cumulo-nimbus cloud formed and lay like a whale across the northern mid-sky in this Yellow-Flower Moon, when there should have been no such clouds at high noon. By the time we had descended the hill to our cars, it was gone.

The people driving back to the village in their long, shiny cars were worried and wondered what it could have meant.

Pronunciation Key

In an unwritten language, pronunciation depends on the ear of the listener, but I have attempted to prepare an informal guide for pronouncing the Osage words and names used in the text.

a	*as in* father	'n	*French nasalized* n
b	*as in* bad	hn	*French explosive* nasal
c	*as* th *in* thin	o	*as in* note
d	*as in* dog	'o	*explosive* o
e	*as in* prey	o'n	*French nasalized* o
'e	*explosive* e	p	*as in* pipe
g	*as in* go	s	*as in* sit
h	*as in* he	sh	*as in* shun
i	*as in* pierce, *close to* ee	t	*as in* ten
	(*Continental* i)	th	*as in* then
'i	*explosive* i	u	*as in* rule
i'n	*nasalized* i	'u	*explosive* u
'i'n	*explosive French nasal* i	w	*as in* wet
k	*something between* k *and* g	x	*rough German* ch, *sounds*
m	*as in* man		*like a German guttural*
n	*as in* no	zh	*as in* azure

There are certain nouns which have been pronounced by English-

787

speaking people for so long that to spell them according to the above key would only cause confusion. I have spelled such nouns and verbs and adjectives in the traditional manner, employing "ee" or "e" for "i," as in "Ki-He-Kah," the original of which was "Ga-Hi-Ga."

Bibliography

Oral Sources

A-Hiu-Xo, Hole-in-His-Wings, Eagle gens (Henry Lookout).

Bird, John L., trader.

Caudill, Josephine Mathews, daughter of William S. Mathews.

Eagle Feather (Mrs. Edna Maze).

Edge, Standley, Caddo.

Finney, Frank F., son of T. M. Finney.

Finney, J. E., trail-trader and scout.

Finney, T. M., trader.

Griffin, Victor, Quapaw.

Hi'n-Ci-Mo'I'n, Yellow-Hair-Walking, Buffalo gens, to William S. Mathews and John L. Bird.

Hiu-Ah-Wah-Kon-Tah, Buffalo Face gens, Big Hill (Alex Tallchief).

I'n-Gtho'n-Ka-Shinkah, Little Panther, Panther-Bear gens, Upland-Forest.

La-Ta-Sah, Big Hill (Clara Wilson).

Little Wing, Buffalo-Face gens, Big Hill, to T. M. Finney and J. E. Finney.

Mathews, John, as told to Susan Mathews Simpson.

Mathews, William S., son of John Mathews.

Miles, Major Laban J., Osage agent, 1878–85 and 1889–93.

Mo'n-Ci-Tse-Xi, Sacred-Arrow-Shaft, Bear gens (Mrs. Fred Lookout).

Mo-Shi-To-Mo'I'n, He-Who-Travels-Above, Eagle gens, to John L. Bird.

No-Pah-Watha, Thunder-Fear, Thunder gens, Upland-Forest.

"Nopawalla" (Henry Pratt).

Old "Aunt Millie," Negro slave nurse of William S. Mathews.

O-Lo-Thi'n-Ka-She, Never-Left-Out, Gentle *Tzi-Sho* gens (Simon Henderson).

Revard, Franklin N., grandson of "Revoir" killed by Cherokees.

Se-Se-Mo'I'n, Trots-as-He-Travels, Buffalo gens, to John L. Bird.

Shonka-Mo'I'n, Walking-Dog (Horse), Gentle *Tzi-Sho* gens, Big Hill, member of Little Old Men, to William S. Mathews.

Si-Zhe-Wah'i, Hesitant-Deer, Deer gens, Upland-Forest (John Abbott).

Simpson, Susan Mathews, daughter of John Mathews.

Ta-Heh-Ska, Deer gens, Thorny-Valley (John Whitehorn).

To-Ka'-Na, Wolverine, Sisseton, and Wapeton Sioux (E. H. Labelle).

To'n-Wo'n-Hi'n (I-Hi), Arrives-at-the-Village, Gentle *Tzi-Sho* gens (Wakon Iron).

Tzi-Sho Hunkah, Big Hill chief, to Laban J. Miles.

Tzi-Sho Shinkah, Tzi-Sho gens (Henry Redeagle).

Tzi-Sho-Wah-Ki-Pa, Meeting-of-the-Lodges, *Tzi-Sho–Wa'h No'n* gens, Big Hill (Fidelis Cole).

Tse-To-Hah, Buffalo-Face gens (Eaves Tallchief), to William S. Mathews.

Ta-Tonka-She'n, Little-Buck (also called *Tah-Zhe-Kah,* Deer-Legs), Deer gens, Upland-Forest (George Pitts).

Tse-Zhi'n-Ga-Wa-Da-I'n-Ga, Playful-Calf (called "Sassy Calf"), Buffalo gens, to William S. Mathews and John L. Bird.

Wah-Tse-Mo'I'n, Star-That-Travels, Bear-Panther gens, to George E. Tinker and John L. Bird.

Wah-Hre-She, Panther gens, to John L. Bird.

Wah-Na-Sha-She, Little-Eagle-That-Gets-What-He-Wants, Eagle gens (Fred Lookout), chief of all the Osages.

Wah-Shinka-Kah-Hu, son of *Shonka-Mo'I'n* ("*Shonka molla*" Joe).

Wah-Tse-Ki-To'n-Pa, Eagle-That-Dreams, Eagle gens (Fred M. Lookout, Jr.)

Weh-Heh-Sa-Ki, Hard Rope, Big Bill, to William S. Mathews.

Xiu-Tha-Wi, One-Eagle, Eagle gens, Little Osage (Mary Lookout Standingbear).

Xu-Tha-Zhu-Dse, Red Eagle, *Tzi-Sho-Shinkah*'s grandson (Harry Redeagle).

Manuscripts and Archival Materials (Other than Federal)

Finney, J. E. Unpublished MS. Stories of his experiences as trail-trader and scout. In private collection of John Joseph Mathews, Pawhuska, Okla.

Foreman Transcripts, in Oklahoma Historical Society, Oklahoma City. Vols. I, II, IV: Letters: Clark to Eaton; Chouteau to Clark; McCoy to Harris; Sumner to Col. Kearny; Hancock to Sumner; Arbuckle to Armstrong; Chouteau to Armstrong; Vashon to Gen. Andrew Jackson; Baller to President Jackson; Stambaugh to Cass; Armstrong to Crawford; Arbuckle to Crawford.

————, ————. Commissioner of Indian Affairs, a-vol. 4.

Gibson, Isaac T. Diary. Unpublished MS. In possession of Dr. David Parsons, Levelland, Texas.

Gilcrease (Thomas) Museum of American History and Art, Tulsa, Okla. Fragment of a letter from N. G. Taylor, commissioner of Indian affairs appointing No Paw Watha (Nopawalla) "chief" of the Little Osages, May 26, 1868. Letter from Calhoun appointing Nathaniel Philbrook as subagent to the Osages. Fragment of a letter giving names of Osages with Bad-Tempered-Buffalo when Major Welborn was killed.

McCoy, Isaac. Journal. Unpublished MS. Kansas Historical Society, Topeka.

Miles, Laban J. Notes as agent to the Osages. In private collection of his granddaughter, Mrs. Eleanor Rost, Topeka, Kan., and of John Joseph Mathews, Pawhuska, Okla.

Parsons, Dr. David. Unpublished MS. Detailed and meticulous account of the removal of Osage Indians from Kansas, 1868–70. In possession of Dr. Parsons, Levelland, Texas.

Schuyler, Lieut. Col. J. Participation of the 7th Cavalry in Battle of the Washita. Letter in University of Oklahoma Archives, Norman.

University of Oklahoma Archives. Letters Received by Office of Indian Affairs, St. Louis Superintendency. Micro-Copies. Clark to Calhoun, 1825; Agent McNair to Clark, 1825; Clark to James Barbour, secretary of war, 1825. Also various letters, 1827–49.

Government Documents, Published and Unpublished

American State Papers. Vol. V, 1832, *Indian Affairs.* Washington, D. C.

Bureau of American Ethnology. *Thirty-sixth Annual Report,* 1914–15. Washington, 1921.

Commissioner of Indian Affairs. *Reports.* E. H. Carruth to Coffin, 1862; W. G. Coffin, 1863–64; Gibson to Hoag, 1871–74; Gibson to Edward P. Smith, 1875; Cyrus Beede to Nickolson, 1876, 1877; Laban J. Miles to Commissioner, 1879, 1881; James I. David to Commissioner, 1886; Carrol H. Potter to Commissioner, 1888; Laban J. Miles to Commissioner, 1890, 1892; H. B. Freeman to Commissioner, 1896; William J. Pollack to Commissioner, 1898, 1899.

Compilation of All Treaties Between the United States and the Indian Tribes. Washington, 1873.

Hodge, Frederick Webb. *Handbook of American Indians North of Mexico.* B.A.E. *Bulletin No. 30.* 2 vols. Washington, 1910.

Indian Office Consolidated Files. Coffin to Dole. Neosho C–596.

Kappler, Charles J. *Indian Affairs: Laws and Treaties,* Vols. II, III. Washington, 1904.

La Flesche, Francis. *A Dictionary of the Osage Language.* Washington, Bureau of American Ethnology, 1932.

———. "The Osage Tribe: Rite of the *Wa-Xo-Se*," B.A.E. *Forty-fifth Annual Report.* Washington, 1930.

———. "The Osage Tribe: Two Versions of the Child-Naming Rite," B.A.E. *Forty-third Annual Report.* Washington, 1928.

National Archives. Bureau of Indian Affairs, Letters Received. Record Group 75. John Sibley, agent for Indian affairs, New Orleans, to General Dearborn, secretary of war, 1807.

———. ———, ———, 1824–26. St. Louis Superintendency.

———. Letter, Joseph McMinn to George Graham. RC–75 BIA–LR SW.

Schoenmakers, John. *Report to the Commission of Indian Affairs of Osage Manual Labor School for 1855 and 1867.*

U. S. Congress, Senate. *Hearings* of Senate Subcommittee on Senate Bill 1399, Feb. 8, 1937, and Departmental Report of May 18, 1937. On peyote.

Newspapers

Arkansas Gazette (Arkansas Post and Little Rock), November 20, 1819, and December 31, 1845.

Kansas City (Kan.) *Times,* April 18, 1957. Article by Sallie Shaffer on Chetopa, Kansas.

The Living Age, Independence, Kan., June, 1881. Clipping.

Oswego (Kan.) *Democrat,* October 16, 1959. Article by Wayne O'Connell, "City Recognizes Old Landmark."

Articles, Periodicals, and Special Publications

American Historical Association. *Annual Report, 1945.* Vol. III: *Spain in the Mississippi Valley, 1755–64; Post War Decade, 1762–91.* Ed. by Lawrence Kinnaird.

Bartles, W. L. "Massacre of Confederates by Osage Indians in 1863," *Kansas Historical Collections,* Vol. VIII. Topeka, Kan.

Dorsey, George A. "The Osage Mourning-War Ceremony," *American Anthropologist,* July, August, September, 1902.

Finney, Frank F. "Old Osage Customs End with the Last Pah-Hue-Skah," *Chronicles of Oklahoma,* Summer, 1958.

———. "The Osage Indians and the Liquor Problem before Statehood," *Chronicles of Oklahoma,* Winter, 1956–57.

Foreman, Grant. "Our Indian Ambassadors to Europe," *Missouri Historical Society Collections* (St. Louis), February, 1928.

Fritz, Henry E. "The Making of Grant's Peace Policy," *Chronicles of Oklahoma,* Winter, 1959–60.

Nebraska State Historical Society Collections, Vol. XX. Ed. by Albert Watkins.

Niles Weekly Register, July 9, 1825.

Osage Magazine, The (Oklahoma City), June, 1910.

Records, Ralph H. "Recollections of the Osages in the 'Seventies," *Chronicles of Oklahoma,* Spring, 1944.

Sibley, Major George C. "Extracts from Diary," *Chronicles of Oklahoma,* March–December, 1927.

———. Reports, in Thwaites' *Early Western Travels (q.v.),* V, 191–94; XVI, 95, 273; XVII, 63, 64.

Turner, G. "Traits of Indian Character," *Niles Register,* July 4, 1818.

Books

Abel, Annie Heloise. *The American Indian as Slaveholder and Secessionist.* Cleveland, Arthur H. Clark, 1915.

Albright, William Foxwell. *From the Stone Age to Christianity.* New York, Doubleday, 1957.

Allsop, Fred W. *Albert Pike: A Biography.* Little Rock, Parke-Harper Co., 1928.

American Guide Series. *Arkansas.* New York, Hastings House, 1941.

———. *Colorado.* New York, Hastings House, 1941.

———. *Kansas.* New York, The Viking Press, 1939.

———. *Missouri.* New York, Duell, Sloan and Pearce, 1941.

———. *Nebraska.* New York, The Viking Press, 1939.

———. *New Mexico.* New York, Hastings House, 1940.

———. *New York.* New York, Oxford University Press, 1940.

———. *Oklahoma.* Norman, University of Oklahoma Press, 1941. Revised ed., 1957.

————. *Tennessee*. New York, The Viking Press, 1939.

————. *Wisconsin*. New York, Duell, Sloan and Pearce, 1941.

Andreas, Alfred Theodore. *History of the State of Kansas*. Chicago, 1883.

Ashley-Smith Explorations and Discovery of a Central Route to the Pacific, 1822–29 (St. Louis, Mo., Fur Company). Ed. by Harrison Clifford Dale. Glendale, Arthur H. Clark, 1941.

Bollig, Richard Joseph. *History of Catholic Education in Kansas, 1836–1932*. Washington, Catholic University of America. 1933.

Bolton, Herbert E., ed. *Athanese de Mézières and the Louisiana-Texas Frontier, 1768–1780*. 2 vols. Cleveland, Arthur H. Clark, 1914.

Bradbury, John. *Travels in the Interior of America, 1809–1811*. Vol. V of Thwaites' *Early Western Travels, q.v.*

Cambridge Ancient History, The. Vol. I, *Egypt and Babylonia to 1580 B.C.* Cambridge, 1923.

Cambridge Modern History, The. Vol. I, *The Renaissance* (1902); Vol. V, *The Age of Louis XIV* (1908); Vol. VI, *The Eighteenth Century* (1909); Vol. VII, *The United States* (1903); Vol. VIII, *The French Revolution* (1904); Vol. XII, *The Latest Age* (1910).

Carter, Hodding. *The Lower Mississippi*. New York, Toronto, Farrar and Rinehart, 1942. Rivers of America Series.

Case, Nelson. *History of Labette County, Kansas*. Topeka, Crane and Co., 1893.

Catlin, George. *Letters and Notes on the Manners, Customs, and Conditions of the North American Indians*. 2 vols. London, 1841.

Charlevoix, Pierre François Xavier de. *History and General Description of New France*. Ed. by John G. Shea. 6 vols. New York, F. P. Harper, 1900.

Corle, Edwin. *The Gila*. New York, Toronto, Farrar and Rinehart, 1951. Rivers of America Series.

Cornelius, E. *The Little Osage Captive*. Boston, Sabbath School Society, 1832.

Cortambert, Louis. *Voyage au pays des Osages*. Paris, Arthus Bertrand, 1837.

Dale, Edward Everett. *The Range Cattle Industry*. Norman, University of Oklahoma Press, 1930.

Davidson, Donald. *The Tennessee: The Old River, Frontier to Secession*. Vol. I. New York, Toronto, Farrar and Rinehart, 1946. Rivers of America Series.

794

Denhardt, Robert Moorman. *The Horse of the Americas*. Norman, University of Oklahoma Press, 1948.

De Smet, Father Pierre-Jean. *Life, Letters, and Travels* .... Ed. by H. M. Chittenden and A. T. Richardson. Part 2: St. Louis to Green River Rendezvous. 4 vols. New York, Francis P. Harper, 1905.

Des Noëttes, Comte Lefebvre. *L'Attelage le Cheval de Selle à Travers les Âges*. Paris, A. Picard, 1931.

Diaz del Castillo, Bernal. *Historia verdadera de la conquista de la Nueva España*. Madrid, Espasa-Calpe, 1928.

Drake, Benjamin. *The Life and Adventures of Black Hawk*. Cincinnati, George Conclin, 1840.

Dobie, J. Frank. *The Mustangs*. Boston, Little, Brown, 1936.

Farnham, Thomas J. *Travels in the Great Western Prairies*. Vol. XXVIII of Thwaites' *Early Western Travels, q.v.*

Farrand, Livingston. *The American Nation: A History*. Vol. II. New York, Harper, 1904.

Favour, Alpheus H. *Old Bill Williams, Mountain Man*. Chapel Hill, University of North Carolina Press, 1936.

Fey, Harold E., and D'Arcy McNickle. *Indians and Other Americans*. New York, Harper and Brothers, 1959.

[Finney, T. M.] *Pioneer Days with the Osage Indians West of '96*, by Wahshowahgaley. Bartlesville, Okla., 1925.

Fitzgerald, Sister Mary Paul. *Beacon on the Plains*. Leavenworth, Kan., Saint Mary College, 1939.

Fitzpatrick, W. S. *Treaties and Laws of the Osage Nation as Passed to November 26, 1890*. Cedarville, Kan., Commercial Press, 1890.

Foreman, Carolyn Thomas. *The Cross Timbers*. Muskogee, Okla., The Star Printery, 1947.

———. *Indians Abroad*. Norman, University of Oklahoma Press, 1943.

———. *Oklahoma Imprints*. Norman, University of Oklahoma Press, 1936.

———. *Park Hill*. Muskogee, Okla., The Star Printery, 1948.

Foreman, Grant. *Advancing the Frontier*. Norman, University of Oklahoma Press, 1933.

———. *Down the Texas Road*. Norman, University of Oklahoma Press, 1936.

———. *The Five Civilized Tribes*. Norman, University of Oklahoma Press, 1934.

———. *Fort Gibson*. Norman, University of Oklahoma Press, 1936.

795

——. *A History of Oklahoma*. Norman, University of Oklahoma Press, 1942.

——. *Indian Removal*. Norman, University of Oklahoma Press, 1932.

——. *Indians and Pioneers*. New Haven, Yale University Press, 1930.

——. *Pioneer Days in the Early Southwest*. Cleveland, Arthur H. Clark, 1926.

Fortier, Alcée. *A History of Louisiana*. 4 vols. New York, Goupil and Co. of Paris, 1904. Vol. I, *Early Explorers and the Domination of the French, 1512–1768*.

Garrard, Lewis H. *Wah-To-Yah and the Taos Trail*. Ed. by Walter S. Campbell. Oklahoma City, Harlow Publishing Co., 1927.

Garraghan, Gilbert J., S. J. *The Jesuits of the Middle United States*. 3 vols. New York, American Press, 1938.

Gittinger, Roy. *The Formation of the State of Oklahoma*. Norman, University of Oklahoma Press, 1939.

Graves, W. W. *Annals of Osage Mission*. St. Paul, Kan., W. W. Graves, 1934.

——. *Father John Schoenmakers*. Parsons, Kan., Commercial Publishers, 1928.

——. *Father Paul Ponziglione*. St. Paul, Kan., W. W. Graves, 1916.

Grinnell, George Bird. *The Fighting Cheyennes*. Norman, University of Oklahoma Press, 1956.

Hamilton, Charles, ed. *Braddock's Defeat*. Norman, University of Oklahoma Press, 1959.

Havighurst, Walter. *The Upper Mississippi*. New York, Toronto, Farrar and Rinehart, 1942. Rivers of America Series.

Hitchcock, Ethan Allen. *Journal of . . . : A Traveler in Indian Territory*. Ed. by Grant Foreman. Norman, University of Oklahoma Press, 1930.

Holbrook, Stewart H. *The Columbia*. New York, Toronto, Farrar and Rinehart, 1956. Rivers of America Series.

Holmes, Vera Brown. *A History of the Americas*. New York, The Ronald Press, 1950.

Horgan, Paul. *Great River: The Río Grande in North American History*. 2 vols. New York, Rinehart and Co., 1954.

Houck, Louis. *History of Missouri*. Chicago, R. R. Donnelly and Sons Co., 1909.

Hyde, George E. *Indians of the High Plains*. Norman, University of Oklahoma Press, 1959.

——. *Red Cloud's Folk*. Norman, University of Oklahoma Press, 1937.

Inman, Colonel Henry. *The Old Santa Fe Trail*. Topeka, Crane and Co., 1916.

Iowa Biographical Series. Ed. by Benjamin F. Shambaugh. Biography of Henry Dodge by Louis Pelzer. Iowa City, The State Historical Society of Iowa, 1911.

Irving, John Treat. *Indian Sketches*. Ed. by John Francis McDermott. Norman, University of Oklahoma Press, 1955.

Irving, Washington. *A Tour on the Prairies*. Ed. by John Francis Mc-Dermott. Norman, University of Oklahoma Press, 1956.

———. *The Western Journals*. Ed. by John Francis McDermott, Norman, University of Oklahoma Press, 1944.

James, Edwin. *Long's Expedition*. Vols. XIV–XVII of Thwaites' *Early Western Travels, q.v.*

Kenton, Edna, ed. *The Indians of North America*. Selected and edited from *The Jesuit Relations and Allied Documents: Travels and Exploration of the Jesuit Missionaries in New France, 1610–1791*, ed. by R. G. Thwaites, *q.v.* 2 vols. New York, 1927.

La Barre, Weston. *The Peyote Cult*. New Haven, Yale University Press, 1938.

La Farge, Oliver. *A Pictorial History of the American Indians*. New York, Crown Publishers, 1956.

La Harpe, Bernard de. *Historical Journal*. In Benjamin F. French, ed., *Historical Collections of Louisiana*, New York, 1851.

La Harpe, J. F. de. *Abrégé de l'Histoire générale: Voyage en Amérique*. Vol. VI. Paris, 1833.

Lankester, Sir Edwin Ray, K.C.B., F.R.S. *Great and Small Things*. London, Methuen and Co., 1923.

Le Page du Pratz. *Histoire de la Louisiane*. 3 vols. Paris, De Bure; 1758. English trans. by Stanley Clisby Arthur. New Orleans, J. S. W. Harmon and Son, 1774.

Lewis, Meriwether, and George Rogers Clark. *Journals*. Ed. by Bernard De Voto. Boston, Houghton, Mifflin, 1953.

———. *Original Journals of Expedition*. Ed. by R. G. Thwaites. 7 vols. New York, Dodd, Mead, 1904–1905.

Lewis, Anna. *Along the Arkansas*. Dallas, The Southwest Press, 1932.

McCoy, Isaac. *History of Baptist Indian Missions*. New York, 1840.

McReynolds, Edwin C. *Oklahoma: A History of the Sooner State*. Norman, University of Oklahoma Press, 1954.

Margry, Pierre. *Découvertes et établissements des français*. 6 vols. Paris, 1876–86.

Mathews, John Joseph. *Talking to the Moon*. Chicago, University of Chicago Press, 1945.

———. *Wah'Kon-Tah: The Osage and the White Man's Road*. Norman, University of Oklahoma Press, 1932.

Maximilian, Prince of Wied. *Travels in the Interior of North America, 1832–34*. Vols. XXII–XXIV of Thwaites' *Early Western Travels, q.v.*

Mississippi Provincial Archives, 1729–1740. French Dominion, Vol. III. Oxford, Mississippi Press (Rowland and Sanders), Dept. of Archives.

Mowat, Farley. *People of the Deer*. Boston, Little, Brown, 1952.

Nasatir, A. P. *Before Lewis and Clark*. Vols. I, II. St. Louis, St. Louis Historical Documents Foundation, 1952.

———. *St. Louis During the British Attack of 1780*. Reprinted from *New Spain and the West*. St. Louis, 1932.

———, and Ernest R. Liljegren, comps. and eds. *Materials Relating to the History of the Mississippi Valley*. Reprinted from *The Louisiana Historical Quarterly*, January, 1938.

Nuttall, Thomas. *A Journal of Travels into the Arkansas Territory During the Year 1819*. Philadelphia, Thos. H. Palmer, 1821.

———. *A Journal of Travels into the Arkansas Territory, October 2, 1818–February 18, 1820*. Vol. XIII of Thwaites' *Early Western Travels, q.v.*

Nye, Captain W. S. *Carbine and Lance: The Story of Old Fort Sill*. Norman, University of Oklahoma Press, 1937.

Osborn, Henry Fairfield. *The Age of Mammals*. New York, Macmillan, 1910.

———. *Men of the Old Stone Age*. London, G. Bell and Sons, 1921.

Pike, Zebulon. *Zebulon Pike's Arkansas Journal*. Ed. by S. H. Hart and A. B. Hulbert. Denver, 1932.

Poncins, Gontran de. *Kabloona*. New York, Reynal and Hitchcock, 1941.

Postgate, Raymond. *Story of the Year 1848*. New York, Oxford University Press, 1956.

Riddle, Kenyon. *Records and Maps of the Old Santa Fe Trail*. Raton, N. M., 1949.

Roe, Frank Gilbert. *The Indian and the Horse*. Norman, University of Oklahoma Press, 1955.

Ross, Alexander. *The Fur Hunters of the Far West*. Ed. by Kenneth A. Spaulding. Norman, University of Oklahoma Press, 1956.

Sandoz, Mari. *The Buffalo Hunters: The Story of the Hide Men*. New York, Hastings House, 1954.

Schoolcraft, Henry R. *The American Indians: Their History, Condition, and Prospects.* Rochester, Wanzer, Foot and Co., 1851.

——. *Indian Tribes of the United States.* 5 vols. Philadelphia, 1851–55.

——. *Travels in the Central Portion of the Mississippi Valley.* New York, 1925.

Sell, Henry Blackman, and Victor Weybright. *Buffalo Bill and the Wild West.* Reprint by Signet Key Books, New York, 1959.

Stites, Raymond S. *The Arts and Man.* New York, London, Whittlesey House, 1940.

Streeter, Floyd Benjamin. *The Kaw.* New York, Farrar and Rinehart, 1941. Rivers of America Series.

Tixier, Victor. *Voyage aux Prairies Osages, Louisiane et Missouri, 1839–40.* Paris, Clermont-Ferrand, 1844. English translation by Albert J. Salvan, ed. by John Francis McDermott, *Tixier's Travels on the Osage Prairies,* Norman, University of Oklahoma Press, 1940.

Thwaites, Reuben Gold, ed. *Early Western Travels, 1784–1897.* 32 vols. Cleveland, Arthur H. Clark, 1904–1907.

——, ed. *The Jesuit Relations and Allied Documents; Travels and Explorations of the Jesuit Missionaries in New France, 1610–1791.* 73 vols. Cleveland, Burrows Brothers, 1896–1901.

Tuttle, Sarah. *Osage Missions.* (Letters on the Chickasaw and Osage missions; letters to cousins Jerome and Delia, signed Cornelia Pelham). Boston, Sabbath School Union, 1831.

Vestal, Stanley. *The Missouri.* New York, Toronto, Farrar and Rinehart, 1945. Rivers of America Series.

Villiers, Baron Marc de. *La découverte du Missouri et l'histoire du Fort d'Orléans (1673–1728).* Paris, H. Champion, 1925.

Vissiers, Paul. *Histoire de la tribu des Osages.* Paris, Charles Béchet, 1827.

Wallace, Ernest, and E. Adamson Hoebel. *The Comanches: Lords of the South Plains.* Norman, University of Oklahoma Press, 1952.

Webb, Walter Prescott. *The Great Plains.* New York, Ginn and Co., 1931.

White, T. H. *The Book of Beasts.* New York, G. P. Putnam's Sons, 1954.

Whitman, William. *The Oto.* New York, Columbia University Press, 1937.

Wissler, Clark. *North American Indians of the Plains.* New York, American Museum of Natural History, 1920.

Woodard, W. E. *The Way Our People Lived.* New York, E. P. Dutton, 1944.

Wright, Muriel H. *A Guide to the Indian Tribes of Oklahoma.* Norman, University of Oklahoma Press, 1951.

Index

Adair, W. P. (Cherokee): 718
Adams, Pres. John Quincy: 510
Adobe Walls: 717 f.
Against-the-Wind: 408
Agriculture: 188, 449–50, 706 f., 719
A'ki-da (soldiers): 158, 736
A'ki-Da Tonkan: see Big Soldier
Alexander, W. B.: 520
Algonkian tribes: 92, 116, 128, 171, 225, 268, 351, 404 f.
Alights-on-Cloud (chief of the Cheyennes): 609
Allotments: refused, 692, 726, 771–72; type of, accepted by Osages, 772–73; *see also Wah-tha-do-bi*
American Board of Commissioners for Foreign Missions: 425, 525
American flag: 402; display of, 591; Osage use of, 631; *see also* flags
American Fur Company: 518, 592
American Revolution: 257, 259–60
Americans: 587; along Missouri River, 240, 251, 253, 259; infiltrate Louisiana country, 289 ff.; contact with Osages, 292 ff.; habits of, 343–44; invade Osage

country, 348, 415; attitude of St. Louisans toward, 368–69; behavior toward Osages, 383–84; aims in Louisiana Territory, 385
Amherst, Sir Jeffrey: 118
Angry Chief (Pawnee chief): 375
Annuities: 706, 725, 729, 731
"Anti-Nebraska" men: 622
Antler-Maker, and the missionaries: 533–34
Apaches: 92, 109, 126 f., 140, 213, 305, 382, 553
A-Pa-Tsi: see Apaches
Arapahoes: 92, 606, 663 ff.
Arbuckle, Gen. (Col.) Matthew: 494, 498, 500 f., 504, 506 f., 510, 512, 514, 565, 578, 581, 601
Arkansas County: 414
Arkansas Osages: *see* Place-of-the-Oaks
Arkansas Post: 246 f., 380, 414, 465, 491
Arkansas River: 110, 137, 187
Arkansas Territory, established: 436
Armstrong, Capt. William: 578, 588, 614

and "wild Indians," 557 ff., 561
ff.; diplomacy of, 563
Dodge, Rev. (of Harmony Mission): 530
Dodge's council (or Fort Gibson council), 1834: 569
Do-Do'n Hunkah (the Sacred-One-of-the-War Movement): 160, 271 ff., 275
Does-Little: 408
Dog People: 34
D'Orléans, Duc (regent of France): 175 f., 184, 195
D'Orléans, Duchess: 206
Dorsey, G. A.: 764
Do-ta'n (Going-for-the-Scalp): 764
Doudna, Maj.: 639, 641 ff.
Douglas, Stephen A.: 623–24
Down-Below-People or Down-Under-People: *see* Little Osages
Down-River-People: 110
Drum Creek, Kan.: 689 ff.
Drum Creek Springs: 667 ff.
Dry Feather: *see* *Wah-Ti-An-Kah*
Du Bourg, Bishop: 537, 546
Duennas: 308, 310–11, 444
Dunlap and Florer (traders of Deep Fork): 714
Dutch (Cherokee warrior leader): 562
Du Tisne, Charles Claude: 124, 178
Dwight of the Cherokees Mission (on the Arkansas River): 464, 476, 485, 494, 496, 525

Eagle Feather: 679
Eagle gens: 279, 330 f., 342
Eagle-That-Dreams: 700, 703
Eastwood, Abraham: 415
Eastwood, Elijah: 415
Eaton, John H.: 550

Education: 722–23, 729; of Osages, 720–21; by force, 730
Edwards, Ninian: 407
Elder, Peter Percival: 643, 645
Ellsworth, Henry L.: 550, 589 ff.
Emigrants: 490–92, 501; *see also* settlers
English (Long Knives): 107, 118, 122, 247, 385, 404; attitudes of, 123; as rivals of French, 212 ff.; and Five Nations, 221; desire for expansion, 222 ff.; encroachments in Louisiana Territory, 237; in Missouri Valley, 251, 253; organized Indian confederacy, 401
Europeans: quality of emigrants in 1740's, 217–18; retributive dreams of, 223–24; types in Mississippi Valley, 284–85

Factory system: 517 f.
Fetish shield: 162, 172
Fever (typhoid or malaria): 201–202; *see also* cholera
Finney, Ed (trail agent with Osages): 714 ff.
Fire Lodge: 453
Flags: 591; *see also* American flags
Florida: 259, 406
Food: 29, 44, 365, 443, 455–56, 457, 478, 560; preparation of, 84, 315–16, 488
Foreign Missions School (Cornwall, Conn.): 531
Forked Horn: *see* *Wah-Ti-An-Ka*
Fort Arbuckle: 616
Fort Belle Fontaine: 357, 395
Fort Carondelet: 285, 355, 362 f.
Fort Cavagnolle: 219
Fort Concho: 718
Fort Detroit: 167, 169, 221

of which *The Osages* is the sixtieth volume, was inaugurated in 1932 by the University of Oklahoma Press, and has as its purpose the reconstruction of American Indian civilization by presenting aboriginal, historical, and contemporary Indian life. The following list is complete as of the date of publication of this volume:

1. Alfred Barnaby Thomas. *Forgotten Frontiers:* A Study of the Spanish Indian Policy of Don Juan Bautista de Anza, Governor of New Mexico, 1777–1787. Out of print.

2. Grant Foreman. *Indian Removal:* The Emigration of the Five Civilized Tribes of Indians.

3. John Joseph Mathews. *Wah'Kon-Tah:* The Osage and the White Man's Road. Out of print.

4. Grant Foreman. *Advancing the Frontier, 1830–1860.* Out of print.

5. John Homer Seger. *Early Days among the Cheyenne and Arapahoe Indians.* Edited by Stanley Vestal.

6. Angie Debo. *The Rise and Fall of the Choctaw Republic.*

7. Stanley Vestal (ed.). *New Sources of Indian History, 1850–1891.* Out of print.

8. Grant Foreman. *The Five Civilized Tribes.* Out of print.

9. Alfred Barnaby Thomas. *After Coronado:* Spanish Exploration Northeast of New Mexico, 1696–1727. Out of print.

10. Frank B. Speck. *Naskapi:* The Savage Hunters of the Labrador Peninsula. Out of print.

11. Elaine Goodale Eastman. *Pratt:* The Red Man's Moses. Out of print.

12. Althea Bass. *Cherokee Messenger:* A Life of Samuel Austin Worcester. Out of print.

13. Thomas Wildcat Alford. *Civilization.* As told to Florence Drake. Out of print.

14. Grant Foreman. *Indians and Pioneers:* The Story of the American Southwest before 1830. Out of print.

15. George E. Hyde. *Red Cloud's Folk:* A History of the Oglala Sioux Indians.

16. Grant Foreman. *Sequoyah*.

17. Morris L. Wardell. *A Political History of the Cherokee Nation, 1838–1907*. Out of print.

18. John Walton Caughey. *McGillivray of the Creeks*.

19. Edward Everett Dale and Gaston Litton. *Cherokee Cavaliers: Forty Years of Cherokee History as Told in the Correspondence of the Ridge-Watie-Boudinot Family*. Out of print.

20. Ralph Henry Gabriel. *Elias Boudinot, Cherokee, and His America*.

21. Karl N. Llewellyn and E. Adamson Hoebel. *The Cheyenne Way:* Conflict and Case Law in Primitive Jurisprudence.

22. Angie Debo. *The Road to Disappearance*. Out of print.

23. Oliver La Farge and others. *The Changing Indian*. Out of print.

24. Carolyn Thomas Foreman. *Indians Abroad*. Out of print.

25. John Adair. *The Navajo and Pueblo Silversmiths*.

26. Alice Marriott. *The Ten Grandmothers*.

27. Alice Marriott. *María:* The Potter of San Ildefonso.

28. Edward Everett Dale. *The Indians of the Southwest:* A Century of Development under the United States. Out of print.

29. Adrián Recinos. *Popol Vuh:* The Sacred Book of the Ancient Quiché Maya. English version by Delia Goetz and Sylvanus G. Morley from the translation of Adrián Recinos.

30. Walter Collins O'Kane. *Sun in the Sky*.

31. Stanley A. Stubbs. *Bird's-Eye View of the Pueblos*.

32. Katharine C. Turner. *Red Men Calling on the Great White Father*.

33. Muriel H. Wright. *A Guide to the Indian Tribes of Oklahoma*.

34. Ernest Wallace and E. Adamson Hoebel. *The Comanches:* Lords of the South Plains.

35. Walter Collins O'Kane. *The Hopis:* Portrait of a Desert People.

36. Joseph Epes Brown. *The Sacred Pipe:* Black Elk's Account of the Seven Rites of the Oglala Sioux.

37. Adrián Recinos and Delia Goetz. *The Annals of the Cakchiquels*. Translated from the Cakchiquel Maya, with *Title of the Lords of Totonicapán*, translated from the Quiché text into Spanish by Dionisio José Chonay, English version by Delia Goetz.

38. R. S. Cotterill. *The Southern Indians:* The Story of the Civilized Tribes before Removal.

39. J. Eric S. Thompson. *The Rise and Fall of Maya Civilization.*

40. Robert Emmitt. *The Last War Trail:* The Utes and the Settlement of Colorado.

41. Frank Gilbert Roe. *The Indian and the Horse.*

42. Francis Haines. *The Nez Percés:* Tribesmen of the Columbia Plateau. Out of print.

43. Ruth M. Underhill. *The Navajos.*

44. George Bird Grinnell. *The Fighting Cheyennes.*

45. George E. Hyde. *A Sioux Chronicle.*

46. Stanley Vestal. *Sitting Bull:* Champion of the Sioux.

47. Edwin C. McReynolds. *The Seminoles.*

48. William T. Hagan. *The Sac and Fox Indians.*

49. John C. Ewers. *The Blackfeet:* Raiders on the Northwestern Plains.

50. Alfonso Caso. *The Aztecs:* People of the Sun. Translated by Lowell Dunham.

51. C. L. Sonnichsen. *The Mescalero Apaches.*

52. Keith A. Murray. *The Modocs and Their War.*

53. Victor W. von Hagen (ed.) *The Incas of Pedro de Cieza de León.* Translated by Harriet de Onis.

54. George E. Hyde. *Indians of the High Plains:* From the Prehistoric Period to the Coming of Europeans.

55. *George Catlin. Episodes from* "Life Among the Indians" *and* "Last Rambles." Edited by Marvin C. Ross.

56. J. Eric S. Thompson. *Maya Hieroglyphic Writing:* An Introduction.

57. George E. Hyde. *Spotted Tail's Folk:* A History of the Brulé Sioux.

58. James Larpenteur Long. *The Assiniboines:* From the Accounts of the Old Ones Told to First Boy. Edited and with an introduction by Michael Stephen Kennedy.

59. Edwin Thompson Denig. *Five Indian Tribes of the Upper Missouri.* Edited and with an introduction by John C. Ewers.

60. John Joseph Mathews. *The Osages, Children of the Middle Waters.*

826

The Osages is set in Granjon, a type carefully designed to be both comfortable to read and aesthetically pleasing. Granjon was designed by George W. Jones in 1924 and, though considerably modified, is based on the Garamond of the Egenolff specimen sheet of 1592. The paper used in this book has an antique wove surface especially appropriate for this type.

UNIVERSITY OF OKLAHOMA PRESS

NORMAN

DATE DUE